Jacob's Wealth

Supplements

to

Vetus Testamentum

Edited by the Board of the Quarterly

VOLUME 146

Jacob's Wealth

An Examination into the Nature and Role of Material
Possessions in the Jacob-Cycle (Gen 25:19–35:29)

By

Paul D. Vrolijk

BRILL

LEIDEN • BOSTON
2011

This book is printed on acid-free paper.

Library of Congress Cataloging-in-Publication Data

Vrolijk, Paul.
    Jacob's wealth : an examination into the nature and role of material possessions in the Jacob-cycle (Gen 25:19–35:29) / by Paul Vrolijk.
        p. cm. — (Supplements to Vetus Testamentum, ISSN 0083-5889 ; v. 146)
    Includes bibliographical references and index.
    ISBN 978-90-04-20329-7 (hardback : alk. paper) 1. Wealth—Biblical teaching.
2. Poverty—Biblical teaching. 3. Jacob (Biblical patriarch) 4. Bible. O.T. Genesis
XXV, 19–35, 29—Criticism, interpretation, etc. I. Title. II. Series.

    BS1199.W35V76 2011
    222'.11083394—dc22

                                                                2011008803

ISSN 0083-5889
ISBN 978 90 04 20329 7

MIX
Paper from
responsible sources
FSC   FSC® C004472
www.fsc.org

PRINTED BY DRUKKERIJ WILCO B.V. - AMERSFOORT, THE NETHERLANDS

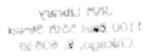

Blessed is he whose help is the God of Jacob,
whose hope is in the Lord his God,
who made heaven and earth, the sea, and all that is in them,
who keeps faith forever

Psalms 146:5–6

CONTENTS

ACKNOWLEDGMENTS

It is a great privilege to study God's word and my study of the Jacob-cycle has been a fascinating journey. This book originates in a PhD dissertation, which was submitted to the University of Bristol (Trinity College Bristol) in 2008. I am greatly indebted to the Revd. Dr. Ernest Lucas, my supervisor, and Prof. Gordon Wenham, who started as my external adviser before moving to Trinity College Bristol himself. Their guidance and encouragement has been of tremendous importance. Trinity is such an inspiring place to be! I thank the Revd. Gervais Angel for his advice and encouragement and Ms Su Brown, Trinity's librarian, who has been such wonderful support in tracking down obscure articles and books. I also would like to thank the library staff at the University of Leiden, the Netherlands, for their professional and courteous assistance on many occasions.

I thank my father for his life-long love and encouragement. I also write this in loving memory of my mum. I thank Janine for her steadfast encouragement over many years. I thank God for giving me such a loving and faithful companion-for-life, mother-of-four. I dedicate this work to her.

I am delighted Brill has decided to publish this work and I thank Prof. Hans Barstad for his editorial advice.

My greatest thanks goes to the God of Jacob, who has been my help (Gen 48:15; Ps 146:5–6). His love forms the Great *Inclusio* for all my life, for all my work, for all my 'being.'

Sigoulès, France   *Soli Deo Gloria*

ABBREVIATIONS

AASOR	*Annual of the American Schools of Oriental Research*
AJSLL	*The American Journal of Semitic Languages and Literatures*
BA	*The Biblical Archaeologist*
BASOR	*Bulletin of the American Schools of Oriental Research*
BDB	Brown, Driver, Briggs
BHS	Biblia Hebraica Stuttgartensia
BI	*Biblical Interpretation*
Bib	*Biblica*
BKC	Bible Knowledge Commentary
BMik	*Beth Mikra*
BN	*Biblische Notizen*
BR	*Bible Review*
BSac	*Bibliotheca Sacra*
BSP	*Bible and Spade*
BTB	*Biblical Theology Bulletin*
BZ	*Biblische Zeitschrift*
BZAW	Beihefte zur Zeitschrift für die alttestamentliche Wissenschaft
CathBQ	*Catholic Biblical Quarterly*
EBC	The Expositor's Bible Commentary
ESV	English Standard Version
ET	*Expository Times*
GKC	Gesenius, Kautch, Cowley
HALOT	The Hebrew and Aramaic Lexicon of the Old Testament
HUCA	*Hebrew Union College Annual*
HTR	*Harvard Theological Review*
HS	*Hebrew Studies*
ICC	International Critical Commentary
IDB	Interpreter's Dictionary of the Bible
Int	*Interpretation*
JAAR	*Journal of the American Academy of Religion*
JANES	*Journal of the Ancient Near Eastern Society*
JAOS	*Journal of the American Oriental Society*
JBL	*Journal of Biblical Literature*
JBQ	*Jewish Bible Quarterly*

JETS	*Journal of the Evangelical Theological Society*
JJS	*Journal of Jewish Studies*
JLR	*Journal of Law and Religion*
JLS	*Journal of Legal Studies*
JNSL	*Journal of Northwest Semitic Languages*
JPJ	*Journal of Psychology and Judaism*
JPS	Jewish Publication Society
JQR	Jewish Quarterly Review
JR	*Journal of Religion*
JRT	*Journal of Religious Thought*
JSOT	*Journal for the Study of the Old Testament*
JSOTSup	Journal for the Study of the Old Testament Supplement Series
JSS	*Journal of Semitic Studies*
JTS	*Journal of Theological Studies*
NBC	New Bible Commentary
NIBC	New International Bible Commentary
NIDOTTE	New International Dictionary of Old Testament Theology and Exegesis
NIV	New International Version
NRSV	New Revised Standard Version
NTT	*Nederlands Theologisch Tijdschrift*
OJLS	*Oxford Journal of Legal Studies*
OTS	*Oudtestamentische Studiën*
ResQ	*Restoration Quarterly*
SCB	*Science and Christian Belief*
SJOT	*Scandinavian Journal of the Old Testament*
TDOT	Theological Dictionary of the Old Testament
ThZ	*Theologische Zeitschrift*
TLOT	Theological Lexicon of the Old Testament
TWOT	Theological Wordbook of the Old Testament
TynBul	*Tyndale Bulletin*
UF	*Ugarit Forschungen*
W&W	*Word & World*
WTJ	*Westminster Theological Journal*
WBC	Word Biblical Commentary
WMANT	Wissenschaftliche Monographien zum Alten und Neuen Testament
VT	*Vetus Testamentum*
ZAW	*Zeitschrift für die alttestamentliche Wissenschaft*
ZTK	*Zeitschrift für Theologie und Kirche*

CHAPTER ONE

INTRODUCTION

And Isaac sowed in that land and reaped in the same year a hundredfold.
The LORD blessed him, and the man became rich, and gained more and
more until he became very wealthy (Gen 26:12–13).

Property is the fruit of labor—property is desirable—is a positive good in
the world. That some should be rich, shows that others may become rich,
and hence is just encouragement to industry and enterprise.—Abraham
Lincoln speech (1864)

The sons of Jacob came upon the slain and plundered the city, because
they had defiled their sister. They took their flocks and their herds, their
donkeys, and whatever was in the city and in the field. All their wealth,
all their little ones and their wives, all that was in the houses, they captured and plundered (Gen 34:27–29).

Property is theft.—Pierre-Joseph Proudhon, *What Is Property?*[1]

1.1   RATIONALE FOR THIS STUDY

Material possessions are an integral part of our lives. Most people
have to work for a living, and much of what seems to matter in our
society revolves around material want and need. Just consider the
vast amount of media coverage concerning wages, pensions, savings,
taxes, debt, the rich, the poor, consumer spending and the immense
amount of advertisement to fuel the latter.[2] Media coverage intensified
in 2008–2009 with the deepfelt effects of global financial turnmoil (the
'banking crisis' and 'credit crunch'). There is also the immense and
persistent inequality between rich and poor, and the great number of
people affected.[3] Poverty, wealth and how the two relate clearly present
us with complex and important challenges.

---

[1] The non-biblical quotes were found in *The Merriam-Webster Dictionary of Quotations*, (Springfield, Massachusetts, USA: Merriam-Webster Inc. Publishers, 1992),
328.

[2] Advertisement spending for 2008 in the USA alone was estimated by Nielsen at
US$ 128 billion and 117 billion for 2009 [cited 25th August 2010]. Online: http://
www.broadcastingcable.com.

[3] For useful statistics [cited 25th of August 2010], online: www.globalissues.org.

What does the Old Testament (OT) say about material possessions?[4] Numerous writers have addressed this question in some form or another; approaches are many and varied. Some approaches are characterized by a selective and highly ideological reading. Not surprisingly quite opposite conclusions can be arrived at (e.g. 'God favours the poor' vs. 'God favours the rich').[5] Alternatively, a more inductive reading of diverse OT texts may offer more satisfactory results. However, within the OT there is a massive amount of material to work with.[6] Relevant passages regarding wealth and poverty appear throughout the OT in basically all genres. These passages present different insights, which at times give the impression of apparent contradiction.[7] In addition, certain texts are quite complex and it is not always clear how the nature and function of material possessions and the attitudes they arouse should be interpreted. Any detailed examination of these texts is a large-scale project.

Many writers who have attempted such large-scale projects start in the book of Genesis.[8] However, when it comes to interpreting patriarchal wealth in Gen 12–50, such projects have often produced unsatisfactory results. For example, the tendency to solely link patriarchal wealth with divine blessing (see below) appears to lack nuance considering the entirety of texts related to this matter (e.g. the pillage of Shechem in Gen 34). More in-depth study into the nature and role of material possessions in Genesis appears necessary.

Although material possessions appear not to be of primary concern to the writer(s)/redactor(s) of Genesis, they are not unimportant either. In Gen 12–50, the amount of textual material regarding

---

[4] A more holistic question than "what does the OT say about wealth or poverty?"

[5] As proposed by certain forms of liberation theology vs. prosperity gospel. For a useful discussion on the semantics of 'God favours the poor', see J.R.W. Stott, *Issues Facing Christians Today* (London, UK: William Collins Sons & Co. Ltd, 1990), 238–239. It is not my aim to offer a critique of liberation theology or 'prosperity gospel.' For a balanced critique of the latter, see A. Perriman, "Faith, Health and Prosperity," (Carlisle, Cumbria, UK: The Evangelical Alliance (UK) Commission on Unity and Truth among Evangelicals/Paternoster Press, 2003). For a useful liberation theology survey see C.L. Blomberg, *Neither Poverty nor Riches* (Leicester, UK: Apollos, 1999), 21–23.

[6] Blomberg's *Neither Poverty nor Riches* offers a good survey of the amount and diversity of OT (and NT) texts on this topic.

[7] E.g. Ps 128:1–4; 37:25–26 vs. 73:12–14.

[8] For example Blomberg, *Neither Poverty nor Riches* and J.R. Schneider, *The Good of Affluence* (Grand Rapids, Michigan, USA: William B. Eerdmans Publishing Company, 2002), although their approaches vary significantly (see below).

possessions is impressive.[9] Besides generic 'possessions' (רְכוּשׁ) there are numerous references to sheep, cattle, donkeys, silver, gold, and slaves and to various related verbs like inheriting, buying and selling.[10] There is of course the important promise God makes to the patriarchs regarding 'the land,' a most prominent piece of possession.[11] Certain passages in Genesis are almost solely devoted to descriptions of possessions and their acquisition (e.g. Gen 23 and 31). A casual reading of Gen 12–50 could give the impression that wealth almost 'happens' to the patriarchs (26:28). On closer reading however, Gen 12–50 is "a story of almost constant struggle," both inside and outside the patriarchal family.[12] Possessions are often at the heart of these struggles and they help to explain certain relationship dynamics (e.g. Jacob vs. Esau). The integral nature of possessions is illustrated by the fact that

---

[9] In Gen 1–11 'possessions' do not feature in a major way.

[10] Appendix A.

[11] The patriarchs: Abraham, Isaac and Jacob as they appear in Genesis. "Despite the fact that 'owning' a land is a rather odd notion" (J. Goldingay, *Old Testament Theology: Israel's Gospel* (2 vols.; vol. 1; Milton Keynes, UK: Paternoster, 2003), 209) and that the land always remained 'YHWH's land' (Lev 25:23; C.J.H. Wright, *Old Testament Ethics for the People of God* (Leicester, UK: Inter-Varsity Press, 2004), 93). Cf. W. Brueggemann, *The Land* (London, UK: SPCK, 2002); J. McKeown, *Genesis* (Grand Rapids, MI, USA: Eerdmans, 2008), 241ff.. "The land theme is so ubiquitous that it may have greater claim to be the central motif in the OT than any other, including 'covenant'" (J.G. Janzen, "Land," in *Anchor Bible Dictionary* (ed. D.N. Freedman; New York, USA: Doubleday, 1996): 146, referring to work by W. Brueggemann, *The Land* (London, UK: SPCK, 1978) and others). C.H.H. Scobie, *The ways of our God: An Approach to Biblical Theology* (Grand Rapids, Mich.: W.B. Eerdmans Pub, 2003). convincingly argues that Brueggemann goes too far by making 'land' the central theme (541, probably referring to Brueggemann's claim that "land is a central, if not *the central theme* of biblical faith" (Brueggemann, *The Land*, 3 italics Brueggemann). E.A. Martens, *God's Design: A Focus on Old Testament Theology* (Leicester, UK: Apollos, 1994), (as mentioned by Scobie, *The ways of our God*, 541) makes 'land' one of four major themes and D.J.A. Clines, *The Theme of the Pentateuch* (Sheffield, UK: Sheffield Academic Press, 1997) identifies 'land' as one of the three big promises in the Pentateuch. For an excellent treatment of the land theme in relation to OT ethics: Wright, *Old Testament Ethics*, 182–211 (and C.J.H. Wright, "אֶרֶץ" NIDOTTE #824, 1:518–524). For a useful bibliography, cf. Wright, *Old Testament Ethics*, 99. For contemporary (evangelical) reflections on 'the land of promise': P. Johnston and P. Walker, eds., *The Land of Promise* (Leicester, UK: Apollos, 2000) and C. Chapman, *Whose Promised Land?* (Oxford, UK: Lion Publishing, 2002).

[12] D. Steinmetz, *From Father to Son: Kinship, Conflict and Continuity in Genesis* (Louisville, Kentucky, USA: Westminster/John Knox Press, 1991), 11. See also J.G. Gammie, "Theological Interpretation by way of Literary and Tradition Analysis: Genesis 25–36," in *Encounter with the Text: Form and History in the Hebrew Bible* (ed. M.J. Buss; Philadelphia, Pennsylvania, USA: Fortress Press, 1979), 118: "there can be little question that the dominant motif in Genesis 25–26 is the motif of strife."

when people move, their belongings move with them. All major movements in Gen 12–50 coincide with the occurrence of רְכוּשׁ (e.g. 12:5).[13] In contrast, the occasions when people move without any possessions appear to have a darker side. Consider Hagar fleeing from Sarah (Gen 16) and her eventual dismissal (Gen 21), Jacob fleeing from Esau (Gen 28) and Joseph being sold by his brothers (Gen 37). Material possessions feature in quite different ways in Genesis.

The interpretive challenges regarding patriarchal wealth are many. Abraham's encounter with Pharaoh (12:10–20) is an interesting case-in-point. Because Abraham fears for his life he devises a scheme to avoid potential conflict in order to protect his life (12:11–13).[14] Ironically, Abraham speaks quite prophetically and indeed is dealt with well because of Sarah and consequently gains substantial wealth (12:16).[15] But as a result of the plagues (12:17), Pharaoh confronts Abraham. Abraham's silence can be interpreted as an admission of guilt[16] and Abraham is escorted out of the country with all he has.[17] Most interpreters are of the opinion that Pharaoh is (mostly) in the right and Abraham is (mostly) in the wrong.[18] But how should Abraham's riches be interpreted? Opinions differ:

---

[13] Appendix A.

[14] C. Westermann, *Genesis 12–36* (trans. J.J. Scullion S.J.; London, UK: SPCK, 1985), 164. For an interesting discussion on the variety of interpretive insights regarding Abraham's conduct, see G.J. Wenham, "The Face at the Bottom of the Well: Hidden Agendas of the Pentateuchal Commentator," in *He Swore an Oath—Biblical Themes from Genesis 12–50* (eds. R.S. Hess, G.J. Wenham and P.E. Satterthwaite; Carlisle, Cumbria, UK: The Paternoster Press, 1994), 186–187.

[15] Note the verbal echoes of Gen 12:13 בַּעֲבוּרֵךְ in 12:16 יֵיטַב־לִי בַעֲבוּרֵךְ הֵיטִיב בַּעֲבוּרָהּ.

[16] Westermann, *Genesis 12–36*, 166. See also R. Davidson, *Genesis 12–50* (eds. P.R. Ackroyd, A.R.C. Leaney and J.W. Packer; Cambridge, UK: Cambridge University Press, 1979), 25. H. Gunkel, *Genesis* (trans. M.E. Biddle; Macon, Georgia, USA: Mercer University Press, 1997), 171; E.A. Speiser, *Genesis* (Garden City, NY, USA: Doubleday & Company, Inc, 1964), 91.

[17] "The reason Abram emerges unpunished is solely that the Pharaoh has experienced the power behind him" (Westermann, *Genesis 12–36*, 166 as quoted by V.P. Hamilton, *The Book of Genesis Chapters 1–17* (ed. R.K. Harrison; Grand Rapids, Michigan, USA: William B. Eerdmans Publishing Company, 1990), 385.

[18] Westermann states that the narrator attributes a clear conscience to the Pharaoh (Westermann, *Genesis 12–36*, 166), contra Waltke: "in spite of the patriarchs' failure of faith, God extends them grace and plunders the real criminal, who we may presume would have killed Abraham to gratify his lust (…). God does not acquit Pharaoh as innocent. In all likelihood, Pharaoh's general behaviour has been the reason for Abraham's fear" (B.K. Waltke, *Genesis* (Grand Rapids, Michigan, USA: Zondervan, 2001), 214–215). The truth probably lies in between these two statements: Abraham has acted unjustly, and as such has not been a blessing to the nations; Pharaoh probably *did* make use of his imperial power to get Sarah into his harem. Abraham might

Early on, 13:2 describes how wealthy Abram became as the first provisional fulfilment of this promise. The rest of the book of Genesis unfolds as a narrative of the various steps and obstacles to inheriting the promise, including the important material portion of that promise, the land of Canaan[19]

Versus:

Abram leaves Egypt a wealthy man, but unlike many other OT individuals whose material prosperity is directly tied to God's blessing, Abram has come upon his wealth through a means other than divine blessing. This is quite an exchange. Abram relinquishes his wife and gains animals and servants.[20]

Resolving this standoff might not be straightforward. Wenham suggests that in OT narrative "it is often very difficult to be sure where the writer and his 'implied reader' stand ethically."[21] Some have tried to defend Abraham's behaviour.[22] Considering the fact that Abraham does not act as a channel of blessing towards Egypt (plagues) it does not seem right to call this wealth "a provisional fulfilment of God's promise" (Blomberg). God's providence might well be at work here, but to label this newly gained wealth a divine blessing seems inappropriate. According to Mazor the listing of Abraham's riches serves as a "deliberate rhetorical signpost" which "causes the reader to become

---

well have had something to fear, but Pharaoh did 'compensate' Abraham well and Pharaoh's unanswered rebuke does make us believe that, according to the narrator, Abraham was the one to get most of the blame.

[19] Blomberg, *Neither Poverty nor Riches*, 36 (referring to God's promise in Gen 12:2–3).

[20] Hamilton, *Genesis 1–17*, 383. Similarly Polzin: "Now this adulterous situation is the means by which Abram acquires a good deal of wealth" (R. Polzin, "'The Ancestress of Israel in Danger' In Danger," *Semeia* 3 (1975): 81–96, 83) and P.D. Miscall, *The Workings of Old Testament Narrative* (Philadelphia, Pennsylvania, USA: Fortress Press, 1983), 42ff.

[21] G.J. Wenham, *Story as Torah: Reading the Old Testament Ethically* (Grand Rapids, Michigan, USA: Baker Academic, 2000), 2. This is illustrated well by Wenham's discussion on various colorful interpretations regarding the morality of the patriarchal family (Wenham, *Story as Torah*, 75–76). Similarly: Wenham, "The Face at the Bottom of the Well," 187. See also M.G. Brett, *Genesis: Procreation and the politics of identity* (London, UK: Routledge, an imprint of the Taylor and Francis Group, 2000), 89.

[22] "The narrative has no interest in defending Abram" (Davidson, *Genesis 12–50*, 26) contra Waltke who states that "only the livestock can be attributed to the gifts of Pharaoh. By the mention of silver and gold, the narrator inferentially points to the Lord as the ultimate Blesser, though the immediate cause may have been various sorts of commercial transactions" (Waltke, *Genesis*, 216), commercial transactions that might well have started with the wealth obtained from Pharaoh!

much more alert and sensitive to the narrator's latent criticism."[23] As Abraham retraces his steps (13:3–4)[24] God is silent.[25] All this suggests that the topic of patriarchal wealth warrants further investigation.[26]

In this study I will limit myself to investigating the Jacob-cycle (Gen 25:19–35:29) and in particular the role of wealth within it. The character of Jacob is of special importance. Twice as much material is dedicated to Jacob, who appears (or is present in the background) in Gen 25–50, compared to Abraham (Gen 12–25).[27] It is from Jacob (renamed Israel in Gen 32) that the twelve tribes trace their origin. Events recorded in Gen 25–50 cover Jacob's entire lifespan.[28] Jacob is the most developed and in-depth character of the three patriarchs[29] and it is Jacob who undergoes "the most extensive and profound character development."[30] In short: Jacob is a fascinating figure to study, and so is his wealth.

---

[23] Y. Mazor, "Scolding Aesthetics," *SJOT* 9 (1995): 297–313, 304.

[24] "A renewal of his lapsed obedience" (D. Kidner, *Genesis* (ed. D.J. Wiseman; London, UK: The Tyndale Press, 1967), 117). "Instinctively Abram sensed his need of forgiveness, cleansing and renewal, and he sought them at the place where he had already owned and worshipped the Lord" (J.G. Baldwin, *The Message of Genesis 12–50* (BST; eds. J.A. Motyer and J.R.W. Stott; Leicester, UK: Inter-Varsity Press, 1986), 39).

[25] Although it is unwise (in most cases) to argue on the basis of silence, the next two conflicts and Abraham's role in them are followed by a specific response from God (Gen 13–14).

[26] See also Miscall, *The Workings of Old Testament Narrative*, 42. Many writers discuss Abraham's, Isaac's and Jacob's wealth under one heading: patriarchal wealth. Although there are certainly similarities between the wealth of the individual patriarchs, there are also some noted differences. However, this probably is a topic of study in itself. Because my focus is on Jacob's possessions, I will only comment on Abraham's and Isaac's wealth in passing.

[27] G. Fischer, "Jakobs Rolle in der Genesis," *BZ* 47, no. 2 (2003): 269–80, 269. Fischer also draws attention to the large number of references to Jacob in the rest of the OT. This number is even larger if we were to include Jacob's new name 'Israel.'

[28] Fischer, "Jakobs Rolle in der Genesis," 272. 'Womb to tomb' (T.L. Brodie, *Genesis as Dialogue: A Literary, Historical and Theological Commentary* (Oxford, UK: Oxford University Press, 2001), 293).

[29] Fischer, "Jakobs Rolle in der Genesis," 272 and B. Vawter, *On Genesis: A New Reading* (London, United Kingdom: Geoffrey Chapman, 1977), 289–90 as quoted by K. Walton, *Thou Traveller Unknown: The Presence and Absence of God in the Jacob Narrative* (Carlisle, United Kingdom: Paternoster Press, 2003), 27. Similarly L.R. Kass, "Love of Woman and Love of God," 107, no. March (1999): 46–54, 46.

[30] S. Spero, "Jacob's Growing Understanding of His Experience at Beth-El," *JBQ* 26, no. 4 (1998): 211–15, 211; Similarly Vawter, *On Genesis*, 289–290; Y. Amit, *Reading Biblical Narratives* (Minneapolis, USA: Fortress Press, 2001), 73; A. Berlin, *Poetics and Interpretation of Hebrew Narrative* (Sheffield, UK: Sheffield Academic Press, 1983), 40. Already noted by B.P. Church, *The Israel Saga* (New York, USA: Macmillan, 1932).

Is there need for another study on the Jacob narrative(s)? Considering the vast amount of work done on Genesis (and on Jacob) in the last fifty (and even twenty) years that is a very good question. However, as the literature survey will show, there appears to be an under-developed area in the studies on Jacob (or Genesis) regarding material possessions. I will now delineate that area in more detail.

1.2 LITERATURE SURVEY

Is there a demonstrable need for more biblical research on Genesis and particular on the Jacob narrative(s) regarding the nature and role of material possessions? I will approach this question from two directions. Firstly, how have biblical scholars who focus on wealth and poverty made use of the Jacob narrative(s)? Secondly, what have biblical scholars, who focus on Genesis and Jacob, written about wealth and poverty? It will become clear that there is an under-explored borderland in between. I will discuss various areas of research in order to survey the contours of this borderland. I realize that the categories which I employ overlap to some extent. What this survey will also show is that there is immense variety in interpretive approaches that are utilized. In section *1.3 Methodology* I will consider the suitability of these various methods in relation to my objectives, but first I will consider how recent scholarship on material possessions has interpreted Genesis and more specifically the Jacob narrative(s).

1.2.1 *Wealth and Poverty*

Over the last thirty years, many (Christian) books and articles have been written on wealth and poverty. However, most of these publications are aimed at a popular level. Not many scholarly works have been written on wealth and poverty, with some notable exceptions.[31] I will discuss the main contributions, especially regarding their use of Genesis and the patriarchal narratives.

---

[31] Quite some work in this area has been done by NT scholars. For example: M. Hengel, *Property and Riches in the Early Church* (London, UK: SCM Press, 1974) and S.E. Wheeler, *Wealth as Peril and Obligation: The New Testament on Possessions* (Grand Rapids, Michigan, USA: Eerdmans, 1995). Blomberg, *Neither Poverty nor Riches* offers a useful introduction and bibliography. Surveying recently published dissertations it is also clear that more work has been done by NT scholars than OT scholars in this area.

In the popular arena, Sider's *Rich Christians in an Age of Hunger* (first published in 1977) is considered by many to be a milestone in the discussion on how Christians are to respond to issues of wealth and poverty.[32] Sider's book contains numerous scriptural references, but only one from Genesis! Sider does not discuss the wealth of the patriarchs at all.[33]

Coming from the opposite direction is Schneider's *The Good of Affluence* (2002),[34] which contains a 'running debate' with Sider.[35] Schneider starts his biblical survey with Genesis, although he applies what I would call a 'Creation perspective' instead of a 'Creation/Fall perspective.'[36] The 'good' of affluence is discussed, but there is no mention of the 'not-so-good' aspects.

In the same book, Schneider also wages war against Blomberg's *Neither Poverty nor Riches: A biblical theology of possessions*. In this very ambitious book, Blomberg aims to write a biblical theology of material possessions based on all relevant parts of Scripture, bringing issues of wealth and poverty together, rather than discussing them apart.[37] This certainly is an attractive approach, but Blomberg only dedicates two pages to the patriarchs as a result.[38] However, what Blomberg says is of interest for our discussion. Blomberg's book also shows how difficult it is to systematize one's findings when so much material is un-earthed. Overall, Blomberg's book is impressive,[39] but it has been

---

[32] In this study I will refer to a later edition of this book: R.J. Sider, *Rich Christians in an Age of Hunger* (Dallas, TX, USA: Word, 1997). Other works in this area have already been mentioned: Stott, *Issues Facing Christians Today*; R. Foster, *Money, Sex and Power* (London, UK: Hodder & Stoughton, 1985).

[33] A very short reference to the goodness of Creation in Gen 1 (Sider, *Rich Christians in an Age of Hunger*, 99).

[34] Also J.R. Schneider, *Godly Materialism: Rethinking Money and Possessions* (Downers Grove, USA: IVP, 1994). For a biting critique on this book: L. Daniel, "Can we talk? About money? Affluent Christians," *Christian Century* February 8 (2003): 26–30, 26–27.

[35] Schneider, *The Good of Affluence*, 12.

[36] Schneider, *The Good of Affluence*, 60–61 and 68–69.

[37] For useful definitions of biblical theology cf. B.S. Rosner, "Biblical Theology," in *New Dictionary of Biblical Theology* (eds. T.D. Alexander and B.S. Rosner; Leicester, England: Inter-Varsity Press, 2000), 10. See also E.A. Martens, "Tackling Old Testament Theology," *JETS* 20, no. 2 (1977): 123–32, 123 as quoted by S.J. Hafemann and P.R. House, eds., *Central Themes in Biblical Theology: Mapping Unity in Diversity* (Nottingham, UK: Apollos, 2007), 16.

[38] Blomberg, *Neither Poverty nor Riches*, 35–37.

[39] Because of its broad set-up and useful bibliography, Blomberg's contribution forms an effective starting point for anybody who wants to study wealth and poverty in the OT (or NT).

criticized by Hughes for lacking an "adequate OT study of poverty and the poor."[40] Hoppe's *There shall be no poor among you: Poverty in the Bible* is seen by Hughes to provide the necessary balance for Blomberg's approach.[41]

It is interesting to see where these different writers put their emphases when it comes to interpreting patriarchal wealth. Blomberg notes that "the riches amassed by the patriarchs are highlighted several times" and that "the wealth of the patriarchs must therefore be understood within its clear covenantal context."[42] Like Blomberg, Schneider notices the link between the theme of prosperity and the promises made to the patriarchs.[43] Schneider also notices 'hardship' endured by the patriarchs, but does not mention the hardship inflicted by the patriarchs on others. In contrast, Hoppe notes that "a common thread in the patriarchal narratives is that people of means and people of power create 'poverty.'"[44] Clearly there is a need to investigate these differences in more detail. Interpretations by Blomberg, Schneider and Hoppe regarding the wealth of the patriarchs (or Jacob) are somewhat unsatisfactory; an in-depth analysis of the nature and role of the material possessions of the patriarchs is lacking.

Also a recent publication, *Tight Fists or Open Hands? Wealth and Poverty in Old Testament Law*, by D.L. Baker (2009) does not focus in any length on the issue of patriarchal wealth in general, or Jacob's wealth in particular.[45] Gen 12–50 appears to be an under-explored area of biblical research regarding wealth and poverty. The question arises whether this is true when we approach these topics from the opposite direction? How much attention has been given to patriarchal wealth

---

[40] D. Hughes, "Book review of 'There shall be no poor among you: Poverty in the Bible' by Leslie J. Hoppe," 30, no. 3 (2005): 107–08, 108 (see also D. Hughes, "Book review of 'Neither Poverty nor Riches: A Biblical Theology of Possessions' by Craig Blomberg," 25, no. 2 (2000): 74).

[41] L.J. Hoppe, *There shall be no poor among you: Poverty in the Bible* (Nashville, Tennessee, USA: Abingdon Press, 2004). Hughes, "Book review of 'There shall be no poor among you: Poverty in the Bible' by Leslie J. Hoppe," 108.

[42] Blomberg, *Neither Poverty nor Riches*, 36.

[43] Schneider, *The Good of Affluence*, 68.

[44] Hoppe, *There shall be no poor among you*, 21.

[45] D.L. Baker, *Tight Fists or Open Hands? Wealth and Poverty in Old Testament Law* (Grand Rapids, MI, USA: Eerdmans, 2009). I would like to thank Dr Baker for allowing me to read part of his manuscript before publication, and for our personal correspondence in this matter.

by scholars who have focussed their efforts on Genesis and on the patriarchs in particular?

1.2.2 Commentaries on Genesis

In this study, extensive use has been made of the large number of commentaries on Genesis. Amongst others from the 20th and 21st century, the 'classic' commentaries by Skinner, Gunkel, Jacob, Speiser, von Rad and Westermann.[46] More recently, substantial commentaries have been written by Hamilton, Wenham and Sarna,[47] and even more recently commentaries focussing on the poetics, narrative and theology of Genesis by Alter, Waltke, Brodie and McKeown.[48] Whereas commentators like Skinner, Gunkel and Speiser occupied themselves almost exclusively with source- and redaction-critical matters, more recent commentators (e.g. Alter, Waltke, Brodie and McKeown) tend to focus almost exclusively on the text in its final form. This is not to say that work on source-critical issues is a thing of the past.[49] However,

---

[46] J. Skinner, *Genesis* (ICC, Edinburgh, UK: T&T Clark, 1910); Gunkel, *Genesis*; B. Jacob, *Das Erste Buch der Tora—Genesis* (Berlin, Germany: Schocken Verlag, 1934); Speiser, *Genesis*; G. von Rad, *Genesis* (trans. J.H. Marks; London, UK: SCM Press Ltd., 1961); C. Westermann, *Genesis 1–11* (trans. J.J. Scullion S.J.; London, UK: SPCK, 1984) and Westermann, *Genesis 12–36*. For a very useful comparison between the commentaries of Gunkel, von Rad and Westermann see Walton, *Thou Traveller Unknown*, 3–5.

[47] W. Brueggemann, *Genesis* (ed. J.L. Mays; Atlanta, Georgia, USA: John Knox Press, 1982); Hamilton, *Genesis 1–17*; V.P. Hamilton, *The Book of Genesis Chapters 18–50* (ed. R.K. Harrison; Grand Rapids, Michigan, USA: William B. Eerdmans Publishing Company, 1995); G.J. Wenham, *Genesis 1–15* (WBC 1; ed. B.M. Metzger, D.A. Hubbard and G.W. Barker; Dallas, Texas, USA: Word Books, Publisher, 1987); G.J. Wenham, *Genesis 16–50* (WBC 2; ed. B.M. Metzger, D.A. Hubbard and G.W. Barker; Dallas, Texas, USA: Word Books, Publisher, 1994) and N.M. Sarna, *Genesis* (JPS Torah Commentary; Philadelphia, USA: Jewish Publication Society, 1989). Besides these commentaries, many more have been used for our research: e.g. N.M. Sarna, *Understanding Genesis* (New York, UK: Schocken Books, 1970); Kidner, *Genesis*; Baldwin, *The Message of Genesis 12–50*; J.E. Hartley, *Genesis* (NIBC 1; Carlisle, Cumbria, UK: Paternoster Press, 2000); A.P. Ross, *Genesis* (BKC 1; eds. J.F. Walvoord and R.B. Zuck; Wheaton, IL, USA: Victor Books, 1983–c1985). and J.H. Sailhamer, *Genesis* (EBC 2; ed. F.E. Gaebelein; Grand Rapids, Michigan, USA: Zondervan, 1992).

[48] R. Alter, *Genesis* (New York, USA: W.W. Norton & Company, 1996); Waltke, *Genesis*; Brodie, *Genesis as Dialogue*; McKeown, *Genesis*.

[49] Take for example J.-D. Macchi and T. Römer, eds., *Jacob: Commentaire à Plusieurs Voix de Gen 25–36—Mélanges offerts à Albert de Pury* (Geneva, Swiss: Labor et Fides, 2001) and A. Wénin, ed., *Studies in the Book of Genesis—Literature, Redaction and History* (Leuven, Belgium: Leuven University Press, 2001). These publications do not limit themselves to source and redaction critical matters.

this rich diversity in methodology is testimony to the developments of the field over the last fifty to a hundred years. Although I will focus on the text in its final form (a 'synchronic reading'), I will engage with various commentators on source-critical matters when deemed relevant. This raises the thorny issue *how* such diverse methods and insights can be combined into an integrated reading. This matter is not easily resolved (see *Section* 1.3 Methodology).

Although most commentators comment on the riches of the patriarchs in selected passages, they do not offer an integrated approach for interpreting material possessions in Gen 12–50 or in the Jacob-cycle. Considering the objectives of a commentary this is certainly understandable, but it does highlight a potential need.

1.2.3   *Old Testament Ethics*

Does the discipline of OT ethics offer such an integrated approach to interpret material possessions in Gen 12–50? A quick survey shows that quite some work has been done on wealth and poverty in the OT,[50] but that most of that work focuses on other parts of the OT, notably the non-narrative part of the Torah, the Prophets and Wisdom literature. Traditionally, the Law given to Moses on Sinai, and the life of Israel in the light of the Law through history have been the focal points for OT ethics.[51] Parry notes that "narrative ethics plays second fiddle to law and wisdom ethics in both the academy and the church."[52]

Janzen in his *Old Testament Ethics* (1994) treats Abraham's dealings with Lot (Gen 13) as an ethical example story. Janzen is careful to

---

[50] Consider for example the work of C.J.H. Wright, *God's People in God's Land* (Exeter, UK: Paternoster Press Ltd, 1990); *Walking in the Ways of the Lord: The Ethical Authority of the Old Testament* (Leicester, UK: Inter-Varsity Press, 1995); *Living as the People of God* (Leicester, UK: Inter-Varsity Press, 1998); Wright, *Old Testament Ethics*). See also: J. Barton, *Ethics and the Old Testament* (London, UK: SCM Press, 2002), 53–57. Note that Wright and Barton differ substantially to what extent the OT is relevant for us today when it comes to property related issues (e.g. Barton, *Ethics and the Old Testament*, 57).

[51] Wenham, *Story as Torah*, 2; R. Parry, *Old Testament Story and Christian Ethics* (Milton Keynes, United Kingdom: Paternoster Press, 2004), xvii. For a useful insight into the field of OT ethics, see *Semeia 66 Ethics and Politics in the Hebrew Bible* (1994) and J.W. Rogerson, "Old Testament Ethics," in *Text in Context: Essays by Members of the Society for Old Testament Study* (ed. A.D.H. Mayes; Oxford, UK: Oxford University Press, 2000).

[52] Parry, *Old Testament Story and Christian Ethics*, xvii. E. Otto, *Theologische Ethik des Alten Testaments* (Stuttgart, Germany: Kohlhammer, 1994) has nothing on ethics implicitly taught in OT narrative (as noted by Wenham, *Story as Torah*, 2).

state that "this story modelling right behaviour is embedded in wider narrative contexts" and that it is necessary to study "how it blends into wider theological themes."[53] However, besides Abraham's generous dealing with Lot in Gen 13, Janzen does not discuss the material possessions of the patriarchs (or Jacob) in an integrated way.

Whereas Gen 13 offers a good example for Janzen's paradigmatic approach, other passages are clearly not as straightforward. Take for example the ethical questions raised by the acquisition of Abraham's riches in Gen 12 (see above) and the pillage of Shechem.[54] To repeat Wenham's comment, it "it is often very difficult to be sure where the writer and his 'implied reader' stand ethically."[55] Yet, generations of Jews and Christians have turned to the OT (including OT narrative) for guidance. "Old Testament narrative books do have a didactic purpose, that is, they are trying to instil both theological truths and ethical ideals into their readers."[56] These elements are very much entwined (see below).[57] In *Story as Torah: Reading the Old Testament Ethically*, Wenham discusses how the ethical stance of the author can be discovered in OT narrative.[58] When it comes to interpreting patriarchal wealth, Wenham places the concerns of Gen 12–50 in the theological framework of human sinfulness and God's grace.

A landmark contribution in the field of OT ethics is C.J.H. Wright's *Old Testament Ethics for the People of God*. In his work over the last decades, Wright has had plenty to say about the responsibilities and challenges of wealth and poverty within God's overall design. Wright's paradigmatic approach enables a holistic study of the theological, social and economic aspects of the life of the people of God (Israel, the Church). Although the book of Genesis is of foundational importance to Wright's paradigmatic proposals, his work contains hardly any references to the Jacob narrative(s).[59]

---

[53] W. Janzen, *Old Testament Ethics* (Louisville, Kentucky, USA: Westminster/John Knox Press, 1994), 14.

[54] Parry's study *Old Testament Story and Christian Ethics* is very much testimony to the ethical complexities of this event. See *Section 4.5*.

[55] Wenham, *Story as Torah*, 2.

[56] Wenham, *Story as Torah*, 3.

[57] This is also clearly reflected in the work of C.J.H. Wright (in the interdependence of the theological, social and economic 'angles' in his paradigm).

[58] Wenham makes use of Genesis and Judges to demonstrate his approach.

[59] I am aware that this comment might sound a bit ungracious in the light of scriptural wealth offered by Wright's work. Lack of grace, or admiration, is certainly not intended.

Although OT ethics offers valuable insights into my area of interest, this study does not entirely fit the confines of that field. My interests are foremost theological, although I do recognize that theology and ethics (especially with a topic like wealth and poverty) are deeply entwined. As Wright states "in the Old Testament (as in the whole Bible) ethics is fundamentally *theological*. That is, ethical issues are at every point related to God—to his character, his will, his actions and his purpose."[60]

In summary: Not much OT ethics work has been done on wealth and poverty in Gen 12–50 or in the Jacob-cycle specifically. Although recently more work has been done on OT narrative ethics (e.g. by Wenham 2000; Parry 2004), this has not yet resulted in an integrated ethical reading regarding material possessions in the Jacob-cycle. There is a clear need to study patriarchal wealth in more detail. I intend to build on what has been done, keeping in mind that theology and ethics are indeed inseparable.[61]

1.2.4 *Monographs on Jacob*

Besides numerous commentaries, plenty of monographs have been written on the whole or part of the Jacob-cycle. Recent monographs that look at the whole of the Jacob-cycle are: *Die Erzählungen vom Patriarchen Jakob—ein Beitrag zur mehrperspectivischen Bibleauslegung* (Recker 2000);[62] *Verheissung und Erfüllung in der Jakoberzählung (Gen 25,19–33,17): Eine Analyse Ihres Spannungsbogens* (Taschner 2000)[63] and *Thou Traveller Unknown: The Presence and Absence of God in the Jacob Narrative* (Walton 2003). The interests of these writers vary. Whereas Taschner focuses on the promise and fulfilment aspects of the Jacob narrative, Walton focuses on the presence and absence of God. Recker's interests are different altogether. Instead of focusing on one particular aspect of the Jacob narrative(s), he has made an inventory of all the methods that have been applied to the Jacob narrative(s) to demonstrate the necessity of a multi-perspective interpretation. The methodologies applied by these writers differ substantially. Where

---

[60] Wright, *Old Testament Ethics*, 23.

[61] Wright, *Old Testament Ethics*, 17; Janzen, *Old Testament Ethics*, 11–12.

[62] C. Recker, *Die Erzählungen vom Patriarchen Jakob—ein Beitrag zur mehrperspektivischen Bibelauslegung* (Münster, Germany: Lit Verlag, 2000).

[63] J. Taschner, *Verheissung und Erfüllung in der Jakoberzählung (Gen 25,19–33,17): Eine Analyse Ihres Spunnungsbogens* (Freiburg, Germany: Herder, 2000).

Taschner takes a synchronic approach to the Jacob-cycle (focussing on the final form of the text), Walton tries to keep diachronic and synchronic methods together. Recker on the other hand aims to bring as many different known techniques together, but does not attempt to integrate them. In these very useful monographs, Jacob's wealth is discussed to some extent, but never in full.

Another set of recent monographs focus on part of the Jacob-cycle: *Had God Not Been on My Side: An Examination of the Narrative Technique of the Story of Jacob and Laban (Genesis 29,1–32,2)* (Sherwood 1990), as the title suggests, examines the narrative technique used to tell the story of Jacob's time with Laban.[64] *Segen für Isaak* (Dieckmann 2003) focuses on Gen 26 and its place within Genesis.[65] Finally, I must mention *Old Testament Story and Christian Ethics: The Rape of Dinah as a Case Study* (Parry 2004), which focuses on the interpretive challenges of Gen 34 for Christian ethics. These monographs make valuable contributions on which I hope to build, yet they do not discuss Jacob's material possessions in much detail.

Besides these monographs, a number of books have been written on the literary qualities of OT narrative, sometimes focussing on Genesis narratives or using parts of the Genesis narrative to demonstrate particular points of interest (e.g. Fishbane 1979; Fokkelman 1991; Alter 1981 and Sternberg 1987).[66] As with the monographs, these books mention Jacob's possessions in part, but never discuss them in full.

---

[64] S.K. Sherwood, *"Had God Not Been on My Side": An Examination of the Narrative Technique of the Story of Jacob and Laban (Genesis 29,1–32,2)* (European University Studies; Series XXIII, Theology, Vol. 400; Frankfurt am Main, Germany: Peter Lang, 1990).

[65] D. Dieckmann, *Segen für Isaak—Eine rezeptionsästhetische Auslegung von Gen 26 und Kotexten* (BZAW 329; Berlin, Germany: Walter de Gruyter, 2003).

[66] M. Fishbane, *Text and Texture* (New York, USA: Schocken Books Inc., 1979; J.P. Fokkelman, *Narrative Art in Genesis* (ed. D.E. Orton; JSOTSup 12; Sheffield, UK: JSOT Press (an inprint of Sheffield Academic Press Ltd), 1991); R. Alter, *The Art of Biblical Narrative* (New York: Basic Books, 1981); M. Sternberg, *The Poetics of Biblical Narrative: Ideological Literature and the Drama of Reading* (Bloomington, Indiana, USA: Indiana University Press, 1987). D.M. Gunn, "Hebrew Narrative," in *Text in Context: Essays by Members of the Society for Old Testament Study* (ed. A.D.H. Mayes; Oxford, UK: Oxford University Press, 2000) maps the developments in the field of Hebrew narrative.

1.2.5 *Monographs on Related Topics*

Besides monographs that focus on aspects of the Jacob-cycle, also certain monographs with a wider focus (e.g. Genesis, Pentateuch), contribute to our topic. A good example is Clines' *The Theme of the Pentateuch*, considered by many to be a key contribution for a better understanding of the Pentateuch as a whole.[67] Clines looks at all the promises made to the patriarchs and their (partial) fulfilment as recorded in Genesis and the rest of the Pentateuch. Some earlier contributions in this area include *Die Verheissungen an die drei Erzväter* (Hoftijzer 1956) and *The Promises to the Fathers: Studies on the Patriarchal Narrative* (Westermann 1980).[68]

An important issue to investigate is the relation between God's promises to the patriarchs and Jacob's wealth. As part of this investigation I will consider the relationship between blessing and wealth in Genesis in more detail. Some of the recent studies done on the topic of 'blessing' are: Grüneberg's *Abraham, Blessing and the Nations: A Philological and Exegetical Study of Genesis 12:3 in its Narrative Context*, in which he investigates God's blessing upon Abraham in Gen 12:3 (the blessing for the nations). It contains a very useful chapter on the various occurrences of √ברך in Genesis.[69] Mitchell has carried out a similar word-study for the whole of the OT in his dissertation *The Meaning of BRK "To Bless" in the Old Testament* (1987).[70] An outstanding recent publication on the topic of blessing that must be mentioned is Frettlöh's *Theologie des Segens* (2005).[71] Although the scope of Frettlöh's project vastly exceeds the Jacob-cycle, her book contains

---

[67] See Wenham, *Genesis 1–15*, xxxiii; Waltke, *Genesis*, 45; Hamilton, *Genesis 1–17*, 42; Brueggemann, *Genesis*, 19; I Provan, V. Philips Long and T. Longman III, *A Biblical History of Israel* (London, UK: Westminster John Knox Press, 2003), 328; McKeown, *Genesis*, 196–197.

[68] J. Hoftijzer, *Die Verheissungen an die drei Erzväter* (Leiden, The Netherlands: Brill, 1956); C. Westermann, *The Promises to the Fathers: Studies on the patriarchal narrative* (Philadelphia, USA: Fortress 1980).

[69] K.N. Grüneberg, *Abraham, Blessing and the Nations: A Philological and Exegetical Study of Genesis 12:3 in its Narrative Context* (BZAW 332; Berlin, Germany: Walter de Gruyter, 2003), chapter 5, 90–122.

[70] C.W. Mitchell, *The Meaning of BRK "To Bless" in the Old Testament* (SBL Dissertation Series 95; Atlanta, Georgia, USA: Scholars Press, 1987).

[71] M.L. Frettlöh, *Theologie des Segens: biblische und dogmatishe Wahrnehmungen* (Gütersloh, Germany: Gütersloher Verlagshaus, 2005).

several references to Genesis. It also contains very good discussions regarding the work of other theologians in this area.[72]

Other recent monographs deal with 'related topics' such as: plot announcement in Genesis (Turner 1990);[73] vows in the Hebrew Bible (Cartledge 1992);[74] reversed primogeniture (Syrén 1993);[75] dreams in Genesis (Lipton 1999);[76] the character of God (Humphreys 2001);[77] and deception in Genesis (Williams 2001).[78]

All these monographs have something to contribute to my study whether it is with regard to methodologies that are applied creatively, or the way these studies enlighten our topic of interest (e.g. how are we to understand deception in Genesis properly and how does that inform our understanding of patriarchal wealth?). These monographs also show the potential for gaining new insight by researching topical areas with a focused approach.

1.2.6   Other Approaches

Scholars from very different areas of discipline have occupied themselves with the patriarchs or with the Jacob narrative(s). Several studies have been carried out to enlighten the sociological, anthropological, cultural and historic settings of the patriarchs and early Israel.[79] All

---

[72] E.g. C. Westermann, *Blessing in the Bible and the Life of the Church* (Philadelphia, USA: Fortress, 1978).

[73] L.A. Turner, *Announcements of Plot in Genesis* (JSOTSup 96; Sheffield, UK: Sheffield Academic Press, 1990).

[74] T.W. Cartledge, *Vows in the Hebrew Bible and the Ancient Near East* (JSOTSup 147; Sheffield, UK: Sheffield Academic Press, 1992).

[75] R. Syrén, *The Forsaken First-Born: A Study of a Recurrent Motif in the Patriarchal Narratives* (JSOTSup 133; Sheffield, UK: Sheffield Academic Press, 1993).

[76] D. Lipton, *Revisions of the Night: Politics and Promises in the Patriarchal Dreams of Genesis* (JSOTSup 288; ed. D.J.A. Clines and P.R. Davies; Sheffield, UK: Sheffield Academic Press, 1999).

[77] W.L. Humphreys, *The Character of God in the Book of Genesis: A Narrative Appraisal* (Louisville, Kentucky, USA: Westminster John Knox Press, 2001).

[78] M.J. Williams, *Deception in Genesis: An Investigation into the Morality of a Unique Biblical Phenomenon* (ed. H. Gossai; New York, USA: Peter Lang Publishing Inc., 2001).

[79] E.g. R. de Vaux, *Ancient Israel* (trans. J. McHugh; London, UK: Darton, Longman & Todd Ltd., 1968); A.R. Millard and D.J. Wiseman, eds. *Essays on the Patriarchal Narratives* (Leicester, UK: Inter-Varsity Press, 1980); Provan, *A Biblical History of Israel*; W.C. Kaiser Jr., *A History of Israel: From the Bronze Age Through the Jewish Wars* (Nashville, TN, USA: Broadman & Holman Publishers, 1998); J.M. Miller and J.H. Hayes, *A History of Ancient Israel and Judah* (London, UK: SCM Press, 1999); and the more recent K.A. Kitchen, *On the Reliability of the Old Testament* (Grand Rapids, Michigan, USA: Wm. B. Eerdmans Publishing Co., 2003).

these could (potentially) provide us with valuable insights concerning the material possessions of the patriarchs.

I also intend to engage with contributions made by feminist theologians. A common critique of feminist scholars on the patriarchal narratives is that they are written with a patriarchal bias, which oppresses women and treats them as chattels. A number of feminist studies have been done on Genesis and on the women in the Jacob narrative(s); I will engage with such studies throughout this book.[80]

Jewish commentators throughout the centuries have commented extensively on Genesis and on the patriarchal narratives.[81] Their approaches and perspectives can be quite different, but their contributions are often thought provoking and refreshing. More recently, various psycho-analytical studies have been conducted on the various players and dynamics in the Jacob narrative(s). It is impossible to engage with all these approaches in detail or offer detailed critiques. However, I aim to be open to what they have to offer regarding our topic of interest.

1.2.7   *Conclusions*

Patriarchal wealth can be studied from many different angles. It is clear that so far no in-depth study on material possessions in Gen 12–50 (or in the Jacob-cycle) has been carried out. Scholars who have approached Gen 12–50 as part of a larger study (e.g. Blomberg,

---

[80] E.g. A. Brenner, ed., *A Feminist Companion to Genesis* (Sheffield, UK: Sheffield Academic Press, 1993). S.P. Jeansonne, *The Women of Genesis* (Minneapolis, USA: Fortress Press, 1990); J.C. Exum, *Fragmented Women: Feminist (Sub)versions of Biblical Narratives* (JSOTSup 163; Sheffield, UK: Sheffield Academic Press, 1993); I. Fischer, *Die Erzeltern Israels: Feministisch-theologische Studien zu Genesis 12–36* (BZAW 222; ed. O. Kaiser; Berlin, Germany: Walter de Gruyter, 1994); and T. Frymer-Kensky, *Reading the Women of the Bible* (New York, USA: Schocken Books, 2002). For an overview of this field of study I refer to J.C. Exum, "Feminist Study of the Old Testament," in *Text in Context: Essays by Members of the Society for Old Testament Study* (ed. A.D.H. Mayes; Oxford, UK: Oxford University Press, 2000); T. Frymer-Kensky, *Studies in Bible and Feminist Criticism* (Philadelphia, USA: The Jewish Publication Society, 2006) and E.W. Davies, *The Dissenting Reader: Feminist Approaches to the Hebrew Bible* (Aldershot, UK: Ashgate, 2003).

[81] In addition to the contributions made to recent literary study of the Hebrew Bible by Jewish scholars (e.g. Alter, *The Art of Biblical Narrative*; Berlin, *Poetics*; M. Sternberg, *Poetics*; S. Bar-Efrat, *Narrative Art in the Bible* (London, UK: T&T Clark International, 1989); see R.W.L. Moberly, *The Bible, Theology and Faith: A Study of Abraham and Jesus* (eds. C Gunton and D.W. Hardy; Cambridge, UK: Cambridge University Press, 2000), 14).

Schneider, and Hoppe) have devoted relatively little attention to patriarchal wealth. Although extensive work has been done in the recent
past (and continues to be done) on Genesis, Jacob and related topics
(e.g. blessing; vows; the forsaken first-born; dreams; presence-absence
of God; characterization of God; deception; ethics etc), it appears that
there is need for an in-depth study on the nature and role of material possessions in Gen 12–50 itself. Considering the large amount of
material, this study will focus on Jacob's possessions as described in
the Jacob-cycle (Gen 25:19–35:29).

But is this topic worthy of a scholarly effort, or is it all a bit 'too
applied?' I am convinced that such an effort is required. The patriarchal narratives offer serious hermeneutical challenges, caused in
part by the fact that it is not always straightforward to determine the
ethical stance of the narrator.[82] Although some biblical scholars have
commented on certain aspects or occurrences of material possessions
in the Jacob-cycle, no integrated study has been produced as of yet.
Scholars, who have commented on patriarchal wealth, have not always
produced satisfactory interpretations because of an apparent lack of
integration and/or depth. Larger constructs (e.g. a biblical theology of
possessions) could benefit from a more in-depth effort on one of its
foundational parts. Finally, topical monographs on other aspects of the
Jacob narrative(s) show that valuable insights can be gained by such a
focussed approach. This is an encouragement for my own endeavour.

As there appears to be an under-explored area for research, and as
the topic seems to be worth the effort, let us see how best to pursue
this investigation.

1.3   Methodology

It is my aim to examine the nature and role of material possessions in
the Jacob-cycle (Gen 25:19–35:29) and to present findings in a comprehensive way. To do this well, a strategy is required that will effectively engage with the various challenges posed by the text. I will start
by clarifying my presuppositions, followed by a short discussion on
assumptions and approaches regarding text and meaning.[83] This will

---

[82] Wenham, *Story as Torah*, 2.
[83] For a comprehensive discussion on presuppositions: W.W. Klein, C.L. Blomberg
and R.L. Hubbard Jr., *Introduction to Biblical Interpretation* (Nashville, Tennessee,
USA: W Publishing Group, 1993), 87–116.

influence which exegetical and interpretive methods are deemed suitable for the study at hand. I will then carry out my own exegesis and interpretation on the entire text of the Jacob-cycle, and will engage with the work of others in the process (Chapters 2–4). Finally, results will be integrated and evaluated (Chapter 5).[84] It is my aim to arrive at an intermediate theological construct that better describes the nature and role of material possessions in the Jacob-cycle than is currently available. I aim to adhere to a scholarly standard of biblical research, and I hope that this project will aid 'comprehension of the faith' and its application.[85] Although presuppositions, understanding regarding text and meaning, and selection of methodology are all interrelated, I will discuss these under separate headings.

1.3.1   *What Sort of Presuppositions?*

Every theologian will readily admit that interpretations, which are totally objective and un-predetermined, are impossible.[86] Every interpreter operates from "a perspective provided by one's preunderstanding."[87] This is not necessarily a bad thing. Osborne rightly notes that preunderstanding "only becomes negative if it degenerates into an a-priori grid that determines the meaning of a text before the act of reading even begins."[88] Osborne thus distinguishes 'presuppositions' (positive preunderstanding) from 'prejudice' (negative preunderstanding).[89] Goldsworthy defines presuppositions as "the assumptions we make in

---

[84] What Barton calls 'an independent system' (J. Barton, *Reading the Old Testament* (London, UK: Darton, Long and Todd Ltd., 2003), 162).

[85] Martens, *God's Design*, 295. See Moberly, *The Bible, Theology and Faith*, 2 on how to keep these last two objectives in balance.

[86] J. Goldingay, "The Study of Old Testament Theology: Its Aims and Purpose," *TynBul*, no. 2 (1975): 37–39, as quoted by R.B. Zuck, E.H. Merrill, and D.L. Bock, *A Biblical Theology of the Old Testament* (Chicago, USA: Moody Press, 1996) in their *Introduction*. Cf. G.R. Osborne, *The Hermeneutical Spiral* (Downers Grove, Illinois, USA: Inter-Varsity Press, 1991), 412–413.

[87] Osborne, *The Hermeneutical Spiral*, 412.

[88] Osborne, *The Hermeneutical Spiral*, 412.

[89] These terms are not applied consistently by practitioners in the field. For example, Thiselton's use of 'presupposition' fits Osborne's definition of 'prejudice,' whereas his use of 'pre-understanding' fits Osborne's use of 'presupposition.' Thiselton traces the attention for the role of presuppositions back to Bultmann's essay "Is Exegesis without Presuppositions Possible?" (R. Bultmann, *Existence and Faith: Shorter Writings of Rudolph Bultmann* (London, UK: Fontana, 1964)). Thiselton notes that Bultmann's use of this phrase goes back to Schleiermacher, and that the phrase 'pre-understanding' (*Vorverständnis*) goes back to Dilthey (A.J. Thiselton, *New Horizons in Hermeneutics* (Grand Rapids, Michigan, USA: Zondervan, 1992), 45).

order to be able to hold some fact to be true."[90] Although such pre-suppositions are inevitable, they are neither static nor unchangeable, but can be challenged and transformed.[91] They can be reshaped by an encounter with the text itself (the OT) if the interpreter is willing to place him- or herself 'in front of the text' (Ricoeur).[92] This cannot happen if the OT is approached as a mere research 'object' from a 'stance of mastery.'[93] Instead, the OT needs to be studied with humility and heard 'on its own terms.'[94] The text of the Jacob-cycle (within Genesis as a whole), provides us with various parameters on how the text should be read (see *Section* 1.3.2). Presuppositions must also be shaped by an open and critical dialogue with other positions that are not 'our own,' with a willingness to adjust one's viewpoint when alternative interpretations prove to be better.[95] In addition, good hermeneutical principles are essential to "control our tendency to read our prejudices into the text."[96]

Although it is impossible to *fully* delineate one's presuppositions, it is good to be aware of their existence and to delineate them as much as we can.[97] Other presuppositions are elusive.[98] This is *exactly* why it is

---

[90] Graeme Goldsworthy, *According to Plan* (Leicester, UK: Inter-Varsity Press, 1991), 54. They are also known as preconceptions or preliminary assumptions (R.W. Yarbrough, "Biblical Theology," in *Evangelical Dictionary of Biblical Theology* (ed. W.A. Elwell; Grand Rapids, Michigan, USA: Baker Books, 2000), 62).

[91] Cf. Thiselton, *New Horizons in Hermeneutics*, 31–35; Klein, *Introduction to Biblical Interpretation*, 91; Osborne, *The Hermeneutical Spiral*, 412–413.

[92] Osborne, *The Hermeneutical Spiral*, 412.

[93] G.D. Fee, *Listening to the Spirit in the Text* (Grand Rapids, Michigan, USA: Wm. B. Eerdmans Publishing Co., 2000), 8.

[94] Some will consider this to be impossible ('vain nonsense,' Hauerwas as quoted by K.J. Vanhoozer, *Is There Meaning in This Text?* (Leicester, UK: Apollos, 1998), 411). See also Fee, *Listening to the Spirit in the Text*, 14 and Osborne, *The Hermeneutical Spiral*, 282.

[95] I aim to engage graciously with anybody with different perspectives than my own. I operate with, what Hays calls, a 'hermeneutic of trust' (R.B. Hays, *The Conversion of the Imagination: Paul as Interpreter of Israel's Scripture* (Grand Rapids, Michigan, USA: Wm. B. Eerdmans Publishing Company, 2005), 190ff.), which is open to 'critical dialogue' (Osborne, *The Hermeneutical Spiral*, 412), even with those who approach the text with a 'hermeneutic of suspicion' (Hays, *The Conversion of the Imagination*, 197ff.).

[96] Osborne, *The Hermeneutical Spiral*, 413.

[97] In the process of reading, the text can challenge subconscious preunderstanding. I assume that the majority of one's presuppositions can be identified over time *if* one is willing to have one's presuppositions examined and tested in the ways described above (cf. Osborne, *The Hermeneutical Spiral*, 412).

[98] See Klein, *Introduction to Biblical Interpretation*, 87ff. and Vanhoozer, *Is There Meaning in This Text?*, 54–55.

important to engage with different angles of observation, to minimize and challenge one's preconceptions. Therefore, I will engage with a broad spectrum of commentators and writers, while keeping the biblical text as my primary frame of reference.

Finally, presuppositions are not just liabilities that impair our vision, they also define who we are and in a strange way enable us to see things that others may not see.[99] My presuppositions will be further clarified by my discussion on 'text,' 'meaning' and 'method(s)' below, and by the rest of this study.[100]

1.3.2   *What Sort of Text?*

Some of my presuppositions relate to the nature of the biblical text. What more can be said about the text of the Jacob-cycle? To answer this, I must discuss the current state of scholarly understanding regarding the shape and meaning of the text, and the various methods to enlighten these. These are complex issues that continue to be subject to scholarly debate. I will sketch the outlines of two different approaches that have dominated biblical scholarship. One approach focuses on the apparent tensions and inconsistencies in the text, while the other approach assumes its inherent unity. Philips Long rightly states that "neither of these assumptions is patently correct, and both should be open to correction in the light of the evidence."[101]

---

[99] "We cannot avoid or deny the presence of preunderstanding in the task of biblical interpretation. Every interpreter comes to study the Bible with prior biases and dispositions. If we ask about the origin or basis of our preunderstanding, we will find it in our prior experiences, conditioning and training—politically social, cultural, psychological, and religious—in short, all our lives up to this point. Even our native language influences our view of reality. All these colour and in many senses determine how we view the world. Each individual processes all these factors to frame a worldview" (Klein, *Introduction to Biblical Interpretation*, 100).

[100] For more background on my position: Klein, *Introduction to Biblical Interpretation*, 87–116, and specifically 111–114, who in turn is very much influenced by B. Ramm, "Biblical Interpretation," in *Hermeneutics* (ed. B. Ramm; Grand Rapids, Michigan, USA: Baker Books, 1987), 18–28. See also E.J. Schnabel, "Scripture," in *New Dictionary of Biblical Theology* (ed. T.D. Alexander and B.S. Rosner; Leicester, England: Inter-Varsity Press, 2000), 32–42; C.L. Blomberg, "The Unity and Diversity of Scripture," also in *New Dictionary of Biblical Theology*; Osborne, *The Hermeneutical Spiral*, 274ff; Yarbrough, "Biblical Theology," 62; J.I. Packer, "Hermeneutics and Biblical Authority," in *Solid Ground* (eds. C.R. Trueman, T.J. Gray and C.L. Blomberg; Leicester, UK: Apollos, 1975), specifically 138–142.

[101] V. Philips Long, "Reading the Old Testament as Literature," in *Interpreting the Old Testament: A Guide for Exegesis* (ed. C.C. Broyles; Grand Rapids, MI, USA: Baker Academic, 2001), 96.

Since the Enlightenment, the historical-critical method has dominated the field of biblical studies.[102] Traditionally, historical criticism
focused mainly on issues related to the pre-history of the text (diachronic study). Understanding the historical setting of the original
author and audience; the history of textual sources, transmission and
editorial composition, are all deemed essential to understand the text
in its current form. Disciplines like source-, form-, and redaction criticism aim to study and clarify such issues.[103] Because numerous issues
remain unsettled, these methods sometimes fail to enhance interpretation of the text in its current (final) form. As a result, some have
abandoned the enterprise altogether to explore completely different
approaches.[104]

Over the last thirty years, scholarly attention has shifted towards
studying the text in its final form. Brodie's comments are illustrative: "The primary path to meaning, and even to history and social
background, is the finished text. The finished text is the number one
artefact."[105] Literary criticism, which shares this sentiment, has produced many fresh insights:[106]

---

[102] Wenham, *Story as Torah*, 5.

[103] For a useful discussion on these various methods and how there relate to each
other, see S.L. McKenzie and S.R. Haynes eds., *To Each Its Own Meaning* (Louisville,
Kentucky, USA: Westminster John Knox Press 1999) and Barton, *Reading the Old
Testament*.

[104] Exum, for example, considers source-criticism *'questionable in any event'*
(Exum, *Fragmented Women: Feminist (Sub)versions of Biblical Narratives*, 94 n. 1,
italics mine). Rendsburg suggests that based on the realization that Genesis is much
more uniform than generally assumed, "the standard division of Genesis into J, E and
P strands should be discarded" (G.A. Rendsburg, *The Redaction of Genesis* (Winona
Lake, Indiana, USA: Eisenbrauns, 1986), 105). For a good overview of the state of
Pentateuchal criticism, see D.A. Knight, "The Pentateuch," in *The Hebrew Bible and
it's Modern Interpreters* (eds. D.A. Knight and G.M. Tucker; Philadelphia, Pennsylvania, USA: Fortress Press, 1985); R.N. Whybray, *The Making of the Pentateuch* (JSOT-
Sup 53; Sheffield, UK: Sheffield Academic Press, 1987); R.N. Whybray, *Introduction
to the Pentateuch* (Grand Rapids, MI, USA: Eerdmans Publishing Company, 1995),
12–13, and more recently G.J. Wenham, "Pondering the Pentateuch: The Search for
a New Paradigm," in *The Face of Old Testament Studies: A Survey of Contemporary
Approaches* (eds. D.W. Baker and B.T. Arnold; Grand Rapids, Michigan, USA: Baker
Books, 2004) and T.D. Alexander, *From Paradise to the Promised Land* (Carlisle, UK:
Paternoster Press, 2002), 42–61.

[105] Brodie, *Genesis as Dialogue*, xi. Similarly D.W. Baker, "Diversity and Unity in
the Literary Structure of Genesis," in *Essays on the Patriarchal Narratives* (eds. A.R.
Millard and D.J. Wiseman; Leicester, UK: Inter-Varsity Press, 1980), 189.

[106] Key contributions of literary criticism to the field of biblical studies have been
mentioned already. See also *The Literary Guide to the Bible* (eds. R. Alter and F. Kermode, *The Literary Guide to the Bible* (London, UK: Collins, 1987).

> As recent literary criticism of the Bible recognizes, the final form of the
> text is not a haphazard product but rather the result of complex and
> meaningful redactional patterning[107]

Because of this focus on the text in its 'final form' (synchronic study) a
divide has opened up between synchronic and diachronic methodologies. Some scholars accept the divide as it is, and do not see a reason
(or possibility) to bring the two together. Others see good reason to
keep the two in conversation.[108] Both method types have their own
applicability, but in their extreme forms suffer from 'blind spots:'

> The purely diachronic approach of the tradition-critical study, (…)
> ignores the poetic function of the narrative, and the purely synchronic
> approach of structuralism, (…) fails to appreciate the distance between
> the interpreter and the text.[109]

Ideally, one would like to avoid such extremes and find synergies
between these two approaches.[110] Although this is acknowledged by
many, the divide remains. Wenham laments that "though most final-
form studies pay lip service to the continuing place of diachronic
study, few have really attempted to create a new synthesis bringing
together the two disciplines."[111] However, this has proved to be a real

---

[107] J.C. Exum, "Who's Afraid of 'the Endangered Ancestress'?," in *The New Literary Criticism and the Hebrew Bible* (eds. J.C. Exum and D.J.A. Clines; Sheffield, UK:
Sheffield Academic Press, 1993), 99.

[108] Cf. J.C. de Moor, ed., *Synchronic or Diachronic? A Debate on Method in Old
Testament Exegesis* (Leiden, The Netherlands: Brill, 1995) for a useful collection of
essays on this topic.

[109] Osborne, *The Hermeneutical Spiral*, 374. See also Philips Long, "Reading the
Old Testament as Literature," 96 as quoted above. Hoftijzer notes that the terms 'synchronic' and 'diachronic' could be ambiguous because they are used in a completely
different way in literary studies. Instead, he prefers the terms 'compositional/redac-
tional' and 'structural' (J. Hoftijzer, "Holistic or Compositional Approach? Linguistic Remarks to the Problem," in *Synchronic or Diachronic? A Debate on Method in
Old Testament Exegesis* (ed. J.C. De Moor; Leiden, The Netherlands: E.J. Brill, 1995),
98). In biblical studies however, 'synchronic' and 'diachronic' appear to have become
entirely accepted terms.

[110] For example, close attention to literary features may well enlighten historical
issues (Clines, *The Theme of the Pentateuch*, as discussed by Wenham, "Pondering
the Pentateuch: The Search for a New Paradigm," 141, and D.M. Carr, *Reading the
Fractures of Genesis—Historical and Literary Approaches* (Louisville, Kentucky, USA:
Westminster John Knox Press, 1996), viii.

[111] Wenham, *Story as Torah*, 141–142. Wenham refers to the work of Moberly as
a good example of a scholar who has tried to develop such a synthesis. Walton (a
Moberly student) has produced such a synthesis for the Jacob narrative. I will comment on his contribution in the course of this study.

challenge.[112] Attempts to bring the two together have met with mixed success.[113]

My study will not produce such a synthesis. I will focus on the text in its final form,[114] but I do not consider historical insights un-important. The history of sources and composition might not be relevant for this study, but an informed historical understanding on issues like 'birthright' and 'blessing' might well be. Proper understanding of such topics requires (wherever possible) knowledge of the historical context(s) in which these texts were written (edited) and received.[115] However, we must negotiate the historical divide with care. In some cases available historical data are 'thin' or non-existent. Considering such uncertainty, certain conclusions must remain tentative. Discipline is required to distinguish hypothesis from fact. Integrating hypotheses within a theological construct is not necessarily problematic, as long as we are willing to label them as such, and to abandon them when better ones come along.[116]

Whatever we consider to be true about the history of the composition of Genesis, it is clear that the author (or final redactor) has made serious efforts to present his material in a coherent form.

> The author/compiler has clearly integrated its apparently diverse contents to provide a literary work which exhibits much greater unity than is generally recognized or acknowledged.[117]

---

[112] Walton, *Thou Traveller Unknown*, 6.

[113] Sometimes synchronic and diachronic readings are merely presented alongside each other, without any effort to integrate them (e.g. E. Boase, "Life in the Shadows: The Role and Function of Isaac in Genesis—Synchronic and Diachronic Readings," *VT* 51, no. 3 (2001): 312–35). A careful and creative attempt to synthesize these approaches is Carr's *Reading the Fractures of Genesis*. Carr's proposals are interesting and his results are well presented, however I was left with the impression that the whole proposal is very tenuous. For a useful discussion of Carr's work, Grüneberg, *Verheissung und Erfüllung*, 6–8.

[114] An approach taken by many modern narrative studies (Wenham, *Story as Torah*, 7). For a similar approach see: Grüneberg, *Verheissung und Erfüllung*; Humphreys, *The Character of God*; Turner, *Announcements of Plot in Genesis*; McKeown, *Genesis*. I agree with Grüneberg that because diachronic hypotheses are often "exceedingly insecure, they will hardly provide much support for arguments concerning the meaning of the final form" (Grüneberg, *Verheissung und Erfüllung*, 11).

[115] Cf. Osborne, *The Hermeneutical Spiral*, 413 on the place of 'critico-historical exegesis.'

[116] A similar sentiment is expressed by D.A. Knight, "Introduction: Ethics, Ancient Israel and the Hebrew Bible," *Semeia* 66 (1994): 1–8, 6.

[117] T.D. Alexander, "Genealogies, Seed and the Compositional Unity of Genesis," *TynBul* 44, no. 2 (1993): 255–70. See also Alter, *The Art of Biblical Narrative* (Chapter 1).

The main structural feature of Genesis is the so-called '*toledot* formula,' which provides a framework in which the various Genesis stories are organized.[118] Five *toledot* statements occur in Gen 1–11. Five occur in Gen 12–50[119] with Gen 12:1–3 seen by many to be the pivot point in Genesis.[120] As such, the history of Israel is placed within a universal backdrop, which describes the formation of the nations going back to creation.[121] Within this macro-structure, various themes appear and are developed. There are the big themes of blessing and curse.[122]

Terino argues for coherence in the Jacob narrative from a linguistic and rhetorical perspective (J. Terino, "A Text Linguistic Study of the Jacob Narrative," *Vox Evangelica* 18 (1988): 45–62). "There is much more uniformity and much less fragmentation in the book of Genesis than generally assumed" (Rendsburg, *The Redaction of Genesis*, 105). Already noted by Church, *The Israel Saga*, 141 (I am indebted to Sherwood, *"Had God Not Been on My Side,"* 3 for this reference). See also Gammie, "Theological Interpretation," 123.

[118] אֵלֶּה תּוֹלְדֹת 'this is the (family) history of,' often discuss the account of the descendants of the named ancestor (e.g. Gen 25:19) (Waltke, *Genesis*, 18). The genealogies provide the continuity framework within which narrative plot is developed and resolved (N. Steinberg, "The Genealogical Framework of the Family Stories in Genesis," *Semeia* 46 (1989): 41–50). See also J.P. Fokkelman, "Genesis," in *The Literary Guide to the Bible* (eds. R. Alter and F. Kermode; London, UK: Collins, 1987), 41; Wenham, *Genesis 1–15*, xxi–xxii; Hamilton, *Genesis 1–17*, 2–10 and Kitchen, *On the Reliability of the Old Testament*, 314. Rendtorff notes that a second framework is provided by notes on the death and burial of the patriarchs by their sons (25:17; 35:29; 49:33 and 50:13; R. Rendtorff, *The Old Testament: An Introduction* (trans. J. Bowden; London, UK: SCM Press Ltd, 1985), 138). Finally, Baker notes that the '*toledot*' formula is by no means the only division marker in Genesis (Baker, "Diversity and Unity in the Literary Structure of Genesis," 195–197), and that it is important to consider both the unity and the diversity of the Genesis material (similarly T.W. Mann, "'All the Families of the Earth': The Theological Unity of Genesis," *Int* 45, no. 4 (1991): 341–53, 342–343).

[119] Six if the "reduplication of 36:1, 9 are counted separately" (Wenham, *Genesis 1–15*, xxi). Cf. Hamilton, *Genesis 1–17*, 2 and Waltke, *Genesis*, 18 (especially n. 5).

[120] "The 'epicentre' of the book's narrative movement, shaping what precedes it as much as what succeeds it" (H. White, *Narration and Discourse in the Book of Genesis* (Cambridge, United Kingdom: Cambridge University Press, 1991), 109).

[121] "Because of this welding of primeval history and saving history, the whole of Israel's saving history is properly to be understood with reference to the unsolved problem of Jahweh's relationship to the nations" (G. von Rad, *Old Testament Theology* (vol. 1; London, UK: SCM Press Ltd., 1979), 164). See also W.J. Dumbrell, *Covenant & Creation* (Exeter, UK: Paternoster Press, 1984), 47ff.; Grüneberg, *Verheissung und Erfüllung*, 1–3; Moberly, *The Bible, Theology and Faith*, 122–126.

[122] 'Blessing' occurs 3x in Gen 1–2, 'cursed' 5x in Gen 3–11. These 'curses' are countered by 5 mentions of 'blessing' in Gen 12:1–3 (Wenham, *Genesis 1–15*, 270; J.G. Janzen, *Genesis 12–50* (Grand Rapids, Michigan, USA: Wm. B. Eerdmans Publishing Company, 1993), 17–18). "Blessing not only connects the patriarchal narratives with each other (cf. 24:1; 26:3; 35:9; 39:5), it also links them with the primeval history (cf. 1:28; 5:2; 9:1). The promises of blessing to the patriarchs are thus a reassertion of

Related to these are God's promises (and their partial fulfilment) to
Abraham and his descendants of land, descendants ('seed')[123] and covenantal relationship (Clines). "Practically everything within chapters
12–50 may be seen as related to these topics."[124] Fokkelman interprets
the "overriding concern of the entire book" as "life-survival-offspring-
fertility-continuity."[125] God's intention for fruitfulness is juxtaposed
with barrenness (e.g. Sarah, Rebecca, Rachel). Yet, towards the end
of Genesis, Jacob's descendants 'were fruitful and multiplied greatly'
(47:23). This theme recurs in Ex 1:7.

The Jacob-cycle is very much embedded in the overall Genesis construct. Also within the Jacob narrative itself, clear structures can be
identified. Fishbane has shown how the Jacob-cycle is organized in
a concentric pattern, with the birth of Joseph and Jacob's decision to
return to Canaan at its centre (Gen 30:22–25), and the key-phrases
'encounter' and 'blessing' occurring throughout the cycle.[126] The various structures within Genesis and within the Jacob-cycle are our guide
on how to interpret the material they contain.[127] In Chapter 2–4 it will
become clear how that might work in practice.

It is within these intentional structures that we are presented with
some fascinating stories. Much work has been done to enlighten its
beauty over the last thirty years.[128] This narrative art operates (and
therefore needs to be analyzed) on various levels.[129] "In Genesis, powerful means of integration are used at the levels of genre, theme, plot,
content and key words."[130] The references to material possessions in

---

God's original intentions for man" (Wenham, *Genesis 1–15*, 275). See also Sailhamer,
Genesis on Gen 12:1–3.

[123] Maybe the most important of the unifying themes (Alexander, "Genealogies, Seed and the Compositional Unity of Genesis"). According to McKeown it is
(McKeown, *Genesis*, 197ff.).

[124] Wenham, *Story as Torah*, 37.

[125] Fokkelman, "Genesis," 41.

[126] Fishbane, 40–62. Many have built on Fishbane's work: e.g. Rendsburg, *The
Redaction of Genesis*; McKeown, *Genesis*, 238–239. See the opening paragraphs of
Chapter 2.

[127] Gammie, "Theological Interpretation," 121; Waltke, *Genesis*, 17–54; Parry, *Old
Testament Story and Christian Ethics*, xix.

[128] Fishbane, *Text and Texture*; Alter, *The Art of Biblical Narrative*; Fokkelman,
Narrative Art in Genesis; Sternberg, *Poetics*.

[129] Fokkelman, *Narrative Art in Genesis*; J.P. Fokkelman, *Reading Biblical Narrative: An Introductory Guide* (trans. Ineke Smit; Louisville, Kentucky, USA: Westminster John Knox Press, 1999). See also Waltke's adaptation of Fokkelman's work
(Waltke, *Genesis*, 31–33).

[130] Fokkelman, "Genesis," 40.

the Jacob-cycle occur within a narrative text, and we need to respect the text for what it is, and how it relates to its various contexts. Barton rightly states that "we cannot extract 'the message' from a narrative text, and then throw away the text itself; a narrative text is its own meaning."[131] Similarly Peterson: "there are, of course, always moral, theological historical elements in these stories that need to be studied and ascertained, but never in spite or in defiance of the story that is being told."[132]

Certain scholars have focused on the *aesthetic* qualities of the text (e.g. Alter), while yet others point to the *didactic* qualities of the text (theology and ethics; e.g. Wenham). Sternberg treats biblical narrative as a "complex multifunctional discourse," which is "functionally regulated by a set of three principles: ideological, historiographic and aesthetic."[133] Longman III identifies three very similar aspects of 'the interpretive task:' literary, historical and theological.[134] Sternberg notes that although these principles form 'natural rivals,'[135] they are inseparably entwined:

> Considering the assortment of its interests, one marvels at the reconciliation of their claims and the interlacing of their teleologies. The three functional principles meet at a junction where they enter into relationships of tense complementarity.[136]

My interests (using Sternberg's phrase) are mainly 'ideological' (theology and ethics).[137] However, it is clear that it will not be straightforward

---

[131] Barton, *Reading the Old Testament*, 163. A similar warning is sounded by Fokkelman: "theologians tend to read the text as message, and to that end separate form from content without realizing that in doing so they violate the literary integrity of the text" (Fokkelman, "Genesis," 36).

[132] E.H. Peterson, *Eat This Book: The Art of Spiritual Reading* (London, UK: Hodder & Stoughton, 2006), 43.

[133] Sternberg, *Poetics*, 41.

[134] T. Longman III, "Literary Approaches to Old Testament Study," in *The Face of Old Testament Studies: A Survey of Contemporary Approaches* (eds. D.W. Baker and B.T. Arnold; Grand Rapids, Michigan, USA: Baker Books, 2004), 115 (earlier published in longer form in T. Longman III, "Literary Approaches and Interpretation," in NIDOTTE 1:103–124. Cf. Wenham's methodology, which includes historical-, literary- and rhetorical criticism (Wenham, *Story as Torah*). Elsewhere, Wenham has described his methodology as "trying to use the methods of Sternberg within a framework akin to von Rad's" (Wenham, "The Face at the Bottom of the Well," 202).

[135] Waltke, *Genesis*, 44.

[136] Waltke, *Genesis*, 44.

[137] "Old Testament narrative books do have a didactic purpose, that is, they are trying to instil both theological truths and ethical ideals into their readers" (Wenham, *Story as Torah*, 3).

to neatly 'extract' ideological content from the text.[138] Added to this challenge is the one noted above, that although the narrator 'teaches by telling stories' (Waltke), the ethical stance of the narrator is not always clear (Wenham).

Whatever our opinion about the history of sources and composition of the Jacob-cycle, it is clear that in its final form its overall shape can be considered coherent.[139] I concur with Brodie that "Genesis was indeed composed with extraordinary complexity and precision."[140] While acknowledging this coherence, I intend to be sensitive to the various ambiguities and tensions in the text. I realize that "the biblical text is something with rough edges, set over against us, not necessarily speaking with one voice, coming to us from a great distance and needing to be weighed and tested even as *it* tests and challenges us."[141] It is within the context of these compositional structures and the rich content and tensions they contain, that I will look at the concept of meaning, especially regarding the nature and role of material possessions in the Jacob-cycle.

1.3.3   *What Sort of Meaning?*

Our assumptions about the 'text' influence our understanding of its 'meaning.' It is to be expected that the diversity of opinion regarding 'text' is matched by a similar diversity regarding 'meaning.' In recent discussions on the issue of 'meaning,' three 'worlds' are being considered: the world of the author; the world of the text; and the world of the reader.[142] The central issues in these discussions are:

- Which of these three 'worlds' has the primary force in determining meaning?
- How do these 'worlds' interact?

---

[138] This leads into the discussion whether meaning is 'extracted' or 'produced' (see below).

[139] Fischer, "Jakobs Rolle in der Genesis," 272.

[140] Brodie, *Genesis as Dialogue*, xv.

[141] Barton, *Reading the Old Testament*, 95.

[142] Some have refined this model by adding the 'implied author' and 'implied' reader, to clarify that we never can get back to the real author or his original audience (cf. Wenham, *Story as Torah*, 8ff.). Such a refinement is indeed welcome, but is not essential for our discussion at hand. See also Osborne, *The Hermeneutical Spiral*, chapter 6.

- If meaning is embedded in the text, what are the best means of 'extraction'?
- Or, is meaning 'produced' in the interplay between reader and text?[143]

Although this is not the place for a detailed discussion, it is important to realize how thinking has changed and developed in this area. Traditionally, the historical-critical method focussed on reconstructing the author's original message ('extraction'). With the ascent of New Criticism, emphasis shifted away from the author and the historical dimensions of the text, to focus almost exclusively on the form and texture of the text. Eventually the emphasis shifted again to approaches focussing heavily on the role of the reader in the process of 'generating' meaning.[144] For some, this development ultimately reached its logical conclusion where 'anything goes.'

It appears that any method that emphasizes one of these worlds at the exclusion of one or the other produces unsatisfactory results. Approaches that bring these three worlds in an *appropriate* conversation seem to offer a way forward. Tate suggests that "the hermeneutical task basically involves mediating between the text and a present situation."[145] However, Tate does not ignore the world of the author: "meaning results from a conversation between the world of the text and the world of the reader, a world *informed* by the world of the author."[146] Historical-critical methods are seen by Tate to provide a useful 'preparatory' function:

> If hermeneutics is willing to bring to bear upon interpretation the scholarship of differing critical approaches, the dialogue will inevitably be more informed, constructive, and pertinent.[147]

---

[143] W.R. Tate, *Biblical Interpretation* (Peabody, Massachusetts, USA: Hendrickson Publishers Inc., 1997), 254–255. See also R.P. Carroll, "The Reader and the Text," in *Text in Context: Essays by Members of the Society for Old Testament Study* (ed. A.D.H. Mayes; Oxford, UK: Oxford University Press, 2000).

[144] A shift has been noted, assigning a greater role back to the author (Osborne, *The Hermeneutical Spiral*, 393–395).

[145] Tate, *Biblical Interpretation*, 254.

[146] Tate, *Biblical Interpretation*, xxiv and 255 (italics mine). See also T.E. Fretheim, *The Pentateuch* (Nashville, Tennessee, USA Abingdon Press, 1996), 37: "The making of meaning, including theological meaning, is a product of the interaction of text and reader." Some scholars propose to change the word 'reader' into 'community' (e.g. Moberly, *The Bible, Theology and Faith*, 6).

[147] Tate, *Biblical Interpretation*, 255.

Considering the fact that interpreters bring various assumptions to the text, Tate describes hermeneutics as a *dynamic* and *productive* enterprise instead of a merely *reproductive* one.[148] Osborne's 'hermeneutical spiral' offers a useful paradigm to describe this dynamic interaction between 'understanding' and text.[149]

My objective to study the nature and role of material possessions in the Jacob-cycle fits Tate's definition of the hermeneutical task as "mediating between the text and a present situation."[150] Besides certain presuppositions I also bring certain questions to the text that will determine (to some extent) what sort of meaning is discovered. Questions like:

- How do possessions function in the narrative?
- What is suggested by the text about the attitudes associated with possessions?
- Does the narrator betray his stance, or are things more ambiguous?
- What elements in the remainder of the text are relevant for a good understanding of the nature and function(s) of material possessions in the narrative?
- Can we systematize our findings to some extent (without reducing the ambiguities or tensions that are evident in the text)?
- How well does this synthesis sit with the text?

Finding answers to these questions is not straightforward. Texts need to be interpreted within their appropriate form and context(s). Being mindful of Sternberg's observations about the text's historiographic, aesthetic and ideological elements being welded together, it will be a challenge to answer these questions inductively. Writing about material possessions was clearly not the primary motive for the author (or redactor), yet material possessions are not unimportant within Genesis either. As a result, we almost have to 'tease' answers on these questions out of the text.

In summary: my study is a dialogue between the world of the reader and the world of the text; a dialogue informed by the world of the author. This interaction between 'the three worlds' is ongoing

---

[148] Tate, *Biblical Interpretation*, 257.
[149] Osborne, *The Hermeneutical Spiral*.
[150] Tate, *Biblical Interpretation*, 254.

throughout the interpretation process of the Jacob-cycle in order that understanding regarding the nature and role of material possessions can grow inductively.[151] The understanding we gain with respect to one passage will influence how we read subsequent passages (the hermeneutical spiral). However, it may well happen that we unearth 'meaning' from different passages that appear to be contradictory.[152] The opening quotes of this chapter show very contrasting views on material possessions. God is clearly involved in some accounts of wealth generation in Genesis, while human struggle and sin appear to be in others. Should we necessarily try to explain or harmonize these apparent contradictions? One possible solution would be to treat material possessions as a multi-dimensional phenomenon. Some of the problems with interpreting patriarchal wealth may simply be explained by the fact that some commentators have ignored this so far.[153]

We must also consider whether a 'dialogical' model of the truth would better explain these apparent contradictions.[154] Newsom, building on the work of Bakhtin, suggests a model

> in which the 'truth' about a difficult issue can only be established by a community of unmerged perspectives, not by a single voice, not even that of God. (…) it resists the attempt to reduce (…) to an assertion, to encapsulate its 'meaning' in a statement, which is still the tendency of much scholarship (…) it balances against the tendency of a synthetic approach to get closure (…) this leaves space for hearing 'unmerged voices' in combination.[155]

---

[151] Walton, *Thou Traveller Unknown*, 6.

[152] Or 'interpretations that refuse closure' (W. Brueggemann, "Biblical Theology Appropriately Postmodern," in *Jews, Christians and the Theology of the Hebrew Scriptures* (eds. A. Ogden Bellis and J.S. Kaminsky; Atlanta, Georgia, USA: Society of Biblical Literature, 2000), 103ff.).

[153] This happens when we say that material possessions are a blessing, while ignoring the other dimensions. This is a form of under-interpretation. A similar thing happens when we say that Genesis is purely ideological writing, while ignoring its historiographic and aesthetic qualities.

[154] In our discussion on Gen 26, I will discuss the work of Brodie, who builds upon work of Newsom (C.A. Newsom, "Bakhtin, the Bible and Dialogical Truth," *JR* 76, no. 2 (1996): 290–306; T.L. Brodie, "Genesis as Dialogue: Genesis' Twenty-six Diptychs as a Key to Narrative Unity and Meaning," in *Studies in the Book of Genesis—Literature, Redaction and History* (ed. A. Wénin; Leuven, Belgium: Leuven University Press, 2001), 310–312), especially Brodie's commentary *Genesis as Dialogue*.

[155] Newsom, "Bakhtin, the Bible and Dialogical Truth," 298.

According to Brodie "truth is richer than any one statement."[156] I will
consider the applicability of these proposals for my topic in the course
of this study.

1.3.4   What Sort of Method(s)?

The great diversity in opinion on 'text' and 'meaning' finds its expression in a rich variety of 'methods.' Where in the past scholars might
have searched for *the* perfect method to analyze a text,[157] "contemporary biblical critics are delighted to have in their repertory a vast array
of methods; their skill is often to know which criticisms best to deploy
with a given text."[158] Longman III notes:

> The cutting edge of the field however, is not only varied in its approach
> to the literary study of the Bible, it is eclectic. That is, it utilizes not one
> but a variety of approaches at the same time.[159]

This is evident in the various approaches taken in studies of the
Jacob narrative(s).[160] No published study on Jacob is exactly the same.
Describing their merits and limitations is well beyond the scope of this
study.[161] Although this rich diversity makes it challenging to compare
and integrate results, I intend to cast my net widely.

The main objective of this study is to investigate the nature and
role of material possessions (and associated attitudes and actions) in
the Jacob-cycle. Considering everything I discussed about text and
meaning, it is clear that answers best appear inductively. So how to go
about this task responsibly? In short, my 'workflow' involves exegesis, interpretation and synthesis. This process is both 'inductive' and
'deductive.' To describe this approach, I find Osborne's descriptions
helpful:

---

[156] Brodie, "Genesis as Dialogue," 314.

[157] Barton even goes so far as to say that "…much harm has been done in biblical
studies by insisting that there is, somewhere, a 'correct' method which, if only we
could find it, would unlock the mysteries of the text" (Barton, *Reading the Old Testament*, 5).

[158] D.J.A. Clines and J.C. Exum, "The New Literary Criticism," in *The New Literary
Criticism and the Hebrew Bible* (eds. J.C. Exum and D.J.A. Clines; JSOTSup 143; Sheffield, UK: Sheffield Academic Press, 1993), 17.

[159] Longman III, "Literary Approaches to Old Testament Study," 111 (earlier published in Longman III, "Literary Approaches and Interpretation," 110). Similarly
J. Goldingay, *Models for Interpretation of Scripture* (Toronto, Canada: Clements Publishing, 1995), 1ff.

[160] Cf. Recker, *Die Erzählungen vom Patriarchen Jakob*.

[161] I will comment on these studies along the way.

> Inductively, the interpretation appears not from an inspired "guess" but from the structural, semantic and syntactical study of the text itself; in other words, it emerges from the text itself, which guides the interpreter to the proper meaning.[162]

And

> Deductively, a valid interpretation emerges by testing the results of the inductive research via a comparison with other scholars' theories and historical or background material derived from sources outside the text. One deepens, alters and at times replaces his or her theory on the basis of this external data, which is tested on the basis of coherence, adequacy and comprehensiveness.[163]

My *starting* point is the text in its final form. For this study I will focus on the Hebrew text as found in *Biblia Hebraica Stuttgartensia* (BHS), unless stated otherwise. English Bible quotations are taken from the *English Standard Version* (ESV), unless I have provided my own translation. For each chapter I divide the text in sub-units, which will first be studied in their own right. This "inductive approach, establishes the internal rhetorical features of cohesion (lexical, semantic and grammatical) as the primary criterion of divisions and discontinuity in the text."[164] Obviously, such features can be interpreted differently by different exegetes. Relevant passages will be studied in their appropriate context(s).[165] The main focus of this study will be on the Jacob-cycle (Gen 25:19–35:29) in the context of Genesis as a whole. In some instances, texts will be considered in a wider 'canonical context.'[166] However, I will spend most time interpreting relevant passages within

---

[162] Osborne, *The Hermeneutical Spiral*, 415. Terino notes that synchronic (linguistic) studies are inherently inductive, as they are "based exclusively on the givenness of the written text" (Terino, "A Text Linguistic Study of the Jacob Narrative," 46). I think his statement is correct if we account for the influence of presuppositions at the same time.

[163] Osborne, *The Hermeneutical Spiral*, 415. Osborne's third component to this process (the 'sociological' one, 415), where "reading communities are involved in an ongoing dialogue," is beyond the scope of my study, although I hope my study might feed into that.

[164] Terino, "A Text Linguistic Study of the Jacob Narrative," 46.

[165] Cf. Klein, *Introduction to Biblical Interpretation*, 161ff.

[166] Wright, *Walking in the Ways of the Lord*, 25. Similarly, L. Ryken, "Literary Criticism of the Bible: Some Fallacies," in *Literary Interpretations of Biblical Narratives* (ed. K.R.R. Gros Louis; Nashville, Tennessee, USA: Abingdon Press, 1974), 34 asserts that "a reading of the Bible that regards the individual parts as complementary takes seriously the Bible's status as story, a progression in which no single moment is self-contained, but is rather part of an overall movement."

their *immediate* context(s), because I think that most improvement regarding the interpretation of material possessions can be gained that way. My literature survey supports that assertion.

Besides making a major investment in the detailed exegesis and 'close reading' of relevant passages, I will engage with the work of other interpreters on many different levels. Some of these interpreters work on the final form of the text; some do not. Although historical-critical methods move us away from the final form of the text, I do not see that as a problem, as long as we return to the interpretive tasks (and challenges) of the text in its final form.

Much has been written about the Jacob-cycle and studies in Genesis continue to be in motion. In some areas there appears to be substantial consensus (e.g. the recognition of shape and symmetry patterns in the Jacob-cycle); in other areas such consensus remains elusive (e.g. the history of composition and setting of earlier forms of the text). As such, my conclusions will be open-ended to some extent. It is my intention to build on what has been achieved, while 'sitting loose' regarding what remains unsettled. I also aim to leave tensions and ambiguities for what they are, in order not to flatten the scriptural witness. The Jacob-cycle is a complex text which contains plenty of tensions, gaps and ambiguities, which are there to make the reader think very hard about what he or she is reading. Such rich texts appear to resist a full disclosure of all their bounties, but always yield more insights for those who spend the extra time and effort.

Despite the numerous methodological challenges that were identified, I find great solace in Barton's suggestion to just 'go ahead and do it' (my paraphrase):

> It is better to attend to the text, produce an interpretation of what it means, and only then go back to analyse the precise level at which the interpretation operates. We cannot be forever trying to watch our own eyes moving.[167]

1.4   SUMMARY

I have outlined the rationale for this study. The literature survey has shown that there is an under-explored research area regarding the

---

[167] Barton, *Reading the Old Testament*, 194.

nature and role of material possessions and associated attitudes and actions in the Jacob-cycle and that it is worthwhile to investigate this area. Subsequently, I discussed various issues regarding text and meaning, and proposed a pragmatic, integrative approach to analyze the text of Jacob-cycle. The rest of this book will demonstrate the application of this approach.

The outline of this study will follow a part of Jacob's life-story and his presence inside and outside the land of Canaan: Chapter 2: *Jacob in Canaan I* (Gen 25:19–28:22); Chapter 3: *Jacob out of Canaan* (Gen 29:1–31:55) and Chapter 4: *Jacob in Canaan II* (Gen 32:1–35:29). This subdivision has proven to be practical, as many relevant encounters (with both man and God) in Jacob's life take place on boundaries.[168] In Chapter 5 I will summarize my findings and will conclude with some methodological reflections.

---

[168] E.g. 28:10–22; 31:25–55, 32:22–32. This is quite similar to the experience of Jacob's descendants (cf. Exodus, Deuteronomy).

JACOB IN CANAAN I (GEN 25–28)

2.1 Introduction

In 1975 Fishbane demonstrated how the episodes in the Jacob-cycle are "aligned in perfectly symmetrical fashion."[1] Rendsburg, building on this work, presents this symmetry as follows:

A   Oracle sought, struggle in childbirth, Jacob born (25:19–34)
   B   Interlude: Rebekah in foreign palace, pact with foreigners (26:1–34)
      C   Jacob fears Esau and flees (27:1–28:9)
         D   Messengers (28:10–22)
            E   Arrival at Haran (29:1–30)
               F   Jacob's wives are fertile (29:31–30:24)
               F'   Jacob's flocks are fertile (30:25–31:1)
            E'   Flight from Haran (31:2–54)
         D'   Messengers (32:1–32)
      C'   Jacob returns and fears Esau (33:1–20)
   B'   Interlude: Dinah in foreign palace, pact with foreigners (34:1–31)
A'   Oracle fulfilled, struggle in childbirth, Jacob becomes Israel (35:1–22)[2]

Gammie notes that Joseph's birth (30:24) and Jacob's decision to return back to Canaan (30:34) stand at the centre of this structure.[3] F and F' describe Jacob's increase of children and wealth (interesting material for our investigation!). E and E' focus on Jacob's struggle with Laban (and its resolution). C and C' focus on Jacob's struggle with Esau (and

---

[1] Rendsburg, *The Redaction of Genesis*, 53. Fishbane's 1975 *JTS* article (M. Fishbane, "Composition and Structure in the Jacob Cycle (Gen 25:19–25:22)," *JJS* 26 (1975): 15–38) was incorporated in his later publication *Text and Texture*. See also Gammie, "Theological Interpretation," 120ff. who independently reached a similar conclusion. '...roughly palistrophically' (Wenham, *Genesis 16–50*, 185).

[2] Rendsburg, *The Redaction of Genesis*, 53–54. Rendsburg basically follows Fishbane with some minor adjustments. Ad B: note that Rebekah never finds herself in a foreign palace!

[3] Gammie, "Theological Interpretation," 123. Cf. Brueggemann, *Genesis*, 211–213; Fokkelman, *Narrative Art in Genesis*, 141; Waltke, *Genesis*, 353.

its resolution).[4] The struggles with Esau and Laban are separated by
Jacob's encounters with divine messengers (D and D').[5] Rendsburg
(and others) have shown how various themes and other textual features further unite the various parts of this palistrophic structure.[6]

> The various segments in the cycle have been assembled with such a
> demonstrable artistry that sound interpretation not only permits but
> requires viewing the segments as integrally related parts of a continuous
> whole. As the parts are viewed in the context of the whole, meanings
> emerge which would not have inhered in them separately.[7]

This is by no means the only way to structure the book of Genesis. Brodie, for example, divides Genesis in twenty-six diptychs, which con-
sist of two panels each that can be seen as 'binary or dialogical.'[8] For
some panels this complementarity is quite obvious: e.g. the increase of
Jacob's children and flock (29:31–30:24 // 30:25–43).[9] In other cases
this is much more difficult to discern, something Brodie himself readily admits.[10] It seems to me that there is much more textual evidence
to support the proposals by Fishbane and Rendsburg. However, I do
not think these insights are mutually exclusive and Brodie's insights
are certainly valuable. I will refer to Brodie throughout this study, but
I will primarily work with the structure(s) as proposed by Fishbane
and Rendsburg.

In this chapter I will analyse Gen 25:19–28:22 (A, B, C and D).
This section starts with the events leading up to the birth of Jacob and
Esau and their growing up together (25:19–28). It ends with Jacob's
journey away from home, when he encounters God for the first time.
The mention of Bethuel and Laban in 25:20 forms an inclusio with
28:2, 5.[11] The episodes in between record Jacob's acquisition of Esau's

---

[4] I prefer 'resolution' instead of reconciliation, as I believe that these resolutions
(with Laban and Esau) are only partial reconciliations at best (see Chapters 3 and 4).
Cf. P.D. Miscall, "Jacob and Joseph Story Analogies," *JSOT* 6 (1978): 28–40, 35–39.

[5] "The vow plays a significant integrative role in tying the Jacob/Laban cycle
together" (Cartledge, 166).

[6] Fokkelman, *Narrative Art in Genesis*; Alter, *The Art of Biblical Narrative*; White,
Narration and Discourse, 205ff.

[7] Gammie, "Theological Interpretation," 123.

[8] Brodie, *Genesis as Dialogue*, xi–xii and Brodie, "Genesis as Dialogue".

[9] Brodie, "Genesis as Dialogue," 306. Or take for example the two-part account
of creation.

[10] Brodie, "Genesis as Dialogue," 309.

[11] Waltke, *Genesis*, 354. Rendsburg notes that the phrase פַדֶּן אֲרָם also occurs in
35:9 (Rendsburg, *The Redaction of Genesis*, 55). It also occurs in 33:18, which makes
these references stand on either side of the interlude Gen 34.

birthright (25:29–34) and of Isaac's blessing (Gen 27). These accounts are juxtaposed with God's generous bestowal of promises and blessing on Isaac (Gen 26) and on Jacob himself (28:10–22), followed by Jacob's response (28:16–22). This interplay between human struggle in all its intensity, divine giving in all its generosity, and human response, creates a tension from which the ensuing stories develop. Concerns about material possessions and well-being are very much at the heart of these texts. I aim to identify these concerns and analyse them in their appropriate contexts.

2.2   Introducing Esau and Jacob (Gen 25:19–34)

2.2.1   Introduction

Gen 25:19–28 describes events before, during and after the birth of Esau and Jacob. Vv. 27–28 serve as transition, setting the scene for vv. 29–34, the sale of Esau's birthright.[12] Structural markers in this section are: the 'toledot formula' (vs. 19); the inclusio formed by the report of Isaac's age (vv. 20, 26); and the prominence of the oracle in the middle (vs. 23).[13] Source critics have identified various sources for this material (J, P and E). However no consensus exists.[14] In its final form, the text is compact and rich, and is highly effective in setting the scene for what follows.[15]

---

[12] Cf. Brueggemann, Genesis, 212. Alternatively, one could divide the section as follows: vv. 19–26 (formed by an inclusio mentioning Isaac's age) and vv. 27–34 (G.W. Coats, Genesis—With an Introduction to Narrative Literature (Grand Rapids, MI, USA: Eerdmans Publishing Company, 1983), 183–188; Walton, Thou Traveller Unknown, 11; J.L. Ska, "Genèse 25, 19–34—Ouverture du Cycle de Jacob," in Jacob: Commentaire à Plusieurs Voix de Gen 25–36—Mèlanges offerts à Albert de Pury (eds. J-D Macchi and T. Römer; Geneva, Swiss: Labor et Fides, 2001); Taschner, Verheissung und Erfüllung, 22ff.; Terino, "A Text Linguistic Study of the Jacob Narrative," 51). Similarly, Wenham speaks of three episodes (Wenham, Genesis 16–50, 172).

[13] Fokkelman, Narrative Art in Genesis, 93. "What food for conflicts is gathered there!" (94).

[14] Cf. Westermann, Genesis 12–36, 406ff.; Brueggemann, Genesis, 205; Wenham, Genesis 16–50, 173; Walton, Thou Traveller Unknown, 11–13; and Ska, "Genèse 25, 19–34."

[15] von Rad, Genesis, 265; Fishbane, Text and Texture, 33; Brueggemann, Genesis, 208; Fokkelman, Narrative Art in Genesis, 94; Wenham, Genesis 16–50, 168ff.; Coats, Genesis, 185.

2.2.2 *Commentary*

25:19–28

In this short passage, many things are achieved. First of all, the story of Isaac and his offspring is set within the whole framework of the book of Genesis. This works on various levels and the many hooks that are provided work both forwards and backwards. This invites the reader to reflect on similarities and differences between the various stories.[16] The section opens with the eighth appearance of the so-called '*toledot* formula' in 25:19.[17] This sets the Jacob-cycle in the context of the other patriarchal stories in Gen 12–50, but also of Gen 1–11, which present us with "*a universal frame of reference*" with "images that set the tone and direction for *reading all that follows.*"[18] The mention of Abraham in this formula is unusual, and reminds us of the whole story surrounding Isaac's birth, and of the promises made to Abraham, many unfulfilled as yet.[19] The verb form הוֹלִיד in 25:19 only appears elsewhere in Genesis in 11:27.[20] According to Wenham "the history of Isaac's family is deliberately compared with that of Abraham."[21] The

---

[16] Alter, *The Art of Biblical Narrative*; Wenham, *Genesis 16–50*, 168. For example, 'barrenness' and 'intercession to alleviate barrenness' occurred in the previous generation and will occur in the next.

[17] See *Section* 1.3.2. See also Walton, *Thou Traveller Unknown*, 11; Alexander, "Genealogies, Seed and the Compositional Unity of Genesis"; Terino, "A Text Linguistic Study of the Jacob Narrative"; Alexander, *From Paradise to the Promised Land*, 111. The Jacob-cycle is marked by two genealogies of 'un-chosen' sons: of Ishmael (25:12–18) and of Esau (36:1–43).

[18] Fretheim, *The Pentateuch*, 44 (italics by the author); T.E. Fretheim, "Which Blessing Does Isaac Give Jacob?," in *Jews, Christians and the Theology of the Hebrew Scriptures* (eds. A. Ogden Bellis and J.S. Kaminsky; Atlanta, Georgia, USA: Society of Biblical Literature, 2000), 280. See also: W.J. Dumbrell, *The Search for Order* (Grand Rapids, Michigan, USA: Baker Books, 1994), 15–37; W.J. Dumbrell, *The Faith of Israel* (Leicester, UK: Apollos, 2002), 13–31; Wenham, *Genesis 1–15*, xxi–xxii; Mann, "All the Families of the Earth." Fischer identifies a number of interesting links between Gen 1–11 and the Jacob narrative (Fischer, "Jakobs Rolle in der Genesis," 276–279).

[19] Wenham, *Genesis 16–50*, 174.

[20] Hiphil, 3rd person, masculine singular of יָלַד TWOT 867 notes that "a man's part in the production of a child is generally represented by the Hiphil, but sometimes the Qal is used."

[21] Wenham, *Genesis 16–50*, 172. Wenham identifies several textual features, which the opening section of the Abraham-cycle has in common with the opening of the Jacob-cycle. Waltke agrees, but discerns substantial differences besides certain similarities (Waltke, *Genesis*, 351). It appears that Waltke is using material from Brueggemann (Brueggemann, *Genesis*, 206), who himself refers to Westermann, *The Promises to the Fathers*, 74–78. Waltke's summary is less nuanced than Westermann's original proposals (cf. Westermann, *Genesis 12–36*, 408–409).

mention of Laban (25:20) anticipates Jacob's traumatic struggle with his uncle.[22] Other links between 25:19–34 and other parts of Genesis have been identified as well.[23]

The main focus of this passage is on events leading up to the birth of Esau and Jacob (vv. 21–23) and the birth itself (vv. 24–26). The struggle in the womb is fierce.[24] Rebekah is at her wits end. The divine oracle (25:23) that follows is placed prominently in the middle of this passage and in the midst of this struggle.

> The crucial point of this story of the birth of twins is not the fact of the birth itself but the future fate of struggle between siblings, which is the burden of the oracular poem.[25]

The juxtaposition of divine revelation and human struggle is something we see throughout the Jacob-cycle. Divine encounters provide vertical input at key moments to a story line that is characterized by human struggle. The prediction that 'the older shall serve the younger' is the 'punch-line' of the oracle.[26] Reversal is a major theme in the Jacob-cycle. In addition, the verb עָבַד ('to serve') is a key-word: it is prominent in Isaac's blessing (Gen 27). It appears in the Jacob-Laban complex and it will feature again in Jacob's encounter with Esau in Gen 32–33.[27] The oracle will probably have done little to ease Rebekah's agony.[28] According to Fokkelman "the short poems in

---

[22] Cf. E-F-F'-E' in Rendsburg's scheme, and Chapter 3. P. Kahn, "Jacob's Choice in Genesis 25:19–28:9," *JBQ* 29, no. 2 (2001): 80–86, having established the relationship of the term *Aramean* to a culture of deception (82), suggests that Gen 25:20 is the opening verse of a *parsha*: will the family raised by Isaac and Rebekah follow the ethical practices of Grandfather Abraham, or of the Grandfather Bethuel and Uncle Laban? Considering the deceit that is practiced by both sides of the family, this does not strike me as a tenable position.

[23] For more in-depth discussions on these links and allusions: cf. Fokkelman, "Genesis"; Fokkelman, *Narrative Art in Genesis*; White, *Narration and Discourse*; Rendsburg, *The Redaction of Genesis*; and Alter, *Genesis*.

[24] The verb רָצַץ (BDB 9276; TWOT 2212; HALOT 8974) that is used to describe the struggle of the children is a strong one ('clashed together', Alter, *Genesis*, 126). Elsewhere the verb is for 'to abuse', 'to crush' the poor (Hamilton, *Genesis 18–50*, 176) and to describe 'skulls being smashed (Jdg 9:53; Ps 74:14; Wenham, *Genesis 16–50*, 174). "Die Söhne *misshandelten* sich in ihrem Bauch" (italics mine; Taschner, *Verheissung und Erfüllung*, 22).

[25] Alter, *Genesis*, 126.

[26] For a detailed analysis of the poetics of the oracle: Fokkelman, *Narrative Art in Genesis*, 89–90; Taschner, *Verheissung und Erfüllung*, 23–29.

[27] See also J. Taschner, *Verheissung und Erfüllung*, 24; Turner, *Announcements of Plot in Genesis*, 120–124. We will discuss these occurrences in more detail below.

[28] Similarly Wenham, *Genesis 16–50*, 175.

Genesis have a special function (...). By serving as crystallization points, they create moments of reflection."[29] This particular 'moment' gives the reader plenty to ponder, even after events have unfolded! Although most scholars agree that the oracle is 'programmatic,'[30] interpretations vary on exactly how.[31] For example, it is not clear whether the oracle represents "a preference on God's part or simply his announcement of what will happen."[32] How one interprets the oracle influences the way one interprets the actions of the various parties that follow. Based on Gen 24, Frymer-Kensky concludes that Rebekah is "a woman of destiny with a divinely ordained role to play." Rebekah fulfils that destiny in Gen 25 and 27 because "oracles are expected to lead to action."[33] Similarly, Jeansonne interprets Rebekah's involvement in Gen 27 positively: she "skilfully completes the task initiated by God."[34] However, Fretheim demonstrates that such divine oracles "do not necessarily cast the future in concrete."[35] "More generally, open-endedness is true of divine pronouncements about the future (e.g., 2 Kgs 20:1–7), at least those that do not entail a divine promise."[36] I will comment on how events in the Jacob-cycle can be interpreted in the light of the birth-oracle, whenever relevant for my topic.

---

[29] Fokkelman, "Genesis," 44.

[30] Fokkelman, "Genesis," 45. "It explains the whole Jacob and Esau story in much the same way as Gen 12:1–3 illuminates the Abraham story" (G.J. Wenham, *Genesis 16–50*, 180). "Clearly, the oracle of designation (25:23) governs the narrative" (W. Brueggemann, *Genesis*, 208). Von Rad describes vv. 21–28 as an 'expository preface to the whole' (von Rad, *Genesis*, 260). Turner takes the birth-oracle together with Isaac's blessing as 'announcement of plot' for the Jacob story (Turner, *Announcements of Plot in Genesis*, 115).

[31] Cf. Turner, *Announcements of Plot in Genesis*, 115ff. for an interesting discussion. I assume that the oracle is 'programmatic', but that its ultimate fulfilment goes well beyond the Jacob-cycle and that it points to the future fate of the peoples of Israel and Edom. Alternatively, Long has suggested that a tribal tradition (vs. 23) and the report of the birth and naming of specific persons (vs. 24), originally were independent (oral) units that were only joined in 'the literary stage of the tradition' (B.O. Long, *The Problem of Etiological Narrative* (BZAW 108; Berlin, Germany: Töpelmann, 1968), 49–50).

[32] Humphreys, *The Character of God*, 163.

[33] Frymer-Kensky, *Reading the Women of the Bible*, 17.

[34] Jeansonne, *The Women of Genesis*, 67. Similarly S. Breitbart, "The Problem of Deception in Genesis 27," *JBQ* 29, no. 1 (2001): 45–47, 46–47, who concludes that Rebekah's acts in Gen 27 were not deceitful.

[35] Fretheim, "Which Blessing?," 283. E.g. Esau will not bow down to Jacob, but Jacob will bow down to Esau! See also Turner, *Announcements of Plot in Genesis*, 115–141 who has performed a detailed study about this issue for the Jacob narrative(s).

[36] Fretheim, "Which Blessing?," 285.

Various interpretations have been offered for Jacob's grasping of Esau's heel (25:26). Some commentators see it as an indication of Jacob's desire to catch his brother and pass him by.[37] Others think that Jacob literally wants Esau's downfall.[38] What is clear is that the struggle will continue outside of the womb.[39] Struggle is indeed a central theme in Genesis,[40] but there is probably more to this birth than meets the eye. Jacob is grasping Esau's heel (עָקֵב), hence the name יַעֲקֹב (Jacob).[41] In 27:36 Esau will exclaim "is he not rightly named Jacob? For he has cheated (וַיַּעְקְבֵנִי)[42] me these two times." Most commentators pick up on this link between 'heel' and 'cheat'/'supplant.'[43] Smith however, draws attention to Jacob's grasping (אֹחֶזֶת). The verb אָחַז has the meaning of 'to grasp', 'to take hold', but also 'to take possession of.'[44] I think Smith's suggestion that the "double meaning of the verb אָחַז enlightens the thrust of the narrative" is a good one.[45] "Perhaps

---

[37] R.B. Chisholm, *From Exegesis to Exposition* (Grand Rapids, Michigan, USA: Baker Books, 1998), 243; R.J. Clifford, "Genesis 25:19–34," *Int* 45, no. October (1991): 397–401, 399.

[38] A. Weiss, "Jacob's Struggle: A Psycho-Existential Exegesis," *JPJ* 18, no. 1 (1994): 19–31, 21. Some have noted that the first descriptions of Esau pertain to his looks (red, hairy), while Jacob is described by his action: 'grasping', drawing attention to his activist (aggressive) nature. "A revealing action as we shall see" (Fokkelman, *Narrative Art in Genesis*, 90). Similar remarks by Taschner, *Verheissung und Erfüllung*, 26 and Clifford, "Genesis 25:19–34," 399.

[39] Wenham, *Genesis 16–50*, 176; cf. T.L. Thompson, "Conflict Themes in the Jacob Narratives," *Semeia* 15 (1979): 5–25; McKeown, *Genesis*, 127.

[40] Fishbane, *Text and Texture*, 45; Westermann, *Genesis 12–36*, 418; Steinmetz, *From Father to Son*, 11; Gammie, "Theological Interpretation," 119. This is probably a better statement than Sailhamer's: "struggle between *brothers* is a central theme in Genesis" (italics mine; cf. Sailhamer, *Genesis* on this passage), as sisters do plenty of struggle as well (Leah vs. Rachel). See also J. Goldingay, *After Eating the Apricot* (Carlisle, Cumbria, United Kingdom: Solway, 1996), 40.

[41] Alternatively: 'may God protect' (von Rad, *Genesis*, 260). Similarly N.M. Sarna, *Genesis* (JPS Torah Commentary; Philadelphia, USA: Jewish Publication Society, 1989), 180.

[42] From the verb עָקַב which can also mean 'to follow closely' or 'over reach' (TWOT 1676; BDB 7344; HALOT 7249). It has the connotation 'to overtake, supplant' (Hamilton, *Genesis 18–50*, 179).

[43] See R.D. Patterson, "The Old Testament Use Of An Archetype: The Trickster," *JETS* 42, no. 3 (1999): 385–94, 390, who suggests that Jacob was 'a deceiver from birth.' Fokkelman warns that the meaning of 'deceive' for the verb עָקַב has probably been derived from and 'lexically enriched' by this narrative (Fokkelman, *Narrative Art in Genesis*, 92, n. 11).

[44] BDB 352; Smith also suggests the meaning 'to inherit' (S.H. Smith, "'Heel' and 'Thigh': The Concept of Sexuality in the Jacob-Esau Narratives," *VT* 40, no. 4 (1990): 464–73, 464).

[45] Smith, "'Heel' and 'Thigh'," 464.

implicit in Jacob's physical act of gripping Esau's heel is the intention
to take possession of the latter's position of power and dominance."[46]
Smith then proposes that עָקֵב is to be taken as a euphemism for genitals[47] and that Jacob's grasping is 'symbolic of his desire to assume'
his brother's 'procreative power.'[48] Having witnessed a birth of twins
myself, I would say that one twin being able to grasp the genitals of
the other strikes me as rather improbable. Smith's proposal has been
critiqued in detail by Malul.[49] Malul argues that there is no reason "for
ascribing a sexual connotation to עָקֵב or to any of the other adduced
terms and expressions in the Jacob traditions."[50] Malul makes a strong
case, supported by substantial legal and anthropological material, to
interpret "the meaning of עָקֵב in the Jacob-Esau traditions as belonging altogether to the idea of succession, which includes notions of both
status, property and inheritance."[51] It is worthwhile to quote Hoebel,
one of Malul's sources, who defines 'property' as an entirely sociological concept:

> The web of social relations with respect to the utilization of some object
> (material or non-material) in which a person or group is tacitly or explic-
> itly recognized as holding quasi-exclusive and limiting demand-rights,
> privilege-rights, powers, and immunities in relation to that object.[52]

Malul continues:

> A person does not transfer to his heir the ownership of a certain prop-
> erty, but rather the whole system of social interactions related to that
> specific property (...) status comes first, and one's succession to a status
> also implies inheritance; the emphasis, however, is on the wider picture
> of the social matrix of statuses in interaction.[53]

---

[46] Smith, "'Heel' and 'Thigh'," 464–465.

[47] Smith refers to Jer 13:22 where the heels suffering violence is a 'parallel senti-
ment' to the "lifting of the skirt, which is a euphemism for exposing one's nakedness"
(Smith, "'Heel' and 'Thigh'," 465). Smith refers to Jeremiah commentaries by R.P.
Carroll (1986) and W.L. Holladay (1986) to support this interpretation of 'heels' in
Jer 13:22.

[48] Smith, "'Heel' and 'Thigh'," 465.

[49] M. Malul, "'Āqēb "Heel' and 'Āqab' "To Supplant" and the Concept of Successions in the Jacob-Esau Narratives," VT 46, no. 2 (1996): 190–212.

[50] Malul refers here to the incident of Jacob wrestling with God at the Jabbok,
where Jacob's hip socket is touched, resulting in a limp. Smith also argues for a sexual
connotation in this case (Malul, "'Āqēb "Heel" and 'Āqab'," 191).

[51] Malul, "'Āqēb "Heel" and 'Āqab'," 193.

[52] E.H. Hoebel, The Law of Primitive Man. A Study of Comparative Legal Dynamics
(Cambridge, UK: 1967), 58 as quoted by Malul, "'Āqēb "Heel" and 'Āqab'," 194.

[53] Malul, "'Āqēb "Heel" and 'Āqab'," 195 (cf. Sarna, Understanding Genesis, 185).
In this context, Malul also discusses the tradition of transferring a piece of land by

Brichto has taken this even further with his proposal that property "was essentially a religious concept, particular real property."[54] Considering the immediate context of the oracle, I find Sarna's summary satisfactory:

> It [the oracle] seeks to interpret the "struggle in the womb" as a contest for priority of birth, as a pre-natal sibling rivalry over the possession of the birthright. This idea is further emphasized by the picture of Jacob emerging from his mother's womb grasping the heel of Esau, as though making a final effort to supplant his brother.[55]

25:27–28

This cameo sets the scene for what follows.[56] Additional questions are raised as well: e.g. when did Isaac start to pray for his wife? How did Rebekah obtain the oracle?[57] Was Isaac familiar with the content of the oracle?[58] Was Jacob aware of the oracle? Why God did choose Jacob over Esau? Many of these questions resist closure.

---

putting your foot down on it (203). This is picked up independently by Dumbrell, *Covenant & Creation*, 72, who refers to W. Zimmerli, *The Old Testament and the World* (London, UK: SPCK, 1976), 69.

[54] H.C. Brichto, "Kin, cult, land and afterlife: a biblical complex," in *Hebrew Union College Annual* (vol. 44 of, 1973), 5.

[55] Sarna, *Understanding Genesis*, 182. I will comment further on Sarna's use of 'supplant' in relation to Gen 27:36.

[56] For example: 'red' will appear again in the episode of the 'birthright sale'; references to 'hairy', 'hunt', 'favouritism', a person who perceives to be at the point of death, and Isaac's 'love for food' will be key-ingredients for the Gen 27 plot. See: Fokkelman, *Narrative Art in Genesis*; Alter, *The Art of Biblical Narrative*; Rendsburg, *The Redaction of Genesis*; Clifford, "Genesis 25:19–34"; White, *Narration and Discourse*. Esau's description as a 'man of the field' invites comparison with Ishmael; both are depicted as 'wild men'. "Though these wild men begin life in the Israelite sphere, they end up as foreigners, outsiders to Israel" (G. Mobley, "The Wild Man in the Bible and the Ancient Near East," *JBL* 116, no. 2 (1997): 217–33, 226–227). Jacob's description as an 'אִישׁ תָּם' is more challenging ('most problematic' Wenham, *Genesis 16–50*, 176). This phrase, which normally has ethical connotations ('innocent', 'integrity' e.g. Job 1:1, 8; see BDB 10564), can also mean 'complete', 'wholesome'. Evans (followed by Hamilton) thinks it does have the ethical meaning here, because Jacob's behaviour is never denounced by the narrator, as Esau's is (C.D. Evans, "The Patriarch Jacob—An Innocent Man," *BR* 2, no. 1 (1987): 32–37; Hamilton, *Genesis 18–50.*, 181–182). Fokkelman thinks it refers to Jacob's "singleness of purpose" (Fokkelman, *Narrative Art in Genesis*, 91). Wenham thinks it refers a 'self-contained, detached personality', hence 'quiet' (Wenham, *Genesis 16–50*, 176). We need to know more about what is still to come to derive a fuller explanation.

[57] Through a priest or a dream? To inquire of YHWH (דָּרַשׁ) is a well attested concept in the Hebrew Bible, especially in the monarchic period, but in this passage it appears to be anachronistic (Walton, *Thou Traveller Unknown*, 16).

[58] Clifford, "Genesis 25:19–34," 399 and M. Reiss, "Archetypes in the Patriarchal Family," *JBQ* 28, no. 1 (2000): 12–19, 14 think it likely she did not.

It is worthwhile to reflect on God's role in this passage. God is first and foremost portrayed as sovereign. Gen 25:19 recalls how God made promises to Abraham and how he enabled Sarah to conceive Isaac. God is the one who hears Isaac's prayer and enables Rebekah to conceive. The divine oracle finds its ultimate fulfilment in the wider context of the OT (e.g. 2 Sam 8:12–14). This points to God's omniscience. Yet the reader might wonder why Rebekah appears to be the ideal, divinely approved partner for Isaac (Gen 24) while she turns out to be barren?[59] The statement that Isaac 'entreated' the LORD (וַיֶּעְתַּר from עָתַר), followed by the statement that 'the LORD granted his prayer' (וַיֵּעָתֶר, the Niphal from the same verb), indicates the efficacy of Isaac's prayer.[60] It is only in vs. 26 that we find out that Isaac and Rebekah had to wait for twenty years. Was Isaac praying for most of this period, and what does that imply for our understanding of effective prayer?[61] Or did Isaac only start praying towards the end of this period?[62] If that is the case, Isaac's assumed piety is placed in a new light. Also, why does this answer to prayer turn out to be such a troublesome pair? The text does not answer these questions. One thing is certain: God's direct involvement is essential to continue the chosen line.[63]

While some aspects of God's workings are clear and attractive, others are more difficult to understand. "At many points the narrative presents the inscrutable, dark side of God."[64] As we examine the nature and role of material possessions in the Jacob-cycle, in the context of various human and divine relationships, we do well to remember the 'inscrutability' of God's nature:[65] "God is omniscient, man is limited,

---

[59] Cf. S. Gillmayr-Bucher, "The Woman of their Dreams: The Image of Rebekah in Genesis 24," in *The World of Genesis. Persons, Places, Perspectives* (ed. P.R. Davies, Clines, D.J.A.; JSOTSup 257; Sheffield, UK: Sheffield Academic Press, 1998), 100; Hamilton, *Genesis 18–50*, 175.

[60] "The tolerative *Niphal* often involves the element of efficacy" (B.K. Waltke and M. O'Connor, *An Introduction to Biblical Hebrew Syntax* (Winona Lake, Indiana, USA: Eisenbrauns, 1990), 389–390); Cf. GKC § 51c on the *Niphal* tolerativum.

[61] "Here it also shows that Isaac intercedes twenty years for his barren wife without losing hope" (Waltke, *Genesis*, 359). Abraham's prayer is for the Philistine women (20:17), but no such prayer is recorded for Sarah. Jacob becomes angry (30:2).

[62] As Merrill appears to suggest (E.H. Merrill, "Fixed Dates in Patriarchal Chronology," *BSac* 137, no. 547 (1980): 241–51, 243).

[63] Cf. McKeown, *Genesis*, 127.

[64] Brueggemann, *Genesis*, 209; cf. Walton, *Thou Traveller Unknown*, 28; T.W. Mann, *The Book of the Torah: The Narrative Integrity of the Pentateuch* (Atlanta, USA: John Knox Press, 1988), 51.

[65] Clifford speaks of 'divine graciousness' that is 'inscrutable and not a little upsetting' (Clifford, "Genesis 25:19–34," 401).

and the boundary is impassable (…) the only knowledge perfectly acquired is the knowledge of our limitations."[66]

In Gen 25:19–28 a web of relationships is introduced, both on a large scale (25:19) and on the family level[67]. The human relationships (and their future development) are described in terms of dominance (vs. 23), struggle (vs. 22, 26) and favouritism (vs. 28). One wonders how the relationship that developed between God and Abraham will take shape for this new generation and how the oracle will be fulfilled.[68] Gen 25:19–28 does not speak specifically about material possessions, although the grasping of the heel might hint in that direction (Malul). I suggest that whatever understanding will be gained regarding material possessions in the texts that follow, should be placed within the context of these relationship concerns.

25:29–34

The central concern of this passage is the transfer of the birthright (בְּכֹרָה). Ska aptly describes this passage as "un premier incident paradigmatique qui donne le 'ton' à l'ensemble."[69] With a minimal number of strokes, a vivid picture is painted of characters and scene.[70] Esau is characterized as exaggerating, carnal, and short-term oriented.[71] Jacob is portrayed as premeditative and ruthless.[72] As soon as the opportunity presents itself (vs. 30), Jacob 'goes in for the kill' (vs. 31).[73] "The way Jacob states his demand suggests long premeditation and a ruthless exploitation of his brother's moment of weakness,"[74] a stark contrast with Abraham's hospitality to complete strangers (Gen 18:1–8). Gen 25:29–34 has a chiastic structure with Esau's protest at its centre (vs. 32, "Behold, I [emphatic] am about to die, what good is to me a

---

[66] Sternberg, *Poetics*, 46–47.

[67] Cf. Walton, *Thou Traveller Unknown*, 27.

[68] Turner, *Announcements of Plot in Genesis*, 115ff.

[69] "A paradigmatic incident which sets the tone for the rest" (my 'free' translation) (Ska, "Genèse 25, 19–34," 11).

[70] "There is not a word too many" (Fokkelman, *Narrative Art in Genesis*, 97).

[71] The 'short-term man' (Fokkelman, *Narrative Art in Genesis*, 95).

[72] Jacob is clearly the aggressor. Reiss's comment that it was from Laban that "Jacob would learn how to be aggressive and manipulative" (Reiss, "Archetypes in the Patriarchal Family," 16) must be rejected. In Laban however, Jacob would meet his match! The show of contrast between the two characters is a characterization technique (Berlin, *Poetics*, 40).

[73] Fokkelman, *Narrative Art in Genesis*, 95.

[74] Wenham, *Genesis 16–50*, 178.

birthright?").[75] Esau's exaggeration is pinched between Jacob's forceful imperatives (מִכְרָה 'sell/exchange' in vs. 31, without the particle of
entreaty[76]; and הִשָּׁבְעָה 'swear' in vs. 33), both combined with the words
כַּיּוֹם....לִי ('today' or 'first'and 'to me' in an emphatic position).[77]

It is fascinating how the different parties speak about the birthright.
While Jacob and the narrator know the birthright is Esau's, Esau never
speaks about the birthright as *his own*: "what good is *a* birthright to
me" (italics mine).[78] After a short exchange it is not his anymore. The
narrator refers to the birthright as *'his* birthright' in vs. 33, but it is
merely *'the* birthright' in vs. 34. Most translations miss this subtle
shift.[79] In 27:36 Esau speaks about *'my* birthright' (בְּכֹרָתִי) and *'my*
blessing' (בִּרְכָתִי), but by then it is too late. Esau releases his birthright
for a pot of stew.[80] White suggests that "transgressive eating is a sign
of the same desire-driven mode of subjectivity in this narrative that
appeared in the story of the Garden of Eden."[81] White does not make
this explicit, but this would place Jacob in the position of the deceiving
snake. Something to ponder.

What makes the birthright so desirable and what is it anyway? The
root בכר appears throughout the OT,[82] but the occurrence of בְּכֹרָה is
rare.[83] We may assume that the position of firstborn came with special
honour and status (cf. 43:33; 49:3). However, Gen 25–27 does not clarify

---

[75] 'Inverted parallelism' (Terino, "A Text Linguistic Study of the Jacob Narrative,"
51). Fokkelman proposes a slightly different structure, but both have Esau's exclamation (vs. 32), pinched between Jacob's demands, at its centre; "hemmed in by his
brother's cunning design" (Fokkelman, *Narrative Art in Genesis*, 95; Terino, "A Text
Linguistic Study of the Jacob Narrative," 52).

[76] In contrast with Esau's request in vs. 30: הַלְעִיטֵנִי נָא. B. Goodnick, "Jacob's
Deception of his Father," *JBQ* 22, no. 4 (1994): 237–40, 239 points out that it can also
express the desire for an immediate response (cf. Isa 1:18), which would make Esau's
demand more urgent than polite.

[77] Hamilton, *Genesis 18–50*, 180 on the translation issues regarding כַּיּוֹם.

[78] Jacob: 'sell me *your* birthright now' vs. 31. The narrator: '...and sold *his* birthright to Jacob' vs. 33.

[79] By translating '*his* birthright', while the suffix is clearly absent. Likewise White,
Narration and Discourse, 213; Fokkelman, *Narrative Art in Genesis*, 95; Hamilton,
Genesis 18–50, 181.

[80] Daube has suggested that Esau was tripped twice: the lentil soup looked like blood
soup: D. Daube, "Fraud on Law for Fraud on Law," *OJLS* 1, no. 1 (1981): 51–60, 55
and D. Daube, *Studies in Biblical Law* (Cambridge, UK: Cambridge University Press,
1947), 191ff.; cf. McKeown, *Genesis*, 129. However, this is not clear from the text.

[81] White, *Narration and Discourse*, 213.

[82] For example, the word בְּכוֹר ('firstborn'; BDB 1221) appears 122x in the OT (B.T.
Arnold, NIDOTE #1144, בכר, 658).

[83] Gen 25:32, 33, 34; 27:36; 43:33; Deut 21:17; and 1 Chr 5:1–2 3x.

this. Explanations rest entirely on Deut 21:17 and on extra-biblical evidence. Numerous ANE sources show that assigning special status to the firstborn was common practice. This could include special honours and a 'double portion' although this was not universal practice:[84]

> This preferential treatment of the eldest son is known throughout the ancient Near East (Mari, Nuzi, Alalakh, Ugarit, Assyria), although the law codes of Lipit-Ishtar (twentieth century B.C.) and Hammurabi (eighteenth century B.C.) both legislate an equal sharing of the inheritance by all the male heirs.[85]

Certain (oft quoted) references on the Nuzi tablets mention the assigning of a double portion, and the possibility of transferring and even selling the birthright.[86] According to Frymer-Kensky in the ANE "the term 'first born' (...) is essentially a description of a particular juridical relationship which may be entered into by contract as well as by birth."[87] This aligns well with Malul's proposal.

Deut 21:15–17 describes the situation where the inheritance is split between sons of two wives ("one loved and the other unloved"). The firstborn, who is the son of the unloved woman, is to receive a double portion (פִּי שְׁנַיִם). However, Esau and Jacob are sons of the same mother! According to Sarna Deut 21:15–17 implies that giving a double portion to the eldest son was standard practice.[88] However, Hiers argues that there is little evidence for that.[89] According to Hiers Deut 21:15–17 describes an exception, and that the double portion

---

[84] Wenham, *Genesis 16–50*, 178; J.S. Kselman, "Birthright," in *Harper's Bible Dictionary* (ed. P.J. Achtermeier; San Fransisco, USA: Harper & Row, 1985), 134; G.N. Knoppers, "The Preferential Status of the Eldest Son Revoked?," in *Rethinking the Foundations: Historiography in the Ancient World and in the Bible—Essays in Honour of John van Seters* (BZAW 294; Berlin, Germany: Walter de Gruyter, 2000), 117ff.; R.H. Hiers, "Transfer of Property by Inheritance and Bequest in Biblical Law and Tradition," *JLR* 10, no. 1 (1993–1994): 121–55, 122.

[85] Kselman, "Birthright," 134. See also Kitchen, *On the Reliability of the Old Testament*, 326.

[86] de Vaux, *Ancient Israel*, 41 and 53; C.H. Gordon, "Biblical Customs and the Nuzu Tablets," *BA* 3, no. 1 (1940): 1–12, 5; S.A. West, "The Nuzi Tablets—Reflections on the Patriarchal Narratives," *BSP* 10, no. 3–4 (1981): 65–73, 72–73; E.A. Speiser, "New Kirkuk Documents Relating to Family Laws," *AASOR* 10, no. 8 (1930): 39; I. Mendelsohn, "On the Preferential Status of the Eldest Son," *BASOR* 156 (1959): 38–40 (I am indebted to Sarna, *Understanding Genesis*, 190, for the last two references).

[87] T. Frymer-Kensky, "Patriarchal Family Relationships and Near Eastern Law," *BA* 44, no. 4 (1981): 209–14, 213.

[88] Sarna, *Understanding Genesis*, 185.

[89] Hiers, "Transfer of Property by Inheritance," 122 and 142ff.

rule does not appear anywhere else (e.g. Num 27). Most commentators who accept the double-portion rule as general practice, assume that the inheritance is split between portions, equal to the number of sons plus one, where the eldest receives the 'double portion.'[90] By adopting Joseph's two sons (Gen 48–49), Jacob in effect gives Joseph this double portion. Several commentators assume that Esau sells his 'extra' share, instead of his whole inheritance.[91] Alternatively, Tsevat has suggested that the inheritance is split in portions equal to the number of sons. The firstborn would receive a double portion. For example: with eight sons, there would be eight portions. The firstborn would receive two and the other seven would divide the remaining six. With two sons, the firstborn would take all, leaving nothing for the younger brother![92] This could explain why there is no blessing for the second son in Gen 27. If that were true, Esau sold his *entire* inheritance with the sale of the birthright. However, arguments can be made that neither proposal fits Gen 25–27. First, there is the risk of cyclical reasoning. The Deuteronomy passage could have been written in the light of the Jacob narrative, instead of the other way around.[93] Secondly, there are indications in Genesis that the owner of the birthright takes all: Isaac did not share his inheritance (25:5–6), which seems to go against Tsevat's proposal.[94] In Gen 27 it appears that 'winner-takes-all.' Jacob was not invited for the proceedings and there was no blessing left for Esau when he sought one. Jacob granting a double portion to his favourite son in the presence of all his brothers could be interpreted as an improvement of the all-or-nothing blessing in Gen 27. However, with Isaac's death the division of his inheritance appears to have become a non-issue.[95] Suggestions have been made that the birthright did not only include honour, status and material benefits, but did also include

---

[90] V.H. Matthews, M.W. Chavalas and J.H. Walton, *The IVP Bible Background Commentary: Old Testament (electronic ed.)* (Downers Grove, IL, USA: InterVarsity Press, 2000), on this passage; Hamilton, *Genesis 18–50*, 185 (although Hamilton suggests that this might have been different in patriarchal times, based on Gen 25:5).

[91] Matthews, *The IVP Bible Background Commentary* on this passage.

[92] M. Tsevat, "בכור," TDOT, 126; example adjusted from Waltke, *Genesis*, 363.

[93] C.M. Carmichael, *Women, Law and the Genesis Traditions* (Edinburgh, UK: Edinburgh University Press, 1979), suggests that this law is written in light of the "ill-treatment of Leah and her son Reuben" (I am indebted to Walton, *Thou Traveller Unknown*, 22 for this reference).

[94] Cf. Hamilton, *Genesis 18–50*, 185.

[95] If we consider 'the land' as inheritance, Gen 36:6–8 tells of Esau moving away. See *Section* 4.6.

certain spiritual (priestly) responsibilities.[96] However, due to the lack of any specific textual evidence we need be careful not to put too much trust in any particular interpretation. We must conclude that we simply do not know much regarding the birthright.[97] In the wider context of the Jacob-cycle, it is probably fair to say that Jacob is driven by the material aspects of the birthright (and the blessing) rather than any assumed spiritual ones.[98]

Although specifics regarding the birthright remain unclear, it is clear that Jacob is determined to get it. When Esau appears to be willing to sell (vs. 32),[99] Jacob insists that Esau swears an oath to make the transferral unconditional and binding. God appears to be completely absent from this scene. Instead, the narrative focuses exclusively on the human players and their relationships. "Jacob gives no indication that he is motivated by, or even aware of, the fact that he stands in any sort of special relationship with God."[100] The only implicit reference to God might be the swearing of an oath. The person, who would swear, would invoke the name of God.[101] According to Fokkelman "Jacob makes so bold as to invite his brother to take the name of God in vain."[102] Jacob appears to use God for his purposes. Esau swore and sold his birthright (vs. 33). According to Tucker the swearing of an oath belongs to the making of a covenant (instead of a contract).[103] This means that we could interpret the stew as a covenant meal. "When Esau's birthright passed to Jacob (Gen 25) the meal provided by Jacob sealed the

---

[96] Brichto, "Kin, cult, land and afterlife," especially 5 and 45–46; Reiss, "Archetypes in the Patriarchal Family," 15.

[97] "What is to be understood by the birthright is not sufficiently clear from the narrative" (von Rad, *Genesis*, 262). Similarly Wenham, *Genesis 16–50*, 178.

[98] Focus on 'wages' in Gen 29 and 31 (Fishbane, *Text and Texture*, 42; Rendsburg, *The Redaction of Genesis*, 65; see Chapter 3).

[99] "The rhetorical question is equivalent to an announcement. It indicates Esau's intention to trade his birthright for some stew" (R.B. Chisholm, "Does God 'Change His Mind'?," *BSac* 152, no. 608 (1995): 387–99, 389).

[100] Humphreys, *The Character of God*, 158.

[101] HALOT 9341; W.L. Holladay, *A Concise Hebrew and Aramaic Lexicon of the Old Testament—Based upon the Lexical Work of Ludwig Koehler and Walter Baumgartner* (Leiden, The Netherlands: Brill, 2000), 8375; G.P. Miller, "Contracts of Genesis," *JLS* 22, no. 1 (1993): 15–45; L. Ryken, J. Wilhoit et al, eds., *Vow, Oath* (*Dictionary of Biblical Imagery*; Downers Grove, IL, USA: InterVarsity Press, 2000), 919; J. Milgrom, *Numbers* (JPS Torah Commentary; Philadelphia, USA: Jewish Publication Society, 1990), 488.

[102] Fokkelman, *Narrative Art in Genesis*, 96.

[103] G.M. Tucker, "Covenant Forms and Contract Forms," *VT* 15, no. 4 (1965): 487–503.

bargain, but was not necessarily the purchase price."[104] If that is so, it
is a meagre affair compared with the covenant meal offered by Isaac
to Abimelech (26:30–31).

The scene concludes succinctly; "he ate, and he drank, and he rose
up, and he left" (vs. 34). White speaks of "the brutal simplicity of
Esau's material urges."[105] It "caricatures once again his unpolished
callousness."[106] The narrator's rare condemnation is severe: "and Esau
despised *the* birthright" (vs. 34).[107]

> It means that he legally relinquished his rights, he abrogated the legal
> relationships, according to which he had had the status of the first-born,
> and stepped outside that status.[108]

Some (Jewish) commentators want to show that Jacob was more suitable to receive the birthright.[109] Although Esau has disqualified himself,
this does not make Jacob an attractive candidate.[110] Waltke probably strikes the right balance: "the characterizations serve to demonstrate Esau's unworthiness without exaggerating Jacob's worthiness."[111]
Although the narrator does not condemn Jacob explicitly, it is clear
from what follows that Jacob's actions regarding birthright and blessing (Gen 27) bring dire consequences.[112]

How does the sale of the birthright relate to the oracle? Interpretations differ. Sarna suggests that "Scripture, therefore, by means of the
oracle story, wishes to disengage the fact of Jacob's election from the
improper means the young man employed in his impatience to for-
malize his predestined, independent, right to the heirship."[113] Sarna
points to Jacob's unhappy biography to support his case. Others see

---

[104] W.T. McCree, "The Covenant Meal in the Old Testament," *JBL* 45, no. 1/2
(1923): 120–28, 123.

[105] White, *Narration and Discourse*, 213.

[106] von Rad, *Genesis*, 262; "calculated to point up Esau's lack of manners and judgment" (Speiser, *Genesis*, 195); "Esau's speech and action mark him as a primitive person" (Berlin, *Poetics*, 39).

[107] "Explicit moral commentary is rare in the Bible" (Wenham, *Genesis 16–50*, 178).
Terino notes that vs. 34b refers specifically to the core of the chiastic structure, the
"crux of the unit" (Terino, "A Text Linguistic Study of the Jacob Narrative," 52).

[108] Malul, "'Āqēb "Heel" and 'Āqab'," 206.

[109] Cf. Walton, *Thou Traveller Unknown*, 26; Goodnick, "Jacob's Deception of his
Father," 237; Breitbart, "The Problem of Deception in Genesis 27," 46.

[110] Cf. Alter, *The Art of Biblical Narrative*, 45.

[111] Waltke, *Genesis*, 361.

[112] L.A. Snijders, "Genesis 27: Het bedrog van Jacob," *NTT* 45 (1991): 183–92,
185–186.

[113] Sarna, *Understanding Genesis*, 183.

it as a first step in the fulfilment of the oracle: "'The elder shall serve the younger.' The exchange of the birthright is the first step in that mysterious inversion" (Brueggemann).[114] "Already the elder is becoming the slave of the younger" (Wenham).[115] In contrast, Turner argues that instead of Esau, it is Jacob who is depicted as "serving or assuming the posture of a servant" in various capacities throughout the Jacob-cycle.[116]

Gen 27 seems to suggest that the birthright was only part of the prize. According to Levine the blessing "counted for more, *probably* because pronouncing the blessing was considered to be the act formally acknowledging the firstborn as the principal heir."[117] The amount of text dedicated to the acquisition of the blessing compared with the birthright, suggests that the blessing was of primary importance.[118]

> The status of first-born was thus wound up with responsibilities and obligations on one hand, and rights, privileges, and prerogatives on the other, including a double portion of the patrimony. *All these were formalized by the father's testamentary blessing.*[119]

Unfortunately, Sarna does not provide sources for the latter statement. Frymer-Kensky suggests that although

> Esau had sold Jacob his birthright, Isaac could have nevertheless have appointed Esau as heir when he announced his intention to make a deathbed announcement with the formulaic phrase "now that I have grown old and know not the day of my death" (Gen 27:2), a phrase used elsewhere for just this purpose (...) *however, we really should await more evidence on this point.*[120]

---

[114] Brueggemann, *Genesis*, 218. See also F.W. Golka, "Bechorah und Berachah: Erstgeburtsrecht und Segen," in *Recht und Ethos im Alten Testament-Gestalt und Wirkung* (eds. S. Beyerle, G. Mayer and H. Strauss; Neukirchener, Germany: Neukirchen-Vluyn, 1999), 135. Golka discusses the links between the episodes, but does not really address this issue.

[115] Wenham, *Genesis 16–50*, 179.

[116] Turner, *Announcements of Plot in Genesis*, 121. More on this in Chapters 3 and 4.

[117] B.A. Levine, "Firstborn," in *Encyclopaedia Judaica (electronic ed.)* (vol. 6; Brooklyn, NY, USA: Lambda Publishers, 1997), followed by Hamilton, *Genesis 18–50*, 185 (italics mine).

[118] Grüneberg, *Abraham*, 18 and n. 22.

[119] Sarna, *Understanding Genesis*, 185, referring to Mendelsohn, "On the Preferential Status of the Eldest Son" regarding the double portion (italics mine).

[120] Frymer-Kensky, "Patriarchal Family Relationships," 213, referring to E.A. Speiser, "I Know Not the Day of My Death," *JBL* 74, no. 4 (1955): 252–56, 252–253 (italics mine).

This would explain why Jacob and Rebekah go to such length to obtain that blessing. Thus the question remains, will Jacob be able to acquire the blessing too? A classic cliff-hanger! This issue is resolved in Gen 27, but first we turn to the events of Gen 26.

2.3   Isaac's Wealth (Gen 26:1–33)

2.3.1   Introduction

Gen 26 is a chapter that traditionally has not received much attention. Considered by some to be an uninspiring copy of the Abraham narrative,[121] or a 'mosaic of Isaac traditions,'[122] it is no wonder that "Gen 26 ist ein Kapital, das oft überlesen wird."[123] So far, Isaac has been fairly passive; a minor and secondary figure in the bigger scheme of things.[124] Although Abraham is mentioned repeatedly in Gen 26, Isaac serves here as a person 'in his own right.'[125]

There is the sticky issue of chronology to consider. Some scholars assume that Gen 26 is placed in chronological order, so that Jacob and Esau were with Isaac and Rebekah in Gerar, although their presence is not mentioned.[126] Others consider it highly unlikely that Isaac could

---

[121] "The Isaac story (26) is strikingly brief and hardly developed at all" (Rendtorff, *The Old Testament: An Introduction*, 135). Van Seters has proposed that the Yahwist narrator "simply constructed a life of Isaac based upon similar episodes in the life of Abraham" (J. van Seters, *Abraham in History and Tradition* (New Haven: Yale University Press, 1975), 183–192 and repeated in J. van Seters, *Prologue to History: The Yahwist as Historian in Genesis* (Louisville, Kentucky, USA: Westminster/John Knox Press, 1992), 268); "the most colourless and least original form" (van Seters, *Abraham in History and Tradition*, 167ff.).

[122] Gunkel, *Genesis*, 293 and von Rad, *Genesis*, 264) following Delitzsch.

[123] Dieckmann, *Segen für Isaak*, 1. Sarna, *Understanding Genesis* does not even comment on this chapter, except in some footnotes.

[124] "The most vague and shadowy of all the patriarchs" (L. Waterman, "Jacob the Forgotten Supplanter," *AJSLL* 55, no. 1 (1938): 25–43, 25). "The pale and schematic patriarch" (Alter, *Genesis*, 131). Isaac is best known as the son of Abraham, and the father of Esau and Jacob (R. Martin-Achard, "Remarques sur Genèse 26," *ZAW* 100 Supplement (1988): 22–46, 22–23); cf. Brueggemann, *Genesis*, 221; Boase, "Life in the Shadows," 313; Waltke suggests that "Isaac's gap seems deliberate (…) and reflects his failure to remain faithful" (Waltke, *Genesis*, 351).

[125] Wenham, *Genesis 16–50*, 194.

[126] Polzin, "'The Ancestress of Israel in Danger' In Danger"; D.J.A. Clines, "The Ancestor in Danger: But not the Same Danger," in *What Does Eve do to Help? And other Readerly Questions in the Old Testament* (ed. D.J.A. Clines; Sheffield, UK: Sheffield University Press, 1990), 79; J. Ronning, "The Naming of Isaac: The Role of the

pretend that Rebekah was his sister with two youngsters around,[127] while yet others adopt a more agnostic stance.[128] Probably the best defence of an achronical reading of Gen 26 comes from Nicol.[129] Central to Nicol's argument stands his contention that the organization of the narratives in Gen 12–50 in three cycles "does not reflect an absolute chronology:"[130]

> In spite of the clear boundary between cycles, however, certain aspects of the way generations overlap have of necessity intruded (…) the form of a series of narrative cycles militates against the presentation of events in an exact chronological order.[131]

Nicol argues that Esau and Jacob were aged fifteen at Abraham's death. However, Abraham's death is reported *before* we read about their birth (21:5; 25:7, 19 and 26). Nicol proceeds by discussing three matters of context that are ignored in Gen 26. There is the absence of Esau and Jacob[132] and the reference to Rebekah's beauty (26:7), which could be considered problematic for a strictly chronological reading.[133] In addition, Gen 25:11 states that God blessed Isaac after Abraham's death, yet in 26:3 he is promised blessing, receives it at vs. 12, which is finally acknowledged by others in vs. 29.[134] "Gen 26 gives no indication that Isaac was rich until vv. 12–16," although Gen 25:5 reports that Isaac was Abraham's sole heir.[135] This would suggest that in Gen 26 Abraham

---

Wife/Sister Episodes in the Redaction of Genesis," *WTJ* 53, no. 1 (1991): 1–28, 2; Hamilton, *Genesis 18–50*, 192; White, *Narration and Discourse*, 204.

[127] Gunkel, *Genesis*, 293; Waltke, *Genesis*, 367; Baldwin, *The Message of Genesis 12–50*, 109; G.C. Nicol, "The Chronology of Genesis: Genesis XXVI 1–33 as 'Flashback'," *VT* 46, no. 3 (1996): 330–38.

[128] Speiser, *Genesis*. Speiser does not discuss the relation with 25:19–34 at all (see above). Alter comments on the relationship between Gen 26 and 27, but does comment on the issue of chronology (Alter, *Genesis*, 131–136). Wenham occupies middle ground: "…Gen 25–26 may well be unchronological at points" (Wenham, *Genesis 16–50*, 187, full quote below). Wenham elsewhere states his position that Gen 26:1–33 take place before the twins were born (Wenham, *Genesis 16–50*, 204).

[129] Nicol, "Genesis XXVI 1–33 as 'Flashback'."

[130] Nicol, "Genesis XXVI 1–33 as 'Flashback'," 334.

[131] Nicol, "Genesis XXVI 1–33 as 'Flashback'," 332.

[132] "There are seven references to Abraham in this chapter, although Isaac's children are not mentioned" (G.C. Nicol, "The Narrative Structure and Interpretation of Gen XXVI 1–33," *VT* 46, no. 3 (1996): 339–60, 352). This is also noted by many other commentators.

[133] "Although such things may be possible in story, and as much is apparently claimed for Sarah in Gen 20" (Nicol, "Genesis XXVI 1–33 as 'Flashback'," 337).

[134] Nicol, "Genesis XXVI 1–33 as 'Flashback'," 337.

[135] Nicol, "Genesis XXVI 1–33 as 'Flashback'," 337.

was not dead yet, or Isaac could have lost everything before coming to Gerar, or was rich already and got richer still, similar to Abraham before the LORD called him (12:4–5).[136] Nicol concludes that Gen 26 "functions something like a 'flashback.'"[137] However, according to Dieckmann there is no textual evidence for this:

> Da stellt sich die Frage, ob es den Leser/inne/n nicht leichter fällt, mit dem plötzlichen Ein- und Ausblenden von Figuren oder mit der Vorstellung umzugehen, dass Jitzchak schon reich nach Gerar kommt und dort weiter und weiter gesegnet wird.[138]

Dieckmann has a good point, but he does not address Nicol's challenges of a chronological reading. Probably more problematic for Nicol's argument is the mention of Abraham's death in 26:18.[139] Although chronology is of importance in Genesis, in Gen 26 it does not appear to be overly important. "The whole is timeless in relation to what precedes and follows it."[140]

The third appearance of a wife/sister tale (A: 12:10–20; B: 20:1–18; C: 26:1, 7–17), including the second appearance of material regarding strife with Philistines over wells (21:22–34),[141] has traditionally received most attention from source-, form- and redaction critics. Source-critics assume the existence of parallel document sources to explain this phenomenon; with J responsible for accounts A and C, and E for account B.[142] Form-critics suggest that the three accounts "developed as oral variants of one original story."[143] However, no consensus exists and much speculation remains. Alexander rightly states that "without independent external evidence any conclusions regarding the origin of the wife/sister accounts must always be hypothetical."[144]

---

[136] The last possibility proposed by Dieckmann, *Segen für Isaak*, 320 and by Ronning, "The Naming of Isaac," 20, who argues that because of Isaac's wealth, it would have been quite easy to conceal Esau and Jacob amongst Isaac's servants.

[137] Nicol, "Genesis XXVI 1–33 as 'Flashback'," 330.

[138] Dieckmann, *Segen für Isaak*, 320.

[139] Cf. Ronning, "The Naming of Isaac," 20.

[140] Vawter, *On Genesis*, 290.

[141] Cf. Coats, *Genesis*, 188–191 and 192–195.

[142] Speiser, *Genesis*, 91; von Rad, *Genesis*, 226, 270.

[143] T.D. Alexander, "Are the Wife/Sister Incidents of Genesis Literary Compositional Variants?," *VT* 42, no. 2 (1992): 145–53, 145.

[144] Alexander, "Are the Wife/Sister Incidents of Genesis Literary Compositional Variants?," 153. For an interesting comparison of source-, form- and redaction criticism on this passage, see Ronning, "The Naming of Isaac." Similarly speculative are various theories about the setting in which this chapter was composed/edited:

Garrett has analysed the parallels between the three episodes in terms of "migration; deception; abduction; deliverance; confrontation and conclusion,"[145] and has noted a pattern in which "a narrative element section is consistently present in two out of the three scenes,"[146] while combinations differ from scene to scene. For example: A and C begin with a famine, but not B; in A and B the wife is taken into the harem, but not in C. Waltke concludes that "this pattern tends to debunk the view that these are doublets of the same event"[147] and that "the accounts differ enough that there is no excuse to think it is the same event told twice."[148] The fact that Gen 26:1 refers to the first incident, and presupposes the second,[149] appears to support that position although this is not considered conclusive by all.

In this context, I must mention the work by Polzin on these chapters in relation to wealth and progeny. Contrary to earlier source and form-criticism that studied the *diachronic* relationships between these episodes, Polzin has focused on "the *synchronic* connections between them, also in relation to their literary context."[150] Polzin suggests that these stories present us with

> Transformations concerning the relationships of wealth and progeny to an adulterous situation (…) and the means by which the monarch discovers the truth of the matter. Both sets of transformations concern the way in which man finds out Yahweh's will and purpose.[151]

---

e.g. A. Marx, "Genèse 26, 1–14A," in *Jacob: Commentaire à Plusieurs Voix de Gen 25–36—Mèlanges offerts à Albert de Pury* (eds. J-D Macchi and T. Römer; Geneva, Swiss: Labor et Fides, 2001), 31 proposes it is a *midrash* on Gen 12, which he places in the time of Jeremiah (p. 32) to offer a radical contrast with Gen 25 and 27, modelling a new way of relationship between nations. For other theories cf. J. Vermeylen, "De Guérar à Béer-Shéva—Genèse 26, 14B–25," in *Jacob: Commentaire à Plusieurs Voix de Gen 25–36—Mèlanges offerts à Albert de Pury* (eds. J-D Macchi and T. Römer; Geneva, Swiss: Labor et Fides, 2001); R. de Hoop, "The Use of the Past to Address the Present: The Wife-Sister Incidents (Gen 12:10–20; 20:1–18; 26:1–16)," in *Studies in the Book of Genesis—Literature, Redaction and History* (ed. A. Wénin; Leuven, Belgium: Leuven University Press, 2001).

[145] D. Garrett, *Rethinking Genesis* (Grand Rapids, Michigan, USA: Baker Book House, 1991), 132 (Cf. Waltke, *Genesis*, 210–211).

[146] Waltke's discussion of Garrett's work (Waltke, *Genesis*, 211). Cf. Hamilton, *Genesis 18–50*, 191, especially n. 15.

[147] Waltke, *Genesis*, 211. Cf. Kidner, *Genesis*, 152–153.

[148] Waltke, *Genesis*, 367; cf. G.C. Nicol, "Story-patterning in Genesis," in *Text as Pretext* (ed. R.P. Carroll; JSOTSup 138; Sheffield, UK: JSOT Press, 1992), 226, who reaches a similar conclusion.

[149] Kidner, *Genesis*, 153.

[150] Polzin, " 'The Ancestress of Israel in Danger' In Danger," 81.

[151] Polzin, " 'The Ancestress of Israel in Danger' In Danger," 81.

These transformations work as follows:

> If in Gen 12 Abram becomes wealthy because of the adulterous situation itself, and if in Gen 20 Abraham increases his wealth because of the removal of such a situation, in Gen 26 Isaac's acquisition of great wealth is not because of the adultery or its removal but only is consequent upon the removal of the potential adultery. In other words, the acquisition of wealth is to the removal of adultery in Gen 26 like the acquisition of progeny is to the removal of adultery in Gen 20.[152]

"God's blessing is seen as a *process* and the process is essentially complete when wealth and progeny are obtained under certain conditions,"[153] a process considered complete for Abraham in Gen 24:1.

> Two conditions appear to be necessary before the obtaining of wealth can be considered a fulfilment of God's promise of blessing: a) wealth must be connected with progeny in some way, and b) the obtaining of wealth must satisfy certain standards set by Yahweh.[154]

Polzin encourages the reader to "reflect on the similarities and differences" between Abraham and Isaac.[155] Polzin requires Gen 26 to be interpreted chronologically in relation to 25:19–34, so that 26:1 functions in a similar way as 24:1. However, Esau's and Jacob's presence in Gen 26 is not completely certain (see above). If wealth and progeny *are* linked in the way proposed by Polzin, it is absolutely mindboggling that Esau and Jacob are not mentioned in Gen 26. In addition, Gen 26 clearly shows that the process of blessing is not complete with the acquisition of wealth and progeny (assuming Esau and Jacob were present), because God's blessing is also experienced in the midst of adversity and in the settlement with Abimelech (*shalom*). It also does not explain why Isaac would experience such an apparent reversal of fortune in Gen 27. Polzin offers us one particular insight regarding wealth in Gen 26, but not an exhaustive analysis, and it does not adequately clarify the relationship between Gen 26 and its immediate context (Gen 25, 27). Miscall, in his discussion of Polzin's work, notes: "The themes of wealth and blessing in Genesis are in need of further

---

[152] Polzin, "'The Ancestress of Israel in Danger' In Danger," 87.
[153] Polzin, "'The Ancestress of Israel in Danger' In Danger," 88.
[154] Polzin, "'The Ancestress of Israel in Danger' In Danger," 89.
[155] Cf. Wenham, *Genesis 16–50*, 187 as quoted at the beginning of *Section 2.3*.

investigation since they go far beyond the limited number of texts that I have been analyzing."[156]

Polzin complains that "one of the more lamentable effects" of efforts that solely focus on comparing these parallel accounts is the "lack of concern for how the individual stories fit into their present literary context."[157] Ronning agrees:

> The critical emphasis on studying the narratives in relation to each other at the expense of their relevance to their respective contexts and to the themes of the patriarchal narratives has obscured the literary genius of the one responsible for giving us the patriarchal narratives in their present form.[158]

Gunkel, Speiser, von Rad and Westermann for example, do not comment at all about the relationship between Gen 26 and the immediate surrounding material.[159] Even in Dieckmann's recent study on Gen 26 this tendency is visible, although he does not neglect it altogether.[160] Ronning even goes as far as saying that "acceptance of the source and form critical explanations for these data tend to prevent discovery of their true role."[161]

So, how does Gen 26 fit in with 25:19–34 and 27? This is not immediately clear. Some earlier scholars did not see many links between Gen 26 and the wider context of the patriarchal narratives.[162] According to Walton "chapter 26 within the 'descendants of Isaac' has little to do with the story of Jacob and Esau."[163] To some extent Gen 26 "looks speciously intrusive"[164] and appears to be "more or less isolated from

---

[156] Miscall, *The Workings of Old Testament Narrative*, 42.

[157] Polzin, "'The Ancestress of Israel in Danger' In Danger," 82. For a similar lament: Exum, "Who's Afraid of 'the Endangered Ancestress'?," 99 and Walton, *Thou Traveller Unknown*, 99.

[158] Ronning, "The Naming of Isaac," 6.

[159] Speiser, *Genesis*, 198–204. For similar approaches, see Gunkel, *Genesis*, 293–298; von Rad, *Genesis*, 263–268; Westermann, *Genesis 12–36*, 420–430; and K. Koch, *The Growth of Biblical Tradition: The Form Critical Method* (trans. S.M. Cupitt; New York, USA: Charles Scribner's Sons, 1969); 111–132.

[160] Dieckmann in a very interesting study on Gen 26 dedicates a mere 8 pages to Gen 26 in its immediate context (Dieckmann, *Segen für Isaak*, 317–324).

[161] Ronning, "The Naming of Isaac," 27.

[162] "…without being harmonized with the subsequent large composition of the patriarchal stories" (von Rad, *Genesis*, 265).

[163] Walton, *Thou Traveller Unknown*, 3.

[164] Hamilton, *Genesis 18–50*, 190; "a misplaced appendix to the history of Abraham" (Skinner, *Genesis*, 355).

its narrative context."[165] There is no mention of Jacob and Esau, and
Isaac and Rebekah are "certainly decades removed from the advanced
age they have attained in chapter 27."[166] Fishbane and Rendsburg note
how Gen 26 and 34 stand opposite each other in the palistrophic
structure of the Jacob-cycle (B and B'), and how both chapters create
an 'interlude' for the events that stand on either side of them.[167] They
also identify various elements Gen 26 and 34 have in common,[168] yet
do not discuss in detail the relationship between Gen 26 and what
immediately precedes and follows it.[169] In his discussion on the similarities between Gen 26, 34 and 38, Fokkelman notes:

> These three texts seem to be intrusions only as long as we ignore the
> fact that they are all separated from the boundary of their cycle by the
> space of one story. Thus they form hooks to the adjoining cycles. If we
> notice this and allow ourselves to be instructed by the key words, we
> can integrate these passages thematically with their context despite their
> superficially digressive character.[170]

Like Fokkelman, Ronning argues that a structural analysis must be
complemented with a thematic one.[171] Since Fishbane/ Rendsburg,
such thematic analysis has been carried out by various scholars (e.g.
Fokkelman, Nicol, Wenham and Waltke). I will discuss their contributions in the course of this chapter.

Some earlier scholars considered Gen 26 to be a collection of independent Isaac traditions.[172] More recent scholarship has focussed on
the coherence of this chapter, which seems to have a clear beginning

---

[165] Nicol, "Genesis XXVI 1–33 as 'Flashback'," 331; Coats, *Genesis*, 189.
[166] Vawter, *On Genesis*, 290.
[167] Fishbane, *Text and Texture*, 46–48; Rendsburg, *The Redaction of Genesis*, 56–59.
In a similar vein, White suggests that the function of Gen 26 is "to permit time to
elapse so that Isaac can be old and blind at the beginning of chapter 27" (White,
Narration and Discourse, 204). This assumes that Gen 26 happened after Gen 25 (see
below).
[168] Fishbane, *Text and Texture*, 47 and Rendsburg, *The Redaction of Genesis*, 57–58
(cf. Wenham, *Genesis 16–50*, 186).
[169] Nicol refers to this aspect of Fishbane's and Rendsburg's work as "less helpful"
(Nicol, "Genesis XXVI 1–33 as 'Flashback'," 330).
[170] Fokkelman, "Genesis," 40; and specifically on Gen 26, Fokkelman, *Narrative Art
in Genesis*, 113–115. For similar comments about the function of Gen 34 cf. Sternberg,
Poetics (chapter 12), and Alter, *The Art of Biblical Narrative* (chapter 1) on Gen 38.
[171] Ronning, "The Naming of Isaac," 26; cf. Fokkelman, "Genesis," 40.
[172] Gunkel, *Genesis*; von Rad, *Genesis* (cf. notes by Wenham, *Genesis 16–50*, 184).

(vs. 1) and a clear end (vs. 33).[173] Nicol treats Gen 26 "as a single story that consists of several interrelated episodes."[174] Van Seters shows how "every episode in Gen 26 presupposes what preceded it."[175] My objectives for this section are to analyse Gen 26:1–33 and then to reflect on how that informs our understanding of the nature and role of material possessions, also in relation to the rest of the Jacob-cycle.[176]

2.3.2   *Commentary*

26:1–6

The opening words of 26:1 are identical to the ones in 12:10.[177] However, the writer clarifies that this famine is a different one from 'the days of Abraham.' Because of the famine Isaac makes his way to Abimelech, king of the Philistines, 'unto Gerar.'[178] Gen 26 mentions Abraham repeatedly. Wenham notes several parallels between Gen 26 and Gen 12–14 and 20–21:[179]

> The parallels with the Abraham story thus show that though the arrangement of material in Gen 25–26 *may well be unchronological at points*, chap. 26 at least is hardly misplaced. Indeed, it serves a most important function, locking together the Abraham and Jacob cycles and highlighting

---

[173] Westermann, *Genesis 12–36*, 423; Wenham, *Genesis 16–50*, 184; Dieckmann, *Segen für Isaak*, 203. I will treat vs. 34 as independent from vv. 1–33 (see Section 2.4 on Gen 27).

[174] Nicol, "Gen XXVI 1–33," 339. Although Nicol's primary concern is "with the text as narrative, and not as a theological or historic document," I believe his work is very useful for my theological purposes.

[175] van Seters, *Abraham in History and Tradition* (cf. Wenham, *Genesis 16–50*, 184).

[176] BHS applies the following subdivision: vv. 1–11 and vv. 12–33. Dieckmann subdivides the first section in two: vv. 1–6 and (6)7–11, but suggests that further subdivision is undesirable (Dieckmann, *Segen für Isaak*, 203). Martin-Achard, "Remarques sur Genèse 26," 31 follows geographic location: vv. 1–22 (Isaac in Gerar) and vv. 23–33 (Isaac in Beersheba). For other variants: cf. Hamilton, *Genesis 18–50*: vv. 1–11; 12–22; 23–33; Wenham, *Genesis 16–50*, 184: vv. 1–6; 7–11; 12–17; 18–22; 23–25; 26–31; 32–33 (These differ from von Rad's seven sections (cf. von Rad, *Genesis*, 265); Waltke, *Genesis*, 365. Events in Beersheba echo to some extent the earlier ones in Gerar. Cf. Wenham, *Genesis 16–50*, 184; Waltke, *Genesis*, 365.

[177] וַיְהִי רָעָב בָּאָרֶץ (Dieckmann, *Segen für Isaak*, 205).

[178] גְּרָרָה is the last word in the sentence. Although most commentators assume that Isaac has arrived in Gerar when the LORD appears to him, this is by no means necessary (the combination of וַיֵּלֶךְ and אֶל־ the locative ה could well represent the sense of movements toward. It could well be that the LORD appeared to him on the way to Gerar ('unto Gerar', JPS) (cf. Dieckmann, *Segen für Isaak*, 210–211).

[179] Wenham, *Genesis 16–50*, 187 (cf. Garrett, *Rethinking Genesis*, 136).

the parallels between Abraham and his son. Its position and content invite the reader to reflect on the similarities and differences between the careers of Abraham and of Isaac.[180]

Then the LORD appeared to Isaac (וַיֵּרָא אֵלָיו יְהֹוָה), a phrase repeated in vs. 24. These are important structural markers. There are only six times in Genesis where it is mentioned that the LORD (or God) 'appeared' (וַיֵּרָא). The LORD (or God) only appears to the patriarchs and the frequency decreases from Abraham onwards: 12:7; 17:1; 18:1; to Isaac in 26:2; 24; and to Jacob (וַיֵּרָא אֱלֹהִים) in 35:9.[181] We see a similar pattern in 'blessing talk' by God.[182] At each appearance the LORD makes important promises. Vv. 2–5 echo earlier encounters with Abraham,[183] and "they are replete with echoes of chap. 22, which Isaac may be presumed to have heard."[184] What makes Gen 26 so important is that the promises God made to Abraham, are now transferred to Isaac.[185] Note that these promises are transferred *by God*, and not by the elder patriarch!

> Auf diese Weise wird dem Leser exemplarisch vor Augen geführt, auf welche Art und Weise der Segen Abrahams auf die nächste Generation übergeht. Es geschieht allein auf die Initiative Gottes hin und folgt dabei ganz offentsichlich einem bestimmten Muster, das in Variationen immer wieder kehrt.[186]

---

[180] Wenham, *Genesis 16–50*, 187 (italics mine). "Each generation, at least to some extent, relives the plot of its predecessor" (D.M. Gunn and D.N. Fewell, *Narrative in the Hebrew Bible* (Oxford, UK: Oxford University Press, 1993), 109.). Wenham elsewhere states his position that Gen 26:1–33 take place before the twins were born (Wenham, *Genesis 16–50*, 204). Cf. Westermann, *Genesis 12–36*, 424: "the purpose of this elaboration is obviously to join Isaac to the Abraham tradition by means of a theological clamp." See also Fokkelman, "Genesis," 40; and Fokkelman, *Narrative Art in Genesis*, 113–115.

[181] Cf. Dieckmann, *Segen für Isaak*, 211.

[182] Cf. Appendix B.

[183] Westermann, *Genesis 12–36*, 425: cf. Gen 12:1–3; 13:14–17; 15; 17; 22:15–18; Coats, *Genesis*, 189.

[184] Wenham, *Genesis 16–50*, 189.

[185] Westermann, *Genesis 12–36*, 424.

[186] Taschner, *Verheissung und Erfüllung*, 200–201; So also Fretheim, "Which Blessing?," 290; Mitchell, *The Meaning of BRK*, 35 ("Blessing was not a family possession or 'heirloom' which people could pass on independently of God (contra J. Pedersen, *Israel: Its Life and Culture* (London, UK: Geoffrey Cumberledge, 1926), 193).

It appears that the promises in vv. 3–4 are conditional on Isaac's compliance with the commandments in vv. 2–3,[187] and are a consequence in themselves of Abraham's obedience (vs. 5):[188]

> Because of Abraham's faithfulness with respect to his son (22:16–18), the remaining promises are transmitted directly by God to Isaac (26:3–5, 24) and to Jacob (28:13–14; 35:11–12; 46:3–4).[189]

According to Waltke this conditional element, which is so strong in vv. 2–5, is absent in vs. 24, because Isaac has proven himself to be obedient by not going down to Egypt.[190] The LORD then promises Isaac "I will be with you and I will bless you." Similar words will be repeated in vs. 24, and will be echoed by Abimelech (vv. 28–29). This is the first instance that God promises *to be with* a patriarch.[191] It implies God's "constant protection and care along the way."[192] According to Frettlöh this promise echoes something of God's original creation blessing.[193] Considering God's intentions with the patriarchs (in the light of Gen 1–11), this is quite reasonable. Fretheim's perspective is complementary:

> Blessing becomes a catchall word throughout Genesis to encompass two realities: 1) God's specific, constitutive promises to the elect family (…); and 2) The general, creational realities such as fertility, various forms of prosperity and success in the socio-political sphere, which all of God's

---

[187] The LORD's instructions contain three elements: "do not go down to Egypt" (cf. 12:10; according to Dieckmann, *Segen für Isaak*, 212 this does not imply criticism on Abraham's journey to Egypt); followed by two Qal imperatives: 'dwell' (שְׁכֹן); 'sojourn' (גּוּר) (cf. D.J. Wiseman, "Abraham in History and Tradition Part I: Abraham the Hebrew," *BSac* 134 (1977): 123–30, 130).The promises "and I will be with you and bless you" (vs. 3b) flow logically from the earlier commandments.

[188] Gen 26:5 is considered by some to be a 'deuteronomistic' addition (e.g. Carr, *Reading the Fractures of Genesis*, 156; cf. Brett, *Genesis*, 87), by others to be a 'priestly' addition (e.g. Wenham, *Genesis 16–50*, 189). For a more in-depth discussion of this matter cf. Dieckmann, *Segen für Isaak*, 245, n. 1. Coats suggests this refers to Abraham's obedience in Gen 22, which makes sense considering the other echoes of that chapter in this context (Coats, *Genesis*, 189–190; see above).

[189] Fretheim, *The Pentateuch*, 95.

[190] Waltke, *Genesis*, 366.

[191] H.D. Preuss, "Ich will mit dir sein," *ZAW* 80 (1968): 139–73. (cf. Hamilton, *Genesis 18–50*, 193; C. Westermann, "Promises to the Patriarchs," in *IDB (Supplementary Volume)* (ed. K. Crim; Nashville, Tennesee, USA: Abingdon, 1976), 140, referring to Maag "the first to draw attention to this promise").

[192] D. Vetter, *Jahwes Mit-Sein: Ein Ausdruck des Segens* (Stuttgart, Germany: Calwer Verlag, 1971), 8–9. See also Preuss, "Ich will mit dir sein," 144 (cf. Westermann, "Promises to the Patriarchs," 141–143).

[193] Frettlöh, *Theologie des Segens*, 374–375 (cf. Vetter, *Jahwes Mit-Sein*).

creatures can mediate and experience independent of their knowledge of God.[194]

This distinction is important for Fretheim's interpretation of Gen 27,[195] but appears to be somewhat blurred in Gen 26. Nicol suggests that the promise 'I will be with you' and 'I will bless you,' "are entirely complementary, two aspects of the one divine initiative for Isaac's benefit that together suggest its completeness."[196] The promise of land, which is quite prominent in this first divine appearance to Isaac,[197] appears to be even stronger and more emphatic than what was promised to Abraham.[198] The mention of a divine oath made to Abraham, is yet another reference to 22:16.[199] As in 12:1–3, the promise of a blessing for the nations appears in a climactic position. [200] Only the promises 'I will be with you,' 'I will bless,' and the promise regarding offspring are repeated in vs. 24.

26:7–11

Isaac 'does as he is told,'[201] and settles in Gerar; he 'meets the conditions of blessing.'[202] However, this act of obedience is followed by a serious error of judgment. Isaac engages in duplicity despite the LORD's assurances.[203] When the men of the place ask him about his wife, a fearful Isaac answers 'she is my sister.'[204] Exum laments:

---

[194] Fretheim, "Which Blessing?," 281; cf. Fretheim, *The Pentateuch*, 48–49.

[195] See *Section* 2.4.

[196] Nicol, "Gen XXVI 1–33," 341 (Nicol refers to Vetter, *Jahwes Mit-Sein*, who has analysed the phrase 'I will be with you' throughout the OT. On Gen 26 he concludes: "das in 26,3.24 im 'Mit-Sein' und 'Segnen' anklang", p. 6). Both Nicol and Frettlöh build here on the work of Vetter: Vetter, *Jahwes Mit-Sein*; D. Vetter, "עם with את," TLOT: 919–921.

[197] '…all these lands;' 2x in vv. 3 and 4.

[198] Wenham, *Genesis 16–50*, 189.

[199] "The only divine oath in Gen 12–25" (Wenham, *Genesis 16–50*, 189).

[200] According to Frettlöh, *Theologie des Segens*, 296 an active blessing role for the patriarchs or for their descendants is not in view; instead the LORD blesses those who bless Israel. Mitchell, *The Meaning of BRK*, 34, disagrees in view of Gen 18:18. Most commentators assume that the patriarchs *are* mediators of this blessing (in some form or another): cf. Grüneberg, *Abraham*. (Abraham as "signally blessed" or "models or pioneers the blessing", 244; cf. Moberly, *The Bible, Theology and Faith*, 124); and those who assume a more active blessing role for the patriarchs: Hamilton, *Genesis 1–17*, 373; Turner, *Announcements of Plot in Genesis*, 104 and 111; Janzen, *Genesis 12–50*, 15; Waltke, *Genesis*, 592; Wenham, *Genesis 16–50*, 255.

[201] Humphreys, *The Character of God*, 160.

[202] Waltke, *Genesis*, 369.

[203] Hamilton, *Genesis 18–50*, 193.

[204] Isaac acts like his father in Gen 12 and 20. It might indeed be better to speak of the 'endangered ancestor' instead of the 'endangered ancestress' in these tales (Clines,

It is not the woman's honour so much as the husband's property rights that are at stake. Still we might expect the patriarch to show some concern for his wife's well-being.[205]

According to Nicol the relationship between Isaac and Abimelech is the main focus of Gen 26.[206] Similarly Taschner: "Die Auseinandersetzung mit den Bewohnern des Landes ist das Thema, dass das gesamte Kapitel wie ein roter Faden durchzieht."[207] The unfolding events show that Isaac had no grounds for fear at all.[208] An "implicit negative assessment of Isaac's actions is provided by Abimelech's unanswered final rebuke of Isaac."[209]

26:12–16

Despite Isaac's failure, but as a result of his obedience to dwell in Gerar,[210] he is blessed abundantly by the LORD.[211] The first expression of that blessing is agricultural success. Isaac sowed in "that land…and reaped (וַיִּמְצָא) in the same year a hundredfold," a spectacular yield.[212] The use of the verb מָצָא in the sense of 'reap' with a crop as object is unique in the OT.[213] In vv. 19 and 32 מָצָא appears in conjunction with

---

"The Ancestor in Danger: But not the Same Danger," 67–68; Exum, "Who's Afraid of "the Endangered Ancestress"?," 94; cf. C.A. Keller, "'Die Gefährdung der Ahnfrau': Ein Beitrag zur gattungs- und motivgeschichtlichen Erforschung alttestamentlicher Erzählungen," *ZAW* 66 (1954): 181–91).

[205] Exum, "Who's Afraid of 'the Endangered Ancestress'?," 94.

[206] Rebekah appears to be a minor character in this episode. "Apart from two occasions where she is named (vv. 7 and 8), every reference to Rebekah in Gen 26 is impersonal, and neither of the principals uses her name" (Nicol, "Gen XXVI 1–33," 350). Nicol notes that Rebekah is referred to as 'wife' six times and 'sister' two times.

[207] Taschner, *Verheissung und Erfüllung*, 201.

[208] Nicol, "Gen XXVI 1–33," 350; Hamilton, *Genesis 18–50*, 195; Wenham, *Genesis 16–50*, 190; Clines, "The Ancestor in Danger: But not the Same Danger," 68; Exum, "Who's Afraid of "the Endangered Ancestress"?," 99; M.J. Williams, *Deception in Genesis: An Investigation into the Morality of a Unique Biblical Phenomenon* (ed. H. Gossai; New York, USA: Peter Lang Publishing Inc., 2001), 17; Kidner, *Genesis*, 153.

[209] Williams, *Deception in Genesis*, 17; cf. Newsom, "Bakhtin, the Bible and Dialogical Truth," 303.

[210] Kidner, *Genesis*, 153; Wenham, *Genesis 16–50*, 191.

[211] "These blessings are certainly not the divine response to model obedience by the patriarch" (Hamilton, *Genesis 18–50*, 200).

[212] בָּאָרֶץ הַהִוא a reference to בָּאָרֶץ in vv. 2–3. Cf. Dieckmann, *Segen für Isaak*, 271. For Calvin such earthy blessings are a visible expression of 'providentia Dei' (cf. J. Calvin, *Institutio Christianae Religionis* (Geneva: 1559), vol. 1, chapter 16; Frettlöh, *Theologie des Segens*, 158–162). Dieckmann, *Segen für Isaak*, 273 has suggested a link between God's blessing in Creation, and this passage, in the verb זָרַע (in the Hiphil in Gen 1:11). For Gunkel the report of Isaac's is 'an immense exaggeration' (Gunkel, *Genesis*, 295), for von Rad 'not an exaggeration' (von Rad, *Genesis*, 266).

[213] Cf. BDB 5549; Hamilton, *Genesis 18–50*, 200; Dieckmann, *Segen für Isaak*, 273.

the discovery of wells. This suggests that these discoveries are a result of blessing as well.[214] The close of vs. 12 יְהֹוָה וַיְבָרֲכֵהוּ could be taken as explanatory:[215] "*and indeed* the LORD blessed him," which is to be preferred over separating these words from vs. 12 and linking them into the next sentence.[216] The second expression of divine blessing is Isaac's ever growing riches (vs. 13):

וַיִּגְדַּל הָאִישׁ וַיֵּלֶךְ הָלוֹךְ וְגָדֵל עַד כִּי־גָדַל מְאֹד

The threefold mention of גָּדֵל (Qal: 'become great') followed by the climactic מְאֹד, gives a sense of tremendous increase of greatness.[217] Isaac's wealth takes the form of "flocks and herds and many servants" (vs. 14). This echoes the report of Abraham's riches in 24:35.[218] The phrase 'the LORD blessed him' is placed emphatically at the centre of this account of Isaac's 'growth'. Harvest success and increase in flocks and servants are a *direct* result of that blessing.[219] But as clear as the link between blessing and riches, so is the link between Isaac's riches and the envy that follows: 'and the Philistines envied him' (vs. 14).[220] Abraham experienced similar tensions and animosity (13:2–7), and Jacob would experience the same too (31:1–2).[221] Dieckmann notes "damit wird der auf Jizchak liegende Segen ambivalent."[222] Is a blessing a blessing if it leads to strife and animosity? Brueggemann notes that

---

[214] D.A. Lutz, "The Isaac Tradition in the Book of Genesis" (Drew University, 1969), 158; Dieckmann, *Segen für Isaak*, 273.

[215] Holladay, HALOT #2098; 2379–5.

[216] This is probably also better than the causal 'because', as in the NIV. Similarly, Hamilton, *Genesis 18–50*, 198, who takes this phrase as the beginning of a new sentence, together with vs. 13.

[217] 'Eine allmähliche Steigerung' (Dieckmann, *Segen für Isaak*, 275). Cf. Brueggemann, *Genesis*, 222; McKeown, *Genesis*, 130.

[218] "The LORD has greatly blessed (בֵּרַךְ...מְאֹד וַיהֹוָה) my master, and he has become great (וַיִּגְדָּל). He has given him flocks and herds (צֹאן וּבָקָר)...male servants...". Westermann argues that the description of Isaac's wealth does not fit the patriarchal period (Westermann, *Genesis 12–36*, 425–426), but that opinion is not taken up by many commentators.

[219] Scholars use different language to describe this link: for some Isaac's riches *is* blessing; for some a *result* of blessing; a *visible sign* of blessing; an *expression* of blessing (*Konkretisierung*) (Dieckmann, *Segen für Isaak*, 273); a *demonstration* of blessing (most clearly Fokkelman, *Narrative Art in Genesis*, 114; cf. Wenham, *Genesis 16–50*, 191).

[220] Envy will also find its way into the patriarchal family: Rachel will envy her sister (30:1) and Joseph's brothers will envy Joseph (37:11).

[221] Wenham, *Genesis 16–50*, 191.

[222] Dieckmann, *Segen für Isaak*, 276; 'a mixed blessing' (Lipton, *Revisions of the Night*, 72).

Gen 26 presents us with two facets of the blessing theme: "the *theological claim* of blessing from Yahweh and blessing as *prosperity judged by worldly standards.*"[223] Human perspectives on blessing may well differ from God's.[224] According to Brueggemann the "narrative in its present form finds no conflict between" these two perspectives. However, this *only* rings true when Abimelech acknowledges that Isaac's blessing is from God that these two facets are fully brought together and *shalom* can be restored (vv. 28–31).[225] Nicol comments that "so long as others do not recognize its source in Yahweh, it is not even real blessing."[226] I propose to rephrase that slightly, by stating that Gen 26 demonstrates how divine blessing finds its 'realization' in a post-Gen 3 world. It is only when God is acknowledged and relationships restored that blessing can be truly experienced for what it was meant to be.[227] The efficacy of divine blessing is not limited to wealth-generation in adverse circumstances, but it can be so impressive that the LORD's involvement can be acknowledged and relationships restored. This is not just about Isaac's wealth! Material wealth can be an outworking of divine blessing, but only brings a sense of completeness (*shalom*, vs. 31) if right relations exist. Taking a wider biblical view, that would include right relationships with God, right relationships with other human beings; and right relationships with the rest of creation. That would be true *shalom*.

For the moment, Isaac's wealth leads only to envy and strife.[228] The narrator tells us that the Philistines had filled the wells dug in the days of Abraham (cf. vs. 18), effectively negating their pact with Abraham.[229] It could be interpreted as a mere act of vandalism,[230] but it might have strategic rationale in order to deter people like Isaac from coming in

---

[223] Brueggemann, *Genesis*, 221.

[224] See Appendix B.

[225] Brueggemann rightly refers to the book of Job as an example where the relationship between divine blessing and prosperity judged by worldly standards is not so straightforward (Brueggemann, *Genesis*, 223).

[226] Nicol, "Gen XXVI 1–33," 357.

[227] Cf. J. McKeown, "Blessings and Curses," in *Dictionary of the Old Testament: Pentateuch* (eds. T.D. Alexander and D.W. Baker; Leicester, UK: Inter-Varsity Press, 2003), 84f.; McKeown, *Genesis*, 131: "It is a mistake to think that blessing is the absence of problems."

[228] Gunkel states that the mention of 'envy' is an insertion to harmonize the Abraham narrative, but he does not give any proof for that (Gunkel, *Genesis*, 293).

[229] Waltke, *Genesis*, 370.

[230] Hamilton, *Genesis 18–50*, 200.

the vicinity of Gerar.[231] There is no clear indication when the filling of wells had taken place,[232] or where these wells were located.[233] However, there is a sense that things are turning hostile. Lack of water is a direct threat to Isaac's well-being and new-'found' wealth (both herds and crops) in an area with meagre rainfall.[234] It sets the scene for frantic well-digging that will dominate the rest of the chapter, and for Isaac's imminent expulsion: Abimelech tells Isaac "go away (לֵךְ) from us, for you are much mightier than we (כִּי־עָצַמְתָּ־מִמֶּנּוּ)" (vs. 16). Abimelech's command לֵךְ echoes Pharaoh's command to Abraham in 12:19, to be repeated by another Pharaoh in Ex 12:31 (וּלְכוּ, now plural), because Isaac's descendants had become too mighty (cf. Ex 1:7,9 [וְעָצוּם מִמֶּנּוּ] and 20).[235]

26:17–22

Isaac does not contend with Abimelech and moves on to 'the valley of Gerar,' presumably not too far away from Gerar itself.[236] There is a sense of loss. Although one may assume that Isaac takes his herds with him, the land which was instrumental in providing Isaac's initial riches must be left behind.[237] Why does Isaac not move further away? The answer is given in vs. 18: Isaac starts opening up the wells that had been dug by his father Abraham, giving them the same names. Isaac appears to know the exact location of these wells.[238] Most scholars think Isaac names these wells in order to 'claim ownership over

---

[231] Westermann, *Genesis 12–36*, 426 (cf. 2 Kgs 3:25); V.H. Matthews, "The Wells of Gerar," *BA* 49, no. 2 (1986): 118–26, 121.

[232] See Dieckmann, *Segen für Isaak*, 281–283 for a discussion on the various possibilities.

[233] "Why would Abraham have dug wells in the land of the Philistines?" (Westermann, *Genesis 12–36*, 426). For several references regarding the geographical location of Gerar and Beersheba, cf. Nicol, "Gen XXVI 1–33," 354, n. 25–26. Vs. 18 suggests that these wells were located in the valley of Gerar.

[234] Annual rainfall falls below 300mm (T.L. Thompson, "The Background of the Patriarchs: A Reply to William Dever and Malcolm Clark," *JSOT* 9 (1978): 25; I am indebted to Hamilton, *Genesis 18–50*, 200 n. 11 for this reference).

[235] Cf. Wenham, *Genesis 16–50*, 191.

[236] Dieckmann, *Segen für Isaak*, 280–281; Matthews, "The Wells of Gerar," 120–121 suggests that the distance between Beersheba and Gerar might have only been 15–20 miles (although we cannot be certain).

[237] Nicol, "Gen XXVI 1–33," 359. Matthews suggests that Isaac's acquiescence is easier to understand, because of his knowledge about the existence of these earlier wells (Matthews, "The Wells of Gerar," 124).

[238] Matthews, "The Wells of Gerar," 123 suggests that such information would be passed on from one generation to another.

them.'[239] According to Wenham this fits in with the 'gradual and partial fulfilment' of the patriarchal promises:

> Genesis notes carefully the acquisition of various territorial rights in the land of Canaan, particularly wells, a burial ground and an altar plot (21:25–34; 23:1–20; 26:12–33; 33:19–30). The narrator is very concerned to point out that these rights were either bought outright or recognized in public legal ceremonies, as was the border with the Aramean Laban (31:52).[240]

Vs. 18 speaks of the death of Abraham, which weakens any argument that assumes Jacob and Esau were not around in Gen 26.[241] When Isaac's servants find (וַיִּמְצְאוּ) a new well, of 'living water', the herdsman of Gerar quarrel (וַיָּרִיבוּ) with Isaac's herdsman. [242] The narrator alludes here to the strife between the herdsmen of Lot and Abraham (13:7).[243] The first two wells Isaac's servants dug are contested by the herdsmen from Gerar, and are abandoned by Isaac. The third well is not contested. And so we have a pattern moving from quarrel (2x) to non-quarrel (וַיָּרִיבוּ vs. 20; וַיָּרִיבוּ vs. 21; וְלֹא רָבוּ vs. 22), which is reflected in the names given to these wells (עֵשֶׂק 'dispute'; שִׂטְנָה 'opposition'; רְחֹבוֹת 'space'). With the naming of the last well Rehoboth, Isaac exclaims "for now the LORD has made room (הִרְחִיב) for us, and we shall be fruitful in the land (וּפָרִינוּ בָאָרֶץ)," echoing God's blessing in creation, as already visible in vs. 12.[244] "At last he confesses the influence of Yahweh in his good fortune."[245] Dieckmann states "immerhin ist aber die ambivalente Wirkung des Segens jetzt unterbunden," but that is only fully realized after Abimelech and Isaac have made peace.[246] With the experience of the LORD's preserving presence

---

[239] Hamilton, *Genesis 18–50*, 201; Matthews, "The Wells of Gerar," 121; Waltke, *Genesis*, 370; Hartley, *Genesis*, 242; Dieckmann, *Segen für Isaak*, 284.

[240] Wenham, *Genesis 16–50*, 22. Cf. Clines, *The Theme of the Pentateuch*.

[241] The mention of Abraham's death, weakens Nicol's argument (cf. Nicol, "The Chronology of Genesis: Genesis XXVI 1–33 as "Flashback"; see above). Abraham was 100 years old when Isaac was born (21:5). Isaac was 60 years old when Esau and Jacob were born (25:26). Abraham died at the age of 175 (25:7). Thus Esau and Jacob were 15 years of age when Abraham died.

[242] מַיִם חַיִּים; a very valuable find! Cf. Waltke, *Genesis*, 370; Hamilton, *Genesis 18–50*, 220.

[243] Sailhamer, *Genesis* on this passage; Dieckmann, *Segen für Isaak*, 284.

[244] Cf. Gen 1:22, 28; 8:17; 9:1; 9:7; 17:7; 17:20; 28:3; 35:11; 47:47; 48:4. Cf. Dieckmann, *Segen für Isaak*, 286.

[245] Nicol, "Story-patterning in Genesis," 221.

[246] Dieckmann, *Segen für Isaak*, 286.

in the midst of strife, Isaac's understanding of what God meant with
"I will be with you and will bless you" must have gained substance and
depth, as witnessed by his speech in vs. 22.[247] In a similar way, Jacob
starts to understand more about God when he experiences strife.[248]

26:23–25a

Isaac then moves on to Beersheba, the end of his journey away from
Gerar. Probably quite some time has elapsed since 26:1.[249] And now
the LORD appears (וַיֵּרָא) to him '*the same night.*' There is a sense
of pertinent involvement. This passage reminds us of two encounters
between the LORD and Abraham, not in the least because the mention
of Abraham at the opening and close of the theophany.[250] The preceding verses recalled the conflict between the herdsmen of Lot and of
Abraham. After that conflict had been resolved, the LORD repeated
his promises of land and offspring to Abraham (13:14–17), and Abraham had built an altar to the LORD (13:18), as Isaac would build one
(26:25).[251] Following Abraham's encounter with foreign kings (Gen
14) the LORD came to Abraham in a vision with the words 'fear not'
(15:1). Possibly both incidents are in mind here.

This is the second divine appearance to Isaac in Gen 26. The land-
promise that featured so prominently in vv. 3–4 and the promise of
blessing for the nations are not repeated here. The other three promises are, although there are some small differences, most notably the
promise of divine presence. Instead of a promise for the future (וְאֶהְיֶה
עִמְּךָ 'I will be with you'), it is now a present reality (כִּי־אִתְּךָ אָנֹכִי
'I am with you'). This is part of a realization pattern that will be further developed with Abimelech's speech in vv. 28–29 (see below).
The LORD also repeats the promise to bless Isaac ('I will bless you').
Considering the fact that Isaac already has been blessed by the LORD
with great wealth (vv. 12–14) and by his success in finding water,
it is clear that the LORD's blessing here transcends these particular

---

[247] 'Isaac's expression of faith'(Wenham, *Genesis 16–50*, 191).
[248] See Chapter 3 and 4.
[249] Nicol, "Gen XXVI 1–33," 356.
[250] For the expression 'God of your father Abraham' see bibliography provided
by Hamilton, *Genesis 18–50*, 205, n. 13. The title 'my servant' is a high accolade (cf.
Deut 34:5; Josh 24:29; Num 14:24; 2 Sam 7:8; Isa 42:1; 49:3; 50:10; 52:13; Waltke,
Genesis, 371).
[251] Cf. Sailhamer, *Genesis* on this passage.

realizations of blessing. There is more to come.[252] Although the second divine speech is much more compact than the first and does not repeat every promise element, its language represents an emphatic confirmation. [253] Isaac responds as his father did before him (vs. 25a).[254]

26:25b–33

Vs. 25b mentions the digging of another well. Together with vs. 32, which reports the completion of this well, it frames the climactic encounter between Abimelech and Isaac in Beersheba (vv. 26–31). Gen 26:1 reports how Isaac "went to Abimelech, king of the Philistines." Now Abimelech with senior officials 'went from Gerar to him' (vs. 26). There is a sense of reversal, mirrored geographically,[255] with Isaac being treated as royalty himself; a force to be reckoned with.[256] When Abimelech arrives, Isaac welcomes him with a complaint (vs. 27). The phrase 'sent me away', וַתְּשַׁלְּחוּנִי (Piel from שָׁלַח) occurs three times in vv. 27–31. Abimelech answers diplomatically, suing for a covenant,[257] arguing that they did not 'touch' Isaac, "and have done nothing but good and have sent you away in peace (בְּשָׁלוֹם וַנְּשַׁלֵּחֲךָ)" (vs. 28–29). The first part of the statement is quite reasonable; the second part is clearly stretching the facts![258] Toward the end of the proceedings, Isaac will send them away (וַיְשַׁלְּחֵם),[259] and 'they departed in peace (בְּשָׁלוֹם)' (vs. 31), the climactic conclusion. [260] Abimelech's statements are highly relevant: "we see plainly that *the LORD has been with you*"[261] at the opening of his speech, and "*you are now the blessed*

---

[252] However, tragedy will follow too: Isaac will be deceived by his wife and son Jacob, which results in Jacob's flight. Similarly, Jacob will experience various tragedies following God's blessing in Gen 35 (see *Section* 4.6).

[253] 'A summary and reaffirmation' (Wenham, *Genesis 16–50*, 192). 'A shorter version of vs. 3–5' (van Seters, *Prologue to History*, 269).

[254] Wenham, *Genesis 16–50*, 192; Hamilton, *Genesis 18–50*, 205; Kidner, *Genesis*, 154.

[255] Nicol, "Gen XXVI 1–33," 355–356.

[256] Van Seters describes this as "the transformation of the patriarch from that of wandering nomadic forefather to that of royalty" (van Seters, *Prologue to History*, 270–271).

[257] "The lord-servant relationship of Gerar and Isaac becomes reversed" (Fokkelman, *Narrative Art in Genesis*, 114).

[258] 'Somewhat of a euphemism' (Wenham, *Genesis 16–50*, 193).

[259] Another element to the reversal theme. Cf. Hamilton, *Genesis 18–50*, 208.

[260] Cf. Nicol, "Gen XXVI 1–33," 359–360.

[261] On the relationship between divine revelation and what is observable: See Polzin, "'The Ancestress of Israel in Danger' in Danger;" R. Polzin, "Literary Unity in Old Testament Narrative: A Response," *Semeia* 15 (1979): 45–49 and P.D. Miscall, "Literary Unity in Old Testament Narrative," *Semeia* 15 (1979): 26–43.

of the LORD" at the very end. This is the theological apex of the narrative.[262] Abimelech refers to the visible aspects of the blessing ('we see plainly'): Isaac's wealth (vv. 12–14) and his success in finding wells.[263] According to Mitchell "God's blessing is a visible sign of his favour that attracts the attention of others and make them desire God's blessing too."[264] This resonates with Grüneberg's and Moberley's proposal that the patriarchs are 'signally blessed.'[265] It is only when the Philistines recognize the source of Isaac's blessedness that they can start sharing in the blessing.[266] Many scholars consider this to be a realization of the 'blessing to the nations.'[267] "The narrator deliberately has Abimelech pick up the language of promise (vs. 3)."[268]

Comparing the three passages that contain these promises, we discern the following pattern:

Gen 26:3	"I will be with you"		"I will bless you"	
	The LORD	FUTURE	GOD	FUTURE
Gen 26:24	"I am with you"		"I will bless you"	
	GOD	PRESENT	GOD	FUTURE
Gen 26:28–29	"the LORD has been with you"		"You are now the blessed of the LORD"	
	ABIMELECH	PAST	ABIMELECH	PRESENT

Although the Gen 26 narrative is compact, there is a clear sense of development; the divine promises made in vv. 2–3 are realized to some extent (and as readers we have to ponder *how*). This realization is also reflected in progressive speech. In vv. 2–3 both promises are in the

---

[262] Cf. Fokkelman, *Narrative Art in Genesis*, 114; Dieckmann, *Segen für Isaak*, 300–301.

[263] Westermann, *Genesis 12–36*, 348. Cf. Hamilton, *Genesis 18–50*, 207; Waltke, *Genesis*, 371; McKeown, *Genesis*, 132–133.

[264] Mitchell, *The Meaning of BRK*, 166.

[265] Grüneberg, *Abraham*, 244; Moberly, *The Bible, Theology and Faith*, 124.

[266] Nicol, "Gen XXVI 1–33," 358.

[267] Wenham, *Genesis 16–50*, 193; Wenham, *Genesis 1–15*, 276–278; Dieckmann, *Segen für Isaak*, 303; Brueggemann, *Genesis*, 224; Taschner, *Verheissung und Erfüllung*, 202. "...signally blessed so that others will notice" (Grüneberg, *Abraham*, 244 on Abraham, now true for Isaac).

[268] Nicol, "Gen XXVI 1–33," 357.

future, yet in vs. 24 the promise *to be with* Isaac is stressed as a present reality. This is matched by Isaac's response in speech (vs. 22) and worship (vs. 25). This development further runs its course as witnessed by Abimelech's speech: "the LORD *has been (was)* with you" (past reality); "*you are now* the blessed of the LORD" (present reality). The realization of God's promises is a dynamic and progressive reality. Any analysis regarding the nature and role of material possessions in Gen 26 must take account of this fact.

Isaac and Abimelech make a covenant marked by a meal and oaths.[269] This sworn pact and the Philistine departure בְּשָׁלוֹם (in *shalom*) form an attractive conclusion to the narrative; a realization of the blessing for the nations. "Jetzt ist wahrhaft Frieden geworden."[270] In this particular context, the translation 'in peace' is a good one, although a state of well-being and security might be in view as well. *Shalom* can be considered one aspect of the blessing Isaac (and the Philistines) experience.[271] However, we should be realistic: although the Philistines depart in *shalom*, which is the best possible outcome for the moment, this might not last (vs. 15). Although the settlement is upheld as desirable,[272] there is no need to become teary-eyed. This did not last. Similarly, as we consider the relations between Jacob's and Esau's descendants over the centuries, it is clear that the reconciliation between their forefathers (Gen 33) did not last either.

The episode is brought to a close with the mention that on 'that same day' Isaac's servants come back with news that another well has been found (מָצָאנוּ מָיִם). With that the climactic engagement with

---

[269] Cf. K.A. Kitchen, "Genesis 12–50 in the Near Eastern World," in *He Swore an Oath—Biblical Themes from Genesis 12–50* (eds. R.S. Hess, G.J. Wenham and P.E. Satterthwaite; Carlisle, Cumbria, UK: The Paternoster Press, 1994), 74–77 on the historical features of such a covenant. Cf. McCree, "The Covenant Meal in the Old Testament" for additional information on 'covenant meals.'

[270] Dieckmann, *Segen für Isaak*, 307.

[271] The concept of *shalom* vastly exceeds that of 'peace.' Meaning is best determined on "the basis of particular contextual usage" (P.J. Nel, "שׁלם #8966," NIDOTTE 4:130–135, cf. G. Gerleman, "שׁלם to have enough," TLOT, 1343). Hempel was the first to suggest that the entire content of blessing is summed up in *shalom* (J. Hempel, *Die israelisch Anschauungen von Segen und Fluch im Lichte altorientalischer Parallelen* (BZAW 81; Berlin, Germany: Walter de Gruyter, 1961), 58–61 as discussed by Mitchell, *The Meaning of BRK*, cf. 181–183; Taschner, *Verheissung und Erfüllung*, 100). Wehmeier has rejected Hempel's proposal, arguing that *shalom* is only one of the benefits God bestows when he blesses (G. Wehmeier, *Der Segen im Alten Testament* (Basel: Friedrich Reinhardt, 1970), 140; cf. Mitchell, *The Meaning of BRK*, 182).

[272] Cf. Wenham, *Story as Torah*, 37–41.

Abimelech and his consorts, which led to *shalom*, is set within the framework of divine provisions, an outworking of divine blessing. The success of Isaac's servants in finding wells can be attributed to divine blessing. The Philistines have ended up with two wells as a result of their quarrelling (one of them with 'living water'!), and Isaac has also ended up with two wells. The blessing of finding water is portrayed in Gen 26 as a mix of human struggle and divine provision, a Creation-Fall perspective that is well worth keeping in mind as we consider the outworking of God's blessing in a fallen world.

2.3.3   *Concluding Remarks*

I will summarize my findings regarding the nature and role of material possessions and associated attitudes and actions in Gen 26 under the headings 'relationships;' 'material possessions' and 'God.' I will also comment on the thematic links between Gen 26 and other parts of the Jacob-cycle.

Relationships
In Gen 26 the main relationships are the one between the LORD and Isaac, and the one between Isaac and Abimelech (and the people they represent).[273] These relationships witness substantial development and even reversal (Isaac-Abimelech). Material possessions are very much at the centre of these relationship developments. Isaac's wealth is *the result* of divine blessing (vs. 12–14), yet the *source* of envy for the Philistines; and the quarrel over wells is very much at the heart of Isaac's engagement with the Philistines in vv. 17–22. Material issues can stand at the beginning, middle and end of relationship change. In the relationship between the LORD and Isaac, we see a dynamic interplay between divine promises (vv. 2–5; 24), divine acts (wealth, wells), and Isaac's response in terms of obedience (vs. 6), failure (vv. 7–9), acknowledgement (vs. 22) and worship (vs. 25). To understand the nature and role of material possessions and associated attitudes and actions properly, we need to account for the dynamic engagement between (relevant) divine revelation and human response. With 'relevant' revelation I mean the following: Gen 26:2–5 is a prominent piece of divine revelation for Isaac, but it is probably not the only one

---

[273] Isaac's relationship with Rebekah appears to be of secondary interest in Gen 26 (cf. Nicol, "Gen XXVI 1–33").

we must take into account. If Esau and Jacob were around in Gen 26 (cf. 25:19–34 and 26:18), God's answer to prayer (25:21) should be considered part of the 'relevant' divine revelation to Isaac as well. In addition, if Isaac indeed witnessed God's speech to Abraham in 22:15–18, also that should be included. It is important to realize that material concerns must be understood in the context of the dynamic engagement between (relevant) divine revelation and human response, and that this might differ (to some extent) from person to person. Isaac had direct divine revelation to go on, Abimelech did not. Yet, Abimelech eventually discerns the LORD's blessing presence in Isaac's life and acts accordingly.

The relationship between Isaac and Abimelech is subject to development too. I have noted the reversal that takes place between vv. 6–11 and vv. 26–29. What started as a relationship of benevolent protection, goes through a phase of turmoil, characterized by 'envy,' 'quarrel' and 'hate,' to result finally in 'covenant' and 'peace.' Both divine and human relationships are very much dynamic. Material possessions and concerns are of integral importance to explain these relationship dynamics and are subject to them at the same time. Anything we say about the nature and role of material possessions (in Gen 26) must take account of this.

Material possessions and associated attitudes lead to strife and separation between Isaac and the Philistines. Following their settlement the Philistines depart בְּשָׁלוֹם (in *shalom*). Similarly, Esau and Jacob will separate after a battle over material advancement (Gen 27). They will find some form of resolution (Gen 33) so that Jacob can arrive 'peacefully' (שָׁלֵם) in Shechem (33:18).[274] As the Philistines and Isaac *de facto* divide the wells between them, so do possessions play a role in the conflict resolution between Esau and Jacob.[275] Like Isaac and the Philistines, Esau and Jacob would not stay close together. As Alter puts it:

> We are prepared for the story in which only one of the two brothers can get the real blessing, in which there will be bitter jealousy and resentment; and which in the long run will end with room enough for the brothers to live peaceably in the same land[276]

---

[274] More on this in *Section* 4.4.
[275] More on this in *Section* 4.4.
[276] Alter, *Genesis*, 135.

Their cohabitation would probably better be described as 'living apart together.' In Gen 26 Isaac deceives Abimelech regarding Rebekah. In Gen 27 Isaac is deceived by Rebekah. Similarly, Jacob will deceive in Gen 27, but is the victim of deceit in Gen 29. It is worthwhile to mention the work of M.J. Williams *Deception in Genesis*:

> In Genesis, deception is justified when it functions to restore *shalom* (e.g. Gen 38:1–26; 42:7–28 and 44:1–34).Conversely, when deception introduces a disruption of *shalom*, it is evaluated negatively (…) Restoration of *shalom*, or "the normal way of life.... in all its aspects, along with all of its tensions" (Westermann 1992, 29), is the only purpose for which deception is justified in the accounts of Genesis.[277]

Both Gen 26 and 27 contain occurrences of deceit, which introduce a disruption of *shalom* (according to Williams), and which are evaluated negatively. However, at the end of both narratives, mention is made of *shalom* (26:31; 33:18). It is clear that Gen 26 is more than a mere 'interlude,' and that actually Gen 26 has quite a lot to do with the story of Jacob and Esau.[278]

Material Possessions

In Gen 26, material possessions are a multi-dimensional phenomenon. At the most basic level, they have a past, a present and a future. Isaac's wealth in vv. 12–14 must be understood in relation to past promises (made to Isaac) and a past relationship between the LORD and Abraham (vs. 3, 5 and 24). There is also a present dimension of experiencing God's blessing reality ('I am with you', vs. 24), and 26:12–14 presents that reality with celebration. [279] There is also a future dimension to consider: Isaac's agricultural wealth will not last, as he is expelled (although he will bring his herds with him). There is the material promise of land, which is so emphatic in vv. 3–4, but which remains something for the future. To apply slightly different labels: possessions can be *indicative* of relationship (e.g. 26:12); they can be *corruptive* of relationship (26:14);[280] and Gen 26 shows we need to look

---

[277] Williams, *Deception in Genesis*, 221. C. Westermann, "Peace (*Shalom*) in the Old Testament," in *The Meaning of Peace: Biblical Studies* (eds. P.B. Yoder and W.M. Swartley; Louisville, Kentucky, USA: Westminster/John Knox, 1992).

[278] Contra Walton, *Thou Traveller Unknown*, 3 as quoted earlier. Cf. Gunn, *Narrative in the Hebrew Bible*, 108–109.

[279] Cf. Brueggemann, *Genesis*, 222.

[280] The *redemptive* aspects of possessions (possessions used to improve a relationship; e.g. 33:11), is not in view in Gen 26, although Isaac's sacrifice could possibly be counted in that category.

at them in a *progressive* way (over a longer time period) to discern what is really going on. It is only when we consider the whole well-digging episode (vv. 15–33) that we start to appreciate the interaction between divine blessing and human struggle, which results in the settlement for peace.

Isaac's wealth is indicative of the LORD's relationship with Isaac (vs. 12!), but it also brings the bad relationship between Isaac and the Philistines to the fore. This is even clearer with the digging of the wells. Through the verb מָצָא there is a clear link between the finding of wells and God's blessing, yet at the same time the wells are also indicative of quarrel and strife, as evident in the naming of these wells. There appears to be a contrast in Gen 26 between wealth that results from divine blessing and almost seems to 'happen' and material advancement that results from human struggle, even though the texts suggest that the latter is also under God's sovereignty (vs. 22). Both perspectives are there, and need to be held in tension. The juxtaposition of material blessing, which is received, and what is fought over, "produce a form of dialogism" in Gen 26,[281] which we also see in the Jacob-cycle at large.[282] At the end of Gen 26 the tension of this dialogism is to some extent reduced, when Abimelech acknowledges the LORD's presence in Isaac's life. This suggests that the dialogism is caused in part by difference in perspective and/or difference in information of the parties involved. Similarly, the dialogism regarding divine blessing vs. human blessing in the Jacob-cycle is explained in part by the fact that Jacob does not yet know the LORD in Gen 27, and that it will take him a long time to learn what it means to be truly blessed. Similarly, I will argue that the struggle between Esau and Jacob is over the tangible part of Isaac's blessing. This is what Esau and Jacob are struggling over.[283] The dialogical nature of Isaac's wealth is also visible in the Jacob-cycle at large. "The paradoxical marks of *gift and conflict* dominate the Jacob narrative."[284]

---

[281] Newsom, "Bakhtin, the Bible and Dialogical Truth," 299; Brodie, "Genesis as Dialogue," 305; Dieckmann, *Segen für Isaak*, 325ff.

[282] Cf. Brueggemann, *Genesis*, 227ff. More in this in Chapter 3 (Jacob's wealth) and Chapter 4, where Jacob's wealth offered as a gift signifies reconciliation (Gen 33), vs. the plunder of war in Gen 34.

[283] Cf. Wenham, *Genesis 16–50*, 187; Waltke, *Genesis*, 354 and 367; Fokkelman, *Narrative Art in Genesis*, 115; Walton, *Thou Traveller Unknown*, 100; Dieckmann, *Segen für Isaak*, 321.

[284] Brueggemann, *Genesis*, 214.

God

At the beginning of Gen 26 the divine promises God made to Abraham are transferred to Isaac. In Gen 28 God will make similar promises to Jacob at Bethel, transferring them again to the next generation. In Gen 27 there is the intense struggle to obtain Isaac's blessing, which itself is linked thematically with the struggle over the birthright (25:29–34).[285] But what is Isaac's blessing all about? Does Isaac transfer God's blessing to his son, or is it something different altogether? Taschner notes that Isaac's behaviour of conflict avoidance and peace-making in Gen 26 also differs markedly with the understanding of blessing in Gen 27 ('ein krasser Gegensatz').[286]

How the divine promises are realized is sometimes tangible (e.g. Isaac's wealth and his success with well-'finding').[287] Sometimes it takes a more hidden or intangible form (protection, covenant with the Philistines). It is interesting to see how commentators attribute different 'outcomes' to these promises. Waltke is probably most inclusive:

> Here the blessing includes protection (26:8–9, 11, 31), enjoyment of his wife (26:8, 11), yield of a hundredfold (26:12–13), herds and servants (26:14), water supply (26:17–22, 32), space (26:22), and triumph over his enemies (26:26–31).[288]

However, the narrative is much less explicit. Brueggemann summarizes blessing in Gen 26 as follows:

> The blessing theme is this-worldly. In its main import, chapter 26 is not concerned with long-range hopes for what will be given in some distant future. Rather, it is celebrative of the present working out of prosperity and well-being in quite visible form. Isaac enjoys *great prosperity, judged by worldly standards*, apart from any theological notion.[289]

Although much of Gen 26 is about human relationships and human struggle, divine revelation provides the framework for this episode. God's revelation does contain substantial promises that imply

---

[285] Wenham, *Genesis 16–50*, 178; Waltke, *Genesis*, 355; Hamilton, *Genesis 18–50*, 185; van Seters, *Prologue to History*, 280–288; Dieckmann, *Segen für Isaak*, 318–319; Walton, *Thou Traveller Unknown*, 110–11.

[286] Taschner, *Verheissung und Erfüllung*, 202. I will address all these questions in *Section* 2.4 and Chapter 3.

[287] Isaac's wealth in vv. 12–14 is clearly labeled as divine blessing by the narrator. Isaac's success in digging wells is also attributed to help from the LORD, through the subtle use of the verb ac'm', yet it takes a while for Isaac to discern and acknowledge that (vs. 22).

[288] Waltke, *Genesis*, 370–371.

[289] Brueggemann, *Genesis*, 222.

'long-range hopes' (the land promise, multiple offspring), but these are indeed not of immediate concern for the human struggle in Gen 26.[290] The fact that Isaac responds to that revelation (although not perfectly), the fact that he credits God for blessing him in the midst of strife (vs. 22), and that he eventually builds an altar and calls on the name of the LORD (vs. 25), plus the fact Abimelech acknowledges the LORD's presence and blessing in Isaac's life mean that Isaac's visible wealth cannot be separated 'from any theological notion. ' There is interaction and development in the relationship between the LORD and Isaac, although the full picture of that relationship's reality might not readily appear.

Finally, Gen 26 offers us a Creation-Fall perspective.[291] According to McKeown "it is a mistake to think that blessing is the absence of problems."[292] The famine and repeated contention over wells form a harsh contrast with the lush reality of the Garden, where water was abundantly present. The human relationship dynamics of fear, deceit, envy, quarrel and hate remind us that we are in post-Gen 3 territory. It is instructive to see how divine blessing unfolds in a fallen world. For some this makes the blessing 'ambivalent' (Dieckmann), but it might also offer a helpful paradigm for understanding the relationship between God's blessing and material possessions in a world in which both blessing and curse are daily realities. Fokkelman's suggestion to consider Gen 26 'demonstration material' (what is a blessing, how does it work?) is a useful one, especially as we turn our attention to the relationship of Gen 26 with other parts of Genesis (and beyond). With this in mind, we now turn to the seedy events of Gen 27.

2.4   ISAAC BLESSES JACOB (GEN 26:34–28:9)

2.4.1   *Introduction*

The episode starts in 26:34 and closes in 28:9; 28:10 marks the next major episode.[293] "The deception of Isaac is set within the framework

---

[290] One wonders, if Esau and Jacob were already born, why that is not mentioned at all in relation to these promises.

[291] Cf. Polzin, "'The Ancestress of Israel in Danger' In Danger," 95, who interprets Gen 12, 20 and 26 in light of divine blessing and curse.

[292] McKeown, *Genesis*, 131.

[293] Walton, *Thou Traveller Unknown*, 100; Wenham, *Genesis 16–50*, 201; Coats, *Genesis*, 206; van Seters, *Prologue to History*, 288ff.

of the problems caused by Esau's marriages"[294] (26:34–35; 28:6–8),
which also provide the rationale to send Jacob away (27:46–28:5). Most
source critics assign 26:34–35 and 27:46–28:9 to P, 27:1–45 to J,[295] and
see the blessings of Isaac in 27 and 28 as two separate and independent
events.[296] However, one needs to come to a conclusion how these texts
relate in their final form, and how they relate to the divine promises in
Gen 26, 28:13–15 and to wider contexts. Many commentators assume
that Isaac is transferring the 'blessing of Abraham' in Gen 27,[297] but I
will discuss various reasons why this is not necessarily the case.[298]

Many scholars have commented on the compositional brilliance of
Gen 27,[299] and on its interaction with the wider context. Although I
will refer to these findings, I do not intend to repeat or summarize
them in detail here. Most commentators identify a "tightly-knit scenic
structure" of five scenes, in which only two characters engage at a
time.[300] Scene 3 (Isaac's blessing of Jacob) stands at the centre of this
structure:

> Scene 1: Isaac and Esau (vv. 1–4)
>   Scene 2: Rebekah and Jacob (vv. 5–17)
>   Scene 3: Isaac and Jacob (vv. 18–29)
>   Scene 4: Isaac and Esau (vv. 20–40)
> Scene 5: Rebekah and Jacob (vv. 41–45)

Scenes 2 and 3 interrupt the expected sequence of events so that Jacob
literally takes the place of his brother. Fishbane and Fokkelman argue
for a sixth scene (Isaac and Jacob, 28:1–5), so that the 'blessings' upon

---

[294] Wenham, *Genesis 16–50*, 202. Cf. Waltke, *Genesis*, 375–376 and 383.

[295] Cf. Walton, *Thou Traveller Unknown*, 100–102; Carr, *Reading the Fractures of Genesis*, 85–88; and Wenham, *Genesis 16–50*, 202–204 for more in-depth discussions. Wenham argues that the arguments to assign 26:34–35 and 27:46–28:9 to P are not weighty (203). L. Schmidt, "Jakob erschleicht sich den väterlichen Segen: Literaturkritik und Redaktion von Genesis 27,1–45," *ZAW* 100, no. 2 (1988): 159–83 continues to defend the former consensus that 27:1–45 are a composite of J and E (cf. von Rad, *Genesis*, 271; Gunkel, *Genesis*, 298ff.).

[296] Cf. Westermann, *Genesis 12–36*, 447–448.

[297] Cf. Boase, "Life in the Shadows"; Walton, *Thou Traveller Unknown*, 111.

[298] Cf. Fretheim, "Which Blessing?"; Snijders, "Genesis 27: Het bedrog van Jacob."

[299] Cf. Fokkelman, *Narrative Art in Genesis*, 97–112; White, *Narration and Discourse*, 214–231; Sternberg, *Poetics*; Taschner, *Verheissung und Erfüllung*, 37, n. 89; Sailhamer, *Genesis, ad loc.*

[300] Walton, *Thou Traveller Unknown*, 111; Taschner, *Verheissung und Erfüllung*, 37–38.

Jacob and Esau stand as mirror images opposite each other. This is quite fitting as we consider the language of these blessings in more detail below. Also, in scene 6, Jacob has now firmly taken the place of Esau as the 'son of the blessing' in scene 1.[301] In addition, Fokkelman argues that "the location of the two poems within the framework of the entire story provides structural proof that the disputed passage 27:46–28:5 forms an organic part of the whole."[302] Whether Fokkelman is correct, or whether we are dealing with five or six scenes is not essential for our discussion; both have their merits.[303] Following a detailed exegesis I will reflect on how these events inform our understanding on the nature and role of material possessions in the Jacob-cycle.

2.4.2 *Commentary*

26:34–35

The announcement of Esau's marriages comes out of the blue. The mention of his age invites comparison with similar events in the Abraham-cycle. When Isaac was forty, he married Rebekah, the result of a careful search instigated by his father.[304] When Abraham was one hundred years old, he got a son, Isaac. In contrast, Isaac got two pagan daughters-in-law. Who is to blame? Has Esau acted in disobedience?[305] Why did Isaac fail to follow his father's example of being pro-active?[306] Gen 28:6–8 will shed additional light on this issue. Esau's decisions embittered his parents in 26:35 (מֹרַת), but Esau will cry out an 'exceedingly great and bitter (וּמָרָה) cry' as a result of the actions of his parents in 27:34.[307] This is one of many reversals in the Jacob-cycle.

---

[301] Fokkelman, *Narrative Art in Genesis*, 97–98; Fishbane, *Text and Texture*, 49–50; Bar-Efrat, *Narrative Art*, 99–100. Note that Gunkel already identified the first four scenes, and treated vv. 41–45 as a transitional conclusion (Gunkel, *Genesis*, 302ff., followed by Brueggemann, *Genesis*, 231ff.).

[302] Fokkelman, "Genesis," 46.

[303] Taschner, *Verheissung und Erfüllung*, 38.

[304] Waltke, *Genesis*, 375.

[305] Waltke, *Genesis*, 375; Sarna, *Genesis*, 189.

[306] Cf. C.F. Pfeiffer, *The Patriarchal Age* (Grand Rapids, Michigan, USA: Baker Book House, 1961), 80; Waltke, *Genesis*, 375; Wenham, *Genesis 16–50*, 205.

[307] Hamilton, *Genesis 18–50*, 211.

27:1–4

Vv. 1–2 introduce a deathbed 'type-scene' (cf. Gen 49–50; Deut 31–34).[308] The fact that Isaac cannot see will be exploited to the full. Isaac's other senses (taste, touch, hearing and smell), although not perfect, appear to be in good working order and endanger Rebekah's and Jacob's ploy at various points. This adds tremendous suspense to the drama. Most commentators assume that Isaac and Esau were executing a well-known custom.[309] Keukens notes various 'irregularities' in the proceedings: Isaac 'does *not* know the day' of his death and indeed will linger for another eighty years (35:28); instead of inviting all his sons, Isaac only invites Esau, and instead of a public ceremony he attempts to conclude his business in secret. Isaac does not intend to give Jacob any share in this blessing, which is evident when no blessing is left for Esau.[310] According to Keukens, these irregularities render the blessing null and void:

> Gen 27,1–45 ist die Geschichte von einem leeren Segen, der nichts anderes als drohenden Fluch bewirkt, weil von allen Familienmittgliedern mit dem Sterbesegen und seinem Zeremoniell nur Spott getrieben wird (Gen 27,12). In der Geschichte wird kein Blinder verspottet, sondern es sind Blinde, die verspotten.[311]

However, it is clear from the text that both Isaac and Esau consider the blessing valid and both realize that a given blessing cannot be revoked.[312] To judge the efficacy of the blessing we need to consider how it is fulfilled for Jacob and his descendants. Following Keukens, Wenham concludes that "the whole procedure is thus flawed from the outset."[313] Hartley's proposal that Isaac reserved the spiritual blessing

---

[308] Alter, *The Art of Biblical Narrative*, 51; Wenham, *Genesis 16–50*, 202; 'Ein 'Idealtyp' (K.H. Keukens, "Der irreguläre Sterbesegen Isaaks—Bemerkungen zur Interpretation von Genesis 27,1–45," *BN* 19 (1982): 43–56, 43); Sternberg speaks of the 'type of the Departing Patriarch' (Sternberg, *Poetics*, 349).

[309] Brueggemann, *Genesis*, 231; Walton, *Thou Traveller Unknown*, 113. Speiser has attempted to link Isaac's phraseology to Hurrian custom (Speiser, "I Know Not the Day of My Death," 252–253; cf. Wenham, *Genesis 16–50*, 205; Frymer-Kensky, "Patriarchal Family Relationships," 231; West, "The Nuzi Tablets," 71). This is disputed by T.L. Thompson, *The Historicity of the Patriarchal Narratives: The Quest for the Historical Abraham* (BZAW 133; Berlin, Germany: Walter de Gruyter, 1974), 285–293, cited by Wenham, *Genesis 16–50*, 206

[310] Wenham, *Genesis 16–50*, 205; Baldwin, *The Message of Genesis 12–50*, 114.

[311] Keukens, "Der irreguläre Sterbesegen Isaaks," 51.

[312] McKeown, *Genesis*, 136–137.

[313] Wenham, *Genesis 16–50*, 202.

for Jacob (cf. 28:3–5) and that this is the reason why he was not invited for the first blessing ritual, appears highly unlikely.[314] Hartley is probably right in assuming that the blessings in Gen 27 and 28 are different things altogether.

Isaac calls Esau and says to him 'my son' (בְּנִי) and he replied 'here I am' (הִנֵּנִי).[315] Jacob will say to Isaac in vs. 18 'my father…הִנֵּנִי' and so verbally supplant his brother. The phrase 'my son' (בְּנִי) appears no less than thirteen times in this passage,[316] and there are sixty-seven (!!) familial relationship references in Gen 27 alone (e.g. 'his father,' 'her son,' 'my brother'). Some of these are quite ironic: "Then Rebekah took the best garments of Esau *her older son*…and put them on Jacob *her younger son*" (vs. 15, also vs. 42). Such apparently redundant information appears to be part of a deliberate tactic by the narrator.[317] The human actors are fully aware of the various familial relationships and of their positions (as evident by their speech), yet act in complete disregard for them. The parental favouritism that was introduced in 25:28 is also brought out this way: Esau is 'his son' (Isaac's; vv. 1, 5 and 20). Rebekah calls Jacob 'my son' (vv. 8, 13 and 43), and he is 'her son' in vs. 17.[318] Note also the similarities of vv. 19 and 32 ('I am Esau your firstborn' vs. 'I am your son, your firstborn, Esau'). All these relationships, of which there is so much awareness, yet such little regard, will be damaged as a result to obtain Isaac's blessing of prosperity and dominion.

Isaac's speech is framed by references to his assumed impending death (vs. 2 and 4), which proves to be far off. Isaac's speech majors on the events of hunting 'game' (צַיִד), and the preparation of 'delicious food' (מַטְעַמִּים) 'as I love' (אָהַבְתִּי), so that his blessing may follow

---

[314] Hartley, *Genesis*, 248. Similar reasoning is followed by some Jewish scholars (e.g. N. Scherman and M. Zlotowitz, *Bereishis/Genesis: A New Translation with a Commentary anthologized from Talmudic, Midrashic and Rabbinic Sources* (New York, USA: Mesorah, 1980), vol. 3: 1020–1029, as cited in Walton, *Thou Traveller Unknown*, 120, n. 68).

[315] Significantly also in Gen 22:1 (Walton, *Thou Traveller Unknown*, 112–113). Cf. Hamilton, *Genesis 18–50*, 211, n. 2.

[316] Cf. Hartley, *Genesis*, 246.

[317] See also K.P. Bland, "The Rabbinic Method and Literary Criticism," in *Literary Interpretations of Biblical Narratives* (ed. K.R.R. Gros Louis; Nashville, Tennessee, USA: Abingdon Press, 1974), 19.

[318] Cf. Hartley, *Genesis*, 246; I. Willi-Plein, "Genesis 27 als Rebekka-geschichte: Zu einem historiographischen Kunstgriff der biblischen Vätergeschichten," 45 (1989): 315–34, 326–327.

(תְּבָרֶכְךָּ). Blessing is clearly the main concern of this passage, but in Gen 27 only human actors utter blessing phraseology.[319] The repeated mention of 'game' and 'delicious food' is important as well.[320] Whereas Isaac once loved Rebekah (24:67), his love for food explains his favouritism of Esau (25:28). "The old man's bondage to his appetite"[321] will enable Rebekah's and Jacob's cynical ploy to succeed (cf. closing words of vs. 9 and 14). The mention of hunting also reminds us of an earlier hunting expedition. [322] White harshly comments: "the 'savoury dish' is thus the quintessence of the hunt and the embodiment of the materialist, violent, desire-driven mentality that goes with it."[323] Although Jacob and Rebekah operate by stealth and cunning instead of violence, it is difficult to see how they are any less 'materialist' or 'desire-driven.'[324] Subsequent events in Jacob's life show that his material well-being was a top-priority.[325] Isaac's focus on 'delicious food' is reminiscent of Esau's urge for instant gratification on the occasion of the sale of 'his' birthright.[326] The narrative seeds that were sown in Gen 25:19–34, now come to full fruition. [327]

The phrase 'my soul' (נַפְשִׁי) begs attention. Earlier scholars suggested an association between blessing and the bestowing of one's energy, life-force and vitality on the receiver of the blessing.[328] Mitchell demonstrates that this link is untenable; "there is no more soul-transfer

---

[319] 23 occurrences in Gen 27; 5 occurrences in 28:1–9. See also Appendix B; Sarna, *Genesis*, 189.

[320] The word 'game' (צַיִד) is repeated eight times and 'delicious food' (from מַטְעַם) six times (cf. Waltke, *Genesis*, 377). "It is not unusual to have the consumption of food and drink as an accompaniment to blessing" (Hamilton, *Genesis 18–50*, 213 and n. 10; cf. Kidner, *Genesis*, 156. Sternberg perceives a subtle echo of Lot's self-indulgence (Sternberg, *Poetics*, 350).

[321] Wenham, *Genesis 16–50*, 206.

[322] Gunn, *Narrative in the Hebrew Bible*, 58.

[323] White, *Narration and Discourse*, 215.

[324] Leaving White's value judgment on hunting aside, how is the slaughter of goats any less violent than the hunting of game?

[325] See Section 2.5 and subsequent chapters of this study.

[326] Brueggemann described 25:29–34 as a contrast between *deferred* and *immediate* material blessing (Brueggemann, *Genesis*, 219).

[327] Cf. Sternberg, *Poetics*, 338–339.

[328] Walton, *Thou Traveller Unknown*, 113. Cf. Pedersen, *Israel: Its Life and Culture*. and Hempel, *Die israelisch Anschauungen von Segen und Fluch im Lichte altorientalischer Parallelen*; Wehmeier, *Der Segen im Alten Testament*, and to some extent C.A. Keller and G. Wehmeier, "ברךto bless," TLOT, 268 and Snijders, "Genesis 27: Het bedrog van Jacob," 189.

in Gen 27 than there is in the texts from Mari, Nuzi and Alalakh."[329]
More recent commentators have simply translated נַפְשִׁי as 'I' or have
interpreted this as indication of Isaac's intense desire to bless Esau.[330]
To determine the nature of Isaac's blessing, it is better to focus on
vv. 27–29 than to deduce meaning from this particular phrase. It is
interesting to see how this phrase is picked up by various parties in the
course of events (cf. vv. 4, 7, 10, 19 and 31).[331] Rebekah is the only one
who does not use the phrase נֶפֶשׁ. Instead she uses 'before the LORD'
(לִפְנֵי יְהוָה, vs. 7), presumably to add gravity to her speech in order to
convince Jacob.[332]

Isaac's and Esau's actions in Gen 27 appear to be in tension with
25:19–34.[333] Several issues are raised: What is the relation between
birthright and blessing, as suggested by the wordplay and 27:36?[334] If
birthright and blessing go together, why does Esau appear to disregard the sale of his birthright to Jacob?[335] Did Isaac know about the
sale of the birthright? Did Isaac know about the birth-oracle?[336] These
are questions over which much scholarly ink has been spilled. I will
suspend judgment on these issues for now.[337] First, we will see to
what lengths Rebekah and Jacob are willing to go to acquire Isaac's
blessing.

---

[329] Mitchell, *The Meaning of BRK*, 81–82.

[330] E.g. 'so that I may bless you' (NRSV) or 'give you my blessing' (NIV). 'I may
solemnly bless you' Alter, *Genesis*, 137 ('an intensive synonym'). Wenham suggests it
expresses Isaac's strong desire to bless Esau (Wenham, *Genesis 16–50*, 206). Similarly
Mitchell: 'So I may wholeheartedly bless you' (Mitchell, *The Meaning of BRK*, 82; cf.
BDB 660a and b). ESV and JPS stick to 'my soul.'

[331] Taschner, *Verheissung und Erfüllung*, 39; Fishbane, *Text and Texture*, 50.

[332] Sternberg, *Poetics*, 392–393; Walton, *Thou Traveller Unknown*, 114; and Hamilton, *Genesis 18–50*, 215–216, although Hamilton points out that such a strategy could
make Jacob more hesitant to participate, which of course it did not.

[333] Cf. Miller, "Contracts of Genesis," 27ff.

[334] As noted by various commentators e.g. Grüneberg, *Abraham*, 17; Wenham,
Genesis 16–50, 178; Hamilton, *Genesis 18–50*, 185; Fokkelman, *Narrative Art in Genesis*, 99. See also *Section 2.2*.

[335] Waltke comments that the relationship between birthright and blessing is
unclear, but that in Esau's mind they are separate issues (Waltke, *Genesis*, 377).

[336] Cf. Sternberg, *Poetics*, 350; Hamilton, *Genesis 18–50*, 212.

[337] Cf. Sternberg, *Poetics*, 186f. on the fascinating topic of 'gaps.'

27:5–17

Vs. 5 serves as transition between scenes.[338] Rebekah overhears Isaac's speech (שָׁמַעַת) similar to Sarah's listening in (18:10).[339] Rebekah exhorts Jacob to take immediate action; scene 1 and 2 vividly display the loyalties as reported in 25:28. Rebekah is firm. It is instructive to study how she reports the events of vv. 1–4 by leaving out certain details and adding others (e.g. לִפְנֵי יְהוָה, vs. 7).[340] Rebekah is using God's name to advance her purposes. Jacob will do likewise in vs. 19. Rebekah's solemn command in vs. 8 is unique for a woman in the OT.[341] Walton notes that for the narrator and his reader the words 'command' and 'obey' would "normally apply to the correct attitude to God and to the Torah."[342] Rebekah outlines her plan (vv. 9–10). Her choice of words and the closing phrase ("so that he may bless you before he dies") are all geared towards a positive response. Jacob is careful and calculating; he does not express any doubt about the morality of Rebekah's proposal, instead he focuses on the risk of being found out (vv. 11–12).[343] Jacob's focus on the downside of the plan ("and bring a curse upon myself and not a blessing")[344] indicates that he is fully aware of the seriousness of this deceit.[345] Rebekah's cavalier response ("let your curse be on me, my son", vs. 13) is interpreted by some as a true piece of heroism,[346] but it was probably a fairly empty gesture, as uttered blessings (and curses) were believed to be irrevocable, as the

---

[338] Hamilton, *Genesis 18–50*, 213 and n. 11; Fokkelman, *Narrative Art in Genesis*, 100, n. 18.

[339] On a further comparison between Sarah and Rebekah, cf. Exum, *Fragmented Women: Feminist (Sub)versions of Biblical Narratives*, 146–147.

[340] Cf. Alter, *The Art of Biblical Narrative*, 88ff.; Hamilton, *Genesis 18–50*, 215–216; Wenham, *Genesis 16–50*, 206–207; Fokkelman, *Narrative Art in Genesis*, 102; 'an artful piece of rhetoric' (Sternberg, *Poetics*, 156).

[341] On מְצַוָּה : the only occurrence of the feminine participle in the OT (Wenham, *Genesis 16–50*, 206).

[342] Walton, *Thou Traveller Unknown*, 115.

[343] Hamilton, *Genesis 18–50*, 216; Walton, *Thou Traveller Unknown*, 215; Fokkelman, *Narrative Art in Genesis*, 103.

[344] Cf. Deut 11:26–28 and 30:1, 19 (Mitchell, *The Meaning of BRK*, 82). On the consequences of being cursed (misfortune): H.C. Brichto, *The Problem of "Curse" in the Hebrew Bible* (JBL Monograph Series 13; Philadelphia, USA: Society of Biblical Literature and Exegesis, 1963), 197–199, as cited by Mitchell).

[345] Cf. Lev 19:14, Ex 21:17 and the curse in Deut 27:18 for those who physically mislead the blind (Wenham, *Genesis 16–50*, 207).

[346] C.G. Allen, "On Me Be the Curse, My Son!," in *Encounter with the Text: Form and History in the Hebrew Bible* (ed. M.J. Buss; Philadelphia, Pennsylvania, USA: Fortress Press, 1979); Jeansonne, *The Women of Genesis*, 67.

subsequent narrative makes clear.[347] However, Rebekah is desperate to see *her* Jacob receive the blessing and she is not easily thwarted, and so takes responsibility for the bulk of the preparation (vv. 13, 14b–17). Jacob's participation by comparison appears limited, expressed by three short verb forms in vs. 14a (וַיֵּלֶךְ וַיִּקַּח וַיָּבֵא). This has been interpreted by some as a lack of enthusiasm,[348] and by others as proof of Jacob's efficient compliance.[349] Preparing the 'tasty food' is only one part of the scheme. Rebekah puts Esau's 'best garments' on Jacob and attaches the goat skins on Jacob's hands and neck to avoid detection, "a clever set of stage props designed to fool the blind."[350] What to think about the morality of Rebekah's and Jacob's actions? White notes that clothing is "virtually never mentioned" in Genesis "except where it serves as a sign of a hidden inner state, or serves to deceive;"[351] e.g. Adam's and Eve's shame (3:7); Joseph's robe as a sign of favouritism (37:3–4), later used to deceive his father (with goat's blood! 38:31–33); Potiphar's wife uses Joseph's robe as a basis for false charges (39:13, 15). And Tamar uses clothing to advance her tactics with Judah (38:14–15).

> Clothing is thus a reflection of the divided nature of corporeal existence. It conceals and reveals in the continuous interplay of intentional deception and unintentional disclosure that is characteristic of the fragmented world "east of Eden". Clothing is never mentioned as an act of simple description.[352]

I agree wholeheartedly with this. However, White omits to mention one piece of clothing that offers a different perspective: the superior piece of clothing provided for Adam and Eve before they leave the Garden (3:20), testimony to human fallenness, but also a sign of divine grace. The use of clothing in Genesis illustrates the duality (Creation/Fall perspective) offered in Genesis regarding material possessions post-Gen 3 ('east of Eden'). And so Jacob, provided with various stealth devices including Rebekah's 'tasty dish,' steps into the next scene. His mother can only do so much; it's now up to him.

---

[347] Cf. Wenham, *Genesis 16–50*, 207.

[348] Wenham, *Genesis 16–50*, 207. Cf. Sternberg, *Poetics*, 384.

[349] Cf. Walton, *Thou Traveller Unknown*, 116. The succession of short verb phrases "reminiscent of the description of Esau's action in 25:34" (White, *Narration and Discourse*, 219).

[350] White, *Narration and Discourse*, 219.

[351] White, *Narration and Discourse*, 220.

[352] White, *Narration and Discourse*, 220.

27:18–29

Rebekah's and Jacob's plan does not go unchallenged.[353] Despite familiar words ('my father... הִנֶּנִּי') Isaac realizes that something is not right;
'Who are you my son?' Immediately, Jacob has to resort to a lie ('I am
Esau your firstborn'); each word geared to ensure that proceedings will
move on. [354] When Isaac wonders about Esau's speedy return, Jacob
has to stoop even lower by enlisting God's involvement in the hunt:
"because the LORD *your* God granted me success."[355] The unfolding
scene is packed with suspense. "Every preparation is needed including
the willingness to lie directly."[356] Excellent work has been done to analyze this scene. There is no need to repeat that here.[357] Despite a tortu-
ous exchange of probing words and actions, Jacob remains undetected.[358]
Jacob's initiative to pour his father some wine appears to provide the
last push to clinch the deal (vs. 25).[359] The mention of wine resonates
with Sternberg's suggestion that Gen 27 contains a subtle echo of
Lot's self-indulgence.[360] An excess of wine caused Noah's drunkenness
(9:20–28). Although there is no mention of drunkenness in Gen 27,
it might be relevant that one of Noah's sons (Ham) dishonoured his

---

[353] 'A long and painful examination' (Fokkelman, *Narrative Art in Genesis*, 103.).
Bledstein identifies eight 'tests' in this scene (A.J. Bledstein, "Binder, Trickster, Heel
and Hairy Man: Rereading Genesis 27 as a Trickster Tale Told by a Woman," in
A Feminist Companion to Genesis (ed. A. Brenner; Sheffield, UK: Sheffield Academic
Press, 1993), 289), and she suggests that Isaac was aware of the deceit, but that this
fitted with his design to discover which son "is clever enough to survive among arro-
gant, powerful men" (287).

[354] Hamilton, *Genesis 18–50*, 220.

[355] Wenham, *Genesis 16–50*, 208; Hamilton, *Genesis 18–50*, 220, discusses this in
connection with the situation mentioned in Lev 6:3; Vawter, *On Genesis*, 303; Walton, *Thou Traveller Unknown*, 116–117, notes possible ambiguity; "is it perhaps true
that God—through the cunning of Rebekah—has indeed helped Jacob?" Hamilton
has noted the use of אֱלֹהִים, cf. Hamilton, *Genesis 18–50*, 220, n. 14 with reference to
Schmidt, "Jakob erschleicht sich den väterlichen Segen," 159–83. See Section 2.5 for
more on the phrase '*your* God.'

[356] White, *Narration and Discourse*, 221.

[357] For some excellent work on this scene: see White, *Narration and Discourse*,
214–224; cf. Taschner, *Verheissung und Erfüllung*, 37–56; Fokkelman, *Narrative Art
in Genesis*, 97–122.

[358] Some commentators assume the opposite, that Isaac knew he was blessing Jacob,
e.g. Bledstein, "Binder, Trickster, Heel and Hairy Man."

[359] In Gen 27, the only act by Jacob that is not in direct response to a command by
Isaac (Taschner, *Verheissung und Erfüllung*, 42).

[360] Sternberg, *Poetics*, 350 (see above). Armstrong has noted other similarities: "like
Lot, Isaac was passive, and like Lot again, he would finally be duped by his own chil-
dren" (K. Armstrong, *In the Beginning: A New Interpretation of Genesis* (New York,
USA: Ballantine Books, 1996), 75).

father and incurred a curse (9:22, 25), something Jacob feared (27:12), whereas Ham's two brothers received a blessing (9:26–27). This link is even more tantalizing when we compare Noah's and Isaac's words of blessing and curse (see below). In the Joseph-cycle, there is mention of 'social drinking,' although wine is not specifically mentioned: Joseph's brothers "drank and were merry with him" (43:34).[361] The context is very much one of 'testing' and deceit (Gen 44).[362] Taschner notes "Der Genuss von Wein wird jedoch in der gesamten Genesis durchweg negativ beurteilt."[363] It appears as if 'wine' (and 'social drinking') in Genesis fulfils a similar role to clothing (as suggested by White). Could this be another physical example of a post-Gen 3 reality ('east of Eden')? Isaac's final 'test' (vs. 26) fails to detect Jacob, and the smell of Esau's garments leads Isaac into his blessing:

<table>
<tr><td>Vs. 28</td><td>May God give to you of the dew of the heaven
    and of the fatness of the earth
    and plenty of grain and new wine</td></tr>
<tr><td>Vs. 29</td><td>Let peoples serve you,
    and nations bow down to you.
Be lord over your brothers,
    and may your mother's sons bow down to you.
Cursed be everyone who curses you,
    and blessed be everyone who blesses you</td></tr>
</table>

The main focus of the blessing is on prosperity (vs. 28) and dominion (vs. 29a). Westermann has commented on the similarities between this blessing and Balaam's third oracle (Num 24:3–9).[364] The prosperity phraseology of Isaac's blessing may well anticipate Israel's settling into the Promised Land.[365] Within the constraints of Genesis, the blessing contains echoes of the birth-oracle (especially לְאֹם only here and in 25:23, and עָבַד).[366] Fokkelman concludes that "the blessing of the deceived Isaac confirms the prenatal oracle,"[367] but we cannot

---

[361] ESV; footnote: Hebrew *and became intoxicated*, cf. BDB 9944).
[362] Later on, when Joseph makes himself known, he will say 'Come near' (45:4) and there is mention of falling upon necks and kissing (45:14–15, cf. 33:4!).
[363] Taschner, *Verheissung und Erfüllung*, 42.
[364] Westermann, *Genesis 12–36*, 440–441. Cf. discussion by Grüneberg, *Abraham*, 18–22.
[365] von Rad, *Genesis*, 273; Wenham, *Genesis 16–50*, 209. For an interesting discussion on an equivalent text in Ugaritic, cf. Hamilton, *Genesis 18–50*, 221.
[366] Noted by many commentators: e.g. Wenham, *Genesis 16–50*, 209; Taschner, *Verheissung und Erfüllung*, 46.
[367] Fokkelman, *Narrative Art in Genesis*, 45.

be sure this is true; "the divine oracle is sufficiently ambiguous."[368]
Esau will never bow down to his brother, whereas Jacob will.[369] The
dominion theme will also feature in Jacob's blessing/ prophecy over
Judah (49:10).[370]

The wording of Isaac's blessing is very different from the patriarchal promises, except the last phrase in 29b, which recalls 12:3a.[371] von
Rad already noted that "the blessing is strangely independent of the
otherwise rather uniformly formulated patriarchal promises."[372] Isaac's
blessing does not mention the patriarchal promises regarding land, offspring or the 'blessing for others.' Some of these are referred to by Isaac
in 28:3–5, implying that Isaac himself understood his blessing in Gen
27 to be something different.[373] Isaac's focus in Gen 27 on prosperity
seems to be more 'earthy' and 'low-level' compared with the content
of God's promises to the patriarchs: e.g. 'fatness of the earth' (הָאָ֫רֶץ
וּמִשְׁמַנֵּי) instead 'all these lands' (כָּל־הָאֲרָצֹת הָאֵל, 26:4), words Isaac
had heard himself. Also, Isaac's emphasis on dominion over others
appears to be quite different from the blessing for the nations (26:5).[374]
A similar discrepancy between high-level and lower-level concerns is
visible in 28:10–22.[375] Indeed, God's thoughts are higher than those of
humans, and so are his ways (Isa 55:8). In 28:3–5 Isaac comes closer
to the language of the patriarchal promises, but still does not mention
the 'blessing for others.' Despite all this, various commentators who
note these differences do not draw the logical conclusions that Isaac's
blessing is something different altogether, and persist in the opinion
that Isaac *does* transfer the patriarchal promises in Gen 27.[376] When

---

[368] Fretheim, "Which Blessing?," 283.
[369] Turner, *Announcements of Plot in Genesis*, 123.
[370] Sailhamer, *Genesis*, ad loc.
[371] Grüneberg, *Abraham*, 19; Mitchell, *The Meaning of BRK*, 81; Walton, *Thou Traveller Unknown*, 118; 'although much less personal' (Wenham, *Genesis 16–50*, 210).
[372] von Rad, *Genesis*, 273.
[373] Fretheim, "Which Blessing?," 289–290.
[374] See *Section* 2.3. According toTaschner Isaac's behaviour of conflict avoidance
and peace-making in Gen 26 differs markedly with the understanding of blessing in
Gen 27: "ein krasser Gegensatz" (Taschner, *Verheissung und Erfüllung*, 202).
[375] See *Section* 2.5.
[376] E.g. Walton, *Thou Traveller Unknown*, who notes the unique language (117), yet
concludes that it is "*unquestionable* that it is the patriarchal promise, the blessing of
Abraham (v. 4) which Jacob *has* gained" (121, italics mine). Wenham, *Genesis 16–50*,
210 notes the different language, and states that in 28:4 "Isaac bestows on Jacob the
blessing of Abraham" (202, see below). Cf. Snijders, "Genesis 27: Het bedrog van
Jacob," 186ff.

we have taken a closer look at events in 28:1–5, I will revisit this issue, and will draw some tentative conclusions.

Having discussed the links with the birth-oracle and other oracles (e.g. Gen 49; Num 24), and having established the fact that Isaac's blessing in Gen 27 appears to be quite different from transferring the patriarchal promises, we still need to decide what this blessing does. The first thing to note is that a blessing, as in Gen 27, is considered a very solemn affair. Miller notes:

> It brings the deity into the transaction (…). A blessing is a testamentary act with binding legal significance. The act of blessing rather clearly fulfils the same function as the oath: *it brings the deity into the transaction and establishes that the actions to be taken are intended to have—and in fact do have—legally binding import.*[377]

This means that the blessing in Gen 27 takes a similar position to the oath in the sale of the birthright in 25:29–34, but the question remains, what exactly does the blessing do? Speiser suggests that there is "strong presumptive evidence that Isaac's blessing was fundamentally a solemn disposal of his property made in the approved fashion of his time and social group."[378] In *Section* 2.3 I argued that Speiser's focus on 'disposal of property' is probably too narrow, and that inheritance was probably more a matter of status, which came with a matrix of responsibilities, obligations, rights, privileges, and prerogatives (including a larger share of the inheritance).[379] If Sarna is right in saying that these were formalized by the father's testamentary blessing,[380] then Esau, having sold his birthright to Jacob, acts deceitfully himself.[381] If Isaac's blessing is indeed about confirming the status of the firstborn and if Isaac would have known about the sale of the birthright, which was confirmed by Esau's oath before God, this would place Isaac's actions in a negative light as well. However, this is not necessarily the case. Isaac's blessing does not say anything about the disposal of property (or

---

[377] Miller, "Contracts of Genesis," 27 (italics mine).

[378] Speiser, "I Know Not the Day of My Death," 254.

[379] See Section 2.1: Sarna, *Understanding Genesis*, 185, referring to Mendelsohn, "On the Preferential Status of the Eldest Son" (regarding the double portion). See also: Waltke, *Genesis*, 377; E.F. Roop, *Genesis* (Kitchener, Ontario, Canada: Herald, 1987), 183.

[380] Sarna, *Understanding Genesis*, 185, referring to Mendelsohn, "On the Preferential Status of the Eldest Son." Also: Levine, "Firstborn"; Hamilton, *Genesis 18–50*, 185.

[381] A thesis followed by various Jewish commentators: e.g. Breitbart, "The Problem of Deception in Genesis 27," 47.

anything regarding an assumed spiritual role of the firstborn either).[382]
Esau clearly states that the birthright belongs to Jacob (vs. 36), which
implies that these are probably not related in the way suggested by
some, unless we should interpret this as an admission of guilt by Esau.
The text does not clarify these issues. Grüneberg suggests an interesting alternative:

> In Genesis 27 there is no reason to think that Isaac will specifically hand
> to Esau the rights of the firstborn; he might prophesy eventual pre-emi-
> nence for him, or ask God to give him pre-eminence (as of course does
> happen), but these are not necessarily incompatible with Jacob having
> the birthright, which brings pre-eminence on the father's death, but not
> necessarily lasting superiority...though possession of the birthright is
> a good start towards acquiring what one hopes to receive as a result of
> the blessing.[383]

Finally, Snijders has concluded that Isaac's blessing in Gen 27 has
nothing to do with transferring the patriarchal promises, and that it is
nothing more than "a rich farmer blessing his heir."[384]

Despite substantial scholarly efforts certain issues regarding Gen 27
remain elusive. How do these uncertainties impact our quest? Does
it matter that we do not understand the exact nature of Isaac's blessing and its relation to the birthright, a concept we do not understand
in detail either? Are these simply details lost to history, which we
might be able to reconstruct to some extent through various forms of
research (archeological, anthropological, sociological, legal etc.)? Or is
the aim and interest of the narrator quite different altogether? Such
questions should remain with us as we follow the unfolding drama of
Jacob's life.

27:30–40

Jacob has scarcely received the blessing, when Esau returns from the
hunt (vs. 30). Jacob left (וַיֵּצֵא) just before Esau arrived back home,
a subtle hint to their birth, where Jacob 'came forth' (יָצָא, 25:26)[385]
just *after* his brother. This time Jacob has beaten his brother to the

---

[382] Brichto, "Kin, cult, land and afterlife," 5.
[383] Grüneberg, *Abraham*, 18.
[384] Snijders, "Genesis 27: Het bedrog van Jacob," 189, an excellent article on the
nature of Isaac's blessing in Gen 27 (knowledge of Dutch will help). See also McKeown,
Genesis, 135–136.
[385] Hamilton, *Genesis 18–50*, 226.

finishing line. Esau's actions and words are a mirror image of Jacob's, signifying reversal:

Jacob (vs. 19)

אָנֹכִי עֵשָׂו בְּכֹרֶךָ
קוּם־נָא שְׁבָה וְאָכְלָה מִצֵּידִי בַּעֲבוּר תְּבָרֲכַנִּי נַפְשֶׁךָ

Esau (vv. 31–32)

יָקֻם אָבִי וְיֹאכַל מִצֵּיד בְּנוֹ בַּעֲבוּר תְּבָרֲכַנִּי נַפְשֶׁךָ
אֲנִי בִּנְךָ בְכֹרְךָ עֵשָׂו

Isaac is rocked to the core and trembles 'very violently' when he realizes that Esau is not the one who has received his blessing, which he cannot revoke (vs. 33). Mitchell, following Thiselton, suggests that "since the testamental blessings were normally pronounced shortly before the father's death, it is likely that there was no socially accepted legal procedure for rescinding them" (cf. Num 30:2 and Judges 11:30–35).[386] Mitchell also suggests that the fact that Jacob received the blessing "despite the invocation of God, must have implied to Isaac that God sanctioned the blessing."[387] Alternatively, Miller suggests that such blessings could not be rescinded in order to minimize the chance of disputes following the death of a clan-leader.[388] This might well be true in most cases, but a blessing deceitfully obtained might still lead to bloodshed (27:41!). Whether Isaac knew the birth-oracle remains open to debate,[389] but Hamilton correctly states that the text does not give any indication that Isaac is motivated by a "sudden insight into the divine will or by a recall of a forgotten divine word."[390] What is clear from the text is that (for whatever reason) Isaac does not rescind the blessing over Jacob despite his deceit.

Now it is Esau's turn for an emotional outburst (vs. 34). Isaac's and Esau's reactions are synchronous:[391]

---

[386] Mitchell, *The Meaning of BRK*, 83; A.J. Thiselton, "The Supposed Power of Words in the Biblical Writings," *JTS* 25 (1974): 283–99, 294. Cf. Gordon, "Biblical Customs and the Nuzu Tablets," 8 on the legality of oral blessings in patriarchal times.

[387] Mitchell, *The Meaning of BRK*, 83. Cf. Pfeiffer, *The Patriarchal Age*, 79, who speaks of the "sanctity of the word."

[388] Miller, "Contracts of Genesis," 29.

[389] Hamilton, *Genesis 18–50*, 212. Boase, "Life in the Shadows," 319 and 321 thinks Isaac did not know the oracle. Sternberg notes that nothing in the text indicates that Isaac was familiar with the oracle (Sternberg, *Poetics*, 350).

[390] Hamilton, *Genesis 18–50*, 226.

[391] Fokkelman, *Narrative Art in Genesis*, 103. The Hebrew words used to describe the emotions in this scene are very strong (Wenham, *Genesis 16–50*, 211).

עַד־מְאֹד	וַיֶּחֱרַד יִצְחָק חֲרָדָה גְּדֹלָה		Isaac (27:33)
עַד־מְאֹד	גְּדֹלָה וּמָרָה	צְעָקָה	Esau (27:34)

The words of this *father*-son team unite them in defeat by the *mother*-son team. One has to be utterly cynical to assume that Isaac knew he was blessing Jacob all along.[392] Three times Esau pleads with his father for a blessing (vs. 34, 36 and 38) and his pleading becomes increasingly desperate.[393] "'Bless me too, my father' (Gen 27:34) are the words of a bewildered, child-like Esau."[394] Finally, Esau 'lifted up his voice and wept' (vs. 38). At the centre of Esau's pleading stands vs. 36. The chiastic structure featuring birthright and blessing serves as a concise summary of the Jacob-cycle up to this point.[395] Although this verse makes it abundantly clear that 25:19–34 and 27 should be read together, it does not settle the uncertainty regarding the nature of the relationship between the birthright and the blessing.

Isaac matches Esau's crescendo of desperation with firmness and ever-increasing gravity regarding the reality and the irreversibility of the blessing he has bestowed on Jacob (vs. 35, 37 and 39–40), all this despite the fact that Jacob took the blessing 'deceitfully' (בְּמִרְמָה vs. 35).[396] Isaac's words in vs. 37 are reminiscent of Noah's pronouncement over his sons. Esau now finds himself in the place of Canaan and will serve his brother (cf. 9:25–27). Although Isaac's words suggest Esau's 'personal subservience to Jacob,'[397] these words were hardly applicable to Esau himself, and appear to point towards a much later

---

[392] E.g. Bledstein, "Binder, Trickster, Heel and Hairy Man."

[393] Cf. Fokkelman, *Narrative Art in Genesis*, 103–104.

[394] Berlin, *Poetics*, 38. Goodnick, "Jacob's Deception of his Father," 239 even interprets this as the main thrust of the passage: "…the words in these scenes are deliberately chosen and not simply chance. They serve to compare different personalities and their reactions to stressful situations."

[395] אֶת־בְּכֹרָתִי לָקָח...לָקַח בִּרְכָתִי; an example of a 'semantic sonant chiasmus' (J.S. Kselman, "Semantic-Sonant Chiasmus in Biblical Poetry," *Bib* 58 (1977): 220, 220; courtesy Hamilton, *Genesis 18–50*, 224, n. 12). See also McKeown, *Genesis*, 137 n. 6 and Sailhamer, *Genesis, ad loc.*

[396] Similar words will appear in Gen 29 and 34, where Jacob and the Shechemites are on the receiving end of deceit (See Chapters 3 and 4). For Jacob's characterization as 'trickster' and how this is picked by later prophets (Jeremiah, Hosea) cf. Patterson, "The Old Testament Use Of An Archetype: The Trickster." But let's not forget Rebekah's initiative and involvement; after all, she is Laban's sister! (cf. Brett, *Genesis*, 88–89; Kahn, "Jacob's Choice in Genesis 25:19–28:9," 83).

[397] הֵן גְּבִיר שַׂמְתִּיו לָךְ (Hamilton, *Genesis 18–50*, 228).

reality.[398] This implies that the scope of Isaac's blessing upon Jacob is more general in scope as well.[399] Ironically, it will be Jacob who appears to do the lion's-share of 'serving' in the Jacob-cycle.[400] Isaac's confirmation of Jacob's blessing culminates in the 'anti-blessing' over Esau (vv. 39–40).[401] The wording echoes the blessing upon Jacob, with the addition of the word מִן in places ("*away* from the fatness of the earth…*away* from the dew of heaven on high", vs. 39). Even the mention of 'dew' and 'fatness' is reversed.[402] The reversal is now complete.

27:41–46[403]

Esau plans to kill Jacob following Isaac's death, but Rebekah is informed about this.[404] We are reminded of Eve, who brought forth two sons, of which the elder would kill the younger (4:8), an ordeal that might repeat itself (27:41–42).[405] Rebekah addresses Jacob in familiar firm fashion (vs. 43). She instructs Jacob to flee to Laban and stay with him 'for a while,' which turns out be somewhat longer. This will be Rebekah's last recorded speech to Jacob; she will not see her beloved son again. Rebekah turns to Isaac to convince him of the merits of her plan (vs. 46). Her emotional address carefully omits mentioning the obvious reasons for this crisis. Instead it focuses on Esau's marriages, which unite Isaac and Rebekah in bitterness (26:35).[406] Rebekah's final

---

[398] Cf. Syrén, *The Forsaken First-Born* who considers these stories an expression of Israel's self-understanding vs. the surrounding nations.

[399] Walton, *Thou Traveller Unknown*, 118.

[400] Turner, *Announcements of Plot in Genesis*, 120–124; Snijders, "Genesis 27: Het bedrog van Jacob," 186; Fretheim, "Which Blessing?," 287.

[401] Fokkelman, *Narrative Art in Genesis*, 98; Coats, *Genesis*, 204. 'Virtually a curse' (Skinner, *Genesis*, 373); or 'a half-blessing': Esau will throw off the yoke eventually (Grüneberg, *Abraham*, 21), cf. 1 Kg 11:14–22, 2 Kg 8:20–22 and 2 Chr 21:8–10 (Hamilton, *Genesis 18–50*, 228); or 'a counter-curse' (Walton, *Thou Traveller Unknown*, 118); cf. Balaam's oracle in Num 24:15ff.

[402] Cf. Waltke, *Genesis*, 381.

[403] It is probably better to speak of three acts (vs. 41: Esau/transition; vv. 42–45: Rebekah and Jacob; vs. 46: Rebekah and Isaac; 28:1–5: Isaac and Jacob) (Wenham, *Genesis 16–50*, 202).

[404] How Rebekah found out while Esau 'said in his heart,' cf. Wenham, *Genesis 16–50*, 212 (cf. *Genesis Rabba* 67.9). Ibn Ezra has suggested that one of Esau's friends reported this to Rebekah (*Ibn Ezra's Commentary on the Pentateuch: Genesis* (trans. H.N. Strickman and A.M. Silver; New York, USA: Menorah Publishing Company, 1988), 272).

[405] And something very similar is about to happen in the Joseph-cycle, as Joseph's brothers contemplate killing Joseph.

[406] Cf. Wenham, *Genesis 16–50*, 213.

outburst reminds us of her groan in 25:22 (genuine grief? exaggeration?). Again, Rebekah gets her way and the scene is set for Jacob's departure.[407]

28:1–5

The final scene is about blessing (28:1 and 6) and instruction (28:1, 5, 6, 10), not rebuke. Jacob's deceit is not mentioned at all. One can speculate why that is, but that cannot detain us here.[408] The mention of Paddan-aram, Bethuel and Laban in vv. 2 and 5 form an inclusio to draw attention to what is at the centre of this encounter, Isaac's words in vv. 3–4.[409] The narrator describes Isaac's action/words as blessing (vv. 1 and 6). The question is, what sort of blessing are we dealing with? The blessing in Gen 27 focuses on 'prosperity' and 'dominion,' the main blessing themes here are 'offspring' (28:4) and 'land' (28:5). Although these four themes are not unrelated, they are not synonymous either.[410] It appears that the blessing themes in Gen 28:3–4 are more high-level than the ones in Gen 27; you first need offspring and land, before promises like 'prosperity of the earth' and 'dominion over others' can gain true significance. Therefore, Walton's suggestion that 28:3–4 can be seen as an 'interpretation' of 27:27–29 does not sound quite right. You would expect an interpretation to work the other way around: 27:27–29 as a specific outcome ('interpretation') of the higher-level promises of offspring and land. This also implies that the blessing referred to in 28:3–4 is more important than the one in Gen 27. There are other reasons as well why these blessings are not related in the way many commentators assume. First of all, Wenham (commenting on Gen 27) states that "fundamental to the whole story is the conviction of the efficacy of the deathbed blessing."[411] Indeed, all players act in full conviction of that efficacy, to the point that they believe that even though the blessing has been taken deceitfully (27:35–36) it cannot be rescinded. If that is the case, why does Isaac see any need to repeat it in 28:3–4? And why does Isaac treat the reception by Jacob

---

[407] 'Rebekah's manipulative language' (Waltke, *Genesis*, 382).

[408] E.g. Did Isaac finally remember the oracle? Did Isaac realize that this was God's will all along? etc.

[409] They also link back to 25:20.

[410] The use of the verbs 'be fruitful' and 'multiply' are also prominent in the creation blessings (1:22, 28) and in the blessing on Noah and his sons (9:1, 7) (McKeown, *Genesis*, 138).

[411] Wenham, *Genesis 16–50*, 216.

of the 'blessing of Abraham' as a desirable future possibility instead of a firm present reality? It appears that Isaac himself considers the 'blessing of Abraham' as something different from his blessing in Gen 27. Secondly, Isaac knows that only God can give Jacob 'the blessing of Abraham' ("May he give the blessing of Abraham to you," vs. 4).[412] This implies that Isaac has not transferred the patriarchal promises in Gen 27, and that he is not transferring them in 28:3–4 either.[413] He merely expresses the wish that Jacob may be the one who receives these promises.[414] This of course is how Isaac received those promises himself.[415] Fretheim's interpretation is insightful:

> But he can finally only commend Jacob to God (28:3–4). It is important to note that he does not claim or imply that his prior blessing to Jacob (27:27–29) has tied God down to extending the special blessing to Jacob. It remains to be seen whether God will in fact finally choose Jacob as the recipient.[416]

It is only in 28:10–22 that God will bestow the patriarchal promises on Jacob, although it is only in 32:29 that Jacob is said to be blessed.[417] Gross, who also interprets 28:3–4 as "an expression of hope that Jacob will be blessed," even puts that realization in Gen 35.[418] Similarly, Westermann and Mitchell, who both have done substantial work on the concept of blessing in Genesis, interpret 28:3–4 as a 'wish or prayer' that Jacob *may* become the recipient of the patriarchal blessing promises.[419] Fretheim comments "Westermann correctly notes that the 'blessing' in 28:3–4 is no longer an effectual word spoken by

---

[412] Contra Boase, "Life in the Shadows," 321 who sees Isaac as "a necessary tool in the passing on of the blessing." Similarly Hamilton, *Genesis 18–50*, 235: "Isaac recognizes his role as that of a link in a chain, a transmitter," and Jeansonne, *The Women of Genesis*, 67: "Rebekah thus plays a crucial role in the ancestral narratives by ensuring the continuation of the promise for future generations."

[413] See also Brett, *Genesis*, 91 who notes the difference in content between Isaac's blessing of Jacob in Gen 27 and the patriarchal promises. Contra Hamilton, *Genesis 18–50*, 235 and Carr, *Reading the Fractures of Genesis*, 85–88, who assume that Isaac does transfer the patriarchal promises here.

[414] Fretheim, "Which Blessing?," 281–282.

[415] Fretheim, "Which Blessing?," 290; Taschner, *Verheissung und Erfüllung*, 200–201.

[416] Fretheim, "Which Blessing?," 283.

[417] Fretheim, "Which Blessing?," 282.

[418] W. Gross, "Jakob, der Mann des Segens. Zu Traditionsgeschichte und Theologie der priesterlichen Jakobsüberlieferungen," *Bib* 49 (1968): 340–41, 340–341 (also cited by Walton, *Thou Traveller Unknown*, 121, n. 70)

[419] Westermann, *Genesis 12–36*, 447–448; Mitchell, *The Meaning of BRK*, 99. Cf. Fretheim, "Which Blessing?," 290.

the father; it has been changed into an optative."[420] Although I agree
with most of Fretheim's thesis regarding Gen 27, the contrast in blessing does not appear to be as clear as suggested by Westermann and
Fretheim. Biblical Hebrew does not have an optative as such, the verb
form וְיִתֶּן (Qal imperfect, jussive in meaning), which appears both in
27:28 ("May God give to you…") and in 28:4 ("May he give the blessing….to you"), could be used as such.[421] Both blessings are phrased
as a wish or prayer, and in both blessings Isaac considers God the
ultimate blessing giver (cf. Heb 11:20), but the overriding difference
is in subject matter and that should be our guide for interpreting the
difference between these blessings.

The "land of your sojournings that God gave to Abraham" (vs. 4)
is somewhat ironic, because Jacob will have to sojourn somewhere
else for the next twenty years. It also demonstrates the necessity for
Jacob to return to Canaan in order for this 'wish' or 'prayer' to be fulfilled. In 28:3–5 Isaac comes closer to the language of the patriarchal
promises, but still does not explicitly mention the 'blessing for others.'
Isaac does express the hope that God Almighty may bless Jacob (28:3).
Ironically, God does not bless Jacob in 28:13–15 (that is for later),
but God does repeat the blessing for 'all the families in the earth' in
28:14. And so, having received two sets of blessings, Jacob sets of for
Paddan-aram (vs. 5).

28:6–9

It turns out that Esau was completely unaware of the distress caused
by his marriages. This sheds new light on the situation and may alter
the stance of readers taken in 26:34–35. It further characterizes Esau
as clueless and insensitive, but it also reveals the complete absence of
communication in Isaac's family.[422] The narrator has distributed cause
and blame very skilfully:

> By switching viewpoints the narrator makes us understand and sym-
> pathise with each party's outlook. We are made to realize that no one in
> this incident is without blame.[423]

---

[420] Fretheim, "Which Blessing?," 290.
[421] Cf. Waltke, *An Introduction to Biblical Hebrew Syntax*, §34.1 *Volitional Forms*,
564.
[422] "Esau was rather slowwitted" (Wenham, *Genesis 16–50*, 214). See Brett, *Genesis*,
88–89 for a different perspective on Esau's marriages.
[423] Wenham, *Story as Torah*, 15.

Esau's desperate move to make amends is as tragic as it is comic. Indeed, "Esau is a figure of tragic irony."[424] Without seeking parental guidance, he blunders again: he aligns himself with another unchosen son, Ishmael. Their *toledots* stand on either side of the *toledot* of the chosen one, Jacob. Esau now has clearly placed himself 'beyond the pale.'[425]

2.4.3   *Concluding Remarks*

Gen 26:34–28:9 is a superb piece of biblical literature. The characterization of the various players is sophisticated and the suspense superb. Considering both the selective way in which the narrator disseminates information, and the information gaps that exist, it is no wonder that this story continues to evoke passionate and widely varying interpretations. Sternberg notes that "where the narrative aims at a complex response, it does not hesitate to mix our feelings about the parties to the conflict by increasing (or decreasing) the appeal of each in relation to a different standard of judgment."[426] Gen 26:34–28:9 is an excellent example of that thesis. How does a complex response look like for this passage? I will discuss this under three headings:

Characterization
Every character invites a mixed response. Isaac is to be pitied for the way Rebekah and Jacob take advantage of him, yet he shares responsibility for the ensuing mess because of his apparent passivity in general, and his favouritism towards Esau in particular. Compared with Abraham, who had organized things so well before his death, Isaac's situation offers a deplorable contrast.[427] However, in 28:1–5 Isaac does take action (manipulated by Rebekah?) and sends Jacob away with a blessing. Esau evokes sympathy as well, although his marriages (especially 28:7ff.) show him as not 'too perceptive.' His pathetic begging and weeping for a blessing do not make him an attractive character either. We discussed Rebekah's important role in Gen 27 already. She appears

---

[424] Waltke, *Genesis*, 383. Cf. Brueggemann, *Genesis*, 234–235; Roop, *Genesis*, 187.
[425] Hamilton, *Genesis 18–50*, 235.
[426] Sternberg, *Poetics*, 55.
[427] Sternberg, *Poetics*, 350. Cf. Keukens, "Der irreguläre Sterbesegen Isaaks," 51; Alter, *Genesis*, 150. Isaac had also not taken the initiative in finding a wife for Esau (cf. 26:34; 28:6–8). See also Lipton, *Revisions of the Night*, 77; Pfeiffer, *The Patriarchal Age*, 80.

to be a very shrewd operator, who despite her underdog position as a woman in patriarchal society, almost single-handedly changes the course of events. However, her willingness to dupe her blind husband, and her complete disregard for Esau's fate, show her ruthless side as well. Finally, there is Jacob. Although he does not appear to be over-enthusiastic about Rebekah's proposal, he goes along and plays his role with conviction. Jacob is willing to abuse God's name, to lie and to deceive his blind father. Above all, he is a person who gets the job done, as with the acquisition of the birthright. Jacob has a ruthless side, which resembles his mother's. Every person in the cast deserves some of our sympathy and some of our disgust. There appear to be no real winners.

Morality

Although some claim that morality is not the interest of the narrative,[428] "the lack of any moral comment by the narrator does not preclude any moral interest."[429] How we judge Isaac's desire to bless just one son in the absence of the other, depends on the understanding of a custom we are not fully familiar with.[430] We do not know enough to reach a definite conclusion. Then there is the uncertainty about Isaac's aware-ness regarding the birth-oracle and the sale of the birthright. Such gaps allow interpreters to reach quite opposing conclusions. Similarly, there is the uncertainty about the relationship between birthright and blessing. Although several proposals have been made, the text does not clarify these issues, hence the difficulties in reaching firm conclu-sions about Isaac's and Esau's morality. Jacob's planned absence for the proceedings however is certainly ominous.

What about Rebekah's morality? Some consider her a villain because she deceives an ailing husband. The fact that she is not mentioned after 27:46, and the fact that not even her death is recorded, is consid-ered evidence by some that Rebekah is 'gapped' because of her deceit-ful role.[431] It is only in 49:31 that her name is mentioned one more time as we find out that Isaac was indeed buried with her. Others

---

[428] E.g. Fretheim, "Which Blessing?," 284.

[429] Walton, *Thou Traveller Unknown*, 115.

[430] Despite various proposals based on archeological evidence (e.g. Gordon, "Bibli-cal Customs and the Nuzu Tablets"; Speiser, "I Know Not the Day of My Death"), we cannot be certain.

[431] Cf. Waltke, *Genesis*, 382; Fokkelman, *Narrative Art in Genesis*, 115ff.

consider her a saint.[432] As we have seen, much depends on how one interprets the nature of the birth-oracle (prescriptive or predictive). We have seen that feminist theologians like Frymer-Kensky and Jeansonne rightly draw attention to Rebekah's importance in influencing the events in Gen 27 and 28, yet because they believe that the oracle demands Rebekah's active involvement, and because of her willingness to 'sacrifice' herself ("on me be the curse"), they consider her to be a heroine instead of a villain. [433] According to Fuchs, Rebekah had to use deception because of "her powerless position in a patriarchal culture."[434] Comparison is made with other powerless characters in the OT (e.g. Tamar, midwives in Ex 1:15ff.). Similarly, White suggests that Rebekah was justified in her "attempt to open a closed system" in subservience to "the contingency of the promissory word and faith, rather than serving the interest of symbiotic personal behaviour and structures of power."[435] Brodie argues that Rebekah occupies such a central position in Genesis that she "appears and acts as if she were a physical manifestation of God's blessings."[436] However, according to Williams deception in Genesis is only approved of if it restores *shalom*.[437] As a result, Tamar's deception can be interpreted as 'justified,' but Rebekah's deception not. Rebekah's (and Jacob's) actions lead to a complete shattering of *shalom*, which will take many years to be restored (if at all).[438] If Fretheim is indeed correct that the blessing in Gen 27 "does not position Jacob for the Abrahamic blessing" and that "Isaac's blessing in Gen 27 does not make God's blessing of Jacob

---

[432] E.g. Allen, "On Me Be the Curse, My Son!"; Jeansonne, *The Women of Genesis*; Frymer-Kensky, *Reading the Women of the Bible*.

[433] Frymer-Kensky, *Reading the Women of the Bible*, 22–23; Jeansonne, *The Women of Genesis*, 67. For an interesting discussion on the contrast between Fokkelman, *Narrative Art in Genesis*. vs. Allen, "On Me Be the Curse, My Son!" on this issue, see Walton, *Thou Traveller Unknown*, 106–108.

[434] E. Fuchs, "Who is hiding the truth? Deceptive Women and Biblical Androcentrism," in *Feminist Perspectives on Biblical Scholarship* (ed. A. Yarbro Collins; Atlanta, USA: Society of Biblical Literature, 1985), and discussed by Jeansonne, *The Women of Genesis*, 67.

[435] White, *Narration and Discourse*, 225, followed and cited by Fretheim, "Which Blessing?," 287.

[436] Brodie, *Genesis as Dialogue*, 115–116.

[437] Williams, *Deception in Genesis*, 18–19 and 221. Although there is no condemnation in the immediate context, compare Gen 29:25–26, where Jacob is on the receiving end of deceit (Fishbane, *Text and Texture*, 55). See also Sarna, *Genesis*, 397–398.

[438] *Shalom* was not really present in this family anyway, but after Gen 27 even less so.

necessary,"[439] then Rebekah is more a tragic than a heroic figure. In that case, she has sacrificed much for nothing.

How do we judge Jacob's morality? Marcus, in his study on traditional Jewish responses to the question of deceit, has identified two responses, a moral one and an amoral one.[440] The amoral one does not see any problem with Jacob's actions, because Esau sold the birthright to him and swore an oath. Hence it was Esau who acted deceitfully.[441] This view assumes that the one who holds the birthright is entitled to the blessing, something that cannot be deduced from the text. It also ignores the 'punishment' Jacob receives through subsequent events (e.g. Gen 29). The moral response acknowledges that Jacob deceived his father, but that he was punished by various events later in life.[442] However, throughout the centuries there have been various attempts to shift blame away from Jacob, in particular to Rebekah, but also to Isaac and Esau.[443] Commentators over the centuries have come up with similar interpretations.[444] Snijders for example takes a stance not too different from Sarna:

> Het is waar dat de verteller het verhaal brengt zonder kreten van afschuw; het vervolg ervan is echter voor de luisteraar een zonneklaar bewijs dat het akelig mis ging in het huis van Isaäk. Immers, in plaats van als een rijke boer op vruchtbare grond te gedijen, trekt Jakob als een berooide zwerver rond en hij zal jarenlang een slavenbestaan leiden. Hij is eerder een gevloekte dan een gezegende.[445]

---

[439] Fretheim, "Which Blessing?," 279.

[440] D. Marcus, "Traditional Jewish Responses to the Question of Deceit in Genesis 27," in *Jews, Christians and the Theology of the Hebrew Scriptures* (eds. A. Ogden Bellis and J.S. Kaminsky; Atlanta, Georgia, USA: Society of Biblical Literature, 2000), 305.

[441] E.g. Breitbart, "The Problem of Deception in Genesis 27."

[442] E.g. Sarna, *Genesis*, 397–398; Sarna, *Understanding Genesis*, 183–184; Bland, "The Rabbinic Method," 19–21. For additional sources cf. Marcus, "Traditional Jewish Responses to the Question of Deceit in Genesis 27," 295, n. 13. Cf. *Section 4.4* on Jacob's return of the 'blessing' in Gen 33.

[443] Marcus, "Traditional Jewish Responses to the Question of Deceit in Genesis 27," 296–297.

[444] Cf. survey by Snijders, "Genesis 27: Het bedrog van Jacob."

[445] Snijders, "Genesis 27: Het bedrog van Jacob," 185–186: "It is true that the narrator tells the story without any trace of denunciation; however what follows is clear evidence for the reader that things went very wrong in the house of Isaac: Instead of being a rich farmer, dwelling on fertile soil, Jacob lives as an outcast tramp, experiencing slave-existence for many years; Jacob appears to be cursed instead of blessed" (my translation).

Such an awareness of the wider context of the Jacob narrative(s) guards against reading Gen 27 purely with a sense of celebration or enjoyment, as suggested by Gunkel:

> Rather, all these narratives were surely originally recounted in praise of the hero and his successors. One cannot have seen sin and shame in these deceits, but only amusing, successful pranks.[446]

Indeed, the dim aftermath of Jacob's deceit is all too clear. However, morality does not seem to be the ultimate benchmark of the story either. The Jacob narrative(s) (and the whole of the OT for that matter) make it abundantly clear that God is willing to work with and through imperfect human beings.[447] This was true for Abraham and Isaac, and will also prove to be true for Jacob. Jacob's life-story demonstrates the entanglement of theological and ethical perspectives, which is so common in OT narrative.[448]

Finally, what to think about God? God does not appear to play an active role at all, yet each human party speaks of Yahweh/God "either in deceit or as deceived."[449] This raises the questions how God is at work in Gen 27, and how God will choose to proceed with his plans for this family that has been torn 'by the ravages of sin.' The last question will be answered by 28:10–22 and by God's ongoing involvement with Jacob and Israel for the sake of all of humanity. For some commentators however, there are questions about God's morality. Some think God is to blame for events in Gen 27:

> God gets what he apparently wants, but at a human cost of strife, separation, and suffering. God's inactivity suggests that responsibility for all this lies only in part with the family members involved.[450]

I am not convinced that 'God gets what he wants.' Again, it depends on how one interprets the birth-oracle, and the nature of the birthright and the blessing in relation to the promises made to Abraham and Isaac. To further reflect on those issues, we need to consider how this passage fits in the wider narrative context.

---

[446] Gunkel, *Genesis*, 301.
[447] Fretheim, "Which Blessing?," 284. See also McKeown, *Genesis*, 128 and Brueggemann, *Genesis*, 217.
[448] Wenham, *Story as Torah*, 3. See Chapter 1.
[449] Humphreys, *The Character of God*, 163.
[450] Humphreys, *The Character of God*, 165.

Plot Development

We have seen how the events surrounding the birth of the twins set the story in motion. The sale of the birth-right gave us a foretaste of the full-blown battle in Gen 27. Every narrative seed that was so carefully sown in 25:19–28 has now come to full fruition. To what extent are the human actors free agents, or has the course of history been solidly cast in stone? It is only when we take a much wider view of Jacob's life (and beyond) that we can start answering those questions. At this point I want to consider the importance of the birth-oracle, the birthright and the blessing once more, this time in view of what happened with Jacob and Esau post Gen 28:5. According to Wenham "fundamental to the whole story is the conviction of the efficacy of the deathbed blessing."[451] And indeed, every participant acts in full conviction of that efficacy. But does God share that perspective? Is the deathbed blessing indeed a 'prophecy whose fulfilment is certain?'[452] Or is the deathbed blessing merely a human institution that can be ignored by a sovereign God in a similar way God ignores human institutions like primogeniture? It has been noted that Isaac's words were not infallible. Various aspects of the birth-oracle and the blessing are sufficiently ambiguous to obscure whether they apply to Jacob and Esau personally or to their descendants. It is clear that aspects of the blessing, which clearly applied personally, did not come to fruition. Esau never bows down to Jacob whereas Jacob does bow down to his brother and does most of the serving in Genesis.[453] Despite a blessing of "dew from heaven and fatness of the earth" Jacob and his family experience a death-threatening famine. Was Goshen the fulfilment of Isaac's prosperity blessing (Gen 47:27), or should we ignore that, and just focus on the Promised Land? Isaac's words for Esau himself appear to have been ineffective: Esau does quite well in Jacob's absence (Gen 32–33).[454] Fretheim notes "God will be at work in Esau's life so that he prospers, and in a way not too different from those blessings

---

[451] Wenham, *Genesis 16–50*, 216.

[452] Wenham, *Genesis 16–50*, 216.

[453] Turner, *Announcements of Plot in Genesis*, 115ff.; Fretheim, "Which Blessing?," 287; McKeown, *Genesis*, 137.

[454] Note the difference between Isaac's blessing and the usual blessing as pronounced by God (Turner, *Announcements of Plot in Genesis*, 125; von Rad, *Genesis*, 278). According to Westermann the Abraham cycle focuses on promise and blessing, whereas the Jacob cycle is more focused on blessing (Westermann, *Genesis 12–36*, 408–409).

promised to Jacob in 27:27–29."[455] As a result, Jacob and Esau will not be able to stay together because of their abundant possessions (36:6–8). Living "away from the fatness of the earth" might have been more applicable for Esau and his descendants after moving away from Jacob.

I have noted the remaining uncertainty regarding birthright and blessing. Are these simply details lost to history, which we might be able to reconstruct to some extent through various forms of research or was the aim and interest of the narrator quite different altogether? Sternberg suggests that the narrator does not know these details, because he has "not the least desire to know" them.[456] In other words, by focusing on these 'missing pieces' of the puzzle, or by speculating about them, we are simply barking up the wrong tree. What seems to support Sternberg is the fact that Isaac's inheritance remains completely unmentioned (unlike Abraham's inheritance, 25:5–6!): "what became of the property remains gapped to the last."[457] What was fought over so hard appears to have become entirely irrelevant. The drive for material blessing at the cost of relationship is very costly and in hindsight might prove to be irrelevant.[458]

Finally, it is interesting to reflect on Gen 27 in the light of the events of Gen 26. Things went so well for Isaac in Gen 26, but things look rather different in Gen 27.[459] What caused this? I will limit myself to consider the relationship between Esau and Jacob in the light of Gen 26. In Gen 26 we looked at Isaac's interaction with the Philistines, which started with deceit but which ended in 'peaceful, covenanted, coexistence.'[460] As we consider the consequences of deceit in Gen 27, we wonder whether Esau and Jacob "might see the possibilities of covenanted reconciliation."[461] Time will tell. For the time being however, the 'chosen one' is on the run to avoid becoming the victim of fratricide. Like Cain, he is a cast out wanderer on his way to the "land of the people of the East" (29:1). Will God answer Isaac's prayer in 28:3–4?

---

[455] Fretheim, "Which Blessing?," 289.
[456] Sternberg, *Poetics*, 184.
[457] Sternberg, *Poetics*, 350.
[458] Cf. McKeown, *Genesis*, 137.
[459] Similarly, Jacob experienced various tragedies after God emphatically confirmed the blessing to him (35:9–13). See *Section* 4.6.
[460] Gunn, *Narrative in the Hebrew Bible*, 109.
[461] Gunn, *Narrative in the Hebrew Bible*, 109.

2.5 Jacob Encounters God (Gen 28:10–22)

2.5.1 Introduction

Many scholars assume that this passage has a long and complex pre-history.[462] Many insights have been generated by this passage.[463] Several textbooks use this passage to demonstrate the workings of source criticism, because of several textual features that are assumed to be favourable for such an endeavour.[464] Most source-critics have assigned this passage to J and E. General consensus (with some variations) is that J was responsible for vv. 13–16 and 19; and E for vv. 10–12, 17–22 (excluding vs. 19).[465] Form and tradition critics also have dedicated much attention to this material. Some of the proposals regarding the redactional process of this text are quite complex (e.g. Blum, Carr, Rendtorff).[466] In short, many assume that it originated in Northern Israel as an etiology of Bethel's sanctuary.[467] That material from Judah was added later on (e.g. patriarchal promises) and that it received its final form in the exile or even later.[468] Conversely, Van Seters argues

---

[462] Westermann, *Genesis 12–36*, 452–453; Walton, *Thou Traveller Unknown*, 29ff.; A.P. Ross, "Studies in the Life of Jacob—Part 1: Jacob's Vision: The Founding of Bethel," *BSac* 142, no. 568 (1985): 224–37, 224 n. 1.

[463] "An entire book could be devoted to recounting them" (Lipton, *Revisions of the Night*, 63).

[464] Cf. Walton, *Thou Traveller Unknown*, 29–31 and van Seters, *Prologue to History*, 289–295 for interesting discussions on this topic.

[465] Cf. Speiser, *Genesis*, 217–218; A. de Pury, *Promesse divine et légende cultuelle dans le cycle de Jacob: Gen 28 et les traditions patriarcales. études bibliques* (Paris, France: Gabalda, 1975), 32–33, 45, 349–350; K. Berge, *Die Zeit des Jahwisten, Ein Beitrag zur Datierung jahwistischer Vätertexte* (BZAW 186; Berlin, Germany: Walter de Gruyter, 1990); W. Richter, "Das Gelübde als theologische Rahmung der Jakobsüberlieferungen," *BZ* 11 (1967): 21–52; Long, *The Problem of Etiological Narrative*, 60; Westermann, *Genesis 12–36*, 453; and Wenham, *Genesis 16–50*, 219.

[466] R. Rendtorff, "Jakob in Bethel: Beobachtungen zum Aufbau and zur Quellenfrage in Gen 28:10–22," *ZAW* 94 (1982): 511–23; Carr, *Reading the Fractures of Genesis*; E. Blum, *Die Komposition der Vätergeschichte* (WMANT; vol. 57; Neukirchen-Vluyn, Germany: Neukirchener Verlag, 1984); E. Blum, "Noch einmal: Jakobs Traum in Bethel—Genesis 28, 10–22," in *Rethinking the Foundations: Historiography in the Ancient World and in the Bible—Essays in Honour of John van Seters* (BZAW 294; Berlin, Germany: Walter de Gruyter, 2000); Rendtorff, "Jakob in Bethel: Beobachtungen" identifies no less than five stages in the editorial expansion of what started as a single story.

[467] Gunkel, *Genesis*, 311–312; E. Otto, "Jakob in Bet-El: Ein Beitrag zur Geschichte der Jakobsüberlieferung," *ZAW* 88 (1976): 165–90; Coats, *Genesis*, 208.

[468] Gunkel for example states that "Jacob's vow in E is more ancient than Yahweh's promise in J" (Gunkel, *Genesis*, 314).

that this section has come into existence by "a single historian, J, and not a complex redactional process."[469] According to Terino the "semantic and rhetorical coherence of this section point to the unity of the original narrative."[470] My objective is to analyse the text in its final form, and how it fits into the wider Jacob narrative. However, as will become clear, issues relating to the pre-history of the text cannot be avoided altogether.

Jacob, the owner of a dubiously acquired birthright and blessing, has to flee empty-handed from his father's house (cf. 32:10).[471] On this flight from Beersheba (Gen 26–27) to Haran (28:1), Jacob encounters God at 'a certain place.' The events of 28:11–22 are well integrated with what precedes and follows.[472] The mention of Haran (instead of Paddan-aram) reminds us of Abraham's calling (cf. 11:32; 12:1–3 and 4). However, Abraham and Jacob are moving in opposite directions when they receive God's promises.[473]

Although many scholars have commented on various aspects of this passage in isolation (e.g. the dream, the 'ladder,' the Bethel etiology), some opt for a more integrated reading. Fokkelman's oft-quoted work on the narrative art of the passage shows that various key-phrases in the passage are arranged palistrophically so that Jacob's response mirrors elements of the vision, and that his vow (vv. 20–22) echoes the divine promises (vv. 13–15).[474] Lipton's more recent study on patriarchal dreams in Genesis suggests that 28:10–22 can be understood as a 'dream report:'[475]

> A study of literature from surrounding cultures show that dream reports were often used as a means of conferring status, or of confirming status that had been called into doubt. I see this as a central concern of Jacob's

---

[469] J. Van Seters, "Divine Encounter at Bethel (Gen 28:10–22) in Recent Literary-Critical Study of Genesis," *ZAW* 110, no. 4 (1998): 503–13, 513 (cf. van Seters, *Prologue to History*, 277–280).

[470] Terino, "A Text Linguistic Study of the Jacob Narrative," 53. Cf. Fokkelman's analysis of this section: Fokkelman, *Narrative Art in Genesis*, 46–81.

[471] "Though he owns the birthright he has purchased and the blessing he has stolen, he has nothing to show for either" (Kass, "Love of Woman and Love of God," 47).

[472] Jacob's journey continues in 29:1. Wenham, *Genesis 16–50*, 219. Cf. Cartledge, *Vows*, 166; Terino, "A Text Linguistic Study of the Jacob Narrative," 52.

[473] Abraham is specifically mentioned in 28:13 and the passage contains various echoes of encounters between Abraham and God.

[474] Fokkelman, *Narrative Art in Genesis*, 46–81. Cf. Wenham, *Genesis 16–50*, 219; Waltke, *Genesis*, 387–388; and Ross, "The Founding of Bethel," 225.

[475] Lipton, *Revisions of the Night*.

dream, which provides the requisite divine validation of his dubiously acquired birthright and blessing.[476]

I will focus on the divine revelation and on Jacob's response, and how both relate to other material in Gen 12–50 (and beyond) regarding material possessions. I will demonstrate that the nature and role of material possessions in the Jacob-cycle can only be understood in the dynamic context of relationship. Gen 28:10–22 is crucial for a proper understanding of the relationship between God and Jacob, and for how that relationship develops over time.

2.5.2   Commentary

28:10–13a

On his journey Jacob comes 'to a certain place' (vs. 11). הַמָּקוֹם appears three times in this verse. Taken together with the three appearances in vv. 16, 17 and 19, there is the sense that this is a highly significant 'place.'[477] The sun had set, only to rise again in the narrative when Jacob's twenty year exile would be over (32:32); "so the happenings of nature attend, underline and symbolize what happens between God and man."[478] Jacob took one of the stones 'of the place,' put it under his head, fell asleep and dreamed.[479] Eight *waw*-consecutive verb forms in vv. 10–12 make place for five participles in vv. 12–13. "The chain of participles bluntly shifts the narrative from the past to the present."[480] This effect is even more striking because of the threefold occurrence of וְהִנֵּה, which is arranged climactically: "Behold…a ladder (סֻלָּם); behold…the angels of God; and behold…the LORD!!"[481] סֻלָּם is a

---

[476] Lipton, *Revisions of the Night*, 64–65.

[477] Wenham, *Genesis 16–50*, 221; "the key word in this story" (Amit, *Reading Biblical Narratives*, 122); Hamilton, *Genesis 18–50*, 238–239; 'a holy place' Westermann, *Genesis 12–36*, 453–454. Wyatt suggests that Jacob's vision has been composed during the exile, where the dreamer confuses Babylon with Jerusalem (N. Wyatt, "Where Did Jacob Dream His Dream?," *SJOT* 2 (1990): 44–57; cf. Walton, *Thou Traveller Unknown*, 45, n. 54; cf. J. Schwartz, "Jubilees, Bethel and the Temple of Jacob," *HUCA* 56 (1985): 63–85, 82–83, who discusses Rabbinic traditions that attempt to identify Bethel with the temple in Jerusalem).

[478] Fokkelman, *Narrative Art in Genesis*, 48–49.

[479] Stones appear in various places in the Jacob narrative (cf. Fokkelman, *Narrative Art in Genesis*).

[480] Hamilton, *Genesis 18–50*, 239.

[481] Cf. Fokkelman, *Narrative Art in Genesis*, 51–52; Ross, "The Founding of Bethel," 228.

hapax legomenon which is translated by some commentators as 'ladder,' but by most as 'ramp or staircase.'[482] Oblath suggests that סֻלָּם can be identified as 'the gate of heaven' and should be understood as "an enclosed Near Eastern gate structure", which is oriented vertically to facilitate traffic between the earthly and the heavenly.[483] Whatever interpretation is preferred, it is quite reasonable to assume that there is a connection between Gen 11:1–9 and 28:10–22.[484] Where the tower-builders of Babel had attempted to build a structure from earth into heaven, here the סֻלָּם was placed '*towards* the earth' (מֻצָּב אַרְצָה); "the contact between heaven and earth exists by the grace of God."[485] Jacob's self-sufficient grasping and scheming invites comparison with the self-sufficient hubris of the tower-builders; but there is also the contrast between human and divine initiative, and the juxtaposition of divine judgment and grace.[486] The 'angels of God' (מַלְאֲכֵי אֱלֹהִים) that are ascending and descending on (or inside) the סֻלָּם are silent participants in the whole.[487] The phrase מַלְאֲכֵי אֱלֹהִים only appears elsewhere in 32:2 (32:1 ET), a clear hint that these passages should

[482] Speiser, *Genesis*, 218; Westermann, *Genesis 12–36*, 454; Hamilton, *Genesis 18–50*, 239–240; J.G. Griffiths, "The Celestial Ladder and the Gate of Heaven (Gen 28:12 and 17)," *ET* 76 (1964/65): 229–30; von Rad, *Genesis*, 279; Wenham, *Genesis 16–50*, 221; Alter, *Genesis*, 149; A.R. Millard, "The Celestial Ladder and the Gate of Heaven (Gen 28:12,17)," *ET* 78 (1966/67): 86–87; Sarna, *Understanding Genesis*, 193. For a comprehensive survey: C. Houtman, "What Did Jacob See in His Dream at Bethel?," *VT* 27 (1977): 337–51.

[483] M. Oblath, " 'To Sleep, Perchance to Dream…': What Jacob Saw at Bethel (Genesis 28:10–22)," *JSOT* 95 (2001): 117–26. See also Ross, "The Founding of Bethel," 228, and the bibliography at n. 15 on the same page.

[484] A 'Kontrastparallele' (Houtman, "What Did Jacob See in His Dream at Bethel?," 351). Cf. Fokkelman, *Narrative Art in Genesis*, 53; Fischer, "Jakobs Rolle in der Genesis," 276; Lipton, *Revisions of the Night*, 99: "Genesis 11 and 28 may be usefully read as 'reflection stories'" (referring to Y. Zakowitz, "Through the Looking Glass: Reflections/Inversions of Genesis Stories in the Bible," *BI* 2 (1993): 139–52 and J.D. Safren, "Balaam and Abraham," *VT* 38 (1988): 105–28). See also McKeown, *Genesis*, 139.

[485] Houtman, "What Did Jacob See in His Dream at Bethel?," 351; cf. Lipton, *Revisions of the Night*, 99–104; Waltke, *Genesis*, 390; Hamilton, *Genesis 18–50*, 240; Humphreys, *The Character of God*, 171.

[486] Jacob "sought to take control of his destiny and make a name for himself" (McKeown, *Genesis*, 139). Lipton notes the fact that the tower-builders did not seek divine approval for their building project, whereas that permission is supposed to be given to Jacob (Lipton, *Revisions of the Night*, 104).

[487] Rashi suggested that the ascending angels had been with Jacob in Canaan, and that the descending angels would accompany Jacob on his journey outside Canaan. Houtman holds that the steady flow of ascending and descending angels depict God's involvement with the world in a more general way (Houtman, "What Did Jacob See in His Dream at Bethel?," 350).

be read in conjunction. Angels appear and are referred to throughout
the Jacob narrative (cf. 48:16). It seems reasonable to interpret the
vision of angels as an 'assurance of God's protection.'[488] Finally, there
is the climactic visual element of the LORD's presence: "and behold
the LORD stood above it" (עָלָיו or: 'upon it,' or 'above him,' or 'beside
him/it').[489] Commentators who favour 'beside/above him' point to the
fact that 'the LORD said' (vs. 13) instead of called, implying that the
LORD stood near Jacob.[490] In addition, Jacob's exclamation "surely
the LORD is in this place" (vs. 16) seems to suggest 'Yahweh's immediate presence.'[491] Besides, the LORD had also 'come down' in Gen 11:5.
However, arguments can be made for the fact that the LORD stood
at the top of the 'staircase.'[492] Whatever interpretations are favoured
regarding the nature of the 'staircase,' or the meaning of 'ascend' and
'descend' of the angels, or the exact position of the LORD, the whole
dramatic experience sets the scene effectively for what follows.[493]

28:13a–15

The magnificent vision breaks into Jacob's dark preoccupation with
fear and uncertainty.[494] "The fact that Jacob is granted the vision of
YHWH highlights how privileged he is, especially after the deception
of his father and brother."[495] We now come to the most important
part of the theophany, the divine speech.[496] Where the first divine

---

[488] Wenham, *Genesis 16–50*, 222, commenting on Rashi's suggestion (see footnote
above). See also: Waltke, *Genesis*, 390; Brueggemann, *Genesis*, 243. Alternatively, Peleg
suggests that the סֻלָּם symbolizes the 'way' to and from the Promised Land (Y. Peleg,
"Going Up and Going Down: A Key to Interpreting Jacob's Dream (Gen 28,10–22),"
ZAW 116, no. 1 (2004): 1–11, 5), and that the "vision in the dream reflects the attitude
towards the patriarchs entering and leaving the Promised Land" (Peleg, "Going Up
and Going Down," 11). However, there does not seem to be anything in the text or in
the immediate context that supports this.

[489] A very old interpretative debate! (cf. Waltke, *Genesis*, 390–391).

[490] Baldwin, *The Message of Genesis 12–50*, 11; Hamilton, *Genesis 18–50*, 241;
Fokkelman, *Narrative Art in Genesis*, 55, n. 24; Westermann, *Genesis 12–36*, 455.

[491] Hamilton, *Genesis 18–50*, 241. Similarly McKeown, *Genesis*, 140. Cf. Fokkelman,
Narrative Art in Genesis, 55, n. 24, who notes that both readings are possible.

[492] Peleg, "Going Up and Going Down," 10; Walton, *Thou Traveller Unknown*, 47;
Wenham, *Genesis 16–50*, 222. Wenham notes that source-critical arguments cannot
settle this matter one way or another (cf. de Pury, *Promesse divine*, 377).

[493] The 'ladder' and the angels do not occur again; they have 'accomplished their
task' (Fokkelman, *Narrative Art in Genesis*, 54). Fokkelman makes the comparison
with Moses' burning bush, 'a mere eye-catcher.'

[494] Baldwin, *The Message of Genesis 12–50*, 118–119.

[495] Walton, *Thou Traveller Unknown*, 47.

[496] Brueggemann, *Genesis*, 243–244.

appearances to Abraham and Isaac had opened with specific instructions, in Jacob's case the LORD starts with identifying himself: "I am the LORD, the God of Abraham your father and the God of Isaac."[497] God identifies himself in relationship terms, not by holy location (cf. 15:1).[498] In 27:20, Jacob (in reply to Isaac) had referred to God as 'the LORD *your* God.' Would the LORD also become Jacob's God?[499] This question could well be the core concern in this encounter. The LORD proceeds by bestowing 'a catena of unconditional' promises on Jacob and his descendants.[500] Some were made to Abraham and Isaac before (vv. 13–14), some are tailor-made for Jacob himself (most of vs. 15).[501] God makes these promises without any reference to Jacob's behavior up to this point.[502] Neither are the promises accompanied by any conditions. This makes this initial encounter between God and a patriarch truly unique.

The familiar promises of land and offspring that follow most closely match those made to Abraham in 13:14–16.[503] Interestingly these were also made in connection with Bethel (cf. 13:3).[504] Jacob hears these words as a single man on the run. Indirectly, God assures Jacob that his mission to Haran to find a wife will be successful.[505] Although all

---

[497] Humphreys, *The Character of God*, 171; Grüneberg, *Abraham*, 83. The phrase 'Abraham your father' indicates Abraham's importance in the family line (cf. 28:4; Walton, *Thou Traveller Unknown*, 48; Grüneberg, *Abraham*, 83). See also Fokkelman, *Narrative Art in Genesis*, 57, n. 28. Lipton suggests that this might imply criticism of Isaac for his favour towards Esau (Lipton, *Revisions of the Night*, 70).

[498] Hartley, *Genesis*, 255; Walton, *Thou Traveller Unknown*, 49. A similar self-identification we see in 15:1, when the LsORD came to Abram in a vision, 'I am your shield,' and in 15:7, "I am the LORD who brought you out from Ur of the Chaldeans to give you this land to possess" (cf. Ross, "The Founding of Bethel," 230).

[499] Taschner, *Verheissung und Erfüllung*, 80; Hamilton, *Genesis 18–50*, 241; Fokkelman, *Narrative Art in Genesis*, 56 and 76. See comments on vv. 16–22 below.

[500] Hamilton, *Genesis 18–50*, 241; cf. Humphreys, *The Character of God*, 172–3; Fokkelman, *Narrative Art in Genesis*, 61.

[501] Some scholars have suggested that these two parts 'reflect different stages of growth,' with the second part of the speech coming from an earlier stage of development (cf. Walton, *Thou Traveller Unknown*, 50).

[502] Humphreys, *The Character of God*, 172; Grüneberg, *Abraham*, 83. "Jacob is not chosen because of his character but in spite of it" (McKeown, *Genesis*, 128). Cf. Brueggemann, *Genesis*, 217.

[503] And to a lesser extent 22:17–18 (cf. Ross, "The Founding of Bethel," 229). Daube has suggested that the phrase 'the land on which you lie' has the same legal meaning as the acts of walking and treading the land (Daube, *Studies in Biblical Law. ad loc*, cited by Malul, "'Āqēb "Heel" and 'Āqab'," 203, n. 38).

[504] Wenham, *Genesis 16–50*, 222; cf. Taschner, *Verheissung und Erfüllung*, 74–75.

[505] Hamilton, *Genesis 18–50*, 242; Wenham, *Genesis 16–50*, 223; Grüneberg, *Abraham*, 83.

these promises are 'indissolubly interwoven,'[506] word-order suggests
that prominence is given to the land promise.[507] Most words, however, are dedicated to the promise of numerous offspring, quite fitting
as we consider the events of Gen 29–30. In the chiasmic structure
identified by Terino (vv. 11b–18a, marked by the taking of stones)
the promise 'you shall spread abroad' stands at its centre, suggesting
that this is the main focus of the divine speech.[508] This is also a further
reflection on the Babel story.[509] Of these first two promises, the one
regarding offspring would be most clearly fulfilled in Jacob's lifetime.
But the climax of the offspring promise is what it will lead to: "and in
you and your offspring shall all the families of the earth be blessed,"
which quotes 12:3 verbatim, adding 'and in your descendants' (echoing 22:18; 26:4).[510] Fokkelman notes that the use of הָאֲדָמָה indicates a
universal blessing that is not limited to those living in הָאָרֶץ of vs. 13.[511]
"Thus Jacob clearly receives the בִּרְכַּת אַבְרָהָם (vs. 4),"[512] a blessing that
can only be bestowed by God himself.[513] Where so much emphasis in
the Jacob story up to this point has been on 'getting' the blessing, now
the emphasis shifts to 'being' the blessing.[514] This is even more striking
when we consider that the LORD does not tell Jacob 'I will bless you'
(cf. 26:3, 24). It will only be in 32:29 that we will read 'and there he
blessed him.'[515] Fokkelman astutely notes that "grammatically Jacob
has been neither subject nor object of *brk* before; curiously enough not
even in 28:14."[516] Hamilton concurs:

---

[506] Fokkelman, *Narrative Art in Genesis*, 60 (cf. 58–59).
[507] Ross, "The Founding of Bethel," 229.
[508] Terino, "A Text Linguistic Study of the Jacob Narrative," 54–55.
[509] McKeown, *Genesis*, 141.
[510] Fokkelman, *Narrative Art in Genesis*, 60. Similarly 12:3 and 22:18 (Grüneberg,
Abraham, 84). Wenham, *Genesis 16–50*, 223. As in 12:3 the Niphal verb form is used,
whose meaning it is difficult to pin-down. Here the passive form is most likely (cf.
Grüneberg, *Abraham*, 84; Waltke, *An Introduction to Biblical Hebrew Syntax*, 378–
391; see Excursus I). In contrast, the Hithpael form is used in 26:4.
[511] Fokkelman, *Narrative Art in Genesis*, 60–61, n. 35 and Grüneberg, *Abraham*,
186. Cf. Hamilton, *Genesis 18–50*, 242 on the use of הָאֲדָמָה in vv. 14 and 15.
[512] Grüneberg, *Abraham*, 83.
[513] Taschner, *Verheissung und Erfüllung*, 79.
[514] Hamilton, *Genesis 18–50*, 242.
[515] See also 35:9 (*Section 4.6*).
[516] Fokkelman, *Narrative Art in Genesis*, 49, n. 6.

Throughout much of his early life, Jacob has all the trappings of one who is declared the family beneficiary (i.e. the birthright and the paternal blessing), but he does not have the blessing of God.[517]

According to Brueggemann the 'blessing for others' expresses "the counter-theme, urging the promise receiver (Jacob) out beyond his own narrow interests."[518] We will learn fairly quickly how successful God has been with this objective (cf. vv. 20–22). Vs. 15 starts with another וְהִנֵּה, establishing a link between the content of vs. 15 and the vision in vv. 12–13a.[519] The promises that follow are meant for Jacob alone and address his most pressing concerns; "six times Yahweh is the subject (...) and six times Jacob is the object."[520] The first three promises ("I am with you…I will keep you…I will bring you back") foreshadow the overall plot of the Jacob story.[521] God's presence will not be limited to specific locations.[522] The promise to bring Jacob back to the land refers back to the land promise in vs. 13, and it appears to be of the utmost importance to God.[523] The latter three promises in vs. 15 are emphatic assurances that God will do what he has promised. The vision of angelic traffic from and to earth appears to function as assurance regarding the promise of divine involvement in Jacob's life.[524] God's personal assurances to Jacob in vs. 15 undergird the promises in vv. 13–14.[525] They also attract Jacob's exclusive attention in vv. 20–22 and will reappear at various stages in the Jacob narrative (e.g. 31:3, 5 and 42).[526]

As we look at the divine speech in its entirety, it is clear that the promises regarding land, offspring and blessing for others, are tightly framed by relationship claims and promises. They form the beginning, the means and the end for the realization of all these promises. There appears to be a hierarchy within the promise material that will

---

[517] Hamilton, *Genesis 18–50*, 220.
[518] Brueggemann, *Genesis*, 244.
[519] Fokkelman, *Narrative Art in Genesis*, 61.
[520] Cf. Grüneberg, *Abraham*, 85; Walton, *Thou Traveller Unknown*, 49; Hamilton, *Genesis 18–50*, 243; Grüneberg, *Abraham*, 85.
[521] Wenham, *Genesis 16–50*, 223; Sailhamer, *Genesis ad loc.*
[522] Walton, *Thou Traveller Unknown*, 49; Waltke, *Genesis*, 392: "unlike the pagan deities of the ancient Near East, God is not limited to a particular land."
[523] Humphreys, *The Character of God*, 171–172.
[524] Grüneberg, *Abraham*, 86; Brueggemann, *Genesis*, 244: "the visual elements are the vessels in which the treasure of promise is given."
[525] Waltke, *Genesis*, 391; cf. Hamilton, *Genesis 18–50*, 243.
[526] Taschner, *Verheissung und Erfüllung*, 76.

become apparent as we consider the rest of Genesis and the Pentateuch.[527] Some promises address the present ('I am with you'), some
the immediate future (offspring) and some the distant future (land).[528]
However, it is only in the context of the relationship dynamics between
God and the patriarchs and their descendants that all these promises
can be understood properly. The transfer of the 'blessing of Abraham'
to Jacob opens up a new phase in God's master-plan.

28:16–22

Jacob's response occurs in stages (vv. 16–22; words-actions-words).
When Jacob awakes, his immediate reaction is one of spontaneous
acknowledgment and reverent fear (vv. 16–17).[529] A much more considered response follows when day breaks. Jacob commemorates his
nocturnal experience by erecting the stone on which he slept as a מַצֵּבָה
and anointing it with oil, by naming the place Bethel (vv. 18–19), and
by making a vow (vv. 20–22).[530] Spero suggests that Jacob's response in
vv. 16–19 is primarily inspired by the visual aspect of the dream, and
that his vow is a response to God's verbal message (vv. 20–22), which
"seems somewhat muted and understandably so."[531] Although Jacob's
vow clearly refers to God's promises in vv. 13–15, Jacob's spontaneous
response in vv. 16–17 and his anointing of the מַצֵּבָה can be seen as a
response to the *entire* dream experience.

I will focus on Jacob's vow, and in passing will comment on the
other elements in his response. Some scholars consider the vow as
secondary, and treat the naming of Bethel as the climax of the original etiology.[532] Westermann even states that "the content of a promise
(v. 15) could scarcely coincide with the content of a vow (vv. 20, 21a)

---

[527] Cf. Clines, *The Theme of the Pentateuch*.

[528] "In passages of direct divine speech, in which God (or the Lord God) is the
subject (e.g. 'I will give to you....'), the result is fascinating. God seems to focus almost
exclusively on the *land* he hopes to give to Abraham and his descendants; and: "There
can be no fulfilment of the land promise unless there is an heir. The promise of the
heir is always in the service of the land promise" (Brueggemann, *Genesis*, 109).

[529] Jacob even seems to reproach himself for his ignorance (Hamilton, *Genesis
18–50*, 244).

[530] מַצֵּבָה: cf. de Vaux, *Ancient Israel*, 285–286. Later such 'pillars' were considered
illicit (cf. Ex 23:24 and 34:14; Dt 7:5, 12:3 and 16:22). The fact that in Genesis this is
considered acceptable practice, testifies to the antiquity of these texts (cf. Hamilton,
Genesis 18–50, 246; Wenham, *Genesis 16–50*, 223).

[531] Spero, "Jacob's Growing Understanding of His Experience at Beth-El," 212.

[532] Richter, "Das Gelübde" (followed by Westermann, *Genesis 12–36*, 458). Otto,
"Jakob in Bet-El: Ein Beitrag zur Geschichte der Jakobsüberlieferung," 169 and 174.

in one and the same text."[533] I fail to see why that is a problem, and I am not alone:

> What can be more natural than for Jacob to make a vow and pledge himself to worship the deity when the divine promise is fulfilled, that is when Jacob has returned to the sanctuary?[534]

Jacob then makes a vow (נֶדֶר), the longest vow in the OT.[535] "The vow was a conditional promise to give something to God, if God first granted a favor."[536] "Vows were chiefly aimed at securing Yahweh's aid, protection, or provision e.g. for success in realizing an ambition."[537] Such vows, often made by people in crisis situations (like Jacob), were binding.[538] Parker notes that "it is expected that the vow will be fulfilled immediately after the condition has been met."[539] This explains the various warnings in the OT that that they should not be made rashly.[540] The language of Jacob's vow (vv. 20–22) is much more formal and considered than his initial response (vv. 16–17). This is not critique but observation. Jacob appears to ignore God's promises of vv. 13–14; instead his sole attention seems to be on God's promises that address his most pressing concerns (vs. 15). Maybe we should not read too much into this, as the other patriarchs did not make "any obvious response to promises relating to the more distant future."[541] However, recalling Brueggemann's statement that the "blessing for others" expresses "the counter-theme, urging the promise receiver (Jacob) out beyond his own narrow interests," we must conclude that for the moment this objective does not receive the desired response.[542] Instead, Jacob takes the wording of vs. 15, and makes God's promises

---

[533] Westermann, *Genesis 12–36*, 458.

[534] de Pury, *Promesse divine*, 438 (also cited by Wenham, *Genesis 16–50*, 224).

[535] On נֶדֶר see R. Wakely, NIDOTTE #5623, 3:37–42; de Vaux, *Ancient Israel*, 465–466. See also Richter, "Das Gelübde"; Humphreys, *The Character of God*, 172; Cartledge, *Vows*, 166–175; Waltke, *Genesis*, 393.

[536] de Vaux, *Ancient Israel*, 465; S.B. Parker, "The Vow in Ugaritic and Israelite Narrative Literature," *UF* 11 (1979): 693–700, 694.

[537] Wakely, NIDOTTE #5623, 3:38.

[538] Parker, "The Vow in Ugaritic and Israelite Narrative Literature," 699.

[539] Parker, "The Vow in Ugaritic and Israelite Narrative Literature," 697.

[540] Wakely, NIDOTTE #5623, 3:38; Waltke, *Genesis*, 397; Hamilton, *Genesis 18–50*, 249.

[541] Grüneberg, *Abraham*, 86 (cf. Fokkelman, *Narrative Art in Genesis*, 75).

[542] Brueggemann, *Genesis*, 244. See also C.J.H. Wright, *The Mission of God* (Leicester, UK: Inter-Varsity Press, 2006), 194f.

ever more specific.[543] Where God promises Jacob to bring him back
'to this land,' Jacob replaces that by "come again to my father's house
in peace" (בְּשָׁלוֹם).[544] Esau's death threat is clearly on his mind. Where
God's promises are conceptual and wide ranging, Jacob's concerns are
much more 'down-to-earth.'[545] Jacob's specification of "bread to eat
and clothing to wear" (cf. Deut 10:18), makes clear how utterly dependent Jacob is on God at this point in time.[546] One last detail: Where
God had promised "I will keep you wherever you go," Jacob specifies
"and keep me in this way (בַּדֶּרֶךְ הַזֶּה) that I go."[547] The word דֶּרֶךְ will
appear again in 32:1, which reports Jacob's return: "Jacob went on his
way (לְדַרְכּוֹ), and the angels of God (cf. 28:12) met him." Consider also
Jacob's speech in 35:3.[548]

Although Jacob focuses on God's promises in vs. 15, there is an
implicit link with vs. 13 as well. God had promised Jacob "the land....
I will give (אֶתְּנֶנָּה) to you and your offspring." Instead, Jacob responds
in vs. 20, "If God....and will *give me* (וְנָתַן־לִי) bread to eat and clothing to wear," and Jacob concludes his vow by promising "and of all
that *you give me* (תִּתֶּן־לִי) I will give a full tenth to you (עַשֵּׂר אֲעַשְּׂרֶנּוּ
לָךְ)." Jacob's promise to tithe is the climax of his vow, signalled by
a switch to direct address.[549] Fokkelman comments that "Jacob frees
himself from the formally solemn tone (...) it is gratitude which breaks
through and requires the intimacy of the dialogue."[550] Jacob's commitment to tithe echoes Abraham's tithe to Melchizedek in Gen 14:20,
and agrees with well-attested tithing practices in the ANE.[551] However, how does Jacob fulfil his tithing commitment? Jacob's return to
Bethel and his building of an altar (35:1–7) is considered by many

---

[543] Cf. Fokkelman, *Narrative Art in Genesis*, 74ff.; Cartledge, *Vows*, 170.

[544] Cf. Jephthah's vow in Jdg 11:31 (Parker, "The Vow in Ugaritic and Israelite
Narrative Literature," 699). "For *shalom* as the *conclusio* of successful negotiations, see
D.J. Wiseman, "'Is it Peace?' Covenant and Diplomacy," *VT* 32 (1982): 325" (cited by
Hamilton, *Genesis 18–50*, 247).

[545] Cf. McKeown, *Genesis*, 141–142.

[546] Cf. Hamilton, *Genesis 18–50*, 247; Speiser, *Genesis*, 218; Fokkelman, *Narrative
Art in Genesis.*, 77; Walton, *Thou Traveller Unknown*, 53.

[547] Fokkelman, *Narrative Art in Genesis*, 77.

[548] See *Section* 4.5 and 4.6.

[549] "He rightly saw his tithe (22b) not as a gift but as giving back" (Kidner, *Genesis*,
158).

[550] Fokkelman, *Narrative Art in Genesis*, 81. Cf. Ross, "The Founding of Bethel,"
233. Cf. Hamilton, *Genesis 18–50*, 249, n. 45 for other instances of the shift from talking *about* God to talking *to* God.

[551] Cf. Waltke, *Genesis*, 394; R.E. Averbeck, "מַעֲשֵׂר," NIDOTTE #5130, 2:1035–55.

scholars to be the fulfilment of his vow,[552] but no specific mention is made of Jacob's tithing in that context.[553] Although it is safe to assume that Jacob made a sacrifice on the newly constructed altar, it is highly unlikely that this sacrifice constituted a tenth of his sizable herds.[554] Waltke's interpretation causes even more problems. Waltke suggests that the use of the Piel (עַשֵּׂר אֲעַשְּׂרֶנּוּ) "may signify that Jacob intends to tithe his increase regularly, not give just a one-time votive offering."[555] Waltke continues to discuss tithing practices in later OT times and its validity for NT Christians.[556] Unfortunately, he does not discuss any of the practicalities that concern Jacob's immediate situation. Many scholars interpret Jacob's pledge to refer to later tithing practice at Bethel's sanctuary, or to tithing in general.[557] According to Wenham Jacob "is also, as father of the nation, setting a pattern for all Israel to follow."[558] In the context of the Jacob-cycle itself, Jacob's commitment is more open-ended. Considering the preceding verses, it is unlikely that Jacob's vow was insincere.[559] However, we cannot be sure whether Jacob did tithe; and if he did not, we do not know the reasons.[560] This uncertainty only adds to the ambiguity of the Jacob character.

The major issue with the translation of this vow is the division of the text between a protasis and an apodosis ('if…then').[561] Jacob's vow can be compared with other vows in the OT and from other cultures

---

[552] Cartledge, *Vows*, 174. More on this in Chapter 4.

[553] Cf. Cartledge, *Vows*, 171–172; Grüneberg, *Abraham*, 88; Parker, "The Vow in Ugaritic and Israelite Narrative Literature," 697 on the expectation that vows should be fulfilled immediately after the condition has been met (as quoted above). See also Milgrom, *Numbers*, 489.

[554] Although no specific mention is made of sacrifice (Grüneberg, *Abraham*, 88; contra Cartledge, *Vows*, 172 who states that "all that is specifically mentioned is the offering of sacrifices on the newly constructed altar."

[555] Waltke, *Genesis*, 394 and Waltke, *An Introduction to Biblical Hebrew Syntax* §24.4i.

[556] Waltke, *Genesis*, excursus 397–398.

[557] Cf. von Rad, *Genesis*, 281; Westermann, *Genesis 12–36*, 460; Milgrom, *Numbers*, 432; Walton, *Thou Traveller Unknown*, 54–55; Hamilton, *Genesis 18–50*, 249; A. Pagolu, *The Religion of the Patriarchs* (JSOTSup 277; Sheffield, UK: Sheffield Academic Press, 1998), 190–191; Wyatt, "Where Did Jacob Dream His Dream?," 56–57 takes the reference to tithing as support to his thesis that Jacob's dream refers to the temple in Jerusalem.

[558] Wenham, *Genesis 16–50*, 225.

[559] Cf. Grüneberg, *Abraham*, 88.

[560] Genesis records Jacob's intention to tithe vs. Abraham doing it (14:20).

[561] Kidner and Sarna, following one option given in *Genesis Rabbah* suggest 'when' instead of 'if' (cited by Grüneberg, *Abraham*, 86, n. 94).

in the ANE.[562] Parker notes that "while the passage is still recognizable
as a vow, its form is in fact more distorted than in all the other cases."[563]
Parker even describes Jacob's vow as 'aberrant.'[564] Most commentators take the last part of vs. 21 as the beginning of the apodosis ('then
the LORD shall be my God').[565] Some opt for the beginning of vs. 22
('then this stone...').[566] Arguments can be made for both.[567] I will only
review the most relevant arguments here. Proponents of taking vs. 22
as the beginning of the apodosis point to a change in verb form at the
beginning of vs. 22; a change from the *waw* plus perfect in vv. 20–21
(the so called 'perfectum consecutivum'),[568] to the imperfect in 22a.[569]
Secondly, in vv. 20–21 the verbs come first in their clauses, while in
vs. 22 it is the other way around.[570] Thirdly, in vv. 20–21 there are
four elements, which refer back to the divine promises in vv-13–15. It
would seem illogical to assign three to the protasis, and one to the apodosis.[571] Opponents to this line of reasoning argue that in vs. 21b, there
is a "change of subject from Elohim to YHWH,"[572] and that elsewhere
in OT prose, the apodosis begins with a *waw* consecutive perfect as
well (cf. 1 Sam 1:11).[573] Finally, Cartledge comments about the unusual
place of the infinite absolute-finite verb construction in the vow, "perhaps a subtle reminder of Jacob's twisted way of doing things."[574]

Besides translation issues, there are some serious theological issues
to consider as well. If the apodosis starts with "then the LORD will
be my God," Jacob's acceptance of the LORD as his God appears to

---

[562] Cf. Num 21:1; Jdg 11:30–31; 1 Sam 1:11; 2 Sam 15:8.

[563] Parker, "The Vow in Ugaritic and Israelite Narrative Literature," 698. Cf. Cartledge, *Vows*, 172.

[564] Parker, "The Vow in Ugaritic and Israelite Narrative Literature," 700.

[565] Most Bible translations (ESV, NIV, NRSV, JPS); Westermann, *Genesis 12–36*,
451; Richter, "Das Gelübde"; Wenham, *Genesis 16–50*, 218; Waltke, *Genesis*, 394;
Grüneberg, *Abraham*, 87, especially n. 97; Walton, *Thou Traveller Unknown*, 52–53.

[566] Hamilton, *Genesis 18–50*, 248; Fokkelman, *Narrative Art in Genesis*, 75–76; Lipton, *Revisions of the Night*, 74–77.

[567] Walton, *Thou Traveller Unknown*, 52.

[568] Fokkelman, *Narrative Art in Genesis*, 75.

[569] Hamilton, *Genesis 18–50*, 248; Fokkelman, *Narrative Art in Genesis*, 75.

[570] "In vs. 22 the verb follows a lengthy subject in the form of a *casus pendens*"
(Hamilton, *Genesis 18–50*, 248).

[571] Fokkelman, *Narrative Art in Genesis*, 75, n. 55.

[572] Walton, *Thou Traveller Unknown*, 52, cf. references in n. 71.

[573] Grüneberg, *Abraham*, 87, n. 97; cf. Cartledge, *Vows*, 143–150; Waltke, *An Introduction to Biblical Hebrew Syntax* §32.2.1, as cited by Grüneberg, *Abraham*, 87; and
Parker, "The Vow in Ugaritic and Israelite Narrative Literature," 694.

[574] Cartledge, *Vows*, 172.

be quite preposterous. Does Jacob's reply in vv. 16–17 and his act of consecration in vv. 18–19 not make it clear that Jacob has accepted the LORD as his God? Lipton notes "if this were indeed a conditional acceptance of God, it would be the only one of its kind in the Bible."[575] However, Walton argues that "it is certainly not unheard of for Israel to choose allegiance to YHWH."[576] Parker classifies Jacob's vow in the same way as Absalom's, service to the deity.[577] Although Jacob's vow is very specific in places, the "ambiguous structure of the sentence," leaves plenty of space for inference.[578] It is this ambiguity that is such an essential element in the characterization of Jacob himself.

In the light of all this, how should we interpret Jacob's vow? Ross takes a fairly positive stance, "Jacob made his vow on the basis of what God had guaranteed to do. So he was taking God at His word and binding himself to reciprocate with his own dedication."[579] This is contra Gunkel, who characterizes such a vow as a 'naive form of prayer,' "naive because one hopes to gain the deity's favor through the prospect of a welcome gift."[580] Spero is less affirmative and comments that "Jacob, in effect, promises to take up the issue later on."[581] Humphreys' assessment of Jacob's vow is fairly negative as well:

> Yahweh offers unconditional support, and a covenant without strings attached. Jacob transposes it into a conditional covenant, with the conditions first and foremost placed on Yahweh (…). For rather than a simple trust, God is met by counter demands that nail down in specifics what he broadly promised.[582]

---

[575] Lipton, *Revisions of the Night*, 74 (and n. 22). Cf. Hamilton, *Genesis 18–50*, 248 for similar reasoning.

[576] Walton, *Thou Traveller Unknown*, 52–53 (cf. 1 Sam 1:11, 2 Sam 15:8, Num 21:2, as cited by Richter, "Das Gelübde," as cited by Walton). See also Grüneberg, *Abraham*, 87. Weiss, "Jacob's Struggle: A Psycho-Existential Exegesis," 29 sees this as a failure by Jacob to genuinely engage with God, and cites this as the reason why Jacob will not meet God in person again till his struggle in the night.

[577] Parker, "The Vow in Ugaritic and Israelite Narrative Literature," 699. See also Sarna, *Genesis*, 200.

[578] Walton, *Thou Traveller Unknown*, 52. Cf. Parker, "The Vow in Ugaritic and Israelite Narrative Literature," 698 as quoted above.

[579] Ross, "The Founding of Bethel," 233.

[580] Gunkel, *Genesis*, 313.

[581] Spero, "Jacob's Growing Understanding of His Experience at Beth-El," 212.

[582] Humphreys, *The Character of God*, 173; Similarly T.J. Whartenby Jr., "Genesis 28:10–22," *Int* 45, no. October (1991): 402–05, 404; Weiss, "Jacob's Struggle: A Psycho-Existential Exegesis," 21.

However, the fact that this vow is conditional should not unduly worry us. Alter comments that "the conditional form of the vow (…) is well attested elsewhere in the Bible and in other ancient New Eastern texts. But its use by Jacob has a characterizing particularity."[583] Sarna notes that "Jacob's vow is unique in that all the desired conditions have already been unqualified promised by God."[584] Cartledge has analyzed this particularity and is quite negative in his overall assessment: "the content of Jacob's vow underscores not only Jacob's distrust but also his reputedly selfish nature."[585] "Jacob's calculating mentality is portrayed in his tendency to spell things out."[586] Cartledge speaks of the "brashness of Jacob's manipulative, manifold, and self-centred petitions."[587] Wenham is far more generous:

> Real experience of God must always result in heartfelt worship; here he gave all he had, the stone and the oil, and promised to give a tenth of all his future income when his affairs improved. To pray for a safe return showed faith, not unbelief.[588]

Similarly, Brueggemann, takes Jacob's response as an act of faith, but "Jacob will be Jacob. Even in this solemn moment, he still sounds like a bargain-hunter."[589] Based on the fact that conditional vows are well-attested in the OT and the ANE, it is probably wrong to interpret the vow as inappropriate, although its wording does characterize Jacob as a careful, calculating type.[590] From the totality of vv. 16–22 there can be no doubt that Jacob considered the LORD as God.[591] What matters is how Jacob understands his relationship with God at this point in time, and how that relationship will be shaped by subsequent events. Fokkelman rightly speaks of a dialogue, which is initiated by God, but which is definitely not one-sided.[592] "For Jacob however, the

---

[583] Alter, *Genesis*, 150. Cf. L.R. Fisher, "Two Projects at Claremont," *UF* 3 (1971): 27–31; Parker, "The Vow in Ugaritic and Israelite Narrative Literature."

[584] Sarna, *Genesis*, 200.

[585] Cartledge, *Vows*, 169.

[586] Cartledge, *Vows*, 170 n. 2 (cf. 30:31!).

[587] Cartledge, *Vows*, 171. Kodell, although less harsh, speaks of 'self-centeredness' as well (J. Kodell, "Jacob Wrestles with Esau (Gen 32:23–32)," *BTB* 10, no. 2 (1980): 65–70, 66).

[588] Wenham, *Genesis 16–50*, 225.

[589] Brueggemann, *Genesis*, 248; cf. Weiss, "Jacob's Struggle: A Psycho-Existential Exegesis," 29; Whartenby Jr., "Genesis 28:10–22," 404; Mann, *The Book of the Torah*, 56.

[590] Cartledge, *Vows*, 174–175.

[591] Hartley, *Genesis*, 258.

[592] Fokkelman, *Narrative Art in Genesis*, 188.

point is that Yhwh will really prove himself to be the *Elōhē Ya'cob*, so that he can do something in return."[593] Grüneberg's assessment is well-balanced:

> Thus it seems that Jacob makes an appropriate response to Yhwh's promises (even one who remains uneasy about aspects of the vow— Jacob will be Jacob—may yet hold that there is demonstrated here as much responsiveness to Yhwh as he is capable of showing).[594]

All in all, vv. 20–22 is an interesting case of 'take and give.'[595] Divine concerns and human understanding regarding material blessing do not always coincide.[596] This passage could serve as a fitting illustration for Isa 55:8: "for my thoughts are not your thoughts, neither are your ways my ways, declares the LORD." Although God's appearance to Jacob at Bethel undoubtedly had an enormous impact on Jacob, Jacob still has much to learn.

2.5.3   *Concluding Remarks*

Gen 28:10–22 is a key-passage in the Jacob-cycle. It is the first encounter between God and Jacob, and it is here that Jacob receives 'the blessing of Abraham.' It is a story of initiation and transformation.[597] A 'certain place' becomes Bethel; a stone becomes a pillar, and a man on the run becomes the holder of great promises. However, the transformation of Jacob will prove to be not only a matter of 'a place' (מָקוֹם), but of a journey (the 'road' דֶּרֶךְ).[598] The relevance of Bethel is that God breaks into the predominantly horizontal elements of the Jacob narrative up to this point. "Bethel is both literally and figuratively an intersection of the divine and human paths."[599] Standing between the Jacob/Esau and Jacob/Laban material, "it is an 'inter-cycle' section that the narrator inserts as a theological peak."[600]

---

[593] Fokkelman, *Narrative Art in Genesis*, 76.
[594] Grüneberg, *Abraham*, 88.
[595] "Jacob is hedging his bets (…) Jacob's opening to the divine is not yet whole-hearted" (Kass, "Love of Woman and Love of God," 47).
[596] Cf. Appendix B.
[597] Fokkelman, *Narrative Art in Genesis*, 69; Hamilton, *Genesis 18–50*, 247; Roop, *Genesis*, 395–396; Waltke, *Genesis*, 394; Blum, "Noch einmal: Jakobs Traum in Bethel— Genesis 28, 10–22," 35; Amit, *Reading Biblical Narratives*, 122–123.
[598] The two readings proposed by Peleg, "Going Up and Going Down."
[599] Mann, *The Book of the Torah*, 55. See also Terino, "A Text Linguistic Study of the Jacob Narrative," 55 as quoted above.
[600] Terino, "A Text Linguistic Study of the Jacob Narrative," 52.

As we survey God's speech it is clear that some elements repeat
what God promised to Abraham and Isaac, but that some elements are
truly unique. No other patriarch receives such emphatic assurance of
God's help and presence. This is even more remarkable when we consider what transpired in Gen 27. However, we must not forget what
God withholds from Jacob at this point: the familiar words 'I will bless
you' are *not* addressed to Jacob just yet. As we consider the nature
and role of material possessions in the Jacob-cycle in the context of
relationship, it is important to realize that any relationship between
God and humans contains both generic and personal aspects, as
clearly demonstrated by the Jacob narrative. Material promises (land)
and material concerns (food, clothing and tithing) are quite central
to the dialogue in this passage. Although the LORD makes awesome
promises to Jacob, we must realize that 'speech' does not equal 'relationship.' It is in the ongoing dialogue between the LORD and Jacob,
between promise and fulfilment, human acknowledgment and worship, that relationship gains depth.[601]

Gen 28:10–22 is indeed a key-passage in the Jacob-cycle; "ein
Grundpfeiler der Architecktur der Jakoberzählung."[602] Jacob's vow
contributes to Jacob's characterization, but more importantly it shapes
the plot of the Jacob-cycle, "dealing with the *making* (28:20–22), *granting* (31:2, 4–16) and *fulfilment* (35:1–7) of a vow."[603] In the following chapters we will reflect on how God's promises were realized in
Jacob's life. It will only be at the end of Jacob's life that we will be
able to survey more fully how this relationship has developed.[604] An
encounter at Bethel does not leave interpreters unaffected either. The
wide variety of interpretations of this passage, and the interpretative
challenges that remain 'unresolved,' testify to the subtlety and ambiguity of Jacob's characterization in the narrative, and this should alert us
that we must tread carefully as we continue our quest to understand
the nature and role of material possessions in the Jacob-cycle. There
will be no simple answers.

---

[601] Cf. Grüneberg, *Abraham*, 87.
[602] Taschner, *Verheissung und Erfüllung*, 82. Cf. Richter, "Das Gelübde," 42ff.;
Blum, *Komposition*, 93; van Seters, *Prologue to History*, 295ff.
[603] Cartledge, *Vows*, 174, summarizing Richter, "Das Gelübde."
[604] Cf. Spero, "Jacob's Growing Understanding of His Experience at Beth-El."

2.6   Reflections on the Boundary

The Jacob-cycle is well-integrated within the narrative framework of Genesis, which provides a universal Creation/Fall backdrop, against which God's particular purposes for Abraham and his chosen line unfold. However, more universal concerns are never far away (e.g. blessing for the nations). Jacob's world is both a post-Gen 3 and a post-Gen 12 reality. Central to Gen 25:19–28:22 is the question how God's promises to Abraham and Isaac will progress to the next generation. The opening scenes offer fascinating perspectives on that issue, but also come with various interpretative challenges. The context for the unfolding drama is formed by various relationship concerns: both divine and human; both inside and outside the chosen family. The various relationships in 25:19–28:22 are multifaceted and are subject to development, both good and bad. "The Jacob story is a complex interplay of the divine will and human fallibility, personality and effort."[605] The 'horizontal' stories of conflict are juxtaposed with 'vertical' narratives of God's involvement.[606]

Concerns over material well-being are very much at the heart of Gen 25–28. Gen 26 demonstrates what could be described as the dialogical nature of material possessions (blessing received vs. source of conflict), while in the other chapters, struggle and conflict dominate. Material possessions and associated attitudes and actions can be described as a multi-dimensional concept, which is best understood in the context of relationship against a Creation/Fall backdrop. Material advancement is something people are willing to fight over very hard. Gen 26 offers the alternative perspectives of reconciliation and peace, which at this point in the story are only distant possibilities for Esau and Jacob.

Gen 25:19–28:22 also raises various questions regarding the relationship between blessing and prosperity. I have argued that such questions should be considered in a wider context. In Gen 12–50 different parties speak about blessing and they do not necessarily mean the same thing.[607] Blessing seems to cover quite a range of issues. We have to be careful with defining 'blessing' too quickly and too tightly, as divine promises and blessing appear to be subject to progressive

---

[605] Walton, *Thou Traveller Unknown*, 126.
[606] Brueggemann, *Genesis*, 211.
[607] Cf. Appendix B.

revelation. Although God certainly shows that he is involved in humanity's concerns, God's concerns differ in places from his human counterparts, who tend to focus on the tangible aspects of blessing instead of the intangible (relationship) and long-term ones (land). Furthermore, human understanding of blessing seems to depend on the degree of relationship a person has with God: the better that relation, the better the understanding. Possessions (as blessing) are best understood within this relationship context. Although it is reasonable to link blessing with possessions in *certain* passages, this does not necessarily mean that *all* possessions are a blessing from God. Blessing is always more than just possessions.

In Gen 25 and 27, Jacob considers material advancement as more important than relationship(s). As a result, relationships within his family are shattered. Ironically, the 'blessed one' leaves his home without family and without any possessions. The birthright and the blessing that were fought over so hard have not brought any immediate benefits, and it remains to be seen how important they are at all. When Jacob has reached 'rock-bottom' a divine vision breaks into his darkness (28:10–15). Despite Jacob's deceit God graciously bestows on him the promises that were first made to Abraham. The specific mention of divine blessing for Jacob is still to come (32:29; 35:9). Jacob's response shows his overriding concern for material well-being, but it is probably as much as he is 'capable of showing now' (Grüneberg). Jacob's journey of faith has begun. God's involvement with Abraham's family continues. The remainder of Jacob's life-story will give us ample opportunity to test Fretheim's proposal that "human beings can neither preserve nor annul God's promises, for God will keep promises; but their words and deeds will have much to say in how these promises move toward fulfilment."[608] And so Jacob, a man with a dark past, holder of divine promises, steps across the boundary of Canaan to go the "land of the people of the east" (29:1).

---

[608] Fretheim, *The Pentateuch*, 100.

CHAPTER THREE

JACOB OUTSIDE CANAAN (GEN 29–31)

3.1 INTRODUCTION

Gen 29–31 tells the story of Jacob's twenty-year stay with Laban. The narrative is structured palistrophically, with the increase of children and riches at its centre (underlined):

C   Jacob fears Esau and flees (27:1–28:9)
    D   Messengers (28:10–22)
       E   <u>Arrival at Haran (29:1–30)</u>
          F   <u>Jacob's wives are fertile (29:31–30:24)</u>
          F' <u>Jacob's flocks are fertile (30:25–31:1)</u>
       E' <u>Flight from Haran (31:2–54)</u>
    D' Messengers (32:1–32)
C' Jacob returns and fears Esau (33:1–20)[1]

It is framed by Jacob's encounters with 'messengers' (D—28:10–22, and D'—32:1–32) and stands between Jacob's flight from Esau, and the encounter with his brother upon his return (C—27:1–28:9, and C'—33:1–20); a 'cycle in a cycle.'[2] The Jacob-Laban narrative is very coherent in itself, but there are also many links with the wider Jacob narrative.[3] Actually, Gen 29–31 cannot be fully appreciated apart from this wider context.

Jacob arrives just by himself, without any possessions, but departs with two wives, two concubines, twelve children, multiple servants and much wealth in the form of flocks (30:43; 31:17–18). In this chapter, I will analyze Jacob's increase in Gen 29–31 in detail. What is the nature and role of material possessions in the Jacob-Laban narrative?

---

[1] From Rendsburg, *The Redaction of Genesis*, 53–54 (I refer to the opening paragraphs of Chapter 2).
[2] Wenham, *Genesis 16–50*, 228.
[3] Wenham, *Genesis 16–50*, 228; Fokkelman, *Narrative Art in Genesis*; Taschner, *Verheissung und Erfüllung*, 85; Walton, *Thou Traveller Unknown*, 127.

What is God's involvement in Jacob's increase? How does this new found wealth 'sit' with regard to the various human relationships? Can we indeed speak of Jacob's 'success' (Rendsburg)?[4] Is it right at this point to call Jacob a blessed man (Taschner)[5] or is it more appropriate to speak of "a life of toil and the establishment of a family (judgment and mercy)" (Fokkelman)?[6] And finally, how will Jacob's wealth feature in the rest of the Jacob-cycle?

Commentators do not agree whether to treat the opening section 29:1–30 as a single narrative unit, or as two (vv. 1–14; 15–30).[7] For our purposes this distinction does not really matter.[8] I will discuss Jacob's arrival in Haran (vv. 1–14) before turning to Jacob's marriages (vv. 15–30) and what follows in Gen 30–31.[9]

3.2   Jacob's Arrival in Haran (Gen 29:1–14)

3.2.1   Commentary

29:1

Jacob seems to have a new spring in his step following Bethel.[10] However, in Gen 29 Jacob does not acknowledge God in any way. Some

---

[4] Rendsburg, *The Redaction of Genesis*, 66.

[5] Is Jacob a "*gesegneten und reichen Mann*"? (Taschner, *Verheissung und Erfüllung*, 85, italics mine).

[6] Fokkelman, *Narrative Art in Genesis*, 49.

[7] Single unit: Westermann, *Genesis 12–36*; Sarna, *Genesis*, and to some extent Brueggemann, *Genesis*: "the opening section (29:1–30) sets the stage, introduces the characters and hints at the conflict to come" (252). Two narrative units: Gunkel, *Genesis*; von Rad, *Genesis*; Speiser, *Genesis*; Wenham, *Genesis 16–50*; Sherwood, "*Had God Not Been on My Side*"; Fokkelman, *Narrative Art in Genesis*; Taschner, *Verheissung und Erfüllung*; Walton, *Thou Traveller Unknown*. Similarly Hamilton, *Genesis 18–50*. The division between the two scenes is sometimes made between vs. 14a and 14b (e.g. Speiser, *Genesis*, 226; Waltke, *Genesis*; Sailhamer, *Genesis*).

[8] Cf. Wenham, *Genesis 16–50*, 228 for a similar sentiment.

[9] Most source critics assign 29:1–14 to J, although originally Dillmann suggested that vs. 1 originated from E (Gunkel, *Genesis*, 316–317). For a more in-depth discussion: Wenham, *Genesis 16–50*, 228 and 233; Blum, *Komposition*, 105–111 and van Seters, *Abraham in History and Tradition*, 205–207.

[10] Cf. Rashi, as quoted by Alter, *Genesis*, 151; Sarna, *Genesis*, 201; Waltke, *Genesis*, 108; Walton, *Thou Traveller Unknown*, 129, n. 8. For various interpretations of the Hebrew idiom 'lifted up his feet' cf. Speiser, *Genesis*, 222; Wenham, *Genesis 16–50*, 229; Hamilton, *Genesis 18–50*, 251 n. 1; Sherwood, "*Had God Not Been on My Side*," 60 n. 20; Sarna, *Genesis*, 201 and 365, and L.J. De Regt, "Hebrew Syntactic Inversions and their Literary Equivalence in English: Robert Alter's Translations of Genesis and 1 and 2 Samuel," *JSOT* 30, no. 3 (2006): 287–314, 289. Feet are mentioned again at

commentators interpret the phrase "land of the sons of the east" as 'eastwards.'[11] However, in the context of Genesis more significance may be inferred by 'the east' (קֶדֶם):

> It was home to Cain and his offspring, the location of the Tower of Babel, the direction Lot went when he separated from Abraham to live in Sodom, and the home of the sons of Abraham who did not inherit the promise.[12]

There are similarities and differences with Cain's story. Cain "went away from the presence of the LORD, and settled in the land of Nod, east of Eden" (4:16) following the murder of his brother. However, when Esau intends to murder his brother (27:41–42), Jacob is the one to 'go east.'[13] The conflict will be resolved differently as well.[14] The allusion to Cain signals that we are firmly in post-Gen 3 territory. Hauge notes that the east is often the place to which the losers in the conflict are exiled.[15] Hauge suggests that there is a link between the land promise and sonship: "the Land motif is the immediate concrete expression for the Sonship: the Son is related to the land, the sons to the Land of Defeat."[16] This is one of several reversals Jacob has to endure as a result of his deceit.[17] However, this reversal will not be permanent (28:15!).

29:2–3

This scene is viewed from Jacob's perspective.[18] Wells were covered with big stones to avoid dust and stones falling in, and to regulate

---

the end of Jacob's life (49:33). "Thus the pilgrimage of Jacob is bracketed by these two statements about lifting his feet" (McKeown, *Genesis*, 143).

[11] Westermann, *Genesis 12–36*, 464, following Jacob, *Genesis*, 585 (as discussed by Wenham, *Genesis 16–50*, 229).

[12] Sherwood, "*Had God Not Been on My Side*," 34.

[13] Cain was not attacked following his fratricide (4:15). Jacob and his sons were not pursued following the pillage of Shechem (35:5).

[14] Fokkelman, "Genesis," 53.

[15] M.R. Hauge, "The Struggles of the Blessed in Estrangement," *ST* 29 (1975): 1–30; 113–46, 15 (I am indebted to Sherwood, "*Had God Not Been on My Side*" for this reference).

[16] Hauge, "Struggles," 15. See also N. Wyatt, "There and Back Again: The Significance of Movement in the Priestly Work," *SJOT* 1 (1990): 61–80, 63. Cf. Gen 24:6!

[17] The others being 'serving' and 'bowing down' to his brother, and in this context Jacob who is watering the flock, and not the 'girl at the well.'

[18] Waltke, *Genesis*, 400; Wenham, *Genesis 16–50*, 230; Alter, *Genesis*, 151. And "behold (וְהִנֵּה) a well in the field, and behold there (וְהִנֵּה־שָׁם), three herds of flocks couching by it" (Sherwood, "*Had God Not Been on My Side*," 21).

the use of a scarce water resource.[19] In Gen 26 wells were a source of contention. Very similar wording to vs. 3 is repeated in vs. 8, where the shepherds explain the procedure for removing the stone to Jacob, and in vs. 10, where Jacob removes the stone to water Laban's flock. This 'three-stroke story'[20] may point to Jacob's eventual conquering of obstacles in the wider Jacob-Laban narrative.[21] The big stone also reminds us of the stone Jacob erected in Bethel.[22] Jacob's successful arrival can be seen in the light of the divine promises made in Gen 28.[23]

29:4–8

Jacob asks the shepherds three questions in quick succession, but their replies are very short. When Jacob appears to have touched a raw nerve by questioning their presence at the well in the middle of the day (question four, vs. 7), they reply at greater length (vs. 8).[24] The shepherds are colourless, flat characters who appear to be utterly passive.[25] They are not even explicitly mentioned as shepherds.[26] They are an effective foil for Jacob, who is characterized as a capable, energetic shepherd, with a (slightly) 'pushy' disposition.[27] Vawter even speaks

---

[19] Gunkel, *Genesis*, 325; H.C. Leupold, *Exposition of Genesis* (Grand Rapids, Michigan, USA: Baker Book House, 1942), 784; Hamilton, *Genesis 18–50*, 252 and Waltke, *Genesis*, 400 both following S.R. Driver, *The Book of Genesis* (London, UK: Methuen, 1916), 269; R. Jamieson, A.R. Fausset and D. Brown, *Commentary Critical and Explanatory on the Whole Bible* (Oak Harbor, WA, USA: Logos Research Systems, Inc., 1871); Matthews, *The IVP Bible Background Commentary*, ad loc; Sarna, *Genesis*, 202.

[20] Fokkelman, *Narrative Art in Genesis*, 125.

[21] Walton, *Thou Traveller Unknown*, 129. "The removal of the stone will seem easy compared to the barriers Jacob will face before he can reach the goal of marrying Rachel, let alone of returning home in peace" (Walton, *Thou Traveller Unknown*, 132).

[22] Sarna, *Genesis*, 202. Walton, *Thou Traveller Unknown*, 129; Fokkelman identifies 'stones' as a unifying theme in the Jacob narrative(s) (e.g. Fokkelman, *Narrative Art in Genesis*, 125).

[23] Waltke, *Genesis*, 398; Fokkelman, *Narrative Art in Genesis*, 123; Wenham, *Genesis 16–50*, 232; Hamilton, *Genesis 18–50*, 253; Walton, *Thou Traveller Unknown*, 129; Humphreys, *The Character of God*, 175.

[24] Sarna, *Genesis*, 202.

[25] 'Shirkers' (Waltke, *Genesis*, 401). "The shepherds who are really too lazy to speak" (von Rad, *Genesis*, 283). Sherwood speaks of an "overall atmosphere of inactivity" (Sherwood, "*Had God Not Been on My Side*," 37).

[26] "Here and in vs. 8 the Hebrew text reads 'flocks' instead of *herdsmen*" (Davidson, *Genesis 12–50*, 151, see also Sherwood, "*Had God Not Been on My Side*," 63 n. 49).

[27] See also Speiser, *Genesis*, 223; Sherwood, "*Had God Not Been on My Side*," 31 and 40; Waltke, *Genesis*, 401, and Alter, *Genesis*, 152.

of "brash self-assuredness which prompts Jacob to offer the shepherds of Haran unsolicited advice on the running of their well."[28] As Jacob makes several inquiries Rachel arrives (vs. 6).[29] "The biblical narrator is careful to expose the hand of divine providence at work in the unfolding drama."[30] While Rachel comes closer, Jacob challenges the shepherds: "Look, it's the middle of the day. It is not time for the cattle to be gathered. Water the flocks and go shepherd!"[31] The shepherds defend themselves by saying that they 'cannot' or 'may not' (לֹא נוּכַל) until all the flocks have gathered (vs. 8).[32] Are they not able physically to lift the stone,[33] or are they bound by local custom to wait till all are gathered?[34]

29:9–12

The overall direction of the passage is towards the meeting with Laban, but Jacob's encounter with Rachel provides the climax for now.[35] The phrase 'his mother's brother' (אֲחִי אִמּוֹ) features no less than three times. Bar-Efrat suggests "that it was Jacob's love for his mother's relatives (…) that caused him to go up and roll the stone single-handed from the mouth of the well."[36] According to Sarna this phrase reminds us of the parental instructions in 27:43 and 28:2 and "contains a hint that this girl is to become his wife."[37] However, there might be more

---

[28] Vawter, *On Genesis*, 318.

[29] הֲשָׁלוֹם לוֹ וַיֹּאמְרוּ שָׁלוֹם Cf. 28:21 and 33:18 for the use of *shalom*. "One need not read into the word *shalom* all the rich nuances it carries elsewhere (…) it is simply polite inquiry" (Hamilton, *Genesis 18–50*, 253).

[30] Sarna, *Understanding Genesis*, 195. See also Hamilton, *Genesis 18–50*, 253; Fokkelman, *Narrative Art in Genesis*, 123–125; Waltke, *Genesis*, 398–399; Humphreys, *The Character of God*, 175.

[31] Paraphrasing Sherwood, "*Had God Not Been on My Side*," 22.

[32] In contrast with Jacob's prevailing (יָכֹל) in 32:26, 29 (MT) (cf. Fokkelman, *Narrative Art in Genesis*, 125).

[33] Hamilton's and Waltke's translation for גְּדֹלָה (vs. 2) as 'enormous' probably pushes the interpretation too much into one direction (Hamilton, *Genesis 18–50*, 251; Waltke, *Genesis*, 400).

[34] Cf. von Rad, *Genesis*, 283 and Sherwood, "*Had God Not Been on My Side*," 42 and notes 67–68 on 64–65, for a comprehensive survey of the various options.

[35] Sherwood, "*Had God Not Been on My Side*," 25. For Westermann this is the climax of vv. 1–14. This is the third mention of the stone in this 'three stroke story' (Fokkelman, *Narrative Art in Genesis*, 125, see above).

[36] Bar-Efrat, *Narrative Art*, 119. Similarly Sternberg: "redundant familial attribution implies motive" (Sternberg, *Poetics*, 538 n. 15).

[37] Sarna, *Genesis*, 202. Similarly Waltke, *Genesis*, 401. For an anthropological perspective that offers quite a different insight on this phrase, see R.A. Jr. Oden, "Jacob as Father, Husband and Nephew: Kinship Studies and the Patriarchal Narratives,"

than meets the eye. The syntax highlights the sight of two 'objects' that moves Jacob into action:[38] "Rachel the daughter *of Laban his mother's brother* and the sheep *of Laban his mother's brother*" (vs. 10):

רָאָה יַעֲקֹב

אֶת־רָחֵל בַּת־לָבָן אֲחִי אִמּוֹ
וְאֶת־צֹאן   לָבָן אֲחִי אִמּוֹ

It is the desired 'acquisition' of Rachel and sheep that will drive the events in Gen 29–31.[39] Rachel and the sheep are 'of Laban' at the beginning of the story, but they will eventually change hands. This verse may also contribute to Jacob's characterization; "Jacob's character—his greed—subtly identified by the text."[40] Kass notes how "Jacob, sharp-eyed, sees Rachel and at the same time sees also the flock. No stranger to the love of gain, he may be attracted by the one as by the other."[41] So Jacob rolls the great stone from the well's mouth, thereby not only breaking with convention, but probably also annoying the shepherds, as Jacob first waters the flock that arrived last. Sherwood identifies five motifs associated with Jacob's initiative: 1) Jacob's love for Rachel; 2) Family affection; 3) Jacob's extraordinary strength; 4) Jacob's job fitness; and 5) Jacob's defiance of local custom.[42] There is nothing mutually exclusive in these motifs, so that it is not necessary to choose just one.[43]

JBL 102, no. 2 (1983): 189–205, 199–200. Oden, based on work by Radcliffe-Brown in 1924, notes the special relationship between a mother's brother and a sister's son in certain cultures, which also has important implication with respect to property.

[38] Cf. Fokkelman, *Narrative Art in Genesis*, 124.

[39] Sherwood, *"Had God Not Been on My Side,"* 49. "Für beides wird Jacob seinem Onkel im weiteren Verlauf des Aufenthaltes in der Fremde dienen" (Taschner, *Verheissung und Erfüllung*, 88). See also Brodie, *Genesis as Dialogue*, 315–316.

[40] J.R. Wilson, "Theology and the Old Testament," in *Interpreting the Old Testament: A Guide for Exegesis* (ed. C.C. Broyles; Grand Rapids, MI, USA: Baker Academic, 2001), 263.

[41] Kass, "Love of Woman and Love of God," 48.

[42] For a comprehensive survey of the various interpretations: Sherwood, *"Had God Not Been on My Side,"* 45–47.

[43] Sherwood, *"Had God Not Been on My Side,"* 47. Although Rachel's beauty is only specifically mentioned in vs. 17 we cannot discount its impact on Jacob in vs. 19. The family connection has indeed been mentioned emphatically in vs. 10 (see above). Jacob's show of strength chimes well with his desire to impress. Jacob's job fitness is something that will be a major theme in rest of the Jacob-Laban narrative. And finally, Jacob has already proven himself to be an effective breaker of man-made customs (Gen 25–27). B. Jacob also opts for a combination: "die Liebe durchbricht alle Regel und gibt Riesenkräfte" (Jacob, *Genesis*, 587). Similarly, von Rad, *Genesis*,

After Jacob has watered the flocks (not a ten-minute job presumably!), Jacob 'kissed Rachel and wept aloud' (vs. 11). Janzen's suggestion that Jacob's weeping is indicative of a transformation that has started to take place inside him, is probably premature.[44] Although the encounter at Bethel did have a substantial impact on Jacob there is nothing in Gen 29 that in any way is indicative of Jacob's transformation. Probably we have to wait much longer for that to become a visible reality.[45] Jacob might have felt great joy over his encounter with Rachel (cf. 28:1–2!), but he first waters the flocks and only then introduces himself.[46] His service might have been aimed to find a way to Rachel's heart. His weeping might contribute to his characterization as a calculating type. From an anthropological perspective it must be noted that certain cultures are "less inhibited in showing their emotions" than we are.[47]

This opening scene introduces various elements that will be developed in more detail later.[48] Sherwood suggests that the well "may also serve as proleptic sexual imagery."[49] Alter comments that "it is especially fitting that this well should be blocked by a stone, as Rachel's womb will be 'shut up' over long years of marriage."[50] Sherwood notes that the stone is described as 'great' (גְּדֹלָה, vs. 2) and that Leah is described

<hr />

284. In contrast, Fokkelman argues that "love calling up gigantic strength is a modern, romantic interpretation" (Fokkelman, *Narrative Art in Genesis*, 124).

[44] Janzen, *Genesis 12–50*, 114.

[45] Cf. Kodell, "Jacob Wrestles with Esau (Gen 32:23–32)," 69. See also *Section 4.3.*

[46] Gunkel, *Genesis*, 318; Fokkelman, *Narrative Art in Genesis*, 124–125; Waltke, *Genesis*, 401; Westermann, *Genesis 12–36*, 466, following Skinner, *Genesis*. Von Rad notes that the watering process would have taken quite some time (von Rad, *Genesis*, 284). See also Fokkelman, *Narrative Art in Genesis*, 124.

[47] Sarna, *Genesis*, 203. See also T.H. Gaster, *Myth, Legend, and Custom in the Old Testament: A Comparative Study with Chapters from Sir James G. Frazer's Folklore in the Old Testament* (New York, USA: Harper & Row, 1969), 193 for a similar anthropological argument (in am indebted to Sherwood, "*Had God Not Been on My Side,*" 48 for this reference).

[48] Brueggemann, *Genesis*, 252; Taschner, *Verheissung und Erfüllung*, 88.

[49] Sherwood, "*Had God Not Been on My Side,*" 36 and 56–57. Similarly Taschner, *Verheissung und Erfüllung*, 86 and Walton, *Thou Traveller Unknown*, 130 (and n. 13), who refers to Alter's observation that there is a pun between 'watered' in vs. 10 (וַיַּשְׁקְ) and 'kissed' in vs. 11 (וַיִּשַּׁק) (Alter, *Genesis*, 152, who followed Sarna, *Genesis*, 202–203). Similar 'sexual imagery' appears in the book of Proverbs (e.g. Prov 5:15–18). I am indebted to Revd Dr Ernest Lucas for this observation.

[50] Alter, *Genesis*, 152. In a similar vein, Janzen suggests that the three flocks around the well symbolize the three women in Gen 29–30 who will bear children before Rachel does, who (so to speak) arrives late on the scene (Janzen, *Genesis 12–50*, 113).

as הַגְדֹלָה in vs. 16, often translated as 'the elder' or 'the older'.[51] The stone may also represent various other obstacles (e.g. Laban's trickery, local customs, changing herding contracts), which Jacob has to remove before he can tap into fertility (children and flocks).[52]

Additional insights are gained by treating Jacob's arrival as a 'type-scene.'[53] It is instructive to reflect on the similarities and differences between Jacob's arrival in Haran, the arrival of Abraham's servant in Gen 24 and Moses' arrival in Midian in Ex 2.[54] I limit myself to comparing Jacob's arrival with Gen 24.[55]

> What a glaring contrast between the well-laden camel train of the grandfather and the lonely, empty-handed Jacob who arrives on foot! Yet Providence is at work in etching the fortunes of the one as surely as in the case of the other.[56]

Why Isaac and Rebekah allowed Jacob to leave empty-handed is not explained.[57] "As a result, Jacob has no bride price to give and will have to reduce himself to a hired hand to secure Rachel."[58] According to Waltke the comparison with Gen 24 "underscores the benevolence of divine providence but puts into relief the contrast between the prayerful servant and the prayerless patriarch."[59] Abraham's servant prayed,

---

[51] Sherwood, "*Had God Not Been on My Side*," 37. Ironically, 'stone' Leah will prove to be more fertile than 'well' Rachel.

[52] Cf. Sherwood, "*Had God Not Been on My Side*," 56–57. See also Jeansonne, *The Women of Genesis*, 71–72.

[53] Alter, *The Art of Biblical Narrative*, 51ff; Alter, *Genesis*, 152; Wenham, *Genesis 16–50*, 229ff; Walton, *Thou Traveller Unknown*, 128–9; Jeansonne, *The Women of Genesis*, 70–71; Mann, *The Book of the Torah*, 57.

[54] The similarities between this scene and Gen 24 and Ex 2 were already noted by Caesarius of Arles (c. 470–543) (ed. M. Sheridan, *Ancient Christian Commentary on Scripture: Genesis 12–50* (ed. T.C. Oden; Downers Grove, Illinois, USA: InterVarsity Press, 2002), 194–195). Caesarius of Arles applied a 'type-scene' approach *avant la lettre*, although the rest of his interpretation was quite different from more modern approaches! See also H. Eising, *Formgeschichtliche Untersuching zur Jakobserzählung der Genesis* (Emsdetten, Germany: Dissertations-Druckenei Heinr. & J. Lechte, 1940), 162–165; Kidner, *Genesis*, 160 n. 1, who notes the comparison between these passages, but does not apply the phrase 'type scene' yet.

[55] Like Abraham's servant, Jacob arrives on his destination virtually instantaneously, despite the four hundred miles journey from Bethel to Haran (Jamieson, *Commentary Critical and Explanatory on the Whole Bible, ad loc*).

[56] Sarna, *Genesis*, 201.

[57] A point raised by Baldwin, *The Message of Genesis 12–50*, 122 and Waltke, *Genesis*, 399.

[58] Waltke, *Genesis*, 399.

[59] Waltke, *Genesis*, 398. Similarly, Vawter, *On Genesis*, 319, Humphreys, *The Character of God*, 174; Hamilton, *Genesis 18–50*, 259 and Walton, *Thou Traveller Unknown*,

but Jacob relies on his own efforts and "seems to stumble into his good fortune unaware of God's presence."[60] Abraham's servant praised God publicly for the success of his mission, but Jacob does no such thing.[61] Waltke suggests that "God's providence becomes a means of discipline to transform Jacob's character (cf. Prov 3:12)."[62] However, it remains to be seen when, and to what extent, that becomes a reality in Jacob's life.

In this opening scene Rachel is silent. For now the only thing that is told us about her is her familial relationship with Jacob (בַּת־לָבָן אֲחִי אִמּוֹ) and that she shepherded her father's flock.[63] We have to wait till vs. 17 to find out more about her appearance, and it is only in 30:1 that she speaks. This supports Sherwood's assertion that the thrust of this opening section is towards the encounter between Jacob and Laban. It is interesting that the actions and characteristics of Rebekah in Gen 24 are now divided between her son and her niece: Jacob is the one who waters the flocks, but Rachel is the one who 'ran' (וַתָּרָץ, only in Gen 24:20, 28 and here), just like her aunt Rebekah had done (24:28).[64] In Gen 24:28 Rebekah reported 'these things' (כַּדְּבָרִים הָאֵלֶּה), while Jacob would tell 'all these things' in vs. 13 (כָּל־הַדְּבָרִים הָאֵלֶּה).

29:13–14

Having heard Rachel's report, Laban 'runs' (וַיָּרָץ) to meet with Jacob (just as he had run out to meet Abraham's servant in 24:29: וַיָּרָץ) and he 'embraced him and kissed him.'[65] von Rad notes the joy of this scene and comments that "the narrator intentionally gives no hint of

---

131–132 note Jacob's self-reliance. In addition, Walton comments that this might also reflect a "greater difficulty in detecting the work of God in the Jacob cycle than the Abraham cycle" (Walton, *Thou Traveller Unknown*, 131–132).

[60] Waltke, *Genesis*, 399.

[61] Sailhamer, *Genesis, ad loc.*

[62] Waltke, *Genesis*, 399. Similarly Kidner: "In Laban Jacob met his match and his means of discipline. Twenty years (31:31) of drudgery and friction were to weather his character" (Kidner, *Genesis*).

[63] Like the shepherds, 'auch Rachel wird kaum charakterisiert' (Eising, *Formgeschichtliche Untersuching*, 163).

[64] Jacob shows himself a true son of Rebekah, who watered the flocks for Abraham's servant (Jacob, *Genesis*, 587). "He shows that same helpfulness as Rebekah in Gen 24" (Fokkelman, *Narrative Art in Genesis*, 124)

[65] "His hospitality was motivated by greed (...) Scripture is here anticipating the character of Laban as it reveals itself later in his relations with Jacob" (Sarna, *Understanding Genesis*, 174). When Laban and Jacob 'part ways' in Gen 31, Laban will only kiss his daughters and grandchildren (Hartley, *Genesis*, 260; see *Section 3.5*).

the knavery and conflict to which the companionship of these people will shortly give rise."[66] However, Sarna notes that the same verb
was used for kissing in 27:26–27 (נָשַׁק) and he suggests that its use
here (vv. 11 and 13) draws "the curtain on that phase of his life while
simultaneously intimating that the next scene is retributive justice for
his offence in the previous one."[67] I will discuss the issue of 'retributive justice' in more detail below, but for the moment I just want to
highlight this as yet another link with the preceding narrative. Most
commentators view Laban's spontaneity with suspicion. "Tricky Laban
knows, even before he has seen Jacob, that a workman is on his way
who is worth his weight in gold."[68] An even stronger impetus must
have been Laban's recollection of the events in Gen 24, where Laban
and his family received rich presents upon the arrival of Abraham's
servant:

> Was his haste this time prompted by the possibility of similar enrich-
> ment? If it was, he was quickly disillusioned, for Jacob was a runaway,
> not a rich emissary with ten camels. And the narrative seems to hint that
> from their first encounter Laban and Jacob's relationship was flawed by
> Laban's concern for material gain.[69]

A suspicious Rashi even suggests that Laban used his embrace of Jacob
for a thorough body-search to find gold.[70] Sherwood wonders whether
Laban is "moved by feelings for his family or is he hoping for more
and better presents," although he is willing to consider that both may
play a role.[71] It will become clear that Laban considers material gain
more important than the quality of familial relationships.

Laban brings Jacob home, where Jacob tells Laban 'all these things.'
This phrase is rather vague. I mentioned the similarity with 24:28,
which refers to events that took place at the well. Rachel probably has
done that already (vs. 12), so 'all these things' could refer to something else.[72] Some commentators think that Jacob gave a full account

---

[66] von Rad, *Genesis*, 284. Similarly Coats: "The principal figures of the story thus
appear without conflict" (Coats, *Genesis*, 213).
[67] Sarna, *Genesis*, 203. See also Sarna, *Understanding Genesis*, 195.
[68] Fokkelman, *Narrative Art in Genesis*, 126.
[69] Wenham, *Genesis 16–50*, 231.
[70] Alter, *Genesis*, 153.
[71] Sherwood, "*Had God Not Been on My Side*," 32. Sarna is not so generous (Sarna,
Genesis, 203).
[72] Fokkelman, *Narrative Art in Genesis*, 126 although we cannot be sure from the
text what Rachel told Laban (Sherwood, "*Had God Not Been on My Side*," 51).

of what transpired in his life up to this point.[73] Others think that this is rather unlikely. Sarna, for example, finds it "hardly credible that Jacob reported that he had cheated his own father and brother."[74] However, Sarna's attempt to fill this gap by suggesting that it is more likely that Jacob told Laban that "misadventures on the journey had brought him empty-handed" cannot be supported from the text.[75] Wenham resists the temptation to fill in the gap:

> The text is vague, and we are left to guess, but it seems likely that Laban discovered plenty about Jacob's past and realized that Jacob had not many financial assets to offer and was very much at Laban's mercy.[76]

Similarly ambiguous is Laban's reply in vs. 14.[77] Laban appears to acknowledge Jacob as family,[78] although earlier suggestions that Laban adopts Jacob as son and heir at this point have been proven to be fallacious.[79] However, there is a subtle interplay between vs. 13 and 14. One's interpretation of 'all these things' in vs. 13 is likely to influence one's interpretation regarding the tone and intention of Laban's

---

[73] E.g. Jacob, *Genesis*, 588 (followed by Fokkelman, *Narrative Art in Genesis*, 126). Kass, "Love of Woman and Love of God," 48 thinks this includes the deception of this father. Leupold, *Exposition of Genesis*, 790–791 suggests that Jacob at this point turned into a "godly man and one repentant of his recent deceit." Weiser suggests that Jacob told Laban "that his father blessed him and on account of this he was forced to flee from his brother's wrath" (A. Weiser, *Pirushe Ha-Torah Le-Rabbenu Avraham ibn Ezra* (Jerusalem, Israel: 1976), as quoted by Strickman, *Ibn Ezra's Commentary on the Pentateuch: Genesis*, 282).

[74] Sarna, *Genesis*, 203. See also Eising, *Formgeschichtliche Untersuching*, 166.

[75] Sarna, *Genesis*, 203.

[76] Wenham, *Genesis 16–50*, 231.

[77] Jacob, *Genesis*, 588; Wenham, *Genesis 16–50*, 231.

[78] W. Brueggemann, "Of the Same Flesh and Bone (Gen 2,23a)," *CathBQ* 32 (1970): 532–42, 537–538.

[79] E.g. Sarna, *Understanding Genesis*, 195 (also Pfeiffer, *The Patriarchal Age*, 79; M. Burrows, "The Complaint of Laban's Daughters," *JAOS* 57, no. 3 (1937): 259–76, 263–264) suggests that Jacob was adopted by Laban (and later replaced as heirs by Rachel's and Leah's younger brothers) but since then, a firm scholarly consensus has formed, which rejects that proposal. See M.J. Selman, "Comparative Customs and the Patriarchal Age," in *Essays on the Patriarchal Narratives* (eds. A.R. Millard and D.J. Wiseman; Leicester, UK: Inter-Varsity Press, 1980), 110 following Thompson, *The Historicity of the Patriarchal Narratives*, 273–280; van Seters, *Abraham in History and Tradition*, 78–81, who in turn follow M. Greenberg, "Another Look at Rachel's Theft of the Teraphim" *JBL* 81 (1962): 239–48. In his JPS commentary on Genesis, Sarna had moved with the consensus as well (Sarna, *Genesis*, 204). See also D. Daube, Yaron, R., "Jacob's Reception by Laban," *JSS* 1 (1956): 60–61, 60–61 and Brueggemann, "Of the Same Flesh and Bone (Gen 2,23a)," 537–538.

reply.[80] If we assume that Jacob indeed told Laban about his deceit of Esau, Laban's reply "surely you are my bone and my flesh" gets an ironic twist, which can only be fully appreciated later.[81] And so, Jacob is accepted into Laban's household and he stays with him for a month (vs. 14). "Jacob is treated like an insider, at least for now."[82]

3.2.2   Concluding Remarks

What stands out in this opening section is the juxtaposition of God's providence (which is subtly implied), and Jacob's self-reliance, which is evident by his actions and the notable absence of prayer or praise (cf. Gen 24). There is also the juxtaposition of Jacob and Laban; Jacob with an eye for Rachel *and* for her father's flock, and Laban, with his implied interest for material gain.[83] The die is cast for a fascinating plot. Let the games begin!

3.3   JACOB MARRIES TWO SISTERS (GEN 29:15–30)

3.3.1   Introduction

Gen 29:15–30 covers the second episode in the Jacob-Laban narrative.[84] If we treat Gen 29:1–30 as a betrothal type-scene, Laban's question in vs. 15 complicates and delays the closing of that scene.[85] In vv. 16–17 Rachel is contrasted with her elder sister Leah. In the remainder of the passage (vv. 18–30) we can discern roughly two palistrophic structures; a micro-structure (vv. 18–20) and a macro-structure (vv. 18–30); both

---

[80] E.g. Fokkelman translates אַךְ in vs. 14 as a sigh of disappointment, following his meeting of an empty-handed Jacob, but when he finds out the reason for Jacob's journey, 'Laban collapses' (Fokkelman, *Narrative Art in Genesis*, 126). Hamilton argues against Fokkelman's interpretation (Hamilton, *Genesis 18–50*, 256 n. 14). For great interpretive balance on vv. 13–14 see Sherwood, "*Had God Not Been on My Side*," 50–53 and Walton, *Thou Traveller Unknown*, 131.

[81] Cf. Fokkelman, *Narrative Art in Genesis*, 126.

[82] Sherwood, "*Had God Not Been on My Side*," 51.

[83] "Der sich immer gleichbleibende Laban ist von Anfang bis Ende meisterhaft charakterisiert, und gerade dieser Typus des selbstsüchtigen, habgierigen, ausbeuterischen, mißtrauischen, aber die Form wahrenden Besitzers mag dem Verfasser aus dem Leben vertraut gewesen sein" (Jacob, *Genesis*, 588). Contra Waltke, *Genesis*, 399, who labels Laban as a 'flat character.'

[84] Some modern translations begin this episode with vs. 14c. See discussion by Sherwood, "*Had God Not Been on My Side*," 75–78.

[85] Walton, *Thou Traveller Unknown*, 133.

have an exchange between Jacob and Laban at their centre.[86] In both instances, Laban's reply takes centre stage, followed by Jacob's compliance. The micro-structure is formed by the mention of Jacob's love for Rachel, and Jacob's service of seven years:

A   'Jacob *loved* Rachel' (vs. 18a)
   B   'I will *serve* you seven years…' (vs. 18b)
      C   Laban' reply 'it is better that I give her to you…' (vs. 19)
   B'   'So Jacob *served* seven years for Rachel' (vs. 20a)
A'   'because of the *love* he had for her' (vs. 20b)

The outer ring of the macro-structure is formed by the mention of Jacob's love for Rachel and of seven years service (vs. 18 and 30). Other structural elements are the notification that Jacob 'went into her' (Leah in vs. 23, וַיָּבֹא אֵלֶיהָ), and similarly 'into Rachel' (vs. 30, וַיָּבֹא אֶל־רָחֵל גַּם); and Laban's gift of Zilpah (vs. 24) and Bilhah (vs. 29) utilizing almost the exact same phraseology, with the phrases לָהּ, and 'to Leah, his daughter' and 'to Rachel, his daughter' in a chiastic arrangement:[87]

וַיִּתֵּן לָבָן לָהּ אֶת־זִלְפָּה שִׁפְחָתוֹ לְלֵאָה בִתּוֹ שִׁפְחָה
(vs. 24)

וַיִּתֵּן לָבָן לְרָחֵל בִּתּוֹ אֶת־בִּלְהָה שִׁפְחָתוֹ לָהּ לְשִׁפְחָה
(vs. 29)

These palistrophically arranged elements highlight the centre of this structure, which is formed by the exchange between Jacob and Laban (vv. 25b–28a), consisting of Jacob's bitter complaint (vs. 25b) and Laban's reply (vs. 26), followed by Laban's proposal (vs. 27) and Jacob's compliance (vs. 28a):

A   "Jacob *loved* Rachel…I will *serve* you" (vs. 18)
   B   "…and he *went in* to her" (vs. 23b)
      C   "*Laban gave his female servant…to his daughter…to be her servant*" (vs. 24)
         D   Jacob's complaint (vs. 25b)
            E   Laban's reply (vs. 26)
            E'   Laban's proposal (vs. 27)

---

[86] Alternatively, Wenham speaks of two scenes ('betrothal' (vv. 15–19) and 'wedding' (vv. 21–30a)) which are both followed by a comment on Jacob's seven year's service (vs. 20 and 30b) (Wenham, *Genesis 16–50*, 234).

[87] This chiastically arranged word-order gets lost in most translations (e.g. ESV, NRSV). Cf. Sherwood, "*Had God Not Been on My Side*," 100.

D'   Jacob's compliance (vs. 28)

C'   *"Laban gave his female servant...to his daughter...to be her servant"* (vs. 29)

B'   "So Jacob *went into* Rachel also" (vs. 30a)

A'   "and he *loved* Rachel more than Leah, and *served* Laban for another seven years" (vs. 30b).[88]

This passage explains how Jacob ended up with four women, in exchange for fourteen years of work. The focus in the narrative is on the bridal week (vv. 22–29), which is placed between the two seven year periods of labour. Laban's desire for selfish gain (expressed through deceit) and Jacob's love for Rachel are the twin-engines that drive the events of this episode. This in turn explains the various tensions that would exist between Jacob and Laban, between Laban and his daughters, and within Jacob's family itself. In this episode, Jacob is confronted with a reversal of his deceit in Gen 27.[89]

3.3.2   *Commentary*

29:15–20

The idyll of the opening scene comes to an abrupt close.[90] With one (apparently sympathetic) gesture Jacob is reduced from family member to hired hand.[91] This sets the tone for the next twenty years. "Because you are my kinsman, should you therefore serve me for nothing? Tell me, what shall your wages be?"[92] Laban probably has discovered quite a lot: 1) Jacob might have mentioned the parental instruction to find a bride; 2) Unlike Abraham's servant, Jacob did not bring anything that could qualify as a 'bride-price;' 3) Jacob's strong affection for Rachel may well have been evident; and 4) Jacob may have shown himself to be a hardworking and capable worker. The text does not give us much

---

[88] For a slightly different version: Sherwood, *"Had God Not Been on My Side,"* 109–110.

[89] Brett, *Genesis*, 89.

[90] Brueggemann, *Genesis*, 253.

[91] Eising, *Formgeschichtliche Untersuching*, 172; Taschner, *Verheissung und Erfüllung*, 90; Wenham, *Genesis 16–50*, 234.

[92] חִנָּם can also mean 'for no purpose' or 'in vain' (Pr 1:17; Mal 1:10; BDB 3252b). "This negative connotation is appropriate because Jacob will soon be cheated by Laban" (Jeansonne, *The Women of Genesis*, 72). Alter and Hamilton assume that Jacob has been working for free so far (Alter, *Genesis*, 153; Hamilton, *Genesis 18–50*, 258).

detail.[93] It is not clear what sort of arrangement Laban has in mind. Does he propose Jacob to become his employee (a herding contract)? Or does he invite Jacob to propose an alternative arrangement for taking care of the bride-price (a marriage contract)?[94] What does become clear is that Laban intends to exploit the situation, and that he has the upper hand.[95] Pulling the rug from under the feet of your opponent is a classic opening move in any negotiation!

The phrases 'serve' and 'wages' in vs. 15 will reverberate throughout the rest of the Jacob-Laban narrative (cf. 30:25ff).[96] This explains in part why this narrative is so important for our understanding of the nature and function of material possessions in the Jacob-cycle. The root עבד can have a "vast range of meanings from the meanest servitude to high political office."[97] What meaning is intended here? Sherwood suggests that Jacob becomes Laban's slave.[98] In support, Vawter notes that Jacob asks Laban's permission to leave with his wives and children in Gen 30:26, which seems to imply that they still belonged to Laban at that point. Note Laban's claim in 31:43.[99] Alternatively, Morrison suggests that the agreements between Laban and Jacob "bear a strong resemblance to Old Babylonian herding contracts."[100] This

---

[93] It is very tempting to fill in the gaps with firm interpretations. E.g. a) the assumption that Jacob's attachment to Rachel was very evident: "in the last few weeks he has observed his attachment to Rachel" (Wenham, *Genesis 16–50*, 234), or b) the assumption that Jacob has worked the full month (Alter, *Genesis*, 153; Hamilton, *Genesis 18–50*, 258), or c) Walton's assertion that Jacob 'is easily taken in' (Walton, *Thou Traveller Unknown*, 133), which seems to ignore Jacob's inferior negotiation position. The text simply does not give such information.

[94] I will discuss herding and marriage contracts in more detail in *Section* 3.5. See also M.A. Morrison, "The Jacob and Laban Narrative in Light of Near Eastern Sources," *BA* 46, no. 3 (1983): 155–64.

[95] Fokkelman, *Narrative Art in Genesis*, 127. See also von Rad, *Genesis*, 286.

[96] "The root 'BD strings nearly all the scenes, the root SKR all of them" (Fokkelman, *Narrative Art in Genesis*, 126). The root עבד appears seven (!!) times in this passage (29:15, 18, 20, 25, 27x2, 30) (cf. Fokkelman, *Narrative Art in Genesis*, 126 and 130; Taschner, *Verheissung und Erfüllung*, 89), and will also appear in 30:26x2, 29, 43; 31:6, 41. מַשְׂכֹּרֶת will appear in 31:7, 41. The root שכר will appear seven (!!) times in Gen 29–31 (Taschner, *Verheissung und Erfüllung*, 89). See also Wenham, *Genesis 16–50*, 234; Rendsburg, *The Redaction of Genesis*, 63–65.

[97] Sherwood, "*Had God Not Been on My Side*," 92. Cf. Westermann's article on עבד in TLOT 2:819–832 and Carpenter's in NIDOTTE #6268, 3:304–309.

[98] Sherwood, "*Had God Not Been on My Side*," 93. Similarly Fokkelman, *Narrative Art in Genesis*, 130.

[99] Vawter, *On Genesis*, 198. See also Sherwood, "*Had God Not Been on My Side*," 121–122 n. 59 and *Section* 3.5.

[100] Morrison, "The Jacob and Laban Narrative," 156. See also Speiser, *Genesis*, 238–239; J.J. Finkelstein, "An Old Babylonian Herding Contract and Genesis 31:38f.,"

would put Jacob in the position of a hired herdsman. This is supported by Van Seters (cf. Gen 30:30).[101] A herdsman, however, might well end up in slavery as a result of accumulated debt.[102] According to Westermann the arrangement reflects "service in the household of a relative conditioned solely by the circumstances."[103] Most commentators agree that Jacob's status as a family member was completely subordinate to his state as hireling, or even slave.

Daube and Yaron suggest that the first part of Laban's speech, introduced by the phrase הֲכִי־אָחִי, should be understood as a question: 'are you my relative?' implying 'you are not,' thereby terminating the family bond that was acknowledged in vs. 14.[104] Sherwood's observation that the phrase 'to stay with' (וַיֵּשֶׁב עִמּוֹ in vs. 14c) is used more often for non-family guests than for family members, could be taken as support for this proposal.[105] Most commentators do not follow Daube and Yaron all the way, but do agree that Laban substantially redefines his relationship with Jacob in vs. 15.[106] Fokkelman concludes that "Laban proclaims the blood-relationship to be irrelevant, that he changes, degrades the uncle-nephew relationship into a lord-servant relationship that makes it poorer."[107] Morrison agrees: "Laban intended to exclude Jacob from the family holdings but to retain his services as a herdsman."[108] Jacob will negotiate wages with Laban at several points. The first exchange focuses on Rachel, whereas subsequent events will focus on cattle (30:25ff.). Fokkelman rightly speaks of "tricky and bitter

---

JAOS 88 (1968): 30–36; J.N. Postgate, "Some Old Babylonian Shepherds and Their Flocks," *JSS* 20 (1975): 1–20.

[101] J. van Seters, "Jacob's Marriages and Near East Customs: A Re-examination," *HTR* 62, no. 4 (1969): 377–95, 390. 'A laborer under contract' (Waltke, *Genesis*, 404).

[102] Morrison, "The Jacob and Laban Narrative," 161. Herding contracts could work quite negatively for the herdsman in poor years.

[103] Westermann, *Genesis 12–36*, 466. Similarly von Rad, *Genesis*, 285.

[104] Daube, "Jacob's Reception by Laban," 61–62. Cf. GKC § 150d, e and discussions by Sarna, *Genesis*, 203; Hamilton, *Genesis 18–50*, 257 n. 1, 258 and Sherwood, *"Had God Not Been on My Side,"* 86.

[105] Sherwood, *"Had God Not Been on My Side,"* 76.

[106] Wenham, *Genesis 16–50*, 234; Hamilton, *Genesis 18–50*, 258; Waltke, *Genesis*, 404; Walton, *Thou Traveller Unknown*, 136; Sherwood, *"Had God Not Been on My Side,"* 87.

[107] Fokkelman, *Narrative Art in Genesis*, 127. See also Wenham, *Genesis 16–50*, 234; Hamilton, *Genesis 18–50*, 258; Walton, *Thou Traveller Unknown*, 113. In contrast, Coats, *Genesis*, 213 does not consider Laban's question negative in itself, although he states that "business relationships should not qualify among relatives."

[108] Morrison, "The Jacob and Laban Narrative," 160.

'wage disputes'" (Gen 30:25–34; 31:36–43).[109] Jacob is "in a position that makes him vulnerable to exploitation."[110]

29:16–17

Vv. 16–17 separate Laban's question from Jacob's reply and provide additional information about Laban's daughters, Leah and Rachel. These verses illuminate Jacob's reply and subsequent events. This interruption also heightens suspense.[111] How will Jacob recover from this blow? The contrast between Laban's daughters is one of age and one of beauty.[112] The contrast between the 'older' (or 'greater' הַגְּדֹלָה) and 'younger' (הַקְּטַנָּה) reminds us of Esau and Jacob (cf. 27:1, 15 and 42) and will come back with a vengeance in vs. 26.[113] The text implies that it is Rachel's beauty that explains Jacob's love for her.[114] Sherwood comments that "Rachel's beauty establishes her in the line of favoured matriarchs."[115] Jacob's love for Rachel provides him with tremendous drive.[116] It also serves as another element of contrast between the two sisters (vs. 30). Favouritism that featured in the previous generation will become a feature of Jacob's family as well.[117] The text does not say whether Jacob's love was reciprocated.[118]

---

[109] Fokkelman, *Narrative Art in Genesis*, 127.

[110] Sherwood, "*Had God Not Been on My Side.*"

[111] Wenham, *Genesis 16–50*, 234.

[112] Although it is not clear whether Leah's eyes were 'weak' (RSV, ESV, JPS, NIV), 'tender' (AV) or 'soft' (רַכּוֹת) (and whatever that might mean: lack of sparkle? Cf. Gunkel, *Genesis*, 319; Jacob, *Genesis*, 589; von Rad, *Genesis*, 286; Sarna, *Genesis*, 204; Wenham, *Genesis 16–50*, 234; Waltke, *Genesis*, 405), or 'lovely' (Speiser, *Genesis*, 225). For an in-depth discussion, see R. Gradwohl, "Waren Leas Augen hässlich?," *VT* 49, no. 1 (1999): 119–24. We cannot be certain (Alter, *Genesis*, 153). However, there is specific mention that Rachel was 'beautiful in form and appearance' (vs. 17), which suggests that Leah was not. Kass sees a contrast here between "the invisible soul and the visible surface" (Kass, "Love of Woman and Love of God," 48). According to Midrashic interpretation Leah's eyes were weak "from crying because she had been told that she was destined to marry Esau" (Strickman, *Ibn Ezra's Commentary on the Pentateuch: Genesis*, 282).

[113] Similarly Walton, *Thou Traveller Unknown*, 134.

[114] Sherwood, "*Had God Not Been on My Side*," 91; Hamilton, *Genesis 18–50*, 259.

[115] Sherwood, "*Had God Not Been on My Side*," 90. See also Ross, *Genesis, ad loc.*

[116] Bar-Efrat, *Narrative Art*, 49. Sherwood notes that "beauty in the Bible is often a sign of God's (and the narrator's) favor, but can also be a source of trouble" (Sherwood, "*Had God Not Been on My Side*," 90). For a critical assessment of Jacob's love, see Kass, "Love of Woman and Love of God": "love of the beautiful Rachel appears (…) to resemble a form of idolatry" (p. 52).

[117] "Jacob's family also becomes divided" (Waltke, *Genesis*, 406). See also Coats, *Genesis*, 213; Jeansonne, *The Women of Genesis*, 74.

[118] Noted by Hamilton, *Genesis 18–50*, 259 and Sherwood, "*Had God Not Been on My Side*," 91.

Laban's question might have been a body-blow, but Jacob claws his way back by proposing to marry Rachel in exchange for seven years of work. Morrison suggests that because of Jacob's proposal to marry Rachel for seven years work, the issues associated with a herding contract and a marriage contract got entwined at the very beginning of the Jacob-Laban narrative and that these will be only fully resolved in the last encounter between the two combatants (31:25–55).[119] Attempts have been made to put a monetary value on Jacob's seven years of work in order to compare these with the size of the bride-price.[120] Most of such analyses conclude that Jacob's offer was extremely generous.[121] This might reflect Jacob's weak negotiation position, and/or his 'high estimation of Rachel.'[122] Waltke's assertion that "Jacob is not interested in money" and that "the Lord graciously gave him the gift of romantic love for a particular woman, which is far better than money" is probably too high-minded.[123] Jacob might also not have been in a hurry to return to Esau although this would go against Rebekah's advice to stay with Laban 'for a few days' (27:44).[124] Other scholars argue that interpretations that heavily rely on historical reconstructions as above may go well beyond the intention of the narrative:[125]

> We must make a distinction between what historical investigation can tell us about practices and laws in the biblical period, whether early or late, on the one hand, and the indications provided by the narrator, which may or may not be historical on the other.[126]

In Chapter 2 I discussed a similar stand-off between various approaches to enlighten the meaning of birthright and blessing. As before, I propose

---

[119] Morrison, "The Jacob and Laban Narrative," 160.

[120] Matthews, *The IVP Bible Background Commentary*, *ad loc*; Wenham, *Genesis 16–50*, 235; Westermann, *Genesis 12–36*, 466–467; Davidson, *Genesis 12–50*, 153. B. Jacob rejects the notion 'bride price' and suggests that it is closer to 'ein Heldenstück', for Jacob to prove himself worthy of the bride (Jacob, *Genesis*, 589; e.g. Joshua 15:16; Judges 1:12; 1 Sam 17:25).

[121] Wenham, *Genesis 16–50*, 235; Gunkel, *Genesis*, 319; Westermann, *Genesis 12–36*, 466; von Rad, *Genesis*, 285; Kidner, *Genesis*, 160.

[122] Matthews, *The IVP Bible Background Commentary*, *ad loc*; Sherwood, "Had God Not Been on My Side," 94; Gunkel, *Genesis*, 328; Eising, *Formgeschichtliche Untersuching*, 171; Westermann, *Genesis 12–36*, 466.

[123] Waltke, *Genesis*, 405. See also my comments on Gen 29:10 above.

[124] Hamilton, *Genesis 18–50*, 259; Fokkelman, *Narrative Art in Genesis*, 127; Sherwood, "Had God Not Been on My Side," 92.

[125] For an excellent discussion on these various options, cf. Sherwood, "Had God Not Been on My Side," 92–94.

[126] Sherwood, "Had God Not Been on My Side," 93.

a balanced approach to tackle similar issues here. I agree with Sherwood that the interpretive issues in Gen 29 can be argued on "the grounds of the narrative irrespective of the historical probabilities."[127] This does not negate the importance of historical investigations in any way (Sherwood's position as well). I agree with Selman that

> When the biblical and non-biblical material is subject to proper control, the way is still open for the social customs of the patriarchal narratives to be legitimately illustrated and supported from a variety of historical contexts in the ancient Near East.[128]

In my opinion, Morrison's work is an example of how historical research can enlighten our understanding of biblical narrative, without imposing a historical framework that is highly precarious.

29:19

This verse offers an interesting insight into the way Laban operates. Laban reply is highly ambiguous.[179] Laban appears to accept Jacob's proposal, but Rachel is not mentioned. We do not know whether Laban already has in mind to palm off Leah, but he certainly keeps his options open (Wenham).[130] Sherwood draws attention the 'insider-outsider game' Laban is playing.[131] Here, Laban sides with Jacob: "it is better that I give her to you than I should give her to any other man." Elsewhere, Laban will treat Jacob as a definite outsider (vs. 26). It is revealing how Laban uses the verb 'to give' (נָתַן). Every time Laban promises to 'give' something, disappointment is in store, as Jacob will learn the hard way. Not surprisingly, fourteen years later, Jacob will retort "you shall not give me anything" in reply to Laban's "what shall I give you?" (30:31). In the course of events, we can reflect on the contrast between human promises 'to give' and on God's (cf. 28:13).[132]

---

[127] Sherwood, "Had God Not Been on My Side," 121 n. 59. See also Sternberg, Poetics, 184 for a similar sentiment.

[128] Selman, "Comparative Customs," 125–126.

[129] von Rad, Genesis, 286; Sherwood, "Had God Not Been on My Side," 95; Fokkelman, Narrative Art in Genesis, 127; Hamilton, Genesis 18–50, 259; Waltke, Genesis, 405; Wenham, Genesis 16–50, 235; Hartley, Genesis, 262.

[130] Fokkelman's suggestion that Laban already plans to give Leah away, including the ploy to squeeze an extra seven years from Jacob, might assume too much (Fokkelman, Narrative Art in Genesis, 127; cf. Eising, Formgeschichtliche Untersuching, 172). Wenham, Genesis 16–50, 235.

[131] Sherwood, "Had God Not Been on My Side," 95.

[132] Cf. Appendix B.

Laban's instruction 'stay with me' (שְׁבָה עִמָּדִי) may imply Laban's intent to keep Jacob indefinitely and has been interpreted as a sign of Laban's authority over Jacob.[133] Scholars have suggested that a marriage like this would keep property in the family, a consideration that surely would have been on Laban's mind if that were the case.[134]

Rachel does not have a say in the matter.[135] And so Jacob serves Laban seven years for Rachel (he thought). Ironically, Jacob is set to serve 'brother' Laban (cf. 27:40; 25:23).[136] Isaac did not travel and did not work for his bride, Jacob does both.[137] The seven years seemed to Jacob 'but a few days', yet another link with Gen 27.[138]

29:21–30

The next exchange between Jacob and Laban takes place seven years later. Although these years seemed to Jacob like a few days, his request in vs. 21 appears to be rather brusque: "give me my wife that I may go in to her."[139] Does this betray Jacob's urgency to consummate the marriage,[140] or is Jacob annoyed that he has to remind Laban of their

---

[133] Walton, *Thou Traveller Unknown*, 134; Sherwood, *"Had God Not Been on My Side,"* 95–96; Jeansonne, *The Women of Genesis*, 72; Speiser, *Genesis*, 225.

[134] Gunkel, *Genesis*, 320; Sarna, *Genesis*, 204; Matthews, *The IVP Bible Background Commentary*, ad loc; Walton, *Thou Traveller Unknown*, 134; Allen Guenther, "A Typology of Israelite Marriage: Kinship, Socio-Economic, and Religious Factors," *JSOT* 29, no. 4 (2005): 387–407, 389.

[135] Cf. von Rad, *Genesis*, 285.

[136] Sarna, *Genesis*, 203; Sherwood, *"Had God Not Been on My Side,"* 87; Taschner, *Verheissung und Erfüllung*, 91.

[137] Walton, *Thou Traveller Unknown*, 133 n. 20.

[138] Cf. 27:44, יָמִים אֲחָדִים; Fokkelman, *Narrative Art in Genesis*, 128; Hamilton, *Genesis 18–50*, 260; Wenham, *Genesis 16–50*, 235; Sherwood, *"Had God Not Been on My Side,"* 96; Alter, *Genesis*, 154; Walton, *Thou Traveller Unknown*, 134; Jacob, *Genesis*, 589.

[139] 'Now then, my wife' (Hamilton, *Genesis 18–50*, 261). See also Sherwood, *"Had God Not Been on My Side,"* 82. "The explicitness of Jacob's statement has triggered maneuvers of exegetical justification in the Midrash, but it is clearly meant to express his—understandable—sexual impatience" (Alter, *Genesis*, 154). For more on Midrashic justification on this passage, cf. Walton, *Thou Traveller Unknown*, 134 n. 24. Noegel identifies a name pun. The phrase 'may go into her' (וְאָבוֹאָה אֵלֶיהָ) suggest the name Leah (לֵאָה), and so when Leah is brought to Jacob, he unknowingly goes into her (וַיָּבֹא אֵלֶיהָ) (S.B. Noegel, "Drinking Feasts and Deceptive Feats: Jacob and Laban's Double Talk," in *Puns and Pundits: Wordplay in the Hebrew Bible and Ancient Near Eastern Literature* (ed. S.B. Noegel; Bethesda, Maryland, USA: CDL Press, 2000), 165).

[140] Alter, *Genesis*, 154; Waltke, *Genesis*, 405; Hamilton, *Genesis 18–50*, 261.

agreement, or both?[141] Wenham detects a 'distinct note of desperation.'[142]
Jacob's demand ('my wife') is characteristic for the rest of this scene.
Leah and Rachel (and Zilpah and Bilhah) are treated as nameless
objects by both Jacob and Laban. Laban's silent compliance is rather
ominous.[143] He gathers all the "men of the place (הַמָּקוֹם) and makes
a feast (מִשְׁתֶּה)" (vs. 22). The word מָקוֹם is used again in vs. 26 where
Laban will use local custom ("it is not done in this place") against
Jacob. Later on Jacob will ask Laban to send him away to 'my own
place' (30:25), which echoes the six-fold use of מָקוֹם in Gen 28:10–22.[144]
Sherwood notes that the expression אַנְשֵׁי הַמָּקוֹם (or something similar) occurs several times in the OT "in contexts in which they are up
to no good and/or represent a danger to the hero," or are "involved
in enforcing mores" (29:26!).[145] The word מִשְׁתֶּה suggests a feast or
banquet, which would feature plenty of drink.[146] Eating and drinking
provided the setting for the deceit of Isaac in Gen 27 and Jacob will
now experience deceit himself.[147] Under the cover of darkness, Leah
is brought to Jacob and he 'went into her' (he does not 'know' her!).[148]
With the ironic 'behold it was Leah' (vs. 25), the narrator reports Jacob's
shock-horror discovery.[149] The heated exchange between Jacob and

---

[141] Leupold, *Exposition of Genesis*, 794; Coats, *Genesis*, 214. Note that Jacob does
not say 'please' (Wenham, *Genesis 16–50*, 235).

[142] Based on three other passages in Genesis (30:1, 47:15, 16) where the verb יְהַב
appears by itself (Wenham, *Genesis 16–50*, 235).

[143] Or even 'sinister' (Hamilton, *Genesis 18–50*, 261).

[144] Brett, *Genesis*, 93.

[145] Cf. Gen 26:7; Judges 19:16; 'men of the town': Gen 19:4, 22 and 1 Kgs 21:11
(Sherwood, "*Had God Not Been on My Side*," 97). Did the shepherds of the opening
scene get their sweet revenge? (Sherwood, "*Had God Not Been on My Side*," 40).

[146] Commentators used to assume that Jacob did not recognize Leah because of the
darkness of the evening and because of her veil (e.g. Westermann, *Genesis 12–36*, 467;
von Rad, *Genesis*, 286; Speiser, *Genesis*, 225; Sarna, *Genesis*, 204; Fokkelman, *Narrative
Art in Genesis,* 129; Brodie, *Genesis as Dialogue*, 314). Jacob's drunkenness probably
was an important factor as well (Coats, *Genesis*, 214; and J.A. Diamond, "The Deception of Jacob: A New Perspective on an Ancient Solution to the Problem," *VT* 34, no.
2 (1984): 211–13, who notes the similarities with the account of Lot's daughters (Gen
19:30ff), who are also referred to as the הַבְּכִירָה and the הַצְּעִירָה. The suggestion that
Jacob was drunk appears to go back to Josephus (Hamilton, *Genesis 18–50*, 262–263).
See also Waltke, *Genesis*, 405 and Matthews, *The IVP Bible Background Commentary*,
ad loc.

[147] Brett, *Genesis*, 89; Recker, *Die Erzählungen vom Patriarchen Jakob*, 210.

[148] Jeansonne, *The Women of Genesis*, 73; Sherwood, "*Had God Not Been on My
Side*," 102.

[149] On the skilful use of 'gaps' by the narrator in this account, see Sternberg, *Poetics*,
242–243. See also Kass, "Love of Woman and Love of God," 49–50.

Laban that follows (vv. 26–27) is the focal point of this scene. Jacob's accusation "why then have you deceived me (רִמִּיתָנִי)?" resonates with 27:35–36.[150] Indeed, "the arch-deceiver has himself been deceived."[151] Although it remains unclear what Laban exactly knows about Jacob's history,[152] Laban's reply, "it is not done in this place to give the younger (הַצְּעִירָה) before the firstborn (הַבְּכִירָה)" (cf. 19:30–38!!), provides the knock-out blow.[153] Jacob is put in his place.[154] When Laban stipulates how Jacob can get 'the other' also, Jacob can do nothing but comply (vs. 28).[155] In the process, Laban seems to have saved himself the cost of a second wedding feast and retains the services of a good worker.[156] Winner takes all! The second seven years of service were undoubtedly not as agreeable for Jacob as the first.[157] Leah, the 'elder' and 'firstborn,'

---

[150] The accusation formula מַה־זֹּאת עָשִׂיתָ לִּי occurs in very similar forms in Gen 12:18; 20:9 and 26:10. This time it is a patriarch who asks the question of a foreigner (Sherwood, "Had God Not Been on My Side," 103; see also Coats, Genesis, 214). Hamilton, Genesis 18–50, 227 and 262; Sherwood, "Had God Not Been on My Side," 104; Fokkelman, Narrative Art in Genesis, 128–129 ('chickens come home to roost'); Mann, The Book of the Torah, 168 n. 9; Alter, Genesis, 154. Miller notes that in both episodes "a parent conspires with a disfavored child to commit fraud by means of an impersonation, and the fraud involves the switch of one child for another" (Miller, "Contracts of Genesis," 31).

[151] Wenham, Genesis 16–50, 236. See also Walton, Thou Traveller Unknown, 135; Fokkelman, Narrative Art in Genesis, 129; Hamilton, Genesis 18–50, 262.

[152] Wenham, Genesis 16–50, 236; Kass, "Love of Woman and Love of God," 50.

[153] The expression לֹא־יֵעָשֶׂה כֵן refers to "serious violations of custom (…) and is tantamount to rebuke" (cf. Gen 34:7; 2 Sam 13:12) (Hamilton, Genesis 18–50, 263; Fokkelman, Narrative Art in Genesis, 129; Sherwood, "Had God Not Been on My Side," 104). "Formally Laban is in the right (…) morally he is a deceiver" (Fokkelman, Narrative Art in Genesis, 129), by not mentioning this to Jacob before. Most commentators, based on historical data, assume that Laban is speaking the truth (cf. Gunkel, Genesis, 320; Westermann, Genesis 12–36, 467; Matthews, The IVP Bible Background Commentary, ad loc; Fokkelman, Narrative Art in Genesis, 129; H. Rand, "Switching Brides: Conspiracy and Cover-Up," JBQ 29, no. 3 (2001): 190–92, 190).

[154] "Cleverness and self-reliance have been partly humbled, all thanks to love" (Kass, "Love of Woman and Love of God," 50).

[155] מַלֵּא שְׁבֻעַ זֹאת (Piel imperative!), literally means 'fulfill these seven' (cf. Speiser, Genesis, 225). Westermann, Genesis 12–36, 467; Kass, "Love of Woman and Love of God," 50; Eising, Formgeschichtliche Untersuching, 173. Later such marriages were forbidden (Lev 18:18). See Kitchen, On the Reliability of the Old Testament, 325–326; Daube, Studies in Biblical Law, 78–79 also quoted by Oden, "Jacob as Father, Husband and Nephew," 192, n. 11; Speiser, Genesis, 227; Sarna, Genesis, 205 and Hamilton, Genesis 18–50, 264, who all comment on the apparent antiquity of this narrative.

[156] Hartley, Genesis, 263; Sherwood, "Had God Not Been on My Side," 83; Westermann, Genesis 12–36, 467.

[157] Westermann, Genesis 12–36, 468. Interestingly, two contrasting periods of seven years will also feature in the Joseph-narrative.

the one with 'weak eyes,'[158] is used to deceive the 'younger' who had deceived his blind father to obtain the blessing, which was reserved for the firstborn.[159] Also, Jacob had duped Isaac in breaking local custom. Now, Jacob is duped and local custom is used against him.[160] And so, Jacob experiences what both Esau and Isaac had experienced before him.[161] These numerous cross-links are hardly accidental. "Damit wird deutlich, dass die Hochzeitepisode als Spiegelbild zur Sterbesegensgeschichte konstruiert ist."[162]

3.3.3 Concluding Remarks

How to interpret Jacob's fate? Again, there is a whole spectrum of interpretations. On one extreme, Jacob's reversal is interpreted as divine judgment. Daube calls it 'justice dispensed from above.'[163] Gammie notes that "the motif of retribution is implicit throughout the cycle." Isaac, Rebekah, Jacob, Laban, Rachel, Simeon and Levi suffer various setbacks as a result of their deceit.[164] It is indeed striking how Jacob is "punished for his deception in taking precedence over his older brother by the very same instruments he used when he deceived."[165] This is even more poignant as we consider the instruments of deceit that are used in Gen 37:31–35. Sarna points to the catalogue of misfortunes experienced by Jacob throughout his life: "In fact, an explicit denunciation could hardly have been more effective or more scathing

---

[158] Sherwood, "*Had God Not Been on My Side*," 88; Bland, "The Rabbinic Method," 19; G.C. Nicol, "Jacob as Oedipus—Old Testament Narrative as Mythology," *ET* 108, no. Nov (1996): 43–44, 43, Nicol, "Story-patterning in Genesis," 231.

[159] For a more in-depth discussion on various other links between Gen 27 and 29, cf. Sherwood, "*Had God Not Been on My Side*," 103–107; Hamilton, *Genesis 18–50*, 262–263.

[160] McKeown, *Genesis*, 144.

[161] Cf. Brodic, *Genesis as Dialogue*, 314.

[162] Taschner, *Verheissung und Erfüllung*, 91. "The plot of chapter 27 is inverted in 29" (Brett, *Genesis*, 89). See also Alter, *Genesis*, 155; Fishbane, *Text and Texture*, 55; Sherwood, "*Had God Not Been on My Side*," 103.

[163] Daube, "Fraud on Law for Fraud on Law," 55. "The crime receives its own, absolutely fitting punishment" (Fokkelman, *Narrative Art in Genesis*, 130). "The event was simply God's decree against Jacob (…) a man reaps what he sows" (Ross, *Genesis*, *ad loc.*).

[164] Gammie, "Theological Interpretation," 119. "A clear case of fitting retribution" (Kass, "Love of Woman and Love of God," 49). "Jacob was getting what he deserved" (Sailhamer, *Genesis, ad loc.*). See also Speiser, *Genesis*, 227.

[165] "'Measure for measure' the ancient rabbis would say" (Bland, "The Rabbinic Method," 19–20).

than this unhappy biography."[166] On the opposite side of the spectrum, scholars have dismissed any ethical dimension to the story. There is no explicit commentary by the narrator, and neither is there any mention of the 'divine perspective.'[167] Gunkel rejects any notion of an 'ethical viewpoint' in this 'humorous narrative,' because the narrator "knows that Jacob will repay the old deceiver his deceit with interest."[168] Niditch warns that "in the case of folklore, the ethics of developed theological perspectives should not be imported anachronistically."[169] This again illustrates how difficult it can be to discover the stance of the narrator. Several commentators opt for middle ground by interpreting Jacob's fate as one of 'poetic justice.'[170] Jacob's fate is indeed 'bittersweet.' Initially we might smile about Jacob's reversal, but the realization of the bitterness of what follows soon sets in. There is no doubt that Jacob has to 'learn his lesson,' but the narrative does not rejoice in Laban's deceit either. Williams comments that "although in this case too, the narrative gives no explicit comment upon the deception, it appears that a negative assessment of Laban's actions is inescapable."[171] Instead of 'retribution and punishment,' Mann prefers to interpret these events as part of "a process of conversion that takes place over the course of Jacob's life (…) a gradual development towards righteousness, a growth marked by setbacks as well as advances."[172] Janzen speaks in this context of 'divine pedagogy.'[173] In subsequent chapters I will reflect in greater depth on Jacob's 'conversion.'

The passivity of the women is another striking feature of this passage. "Both Rachel and Leah are the passive objects of Jacob's and

---

[166] Sarna, *Understanding Genesis*, 184.

[167] Walton, *Thou Traveller Unknown*, 136. See also Humphreys, *The Character of God*, 175.

[168] Gunkel, *Genesis*, 319. Gunkel neglects that there is an intended parallel with Gen 27 (Walton, *Thou Traveller Unknown*, 136). See also Brueggemann, *Genesis*, 250–251.

[169] S. Niditch, *Underdogs and Tricksters: A Prelude to Biblical Folklore* (San Fransisco, USA: Harper and Row, 1987), 49–50 (also discussed by Brett, *Genesis*, 92).

[170] Kodell, "Jacob Wrestles with Esau (Gen 32:23–32)," 67; Wenham, *Genesis 16–50*, 236; Brett, *Genesis*, 89–90; Brodie, *Genesis as Dialogue*, 314 (following Armstrong, *In the Beginning*, 85); Alter, *Genesis*, 155.

[171] Williams, *Deception in Genesis*, 20. See also Fokkelman, *Narrative Art in Genesis*, 160. There is a similarity between the fate of Laban and that of Babylon and Assyria in later history. All were used by God to discipline his chosen one(s), yet all received their own punishment in the end as well.

[172] Mann, *The Book of the Torah*, 56.

[173] Janzen, *Genesis 12–50*, 115. Similarly Ross, *Genesis, ad loc.*

Laban's actions."[174] As their names might suggest, they are traded as cattle.[175] Daughters did not have much say in these matters (e.g. von Rad). "Females were used, through marriage contracts, to obtain wealth and prestige for the family."[176] The view that it might have been culturally acceptable to treat daughters as property items has been discredited,[177] but Laban's callous actions and speech ("we will give you the other also" vs. 27) appear to go a step further.[178] Many years later, Leah and Rachel will use language of commerce to describe this episode (cf. 31:15 'he has sold us').[179] Zilpah and Bilhah are in an even lower category. They are objects of trade like Rachel and Leah, but they never get a voice.[180] Giving away slave-girls as part of a dowry was an accepted practice in the ANE.[181] Morrison describes a dowry as "a sort of pre-mortem inheritance or the daughter's share of the family estate."[182] Dowries could include slave-girls, but more often consisted of items such as 'clothing, furniture and money.'[183] The absence of any mention of such gifts has been interpreted as a sign of Laban's greed.[184] Morrison insists that Laban did not provide his daughters with a dowry, and that this is central to Leah's and Rachel's complaint in 31:14–15.[185] Wenham on the other hand, notes that in the OT details of the dowry are not mentioned except when they are 'exceptionally

---

[174] Sherwood, "*Had God Not Been on My Side,*" 84 and 99. "They are treated as objects for money" (Waltke, *Genesis,* 404).

[175] Rachel's and Leah's names mean 'ewe lamb' and 'wild cow' (Noegel, "Drinking Feasts," 164 and 172; cf. Skinner, *Genesis,* 383; Jacob, *Genesis,* 589; Rendsburg, *The Redaction of Genesis,* 65; Sarna, *Genesis,* 202–203; Waltke, *Genesis,* 405).

[176] Matthews, *The IVP Bible Background Commentary* on Gen 29:26–30. See also Exum, "Who's Afraid of 'the Endangered Ancestress'?," 94.

[177] Cf. von Rad, *Genesis,* 285.

[178] Jeansonne, *The Women of Genesis,* 73.

[179] von Rad, *Genesis,* 287; Waltke, *Genesis,* 405.

[180] Besides being structural markers (see above; Sherwood, "*Had God Not Been on My Side,*" 101), the mention of Zilpah and Bilhah is also anticipatory of what follows in the next passage (Sarna, *Understanding Genesis,* 196; Coats, *Genesis,* 214; Waltke, *Genesis,* 406).

[181] Pfeiffer, *The Patriarchal Age,* 81; Sarna, *Understanding Genesis,* 196; West, "The Nuzi Tablets," 70; Selman, "Comparative Customs," 127 and 137; Sarna, *Genesis,* 205; Wenham, *Genesis 16–50,* 236; Waltke, *Genesis,* 406; Kitchen, *On the Reliability of the Old Testament,* 325; Speiser, *Genesis,* 227.

[182] Morrison, "The Jacob and Laban Narrative," 160. See also Wenham, *Genesis 16–50,* 236 and Kitchen, *On the Reliability of the Old Testament,* 325.

[183] Wenham, *Genesis 16–50,* 236. Wenham notes that the dowry system provided financial security for women.

[184] Morrison, "The Jacob and Laban Narrative," 160ff.; von Rad, *Genesis,* 287.

[185] Morrison, "The Jacob and Laban Narrative," 160–161.

valuable.' Wenham concludes that Laban treats his daughters 'gener-ously' in this matter.[186] Again we have to be careful in not reading too much into the text. If we limit ourselves to the text, it is clear that Leah and Rachel had one servant each, while Rebekah had more than one (24:61), although no precise number is given. Maybe this is a hint that Laban has become "greedier in the ensuing years—a detail that adds to the characterization of Laban."[187]

Finally, we must reflect on the strong enticement of selfish gain. Concern over or craving for material advancement (in some form or another) is such an essential element in understanding the motivation of various players in so many of the Genesis narratives.[188] In Gen 29, Laban is not only willing to cheat Jacob, but he also seems to lack any concern about the fate his daughters.[189] Leah ends up as 'unloved' or 'hated' (29:31). Rachel's marriage will be forever marred by the pres-ence of her sister. A bitter rivalry will develop between the two, which will influence relationships into the next generation. All this, sacrificed for the sake of selfish gain. Laban's actions are clear testimony to the strong pull of material advancement to the detriment of human rela-tionships.[190] Exactly the same could be said of Jacob in Gen 25 and 27. Jacob put material advancement over relationship and was willing to employ deceit to get his way. Here he suffers at the hand of another man who demonstrates identical behaviour. As in Gen 25 and 27, vari-ous relationships suffer.[191] When Jacob looks at Laban, he sees himself. The next episode will show what damage can be caused by this.

---

[186] Wenham, *Genesis 16–50*, 236. This is a minority position.

[187] Sherwood, *"Had God Not Been on My Side,"* 100. Cf. A. Dillmann, *Genesis* (Edinburgh, UK: T&T Clark, 1897), 237; von Rad, *Genesis*, 287; Leupold, *Exposition of Genesis*, 796.

[188] We have already seen this with Jacob's acquisition of birthright and blessing and with the Philistine envy over Isaac's success. In Gen 32 we will discuss Jacob's concern as he is about to meet with Esau and in Gen 34 we will reflect on the Shechemites' motives in agreeing to be circumcised (Chapter 4). For a more in-depth discussion on the cumulative effect of these stories, see Chapter 5.

[189] For a completely different interpretation, where Rachel and Leah actively par-ticipate in the ruse, see Rand, "Switching Brides: Conspiracy and Cover-Up."

[190] Walton rightly speaks of "the tragedy of breakdown in family relationships caused by the greed of one man" (Walton, *Thou Traveller Unknown*, 137).

[191] Comparing human relationships in Gen 27 and 29: "Die Qualität der Beziehun-gen unterscheidet sich jedoch in nichts" (Taschner, *Verheissung und Erfüllung*, 91).

3.4 JACOB'S CHILDREN (GEN 29:31–30:24)

3.4.1 *Introduction*

The account of the birth of Jacob's children flows seamlessly from the preceding episode and moves towards the climactic birth of Joseph (30:34), which will trigger Jacob's decision to return home (30:25).[192] Earlier source-critics have come up with various proposals to divide the text in J and E segments (with an occasional pinch of P). Some of these proposals are rather complex, assigning verse-by-verse fragments to different sources.[193] However, no consensus has been reached.[194] More recent commentators tend to focus on the inherent unity of the passage. Westermann suggests that the 'basic narrative is from J' and Sherwood notes that its unity is "well-enough agreed upon by commentators not to need much defence."[195] Wenham speaks of a "tightly integrated and powerful narrative on its own."[196] This passage is the first of two sections (or 'panels') that stand at the centre of the Jacob-cycle. According to Brodie, these "panels (…) have a deep-seated complementarity."[197] Both focus on fertility; first of Jacob's wives and then of his flocks.[198] The first panel is "framed by the rivalry between two women—Leah and Rachel," which mirrors the conflict between Esau and Jacob.[199] The increase of herds (30:25–31:1) is framed by the

---

[192] The resolution of Rachel's barrenness; according to Coats the main concern of the passage (Coats, *Genesis*, 214–215).

[193] "Its extraordinary literary compositeness must be catalogued almost from verse to verse" (von Rad, *Genesis*, 288). See also Hamilton, *Genesis 1–17*, 16 (who follows Speiser) and Gunkel, *Genesis*, 321. For a recent adherent of the J-E hypothesis see A. LaCocque, "Une Descendance Manipulée et Ambiguë (Genèse 29,31–30,24)," in *Jacob: Commentaire à Plusieurs Voix de Gen 25–36—Mèlanges offerts à Albert de Pury* (eds. J-D Macchi and T. Römer; Geneva, Swiss: Labor et Fides, 2001).

[194] "The boundaries between J and E are sometimes indistinct" (Speiser, *Genesis*, 232).

[195] Westermann, *Genesis 12–36*, 472. See also discussion by Wenham, *Genesis 16–50*, 242–242. Sherwood, *"Had God Not Been on My Side,"* 138.

[196] Wenham, *Genesis 16–50*, 240. See also Blum, *Komposition*, 111. This is not agreed by all: Walton for example occupies middle ground between the diversity and unity extremes (Walton, *Thou Traveller Unknown*, 144).

[197] Brodie, *Genesis as Dialogue*, 316.

[198] Section F and F', see Rendsburg, *The Redaction of Genesis*, 65–66 and the opening paragraphs of Chapter 2 and of this chapter.

[199] Wenham, *Genesis 16–50*, 245; Sherwood, *"Had God Not Been on My Side,"* 159; Janzen, *Genesis 12–50*, 117; Brodie, *Genesis as Dialogue*, 317; Alter, *Genesis*, 159; McKeown, *Genesis*, 145. Ogden Bellis rightly notes there is more conflict in this passage than just sibling rivalry (A. Ogden Bellis, "A sister is a forever friend: reflections on the story of Rachel and Leah," *JRT* 55–56, no. 2–1 (1999): 109–15, 113–114).

"rivalry of two men—Jacob and Laban."[200] I will analyze the text in the following subsections, before discussing the passage as a whole:

1. 29:31–35 :Leah gives birth to four sons;
2. 30:1–8   :Bilhah gives birth to two sons;
3. 30:9–13 :Zilpah gives birth to two sons;
4. 30:14–21 :Jacob is hired by Leah; Leah gives birth to two sons and a daughter;
5. 30:22–24 :Rachel bears a son.[201]

3.4.2   Commentary

29:31–35

The consequences of Laban's deceit now unfold.[202] Jacob's preference for Rachel over Leah is noted by the LORD (vs. 31).[203] According to Alter, the phrase 'hated' (שְׂנוּאָה) is a "technical, legal term for the unfavoured co-wife."[204] Leah's hurt pervades this passage (e.g. 29:33).[205] Leah's womb is opened, but Rachel is barren.[206] The narrator seems to imply that this is because of Jacob's failure to love Leah.[207] Rachel's

---

[200] Brodie, *Genesis as Dialogue*, 315.

[201] "The accounts of the births is arranged according to maternal origin" (Sarna, *Genesis*, 206). According to Frankel, these groupings "represent primarily a geopolitical situation of a much later period" (R. Frankel, "The Matriarchal Groupings of the Tribal Eponyms: A Reappraisal," in *The World of Genesis. Persons, Places, Perspectives* (eds. P.R. Davies and D.J.A. Clines; JSOTSup 257; Sheffield, UK: Sheffield Academic Press, 1998)). For alternative subdivisions, see Wenham, *Genesis 16–50*, 240 and Fokkelman, *Narrative Art in Genesis*, 132.

[202] Laban is not mentioned at all, "the stronger however is his influence" (Fokkelman, *Narrative Art in Genesis*, 131).

[203] 'When X saw' marks the opening of the first three sections (29:31; 30:1 and 9). See also Wenham, *Genesis 16–50*, 241.

[204] Alter, *Genesis*, 155. Cf. Deut 21:15ff (von Rad, *Genesis*, 289). See also Jeansonne, *The Women of Genesis*, 74–75.

[205] The account of Jacob's marriages helps to show why in later times it was forbidden to marry two sisters in each other's lifetime (Lev 18:18) (Kidner, *Genesis*, 161). Kidner takes this as an indication for the antiquity of this text. "In Scripture, most polygamous families experience deep, bitter conflicts" (Hartley, *Genesis*, 265). Similarly Wenham, *Story as Torah*, 152.

[206] For a study on the development of the barrenness theme in the patriarchal narratives see M.E. Donaldson, "Kinship Theory and the Patriarchal Narratives: The Case of the Barren Wife," *JAAR* 49, no. 1 (1981): 77–87 and Oden, "Jacob as Father, Husband and Nephew," 199.

[207] Ogden Bellis, "A sister is a forever friend," 110. See also Humphreys, *The Character of God*, 175–176; Janzen, *Genesis 12–50*, 115; Berlin, *Poetics*, 52 and J. Ross-Burstall, "Leah and Rachel: A Tale of Two Sisters," *W&W* 14, no. Spring (1994): 162–70, 165.

beauty stands in line with Sarah's and Rebekah's, and so does her bar-renness, which comes to an end when God 'opens her womb' in 30:22. God's opening of wombs frames this passage (29:31, 30:22).[208] God's fingerprints might have been all over 29:1–30, but vs. 31 is the first explicit reference to his involvement since Bethel. The LORD/God is a silent but sovereign actor in this episode. His involvement is expressed in six verbs; three concern Leah and three concern Rachel.[209] In the end there is a sense of balance.[210] The bulk of God's initial attention, and a 'bumper-crop' of children, is bestowed on the 'despised' Leah. Rachel has to wait. The sisters make several statements about God's involvement as well, but these are all highly subjective.[211] Sometimes they align with the narrator's (e.g. 29:32), but not necessarily (e.g. 30:18). God's concern for, or involvement with, Zilpah and Bilhah is not mentioned.[212]

The birth reports of Leah's first four sons contain the following ele-ments: 'conceived;' 'bore;' 'said;' 'named.'[213] They express Leah's strug-gle and longing for Jacob's love (29:32, 34; also 30:20).[214] The name Joseph expresses Rachel's struggle and desire for children.[215] "Each

---

[208] Waltke, *Genesis*, 408. See also Sherwood, *"Had God Not Been on My Side,"* 138; Wenham, *Genesis 16–50*, 248. Jacob's role in Leah's conception is omitted, and Jacob is not involved in the naming of his children. Jacob is only referred to twice, but not by name ('my husband' 29:32, 34).

[209] God-Leah: 'Saw' and 'opened' in 29:31; and 'listened' in 30:17. God-Rachel: 'Remembered,' 'listened' and 'opened,' all in 30:22.

[210] Similarly Brueggemann, *Genesis*, 255: "The narrative is a delicate balance." See also Humphreys, *The Character of God*, 177.

[211] Humphreys, *The Character of God*, 177. 'Colored by their emotions' (Walton, *Thou Traveller Unknown*, 146). "…intensely 'subjective' cries of pride and expecta-tion" (Fokkelman, *Narrative Art in Genesis*, 133). See also Sherwood, *"Had God Not Been on My Side,"* 149. Many names contain a theophoric element (Waltke, *Genesis*, 408), but "at the same time a malicious shaft to the co-wife" (Fokkelman, *Narrative Art in Genesis*, 133).

[212] Cf. Jeansonne, *The Women of Genesis*, 76 and 135 n. 22.

[213] See also Waltke, *Genesis*, 407–408. The verb הָרָה ('to conceive' BDB 2470) appears 9x in Gen 29–30. It will reappear in Gen 38 (5x). The verb יָלַד ('to bear' BDB 3934) appears 18x in this passage. The birth reports in Gen 30 contain similar elements, but not necessarily all of them. The sequence in Reuben's naming is slightly different. For more detail, cf. Hamilton, *Genesis 18–50*, 267 n. 8; Long, *The Problem of Etiological Narrative*, 30–33.

[214] Sternberg, *Poetics*, 330–331. Ross-Burstall calls them 'prayers of lament' (Ross-Burstall, "Leah and Rachel: A Tale of Two Sisters," 166).

[215] Each son becomes the eponymous ancestor of a tribe of Israel, but Gen 29–30 is not concerned with that at all, unlike Gen 49 (Sarna, *Genesis*, 206; contra Fran-kel, "The Matriarchal Groupings of the Tribal Eponyms: A Reappraisal"). Cf. Walton, *Thou Traveller Unknown*, 145.

woman wants what the other has."[216] Intense desires drive the narrative forward.[217] von Rad describes the name-giving as a "delicate and very free etymological game in which the narrator sparkles, but which we are aesthetically unable to imitate."[218] Alter speaks of "ad hoc improvisations (…) essentially, midrashic play on the sound of names."[219] Reuben for example sounds like 'see a son.'[220] Leah however, makes the link between the verb רָאָה ('to see') and the phrase בְּעָנְיִי ('upon my affliction').[221] Likewise Simeon is a name play on 'has heard' (שָׁמַע). The mention of 'sight' and 'sound' allude to Hagar's story, where God is also the one who 'sees' (16:13) and 'hears' (21:17x2). Note that the LORD 'saw' that Leah was hated (29:31) and that God 'heard Leah' (30:17).[222] This interpretation gains further credence when Rachel starts to behave like Sarai (30:3). This might suggest that at the heart of the struggle lies a deep-seated concern about who will 'produce' Jacob's heir.[223] Taschner draws attention to Judges 11 and Deut 21:15–17: "Bei den anderen Erzählungen, die von einer vergleichbaren Rivalität zweier Frauen handeln, geht es jedesmal im Grunde um Erbschaftsfragen."[224] Similarly Brenner:

> The chief aspiration which informs these women's being, as delineated by the narratives, is biological motherhood and its benefits. Such

---

[216] Waltke, *Genesis*, 411. See also A. Brenner, "Female Social Behaviour: Two Descriptive Patterns within the 'Birth of Hero' Paradigm," *VT* 36, no. 3 (1986): 257–73, 262.

[217] Wenham, *Genesis 16–50*, 240.

[218] "The names and their puns can only be understood altogether in the original and cannot be transferred to English" (von Rad, *Genesis*, 289). Cf. Hamilton, *Genesis 18–50*, 267 and A. Strus, "Étymologies des noms propres dans Gen 29:32–30:24: valeurs littéraires et fonctionelles," *Salesianum* 40 (1978): 57–72 for more detail.

[219] Alter, *Genesis*, 156.

[220] '…the obvious explanation' (von Rad, *Genesis*, 289).

[221] Sarna, *Genesis*, 206; Walton, *Thou Traveller Unknown*, 139; Hamilton, *Genesis 18–50*, 266–267; Fokkelman, *Narrative Art in Genesis*, 134.

[222] "Leah begins to resemble Hagar" (Sherwood, *"Had God Not Been on My Side,"* 146, 154 and 170). See also Fokkelman, *Narrative Art in Genesis*, 134; Wenham, *Genesis 16–50*, 243; Waltke, *Genesis*, 410; Hamilton, *Genesis 18–50*, 267; Brenner, "Female Social Behaviour," 262. Alter suggests that the mention of 'sight' and 'sound' in these names refers to the "two senses that might have detected him [Jacob] in the deception of his father," if blindness and deception by smell and touch had not stood in the way (Alter, *Genesis*, 156).

[223] "Rachel, afraid she would lose her status as favorite wife to her fertile sister, was desperate to produce heirs" (K. Spanier, "Rachel's Theft of the Teraphim: Her Struggle for Family Primacy," *VT* 42, no. 3 (1992): 404–12, 407, as quoted in Taschner, *Verheissung und Erfüllung*, 92 n. 33).

[224] Taschner, *Verheissung und Erfüllung*, 93.

a motivation should be distinguished from so-called maternal love or wifely affection. We have seen that even biological motherhood is not sufficient, and that the fight to ensure the economic status of the son assumes central place after the birth. Therefore, the conduct of the women involved should be judged as—and apparently is intended to be judged as—an act born out of calculations of power politics rather than mere emotion or similar consideration.[225]

The ferocity of the 'power politics' is demonstrated by the name-giving battle.[226] "Laban treats his daughters as pawns in an economic struggle, and now his daughters seem to view their children as pawns in a family conflict."[227] Brenner's conclusions deserve careful consideration. As shown in Chapter 2, material well-being is an integral part of 'inheritance.' Although material possessions are not explicitly mentioned in the birth narratives, concerns about material well-being, security or advancement might never be never far away.[228] It will only become clear much later how the latent concerns regarding Jacob's inheritance will be resolved.[229] However, we must be careful not to exaggerate such concerns. Leah's name-giving also suggest that she was genuinely concerned about Jacob's affection, not merely about who would 'produce' Jacob's heir.[230] For Brueggemann, the conflict over descendants (and property; Gen 31) points to deeper concern; "it is a battle over the future which the combatants want to take into their own hands."[231]

With the birth of Levi, Leah expresses hope that Jacob will 'be attached' to her.[232] The birth of Judah (possibly 'may Yah be praised')

---

[225] Brenner, "Female Social Behaviour," 264, as quoted by Sherwood, "*Had God Not Been on My Side*," 184 n. 9.

[226] Cf. Fokkelman, *Narrative Art in Genesis*, 133.

[227] Waltke, *Genesis*, 412.

[228] More on the link between child-bearing and economic security: cf. Ogden Bellis, "A sister is a forever friend," 111.

[229] In Gen 49 all of Jacob's sons are present as he tells them "what shall happen in days to come" (49:1). With the division of the Promised Land it becomes clear that all of Jacob's sons share in the inheritance, in some form or another. Note that Joseph's descendants receive a 'double portion' through Jacob's adoption of Joseph's sons Ephraim and Manasseh (Gen 48). Cf. Sherwood, "*Had God Not Been on My Side*," 141; Hauge, "Struggles," 12–13; Frymer-Kensky, "Patriarchal Family Relationships," 214.

[230] In the ANE it was considered important to bear sons, in order to be a proper wife (cf. Hannah's plight in 1 Sam 1–2). I am indebted to discussions with Prof. G. Wenham and Revd. G. Angel in this matter.

[231] Brueggemann, *Genesis*, 260.

[232] Alter, *Genesis*, 157; Hartley, *Genesis*, 264; Waltke, *Genesis*, 410; Hamilton, *Genesis 18–50*, 268; Westermann, *Genesis 12–36*, 473.

is the climax of this first burst of childbearing.[233] "This time I will praise the LORD" Leah exclaims.[234] Gen 29:31–35 moves from distress towards praise, by means of the LORD's intervention.[235] The despised Leah bears Levi and Judah in whom Israel's priesthood and kingship have their origin.[236] In mysterious ways, Jacob's marriage to Leah was 'part of God's plan.'[237] After the birth of Judah, Leah 'ceased bearing.' This has been interpreted as temporary infertility[238] or as an indication that intercourse ceased (cf. 30:14ff).[239]

30:1–8

Rachel envies her sister (30:1). The Philistines had envied Isaac (26:14); now envy becomes part of Jacob's family (37:11).[240] Rachel's violent outburst "give me children or I shall die"[241] reminds us of Rebekah (25:22, 27:46) and of Esau (25:32).[242] Rachel's demand 'give me' (הָבָה־לִּי) is virtually identical to Jacob's in 29:21 (הָבָה).[243] Birds of a feather flock together![244] Jacob retorts in anger (30:2). Only God can 'open wombs' (cf. 29:31).[245] The love idyll turns bitter with accusation and rebuke.[246] Armstrong even concludes that "this was no

---

[233] A.R. Millard, "The Meaning of the Name Judah," *ZAW* 86, no. 216–218 (1974). See also discussion by Hamilton, *Genesis 18–50*, 268.

[234] "A cry of praise as a conclusion of a psalm of praise" (Westermann, *Genesis 12–36*, 473).

[235] It resembles "the piety of Israel, particularly as expressed in the psalms" (Walton, *Thou Traveller Unknown*, 138). See also Ross-Burstall, "Leah and Rachel: A Tale of Two Sisters," 163.

[236] See also Hamilton, *Genesis 18–50*, 268; Waltke, *Genesis*, 409.

[237] Walton, *Thou Traveller Unknown*, 136

[238] Wenham, *Genesis 16–50*, 243; Coats, *Genesis*, 215; Brenner, "Female Social Behaviour," 262; Alter, *Genesis*, 157.

[239] Wenham, *Genesis 16–50*, 240; Waltke, *Genesis*, 410; Hamilton, *Genesis 18–50*, 268; Ogden Bellis, "A sister is a forever friend," 112; Alter, *Genesis*, 157.

[240] Jeansonne, *The Women of Genesis*, 76; Sherwood, "*Had God Not Been on My Side*," 157.

[241] This is possibly meant to foreshadow Rachel's premature death (Alter, *Genesis*, 158).

[242] "...an impetuousness reminiscent of her brother-in-law Esau" (Alter, *Genesis*, 158).

[243] Hamilton, *Genesis 18–50*, 270; Sherwood, "*Had God Not Been on My Side*," 157.

[244] Captured so well by Fokkelman, who regularly refers to Rachel as "Jacoba" (e.g. Fokkelman, *Narrative Art in Genesis*, 139), interestingly a name still in use in the Netherlands. "Rachel is very much Jacob's counterpart" (Janzen, *Genesis 12–50*, 118).

[245] "'Am I in God's place' asked the king of Israel when faced with another impossible demand (2 Kgs 5:7)" (Wenham, *Genesis 16–50*, 244; Also Westermann, *Genesis 12–36*, 474).

[246] Hamilton, *Genesis 18–50*, 270; Coats, *Genesis*, 215; Kass, "Love of Woman and Love of God," 51. Ogden Bellis sees this as a typical example of miscommunication

marriage made in heaven."[247] Unlike Rebekah, Rachel is not reported to have enquired of the LORD, although her words in vs. 6 have been interpreted as such.[248] Unlike Isaac, Jacob does not pray to the LORD either.[249] Rachel now adopts Sarai's tactic (30:3). Bilhah, by Kitchen described as 'insurance policy,'[250] is offered to Jacob as 'a wife' (30:4), in order to 'produce' a son and heir.[251] The phrase וְתֵלֵד עַל־בִּרְכַּי most likely refers to adoption.[252] Like Abraham (16:2–4a), Jacob's compliance is silent and immediate.[253] From Gen 16–21 we know this is not a desirable option.[254] Twice Bilhah conceived and bore Jacob a son (30:5, 7).[255] According to Guenther, "the children born to Bilhah were considered Rachel's in every respect (*including inheritance*), in as much as Bilhah remained Rachel's slave."[256] Rachel counters Leah's name-giving and Jacob's retort by her naming of Dan and Naphtali.[257]

---

between the sexes, where women seek sympathy, while men understand such statements as 'requests for solutions to problems' (Ogden Bellis, "A sister is a forever friend," 110).

[247] Armstrong, *In the Beginning*, 86. See also Kass, "Love of Woman and Love of God," 50–51: "…erotic love of the sort Jacob felt for Rachel may *not* be the best foundation for marriage and family life."

[248] Cf. "God (…) has also heard my voice" in 30:6 (Wenham, *Genesis 16–50*, 245; Waltke, *Genesis*, 411). Also, God 'heard her' in 30:22. Alter takes this as indicative of prayer (Alter, *Genesis*, 162).

[249] Waltke, *Genesis*, 408; Walton, *Thou Traveller Unknown*, 139; Kass, "Love of Woman and Love of God," 51; Ogden Bellis, "A sister is a forever friend," 110. Waltke interprets Jacob's outburst as "a theological certitude but also as an abdication of his role as a godly leader" (p. 411).

[250] Kitchen, *On the Reliability of the Old Testament*, 325. See also Selman, "Comparative Customs," 127.

[251] Brenner, "Female Social Behaviour," 261. For more on the background of this custom, see Frymer-Kensky, "Patriarchal Family Relationships," 211–212. For more on the multiple puns in Rachel's speech, cf. Noegel, "Drinking Feasts," 165.

[252] H.F. Richter, "'Auf den Knien eines andern gebären'? (Zur Deutung von Gen 30:3 und 50:23)," *ZAW* 91 (1979): 436–37, 436–437; Wenham, *Genesis 16–50*, 244; de Vaux, *Ancient Israel*, 51; W.D. Reyburn and E.M. Fry, *A Handbook on Genesis* (New York, USA: United Bible Societies, 1997), 684; Alter, *Genesis*, 159; Hamilton, *Genesis 18–50*, 270; von Rad, *Genesis*, 186; Speiser, *Genesis*, 230; Gunkel, *Genesis*, 325; Sarna, *Genesis*, 207–208.

[253] Brenner, "Female Social Behaviour," 262.

[254] Armstrong, *In the Beginning*, 86; Kass, "Love of Woman and Love of God," 51.

[255] The phrase לְיַעֲקֹב might have been added to indicate that these sons were acknowledged as full sons of Jacob (Sherwood, "*Had God Not Been on My Side*," 159, following E. Munk, *The Call of the Torah: An Anthology of Interpretation and Commentary on the Five Books of Moses* (Jerusalem, Israel: Feldheim, 1980), 656).

[256] Guenther, "A Typology of Israelite Marriage," 390 (italics mine). See also Kitchen, *On the Reliability of the Old Testament*, 325–326.

[257] Sherwood, "*Had God Not Been on My Side*," 159; Ogden Bellis, "A sister is a forever friend," 111.

Rachel celebrates Dan's birth as 'vindication;' 'the LORD has judged/ vindicated me' (vs. 6).[258] Naphtali is commentary on Rachel's 'divine struggle' with Leah.[259] According to Rachel God is involved in this (cf. 29:31; 30:2), and she has 'prevailed.' Similarly, Jacob would prevail in his struggle with God (32:26, 29 MT).[260] Yet another thing Rachel and Jacob have in common.

30:9–13

In a 'tit for tat,' Leah offers Zilpah to Jacob.[261] 'Hagar-Leah' is turning into 'Sarai-Leah.'[262] Zilpah also bears two sons. Brenner speaks of 'feverish heir-oriented activity.'[263] Leah's naming lacks any reference to God or to Jacob.[264] Gad alludes to 'good luck' or 'fortune.' Asher expresses Leah's 'happiness' or 'joy' (vs. 13).[265] Leah might have been driven by a desire to find 'security in numbers;' to ensure that her desired heir would have "many full brothers to take one's side should a dispute over the inheritance arise."[266] If one is not convinced about this, her actions are still illustrative of the fierce battle for Jacob's affection.

30:14–21

The exchange between Leah and Rachel stands at the centre of Gen 29:31–30:24.[267] It is the first, and in Gen 29–30 only, conversation between the sisters.[268] Simmering resentment now turns into open

---

[258] Wenham, *Genesis 16–50*, 244.

[259] Translated by most modern translations as 'mighty wrestlings' or something similar (e.g. ESV, JPS, NRSV; cf. Reyburn, *A Handbook on Genesis*, 686; Wenham, *Genesis 16–50*, 245). For a more in-depth discussion, cf. references by Hamilton, *Genesis 18–50*, 271 n. 14–15.

[260] Hamilton, *Genesis 18–50*, 272; Wenham, *Genesis 16–50*, 245; Fokkelman, *Narrative Art in Genesis*, 136; Fishbane, *Text and Texture*, 57; Mann, *The Book of the Torah*, 57; Walton, *Thou Traveller Unknown*, 140.

[261] E.g. Wenham, *Genesis 16–50*, 245; Waltke, *Genesis*, 412.

[262] Sherwood, "*Had God Not Been on My Side*," 161–162.

[263] Brenner, "Female Social Behaviour," 262.

[264] Wenham, *Genesis 16–50*, 246; Waltke, *Genesis*, 412.

[265] For more on these names: Alter, *Genesis*, 159; Wenham, *Genesis 16–50*, 246; Strus, "Étymologies," 67–68.

[266] Sherwood, "*Had God Not Been on My Side*," 142. "…the rights of the firstborn are fragile" (Brett, *Genesis*, 90–91).

[267] 'The climax of the story' (Sherwood, "*Had God Not Been on My Side*," 163). "…an exchange of words and of things" (Sherwood, "*Had God Not Been on My Side*," 147).

[268] Jeansonne, *The Women of Genesis*, 77.

confrontation. The conversation revolves around mandrakes found by Reuben.[269] Mandrakes (דּוּדָאִים) were considered an aphrodisiac and were thought to enhance fertility.[270] Rachel is desperate to conceive and Leah is equally desperate to regain access to Jacob.[271] The exchange is awkward. Although Rachel seems to 'control' Jacob, she desperately wants what Leah has, hence her polite request (תְּנִי־נָא; vs. 14).[272] Leah reacts angrily (vs. 15a). Pent-up frustration bursts forth. In response, Rachel offers Jacob's 'services' in exchange for the mandrakes. Fokkelman calls it a 'creative compromise.'[273] The root שׂכר now emerges at the heart of Jacob's family. In 30:16 Leah tells Jacob: "you must come in to me (cf. 29:23!), for I have hired (שָׂכֹר שְׂכַרְתִּיךָ) you."[274] Again, Jacob's compliance is silent.

> The family's life is rotten and broken by the dehumanizing atmosphere of SERVICE-WAGES. Things have come so far that the enslaved and oppressed wife must 'hire' (שׂכר) her husband to have intercourse, but it does not bring her the loving communications which gives recognition.[275]

Despite this "confused and complex web of mixed motives and situations" God hears Leah (30:17).[276] Leah conceives and bears Jacob her fifth son. Leah interprets this as God's reward for offering Zilpah to Jacob; "God has given me my wages" (שְׂכָרִי), so she called his name Issachar (יִשָּׂשכָר). Various possibilities for the meaning of Issachar have

---

[269] Reuben is probably not of an age yet where he can fully appreciate the role of mandrakes in the "feverish heir-oriented activities" (contra Sherwood, "*Had God Not Been on My Side*," 143).

[270] Wenham, *Genesis 16–50*, 246; Alter, *Genesis*, 160; Hamilton, *Genesis 18–50*, 274–275; Waltke, *Genesis*, 412–413.

[271] This explains why the mandrakes were of relevance for both women (cf. Taschner, *Verheissung und Erfüllung*, 93).

[272] Cf. Jeansonne, *The Women of Genesis*, 78; Niditch, *Underdogs and Tricksters*, 98.

[273] Fokkelman, *Narrative Art in Genesis*, 137. Similarly Ogden Bellis, "A sister is a forever friend," 112.

[274] The combination of the perfect and the infinitive absolute is indicative of the intensity of Leah's desire (Wenham, *Genesis 16–50*, 247).

[275] Fokkelman, *Narrative Art in Genesis*, 137. Fokkelman also notes that although Jacob 'lies with her,' he does not 'know her' (137). Leah's idiom suggests that "Jacob had been sexually boycotting Leah" (Alter, *Genesis*, 160), except on the occasions when he fathered her children. Sarna notes that the verb שָׁכַב, "when employed in Genesis with a sexual nuance, never connotes a relationship of marital love but is invariably used in unsavory circumstances" (Sarna, *Genesis*, 209; also Waltke, *Genesis*, 413). Cf. Gen 19:32ff; 26:10; 34:2, 7; 35:22. See also 1 Sam 2:22; 2 Sam 13:11, 14 (TWOT 2381).

[276] Walton, *Thou Traveller Unknown*, 147.

been offered.[277] Above all it is a painful allusion. Jacob will be tainted forever as a 'man of wages.'[278] For Fokkelman this name is the most important name of the whole story (after that of Jacob himself).[279]

The exchange between Leah and Rachel is a mirror image of the sale of the birthright (25:29–34).[280] The phrase מִן־הַשָּׂדֶה (30:16) reminds us of 25:29 where Esau came in 'from the field.'[281] In both cases the younger person takes the initiative and proposes an exchange.[282] Fokkelman concludes that the rivalry between the sisters mirrors the rivalry between Esau and Jacob; it is a battle over primacy.[283] There is more. Where Jacob experienced a reversal for his deceit of Isaac and Esau in Gen 29, Jacob now experiences another reversal. The sisters were mere 'objects of trade' in 29:15–30, here "Jacob himself is demeaned by being made an object of reward, to be bartered away."[284] Note that Jacob's name is not mentioned, just like Leah's and Rachel's names were not mentioned in 29:15–30. Jacob has now reached the same level of passivity as Zilpah and Bilhah (Rachel's and Leah's possessions!); a passive instrument in the procreation war, which culminates in the birth of 'Issachar.'[285] This reversal is probably *the* low-point of the Jacob-cycle, although there are several episodes to choose from.[286]

Ironically, Rachel gets the mandrakes but Leah gets the children. God gives new life, not the mandrakes![287] Following Issachar, two more children are born to Leah; Zebulon and Dinah, the only daughter. Zebulon is a name-play on 'honour:' "now my husband will honour

---

[277] Cf. Wenham, *Genesis 16–50*, 247 (following Strus, "Étymologies," 68 n. 32); Hamilton, *Genesis 18–50*, 275; Alter, *Genesis*, 161; Hartley, *Genesis*, 267; HALOT 443.

[278] Fokkelman, *Narrative Art in Genesis*, 137–138; von Rad, *Genesis*, 290; Alter, *Genesis*, 161; Waltke, *Genesis*, 413; Noegel, "Drinking Feasts," 166; Hamilton, *Genesis 18–50*, 275; Sarna, *Genesis*, 210, who refers to Gen 49:14–15.

[279] Fokkelman, *Narrative Art in Genesis*, 138.

[280] Fokkelman, *Narrative Art in Genesis*, 139–141. Also Taschner, *Verheissung und Erfüllung*, 92–93.

[281] Hamilton, *Genesis 18–50*, 275 and his reference to S. Ben-Reuven, "Mandrakes as Retribution for Buying the Birthright (Hebrew)," *BMik* 28 (1982/83): 230–31 in n. 10. See also Sherwood, "*Had God Not Been on My Side*," 169; Niditch, *Underdogs and Tricksters*, 91.

[282] Fokkelman, *Narrative Art in Genesis*, 140; Taschner, *Verheissung und Erfüllung*, 94.

[283] Fokkelman, *Narrative Art in Genesis*, 149.

[284] Walton, *Thou Traveller Unknown*, 141. In addition, Joseph would be traded by his brothers to strangers in Gen 37.

[285] Brenner, "Female Social Behaviour," 262. It must be noted that 'hired' refers to a temporary arrangement (cf. Westermann, *Genesis 12–36*, 476).

[286] So also Walton, *Thou Traveller Unknown*, 176.

[287] Sarna, *Genesis*, 207; Sherwood, "*Had God Not Been on My Side*," 154.

me" (יִזְבְּלֵנִי). Leah never ceases in her hope for Jacob's acceptance and love.[288] No explanation is given for Dinah's name, possibly because Dinah 'was merely a daughter.'[289] Armstrong calls Dinah's birth a 'non-event' and suggests that Jacob "disliked Dinah all her life, simply because she was Leah's daughter."[290] Leah bears more children than the other three women combined.[291]

30:22–24

'Then God remembered Rachel.'[292] The narrator does not tell us why. Some scholars think that God heard Rachel (cf. 30:17) and opened her womb because she had allowed Leah access to Jacob.[293] Rachel might have become oppressed herself.[294] Rachel's exclamation "God has taken away (אָסַף)[295] my reproach" (vs. 23) may hint in that direction.[296] The words that have been used so often in conjunction with others ('conceived,' 'bore a son,' 'said,' and 'called his name') now finally apply to Rachel herself.[297] However, Rachel's longing is only partially fulfilled.

---

[288] Ogden Bellis, "A sister is a forever friend," 110. Leah's yearning here echoes her plea after the arrival of the third son (Sarna, *Genesis*, 210). See also Jeansonne, *The Women of Genesis*, 75.

[289] Jeansonne, *The Women of Genesis*, 135 n. 28; N. Graetz, "Dinah the Daughter," in *A Feminist Companion to Genesis* (ed. A. Brenner; Sheffield, UK: Sheffield Academic Press, 1993), 307; Wenham, *Genesis 16–50*, 248; Hamilton, *Genesis 18–50*, 271.

[290] Armstrong, *In the Beginning*, 87. See *Section 4.5*. Similarly, Laban had more respect for custom and greed than for Rachel's affections (I am indebted to the Revd. G. Angel for this insight).

[291] Sarna, *Genesis*, 206.

[292] As God remembered Noah (8:1) and Abraham (19:29), he now remembers Rachel. Similarly, God would remember his covenant with Abraham, Isaac and Jacob when he would hear the groaning of the people of Israel (Ex 2:24). Cf. Brueggemann, *Genesis*, 255; Wenham, *Story as Torah*, 24; Brodie, *Genesis as Dialogue*, 318; McKeown, *Genesis*, 146. "This is the climax of 29:31–30:24" (Waltke, *Genesis*, 414). For Brueggemann this is the turning point of the Jacob-Laban narrative (Brueggemann, *Genesis*, 259).

[293] Ogden Bellis, "A sister is a forever friend," 110; Fokkelman, *Narrative Art in Genesis*, 140–141; Waltke, *Genesis*, 416.

[294] "Now Yahweh responds to Leah's sense of triumph by remembering Rachel" (Janzen, *Genesis 12–50*, 117). Similarly Sherwood, *"Had God Not Been on My Side*," 173.

[295] Another name-play (Kidner, *Genesis*, 162; Janzen, *Genesis 12–50*, 118; Leupold, *Exposition of Genesis*, 816; Sarna, *Genesis*, 210).

[296] The word חֶרְפָּה can be translated 'taunt' in contexts where "an adversary reproaches with scorn or insults" (TWOT 749a). The name-giving battle might well fit that description.

[297] Alter notes "a rapid-fire chain of uninterrupted verbs" (Alter, *Genesis*, 162). This reminds us of the conclusion of the sale of the birth-right in 25:34 (see *Section 2.2*).

In 30:1 she had exclaimed 'give me sons.'[298] Joseph's name is fitting;
"may the LORD add (יֹסֵף) to me another son." Tragically, the fulfilment of her longing coincides with her death (35:16–20).[299] Despite
large offspring, unfulfilled hopes linger; Leah's for Jacob's love and
Rachel's for additional offspring.[300] Jacob now has twelve children
(eleven sons and one daughter); an almost perfect number, but not
quite.[301] The birth of Benjamin will 'complete the set' (35:17–18).

3.4.3 Concluding Remarks

Material possessions are not the primary focus of this passage. However, concerns about material advancement or security are never far
away. First of all, the context in which the conflict between Rachel
and Leah is set, and in which many children are born, finds its origin
in Laban's greed (29:15–30). Secondly, it is clear from the parallels
with the Sarai-Hagar episode that the big (unvoiced) concerns in the
entire passage are 'who will produce Jacob's heir?' and 'who will be
excluded?' (e.g. Ishmael and Esau).[302] This will only be resolved much
later (Gen 49). Although Leah genuinely strives for Jacob's affection,
inheritance related concerns must not be ignored altogether. Thirdly,
the barter-agreement between Leah and Rachel, which reduces Jacob
to an object of trade, stands at the centre of Gen 29:31–30:24. This
links in with the much bigger question of slavery (e.g. Bilhah and Zilpah). However, this does not seem to be of interest to the narrator, and
it also vastly exceeds the scope of this study.[303]

The setting in which these children are born is far from ideal: Most
human relationships appear to be troubled and complicated; Jacob's

---

[298] Alter, *Genesis*, 162; Kass, "Love of Woman and Love of God," 51.

[299] Walton, *Thou Traveller Unknown*, 144. The word 'ironically' is not quite appropriate to describe Rachel's death (e.g. Brenner, "Female Social Behaviour: Two Descriptive Patterns within the 'Birth of Hero' Paradigm," 263; Waltke, *Genesis*, 411).

[300] Sherwood, *"Had God Not Been on My Side,"* 139–141. See also Brenner, "Female
Social Behaviour: Two Descriptive Patterns within the 'Birth of Hero' Paradigm" and
Morrison, "The Jacob and Laban Narrative."

[301] N. Jay, "Sacrifice, Descent and the Patriarchs," *VT* 38, no. 1 (1988): 52–70, 64.

[302] Sherwood, *"Had God Not Been on My Side,"* 145–146.

[303] Slavery was an accepted feature of life in the ancient Near East (cf. Pfeiffer,
The Patriarchal Age; 108; de Vaux, *Ancient Israel*, 80–90; Kitchen, "Genesis 12–50
in the Near Eastern World," 78–79; Kitchen, *On the Reliability of the Old Testament*,
325–326). For an in-depth discussion on this topic, see G. Chirichigno, *Debt-Slavery
in Israel and the Ancient Near East* (Sheffield, UK: Continuum Publishing, 1993) (I am
indebted to Professor Gordon Wenham for this reference).

marriages were the result of deceit; Leah is 'hated;' child bearing becomes a matter of competition and children become pawns in the battle for Jacob's favour (as evident by their names);[304] although the births bring some joy, there is plenty of unfulfilled longing and strife;[305] some children are born to full wives, others to concubines; favouritism for wives translates into favouritism for children;[306] and, looking ahead, Jacob will suffer at the hand of his children.[307] However, the LORD/God is clearly involved (29:31; 30:17, 22). This can be seen as a first step in the fulfilment of God's promise to Jacob at Bethel (28:14).[308] Human manipulation is a factor as well (e.g. the births through Bilhah and Zilpah). Walton speaks of "the juxtaposition of the human and the divine,"[309] although sometimes it more resembles a head-on collision. According to Humphreys "there are links, but not a full merger, between God's activity and that of the other characters in the narrative."[310]

> The stories of the matriarchs reveal the patriarchal goal of having sons to add to man's prestige and material well-being. However, they also present the prominent perspective that the God who calls Abraham out of Ur keeps the promise of descendants and is a powerful God of fertility.[311]

Is it right to interpret these births as blessing? So often in the OT fertility is associated with blessing. Is such an association valid here? Is Leah blessed or cursed? "Leah's joy in her blessed fertility was never unalloyed."[312] In addition, specific references to blessing are absent in the text. Neither does 'creation language' occur.[313] On the other hand, God is clearly involved in the midst of a complex setting characterized

---

[304] "The anger and rivalry expressed in the names of his sons showed that the conflict and hatred were etched deeply into their identity" (Armstrong, *In the Beginning*, 88). See also Sternberg, *Poetics*, 468–469.

[305] "Fruitfulness leads to renewed tension" (Humphreys, *The Character of God*, 176).

[306] This becomes painfully clear when Jacob prepares to meet Esau (cf. 33:1–3). See also Wenham, *Story as Torah*, 96.

[307] E.g. the pillage of Shechem by Simeon and Levi (34:30); Reuben's trespass (35:22); and the deceit by his children following the sale of Joseph (32–34). Cf. Armstrong, *In the Beginning*, 87–88; Wenham, *Genesis 16–50*, 249.

[308] Hartley, *Genesis*, 264; Wenham, *Genesis 16–50*, 249; Taschner, *Verheissung und Erfüllung*, 97–98.

[309] Walton, *Thou Traveller Unknown*, 146. See also Brueggemann, *Genesis*, 255 ("the narrative is a delicate balance"). See also Brett, *Genesis*, 90.

[310] Humphreys, *The Character of God*, 179.

[311] Jeansonne, *The Women of Genesis*, 79.

[312] Armstrong, *In the Beginning*, 87.

[313] E.g. 'fruitful' in Gen 1:28; 47:27 and Ex 1:7.

by human love, hate, strife and sin. Looking at the meta-narrative one could say that God moves his plan forward, although that might not be easily discerned in the immediacy of the fracas.[314] It therefore seems insufficient to describe the births as straightforward blessing. Mann calls "the frenetic sexual activity is clearly a manifestation of the divine blessing," yet "'Israel' has emerged out of the intense struggle between Rachel and Leah, just as 'Israel' will emerge from the struggle between Jacob and God in chapter 32."[315] I prefer to describe the fertility of the women and the resulting births as a "clear manifestation of divine blessing," whereas the "frenetic sexual activity," in view of the pervasive strife and associated language (cf. 30:16!), does not fit that description.[316] This passage demonstrates yet again the Creation-Fall perspective that pervades the patriarchal narratives. It is within this context that people live with the consequences of greed and worry about inheritance and fight for primacy. Indeed, "it seems impossible for humanity, in its exile from Eden, to enjoy unmixed blessing."[317]

3.5 JACOB'S WEALTH (GEN 30:25–31:1)

3.5.1 Introduction

The rivalry between two women makes place for a contest between two men.[318] In the previous section, any concerns about material advancement and security were unvoiced. Here they take centre stage. The focus in this passage is on Jacob's acquisition of great wealth at the expense of his uncle. Joseph's birth triggers Jacob's decision to return home (30:25a). The conversation between Jacob and Laban that follows, results in a new labour agreement. Over a period of six years Jacob becomes wealthy as a result of an ingenious breeding method. This leads to tensions with Laban's family, which results in Jacob's flight (Gen 31). Source-critics have come up with various proposals to

---

[314] Brenner, "Female Social Behaviour: Two Descriptive Patterns within the 'Birth of Hero' Paradigm," 263; Kass, "Love of Woman and Love of God," 51.

[315] Mann, The Book of the Torah, 57. Similarly Waltke, Genesis, 415; Taschner, Verheissung und Erfüllung, 97.

[316] Cf. von Rad, Genesis, 286: "God's work descended deeply into the lowest worldliness and there was hidden past recognition."

[317] Armstrong, In the Beginning, 86.

[318] Sherwood, "Had God Not Been on My Side," 199; Brodie, Genesis as Dialogue, 315; Recker, Die Erzählungen vom Patriarchen Jakob, 213; Janzen, Genesis 12–50, 119.

divide the text in J and E segments. More recent commentators tend to focus on the inherent unity of the passage.[319] The text in its final form moves from speech (vv. 25b–34), to actions (vv. 35–42a), to results (42b–43 and 31:1). Although the storyline is fairly straightforward, the text itself is not.[320] Sherwood describes the Hebrew as "notoriously difficult to make sense of."[321] In addition, there are plenty of ambiguities and other difficulties to keep the reader guessing (e.g. Jacob's breeding method).[322] Some scholars suggest that all this is deliberate narrative strategy.[323] Others think that these challenges are the result of 'expanding and explanatory glosses.'[324] Still others 'merely gloss over the difficulties.'[325] Brueggemann goes as far as saying that "verses 31–41 describe a series of actions which are beyond explanation. They need not be understood but only narrated."[326] Although this seems true for several issues, there is plenty that can be 'understood.'

3.5.2 Commentary

30:25–34

Following Joseph's birth, Jacob requests Laban to allow him to go home with his wives and children. The phrase אֶל־מְקוֹמִי וּלְאַרְצִי ('my place and my land,' vs. 25) is highly significant in view of Bethel.[327] Jacob's request is a mix of fortitude and deference. Jacob's speech (two

---

[319] E.g. Taschner, *Verheissung und Erfüllung*, 106–107.

[320] "As a whole the narrative is well arranged" (von Rad, *Genesis*, 293).

[321] Sherwood, *"Had God Not Been on My Side,"* 200. See also Westermann, *Genesis 12–36*, 479. "This difficult text must 'mature' before we can explain the whole by means of the parts in a well-founded literary way" (Fokkelman, *Narrative Art in Genesis*, 144). See also Fokkelman's philological elaborations of the text pp. 145–148.

[322] S.B. Noegel, "Sex, Sticks and the Trickster in Gen 30:31–43," *JANES* 25 (1997): 7–17, 7–8. "It would be convenient to speak of 'geep' or 'shoats' especially since the distinction between the two types of animals appears to be unimportant" (Lipton, *Revisions of the Night*, 115).

[323] Suggested as a possibility by Sherwood, *"Had God Not Been on My Side,"* 245 and Noegel, "Sex, Sticks and the Trickster," 16.

[324] Westermann, *Genesis 12–36*, 480 (followed by Walton, *Thou Traveller Unknown*, 155). "Unfortunately, this text has survived in deteriorated fashion" (Miller, "Contracts of Genesis," 33). Similarly Gunkel, *Genesis*, 327 and Speiser, *Genesis*, 239.

[325] Noegel, "Sex, Sticks and the Trickster," 7 and references in n. 7.

[326] Brueggemann, *Genesis*, 257.

[327] Wenham, *Genesis 16–50*, 254. See also Brett, *Genesis*, 93; Waltke, *Genesis*, 418; Walton, *Thou Traveller Unknown*, 150.

imperatives followed by a cohortative) is devoid of any niceties.[328] This may betray Jacob's feelings towards Laban, and/or may be intended to press Laban into action. Yet the verb 'to serve' reappears three times. The fact that Jacob uses this verb in his request suggests a situation of slavery.[329] Although *"de jure* his wives and children belong to Jacob, *de facto* Laban regards them as his."[330] Jacob's status might have been closer to that of a hired hand, but Laban treats him like a slave (cf. 31:43).[331] Partial deference may also be part of Jacob's strategy.

Jacob's request (שַׁלְּחֵנִי) resonates with earlier episodes. In 12:20, Pharaoh sent Abram away (וַיְשַׁלְּחוּ) "with his wife and all that he had". The description of Jacob's wealth in 30:43 resembles that of Abram in 12:16. In Gen 24 Abraham's servant had requested Laban to send him off with Rebekah (cf. 24:54, 56 and 59).[332] Finally, there is Rebekah's speech in 27:45, where she promised Jacob that she would send for him (וְשָׁלַחְתִּי) after a few days (cf. 29:20). Looking ahead, Moses would ask Pharaoh several times to let the Israelites (slaves!) depart (e.g. שַׁלַּח in Ex 5:1).[333] Similar to Jacob and Abram, the Israelites would come out with plenty of possessions (Ex 3:21–22; 12:35–36).[334]

It is not clear whether it was Jacob's intention to achieve a new work-agreement instead of just going home with his family.[335] However, Jacob seems to know what to ask for when Laban opens the negotiation, and he immediately goes to work when the new agreement is in place (vs. 37ff.).[336] This suggests that Jacob had well and truly premeditated his negotiation objectives and strategy.[337] This fits well with the characterization of Jacob in the narrative so far (cf. 25:29ff). The

---

[328] Wenham, *Genesis 16–50*, 254; "Now he is once again aggressive and shrewd" (Waltke, *Genesis*, 417).

[329] von Rad, *Genesis*, 294 refers to Ex 21:4–6 which states that a freed slave is not allowed to bring his wives and children with him (cf. 31:43). See also Sarna, *Genesis*, 211.

[330] Waltke, *Genesis*, 418 (abbreviated).

[331] Speiser, *Genesis*, 235–236; Waltke, *Genesis*, 418; Sherwood, *"Had God Not Been on My Side,"* 211; Taschner, *Verheissung und Erfüllung*, 98.

[332] Sherwood, *"Had God Not Been on My Side,"* 210. Cp. Jacob's arrival in Haran with Gen 24 (see *Section 3.2*).

[333] Janzen, *Genesis 12–50*, 120.

[334] Brueggemann, *Genesis*, 258; Waltke, *Genesis*, 418.

[335] Also noted by Walton, *Thou Traveller Unknown*, 152 and Brodie, *Genesis as Dialogue*, 318.

[336] "Jacob's actions, from vs. 37 onward, betray a steady hand" (Fokkelman, *Narrative Art in Genesis*, 149). Similarly Sherwood, *"Had God Not Been on My Side,"* 230.

[337] Similarly Gunkel, *Genesis*, 330 and Brodie, *Genesis as Dialogue*, 318.

negotiation that follows resembles the engagement of two experienced *judokas* circling each other; both hesitant to make the first move.[338] The somewhat garbled nature of Laban's reply suggests that Jacob's request has taken him by surprise.[339] Laban regains his footing rather quickly. His polite opening statement ignores Jacob's request.[340] Laban wants to retain Jacob's services.[341] Instead of discussing departure Laban invites Jacob to 'name his wages.' Laban "is deferential to the point of being obsequious,"[342] which taunts Jacob's dependence at the same time.[343] The mention of 'service' and 'wages' (also in vv. 32–33) reminds us of the earlier negotiation between the two (29:15–19).[344] Vv. 38–42 contain several hints of Laban's deceit in Gen 29. The second negotiation and its aftermath therefore, must be seen in conjunction with the first.[345] Scholars disagree about the translation of נִחַשְׁתִּי (vs. 27). Most translations opt for 'I have learned by divination' (44:5, 15).[346] Some scholars have challenged that rendering, because divination is normally applied to determine the future.[347] Wenham finds it unlikely that Laban would "resort to divination when he was prospering."[348] Waldman and Finkelstein have proposed a connection between נִחַשְׁתִּי and the Akkadian cognate 'to prosper.'[349] Thus Laban

---

[338] The *judo* metaphor is also used by Fokkelman in his commentary on vs. 37ff. (Fokkelman, *Narrative Art in Genesis*, 150).

[339] Dillmann, *Genesis*, 245; Jacob, *Genesis*, 602; Gunkel, *Genesis*, 329; von Rad, *Genesis*, 295; Westermann, *Genesis 12–36*, 481; Sherwood, "*Had God Not Been on My Side*," 212; Fokkelman, *Narrative Art in Genesis*, 142–143. According to Alter this might also indicate that Laban knows that he owes Jacob (Alter, *Genesis*, 163).

[340] "Oriental diplomatic courtesy and cunning (cf. chap. 23)" (von Rad, *Genesis*, 295). See also Taschner, *Verheissung und Erfüllung*, 98; Sherwood, "*Had God Not Been on My Side*," 201; Wenham, *Genesis 16–50*, 254; A. Pollak, "Laban and Jacob," *JBQ* 29, no. 1 (2001): 60–62, 61.

[341] Mann, *The Book of the Torah*, 57.

[342] Sarna, *Genesis*, 211. Similarly Skinner, *Genesis*, 390.

[343] Sherwood, "*Had God Not Been on My Side*," 213.

[344] Fokkelman, *Narrative Art in Genesis*, 142. See *Section 3.2*.

[345] Brueggemann, *Genesis*, 249; Noegel, "Sex, Sticks and the Trickster," 14ff.; "…it is a good thing to have 29.15ff. side by side with this text all the time" (Fokkelman, *Narrative Art in Genesis*, 142).

[346] E.g. ESV, NIV, NRSV.

[347] E.g. Hamilton, *Genesis 18–50*, 282; Finkelstein, "An Old Babylonian Herding Contract and Genesis 31:38f.," 34 n. 19.

[348] Wenham, *Genesis 16–50*, 254.

[349] N.M. Waldman, "A Note on Genesis 30:27b," *JQR* 55 (1964): 164–65; Finkelstein, "An Old Babylonian Herding Contract and Genesis 31:38f." This is followed by Sarna, *Genesis*, 211; Hamilton, *Genesis 18–50*, 282; Wenham, *Genesis 16–50*, 254 and Alter, *Genesis*, 163. See also HALOT 690. Sarna notes that other translations like

would be saying 'I have become prosperous' or 'I have grown rich,' which fits the context. Laban's 'divination' is ironic:

> There is something unusual about Laban's practice and this serves to characterize him. Laban is a man who is suspicious of good fortune. There is further irony in the fact that the heathen Laban has learned of Yhwh's blessing through divination.[350]

How to interpret "the LORD has blessed me because of you?"[351] Laban used similar language when he addressed Abraham's servant as the 'blessed of the LORD' (24:31). Back then, Laban's words did not primarily function as a theological statement,[352] but appeared to be sheer flattery that flowed from his covetousness and greed (24:30!). The same is probably true here.[353] Laban appears to use pious language to advance his cause.[354] Sherwood suggests that by speaking about the LORD's blessing, Laban aims to take credit away from Jacob to weaken Jacob's position.[355] Humphreys calls the remarks about the LORD's blessing "almost polite asides in a prelude to complex negotiations laced by a pattern of continued deceit and counter deceit."[356] When we view the blessing on Laban's household in connection with God's promise to Abram in 12:3, the following must be noted. Laban's statement is rather different from (for example) Abimelech's address to Isaac in 26:29.[357] Laban, in contrast, focuses on his own blessedness.[358] If Jacob now is 'the blessed of the LORD,' then the fact that Laban is not, and has not been, a blessing to Jacob will likely reverse Laban's 'blessed' situation.[359]

"I have learned by experience" are etymologically and semantically insupportable (Sarna, *Genesis*, 211).

[350] Sherwood, *"Had God Not Been on My Side,"* 215. Jacob, *Genesis*, 602 speaks of Laban's 'religiöse Zweispältigkeit.'

[351] This is discussed to some extent in Appendix B.

[352] Unlike the narrator's statement in 24:1.

[353] In Brueggemann's opinion "a theological statement is also made. Yahweh is the giver of prosperity" (Brueggemann, *Genesis*, 256). However, I think he takes Laban's statement too much at face value.

[354] "A backhanded way of saying that he cannot afford to let Jacob go" (Wenham, *Genesis 16–50*, 258).

[355] Sherwood, *"Had God Not Been on My Side,"* 205.

[356] Humphreys, *The Character of God*, 179.

[357] Wenham, *Genesis 16–50*, 255 and 259; Frettlöh, *Theologie des Segens*, 296 and 302.

[358] Westermann, *Genesis 12–36*, 484.

[359] Waltke, *Genesis*, 419. See also Taschner, *Verheissung und Erfüllung*, 101–102, who reflects on Laban's and Jacob's fate in connection with Isaac's blessing in 27:27–29.

Jacob does not accept Laban's invitation just yet.[360] Instead, Jacob reminds Laban how he 'served' him, how his livestock has fared with him, and how Laban's meagre holdings have 'increased abundantly' (וַיִּפְרֹץ לָרֹב).[361] Jacob acknowledges the LORD's involvement, but he also firmly turns the attention back to himself.[362] Like Laban, Jacob does not appear to make a theological statement primarily, but appears to counter Laban's pious diversionary tactic. This interpretation gains weight as we consider the apparent inconsistency between words and actions of both men in what follows:

> Jacob and Laban acknowledge God's role in Laban's good fortune, and agree that this is because God is with Jacob. Nevertheless, the two men take action to insure the result each seeks.[363]

Contrary to the births narrative, God's involvement in the increase of Jacob's herds is not explicitly mentioned.[364] Jacob will make claims about divine involvement in 31:4–13, but it remains to be seen whether his statement can be trusted.[365] In vs. 30b we discover Jacob's key-concern: "but now when shall I provide for my own household also?" Again, Laban carefully avoids making the first move and responds with another question, "what shall I give you?" (vs. 31a). Sherwood asks the intriguing question whether the reader is supposed to think of Deut 15:12–14:[366]

> If your brother, a Hebrew man or a Hebrew woman, is sold to you, he shall serve you six years, and in the seventh year you shall let him go free from you. And when you let him go free from you, you shall not let him go empty-handed. You shall furnish him liberally out of your flock, out

---

[360] Alter, *Genesis*, 163.

[361] Similar phraseology echoes God's promise of 28:14 and will be applied to Jacob's 'new-found' wealth in 30:43. It will also reappear in Ex 1:12 (Wenham, *Genesis 16–50*, 259). See also Waltke, *Genesis*, 419; Hamilton, *Genesis 18–50*, 279 and 284; Sherwood, "*Had God Not Been on My Side*," 200; Walton, *Thou Traveller Unknown*, 151.

[362] Westermann, *Genesis 12–36*, 481.

[363] Humphreys, *The Character of God*, 179–180. See also Brett, *Genesis*, 94.

[364] Brodie, *Genesis as Dialogue*, 318. Similarly Walton, *Thou Traveller Unknown*, 156; Brett, *Genesis*, 94; J.D. Pearson, "A Mendelian Interpretation of Jacob's Sheep," *SCB* 13, no. 1 (2001): 51–58, 52; Mann, *The Book of the Torah*, 58; Humphreys, *The Character of God*, 179. Brodie sees this variation, from divine to human, as one aspect of the texts' complementarity.

[365] Cf. *Section 3.6*.

[366] Sherwood, "*Had God Not Been on My Side*," 219. See also Wenham, *Genesis 16–50*, 255; Waltke, *Genesis*, 418 and Sarna, *Genesis*, 211, who refers to 31:38–42, where Jacob uses an identical formula "you would have sent me away empty-handed."

of your threshing floor, and out of your winepress. As the LORD your God has blessed you, you shall give to him.

Considering the length of Jacob's service and Laban's acknowledgment of the LORD's blessing, it is indeed interesting to reflect on the juxtaposition of Laban's tightfistedness with God's intended generosity, as revealed to later generations. The consequences of Laban's lack of generosity (in light of Deut 15:12–14) are an apt demonstration of how 'story' can function as *Torah*.[367] Before further engaging in such reflections, we need to take a closer look at Jacob's proposal and its aftermath. Jacob's reply "you shall not give me anything" is a classic bargainer's ploy.[368] It may also reflect Jacob's hard-gained experience of how Laban 'gives' (cf. 29:19).[369] Finally, Jacob makes an almost reluctant first move; "if you will do this for me." The text that follows 'bristles with difficulties.'[370] It is not immediately clear whether Jacob requests an immediate payment, or whether he has a future payment in mind. Jacob's speech in vs. 32 (הַיּוֹם) seems to indicate an immediate payment (assuming it is Jacob who separates the animals), but vs. 33 (בְּיוֹם מָחָר) seems to support the understanding of a future payment.[371] It is also not clear who is supposed to separate the animals. Sherwood speaks of a "vagueness of language that characterizes this pericope."[372] The main problem stems from the word הָסֵר which can be taken as an infinite absolute or as an imperative.[373] As a result, it is not clear whether Jacob suggests he does the separation, or whether he asks Laban to do so. Sherwood suggests that "the impression is given that, whereas Jacob intended to do the separating, the ambiguity of his הָסֵר gives Laban the opening he needs to carry out the separation himself."[374] By now we should know Laban well enough to realize that

---

[367] Cf. Wenham, *Story as Torah*.

[368] Alter, *Genesis*, 164. Sailhamer sees an allusion to Abraham's refusal to accept anything from the king of Sodom (14:21) (Sailhamer, *Genesis*, ad loc.).

[369] See *Section 3.3* and Sherwood, *"Had God Not Been on My Side,"* 220: "Laban is not a person who *gives* anything away."

[370] Sherwood, *"Had God Not Been on My Side,"* 220.

[371] Sherwood, *"Had God Not Been on My Side,"* 226. See also Hamilton, *Genesis 18–50*, 280 n. 15.

[372] Sherwood, *"Had God Not Been on My Side,"* 220.

[373] Hamilton, *Genesis 18–50*, 279 n. 13; Sherwood, *"Had God Not Been on My Side,"* 221. Taschner, *Verheissung und Erfüllung*, 99 n. 59, based on GK §113h, does not agree with Sherwood's analysis. Considering the broken syntax of the exchange, I think Sherwood's analysis remains an option.

[374] Sherwood, *"Had God Not Been on My Side,"* 221.

he is likely to exploit such an opportunity to 'the max.'[375] The description of the animals is not straightforward either. This aspect of the narrative becomes even more complex as additional terms are introduced in what follows. Much has been written about the different phrases used to describe the animals and their colour.[376] It is reasonable to assume that sheep were mainly white and goats were mainly black.[377] Thus Jacob asks a small percentage; twenty to twenty-five percent of the flocks at the most.[378] Jacob also provides Laban with a straightforward method for auditing.[379] Any normal coloured animal that will be found in Jacob's flock, 'shall be counted stolen' (vs. 33). The root גנב will be an important feature of the final episode of the Jacob-Laban narrative.[380] Laban is quick to agree, although his assent (as in 29:19) is again somewhat ambiguous.[381]

---

[375] Sherwood, "*Had God Not Been on My Side*," 229.

[376] I will not repeat that in detail here. I refer to Fokkelman, *Narrative Art in Genesis*, 145–150; Taschner, *Verheissung und Erfüllung*, 99–100; Sherwood, "*Had God Not Been on My Side*," 222–224 (and references there); A. Brenner, *Colour Terms in the Old Testament* (JSOTSup 21; Sheffield, UK: Sheffield Academic Press, 1982), 169 and 171; and Blum, *Komposition*, 114–116 for more details. In light of 31:7 ("your father…changed my wages ten time"), von Rad, *Genesis*, 294 and Morrison, "The Jacob and Laban Narrative," 158 have suggested that the various colour descriptions indicate changes in contract. However, this is not evident from the text of this passage.

[377] Hamilton, *Genesis 18–50*, 282–283; Pearson, "A Mendelian Interpretation," 53 (and reference there: L. Piper, Ruvinski, A., *The Genetics of Sheep* (Wallingford Oxfordshire, UK: CABI Publishing, 1997); S. Mongold, "Color Genetics in Icelandic Sheep," 42, no. 6 (1997): 11–16).

[378] "Thus Jacob is requesting the irregular, abnormal parts of Laban's flock" (Hamilton, *Genesis 18–50*, 283). See also J. Feliks, "Biology," in *Encyclopaedia Judaica (electronic ed.)* (vol. 4; Brooklyn, NY, USA: Lambda Publishers, 1997); Finkelstein, "An Old Babylonian Herding Contract and Genesis 31:38f.," 33–35; Matthews, *The IVP Bible Background Commentary, ad loc*; Morrison, "The Jacob and Laban Narrative," 161. According to Miller "Jacob has moved from the position of employee to that of co-owner with a claim on the profits of the enterprise" (Miller, "Contracts of Genesis," 34). However, Jacob himself still speaks of 'wages' (vv. 32–33). This was simply how herding contracts worked (cf. Morrison, "The Jacob and Laban Narrative"; Finkelstein, "An Old Babylonian Herding Contract and Genesis 31:38f."; Postgate, "Some Old Babylonian Shepherds and Their Flocks").

[379] "This clear and controllable offer (…) would appeal to the avaricious Laban" (Westermann, *Genesis 12–36*, 482). See also Miller, "Contracts of Genesis," 34.

[380] Cf. 31:19, 20, 26, 27, 30, 32, 39x2. Westermann, *Genesis 12–36*, 482; Hamilton, *Genesis 18–50*, 283; Fokkelman, *Narrative Art in Genesis*, 163.

[381] Fokkelman, *Narrative Art in Genesis*, 144; Sherwood, "*Had God Not Been on My Side*," 205.

30:35–36

Words flow into actions. However, it only becomes clear in vs. 36 that it is Laban who separates the odd-coloured animals.[382] Some commentators speak of deceit,[383] but it might not be that straightforward.[384] Although the reader might have assumed that Jacob was supposed to do the separation, and although the description of the animals seems to differ slightly from Jacob's description (vs. 32), Sherwood demonstrates that Jacob left enough room for Laban "to exegete it in his favour."[385] It is probably better to speak of a blatantly selfish interpretation of an ambiguous agreement than of deceit. Although Jacob fully lived up to earlier agreements, Laban's actions betray his mistrust.[386] He does not leave any detail of the new agreement unattended. "Laban is greedy, suspicious and cautious."[387] Once the odd-coloured animals are separated, Laban entrusts them to his sons and puts a three days journey between them and Jacob.[388] Laban clearly intends to minimize Jacob's future holdings.[389] Ironically, this plays to the advantage of Jacob, who can now put his plan to work without any interference.[390] Jacob still has the whole of Laban's remaining flock to breed from.[391] It would have been better for Laban if he had just given Jacob what he had asked for.[392] Live and learn!

---

[382] Sherwood, "*Had God Not Been on My Side*," 227. Some translations already provide that information in vs. 35 (e.g. ESV; NRSV).

[383] E.g. Mann, *The Book of the Torah*, 58; Waltke, *Genesis*, 419.

[384] "The text does not treat this as a breach of contract" (Miller, "Contracts of Genesis," 34). See also Sherwood, "*Had God Not Been on My Side*," 227.

[385] Sherwood, "*Had God Not Been on My Side*," 225. Similarly Speiser, *Genesis*, 238.

[386] Sherwood, "*Had God Not Been on My Side*," 225. Leupold, *Exposition of Genesis*, 822.

[387] Sherwood, "*Had God Not Been on My Side*," 205.

[388] The narrator slips in a piece of information about Laban's sons, who will play a role in the following episode (31:1ff.).

[389] Cf. Brett, *Genesis*, 94; Hamilton, *Genesis 18–50*, 283; Alter, *Genesis*, 164; Ross, *Genesis, ad loc.*

[390] Fokkelman, *Narrative Art in Genesis*, 149; Wenham, *Genesis 16–50*, 255; Waltke, *Genesis*, 419; Hamilton, *Genesis 18–50*, 283; Walton, *Thou Traveller Unknown*, 154. This would also facilitate Jacob's flight in Gen 31 (31:22!). "Thus the cunning man was betrayed by his own caution" (von Rad, *Genesis*, 296).

[391] Sherwood, "*Had God Not Been on My Side*," 225.

[392] Sherwood, "*Had God Not Been on My Side*," 225.

30:37–42a

The reader might fear for Jacob's chances to succeed.[393] Jacob's thoughts or feelings are not mentioned.[394] Instead, it is Jacob's drive and determination that characterize what follows.[395] Jacob goes to work immediately. Laban made the first move, but Jacob like an expert *judoka* now fully utilizes the energy of his opponent to 'take him over.'[396] The details of Jacob's breeding method have puzzled generations of scholars. Although various aspects of this story avoid closure, several insights have been gained that clarify our understanding.

The first set of insights focus on the 'poetics' of the narrative. The text contains several puns on the name Laban, which means 'white' in Hebrew (לָבָן).[397] In vs. 35, Laban had taken the female goats, "every one that had white on it" (כָּל אֲשֶׁר־לָבָן בּוֹ).[398] In vs. 37 Jacob takes 'fresh sticks of poplar' (לִבְנֶה) and peels 'white streaks' (לְבָנֹות) on them,[399] exposing 'the white' (הַלָּבָן) on the sticks.[400] According to Sarna this "conveys the idea of Jacob beating Laban at his own game."[401] In Gen 25:29–34 Jacob had defeated 'Edom' (אֱדֹום) with red (אָדֹם), here Laban is defeated with white (לָבָן).[402] There are several other allusions to earlier scenes. Laban's deceit of Jacob took place during a drinking feast (מִשְׁתֶּה, 29:22). Jacob's manipulation of the flocks took place when they came 'to drink' (לִשְׁתֹּות, 30:38).[403] There are various references to 'service' and 'wages' that connect this scene with the previous

---

[393] E.g. von Rad, *Genesis*, 296. "Just what is Jacob up to?" (Sherwood, "*Had God Not Been on My Side*," 202 and 229, following Gunkel, *Genesis*).

[394] Pearson suggests that "Jacob must have been very upset on finding that he was starting with no animals of the desired characteristics. He must have been delighted after the first year's breeding to find such new animals, indeed it may have provoked him in telling his wife of the visit of the angel" (Pearson, "A Mendelian Interpretation," 54). However, none of this is apparent in the text.

[395] Fokkelman, *Narrative Art in Genesis*, 149.

[396] Fokkelman, *Narrative Art in Genesis*, 150.

[397] Brenner, *Colour Terms in the Old Testament*, 83–85.

[398] Fokkelman, *Narrative Art in Genesis*, 149–150.

[399] This way, Jacob will 'strip' Laban of his possessions (Sherwood, "*Had God Not Been on My Side*," 231).

[400] Noegel, "Sex, Sticks and the Trickster," 16; Sherwood, "*Had God Not Been on My Side*," 230; Fokkelman, *Narrative Art in Genesis*, 150; Rendsburg, *The Redaction of Genesis*, 65; von Rad, *Genesis*, 297; Speiser, *Genesis*, 237; Davidson, *Genesis 12–50*, 166; Hamilton, *Genesis 18–50*, 283.

[401] Sarna, *Genesis*, 212. This is followed by Alter, *Genesis*, 164.

[402] Fokkelman, *Narrative Art in Genesis*, 150; Waltke, *Genesis*, 420. See *Section 2.2*.

[403] Noegel, "Sex, Sticks and the Trickster," 16.

two.[404] As noted before, the fertility theme connects the central scenes in the Jacob-Laban narrative.[405] The verb יָלַד that occurs throughout 29:32–30:23 is also used in 30:39.[406] There are similarities between the use of mandrakes and the peeled rods.[407] Finally, where Laban had given the "fertile but weak-eyed Leah ('cow') instead of Rachel ('ewe lamb')," Jacob gets even by only allowing the "younger and weaker of Laban's flock to reproduce,"[408] thus giving the weaker stock to Laban.[409] According to Noegel "this is more than a literary parallel, for by connecting Jacob's wives with Jacob's flocks and by mirroring one act of deception with another, the redactor administers a lesson in *lex talionis*."[410] "Thus Jacob fights Laban with his own weapons and defeats him."[411] The phrase 'poetic justice' is now applied to describe Laban's fate.[412]

The inherent strength of interpretations that focus on the 'poetics' of the narrative, is that they rely predominantly on what is evident in the text. In a way, the results 'speak for themselves.' Unfortunately, they do not answer all questions.[413] It is interesting to consider whether 30:37–41 solely has narrative quality (e.g. Brueggemann), or not. Was Jacob's method merely a form of 'white magic' or 'superstition', or do

---

[404] See also Fokkelman, *Narrative Art in Genesis*, 142; Noegel, "Sex, Sticks and the Trickster," 16.

[405] "The fertility of the flocks is paralleled by the growth of Jacob's family" (Morrison, "The Jacob and Laban Narrative," 163).

[406] Rendsburg, *The Redaction of Genesis*, 65; Noegel, "Sex, Sticks and the Trickster," 16.

[407] See below. See also Fokkelman, *Narrative Art in Genesis*, 147; Fishbane, *Text and Texture*, 40–62; and Rendsburg, *The Redaction of Genesis*, 65. Also quoted by Noegel, "Sex, Sticks and the Trickster," 7–8.

[408] Noegel, "Drinking Feasts," 173. See also Sherwood, *"Had God Not Been on My Side,"* 240.

[409] Sherwood, *"Had God Not Been on My Side,"* 240. See also Roop, *Genesis*, 201. Alter notes that, as in the stealing of the blessing, Jacob is embarked on a plan of deception that involves goats (Alter, *Genesis*, 164). Although this is an interesting parallel, it remains to be seen whether it is correct to describe Jacob's actions in this episode as deception (see below).

[410] Noegel, "Drinking Feasts," 173. See also Noegel, "Sex, Sticks and the Trickster," 16. For more background on *lex talionis* see P.J. Nel, "The Talion Principles in Old Testament Narratives," *JNSL* 20, no. 1 (1994): 21–29. (courtesy Noegel, "Drinking Feasts"). Laban was "due to be repaid in kind for his machinations" (Speiser, *Genesis*, 238).

[411] Fokkelman, *Narrative Art in Genesis*, 150.

[412] E.g. Brett, *Genesis*, 94.

[413] I leave aside whether all our questions could or should be answered. As noted before, there are plenty of issues in the interpretation of the Jacob-cycle that remain undecided. See also my earlier discussion on the function of 'gaps' in *Section 2.3*. See also Sternberg, *Poetics*, 55 and Chapter 7, especially pp. 258–263.

some parts (or all of it) make sense? Answers to such questions could help us to determine whether supernatural means were required to achieve Jacob's success. This in turn could help us to determine whether Jacob's claim of divine involvement in Gen 31 is open for challenge. These questions cannot be answered by 'poetics' alone. Commentators who conclude that Jacob's methods do not make sense, require divine involvement to explain his success. They are also more likely to assume that Jacob speaks the truth in 31:4–13.[414] Scholars, who think that Jacob could have achieved his success without divine intervention, often view Jacob's credibility in 31:4–13 differently. This also would allow for an interpretive position that acknowledges God's involvement as the ultimate source of fertility and prosperity, but leaves undecided whether God was involved as Jacob led his wives to believe.

Another set of interpretive approaches could be described to some extent as 'scientific.'[415] Kidner suggests that Jacob acts "on the common belief that a vivid sight during pregnancy or conception would leave its mark on the embryo."[416] Although this thesis is widely cited,[417] Noegel offers several reasons why it probably should not be used to explain the events in Gen 30. Noegel's main objection is based on the fact that "the earliest sources for this magical belief do not appear to antedate the fifth century CE," although there are several relevant texts that are older, in which one would expect to find references to such a belief if it was around at that time.[418] There are alternative explanations. According to Sarna, the trees mentioned were "used in the ancient world for medicinal purposes, could have had the effect of hastening the onset of the estrous cycle in the animals and so heightened their readiness to copulate."[419] However, these proposals in themselves cannot explain

---

[414] E.g. Waltke, *Genesis*, 420; 'Clearly God intervened' (Kidner, *Genesis*, 163). Hamilton is more careful: "But *perhaps* such knowledge has been given him by God, just as his son's capacity to interpret dreams was a gift from God" (Hamilton, *Genesis 18–50*, 284; italics mine).

[415] I realize that the phrase 'scientific' is a rather broad term, considering the proposals that have been classified under this term. Alternatively, one could label this category as 'non-poetic' approaches.

[416] Kidner, *Genesis*, 163. Similarly Westermann, *Genesis 12–36*, 483. See also discussions by Sarna, *Genesis*, 212; Pearson, "A Mendelian Interpretation," 52 and Noegel, "Sex, Sticks and the Trickster," 8–9.

[417] E.g. von Rad, *Genesis*, 296.

[418] Noegel, "Sex, Sticks and the Trickster," 9.

[419] Sarna, *Genesis*, 212.

Jacob's extraordinary success. For that we need to understand the laws of heredity:

> Scientifically, the required results could be achieved by the successive interbreeding of the monochrome heterozygotes, or the single coloured animals that carried recessive genes for spottedness. Such animals are detectable by the characteristic known as heterosis, or hybrid vigour.[420]

Although the laws of heredity were only formulated by Gregor Mendel in 1865AD, it is apparent that Jacob and Laban had some understanding of selective breeding.[421] Laban appears to act on such knowledge when he removes the odd-coloured sheep and goats.[422] How much did Jacob know, and to what extent was this common knowledge? Feliks interprets the facts as follows:

> In the flock tended by Jacob (...) a third of them were pure monochromes (homozygotes) and two-thirds heterozygotes, that is, they contained the gene of "spottedness." And since the gene of "monochromeness" is dominant, all the sheep appeared monochrome. In order to obtain spotted young, Jacob had to see that only the heterozygotes were crossed among themselves, and these according to the laws of heredity bore 25% spotted sheep, which became Jacob's property. But all this was on condition that the monochrome heterozygotes were not crossed with the monochrome homozygotes, from which only monochrome sheep would be born. (...) all the he-goats were monochrome but in some the characteristic of "spottedness" was recessive. This characteristic could be detected by the phenomenon of the hybrid's excessive potency (hybrid vigor-heterosis), that is, the monochrome sheep carrying the genes of "spottedness" conceived earlier than the homozygotes. Those that showed this hybrid vigor-heterosis are called in the Pentateuch *mekusharot* ("the stronger") and the others *atufim* ("the feebler"). Jacob handed over to Laban all the homozygote monochromes which had not revealed heterosis—these in addition to the spotted ones which Laban had received when the flocks were divided.

Hence Laban was left with a total of 75% of all the sheep, while Jacob got 25% of them, a percentage which Laban had not expected and which no

---

[420] Sarna, *Genesis*, 212. See also Feliks, "Biology" and Pearson, "A Mendelian Interpretation," 53 (and references quotes there) for more in-depth discussions.

[421] Feliks, "Biology," 1022.

[422] Pearson, "A Mendelian Interpretation," 53. "Selective breeding was already current in antiquity" (Kitchen, *On the Reliability of the Old Testament*, 337–338 and cited references in n. 77 and n. 78 on p. 573).

shepherd could have obtained without a precise knowledge of the laws of heredity.[423]

Feliks accepts Jacob's statement that he gained this knowledge in a dream (31:12).[424] He further assumes that Jacob merely applied the peeled rods in order to disguise his method of selection, which was unknown to Laban. Overall, Feliks' proposal is useful. However there are some problems as well. Although Feliks is right in saying that Jacob's twenty-five percent of the flock would be much higher than expected by Laban,[425] it is too low to explain Jacob's excessive wealth (vs. 43) and Laban's apparent destitution (31:1). Seventy-five percent of 'feebler' animals still accounts for plenty of wool and meat! Also, the knowledge Jacob claims to have gained in a dream (cf. 31:10–12) does not appear to be too different from the knowledge that caused Laban to separate the right kind of animals from the flock.

Pearson, starting from the same genetic baseline as Feliks,[426] arrives at a very different outcome. Pearson leaves aside whether Jacob gained his insight by means of a dream (31:10–12). After all, Jacob would have gained a lot of experience in his fourteen years in Haran (in addition to what he knew already).[427] According to Pearson "some understanding of inherited characteristics was known at the time of Jacob."[428] Jacob apparently had learned that "the chances of producing a lamb with a desired characteristic were greatly enhanced by serving the female with a male exhibiting the desired characteristics (31:10–12)."[429] By making some reasonable assumptions regarding Jacob's management with respect to culling and selective breeding, Pearson demonstrates that over a period of six years, almost ninety-five (!!) percent of animals would have had the desired characteristics.[430] This result fits much better with the complaint that Jacob had taken *all* of Laban's wealth (31:1). Morrison's observation adds further support:

---

[423] Feliks, "Biology," 1024–1025.
[424] Feliks, "Biology," 1025.
[425] Feliks, "Biology," 1026.
[426] See also Piper, *The Genetics of Sheep* and Mongold, "Color Genetics in Icelandic Sheep" as referred to by Pearson, "A Mendelian Interpretation," 53.
[427] Pearson, "A Mendelian Interpretation," 53.
[428] Pearson, "A Mendelian Interpretation," 53.
[429] Pearson, "A Mendelian Interpretation," 56.
[430] Pearson, "A Mendelian Interpretation," 54–55.

It is also interesting that the time allowed for this period of Jacob's service, six years, is close to the six-and-a-half-year turnover time demonstrated by the Nuzi flocks. Within such a time, all of the original flock
belonging to Laban could have died off and been replaced by the abnormally coloured livestock that were Jacob's.[431]

According to Pearson, the peeled rods were simply used to construct
pens in order to prevent the white rams getting at the ewes.[432] Although
I think Pearson's overall proposal has great merit, I am not convinced
by his suggestion regarding the use of the rods in view of 30:37ff.

This brings us to Noegel who has come up with a novel solution
to explain the use of the rods. The translation of אֶל־הַמַּקְלוֹת 30:39))
proves to be the *crux* of the matter. Some translations have 'in front of
the sticks/branches.'[433] Others translate it as 'at the sight of the rods.'[434]
Noegel argues for a literal translation of 'upon the rods:'[435]

> When we read Gen 30:39 in this vein the passage depicts Jacob employ
> ing the poplar rod not as a fertility symbol or aphrodisiac, but rather as a
> type of *"phallus fallax."* That is, Jacob allowed only the animals which he
> did not want to sire offspring to "become heated upon the rods". Herd
> ers and veterinarians acquainted with the breeding pattern of sheep and
> goats are well aware that while in estrus, ewes often are inclines to rub
> their vulvas on trees or sticks.[436]

Also

> Jacob allows the stronger of Laban's animals to mate upon the rods so
> that they produce no young, while allowing the weaker of Laban's flock
> to produce without interruption.[437]

Noegel also comments on the similarities between the mandrakes in
the previous scene and the rods here.[438] According to Waltke these are

---

[431] Morrison, "The Jacob and Laban Narrative," 158.

[432] Pearson, "A Mendelian Interpretation," 58.

[433] E.g. ESV, NRSV, NIV.

[434] E.g. JPS.

[435] Noegel, "Sex, Sticks and the Trickster," 10. See also references in n. 24–25 (same
page) to personal communications with Dr. Haupt and Dr. Hogue, professors of animal behavior, Cornell University.

[436] Noegel, "Sex, Sticks and the Trickster," 10. Noegel also suggests that רְהָטִים
could be understood as 'flowing hair' (cf. Ct 7:6; BDB 8941 and 8943) instead of
'runnels'; "...then the passage would describe how Jacob fashioned models of goats'
genitalia or of entire animals" (Noegel, "Sex, Sticks and the Trickster," 14).

[437] Noegel, "Sex, Sticks and the Trickster," 13.

[438] Cf. Fokkelman, *Narrative Art in Genesis*, 147; Fishbane, *Text and Texture*, 40–62;
and Rendsburg, *The Redaction of Genesis*, 65.

proof of Rachel's and Jacob's superstition.[439] Feliks considers the rods "only a dodge, a gesture to popular belief."[440] Noegel sees irony:

> The mandrakes and the rods are understood better not as aphrodisiacs, but rather as 'fertile items of irony.' The mandrakes are eaten by the barren Rachel, but it is Leah who conceives. The rods perform a similar function. They are meant to inspire Laban's older animals to copulate, but to no effect.[441]

In summary, studies that utilize a 'scientific approach' (e.g. Pearson), aim to demonstrate that Jacob could have achieved his success to some extent without supernatural means. However, they all make assumptions (however reasonable), that are not evident in the text. What also remains unclear is how much of this could have been known by the story's original audience. Although several issues remain undecided,[442] it is clear from the text that Jacob succeeds in breeding the right type of animals and so transfers them to his ownership. In addition, Jacob ensures that the strong animals are his, and the 'feeble' go to Laban (vv. 41–42).[443]

30:42b–31:1

Against all odds, Jacob becomes rich at the expense of his uncle, and so provides for his 'household' (vs. 30). The description of Jacob's spectacular wealth forms the climax of this episode: וַיִּפְרֹץ הָאִישׁ מְאֹד מְאֹד[444] Again, various earlier episodes come to mind. The roots פרץ and רבב that were used to describe Laban's riches in vs. 30 now apply to Jacob's wealth.[445] The phrase וַיִּפְרֹץ also reminds us of God's promise in 28:14 regarding offspring (the main interest of the previous episode).[446] Therefore, vs. 43 can be considered as a conclusion

---

[439] "Both tarnish their faith with superstitious practices" (Waltke, *Genesis*, 421).

[440] Feliks, "Biology" as quoted by Alter, *Genesis*, 165.

[441] Noegel, "Sex, Sticks and the Trickster," 14.

[442] Especially regarding vv. 39–40: cf. Sherwood, "*Had God Not Been on My Side*," 233–238; Blum, *Komposition*, 608.

[443] Wenham, *Genesis 16–50*, 257. Wenham makes the theological point, that Jacob is portrayed as a "benevolent ruler of the animal kingdom, thus reaffirming God's primal intentions for the world" (Wenham, *Story as Torah*, 30). Although I agree that Jacob's selective breeding demonstrates man's dominion over creation, I am not sure we can drive the point that far.

[444] 'Thus the man increased greatly' (ESV) or 'grew exceedingly prosperous' (NIV).

[445] Sherwood, "*Had God Not Been on My Side*," 240.

[446] Wenham, *Genesis 16–50*, 257. The phrase לוּז as a word for 'almond' (30:37) is unique in the MT (Sherwood, "*Had God Not Been on My Side*," 230). It might

and summary statement for this and the previous episode.[447] Although
God's involvement in Jacob's breeding project is not specifically mentioned, the reader gets the impression that its outcome aligns with
God's promises at Bethel. Brueggemann detects a "formula of inversion (vv. 42–43), which affirms the increase of God's chosen one," and
attributes Jacob's wealth to "the watchfulness of God over his decree
(25:23)."[448] Westermann reflects on the relationship between divine
blessing, prosperity and justice:

> Laban misuses the blessing by exploiting Jacob's ability for himself alone.
> It cannot be Yahweh's blessing where one gets all, the other nothing.
> Yahweh, the God of Jacob, is clearly with the weak who is being abused
> by the strong.[449]

However, the nature and extent of God's involvement is not specified
by the narrator, and it remains to be seen whether it will be clarified
by subsequent events.[450]

The description of Jacob's wealth resembles earlier descriptions of
wealth accumulations by Abraham and Isaac. According to Wenham
this betrays the positive attitude of Genesis towards wealth.[451] Three
episodes come to mind. In Gen 12:16 Pharaoh dealt well with Abram
after he had taken Sarai into his house. Abram's wealth is described in
terms of flocks, herds, male and female servants, donkeys and camels.[452]
In *Section* 1.1 I demonstrated that opinions about Abram's wealth
in 12:16 are divided. I concluded that it does not seem right to call
Abram's wealth "a provisional fulfilment of God's promise" just yet.
God's providence might well be at work, but to label Abram's newly
gained wealth a divine blessing seems inappropriate. In Gen 24:35
Abraham's servant reports how the LORD had blessed Abraham, and
how he has given him "flocks and herds, silver and gold, male and
female servants, camels and donkeys." In this episode there is explicit
mention of God's blessing (cf. 24:1). The allusion to Gen 24 recalls the

---

be another reference to Bethel, which was formerly called Luz in 28:19 (לוּז). 'Who
knows?' (Fokkelman, *Narrative Art in Genesis*, 150). See also Hamilton, *Genesis 18–50*,
284; Sarna, *Genesis*, 213.
    [447] Sherwood, *"Had God Not Been on My Side,"* 241.
    [448] Brueggemann, *Genesis*, 257.
    [449] Westermann, *Genesis 12–36*, 484.
    [450] Fokkelman, *Narrative Art in Genesis*, 149.
    [451] Wenham, *Story as Torah*, 92.
    [452] Wenham, *Genesis 16–50*, 257; Sherwood, *"Had God Not Been on My Side"*, 240–
241; Sailhamer, *Genesis, ad loc.*

opening of the betrothal type-scene when Jacob had arrived empty-handed in Haran. Things have changed considerably since. Finally, the description of Jacob's wealth reminds us of Isaac's wealth in 26:12–14. Sherwood notes that Isaac's wealth resulted in Philistine envy, which seems similar to the grumblings of Laban's sons (31:1).[453] And indeed, "while his [Jacob's] magical breeding methods would make Mendel smile, the results are not amusing to Laban and his sons."[454] As with the Philistines, envy and tension set the scene for impending separation. Similar to the covenant between Isaac and Abimelech, there will be a settlement between Jacob and Laban, following a period of separation.

3.5.3   Concluding Remarks

Although various challenges remain, a number of insights emerge that inform our understanding of the nature and role of material possessions in the Jacob-cycle. To do justice to the composite nature of this understanding, I will summarize my thoughts along three relational axes: i) Jacob-Laban; ii) Jacob-God; iii) Jacob-Isaac-Abraham:[455]

Jacob-Laban
Much has changed since Jacob's arrival. After Jacob's decision to return to his 'place and land,' things are turning Jacob's way at the expense of Laban.[456] Jacob was no match for Laban's deceit in Gen 29. Now Laban receives his 'comeuppance.'[457] Both episodes can be seen as vivid lessons in *lex talionis*.[458] The battle for material advancement

---

[453] Sherwood, "*Had God Not Been on My Side*," 241. Cf. Coats, *Genesis*, 217.

[454] Mann, *The Book of the Torah*, 58.

[455] At this point, the reader might want to re-read my summary in *Section* 3.4.3, because my conclusions there align well with my reflections regarding Jacob's new-found wealth.

[456] This decision is the turning point of the story (Gunkel, *Genesis*, 326). "The architectonic pivot of the Cycle" (Fishbane, "Composition and Structure in the Jacob Cycle (Gen 25:19–25:22)," 32). "The point at which (…) Jacob's anabasis begins" (Sherwood, "*Had God Not Been on My Side*," 209).

[457] Walton, *Thou Traveller Unknown*, 156; Wenham, *Genesis 16–50*, 259. Similarly Mann, *The Book of the Torah*, 58; Miller, "Contracts of Genesis," 36; and Ross, *Genesis, ad loc*. This story undoubtedly has given many readers and listeners 'a great sense of satisfaction' (Wenham, *Genesis 16–50*, 259).

[458] See also Sherwood, "*Had God Not Been on My Side*," 208. According to the Revd. G. Angel it is better to speak of the Greek concept of *nemesis*, because *lex talionis*, strictly speaking, is a rule for making legal judgment. *Nemesis* applies to revenge or getting paid back for one's evil deeds.

in Gen 30 therefore, can be seen as a vehicle to dispense justice to Laban. To what extent God is an active participant in this remains unclear.[459] Some commentators speak of Jacob's deception,[460] but it is probably better to describe his actions here as cunning ingenuity:[461]

> The text is sufficiently coherent as to suggest that Jacob's wealth comes as the result of his own cunning initiative. The narrator does not suggest any direct divine involvement, but the implication seems to be that Jacob deserved his wealth, and the suggestion of poetic justice is reinforced by the use of the word *lavan* (white/Laban).[462]

Jacob-God

The LORD is only mentioned at the opening of the negotiation between Jacob and Laban (30:27, 30). God's influence however, may be inferred in several ways. First, there is God's involvement as the giver of life. The fertility theme connects this episode with the previous one.[463] In the previous episode, God's involvement is explicitly mentioned.[464] In this one it is not. Pearson demonstrates that 'direct divine intervention was unnecessary' to explain Jacob's success.[465] According to Walton "the divine has retreated into obscurity, and Jacob seizes the situation for himself employing all means to advance his cause."[466] Although ultimately fertility must be ascribed to God, both episodes show the importance of human involvement.[467]

---

[459] Probably things are not as clear-cut as suggested by Westermann, *Genesis 12–36*, 484 (see above).

[460] E.g. Mann, *The Book of the Torah*, 58; Fokkelman, *Narrative Art in Genesis*, 151. Westermann disagrees: "It cannot be described as deception" (Westermann, *Genesis 12–36*, 482). Interestingly, also Williams, *Deception in Genesis* does not categorize this episode as a 'deception' narrative.

[461] E.g. Brett, *Genesis*, 94; Armstrong, *In the Beginning*, 89; Gunkel, *Genesis*, 328; Westermann, *Genesis 12–36*, 484; Taschner, *Verheissung und Erfüllung*, 102; Brodie, *Genesis as Dialogue*, 318. Sailhamer even speaks of 'Jacob's wise dealings with Laban.'

[462] Brett, *Genesis*, 94.

[463] Cf. Brodie, *Genesis as Dialogue*, 315–316.

[464] "So far Yahweh has not been involved in the story overtly, except in the opening and closing of wombs" (Mann, *The Book of the Torah*, 58).

[465] Pearson, "A Mendelian Interpretation," 52.

[466] Walton, *Thou Traveller Unknown*, 156. Similarly Humphreys, *The Character of God*, 180 and Brodie, *Genesis as Dialogue*, 318.

[467] Wenham sees Jacob's success in relation to man's dominion over other creatures as ordained by God in Gen 1:28 (Wenham, *Story as Torah*, 26 and 30).

We can also think of God as promise-keeper.[468] Jacob's increase aligns with God's promises of offspring and presence (28:14–15).[469] However, in contrast to God's involvement in the birth of Jacob's children, which is specifically mentioned, it is not clear to what extent God is involved in Jacob's wealth-increase. Besides various hints of God's involvement, there is great emphasis on various human initiatives in both episodes. As with the births of Jacob's children, the activities associated with the increase of Jacob's flocks are portrayed as all-consuming activities for the participants. It is by no means straightforward to discern God's presence in this human context of struggle, intrigue, trickery and harsh disappointment. Considering the larger story-line in Genesis God seems to advance his plans, even despite the human actors.[470] When we take a closer look at individual events however, we may know the beginning and the end, but it is often impossible to determine how God has been at work in between.[471] I agree with Humphreys that "there are links, but not a full merger, between God's activity and that of the other characters in the narrative."[472]

Jacob-Isaac-Abraham
When we compare Jacob's riches with those of Isaac and Abraham, there are similarities but also differences. As noted before, such contrasts are a feature of the patriarchal narratives. According to Sherwood "the casting of Laban in the role of foreign adversary puts Jacob in the role of patriarch in the line of Abraham and Isaac."[473] Jacob like his forebears eventually overcomes various adverse situations. I noted the similarities between plot-development in Gen 26 and in the Jacob-Laban narrative. Jacob's wealth however, seems very different from Isaac's, which was a direct result of the LORD's blessing (26:12) and

---

[468] This aligns with Brueggemann's comment about God's "watchfulness of God over his decree" (Brueggemann, *Genesis*, 257; see above).

[469] Taschner, *Verheissung und Erfüllung*, 102; Sailhamer, *Genesis, ad loc.*

[470] Humphreys, *The Character of God*, 179.

[471] von Rad attributes different perspectives on God's involvement in Jacob's wealth generation to different sources (von Rad, *Genesis*, 297; see n. 508 below).

[472] Humphreys, *The Character of God*, 179. Lucas' comments on the book of Proverbs, equally apply to Genesis: "as elsewhere in the Hebrew Bible, there is an unresolved tension between human freedom and responsibility and divine sovereignty" (E. Lucas, "Proverbs: The Act-Consequence Nexus," in *Postgraduate Seminar, 6th February 2007* (Trinity College Bristol, 2007), 8).

[473] Sherwood, "*Had God Not Been on My Side*," 206. Sherwood follows Hauge, "Struggles," 119.

almost just seems to 'happen.' The acquisition of Jacob's wealth is much more involved. Possibly this must be attributed to the consequences Jacob suffered as a result of his deceit. As a result, questions about God's involvement in the acquisition of Jacob's riches linger into the next episode.

To conclude: the change of Jacob's fortune, as evident in the increase of his wealth, is the main concern of this key-episode at the heart of the Jacob-Laban cycle. Material possessions and associated attitudes and actions are key-ingredients to the narrative. They also explain the various relationship dynamics and their development. They are at the heart of the struggle between Jacob and Laban, and they are testimony to Jacob's success. The intensity of the struggle is illustrative for the power of material advancement as a motivating force. As noted before, a Creation-Fall perspective pervades the patriarchal narratives. It is within this setting that people live with the consequences of greed and fight for material advancement. Yet God moves his plan forward, although that might not be easily discerned in the immediacy of the fracas.

3.6   Jacob's Flight (Gen 31:2–32:1)

3.6.1   *Introduction*

The tensions that result from Jacob's wealth (31:1–2), and a short address by God (vs. 3) trigger Jacob's decision to leave.[474] As before, Jacob has to overcome various obstacles. Jacob overcomes these obstacles and completes the transformation from a destitute refugee to a *paterfamilias*,[475] who is able to establish an international border.[476] Jacob's encounter with angels (32:1) reminds us of Bethel (28:11–22)

---

[474] Cf. C. Mabee, "Jacob and Laban: The Structure of Judicial Proceedings (Genesis XXXI 25–42)," *VT* 30 (1980): 192–207, 192.

[475] "The transformation of Jacob, the empty-handed fugitive, into a man of means and well-being" (Brueggemann, *Genesis*, 259). See also Mabee, "Judicial Proceedings," 194.

[476] Between Laban the Aramean and himself (Sherwood, "*Had God Not Been on My Side*," 277). For ANE parallels of boundary treaties cf. R. Frankena, "Some Remarks on the Semitic Background of Chapters xxix–xxxi of the Book of Genesis," *OTS* 17 (1972): 53–64, 64.

and anticipates his next confrontation(s).[477] Gunkel, Speiser and von Rad assign most of Gen 31 to E, with a few insertions from J and one (vs. 18) from P.[478] In contrast, Westermann concludes that most of Gen 31 must be ascribed to J.[479] According to Wenham there are "wide differences of opinion as to how much should be ascribed to J, especially in the latter part of the chapter."[480] Again, no clear consensus exists. Gen 31 has several ties with previous episodes in the Jacob-Laban narrative, but also with the wider Jacob-cycle and beyond.[481] Sherwood calls it 'a grand finale.'[482] All characters (including the herds) make a final joint appearance, and the drawn-out conflict between Jacob and Laban gets resolved. God, who appears to have been largely absent, intervenes at key-moments (vv. 3 and 24). God is also referred to in major speeches by Jacob, his wives and Laban. However, it is challenging to discern the speakers' reliability. The narrative art of Gen 31 is rich. Besides shreds of irony and sarcasm, there is plenty of suspense.[483] Material possessions and concerns are key-ingredients of the narrative. I will comment on this episode, before summarizing my findings for the Jacob-Laban narrative as a whole.

3.6.2 Commentary

31:1–3

These verses are the transition from the climax in 30:43[484] to Jacob's decision to return home (31:4ff).[485] Jacob arrives at his decision in

---

[477] Wenham, *Genesis 16–50*, 280. Brodie considers this 'panel' about the confrontation between Jacob and Laban (31:1–32:2) as complementary to Jacob's engagement with Esau (32:3–33) (Brodie, *Genesis as Dialogue*, 322–323). See Chapter 4.

[478] Speiser, *Genesis*, 248; Gunkel, *Genesis*, 331; von Rad, *Genesis*, 300; Wenham, *Genesis 16–50*, 268 (e.g. Richter, "Das Gelübde," 45ff.). Cf. Walton, *Thou Traveller Unknown*, 157–160 for an enlightening survey.

[479] Westermann, *Genesis 12–36*, 490. Similarly, but not identical, Coats, *Genesis*, 221.

[480] Wenham, *Genesis 16–50*, 268.

[481] Sherwood, *"Had God Not Been on My Side,"* 276.

[482] Sherwood, *"Had God Not Been on My Side,"* 275. Similarly Sarna, *Genesis*, 213.

[483] Will Jacob convince his wives to go with him? Will Jacob be able to depart undetected? Will Laban and retinue manage to catch up? What will Laban do to Jacob? Will the *teraphim* be found? How will the dispute between Jacob and Laban be settled? Cf. Sherwood, *"Had God Not Been on My Side,"* 279–281; Walton, *Thou Traveller Unknown*, 177.

[484] In *Section* 3.4 I mentioned some reasons for including 31:1 with the previous episode. As mentioned before, there are similarities with the Philistine envy in 26:14 (Waltke, *Genesis*, 423).

[485] Jacob's return home foreshadows the exodus (e.g. Brueggemann, *Genesis*, 258; Waltke, *Genesis*, 424; Wenham, *Genesis 16–50*, 277; Brodie, *Genesis as Dialogue*, 326). Cf. Fokkelman, *Narrative Art in Genesis*, 156.

three steps: Jacob 'hears' the complaint of Laban's sons; he 'sees' a change in Laban's attitude; and finally he is addressed by the LORD himself. This is the first time since Bethel that God addresses Jacob; again at a time of crisis.[486] Some commentators see the introduction of the divine in Gen 31 as a refinement of what has preceded (e.g. Blum).[487] Others see it as a weakness (e.g. Coats).[488] In the narrative however, it is decisive. The LORD's speech is short but significant. For Brueggemann "the call of God governs the entire narrative."[489] God's command resembles the one to Abram in 12:1–3[490] and his promise echoes Bethel ('I will be with you'; עִמָּךְ).[491] This balances the statement that Laban was 'not with him' (Jacob; עִמּוֹ) in vs. 2.[492] This juxtaposition of God and Laban will be an important feature of Jacob's speech to his wives (vv. 4–13).[493]

31:4–13

Will Jacob be able to take his family and his possessions with him? His first obstacle is to convince Rachel and Leah. We may assume that they realize that fleeing will not be without risk.[494] Jacob calls them together for a private discussion.[495] Jacob's speech echoes vv. 2–3 and juxtaposes 'your father' with the God of 'my father.'[496] The key-words 'service' and

---

[486] Mann, *The Book of the Torah*, 58; Baldwin, *The Message of Genesis 12–50*, 128; Kass, "Love of Woman and Love of God," 52; Lipton, *Revisions of the Night*, 143.

[487] Blum, *Komposition*, 118ff. Cf. Lipton, *Revisions of the Night*, 136.

[488] Coats, *Genesis*, 222. Cf. Walton, *Thou Traveller Unknown*, 180.

[489] Brueggemann, *Genesis*, 257. Brueggemann also notes various similarities with the Exodus (p. 258).

[490] Both 'land' (אֶרֶץ) and 'kindred' (מוֹלֶדֶת, see also 24:4 and 7) feature in 12:1–3 (Wenham, *Genesis 16–50*, 269; Brett, *Genesis*, 94; Janzen, *Genesis 12–50*, 120; Sherwood, "Had God Not Been on My Side," 291). Like God's calling of Abram, this one calls for an abrupt departure (Brueggemann, *Genesis*, 257).

[491] Alter, *Genesis*, 166; Hamilton, *Genesis 18–50*, 288; Sarna, *Genesis*, 213; Taschner, *Verheissung und Erfüllung*, 109; Fokkelman, *Narrative Art in Genesis*, 152; Sherwood, "Had God Not Been on My Side," 291.

[492] Fokkelman, *Narrative Art in Genesis*, 152; Hamilton, *Genesis 18–50*, 288; Waltke, *Genesis*, 423.

[493] Fokkelman, *Narrative Art in Genesis*, 154; Wenham, *Genesis 16–50*, 270.

[494] Cf. Wenham, *Genesis 16–50*, 270.

[495] Note the word-order. Cf. Waltke, *Genesis*, 424. Bilhah and Zilpah still do not have a voice (Cf. Humphreys, *The Character of God*, 268 n. 18).

[496] Jacob never mentions Laban's name, but consistently refers to him as 'your father' (Hamilton, *Genesis 18–50*, 288). See also Waltke, *Genesis*, 424.

'wages' reappear as well (vv. 6–8).[497] Jacob contrasts Laban's maltreatment with God's interventions (e.g. vs. 7),[498] with the consequence that "God has taken[499] away the livestock of your father and given them to me" (vs. 9).[500] Jacob's justification in effect addresses the complaint of Laban's sons (vs. 1).[501] However, this is not the 'clincher' for obtaining a favourable decision. God's (alleged) command in vs. 13 will serve to that end.[502] Jacob gives God all the credit and reduces his own involvement to nil, while portraying himself as the suffering and aggrieved party.[503] In vs. 10 Jacob intensifies his appeal by elaborating on God's involvement. Jacob recounts a dream in which he sees goats 'mating' the flock, literally, 'the goats ascending the flock' (הָעַתֻּדִים הָעֹלִים עַל־הַצֹּאן). This echoes Jacob's Bethel-experience, where angels 'were ascending' (מַלְאֲכֵי אֱלֹהִים עֹלִים).[504] Jacob does not clarify *how* the vision affected the transfer of Laban's wealth to Jacob and he avoids mentioning the 'peeled rods' (30:37–42). Instead, Jacob reports the appearance of the angel of God, who has "seen all that Laban is doing."[505] Verse 13 forms the climax of Jacob's appeal. Jacob tells his

---

[497] Fokkelman, *Narrative Art in Genesis*, 153; Rendsburg, *The Redaction of Genesis*, 64; Fokkelman, *Narrative Art in Genesis*, 179; Taschner, *Verheissung und Erfüllung*, 110.

[498] Waltke, *Genesis*, 425; Humphreys, *The Character of God*, 182; Hamilton, *Genesis 18–50*, 288; Fokkelman, *Narrative Art in Genesis*, 154; Wenham, *Genesis 16–50*, 270.

[499] וַיַּצֵּל Hiphil of נָצַל, could be translated as 'snatched away,' 'delivered' or 'salvaged.' Also in 31:16 (cf. BDB 6281; HALOT 6314; Hamilton, *Genesis 18–50*, 286 n. 11; Janzen, *Genesis 12–50*, 121). A nice ironic touch (?); poor cattle saved from bad Laban. See also 32:12 (Hiphil imperative); 32:31 (Niphal); 37:21; and 37:22, where deliverance is in view. Note also the frequent occurrence of נָצַל in the book of Exodus (cf. Strickman, *Ibn Ezra's Commentary on the Pentateuch: Genesis*, 298).

[500] According to Sarna "this is a legal formula for the conveyance and transfer of property" (Sarna, *Genesis*, 214 and n. 3 on 365–366 and Waltke, *Genesis*, 425, both following J. Greenfield, "Našu-nadānu and Its Congeners," in *Essays on the Ancient Near East in Memory of J.J. Finkelstein* (ed. M. de Jong Ellis; Hamden, Conn., USA: Archon, 1977)).

[501] Cf. Eising, *Formgeschichtliche Untersuching*, 197.

[502] Fokkelman, *Narrative Art in Genesis*, 156; Wenham, *Genesis 16–50*, 272.

[503] Brueggemann, *Genesis*, 258; Hamilton, *Genesis 18–50*, 289; Fokkelman, *Narrative Art in Genesis*, 159, 162. Lipton draws attention to 15:4 where "as in the dream of the flocks, God assumes responsibility for something that had previously been presented as human endeavour" (Lipton, *Revisions of the Night*, 136).

[504] עֹלִים in 28:12. הָעֹלִים in 31:10 and 12 (cf. Wenham, *Genesis 16–50*, 272). According to Novak this signifies a spiritual low for Jacob. Where Jacob had been dreaming of angels, now he dreams of mating animals (S. Novak, "Jacob's Two Dreams," *JBQ* 24, no. 3 (1996): 189–90, 190).

[505] Cf. Ex 2:25. "This term frequently is used to express God's compassionate response to a suffering victim" (Sarna, *Genesis*, 214 and 366 n. 4; cf. Ex 3; Wenham, *Genesis 16–50*, 272).

wives that God identified himself as the God of Bethel, where Jacob had anointed a pillar and made a vow. Jacob thus presents himself as under obligation.[506] The divine speech, as reported by Jacob, concludes with no less than three imperatives (in contrast to the one in vs. 3). The reader might wonder what to make of all this new information. How to explain the differences from the account in Gen 30?[507] Is Jacob selective or deceptive? Source-critics have explained the differences by assigning these passages to different sources (30:37–43 to J; 31:4–13 to E),[508] but that does not help to clarify the text in its final form.[509] Alter acknowledges the apparent inconsistencies, but suggests that the text 'makes perfect narrative sense.'[510] After all, Jacob's objective is to convince his wives to join him, so he appears to emphasize certain events while ignoring others.[511] Other scholars see the second passage as a theological interpretation of the first (e.g. Rendtorff; Waltke; Brueggemann).[512] However, if we think we can make sense of some discrepancies, other issues remain:

- Jacob seems to collapse two appearances of God into one.[513] The first part of his dream (regarding the mating of the flock) has not been reported by the narrator;
- The second part of Jacob's dream, regarding God's commandment to leave, seems to be an embellished version of the LORD's speech in vs. 3 (e.g. three imperatives vs. one; plus the reference to Bethel);[514]

---

[506] Sherwood, *"Had God Not Been on My Side,"* 299; Sarna, *Genesis,* 215; Wenham, *Genesis 16–50,* 272.

[507] "The narrative (…) is confusingly inconsistent with what has preceded it" (Lipton, *Revisions of the Night,* 115).

[508] E.g. von Rad, *Genesis,* 297: "The Elohist is here much more intelligible and simple. He considers Jacob's increasing wealth as God's blessing (31.9ff.). But it is not certain that the Yahwist also shares his view". See also Hamilton, *Genesis 18–50,* 288 n. 21.

[509] Cf. Walton, *Thou Traveller Unknown,* 169.

[510] Alter, *Genesis,* 167. Cf. Westermann, *Genesis 12–36,* 491 who downplays any contradiction for the listeners.

[511] Cf. Fokkelman, *Narrative Art in Genesis,* 156–157.

[512] R. Rendtorff, *Das überlieferungsgeschichtliche Problem des Pentateuch* (BZAW 147; Berlin, Germany: Walter de Gruyter, 1977), 58; Waltke, *Genesis,* 422 and 435; Brueggemann, *Genesis,* 257–259.

[513] Sarna, *Genesis,* 214; Waltke, *Genesis,* 425–426; Lipton, *Revisions of the Night,* 130.

[514] Cf. Hamilton, *Genesis 18–50,* 289; Wenham, *Genesis 16–50,* 271.

- It is difficult to harmonize the timing of this dream with narrated events. The part of the dream regarding the mating of the flock must have taken place before Jacob's negotiation with Laban in 30:25–34. Jacob's complaint that Laban changed his wages ten times (31:7) must refer to the period after the agreement was put in place. God's intervention then, as reported by Jacob, cannot be in response to the injustice of changing wages, because that simply has not occurred yet. Something that seems to be in tension with Jacob's words in 31:8. Note also that the LORD's address to Jacob took place after the acquisition of Jacob's wealth (31:3);
- Jacob's speech suggests that Laban changed wages several times, and that every time newborn flock would follow the newly agreed pattern. This aspect of the story is not reported in 30:37–43;
- Jacob does not explain how the sight of the odd-coloured animals in vv. 10–12 impacts the wealth-transfer from Laban to Jacob. The language is lofty ("lift up your eyes and see"), but in itself does not explain Jacob's breeding success. Is Jacob pulling the wool over his wives' eyes?

How to address these challenges? A lot depends on whether one trusts Jacob or not.[515] Jacob fills in some of our 'gaps,' but it is not certain that he does so reliably.[516] "After all, Jacob is hardly a reliable witness on his own behalf."[517] Sternberg suggests various ways in which 'gaps' can be filled.[518] There is great diversity in opinion regarding Jacob's reliability as a 'gap-filler,' ranging from 'total trust' to 'total mistrust.' Both positions bring their own challenges. Scholars who accept Jacob's version of events can address some, but not all of the above mentioned problems. Scholars, who do not trust Jacob, are willing to accept the fact that Jacob breaks the third commandment, something that must have been difficult to accept for the original Torah-abiding audience of Genesis.[519] I will briefly discuss these different perspectives before reaching some (tentative) conclusions.

Waltke is representative of those who fully accept Jacob's version of events. He not only trusts Jacob, but also sees great merit in Jacob's

---

[515] Cf. Fokkelman, *Narrative Art in Genesis*, 161.
[516] Cf. Sherwood, *"Had God Not Been on My Side,"* 287.
[517] Sherwood, *"Had God Not Been on My Side,"* 296 and 357 n. 36.
[518] Sternberg, *Poetics*, 258–263.
[519] Walton, *Thou Traveller Unknown*, 162.

conduct. Waltke criticized Jacob's passivity and lack of (spiritual) leadership in earlier episodes. But here, according to Waltke, Jacob demonstrates that he is a changed man:

> For the first time in this act, he emerges as a man of public faith, and he takes the leadership of his home. He acts promptly upon God's command to return to the Promised Land (31:3–4), bears witness first to his wives of God's presence and provisions and then finally to Laban's whole family, and willingly undertakes the dangerous and difficult journey in obedience to God.[520]

Waltke acknowledges that Jacob seems to collapse two dreams into one, but does not dwell on the possible implications of that observation.[521] According to Waltke, Jacob's appeal to divine inspiration and the divine addresses to Jacob and Laban (vs. 3 and 24) validate Jacob's version of events.[522] Maybe the only thing we can say is that God wants Jacob to return home (cf. 28:15), and that God sides with Jacob over against Laban. Humphreys compares this with "earlier accounts of God's preference for Abraham over against Pharaoh and Abimelech. In those episodes the narrator, while stressing that God is on Abraham's side, never suggests Abraham's was the just side."[523] Likewise, God appeared to Jacob in Bethel following his deceit in Gen 27. God's appearance there signifies God's election and grace. It does not mean that everything Jacob had done up to that point was truthful or approved of by God. We must be careful not to make too much of the alleged transformation that had taken place within Jacob at this point.[524] Undoubtedly, Jacob had learned a lot, but it is only in 32:9 that the narrator tells us that Jacob prays to God, and this comes at a time when Jacob fears that his planning and scheming (32:3–8) might not suffice. Jacob's life-changing encounter at Peniel is still to come.[525]

Not everyone is convinced of Jacob's reliability. Armstrong thinks that Jacob must have been confused: "He had sometimes interpreted a bright (and dubious) idea of his own, such as the duping of Laban,

---

[520] Waltke, *Genesis*, 422–423.
[521] Waltke, *Genesis*, 425–426.
[522] Waltke, *Genesis*, 425.
[523] Humphreys, *The Character of God*, 183.
[524] Waltke, *Genesis*, 422. Waltke later on qualifies that by speaking of Jacob's "slowly developing faith" (Waltke, *Genesis*, 435). See also Kodell, "Jacob Wrestles with Esau (Gen 32:23–32)," 69; Mann, *The Book of the Torah*, 56.
[525] Gen 32:22–31. More on this in Chapter 4.

as divine inspiration (31:9–13)."[526] Other commentators focus on the rhetorical qualities of Jacob's speech: "Jacob has inflated the facts in order to persuade his wives that the 'Elohim of my father' is behind his success" (Brett).[527] Similarly Humphreys, who describes God's portrayal by Jacob as a 'construct;' God has been made a "character in a story within a story;"[528] "a powerful rhetorical force in the decision he presents his wives;"[529] "a story designed to convince them to throw their lot with him."[530]

Lipton argues it is not sufficient to study Jacob's dream as a mere 'gap-filler:'[531]

> The question whether or not Jacob's dream is to be understood as having actually occurred is unlikely to have been the cause of much insomnia in the ancient world; the narrator was merely using a standard, and thoroughly acceptable rhetorical device.[532]

According to Lipton, the fact that the dream's rhetorical value has been emphasized in the narrative, suggests that it belongs to "that tradition of ancient Near Eastern tradition of dreams whose purpose was to validate the claims and confirm the position of their (usually royal) dreamers."[533] She suggests that Jacob's fabrication may lie in the fact that he presents two dreams as one.[534]

Whatever one concludes about Jacob's reliability, uncertainties remain.[535] Jacob's rebuttal and Laban's reply (vs. 36ff.) shed some new light on these questions, but they do not clarify everything. Sherwood's conclusion is tentative: "So, in the end, *I am inclined* to follow the Midrash and see the narrative of the dream as genuine gap-filling."[536] Conversely, there is the possibility that Jacob's speech could be classified as (what Sternberg calls) a 'half-direction,' "fillings voiced by characters, often unreliably."[537] Whatever we decide about Jacob's

---

[526] Armstrong, *In the Beginning*, 89.
[527] Brett, *Genesis*, 95. Similarly Eising, *Formgeschichtliche Untersuching*, 205 and 209; Kass, "Love of Woman and Love of God," 52.
[528] Humphreys, *The Character of God*, 181.
[529] Humphreys, *The Character of God*, 182.
[530] Humphreys, *The Character of God*, 182.
[531] Lipton's critique of Sherwood's approach (Lipton, *Revisions of the Night*, 115).
[532] Lipton, *Revisions of the Night*, 130.
[533] Lipton, *Revisions of the Night*, 143.
[534] Lipton, *Revisions of the Night*, 130.
[535] See also Walton, *Thou Traveller Unknown*, 162 and 168.
[536] Sherwood, "*Had God Not Been on My Side*," 302 (italics mine).
[537] Sternberg, *Poetics*, 259.

reliability, it is clear that the justification of his wealth is at the heart of his argument (vs. 9), and this is perceived flawlessly by his wives, as we will now see.

31:14–16

Rachel's and Leah's response is firm.[538] They are willing to cut off the allegiance with their father (vs. 14).[539] Their motivation is a powerful mix of perceived ill-treatment and various material considerations. The sisters speak with one voice.[540] Unlike Sarah and Hagar, they have managed to overcome their differences to form a unified front.[541] "The strife between the two sisters is nowhere explicitly resolved, but finds surcease in their joint agreement to leave their father (Gen 31:14–16)."[542] Multiple complaints are voiced: there is 'no inheritance left for them' (vs. 14);[543] their father has 'sold them' (vs. 15);[544] and he has 'devoured their money' (vs. 15). Although they give Jacob their full assent,[545] the differences between their interpretation of events and Jacob's are subtle but telling.[546] The interpretation of their speech hinges on the meaning of 'we' and 'us' in vv. 14–16. Although some instances would allow for Jacob's inclusion (e.g. "are we not regarded by him as foreigners?"), vs. 15 ("he has sold us") suggests that 'us' only refers to Rachel and Leah. This means, that where Jacob was the aggrieved party in his speech, Rachel and Leah present themselves as such in theirs.[547] As a result, God has not transferred Laban's wealth to Jacob ('to me'! vs. 9),

---

[538] "They respond with alacrity and vigor" (Wenham, *Genesis 16–50*, 272).

[539] 'Have we any share…?' is a formula to renounce allegiance (cf. 2 Sam 20:1; 1 Kgs 12:16) (Sarna, *Genesis*, 215; Westermann, *Genesis 12–36*, 492; Fokkelman, *Narrative Art in Genesis*, 162; Janzen, *Genesis 12–50*, 121).

[540] A shared lot has brought them closer together. What started in 30:14–16 seems to have further developed (see *Section* 3.3). According to Brodie, this "apparent mutual reconciliation seems to intimate the forthcoming Jacob-Laban reconciliation" (Brodie, *Genesis as Dialogue*, 327).

[541] Sherwood, "*Had God Not Been on My Side*," 306. This is one of many stories in Genesis that move from conflict to some form of resolution or accommodation (cf. Recker, *Die Erzählungen vom Patriarchen Jakob*, 213). See also Coats, *Genesis*, 218.

[542] Gammie, "Theological Interpretation," 118. Similarly Ogden Bellis, "A sister is a forever friend," 113.

[543] Their rhetorical question assumes a negative answer (Reyburn, *A Handbook on Genesis, ad loc*).

[544] The women see themselves reduced to chattel by their father (Alter, *Genesis*, 168; see *Section* 3.2).

[545] Closing imperative of vs. 16! Cf. Fokkelman, *Narrative Art in Genesis*, 157.

[546] "They accept Jacob's reconstruction of the situation in general, but they build upon it with their own particular spin" (Humphreys, *The Character of God*, 183).

[547] Cf. Humphreys, *The Character of God*, 183.

but to Jacob's wives and their children (vs. 16)![548] As in Jacob's speech, God's involvement is invoked to add weight to the argument.[549]

A striking feature of their response is the centrality of material considerations.[550] Some of these are clear enough; some are not. 'Being sold' must refer to the events in 29:15–30,[551] whereas 'being treated as foreigners' seems to indicate general ill-treatment.[552] References to 'inheritance' (vs. 14) and 'devoured our money' however, are less straightforward. Some scholars suggest that if no sons had been born to Laban, Rachel and Leah would have shared in the inheritance. With sons on the scene (30:35; 31:1) there will be no share for them.[553] Others suggest that the gift of Bilhah and Zilpah represented their share in the inheritance, so there is nothing more to come. Alternatively, God had taken away Laban's wealth and given it to Jacob, so that there would be nothing left for them; the same concern as expressed by their brothers in 31:1.[554] However, by joining Jacob, they and their sons can share in the transferred wealth. The phrase 'he has devoured our money' has been interpreted differently as well. Sarna and Morrison argue that this complaint refers to a dowry that was never paid.[555] Others think it refers to the wealth they would eventually share in, but which has now disappeared. Our interpretation of these issues influence our thinking about Rachel and Leah. Is their complaint justified, or is it indicative of mixed motives or greed?[556] It is impossible to fully reconstruct the

---

[548] Taschner, *Verheissung und Erfüllung*, 114. As in vs. 9 the legal 'taken away' is used by the speakers. "The Hebrew includes the idea of 'plunder' (see Ex. 12:36)" (Waltke, *Genesis*, 426).

[549] Humphreys, *The Character of God*, 183.

[550] Brett, *Genesis*, 95; E. Fuchs, "For I Have the Way of Women: Deception, Gender, and Ideology in Biblical Narrative," *Semeia* 42 (1988): 68–83, 72.

[551] Burrows, "The Complaint of Laban's Daughters," 265; Hamilton, *Genesis 18–50*, 289; Sarna, *Genesis*, 215; Waltke, *Genesis*, 426; Westermann, *Genesis 12–36*, 492.

[552] Burrows, "The Complaint of Laban's Daughters," 264–265.

[553] Normally, only sons would inherit in the ANE (Wenham). For more background cf. Hiers, "Transfer of Property by Inheritance," 128; Sherwood, *"Had God Not Been on My Side,"* 303 and references there.

[554] Fokkelman, *Narrative Art in Genesis*, 157. Cf. Sherwood, *"Had God Not Been on My Side,"* 288.

[555] Sarna, *Genesis*, 215. Morrison, "The Jacob and Laban Narrative," 161. See *Section 3.3* regarding Laban's disputed generosity (cf. Wenham, *Genesis 16–50*, 272). See also Hamilton, *Genesis 18–50*, 289–290 and Thompson, *The Historicity of the Patriarchal Narratives*, 274–275; Burrows, "The Complaint of Laban's Daughters," 265–266.

[556] For example, if Wenham is correct that the gift of slave-girls represented a generous dowry, then Rachel's and Leah's speech gives an impression of ingratitude and possibly greed.

backgrounds of their complaint(s).[557] However, as before, an understanding of the historical issues concerning inheritance and marriage
customs, although of interest, is probably not essential for discerning
the main thrust of the narrative. What is clear is that Rachel's and
Leah's feelings are strong enough to throw in their lot with Jacob,
and that their key-motivators are of a pragmatic and material nature,
which drive them away from Laban. No love lost there. However, their
decision does not appear to be a matter of romance either.[558] Pragmatism rules! What this episode illustrates is how material possessions,
and the associated attitudes and actions help to explain the various
relationship dynamics (both positive and negative). Laban's greed for
material advancement results in Rachel's and Leah's ill-treatment.[559] In
turn, various material considerations lead them to decide to leave their
father's house, which strengthens the unity within Jacob's family.[560]

31:17–21
Rachel's and Leah's agreement leads to an immediate departure. Jacob
'arose' and set his sons and wives on camels (vs. 17; cf. 24:61).[561] The
verb 'arose' (וַיָּקָם; in vv. 17 and 21) echoes God's command to him
(קוּם; 31:13).[562] The scene reminds us how Rebekah and her young
women 'arose' and rode on 'camels' (24:61). Finally, 'fled' and 'arose'
(vs. 21) recall Rebekah's words before Jacob's flight to Haran (27:43).[563]
Jacob is on the run again, but the camels are testimony to Jacob's new
wealth (cf. 30:43).[564]

---

[557] Cf. Hamilton, *Genesis 18–50*, 290 and reference in n. 26.

[558] "Laban's daughters are not motivated by romantic attachment to Jacob" (Sherwood, "*Had God Not Been on My Side*," 303).

[559] "Part of the hidden price of covetousness" (cf. Hab 2:6–8) (Kidner, *Genesis*, 165).
"Laban's greed for blessing, and his unjust treatment of the one who bears it, have
produced his own financial ruin and alienated him from Jacob and from his own
daughters" (Mann, *The Book of the Torah*, 58).

[560] I do not suggest here that as a result there is perfect harmony in Jacob's family.
However, they are now probably more united than ever before.

[561] No mention of Dinah (Hamilton, *Genesis 18–50*, 290).

[562] Fokkelman, *Narrative Art in Genesis*, 163.

[563] Sarna, *Genesis*, 217; Fokkelman, *Narrative Art in Genesis*, 163. Cf. Walton, *Thou
Traveller Unknown*, 163. Jacob's move is a reversal of that flight.

[564] "Yet, despite his prosperity, he leaves as he came, in flight from mortal danger"
(Kass, "Love of Woman and Love of God," 52; Cf. Taschner, *Verheissung und Erfül-
lung*, 108). Jacob had arrived on foot whereas Abraham's servant had arrived by camel
(Gen 24; see *Section 3.1*).

Verse 18 dwells on Jacob's possessions. Jacob leaves with 'all he has' (vs. 18 and 21). Twice the phrase 'that he had acquired' is used (אֲשֶׁר רָכָשׁ) and there is the repeated use of the third person pronominal suffix (his sons; his wives; his livestock; his property; his possessions).[565] The narrator wants to stress that everything belongs to Jacob and that it was legitimately acquired.[566] This will be refuted by Laban in vs. 43, but the narrator leaves us in no doubt about his opinion.[567] As noted in *Section* 1.1, all major movements in Gen 12–50 coincide with the occurrence of רְכוּשׁ.[568] Jacob's flight is no exception (vs. 18). I noted the similarities between the LORD's command in vs. 3 with his command to Abram in 12:1–3. The phrase 'that he acquired' (אֲשֶׁר רָכָשׁוּ; 12:5) reappears in 31:18. Jacob's obedience to the LORD's command is set alongside Abram's.[569] This invites us to reflect on the significance of Jacob's move.[570] Looking ahead: as Jacob amassed his wealth abroad, so Israel would come out of Egypt with many possessions (Ex 3:22; 12:35–36).[571]

Laban's sheep shearing (vs. 19) provides the perfect cover for Jacob's flight.[572] The detailed report of Jacob's possessions (and their legitimate acquisition) is now balanced by the introduction of a key-verb: 'to steal.'[573] Rachel stole her father's *teraphim* (vs. 19)[574] and Jacob 'stole

---

[565] Hamilton, *Genesis 18–50*, 291; Fuchs, "For I Have the Way of Women," 74.

[566] Sarna, *Genesis*, 215; Hamilton, *Genesis 18–50*, 291; Fokkelman, *Narrative Art in Genesis*, 162; Alter, *Genesis*, 169.

[567] Sherwood speaks aptly of 'the battle of pronominal suffixes' (Sherwood, "*Had God Not Been on My Side*," 306).

[568] Cf. 12:4; Appendix A.

[569] Wenham, *Genesis 16–50*, 273. See also Fokkelman, *Narrative Art in Genesis*, 162; Waltke, *Genesis*, 424.

[570] Fokkelman, *Narrative Art in Genesis*, 163.

[571] Cf. A.P. Ross, *Creation and Blessing: A Guide to the Study and Exposition of Genesis* (Grand Rapids, MI, USA: Baker Books, 1996), 517–518.

[572] Already noted by Rashi (Alter, *Genesis*, 169). See also Waltke, *Genesis*, 427; Sherwood, "*Had God Not Been on My Side*," 307; Sarna, *Genesis*, 216; and Frankena, "Semitic Background," 57. Maybe it is indicative of the family schism that Jacob was not invited for this festive occasion (Skinner, *Genesis*, 396).

[573] גָּנַב in vs. 19, 20, 26, 27, 30, 32, 39 and גָּזַל in vs. 31. Cf. Fishbane, *Text and Texture*, 56; Fokkelman, *Narrative Art in Genesis*, 167; Hamilton, *Genesis 18–50*, 291; Wenham, *Genesis 16–50*, 267.

[574] הַתְּרָפִים. 'Teraphim' (JPS). Translated as 'idols' by the Aramaic Targums and the Septuagint (τὰ εἴδωλα). Possibly it is a derogatory term; "it may be a contemptuous substitution word" (Sarna, *Genesis*, 216). Translated as 'household gods' by the ESV, NRVS and NIV (also in vs. 34 and 35). According to van der Toorn, this latter translation "suffers from a one-sided use of Mesopotamian material" (K. van der Toorn, "The Nature of the Biblical Teraphim in the Light of the Cuneiform Evidence," *CathBQ* 52

the heart of Laban' (vs. 20).[575] Jacob and Rachel are linked by this verb.[576] According to Fuchs this suggests both similarity and contrast. Whereas Jacob's figurative stealing "is presented as an act of self-defence, Rachel's unexplained deception seems arbitrary."[577] Fuchs suggests that because of the absence of any motivation or explanation, the narrator causes Rachel (and other women in the patriarchal narratives) to be perceived as ambiguous and deceptive.[578]

Biblical references to *teraphim* are few. Scholars have relied on extrabiblical material to elucidate its meaning. However, such evidence 'can only be suggestive.'[579] According to Alter, the *teraphim* were probably "small figurines representing the deities responsible for the well-being and prosperity of the household."[580] Some scholars think that the holder of the *teraphim* possessed the paternal authority of the head of the house.[581] As such, they were associated with the inheritance or legal title of the estate:[582]

> Rachel completes Jacob's emancipation by adding to the material possessions he took over from her father's estate the symbolic tokens of the transition. The possession of the house-gods means (…) the possession of the house, hence her right to take the child from the father and hand it over to the husband.[583]

This has been disputed by Greenberg and others.[584] Others suggest that the *teraphim* were used for divination and that by stealing them

---

(1990): 203–22, 222). They are referred to as 'gods' (אֱלֹהִים) by Laban and Jacob in vs. 30 and 32.

[575] Translated by the ESV as 'deceived.' See also Waltke, *Genesis*, 427.

[576] "Rachel is a true Jacoba, related by nature to Jacob. This is expressed in parallel thefts" (Fokkelman, *Narrative Art in Genesis*, 163). See also Janzen, *Genesis 12–50*, 122; Walton, *Thou Traveller Unknown*, 163–164.

[577] Fuchs, "For I Have the Way of Women," 74. See also Hamilton, *Genesis 18–50*, 296. According to Williams Jacob's deception "receives a positive assessment by the narrator, or, at the very least, not a negative assessment" (Williams, *Deception in Genesis*, 22). Similarly Mabee, "Judicial Proceedings," 194.

[578] Fuchs, "For I Have the Way of Women," 77–81. See also Fuchs, "Who is hiding the truth? Deceptive Women and Biblical Androcentrism."

[579] Toorn, "The Nature of the Biblical Teraphim," 205.

[580] Alter, *Genesis*, 169. See also Fokkelman, *Narrative Art in Genesis*, 163–164 (following Speiser, *Genesis*, 250–251).

[581] Morrison, "The Jacob and Laban Narrative," 161; Spanier, "Rachel's Theft."

[582] Kidner, *Genesis*, 165; Speiser, *Genesis*, 250–251; West, "The Nuzi Tablets," 70–71; Pfeiffer, *The Patriarchal Age*, 79.

[583] M. Bal, "Tricky Thematics," *Semeia* 42 (1988): 133–55, 152.

[584] Greenberg, "Another Look at Rachel's Theft of the Teraphim." See also Selman, "Comparative Customs," 110 quoting Thompson, *The Historicity of the Patriarchal Narratives*, 272–278; van Seters, *Abraham in History and Tradition*, 93–94.

Rachel aims to avoid detection.[585] According to van der Toorn they were 'ancestor statuettes' that had their place in 'family ritual' and 'necromantic queries.'[586] In view of this diversity, Sarna concludes that the nature and function of the *teraphim* "remain largely obscure, as does Rachel's motivation."[587] Mabee argues that "it is the stealing of another's property that matters."[588] Rachel's theft seriously endangers Jacob's flight.[589] According to Fokkelman Laban might not have pursued Jacob, were it not for the *teraphim*.[590] Although we may deduce from Jacob's rash vow (vs. 32) that Rachel's theft was indeed a serious offence,[591] the narrator does not offer an explicit evaluation.[592] So Jacob flees with all he has and crosses the Euphrates (vs. 21).[593] This marks an important moment in Jacob's life.[594]

31:22–24

Laban and his kinsmen pursue Jacob for seven days. Jacob has a three-day's head-start (30:22). Considering the distance from Haran to Gilead, most commentators take these numbers as symbolic, approximate or formulaic, conveying the 'terrific speed of the chase.'[595] Jacob's

---

[585] Speiser, *Genesis*, 245; Kass, "Love of Woman and Love of God," 52; Sherwood, "*Had God Not Been on My Side,*" 309 and references there. Some commentators note a link with the Joseph-cycle where an item that was used for divination was allegedly stolen (cf. Mabee, "Judicial Proceedings," 201 n. 2). See also Sarna, *Genesis*, 216 and 366 n. 7. For a more in-depth discussion on the *teraphim* cf. Taschner, *Verheissung und Erfüllung*, 115–123; Sherwood, "*Had God Not Been on My Side,*" 307–311; Hamilton, *Genesis 18–50*, 293–295; Jay, "Sacrifice, Descent and the Patriarchs," 65–66.

[586] Toorn, "The Nature of the Biblical Teraphim," 222. See also Wenham, *Genesis 16–50*, 273.

[587] Sarna, *Genesis*, 216. See also Alter, *Genesis*, 169; Waltke, *Genesis*, 427; and Fuchs, "For I Have the Way of Women" (see above). Kass suggests that Rachel is "hedging her bet on Jacob's God" (Kass, "Love of Woman and Love of God," 52).

[588] Mabee, "Judicial Proceedings," 195.

[589] Kidner, *Genesis*, 165; Kass, "Love of Woman and Love of God," 53.

[590] Fokkelman, *Narrative Art in Genesis*, 163.

[591] Fokkelman, *Narrative Art in Genesis*, 164.

[592] Williams, *Deception in Genesis*, 23. Cf. Fuchs, "For I Have the Way of Women." (see above).

[593] Literally 'the river' (אֶת־הַנָּהָר), "a term which refers specifically to the Euphrates" (Alter, *Genesis*, 169).

[594] Fokkelman calls it 'his Rubicon.' Fokkelman also notes that the description of the crossing has four words in common with 'the famous Jabbok-scene' (Fokkelman, *Narrative Art in Genesis*, 163).

[595] Alter, *Genesis*, 170. The distance from Haran to Gilead is approximately 300–400 miles. Cf. Sarna, *Genesis*, 217; Wenham, *Genesis 16–50*, 274; Alter, *Genesis*, 170; Hamilton, *Genesis 18–50*, 299. Gunkel takes the apparent difficulty to harmonize time and distance as indicative of two sources (Gunkel, *Genesis*, 335).

restrained pace enables Laban to catch up.[596] Just before Laban over-takes Jacob, God appears to Laban the Aramean[597] in a dream and says: "Be careful not to say anything to Jacob, either good or bad" (cf. 24:50).[598] According to Fokkelman, the repetition of this uncommon phrase is no coincidence.[599] "What Laban saw in Gen 24 willingly and of his own accord, must now be impressed upon him threateningly by God."[600] God intervenes at a critical time.[601] "Again God places himself squarely on the side of his elect, regardless of the balance of justice in the relations between his elect and the other."[602] According to Hamilton, God does not impose silence, but Laban is "not to prosecute and take (legal) action against Jacob."[603] God restrains Laban.[604] According to Lipton Laban is changed by the dream, which leads him to propose a covenant (31:44).

> Laban's dream (...) confirms that God is protecting the patriarch. Laban himself is forced to acknowledge this, and his subsequent report of the dream (31:29) is one of the means by which the patriarch can witness God's intervention on his behalf.[605]

The dream also reflects a change in Jacob's status.[606] God's appear-ances to Jacob confirmed his relationship with God (e.g. 28:12ff; 31:3). However, in Gen 12–50 "it is not enough that the protagonist himself is aware of his special relationship with God; it is crucial that those

---

[596] Baldwin, *The Message of Genesis 12–50*, 131; Fokkelman, *Narrative Art in Genesis*, 164.

[597] This sets the scene for the encounter between Jacob and Laban as one 'between national entities' (Alter, *Genesis*, 169). Similarly Waltke, *Genesis*, 427; Sarna, *Genesis*, 216.

[598] Cf. 24:50. Alter suggests that the idiom means "lest you speak…anything at all" (Alter, *Genesis*, 170).

[599] Fokkelman, *Narrative Art in Genesis*, 165; Lipton, *Revisions of the Night*, 155; Janzen, *Genesis 12–50*, 123.

[600] Fokkelman, *Narrative Art in Genesis*, 165.

[601] Cf. 20:3, where God appeared to Abimelech (Sarna, *Genesis*, 217; Hamilton, *Genesis 18–50*, 299; Humphreys, *The Character of God*, 184; Taschner, *Verheissung und Erfüllung*, 110). Abimelech's dream "clearly represents the closest parallel" (Lipton, *Revisions of the Night*, 150).

[602] Humphreys, *The Character of God*, 184.

[603] Hamilton, *Genesis 18–50*, 299 and n. 28. Similarly Sherwood, "*Had God Not Been on My Side*," 315.

[604] "God has corked the bottle of his aggressiveness" (Fokkelman, *Narrative Art in Genesis*, 166). Cf. Hamilton, *Genesis 18–50*, 299; Walton, *Thou Traveller Unknown*, 164.

[605] Lipton, *Revisions of the Night*, 171. See also Brett, *Genesis*, 96.

[606] Lipton, *Revisions of the Night*, 171.

around him are also aware of it."[607] God's appearance to Laban and his acknowledgement (31:29) serve that purpose.

31:25–32

Laban finally overtakes Jacob. The image of pitched tents signals impending confrontation.[608] At the heart of this long scene (31:26–54) stands the judicial dispute between Laban and Jacob and its resolution.[609] During the proceedings the "relative standing between Laban and Jacob changes fundamentally."[610] Laban starts as the *paterfamilias* who summons his son-in-law to explain himself. At the end, Jacob and Laban "operate on a more equal footing"[611] with Jacob head of his own household.[612] The scene can be subdivided as follows:

31:26–30: <u>Long speech</u> by Laban
    31:32–32a: *Short reply* by Jacob

    <u>Turning point:</u> 31:33–35: Laban's failed search

31:36–42: <u>Long speech</u> by Jacob
    31:43–44: *Short reply* by Laban; proposal for covenant[613]

Initially, Laban is on the offensive and Jacob is on the defensive. Laban's failure to find the *teraphim* is the turning point.[614] After this Jacob goes on the attack and Laban is pressed into a more defensive role. Laban opens with almost identical words to those Jacob had used in 29:25:

---

[607] Lipton, *Revisions of the Night*, 121. Consider Pharaoh to Abraham (12:17); Abimelech to Abraham (20:3ff); Abimelech to Isaac (26:28); and Pharaoh to Joseph (41:38–39). See also Fokkelman, *Narrative Art in Genesis*, 142.

[608] Sarna suggests that the dual use of the verb תָּקַע ('to thrust, drive in (pegs);' cf. Jer 6:3) is "intended to convey something of the hostile atmosphere that pervades the scene" (Sarna, *Genesis*, 217). Similarly Hamilton, *Genesis 18–50*, 300; Waltke, *Genesis*, 428.

[609] Mabee, "Judicial Proceedings"; Wenham, *Genesis 16–50*, 274.

[610] Wenham, *Genesis 16–50*, 274.

[611] Wenham, *Genesis 16–50*, 274; Sarna, *Genesis*, 221; Hamilton, *Genesis 18–50*, 313; Mabee, "Judicial Proceedings," 194.

[612] "The intention of the judicial narrative portion of our pericope is legally to establish a new family unit, to be governed henceforth by a new *paterfamilias* (Jacob)" (Mabee, "Judicial Proceedings," 205).

[613] Fokkelman, *Narrative Art in Genesis*, 164.

[614] "The narrator focuses our attention (…) as though as though the outcome of the whole interaction turns on this central scene" (Janzen, *Genesis 12–50*, 122).

'what have you done' (מַה־זֹּאת עָשִׂיתָ vs. מֶה עָשִׂיתָ here).[615] Use of this phrase by Laban signifies reversal[616] and is a building block for the palistrophic structure of the Jacob-Laban cycle.[617] Laban's indictment can be summarized as follows:

> Jacob stands accused of two counts of 'robbery' (*gnb*). First, he has 'stolen Laban's heart' by leading away (*nhg*) his daughters (secretly) as captives of the sword (v. 26). Second he has stolen Laban's 'gods' (v. 30) (…). The overall crime of which Jacob stands accused is best termed fraud or breach of trust.[618]

Laban complains that Jacob did not observe the proper formalities for leaving (vv. 26–28). However, his climactic complaint is that Jacob had stolen his 'gods' (vs. 30).[619] Some of Laban's complaints are preposterous. His accusation that Jacob has taken 'my daughters' by force (vs. 26),[620] is ironic in view of Rachel's and Leah's tacit agreement to flee (vv. 14–16).[621] It also juxtaposes Jacob's violence that is entirely imagined, with Laban's, which is for real (vs. 29).[622] Laban's expression of regret, having been denied the opportunity to send Jacob on his way with 'mirth and songs' (vs. 27), is ironic too.[623] Laban repeats God's words *ad verbatim*, indicating their efficacy in restraining Laban.[624] Laban's final complaint however, is entirely based on fact and offers the most dangerous threat to Jacob and his family.[625] Jacob addresses the first set of complaints by mentioning his fear of losing his wives (vs. 31).[626] Jacob counters Laban's accusation of theft with a rash vow:

---

[615] Waltke, *Genesis*, 429; Sarna, *Genesis*, 218. Also, cf. 3:13; 4:10; 12:18; 20:9; 26:10 (Wenham, *Genesis 16–50*, 275). See also Noegel, "Drinking Feasts," 176–177.

[616] Cf. Fuchs, "For I Have the Way of Women," 70.

[617] Another one is the kissing in 31:55 vs. 29:11 and 13 (see below).

[618] Mabee, "Judicial Proceedings," 194–195.

[619] Wenham, *Genesis 16–50*, 274; Hamilton, *Genesis 18–50*, 301; von Rad, *Genesis*, 304. Contra Mabee, "Judicial Proceedings," 194 (see below).

[620] "Not 'your wives' of course" (Fokkelman, *Narrative Art in Genesis*, 167).

[621] Waltke, *Genesis*, 429.

[622] Alter, *Genesis*, 170.

[623] "The extravagance of this fantastic scene conjured up by a past master of fleecing is self-evident" (Alter, *Genesis*, 171). Similarly Waltke, *Genesis*, 429.

[624] Cf. Fokkelman, *Narrative Art in Genesis*, 167; Hamilton, *Genesis 18–50*, 301.

[625] Laban's *coup de grace* (Sarna, *Genesis*, 218).

[626] "The use of fear to justify a course of action is as ancient as Gen 3:10" (Hamilton, *Genesis 18–50*, 301). Cf. 20:11 (Janzen, *Genesis 12–50*, 124). 'Fear' is also central in the complementary 'panel' of Gen 32–33 (Brodie, *Genesis as Dialogue*, 322).

"Anyone with whom you shall find your gods shall not live" (vs. 32).[627] Jacob continues: "in the presence of *our* kinsmen" (nice rhetorical touch!), "point out what I have that is yours, and take it."[628] The burden of proof now lies with Laban. The narrator clarifies that Jacob is unaware of Rachel's theft (vs. 32b).[629] The combination of Jacob's vow with ignorance creates tremendous tension.[630]

31:33–35

The narrator skilfully builds up suspense.[631] When Laban has searched through a whole series of tents, he finally ends up in Rachel's, who has hidden the *teraphim* in a camel's saddle and sits on them (vs. 34). Laban's search is methodical:

> What Laban does is "feel all things, one by one". An effective choice of words, this iterative *pi'el* of *mšš* (vv 34, 37), because the verb had already been used in Gen 27. There, Jacob's father was trying to learn the truth about his son by... feeling, but in vain because of a trick of Jacob's.[632]

Rachel deceives her father by saying that she cannot rise because of her menstrual period.[633] This highlights interesting parallels with Jacob's

---

[627] "A cruel 'irony of fate'" (Sternberg, *Poetics*, 164). Cf. 44:9, where a similar threat occurs "in conjunction with the allegation of theft of a sacred object" (Sarna, *Genesis*, 218; Mabee, "Judicial Proceedings," 199; see also Waltke, *Genesis*, 430; Sternberg, *Poetics*, 305). Some commentators associate Jacob's words with Rachel's early death (cf. G. Tucker, "Jacob's Terrible Burden: In the Shadow of the Text," *BR* 10, no. June (1994): 20–28 and 54, 22; Daube, "Fraud on Law for Fraud on Law," 55; Fuchs, "For I Have the Way of Women," 80). In Alter's opinion, "his peremptory words at least foreshadow her premature death in child birth" (Alter, *Genesis*, 171). See also Alter, *The Art of Biblical Narrative*, 173 where he formulates this thesis more firmly. "Like Jephtah (Judg 11:30–31), he makes a rash statement that endangers one he loves" (McKeown, *Genesis*, 150). Hepner points to an intertextuality with 37:33, where Jacob cries out "*torn, yes torn to pieces* is Joseph" (טָרֹף טֹרָף), thus indicating Jacob's belief that Joseph had died because of Jacob's oath regarding the *teraphim* (G. Hepner, "Verbal Resonance in the Bible and Intertextuality," *JSOT* 26, no. 2 (2001): 3–27, 10).

[628] The verb הַכֶּר; hiphil imperative 'point out,' 'make recognition') previously figured in Jacob's deception of Isaac (27:23) (Alter, *Genesis*, 171; Hamilton, *Genesis 18–50*, 302 n. 37). That this is no accident will become clear by the use of another verb in vs. 34 (see below).

[629] Berlin, *Poetics*, 38.

[630] Kidner, *Genesis*, 166; Fokkelman, *Narrative Art in Genesis*, 169; Wenham, *Genesis 16–50*, 276.

[631] Hamilton, *Genesis 18–50*, 303; Fokkelman, *Narrative Art in Genesis*, 170.

[632] Fokkelman, *Narrative Art in Genesis*, 170. See also Fishbane, *Text and Texture*, 51; Walton, *Thou Traveller Unknown*, 165.

[633] "A woman would simply have checked, a man would not dream of trying" (Bal, "Tricky Thematics," 151). See also N. Steinberg, "Israelite Tricksters: Their Analogues

deceit in Gen 27.[634] In both episodes the father is deceived by a younger sibling; both Rebekah and Rachel act without prompting by a male;[635] both scenes involve 'feeling' without exposing; both result in receiving a blessing obtained by deceit (cf. 31:55).[636] The fact that *teraphim* have been associated with inheritance offers another interesting parallel, but this association has been disputed (see above). What is clear is that Rachel and Jacob are a natural combination; "birds of a feather flock together." Rachel relegates Laban's 'gods' to the position of menstrual cloths.[637] Alter notes the ironic contrast between "the impotence of an irate father" versus "his biologically mature daughter," who had suffered years of "uninterrupted menses before she was able to conceive and bear her only son."[638] There is also 'a playful yet important contrast' between Jacob's God, who intervenes at key-moments and who seems in over all control, versus Laban's 'gods' who can do nothing.[639] Laban's search leads to triple nothing; 'he did not find them' (וְלֹא מָצָא; 3x).[640]

31:36–42

Initially, Rachel's theft poses a major threat to Jacob (Kidner, Fokkelman). Ironically, the missing *teraphim* divert attention away from the grumbling over the acquisition of Jacob's wealth that led to Jacob's departure. According to Mabee "Rachel's theft plays absolutely no role in motivating the judicial encounter (...) this makes the view that the dispute is centred on the theft and Laban's inability to find the gods difficult to defend."[641] Mabee probably expresses himself too strongly here. It may well be that larger grievances lurk beneath the surface

---

and Cross-Cultural Study," *Semeia* 42 (1988): 1–13, 7 and 9, on Rachel as trickster and the relation between trickery and role-reversal. Cf. E.M. Good, "Deception and Women: A Response," *Semeia* 42 (1988): 117–32, 121.

[634] Note also the use of the verb נָכַר in 27:23 and 31:32 (see above). Cf. Alter, *Genesis*, 171.

[635] I am indebted to the Revd G. Angel for this insight.

[636] Cf. Fishbane, *Text and Texture*, 51 and 56; Armstrong, *In the Beginning*, 89; Waltke, *Genesis*, 430; Hamilton, *Genesis 18–50*, 303; Jacob, *Genesis*, 620; Wenham, *Genesis 16–50*, 267.

[637] Alter, *Genesis*, 172; Waltke, *Genesis*, 430; Hamilton, *Genesis 18–50*, 303; Fokkelman, *Narrative Art in Genesis*, 170; Brett, *Genesis*, 96.

[638] Alter, *Genesis*, 172.

[639] Brueggemann, *Genesis*, 259. Similarly Sarna, *Genesis*, 219.

[640] Fokkelman, *Narrative Art in Genesis*, 171.

[641] Mabee, "Judicial Proceedings," 194.

(e.g. paternal authority; lost wealth),[642] but the accusation regarding the missing *teraphim* is the climax of the indictment.[643] It is this accusation which evokes Jacob's strongest defence. It is only when this accusation backfires that Laban lamely states his claim on Jacob's wives, children and flocks (vs. 43). By then he has lost all credibility.[644] The accusation regarding the theft of his 'gods' forms the main thrust of Laban's indictment. His failure to find them seems to diffuse his entire argument.

The undetected *teraphim* now become a catalyst for Jacob's transformation.[645] Laban strikes a foolish figure.[646] "According to ancient law, the futility of Laban's search for his property constitutes presumptive proof of Jacob's innocence."[647] The balance of power now swings to Jacob, who takes Laban to task (וַיָּרֶב from רִיב).[648] The verb רִיב also features in the conflict between the herdsmen of Abraham and Lot (13:7), and between the Philistine herdsmen and Isaac's (26:20, 21, 22).[649] These are significant links. רִיב has also been associated with legal proceedings.[650] "Jacob's speech is manifestly cast as a rhetorically devised plea of defence against a false accusation."[651] Laban as *paterfamilias* considers himself to be judge, but Jacob puts the kinsmen in that role. In vs. 32 Jacob spoke about 'our kinsmen' in vs. 32. Here he speaks of 'my kinsmen and your kinsmen' (vs. 37). This might be indicative of the impending rift.[652] At the core of Jacob's rebuttal is his

---

[642] According to Pollak this goes back to the labour contract: "Rachel steals her father's household gods and Laban uses this as an excuse to pursue Jacob and his family and to attempt to abrogate the contract" (Pollak, "Laban and Jacob," 62).

[643] von Rad, *Genesis*, 304; Kass, "Love of Woman and Love of God," 52–53.

[644] Hamilton, *Genesis 18–50*, 313.

[645] "The folly of Rachel in stealing the household gods enables Jacob to win his lawsuit" (Waltke, *Genesis*, 435).

[646] Fokkelman, *Narrative Art in Genesis*, 170–171.

[647] Sarna, *Genesis*, 219.

[648] von Rad, *Genesis*, 305; Coats, *Genesis*, 220.

[649] Hamilton, *Genesis 18–50*, 305. See *Section* 3.7.

[650] Cf. Mabee, "Judicial Proceedings"; Westermann, *Genesis 12–36*, 495 and references there; Walton, *Thou Traveller Unknown*, 161; Fokkelman, *Narrative Art in Genesis*, 168.

[651] Alter, *Genesis*, 172. "What is my offense/crime (פִּשְׁעִי)?" (vs. 36) BDB 7921, "refers in the first instance to property offenses (e.g. Ex 22:8[9])" (Wenham, *Genesis 16–50*, 276).

[652] Hamilton, *Genesis 18–50*, 306; Fokkelman, *Narrative Art in Genesis*, 174.

impeccable service record of twenty years.[653] Many scholars comment
on the apparent one-sided nature of Laban's labour contract:

> Laban's terms for Jacob's care of his flocks—making Jacob bear the
> loss of sheep and goats killed by wild animals—were harsher than the
> requirements of both Mesopotamian and biblical law (Gen 31:38–39).[654]

Arguing from a stellar track-record, Jacob aims to justify "that all the
goods now in his possession (including Laban's daughters) are right-
fully his" (vs. 41).[655] Jacob repeats the words he had spoken to his
wives; "you have changed my wages ten times" (vs. 7 and 41).[656] Understandably, he omits the blunt accusation that Laban tricked him.[657] As
before (vs. 13), Jacob's closing argument includes an appeal to divine
intervention (vs. 42).[658] If it were not for God, "you Laban would have
sent me away empty-handed!"[659] Laban does not deny Jacob's claims.
According to Waltke, 'Laban's silence condemns him.'[660] Alternatively,
Laban might recognize the futility of further arguing. Whether Jacob's
account is wholly accurate or whether it contains some level of hyper-
bole remains uncertain.[661] Despite such uncertainties, "our attitude to
Jacob is gradually softened."[662] The reader might have queried Jacob's
facts in the speech to his wives, but God's dream appearance to Laban

---

[653] Walton, *Thou Traveller Unknown*, 132; Alter, *Genesis*, 152; Hamilton, *Genesis 18–50*, 306–308.

[654] D.L. Baker, "Safekeeping, Borrowing and Rental," *JSOT* 31, no. 1 (2006): 27–42, 34. See also Alter, *Genesis*, 173; Morrison, "The Jacob and Laban Narrative," 157; Waltke, *Genesis*, 432; Hamilton, *Genesis 18–50*, 308; Wenham, *Genesis 16–50*, 277.

[655] Mabee, "Judicial Proceedings," 204. Note the recurrence of 'served' and 'wages' (cf. Rendsburg, *The Redaction of Genesis*, 63–65). Laban's obsessions with property may be inferred from vv. 38–39 (Fokkelman, *Narrative Art in Genesis*, 175).

[656] Herding contracts would be reviewed annually (Postgate, "Some Old Babylonian Shepherds and Their Flocks," 2; Morrison, "The Jacob and Laban Narrative," 158; Hartley, *Genesis*, 272).

[657] Alter, *Genesis*, 173.

[658] Cf. Mann, *The Book of the Torah*, 58. 'Everything is credited to God' (Brueggemann, *Genesis*, 258). Gunkel has noted similarities with Ps 124 (Gunkel, *Genesis*, 339). For Westermann, the climax of this episode (Westermann, *Genesis 12–36*, 501). Similarly Wenham, *Genesis 16–50*, 278: "This last remark (…) is much more than the deci-sive climax to his speech of self-justification. It is the summary of the whole story of Jacob's life, at least in Harran."

[659] The same term appears in Deut 15:13–14 (see comments on 30:31; cf. Sarna, *Genesis*, 211). See also Ex 3:21 (Wenham, *Genesis 16–50*, 277; Sherwood, "*Had God Not Been on My Side*," 338; Brueggemann, *Genesis*, 258; Waltke, *Genesis*, 432).

[660] Waltke, *Genesis*, 423.

[661] Walton criticizes Fokkelman for playing down the difficulties for the reader in this matter (Walton, *Thou Traveller Unknown*, 162).

[662] Walton, *Thou Traveller Unknown*, 167.

and Laban's unreasonable attitude to Jacob (e.g. vs. 43), results in a growing sympathy for Jacob. Possibly this is the sort of 'complex response' the narrator is aiming for.[663]

31:43–32:1[664]

Roles have reversed: "Laban, originally the plaintiff has become the criminal. Jacob, originally the criminal, has become the plaintiff."[665] Having received the full brunt of Jacob's accusation, Laban's defence is rather pathetic.[666] Laban still claims title to Jacob's wives, children and flocks (vs. 43), but possibly realizing the weakness of his position due to his failure to recover the *teraphim*, he proposes to make a covenant. "When foreigners seek to make covenants or oaths with the patriarchs, it is an acknowledgment of the latters' superiority (cf. 21:22–24; 26:26–31."[667] Jacob now achieves a similar position to that of Isaac and Abraham. In response, Jacob takes a stone and sets it up as a pillar (vs. 43). Jacob had done the same at Bethel.[668] This suggests that events should be seen in light of 28:10–22.[669] Laban and Jacob now act on an equal footing.[670] The monument is named by both parties,[671] and will mark the border between Jacob and Laban 'the Aramean' (31:24).[672] This can be seen as an initial contour in the fulfilment of

---

[663] Cf. Sternberg, *Poetics*, 55 (as quoted before).

[664] Throughout this study I follow the MT verse-numbering (see *Section* 4.2.1); e.g. 32:1; ET 31:55......32:33; ET 32:32.

[665] Hamilton, *Genesis 18–50*, 308.

[666] Sarna, *Genesis*, 220; Hamilton, *Genesis 18–50*, 313.

[667] Wenham, *Genesis 16–50*, 279. Similarly Waltke, *Genesis*, 433. Cf. Fokkelman, *Narrative Art in Genesis*, 187.

[668] מַצֵּבָה Cf. 28:18, 22 and comments there. See also 31:13. Noegel detects a 'punning *inclusio*' with 29:10, where Jacob 'rolled' (from גָּלַל) the 'stone' (אֶבֶן) off Laban's well (Noegel, "Drinking Feasts," 179; cf. Rendsburg, *The Redaction of Genesis*, 64; Wenham, *Genesis 16–50*, 267).

[669] Janzen, *Genesis 12–50*, 125; Brodie, *Genesis as Dialogue*, 329.

[670] Sarna, *Genesis*, 221; Hamilton, *Genesis 18–50*, 313; Mabee, "Judicial Proceedings," 194; Wenham, *Genesis 16–50*, 274.

[671] "In legal terms, it means that he [Laban] tacitly acknowledges Jacob as constituting a separate, independent social entity of equal status. This is reflected in narrative in several ways: there are two tone markers, two means, two place-names; the deity is twice invoked, and by two separate names" (Sarna, *Genesis*, 221). Source-critics have taken these duplications as proof for multiple sources (J and E), although no consensus exists on how particular sections can be attributed to a particular source (cf. Hamilton, *Genesis 18–50*, 312; Wenham, *Genesis 16–50*, 279; Speiser, *Genesis*, 248; von Rad, *Genesis*, 307; cf. Walton, *Thou Traveller Unknown*, 170–171).

[672] Sherwood, *"Had God Not Been on My Side,"* 277.

the land promise.[673] The covenant is sealed by oath, sacrifice and meal.[674] Jacob's invitation to 'share a meal' in vs. 54 (לֶאֱכָל־לָחֶם), can be connected with his vow in 28:20 ("and give me bread to eat"; לֶחֶם לֶאֱכֹל). "God has fulfilled the desires of Jacob's heart physically. He does have bread to eat."[675] However, "Jacob is returning to his father's house not just with basic food and clothing but with considerable wealth."[676] The next morning Laban "kissed his grandchildren and his daughters and blessed them" (32:1). Kissing frames the Jacob-Laban cycle.[677] No kissing with Jacob this time![678] And so Laban and Jacob part ways.[679]

3.6.3   Concluding Remarks

Material possessions and material concerns are critical ingredients for this episode:

- They appear in every speech of this episode;
- Jacob's wealth is cause of concern for Laban's sons (31:1);
- Jacob's speech to his wives is aimed to justify his wealth;
- Material concerns cause Rachel and Leah to flee with Jacob;
- The narrator dwells on Jacob's possessions and on the legitimate way they were acquired (vv. 17–18); in contrast to the multiple references to 'stealing;'
- Undoubtedly, Jacob's vast herds are a factor in allowing Laban and his armed group to catch up;
- In the final confrontation between Jacob and Laban, 'wages' and 'who owns what' are at the heart of the dispute yet again;

---

[673] Taschner, *Verheissung und Erfüllung*, 129; Wenham, *Story as Torah*, 22. "Family struggle is made an etiology for political history" (Alter, *Genesis*, 175. See also Brett, *Genesis*, 96).

[674] Cf. McCree, "The Covenant Meal in the Old Testament"; Sarna, *Genesis*, 221; Kidner, *Genesis*, 167; Alter, *Genesis*, 176; Waltke, *Genesis*, 434–435; Hamilton, *Genesis 18–50*, 315. "With this ceremony of irrevocable contract, the labour negotiation between Laban and Jacob had come to a truly final conclusion" (Pollak, "Laban and Jacob," 62).

[675] Hamilton, *Genesis 18–50*, 316.

[676] Brett, *Genesis*, 97.

[677] Cf. 29:11, 13; 31:55. Brueggemann, *Genesis*, 249. See also Rendsburg, *The Redaction of Genesis*, 64.

[678] Hartley, *Genesis*, 278.

[679] Nachman Levine, "The Curse and the Blessing: Narrative Discourse Syntax and Literary Form," *JSOT* 27, no. 2 (2002): 189–99, 194–195.

- Material possessions that were at the heart of the struggle between Jacob and Laban implicitly feature in its resolution. Jacob is allowed to keep all he has.

3.7   SUMMARY

The Jacob-Laban cycle offers a fascinating mix of perspectives, subtle insights and dramatic developments which are communicated through narrative art of the highest level. It displays great inner cohesion with individual episodes tightly integrated with the rest of the Jacob-Laban narrative and beyond:[680]

> At each stage we deal with individuals and their stories piecemeal, each with a plot and integrity of its own. But then each is part of a whole, each story part of the main story, and the complex web of intertextuality invites the reader to see everything together.[681]

It is now time to 'see everything together.' I will summarize my findings for Gen 29–31 under now familiar headings:

Relationships
Jacob's stay in Haran takes place against a background of shattered relationships and unresolved conflict (Gen 27). Although Jacob's arrival is marked by familial bonhomie, the relationship between Jacob and Laban is soon reduced to one of 'service' and 'wages.' This relationship further deteriorates when Laban causes Leah (instead of Rachel) to spend the wedding night with Jacob, resulting in a double marriage. Laban's deceit can be seen as a conduit of *lex talionis* for Jacob's deceit in Gen 27. Laban will suffer his comeuppance through the loss of wealth and the separation from his daughters and grandchildren.[682] Consequences of deceit in Genesis have serious repercussions. Laban's

---

[680] Wenham, *Genesis 16–50*, 228; Fokkelman, *Narrative Art in Genesis*; Taschner, *Verheissung und Erfüllung*, 85; Walton, *Thou Traveller Unknown*, 127. See opening comments of this chapter.

[681] Walton, *Thou Traveller Unknown*, 173.

[682] Noegel, "Drinking Feasts," 178–179. Described as 'poetic justice' by others. "Laban's greed robs him, leaving him without wealth or daughters and their children" (Waltke, *Genesis*, 436). Laban was "paying part of the hidden price of all covetousness (Hab 2:6–8)" (Kidner, *Genesis*, 165). See also Sarna, *Genesis*, 219 who describes Rachel's deceit as 'a final act of retribution.' Similarly Kass, "Love of Woman and Love of God," 53.

deceit plants conflict in the midst of Jacob's own family that will linger for the rest of Jacob's life. The resolution of this conflict is a central theme in the Joseph-cycle.

All human relationships in Gen 29–31 move from stability to conflict (e.g. Jacob-Laban; Leah-Rachel), before moving to some form of resolution. Coats is probably too pessimistic by interpreting the Jacob story as one of 'family conflict without reconciliation.'[683] However, the opposite statement would be too positive. According to Brueggemann "the entire narrative of Jacob and Laban (…) is one long recital of conflict (…) even at the end, there is only a truce, not a resolution."[684] I think Recker achieves the right balance:

> In vielen Facetten und auf spannende Weise spielen die Erzähler der Genesis Konfliktsituationen durch mit dem Ziel, einen modus vivendi, eine Situation des Ausgleichs der widerstrebenden Kräfte zu finden, sei es indem man sich im Einvernehmen trennt oder sei es indem man das Zusammenleben auf eine neue Art klar und unmißverständlich regelt.[685]

The final settlement between Jacob and Laban is testimony to what Genesis seems to consider a desirable form of national engagement. Philistines, Edomites and Arameans might be troublesome, but to reach some form of settlement with them is better than to engage in ongoing conflict.[686]

Material Possessions
Jacob's increase of children and flocks are at the heart of the Jacob-cycle. Jacob, arrives in Haran as a destitute refugee, but leaves a rich man. Material possessions and concerns about material advancement and security are present in every episode of the Jacob-Laban cycle. At some point Jacob, Laban, Laban's sons and daughters all express material desires or concerns (by word or deed). At low-points in the narrative, humans are treated as nameless possessions (cattle?); Leah and Rachel in Gen 29, and Jacob in Gen 30.[687] In addition, in every conflict material desires and/or concerns play a role:

---

[683] Coats, *Genesis*, 220 and 222 ("Jacob and Laban agree to be enemies"). See also Walton, *Thou Traveller Unknown*, 180.
[684] Brueggemann, *Genesis*, 251.
[685] Recker, *Die Erzählungen vom Patriarchen Jakob*, 213.
[686] Cf. Wenham, *Story as Torah*, 39 and 148.
[687] Bilhah's and Zilpah's fate may illustrate this point as well, but they are only of peripheral interest to the narrator.

- The conflict between Jacob and Laban finds its origin in Laban's greed;
- The conflict between Leah and Rachel is a result of Laban's wedding arrangements, which originate in Laban's greed;
- Inheritance-related concerns may play a part in the ensuing battle to generate Jacob's offspring;
- Jacob's wealth leads to tension with Laban and features predominantly in their final settlement;
- The only time in the narrative where Laban's sons get a voice, they express their dissatisfaction with the increase of Jacob's wealth;
- In Jacob's speech to his wives and in their response, Jacob's wealth is at the heart of the matter.

Attitudes and actions associated with material possessions are indicative of the state of the various relations in Gen 29–31 and of their development. Material possessions and associated attitudes are at the heart of the various conflicts, but they also feature as an essential element in finding resolution. Rachel's decision to 'share' Jacob with Leah seems to have been a turning point in their relationship, as evident in their united stance at the time of Jacob's flight. In the conflict between Jacob and Laban, striving for material gain at the expense of 'relationship' is a recurring feature. However, Laban's decision to allow Jacob to keep his possessions (following divine intervention) is an essential element in the resolution of their conflict. This seems to be the pattern in Genesis. The 'natural state' appears to be one where 'relationship' takes precedence over 'material possessions and/or concerns.' As soon as material concerns, desires or attitudes take precedence over 'relationship,' conflict is inevitable. Examples of this are the conflict between the herdsmen of Abraham and Lot (Gen 13); the conflict between Philistine and Isaac's herdsmen (Gen 26); the battle over birthright and blessing between Jacob and Esau; the conflict between Jacob and Laban; and the conflict between Leah and Rachel (Jacob being the 'object' of contention). As noted before, the root ריב occurs in three places in Genesis: In 13:7 (Abraham-Lot); 26:20, 21, 22 (Isaac-Philistines); and 31:36 (Jacob-Laban). In every one of these episodes, material possessions and/or concerns about material security or wellbeing (e.g. wells) are at the heart of the conflict. Every one of these conflicts is eventually resolved, and each resolution involves a concession of a material nature. A paradigmatic example of conflict resolution is Gen 13, where Abraham's and Lot's herdsmen quarrel over wells.[688] Abraham takes the generous initiative to resolve that conflict (13:8–9). God's approval may be inferred by the fact that God immediately appears to Abraham following the resolution of that conflict with an emphatic confirmation of God's promises to him.[689] "God repays both deception and acts of kindness in kind."[690] In Gen 26, the strife is again over wells. Abimelech proposes to make a covenant, which includes a sharing of the wells that have been discovered. This is not spelled out in the agreement, but is in effect what happens.[691] Another possible example is Rachel's conception, following her willingness to share Jacob with Leah.[692] In the final settlement between Jacob and Laban, Laban allows Jacob to keep everything he has. What these three stories have in common is that conflict arose when material concerns/possessions took precedence over relationship, and that these conflicts reached some form of resolution when concessions were made, restoring the proper balance between material concerns and relationship values. The conflict between Jacob and Esau, and its resolution will very much demonstrate this as well.[693]

At the beginning of this chapter I asked the questions whether it is right to speak of Jacob's 'success' (Rendsburg)[694] and whether it is appropriate to describe Jacob as 'blessed' (Taschner).[695] In the context of the various human relationships in Gen 29–31 we have seen that material possessions are at the heart of conflict and of conflict resolution. In Armstrong's opinion

> Jacob was able to achieve the outer marks of a blessed life but not the interior harmony and liberation of blessing, and this failure vitiated the rest. His abundant progeny had been conceived in an atmosphere of hatred, and his wealth achieved by the guile of the serpent.[696]

Jacob worked really hard for his wealth (cf. 31:38–42), but to address Jacob's blessedness in more depth, we need to consider God's involvement.

---

[688] Janzen, *Old Testament Ethics*, 9–12.
[689] See *Section* 1.1.
[690] Noegel, "Drinking Feasts," 179.
[691] See *Section* 2.3.
[692] See *Section* 3.4.
[693] See Chapter 4.
[694] Rendsburg, *The Redaction of Genesis*, 66.
[695] Taschner, *Verheissung und Erfüllung*, 85.
[696] Armstrong, *In the Beginning*, 89.

God

The Jacob-Laban narrative is framed by Jacob's encounter with divine messengers[697] and must be seen in light of God's promises at Bethel.[698] In Gen 29–31 God's involvement differs markedly from episode to episode.[699] In some episodes God does not seem to be present, although his 'fingerprints are all over' (e.g. 29:1–14).[700] Sometimes God seems to be entirely absent (e.g. 30:25–43). In other episodes his role is explicitly mentioned (e.g. 29:31; 30:22; 31:3 and 24). It is only at the end of his twenty-year stay in Haran that Jacob is addressed by God again (31:3). What is God's involvement in Jacob's increase? In the child-bearing episode God is portrayed as the giver of life. The same must be true for the sheep-bearing episode (cf. Gen 1:20–25), although God's involvement is not specifically mentioned. This might illustrate the 'deep-seated complementarity' of these two panels (Brodie). Gen 30:25–43 emphasizes the human involvement in the acquisition of Jacob's wealth. Although God is the giver of all life (cf. 29:31–30:24), supernatural means were probably not required to explain Jacob's extraordinary success, despite Jacob's rhetoric that suggests otherwise (Gen 30 vs. 31). Walton comments on this contrast that "in one case, it is Jacob's cunning and skill that brings about success, in the others it is God's blessing. Perhaps in the end, we are meant to see the two aspects as being two sides of the same coin."[701] This would be close to a dialogical understanding à la Brodie.[702] Walton also suggests that this "un-clarity points to the complex task of discerning God's part in human affairs."[703] God's role is much clearer towards the end

---

[697] 28:12–15; 32:1–3 (Fishbane, *Text and Texture*, 53–54; Rendsburg, *The Redaction of Genesis*, 62–63).

[698] Brett, *Genesis*, 97.

[699] For a more in-depth analysis cf. Eising, *Formgeschichtliche Untersuching*, 416–427; Walton, *Thou Traveller Unknown*, Chapter 5 (especially 177–180) and Humphreys, *The Character of God*, Chapter 7. Walton notes a greater difficulty in detecting the work of God in the Jacob cycle than the Abraham cycle (Walton, *Thou Traveller Unknown*, 131–132).

[700] Brueggemann describes God as 'this hidden but effective inverter' (Brueggemann, *Genesis*, 259).

[701] Walton, *Thou Traveller Unknown*, 179. One could argue that for cunning to succeed, God's aid is needed in a theo-centric worldview (I am indebted to the Revd G. Angel for this suggestion).

[702] Brodie, *Genesis as Dialogue*, 315–319. Lipton (following Y. Amit, "The Dual Causality Principle and its Effect on Biblical Literature," *VT* 37, no. 4 (1987): 385–400) speaks of 'dual-causality' (Lipton, *Revisions of the Night*, 140ff.).

[703] Walton, *Thou Traveller Unknown*, 168.

of the Jacob-Laban narrative, where God's intervention (31:24) must account for the fact that Jacob can keep all his possessions and continue his journey. The narrative suggests that God was indeed involved in every phase of Jacob's wealth generation, but that his involvement is sometimes more identifiable than at other times. In view of God's promises at Bethel (28:13–15), we must conclude that God has indeed been 'with Jacob' and that the promise of offspring has taken a giant leap forward. God is also well on his way to bring Jacob back to the Promised Land. Even the land-promise seems to have moved forward with the agreement over a border between Laban and Jacob. God has provided so much more than Jacob's basic demands of "bread to eat and clothing to wear" (28:20–22).

Traditionally, fertility and prosperity have been considered expressions of divine blessing.[704] Considering the level of conflict in Gen 29–31 however, it seems too simple to label Jacob's wealth and offspring as unalloyed blessings. As with the birth of children, Jacob's wealth is the result of a complex interplay between human and divine involvement.[705] One exponent of that interplay is the interaction between divine revelation and human response.[706] At the end of *Section* 3.4.3 I concluded that the child-bearing episode demonstrates the Creation-Fall perspective that pervades the patriarchal narratives. The same is true for the acquisition of Jacob's wealth. Indeed, "it seems impossible for humanity, in its exile from Eden, to enjoy unmixed blessing."[707]

Finally, a reflection on Jacob's relationship with God: although Jacob probably has learned some valuable lessons during his difficult stay in Haran it seems too early to speak of a visible transformation in Jacob's character.[708] In the next chapter, Jacob is forced to abandon his fierce self-reliance and it is probably at that stage that we can really speak of transformation, accompanied by an altogether different blessing (32:29).

---

[704] See *Section* 2.2.
[705] Cf. Humphreys, *The Character of God*, 179.
[706] E.g. God's command to Jacob in 31:3, and Jacob's response, and God's instruction to Laban (31:24) and his response.
[707] Armstrong, *In the Beginning*, 86.
[708] Cf. Waltke, *Genesis*, 399; Mann, *The Book of the Torah*, 58–59 and 168 n. 11; Wenham, *Genesis 16–50*, 237.

CHAPTER FOUR

JACOB IN CANAAN II (GEN 32–35)

4.1 INTRODUCTION

The story line that was interrupted by Jacob's flight is now resumed (27:41ff.).[1] Jacob has to face his brother. In the palistrophic structure of the Jacob-cycle, Gen 32–35 stands opposite Gen 25–28 and brings the cycle to a close.[2] Themes that were introduced and developed in Gen 25–28, now re-emerge and move towards their conclusion.[3] Gen 32 progresses slowly towards Jacob's climactic meeting with Esau (33:1–17).[4] However, Jacob's struggle with 'a man' (32:22–32) that immediately precedes this is the most profound and mysterious episode in the entire cycle.[5] Therefore it is probably better to speak of a twin-peak climax.[6] According to Walton "it is evident from the structure [in Gen 32–33] that a divine-human contrast is in operation."[7] Gen 33:18–20 can be seen as a conclusion of Jacob's return to the Promised Land and as a bridge to the episode with the Shechemites (Gen 34).[8] Within the Jacob-cycle Gen 34 stands opposite Isaac's encounter with

---

[1] Although there are similarities between the resolutions of the Jacob-Laban conflict (Gen 31) and the Jacob-Esau conflict (Gen 32–33) there is nothing evident in the former that addresses the latter (Cf. Wenham, *Genesis 16–50*, 287; Brodie, *Genesis as Dialogue*, 324–325; Brueggemann, *Genesis*, 260).

[2] Rendsburg, *The Redaction of Genesis*, 53–54. Rendsburg basically follows Fishbane, *Text and Texture* with some minor adjustments. See the opening paragraphs of Chapter 2.

[3] Cf. Wenham, *Genesis 16–50*, 288; Coats, *Genesis*, 228; van Seters, *Prologue to History*, 302; Taschner, *Verheissung und Erfüllung*, 140; Rendsburg, *The Redaction of Genesis*, 59–63; Fishbane, *Text and Texture*, 51–52.

[4] Twenty years with Laban were covered by three chapters. Now two chapters are taken to cover two-three days. This slowing down appears to be a deliberate narrative strategy to prepare us for the climax of the cycle (cf. Taschner, *Verheissung und Erfüllung*, 144; von Rad, *Genesis*, 257; Eising, *Formgeschichtliche Untersuching*, 144; Fokkelman, *Narrative Art in Genesis*, 195).

[5] "One of the Bible's most imposing religious encounters" (Brueggemann, *Genesis*, 261).

[6] Cf. Brueggemann, *Genesis*, 262.

[7] Walton, *Thou Traveller Unknown*, 181. Similarly Brueggemann, *Genesis*, 261; Waltke, *Genesis*, 437; Westermann, *Genesis 12–36*, 504.

[8] "It is characteristic of Genesis to have a trailer for what follows at the close of the previous section (e.g. 4:25–26; 9:18–29; 32:2–3 [1–2])" (Wenham, *Genesis 16–50*, 287).

the Philistines in Gen 26, and serves a similar function. Gen 35 brings the Jacob-cycle to a close.

So many scholars have commented on the complex origins and developmental history of Gen 32–35 that it is difficult to summarize succinctly the multitude of source- and redaction critical insights that have been generated.[9] My main focus will be to make sense of the text in its current form.[10] I will demonstrate that (again) material possessions and associated attitudes and actions are key-ingredients to the narrative. I will study these in their own right, but I will also test the validity of the various proposals that were derived in earlier chapters. Many things that have been discovered so far will be confirmed, but there are some new twists as well (Gen 34!).

4.2 Jacob Prepares to Meet Esau (Gen 32:2–22)

4.2.1 *Introduction*

This section can be subdivided into four parts that contrast the 'vertical' and 'horizontal' dimensions of the narrative.[11] The high level of continuity of the narrative in its final form is recognized and agreed upon by most scholars.[12] The tendency among earlier and later source-critics is to assign this entire passage to J.[13] Jacob's encounter with angels (32:2–3) and prayer (32:10–13) are juxtaposed with Jacob's practical arrangements for his meeting with Esau (32:4–9 and 32:14–22). Another fearful meeting awaits him, which will take him entirely by surprise (32:23–33).[14] The binary nature of this narrative is evident throughout Gen 32–33: two camps; two meetings; two brothers.

---

[9] Cf. Wenham, *Genesis 16–50*, 288–289.

[10] E.g. von Rad, *Genesis*, 309–310; Brueggemann, *Genesis*, 261; Walton, *Thou Traveller Unknown*, 194.

[11] Throughout this study I follow the MT verse-numbering. For Gen 32, the verse-numbering in the English text (ET) is one lower than the MT; e.g. 32:1; ET 31:55....32:33; ET 32:32.

[12] E.g. Skinner, *Genesis*, 412. See also Wenham, *Genesis 16–50*, 289.

[13] Cf. Wenham, *Genesis 16–50*, 289; Coats, *Genesis*, 223. Gunkel and Speiser assume that the Mahanaim episodes is from E (Gunkel, *Genesis*, 342; Speiser, *Genesis*, 255).

[14] According to Westermann, Jacob's two encounters with the divine are "clearly recognizable as originally independent narratives" (Westermann, *Genesis 12–36*, 504. Cf. Coats, *Genesis*, 228; Speiser, *Genesis*, 255).

It seems as if Jacob's story is played out on two levels that must be interpreted in conjunction with each other.[15]

4.2.2 *Commentary*

32:2–3

Following Laban's departure, Jacob 'went on his way' (cf. 28:20) and is met by 'the angels of God.'[16] There are textual arguments to include these verses with the previous section,[17] but they can also been seen as introduction of what follows. Both positions have merit.[18] Gen 32: 2–3 has several links with Gen 28:10–22.[19] The encounters with 'angels of God' separate the Jacob-Laban narrative from the Jacob-Esau narrative.[20] Both occur on the border of the Promised Land.[21] The relatively rare verb פָּגַע occurs in 28:11 and 32:2.[22] In both instances, Jacob expresses something about his experience, and names the place using the exact same formula (28:19; 32:3).[23] According to Kidner, the Mahanaim experience offers Jacob "a reminder and new foretaste of Bethel."[24] There are also differences, and here we come to consider the

---

[15] Cf. Speiser, *Genesis*, 256; Armstrong, *In the Beginning*, 90; E. Fox, *Genesis and Exodus: A New English Rendition with Commentary and Notes* (New York, USA: Schocken Books, 1983), 131; Waltke, *Genesis*, 438.

[16] "The words 'go' and 'way' are nowhere[else] together in the story of Jacob, except in…Jacob's vow at Bethel, 28.20" (Fokkelman, *Narrative Art in Genesis*, 197). Cf. Walton, *Thou Traveller Unknown*, 182.

[17] According to Sailhamer, the chiastic arrangement of וַיֵּלֶךְ וַיָּשָׁב לִמְקֹמוֹ וְיַעֲקֹב הָלַךְ לְדַרְכּוֹ לָבָן suggests that this section belongs to the previous scene (cf. Sailhamer, *Genesis*, notes on 32:1–2). See also discussion in Wenham, *Genesis 16–50*, 266 and 286.

[18] Cf. Mann, *The Book of the Torah*, 59.

[19] Cf. Fokkelman, *Narrative Art in Genesis*, 197–199; Taschner, *Verheissung und Erfüllung*, 141; Terino, "A Text Linguistic Study of the Jacob Narrative," 52 and 58–59; Richter, "Das Gelübde als theologische Rahmung der Jakobsüberlieferungen," 42ff.; Rendsburg, *The Redaction of Genesis*, 62–63.

[20] מַלְאֲכֵי אֱלֹהִים; This phrase only appears in Genesis in 28:12 and 32:2. Cf. Hamilton, *Genesis 18–50*, 317; Westermann, *Genesis 12–36*, 505; Taschner, *Verheissung und Erfüllung*, 141.

[21] Cf. von Rad, *Genesis*, 309; Fokkelman, *Narrative Art in Genesis*, 198; Alter, *Genesis*, 177; Waltke, *Genesis*, 437. Sailhamer suggests this resonates with the angel guarding the Garden of Eden (3:24) (Sailhamer, *Genesis, ad loc.*)

[22] Only other occurrence in Genesis is 23:8.

[23] Fokkelman, *Narrative Art in Genesis*, 198; Westermann, *Genesis 12–36*, 505. Long, *The Problem of Etiological Narrative*, 39–40; Hamilton, *Genesis 18–50*, 317. Cf. Jacob's naming of Peniel (Waltke, *Genesis*, 439).

[24] Kidner, *Genesis*, 167. Before Jacob could return to Bethel, he had to address his past (cf. Kidner, *Genesis*, 167; Baldwin, *The Message of Genesis 12–50*, 134). See *Section 4.5*.

anticipatory quality of this episode. In Bethel, God appears to Jacob and makes specific promises. This does not happen at Mahanaim.[25] Gen 28:17 notes that Jacob 'was afraid.' Such fear appears to be absent in the Mahanaim encounter, but is associated with Esau's approach a few verses later (32:9, 13).[26] Bethel was predominantly an affirming experience for Jacob, but the Mahanaim encounter seems more ambiguous. Several commentators assume that the angels signify 'safe conduct,' but maybe there is more to consider.[27] After angels of God (מַלְאֲכֵי אֱלֹהִים) meet with Jacob, he sends 'messengers' (מַלְאָכִים; vs. 4, 7) to Esau.[28] The military language ('camp') resonates with Esau's approaching militia of four hundred men.[29] The verb פָּגַע may have threatening connotations.[30] The angels are silent, and so is Esau. Esau's silence is interpreted as ominous by Jacob (vv. 8–9). After all, Esau's last recorded words constituted a murderous threat (27:41).[31] As a result, Jacob splits his party 'into two camps' (לִשְׁנֵי מַחֲנוֹת; vs. 8). Note Jacob's earlier naming of מַחֲנָיִם; dual for 'camps' (32:3).[32] Waltke suggests that Jacob's safe passage past the angels assures him of "God's protective presence (...), while also preparing him to be on his guard."[33] Houtman concludes that it is not evident "whether the encounter with the messengers of

---

[25] At Peniel (32:22–32) Jacob will encounter the divine again. Both the Mahanaim and Peniel episodes link back to Bethel. Note that the sun that set in 28:11, arises in 32:31 (cf. Fokkelman, *Narrative Art in Genesis*, ad loc; see below).

[26] Hamilton, *Genesis 18–50*, 317.

[27] Brueggemann, *Genesis*, 262. Cf. Strickman, *Ibn Ezra's Commentary on the Pentateuch: Genesis*, 310; Kidner, *Genesis*, 167; Hartley, *Genesis*, 281. Note the parallel with Josh 5:13–15 (Westermann, *Genesis 12–36*, 505).

[28] Some commentators suggest that the sight of angels inspire Jacob to send messengers to Esau (cf. Fokkelman, *Narrative Art in Genesis*, 199; Waltke, *Genesis*, 441).

[29] Fokkelman even translates מַחֲנֵה אֱלֹהִים זֶה as 'this is God's army' (Fokkelman, *Narrative Art in Genesis*, 198).

[30] E.g. Num 35:21; Josh 2:16; Ruth 2:22. C. Houtman, "What Did Jacob See in His Dream at Mahanaim?," *VT* 28 (1978): 37–44, 39–40; Hamilton, *Genesis 18–50*, 317; Waltke, *Genesis*, 440 n. 193; Mann, *The Book of the Torah*, 59. According to Waltke, Gen 32:1 grammatically and contextually best suits this threatening aspect of the verb (441).

[31] Sailhamer, *Genesis*, ad loc.

[32] "In the beginning of the narrative the dual of the name is given no significance" (Hamilton, *Genesis 18–50*, 318). Similarly Eising, *Formgeschichtliche Untersuching*, 102 and Taschner, *Verheissung und Erfüllung*, 141. According to Kidner this refers to Jacob's realization that his own camp was matched by another (Kidner, *Genesis*, 167). See also Houtman, "What Did Jacob See in His Dream at Mahanaim?," 40–42; Fokkelman, *Narrative Art in Genesis*, 199; Waltke, *Genesis*, 441; Alter, *Genesis*, 177; Janzen, *Genesis 12–50*, 127; Brett, *Genesis*, 98.

[33] Waltke, *Genesis*, 441 quoting Roop, *Genesis*, 209.

God has a hostile or amicable character."[34] This uncertainty may well be intentional.[35] The interaction between the allusions to Bethel, which are positive and hopeful, and the perceived threat of Esau, that will soon present itself, create palpable tension and suspense. It is within this tension that events unfold.[36] At this point, Jacob (and the reader) must reflect on God's promises and proven faithfulness in the face of Esau's (perceived) threat. Which will prevail? "Gottes Glaubwürdigkeit steht angesichts der herannahenden Bedrohung durch Esau genau an diesen Punkt der Jakoberzählung auf dem Spiel."[37] Will God safeguard Jacob's 'peaceful' return home (בְּשָׁלוֹם; 28:21) or not?[38]

32:4–9

Jacob takes the initiative to engage Esau, but is careful to keep a safe distance.[39] First he sends messengers 'before him' (vs. 4), followed by droves of cattle accompanied by servants later on (vs. 17ff.).[40] It is only after his nocturnal struggle (32:23ff.) that Jacob goes 'before' somebody else (33:3).[41] The description of the messengers' destination is interesting: "to Esau his brother in the land of Seir, the country of Edom." How Jacob knew where to find his brother is beyond the narrative, but the description of Esau as 'his brother'[42] and the mention of the land of Seir and the country of (שָׂדֶה lit. 'field') Edom evoke memories

---

[34] Houtman, "What Did Jacob See in His Dream at Mahanaim?," 38. Similarly Gunkel, *Genesis*, 343; Mann, *The Book of the Torah*, 59; Walton, *Thou Traveller Unknown*, 182. Westermann and Wenham assume that the most likely option is amicable (Westermann, *Genesis 12–36*, 505; G.J. Wenham, *Genesis* (NBC; Leicester, UK: Inter-Varsity Press, 1994), 281).

[35] "J characteristically leaves it open what this means for Jacob in his present situation" (Westermann, *Genesis 12–36*, 505).

[36] Cf. Bar-Efrat, *Narrative Art*, 123.

[37] Taschner, *Verheissung und Erfüllung*, 141. "…will God sustain Jacob now, too, 'on the way that he goes'?" (Fokkelman, *Narrative Art in Genesis*, 197; cf. 199).

[38] A mention of שָׁלֵם only appears in 33:18, which follows Jacob's encounter with Esau (see *Section* 4.4.2). Cf. Fokkelman, *Narrative Art in Genesis*, 198; Taschner, *Verheissung und Erfüllung*, 149.

[39] "Long-suppressed memories from his ignoble past intrude upon his consciousness" (Sarna, *Genesis*, 223).

[40] '…before him' (vs. 4); "pass on ahead of me and put a space between drove and drove" (vs. 17); "…and moreover he is behind us" (vs. 19 and 21); "…the present that goes ahead of me" (vs. 21); "…and the present passed on ahead of him" (vs. 22). Cf. Brodie, *Genesis as Dialogue*, 331; Hamilton, *Genesis 18–50*, 325; Fokkelman, *Narrative Art in Genesis*, 205–206.

[41] Cf. *Section* 4.3.

[42] 32:5, 8, 13, 15, 19; 33:3 (cf. Taschner, *Verheissung und Erfüllung*, 145). Note also the multitude of such descriptions in Gen 27 (see Chapter 2).

of the birth narrative and of Jacob's acquisition of the birthright and
the blessing.[43] Jacob's message is well-crafted and polite.[44] The phrases
'lord' and 'servant' appear at odds with Isaac's blessing (Gen 27). Contrary to Isaac's prediction, Jacob features in the role of 'servant' and
Esau as 'lord.'[45] This contrast appears throughout the narrative (32:19,
21; 33:5, 8, 15) and finds its climax in Jacob's sevenfold bowing as he
approaches Esau (33:3).

Jacob starts by reporting his stay with Laban. "Jacob is careful to
emphasize the reason for the delay of his return, and he cautiously
avoids any reference to the alacrity of his departure in the first place."[46]
The second part of Jacob's message pertains to his possessions. On first
impression it seems strange that Jacob mentions these here. According to Hamilton, Jacob suggests that these are 'Esau's for the taking.'[47]
Wenham thinks that Jacob does not boast, but seeks to impress his
brother in order to find favour.[48] Jacob is indeed restrained in his
description. He subtly employs singulars to describe his possessions.[49]
He also omits the mention of camels (vs. 9), which were indicative
of great wealth.[50] Jacob seems careful not to overstate his riches. It
seems that Jacob wants to give Esau "enough information to arouse
his interest, but not exhaustive information to give his hand away."[51]

---

[43] Hamilton, *Genesis 18–50*, 320; Sarna, *Genesis*, 224; Taschner, *Verheissung und Erfüllung*, 142; Fokkelman, *Narrative Art in Genesis*, 199–200; Waltke, *Genesis*, 442.

[44] For a very different perspective, cf. J.M. Cohen, "The Jacob-Esau Reunion," *JBQ* 21, no. July (1993): 159–63. According to Sarna, it "conforms to the standard episto-lary style of the ancient Near East" (Sarna, *Genesis*, 224; cf. Speiser, *Genesis*, 254; Alter, *Genesis*, 178). In Brueggemann's opinion it is "the kind of deference appropriate to a wrong-doer in the face of the offended" (Brueggemann, *Genesis*, 263). Gunkel sug-gests that the original audience of this story would have "enjoyed Jacob's great skill in flattery" (Gunkel, *Genesis*, 346).

[45] Cf. Turner, *Announcements of Plot in Genesis*, 115–141 and 175–183; Taschner, *Verheissung und Erfüllung*, 143 and 145; Fokkelman, *Narrative Art in Genesis*, 200; Brett, *Genesis*, 98.

[46] Hamilton, *Genesis 18–50*, 321. See also Sarna, *Genesis*, 224; Waltke, *Genesis*, 442.

[47] Hamilton, *Genesis 18–50*, 321. "Jacob obliquely hints that he has the wherewithal to pay off his brother, if need be" (Sarna, *Genesis*, 224). Similarly Jacob, *Genesis, ad loc* and von Rad, *Genesis*, 312.

[48] Wenham, *Genesis 16–50*, 290. Cf. Hartley, *Genesis*, 281; Janzen, *Genesis 12–50*, 127.

[49] Speiser, *Genesis*, 254; Hamilton, *Genesis 18–50*, 321.

[50] Note that the camels are mentioned in vs. 7! According to Waltke, Jacob "under-states his wealth" by this omission (Waltke, *Genesis*, 442). Similarly Sarna, *Genesis*, 224. Cf. Wenham, *Genesis 16–50*, 142 and Wenham, *Genesis 1–15*, 289; Waltke, *Gen-esis*, 442 (and his comments regarding camels in Gen 24 on p. 328).

[51] Hamilton, *Genesis 18–50*, 321.

If we consider this in conjunction with Jacob's elaborate gift later on (vv. 14–22), this suggests a careful and well meditated approach, designed to achieve maximum effect. The close of Jacob's message reveals his ultimate aim: "that I may find favour (חֵן) in your sight." It is Esau's forgiveness and acceptance that Jacob desperately seeks (cf. 32:21–22; 33:8).[52] The word favour (חֵן) is a key-word in the narrative (33:8, 10 and 15). There is an interesting wordplay with two other words that appear throughout this section: 'camp' (מַחֲנֶה) and 'gift/tribute' (מִנְחָה) (see below).[53]

The messengers immediately report back, but merely state that Esau is on his way to meet Jacob together with four hundred men.[54] Isaac 'blessed' Esau with the words "by your sword you shall live and you shall serve your brother" (27:40a).[55] However, Esau seems to have done quite well (cf. 33:9), while Jacob is the one who places himself in the servant position. Jacob interprets Esau's approach as ominous and is distressed (vs. 9 and 12). Esau's intention to harm Jacob may be inferred, but cannot be proven from the text.[56] If Esau intends to harm Jacob, why does he allow the messengers to return unharmed? This certainly would preclude a surprise attack.[57] Does Jacob expect the worst because of his own guilty conscience?[58] The reader shares Jacob's uncertainty.[59]

Jacob's response is practical.[60] He decides to divide his people and his herds (including camels!) into two camps. The reader is given a

---

[52] "The only possible thing left to restore the relationship (…) that Esau should forgive his cheating brother" (Fokkelman, *Narrative Art in Genesis*, 201). See also Brodie, *Genesis as Dialogue*, 331; Brueggemann, *Genesis*, 263; Hamilton, *Genesis 18–50*, 321.

[53] Cf. Wenham, *Genesis 16–50*, 289; Taschner, *Verheissung und Erfüllung*, 146; Fokkelman, *Narrative Art in Genesis*, 205; Alter, *Genesis*, 177; Hartley, *Genesis*, 280; Waltke, *Genesis*, 439.

[54] Elsewhere in the OT, four hundred men constitute a standard military unit (1 Sam 22:2; 25:13 and 30:10, 17) (Sarna, *Genesis*, 224; Alter, *Genesis*, 178). The encounter between the messengers and Esau is entirely gapped.

[55] Westermann, *Genesis 12–36*, 507.

[56] Cf. Westermann, *Genesis 12–36*, 507.

[57] Fokkelman, *Narrative Art in Genesis*, 201; Wenham, *Genesis 16–50*, 289; Hamilton, *Genesis 18–50*, 322.

[58] Fokkelman, *Narrative Art in Genesis*, 201; Sarna, *Genesis*, 224; Waltke, *Genesis*, 443.

[59] Sailhamer, *Genesis*, ad loc; Fokkelman, *Narrative Art in Genesis*, 197–198; Waltke, *Genesis*, 442.

[60] Westermann thinks that originally Jacob's prayer started here, but that would take away from Jacob's characterization as a highly complex personage (Westermann, *Genesis 12–36*, 507–508). Kidner describes Jacob's reaction as 'characteristically energetic' (Kidner, *Genesis*, 168).

rare disclosure of Jacob's rationale in vs. 9 (also vs. 21). If Esau attacks one camp then the other might escape.[61] In Fokkelman's opinion this is "no more than an emergency dressing (…) It is a poor stratagem: one half of the troop is to be jeopardized for the salvation of the other."[62] Instead of poor decision making, it may show Jacob's lack of options.[63] Because of his agreement with Laban he cannot return and cross the newly instituted border that is behind him.[64] A move sideways does not offer any respite either. The slow pace of his big retinue would have been no match for the speed of Esau's militia.[65] Cautiously moving forward seems to be the only option. Jacob seems to have reached the limits of his self-sufficiency. Or has he?

This scene shows us something of the responsibilities and worries that come with great wealth.[66] When Jacob is not striving and toiling for gaining wealth, he is worrying about how not to lose it all. Almost nowhere in Genesis is Jacob's wealth associated with unalloyed 'peace.' There is another side to this. In a way, it is *because* of the size of Jacob's possessions that he is 'forced' to face Esau. This is comparable to Gen 31, where the speed limitation of Jacob's caravan allowed Laban to catch up. Jacob did not have any other option than to face his opponent and come to a resolution. The same is true here. Jacob can run, but he cannot hide. Jacob *has* to face his past. This episode might point to mechanisms that exist in the natural order to (self-) correct imbalances and injustice. People who pursue material advancement at the expense of various relationships will have to face the consequences of their actions at some point, exactly because the acquisition and use of material possessions are so entwined with various relationships in the first place.[67]

---

[61] Cf. Kitchen, *On the Reliability of the Old Testament*, 338 and 573 n. 84 for more on this practice. Cf. Walton, *Thou Traveller Unknown*, 183 n. 9.

[62] Fokkelman, *Narrative Art in Genesis*, 201; 'half-measures' (Westermann, *Genesis 12–36*, 508).

[63] Cf. Sarna, *Genesis*, 224.

[64] Sarna, *Genesis*, 224

[65] Westermann, *Genesis 12–36*, 507.

[66] The book of Ecclesiastes will have to say more on this!

[67] Jacob's responsibilities and worries to some extent resonate with the sentiments of Ecclesiastes (cf. Blomberg, *Neither Poverty nor Riches*, 61–62 and references quoted there).

32:10–13

Jacob's first response was a practical one. Now he turns to prayer.[68] That sequence is interesting in itself. There might be a similarity with Jacob's kissing of Rachel and his emotional weeping only *after* he had watered the flocks.[69] Jacob's address to God is stylized as was his message to Esau.[70] At the heart of Jacob's prayer is a genuine cry for deliverance: "deliver me (Hiphil imperative הַצִּילֵנִי) from the hand of my brother" (vs. 12).[71] The potential of another fratricide (cf. 4:2–14) and of the suffering of innocent women and children contribute to the emotional appeal for God's intervention.[72] Jacob assumes the worst and paints a dark picture of his predicament.[73] Jacob's appeal is embedded in measured rhetoric where Jacob both recalls what God has done and what God has said. Jacob refers in various ways to God's promises regarding land; offspring and assistance (cf. 28:13–15).[74] The phrase "God of my father Abraham and the God of my father Isaac" resembles God's address *to* Jacob at Bethel (28:13).[75] This reminds God (and the reader) of God's relationship with, and promises to, Abraham and Isaac and his faithfulness to both.[76] Sarna calls Jacob's prayer "an expression of absolute faith in a living God."[77] However, Frey notes "noch wagt er nicht, ihn *seinen* Gott zu nennen."[78] Jacob reminds

---

[68] Cf. Hamilton, *Genesis 18–50*, 322. Some scholars consider Jacob's prayer the climax of this scene (e.g. von Rad, *Genesis*, 313; Westermann, *Genesis 12–36*, 507; Fokkelman, *Narrative Art in Genesis*, 202). Taschner eloquently argues against that: Taschner, *Verheissung und Erfüllung*, 147–148.

[69] See *Section 3.2*.

[70] "Jacob is deferential to God, as he is to Esau" (Brueggemann, *Genesis*, 264). For more on the structure of this prayer, see Hamilton, *Genesis 18–50*, 322–323.

[71] Westermann, *Genesis 12–36*, 508; Fokkelman, *Narrative Art in Genesis*, 204. According to Westermann, Jacob's original prayer was 'a simple cry for help' (vs. 12). Westermann considers vv. 10–11 and 13 as later additions. In his opinion, the prayer as a whole did not belong to the original narrative. Similarly Coats, *Genesis*, 226. See also Wenham, *Genesis 16–50*, 290; Baldwin, *The Message of Genesis 12–50*, 136; Brueggemann, *Genesis*, 265; Janzen, *Genesis 12–50*, 128; Walton, *Thou Traveller Unknown*, 185.

[72] Cf. Wenham, *Genesis 16–50*, 291.

[73] Cf. Humphreys, *The Character of God*, 189; Westermann, *Genesis 12–36*, 509.

[74] Cf. Fokkelman, *Narrative Art in Genesis*, 202–203; R. Rendtorff, *The Canonical Hebrew Bible: A Theology of the Old Testament* (trans. D. Orton; Leiden, The Netherlands: Deo Publishing, 2005), 25.

[75] Jacob "means to hold God to the promise" (Waltke, *Genesis*, 443).

[76] Cf. Wenham, *Genesis 16–50*, 290. See also Walton, *Thou Traveller Unknown*, 184.

[77] Sarna, *Genesis*, 225.

[78] H. Frey, *Das Buch des Kampfes* (Stuttgart, Germany: Calwer Verlag, 1938), *ad loc*

God that his current situation is a direct result of God's instruction to him to return home.[79] However, God's promise 'I will be with you' is changed by Jacob into 'that I may do you good' (vs. 10). The intensified version of this phrase is repeated in vs. 13 ('I will surely do you good').[80] According to Taschner this demonstrates Jacob's intense desperation.[81] Sarna notes that this change of words "has no parallel in the divine promises."[82] It might be an innocent paraphrase,[83] but it can also be Jacob's *interpretation* of God's promise.[84] As we have seen before, there might be a difference between God's promise, and Jacob's interpretation of that promise.[85] Some commentators even suggest that Jacob, despite his dire situation, continues to manipulate God whenever he can:[86]

> Jacob, in keeping with his stance as a bargainer (who at Bethel stipulated that God must provide him food and clothing) substitutes a verb that suggests material bounty.[87]

Jacob now humbles and commits himself to God's grace and faithfulness by describing himself as unworthy (קָטֹנְתִּי) (vs. 11). In 27:15 and 42 Jacob was described as 'the younger' (הַקָּטָן), a status he so desperately tried to struggle himself out of,[88] but now he has to admit: קָטֹנְתִּי.[89]

---

as quoted by Fokkelman, *Narrative Art in Genesis*, 203. See also Taschner, *Verheissung und Erfüllung*, 149. Cf. Jacob's words towards the end of his life: "The God before whom my father's Abraham and Isaac walked, the God who has been my shepherd all my life long to this day" (48:15). It is in 33:20 where Jacob builds an altar and called it El-Elohe-Israel. Finally, God has become Israel's/Jacob's God (see below).

[79] Wenham, *Genesis 16–50*, 290; Hartley, *Genesis*, 282; Brueggemann, *Genesis*, 264. Jacob's wording closely resembles 31:3.

[80] "This is an important nuance usually lost in translation" (Brueggemann, *Genesis*, 265).

[81] Taschner, *Verheissung und Erfüllung*, 147.

[82] Sarna, *Genesis*, 225. Similarly Westermann, *Genesis 12–36*, 509; Hamilton, *Genesis 18–50*, 323.

[83] Wenham, *Genesis 16–50*, 291. Similarly van Seters, *Prologue to History*, 301–302; Westermann, *Genesis 12–36*, 509: "the purpose of this modification is obviously to compass several promises in one statement."

[84] Sarna, *Genesis*, 225.

[85] A similar thing is true in Genesis for God's blessing pronouncements and human interpretation of blessing (cf. Appendix B).

[86] Humphreys, *The Character of God*, 188. See also Brett, *Genesis*, 97.

[87] Alter, *Genesis*, 179. Cf. HALOT 3743 'do good to someone' (Hiphil imperfect); BDB 3917. 'Make it advantageous for you' (Speiser, *Genesis*, 255).

[88] Cf. Hamilton, *Genesis 18–50*, 323; Brueggemann, *Genesis*, 264.

[89] Fokkelman, *Narrative Art in Genesis*, 203. See also Hamilton, *Genesis 18–50*, 323; Armstrong, *In the Beginning*, 90. Walton notes that de Pury "sees the prayer as expressing the kerygma of the Yahwist that divine blessing operates over and against

Mann wryly comments that "if there is a moment of righteousness in Jacob's life, it is surely here."[90] This truly is a momentous day:

> On one and the same day in his life he asks his brother for mercy, as a servant asks his lord, and he confesses to be dependent on God's חֶסֶד and אֱמֶת, as a servant of God.[91]

Jacob acknowledges what God has done for him in material terms (offspring and possessions): "with only my staff I crossed this Jordan and now I have become two camps" (vs. 10). Jacob talks about his possessions in a relationship context. Towards Esau, he seems to imply that his possessions are available for Esau, to make amends. In his prayer, Jacob attributes his possessions to God's "deeds of steadfast love and faithfulness;" supreme relationship qualities. Jacob's humbling of himself and his grateful acknowledgment to God 'pave the way' for Jacob's cry for deliverance (vs. 12).[92] Jacob concludes his prayer by emphatically reminding God of his word (vs. 13), or at least Jacob's version of it. Jacob's closing words regarding promised offspring ("as the sand of the sea") appear nowhere else in the Jacob narrative, but resemble God's words in 22:17, where God emphatically repeats and intensifies his promises to Abraham following the near sacrifice of Isaac; the climax of the Abraham-cycle.[93] Thus Jacob returns where he started, God's faithfulness to Abraham and Isaac.

Jacob's prayer is significant. It captures perfectly the tension in the narrative[94] and is relevant theologically because of its juxtaposition of the patriarchal promises with imminent human threat.[95] It is Jacob's first recorded prayer and it is the only 'extended prayer' in Genesis.[96] Brueggemann describes it as "the voice of a man accustomed to

---

the unworthiness of the patriarch" (Walton, *Thou Traveller Unknown*, 184 n. 11; cf. de Pury, *Promesse divine*, 102).

[90] Mann, *The Book of the Torah*, 60.

[91] Fokkelman, *Narrative Art in Genesis*, 203. The reference to God's "deeds of steadfast love and faithfulness" can be considered as "characteristic of OT prayer (cf. 2 Sam 7:19; Gen 19:19; 24:12, 14; frequently in the Psalms)" (Wenham, *Genesis 16–50*, 291). See also Waltke, *Genesis*, 443; Brueggemann, *Genesis*, 264–265.

[92] Fokkelman, *Narrative Art in Genesis*, 203.

[93] Wenham, *Genesis 16–50*, 99; Wright, *The Mission of God*, 205; Moberly, *The Bible, Theology and Faith*, 71.

[94] Cf. Taschner, *Verheissung und Erfüllung*, 146.

[95] Cf. K. Elliger, "Der Jakobskampf am Jabbok," *ZTK* 48 (1951): 1–31, 18–20 as discussed by Walton, *Thou Traveller Unknown*, 184.

[96] Brueggemann, *Genesis*, 263; Waltke, *Genesis*, 443.

stating his best case."[97] It certainly is 'a model of persuasive rhetoric,' not dissimilar to Jacob's vow in Bethel (28:20–22).[98] As with Jacob's vow, scholarly opinion is diverse. Some commentators consider it an example of piety and faith.[99] Sailhamer for example, suggests that it was Jacob's prayer that changed the course of events. The narrative however, does not make that explicit in any way.[100] Other commentators are more reserved in their endorsement.[101] Janzen for example, wonders whether Jacob is "using the rhetoric he thinks will work with God?" "If he is sincere, this is a Jacob we have not seen before."[102] Like Jacob's vow, Jacob's prayer is a complex mix. Jacob is deeply aware of the limitations of self-sufficiency in the face of imminent threat. Yet, Jacob does not abandon practical arrangements altogether. This is quite characteristic:

> We do not have two Jacobs here; we have only the one man, at once cal-culating and contrite, an inextricable combination expressed by the posi-tion of Jacob's prayer in between his two precautionary manoeuvres.[103]

Jacob seems to have made substantial progress in his relationship with God,[104] but his prayer is probably not entirely on God's terms yet:

> Jacob co-opts God's assurance and promise into his own terms for the specific future he seeks. That Jacob can do this, and at the same moment stress his own significance, is a rhetorical ploy that leaves God little room for response other than to accept Jacob's construction. That, or confront him in a new and unexpected way.[105]

---

[97] Brueggemann, *Genesis*, 265. Cf. Gunkel, *Genesis*, 346.

[98] Janzen, *Genesis 12–50*, 128. See also Humphreys, *The Character of God*, 188–190; M. Greenberg, *Biblical Prose Prayer* (Berkeley, USA: University of California, 1983), 14 (as quoted by Hamilton, *Genesis 18–50*, 324); Brueggemann, *Genesis*, 265; Fokkel-man, *Narrative Art in Genesis*, 202–203.

[99] E.g. Sailhamer, *Genesis*, ad loc; Sarna, *Genesis*, 225; Waltke, *Genesis*, 443; C.J. Sedgwick, "Victory through Defeat," *ET* 110, no. 10 (1999): 325–26, 325; Baldwin, *The Message of Genesis 12–50*, 135; Kidner, *Genesis*, 168.

[100] Cf. Brueggemann, *Genesis*, 265.

[101] E.g. Mann, *The Book of the Torah*, 60; Janzen, *Genesis 12–50*, 128; Humphreys, *The Character of God*, 188.

[102] Janzen, *Genesis 12–50*, 128.

[103] Mann, *The Book of the Torah*, 60. See also Wenham, *Genesis 16–50*, 291; Ross, *Creation and Blessing*, 543–544.

[104] Cf. Fokkelman, *Narrative Art in Genesis*, 204; Waltke, *Genesis*, 443; Brodie, *Genesis as Dialogue*, 331; von Rad, *Genesis*, 313, who describes the prayer as "an expres-sion of a purification taking place in Jacob."

[105] Humphreys, *The Character of God*, 188. "His prayer is a mixture of the old Jacob and the new" (Kodell, "Jacob Wrestles with Esau (Gen 32:23–32)," 67).

Jacob has grown, but still has more growing to do. The fact that God will confront Jacob the way he does (32:23–33) points in that direction.

32:14–22

The mention that Jacob 'stayed [there] that night' (vs. 14 and 22) brackets this scene.[106] Jacob reverts to his preparations for meeting Esau. Some commentators assume that for practical reasons this must have taken place by day-light,[107] but the narrator seems to emphasize that it took place by night (vs. 14, 22 and 23).[108] Darkness certainly resonates with Jacob's mood. Brodie suggests that "facing Esau is like facing the darkness."[109] The darkness will only specifically lift after Jacob has struggled with 'a man' (32:32).[110] The gift (מִנְחָה) Jacob prepares is impressive. It consists of five-hundred and fifty animals (vv. 15–16).[111] "It seems to involve a real letting go."[112] In Hartley's opinion "Jacob acknowledged that he had inflicted great damages on Esau by having usurped the birthright and the blessing."[113] Fokkelman is quite positive about Jacob's prayer, but is less so regarding his gift:

> The reconciliation Jacob now attempts is still impure, for it remains in fact an effort to bribe Esau with gifts. Jacob has still to recognize that his stand on the back line (which is a refusal to take responsibility, 32:18, 20) must be replaced by a position up front (acknowledgment of guilt and a plea for forgiveness, 33, 2, 10–11). But that does not happen until chapter 33.[114]

The size of Jacob's gift also reinforces our sense of Jacob's immense wealth (cf. 30:43).[115] מִנְחָה can be translated as 'gift,' 'tribute' or 'offering.'[116] All three meanings are alluded to in the text. Normally,

---

[106] From the verb לוּן. A similar phrase appears in 28:11 and 31:54.

[107] E.g. Armstrong, *In the Beginning*, 90.

[108] Wenham, *Genesis 16–50*, 291; Hamilton, *Genesis 18–50*, 328; Taschner, *Verheissung und Erfullung*, 141–142; Fokkelman, *Narrative Art in Genesis*, 205: "Jacob has entered the longest night of his life."

[109] Brodie, *Genesis as Dialogue*, 331.

[110] "The sun rose upon him…" (cf. Fokkelman, *Narrative Art in Genesis*, 48–49 and 205). See *Section 2.5*. Cf. Speiser, *Genesis*, 256.

[111] "Each drove with a proportionate number of males to ensure maximum increase" (Baldwin, *The Message of Genesis 12–50*, 136).

[112] Brodie, *Genesis as Dialogue*, 331. See also Wenham, *Genesis 16–50*, 292; Westermann, *Genesis 12–36*, 510.

[113] Hartley, *Genesis*, 282.

[114] Fokkelman, "Genesis," 50.

[115] Cf. Sailhamer, *Genesis, ad loc.*

[116] Cf. Hamilton, *Genesis 18–50*, 325, especially n. 9; Rendtorff, *The Canonical Hebrew Bible*, 509.

an interpreter needs to guard against the fallacy of 'totality transfer' (Barr),[117] but Sarna argues that "the ambiguity in its repeated use here is intentional. Esau is free to interpret it as he wishes."[118] Although Jacob does not stand in a formal vassal relationship with Esau, the recurrent use of 'lord' and Jacob's bowing hint in that direction.[119] However, Jacob's desire in vs. 20 "that I may appease his face" (אֲכַפְּרָה פָנָיו) seems to have sacrificial overtones.[120] Jacob expresses a hope to make 'atonement' (כפר).[121] According to Kidner, this illustrates Jacob's (yet incomplete) understanding of what is required to receive forgiveness:

> Jacob's sacrificial terms unconsciously illustrate the gulf between man's thinking and God's. The pagan approaches his deity as Jacob now approaches Esau (cf. 33:10), reckoning that 'a man's gift makes room for him' (Pr 18:16). (...) As Jacob would soon discover, grace, not negotiation, is the only solvent of guilt.[122]

Jacob's instructions are specific. The droves have to travel separately, and every servant receives instructions how to address 'my lord Esau' on behalf of 'your servant Jacob.' Jacob is ever 'behind.' The size, spacing and wording that accompany Jacob's gift are employed to achieve the maximum desired effect.[123] Jacob's aim is disclosed in the second half of vs. 21, which can be seen as a restatement of Jacob's desire in vs. 6, to 'find favour' (חֵן). Again we are offered a rare insight into Jacob's thinking:

אֲכַפְּרָה פָנָיו
בַּמִּנְחָה הַהֹלֶכֶת לְפָנָי
וְאַחֲרֵי־כֵן אֶרְאֶה פָנָיו

---

[117] James Barr, *The Semantics of Biblical Language* (London, UK: SCM, 1983).

[118] Sarna, *Genesis*, 225.

[119] Cf. Alter, *Genesis*, 179–180; Waltke, *Genesis*, 444; Janzen, *Genesis 12–50*, 127; Matthews, *The IVP Bible Background Commentary*, ad loc. "A magnificent gift that bears the stamp of paying tribute" (Sarna, *Genesis*, 225). Hamilton and Waltke argue against the translation 'tribute' (Hamilton, *Genesis 18–50*, 325; Waltke, *Genesis*, 444).

[120] Wenham, *Story as Torah*, 106. Wenham discusses Jacob's generosity in the context of God's generosity as expressed in his compassion and mercy and forgiveness.

[121] Fishbane, *Text and Texture*, 52; Wenham, *Genesis 16–50*, 291; Wenham, *Story as Torah*, 106; Janzen, *Genesis 12–50*, 129; Kidner, *Genesis*, 168; Waltke, *Genesis*, 444; Brueggemann, *Genesis*, 266; Hamilton, *Genesis 18–50*, 326; Westermann, *Genesis 12–36*, 510.

[122] Kidner, *Genesis*, 168. I will return to Kidner's observation in *Section* 4.4.

[123] "Esau is bound to be overwhelmed by it all" (Sarna, *Genesis*, 225). Jacob "prudently tries to pacify his adversary with a smothering of gifts" (Waltke, *Genesis*, 438). Cf. Gunkel, *Genesis*, 347.

אוּלַי יִשָּׂא פָנָי

[124]וַתַּעֲבֹר הַמִּנְחָה עַל־פָּנָיו

The five-fold allusion to the word 'face' (פָּנֶה) is central here; a word that will also be a key-feature of the following two episodes (32:31; 33:8, 10).[125] Vs. 21, which brings this scene to a close, vividly captures the movement that is now in progress. Jacob himself stays in the camp (מַחֲנֶה). His present (מִנְחָה) is passing ahead of him, in the hope of appeasing his brother. Taschner astutely observes "Jakob macht aus seinem Lager (מחנה) eine Gabe (מנחה), um Gnade (חן) vor den Augen seines Bruders zu finden."[126] A movement that is also succinctly captured in vs. 19. This is a reversal of what we have seen in Gen 25 and 27, where Jacob sacrificed the relationship with his brother to obtain birthright (בְּכֹרָה) and blessing (בְּרָכָה).[127] Now, he takes from his camp (מַחֲנֶה) a present (מִנְחָה) in the hope to restore that relationship (חֵן).

4.2.3   Concluding Remarks

In chapter 3, I suggested that conflict over material possessions or well-being is often at the heart of conflict in Genesis, and that material gestures (of some sort) are an integral part of any conflict resolution. As events unfold, we will see that this is also true for the resolution of the Jacob-Esau conflict. This also seems to be reflected in the Hebrew wordplay between מִנְחָה ,מַחֲנֶה and חֵן. Has Jacob done everything he could to appease his brother? In the darkness of night Jacob probably remains anxious that it might not be enough.[128] Jacob's immense wealth and calculated generosity cannot buy him 'peace of mind.'[129]

---

[124] Taschner, *Verheissung und Erfüllung*, 148. Similarly Fox, *Genesis and Exodus*, 139 (as quoted by Armstrong, *In the Beginning*, 91).

[125] Cf. Brueggemann, *Genesis*, 266; Hamilton, *Genesis 18–50*, 326; Speiser, *Genesis*, 255; von Rad, *Genesis*, 314; Coats, *Genesis*, 227; Sarna, *Genesis*, 226; Armstrong, *In the Beginning*, 91; Mann, *The Book of the Torah*, 60; Hartley, *Genesis*, 280; Alter, *Genesis*, 189; Janzen, *Genesis 12–50*, 128; Waltke, *Genesis*, 439; Fokkelman, *Narrative Art in Genesis*, 206 and 220; Walton, *Thou Traveller Unknown*, 185. This includes the preposition לְפָנָיו which occurs four times (32:3, 16, 17,20) Waltke, *Genesis*, 439 n. 189.

[126] Taschner, *Verheissung und Erfüllung*, 146. I agree with Taschner that this is better than Fokkelman's suggestion that "it is an important step towards חן to use a מנחה instead of a מחנה" (Fokkelman, *Narrative Art in Genesis*, 205).

[127] Cf. 33:11 where Jacob will return the בְּרָכָה (*Section* 4.4).

[128] Fokkelman speaks of a certain 'two-facedness' of Jacob's preparations (Fokkelman, *Narrative Art in Genesis*, 212).

[129] "Jacob's main motivation is not penitence but fear" (McKeown, *Genesis*, 154).

4.3   Jacob Wrestles with 'a Man' (Gen 32:23–33)

4.3.1   *Introduction*

Jacob's mysterious struggle with 'a man' at Peniel is probably the most profound event in the entire Jacob-cycle.[130] Scholars have made numerous suggestions regarding the pre-history of this text.[131] Earlier source-critics assigned most of this passage to J and E, but the more recent consensus is to assign it to J in its entirety.[132] Various scholars have demonstrated the basic unity of this passage, and their findings have gained wide acceptance.[133] This is the central scene in Jacob's return to Canaan and it separates Jacob's preparations for his meeting with Esau from the meeting itself.[134] Jacob's struggle with 'a man' and Jacob's reunion with his brother are textually and thematically linked in various ways (e.g. 32:31 and 33:10).[135] This suggests

---

[130] "This culminating moment of his life story" (Alter, *Genesis*, 180). Cf. Fokkelman, *Narrative Art in Genesis*, 209; R.S. Hendel, *The Epic of the Patriarch: The Jacob Cycle and the Narrative Traditions of Canaan and Israel* (Atlanta, Georgia, USA: Scholars Press, 1987), 103. Much has been written on this episode. Cf. sub-bibliography Wenham, *Genesis 16–50*, 292.

[131] Westermann, *Genesis 12–36*, 515; Gunkel, *Genesis*, 349–350; von Rad, *Genesis*, 314–315 and 319; Walton, *Thou Traveller Unknown*, 66. For a helpful overview of the rich history of interpretation of this passage cf. A.P. Ross, "Studies in the Life of Jacob—Part 2: Jacob at the Jabbok, Israel at Peniel," *BSac* 142, no. 568 (1985): 338–54, 339–341; Ross, *Creation and Blessing*, 547; D.F. Pennant, "Genesis 32: Lighten Our Darkness, Lord We Pray," in *He Swore an Oath—Biblical Themes from Genesis 12–50* (eds. R.S. Hess, G.J. Wenham and P.E. Satterthwaite; Carlisle, Cumbria, UK: The Paternoster Press, 1994) and especially W.T. Miller, *Mysterious Encounters at Mamre and Jabbok* (Brown Judaic Studies 50; ed. J. Neusner; Chico, Ca, USA: Scholars Press, 1984).

[132] Cf. von Rad, *Genesis*, 315; Wenham, *Genesis 16–50*, 289; Blum, *Komposition*, 143ff.; Coats, *Genesis*, 231; Ross, "Studies in the Life of Jacob—Part 2 Peniel," 340; Westermann, *Genesis 12–36*, 515 and 520–521; Walton, *Thou Traveller Unknown*, 67–72. For a comprehensive survey of E and J adherents, cf. Ross, *Creation and Blessing*, 548.

[133] R. Barthes, "La lutte avec l'ange: analyse textuelle de Gen 32:23–33," in *Analyse structurale et exégèse biblique* (eds. R. Bovon and T. Barthes; Neuchâtel: Delachaux et Niestlé, 1971); Blum, *Komposition*, 143ff.; A. de Pury, "Jakob am Jabbok, Gen. 32,23–33 im Licht einer alt-irischen Erzählung," *ThZ* 35 (1979): 18–34; Wenham, *Genesis 16–50*, 294; Walton, *Thou Traveller Unknown*, 72–75. See also Ross, *Creation and Blessing*, 550–551 and H. White, "French Structuralism and OT Narrative Analysis: Roland Barthes," *Semeia* 3 (1975): 99–127.

[134] Wenham, *Genesis 16–50*, 293. Although it is an interlude, it does not provide any breathing space (Fokkelman, *Narrative Art in Genesis*, 208).

[135] In addition, the verbs 'to wrestle' (אָבֵק in 32:24) and 'to embrace' (חָבַק in 33:4) sound similar. "Two verbs that rhyme are chosen to describe the start of Jacob's encounters" (Hamilton, *Genesis 18–50*, 329).

that they must be interpreted in conjunction with each other.[136] This passage also has various links with wider contexts. Within the palistrophic structure of the Jacob-cycle, it stands opposite Jacob's encounter with God at Bethel.[137] Jacob wrestles with many opponents to achieve blessing. "This passage shows him wrestling with Yahweh as the one who truly holds the key to that blessing."[138] Speiser draws a parallel with Abraham's test in Gen 22.[139] It can even be seen as representative for the entire Jacob-cycle, as Jacob continues his struggle for blessing that started in the womb (25:22).[140] This is also the first time in the OT that the name Israel is mentioned, a highly relevant passage from that point of view as well.[141]

The episode can be divided into three parts: the fight (vv. 23–26),[142] the dialogue (vv. 27–30) and its aftermath (vv. 31–32).[143] The central dialogue carries most weight.[144] Barthes identifies the following parallel arrangement in the dialogue structure:

> Vs. 28, God asks Jacob's name—Jacob's response—vs. 29, name changed
> Vs. 30, Jacob asks God's name—Indirect response—vs. 31, place name changed.[145]

---

[136] Cf. von Rad, *Genesis*, 315; Kodell, "Jacob Wrestles with Esau (Gen 32:23–32)," 65 and 70; Brueggemann, *Genesis*, 266ff. and 272–273; Coats, *Genesis*, 229 and 231; Mann, *The Book of the Torah*, 60–61; Brett, *Genesis*, 99–100; Taschner, *Verheissung und Erfüllung*, 156; E.M. Curtis, "Structure, Style and Context as a Key to Interpreting Jacob's Encounter at Peniel," *JETS* 30 (1987): 129–37, 135ff. See also the end of *Section 4.3*.

[137] See opening Chapter 2 (cf. Fishbane, *Text and Texture*, 54–55; Rendsburg, *The Redaction of Genesis*, 62–63). Fokkelman, *Narrative Art in Genesis*, 208 and 213; Westermann, *Genesis 12–36*, 515; Taschner, *Verheissung und Erfüllung*, 155; Humphreys, *The Character of God*, 191; Waltke, *Genesis*, 447–448; Bar-Efrat, *Narrative Art*, 135.

[138] McKeown, *Genesis*, 156.

[139] Speiser, *Genesis*, 256. See also Pennant, "Genesis 32," 178.

[140] Alter, *Genesis*, 180; Sailhamer, *Genesis, ad loc*; Walton, *Thou Traveller Unknown*, 75. "The episode arguably functions as a parable for Jacob's whole life, which has been characterized by struggle, deception, quests for blessing, and bargains with a divinity who seems to be identifiable by no single name" (Brett, *Genesis*, 99).

[141] S. Gevirtz, "Of Patriarchs and Puns: Joseph at the Fountain, Jacob at the Ford," *HUCA* 46 (1975): 33–54, 50; Taschner, *Verheissung und Erfüllung*, 150; Walton, *Thou Traveller Unknown*, 84–85.

[142] Vv. 22–24a set the scene for the fight.

[143] Cf. S.A. Geller, "The Struggle at the Jabbok," *JANES* 14 (1982): 37–60, 41; Wenham, *Genesis 16–50*, 294; Ross, *Creation and Blessing*, 551; Fokkelman, *Narrative Art in Genesis*, 210; Hamilton, *Genesis 18–50*, 328.

[144] Fokkelman, *Narrative Art in Genesis*, 213; Walton, *Thou Traveller Unknown*, 79 n. 27. Dialogue also takes centre stage in the encounter between Esau and Jacob that follows.

[145] Barthes, "La lutte avec l'ange," 35. See also Brueggemann, *Genesis*, 268; Geller, "The Struggle at the Jabbok," 56; Wenham, *Genesis 16–50*, 294; Ross, *Creation and Blessing*, 550; White, "French Structuralism," 114.

The blessing Jacob receives in the form of a name change clearly is the climax of the dialogue and of the episode as a whole.[146] The passage also contains wordplays between Jabbok (יַבֹּק), Jacob (יַעֲקֹב), and the verb 'to struggle' (אָבֵק).[147] These words resonate with the dislocation of Jacob's hip (from the verb יָקַע).[148] Besides struggle in a particular location, the passage deals with transition. Occurrences of the verb עָבַר ('cross over' or 'pass by' in vs. 23, 24x2, and 32) frame this passage.[149] Taken together, these themes can be seen as symptomatic for Jacob's life-story; transformation in the midst of struggle, epitomized by Jacob's new name—Israel.[150]

4.3.2   Commentary

32:23–25a

Jacob decides to cross the Jabbok in the same night that various droves of cattle are on their way to Esau.[151] To do this with his whole family and 'everything else that he had' amidst darkness, must have been a substantial and dangerous undertaking.[152] According to Sarna, Jacob aims to "better exploit the immediate psychological advantage gained

---

[146] Barthes, "La lutte avec l'ange," 35–36; Coats, *Genesis*, 230; Wenham, *Genesis 16–50*, 294; Sarna, *Genesis*, 227; Janzen, *Genesis 12–50*, 129; Ross, *Creation and Blessing*, 550; Hamilton, *Genesis 18–50*, 328; Hendel, *The Epic of the Patriarch*, 103; Curtis, "Structure, Style and Context;" Walton, *Thou Traveller Unknown*, 79, n. 27; Fox, *Genesis and Exodus*, 135 as quoted in Waltke, *Genesis*, 439; Taschner, *Verheissung und Erfüllung*, 154.

[147] R. Martin-Achard, "Un exégète devant Gen 32:23–33," in *Analyse structurale et exégèse biblique* (eds. R. Barthes and T. Bovon; Neuchâtel: Delachaux et Niestlé, 1971), 47; Gevirtz, "Of Patriarchs and Puns," 51; B. Weber, "Nomen est Omen: Einige Erwägungen zu Gen 32:23–33 und seinem Kontext," *BN* 61 (1992): 76–83, 78; Fokkelman, *Narrative Art in Genesis*, 210; Wenham, *Genesis 16–50*, 295; Sarna, *Genesis*, 227; Hamilton, *Genesis 18–50*, 329; Janzen, *Genesis 12–50*, 129–130; Ross, *Creation and Blessing*, 549; Taschner, *Verheissung und Erfüllung*, 152.

[148] It might be relevant that elsewhere יָקַע 'refers to alienation between parties' (Janzen, *Genesis 12–50*, 130). Cf. BDB 4117; TWOT 903; 'turn away in disgust' HALOT 3933.

[149] Barthes, "La lutte avec l'ange," 32–33; Blum, *Komposition*, 143; Fokkelman, *Narrative Art in Genesis*, 212; Taschner, *Verheissung und Erfüllung*, 151–152; Walton, *Thou Traveller Unknown*, 88.

[150] Cf. Kodell, "Jacob Wrestles with Esau (Gen 32:23–32)," 66ff.; Janzen, *Genesis 12–50*, 129–131; Mann, *The Book of the Torah*, 61; Sailhamer, *Genesis, ad loc.*

[151] See comments in *Section 4.2*.

[152] Wenham, *Genesis 16–50*, 292; von Rad, *Genesis*, 315. "A toilsome operation" (Fokkelman, *Narrative Art in Genesis*, 213). Commentators have wondered why Dinah is not mentioned (e.g. Hamilton, *Genesis 18–50*, 328). According to Sarna only Jacob and his eleven sons are mentioned because they are "the principal actors in the

from the mollifying effect of the tribute."[153] Others suggest that Jacob wants to be alone for meditation and prayer.[154] The narrator does not disclose Jacob's rationale. "Part of the richness of the story is that it tells us absolutely nothing about the motivation of the characters."[155] Yet the circumstances suggest major restlessness on Jacob's part.[156]

If we could view the scene from above, we would see a long caravan of various droves 'by themselves' (לְבַדּוֹ; vs. 18), followed by Jacob's family and remaining possessions.[157] At the tail end, there is Jacob all 'by himself' (לְבַדּוֹ).[158] It is not clear on what side of the river Jacob now finds himself. Vs. 24 suggests that Jacob has crossed the stream, but vs. 25 seems to contradict this.[159] It could well be that Jacob 'criss-crossed the Jabbok several times.'[160] However, this is just one of many ambiguities in the passage (see below).[161] Jacob is now separated from his family and possessions. According to Waltke, "Jacob's solitude serves an important spiritual purpose. Jacob must encounter God alone, without possessions or protection."[162] Events associated with the increase of Jacob's offspring and wealth stood at the heart of the Jacob-Laban narrative.[163] Yet here, in what is considered by many to

---

evolution of the nation." Jacob is about to become Israel "the personification of the tribal confederation" (Sarna, *Genesis*, 226). Similarly Waltke, *Genesis*, 445.

[153] Sarna, *Genesis*, 227.

[154] Kidner, *Genesis*, 168; Baldwin, *The Message of Genesis 12–50*, 137; Hartley, *Genesis*, 283.

[155] Mann, *The Book of the Torah*, 61. Such lack of clarity explains in part the 'rich expository possibility' of this passage (Brueggemann, *Genesis*, 266).

[156] Cf. Wenham, *Genesis 16–50*, 292; Fokkelman, *Narrative Art in Genesis*, 211–212. "A matter of great urgency" (Sarna, *Genesis*, 226). "Anxiety may have produced insomnia" (Hamilton, *Genesis 18–50*, 328).

[157] The last thing Jacob separates from are his possessions (cf. Hamilton, *Genesis 18–50*, 327).

[158] Hamilton, *Genesis 18–50*, 329.

[159] Martin-Achard, "Un exégète devant Gen 32:23–33," 47; Walton, *Thou Traveller Unknown*, 66. Gunkel, *Genesis*, 347 assigns vs. 24 to J and vs. 25 to E. Cf. Wenham, *Genesis 16–50*, 292; Taschner, *Verheissung und Erfüllung*, 151; S. Frolov, "The Other Side of the Jabbok: Genesis 32 as a Fiasco of Patriarchy," *JSOT* 91 (2000): 41–59, 46–47. Frolov interprets Jacob's movement as flight and labels this scene as the 'fiasco of patriarchy.'

[160] Hamilton, *Genesis 18–50*, 329.

[161] Cf. Barthes, "La lutte avec l'ange," 32. Not all commentators are satisfied with that interpretation (e.g. Walton, *Thou Traveller Unknown*, 80).

[162] Waltke, *Genesis*, 445. "There is an evoking therefore of a complete letting go or a complete separation from everyone and everything" (Brodie, *Genesis as Dialogue*, 331).

[163] Stories about the increase of offspring and wealth stand at the centre of the Jacob-Laban narrative (Chapter 3) and of the Jacob-cycle as a whole (see opening comments Chapter 2).

be the climactic episode of the Jacob-cycle, Jacob is separated from everything he strived for so hard. The fact that Jacob still longs for a blessing (vs. 27) will make us reflect in more detail on the relationship between offspring, possessions and blessing. So Jacob is left alone. We have to go back to Bethel to see Jacob in a similar bare state. As in Bethel, the only thing from which Jacob seems inseparable is the unresolved conflict with Esau.

32:25b–26

'A man' struggles with Jacob throughout the night till day break, and 'he' (the man) was not able to overcome 'him' (Jacob; vs. 26).[164] The report about the struggle is short. The focus is clearly on the dialogue that follows. There are several ambiguities in this episode. First of all there is the identity of Jacob's opponent. In vs. 25 he is called 'a man' (אִישׁ) "purposely a very general meaningless word has been chosen which suggests a mystery but reveals nothing."[165] In vs. 31 Jacob will identify his opponent as 'God' (אֱלֹהִים).[166] Alternatively, Sarna translates אֱלֹהִים in vs. 29 as 'divine being', but as 'God' in Gen 33.[167] According to Janzen "from the explanation of the new name (32:28b), this figure may be divine, human, or both."[168] Based on certain assumptions regarding the pre-history of the text, some commentators even detect a demonic element.[169] Indeed there is a sense that we are dealing with an inscrutable and dark mystery,[170] but to allow for an inclusion of a demonic element in the interpretation of the text as it stands seems

---

[164] We find out later that this is 'the man' who is not able to overcome Jacob (see below).

[165] Fokkelman, *Narrative Art in Genesis*, 213. Similarly Brueggemann, *Genesis*, 267.

[166] Hosea 12:4 identifies him as an angel (cf. Sarna, *Genesis*, 227; Hamilton, *Genesis 18–50*, 330; Ross, "Studies in the Life of Jacob—Part 2 Peniel," 338). Taschner suggests that because Jacob is the one who identifies the opponent (and not the narrator himself), the narrator subtly distances himself from Jacob's identification (J. Taschner, "Mit Wem Ringt Jakob in der Nacht?—Oder: Der Versuch, mit Rembrandt eine Leerstelle anzuleuchten," *BI* 6, no. 3/4 (1998): 367–80, 367 + n2).

[167] Cf. Sarna, *Genesis*, 227 and *Excursus* 10, 383ff. See also: Miller, *Mysterious Encounters at Mamre and Jabbok*, 114; Brodie, *Genesis as Dialogue*, 332.

[168] Janzen, *Genesis 12–50*, 130. See also F.C. Holmgren, "Holding Your Own Against God! Genesis 32:22–32 (In the Context of Genesis 31–33)," *Int* 44 (1990): 5–17, 8. Based on parallels with the Oedipus myth, Nicol suggests that Jacob's opponent can in some way be identified with Isaac (Nicol, "Jacob as Oedipus—Old Testament Narrative as Mythology," 44).

[169] Cf. Westermann, *Genesis 12–36*, 516; Brodie, *Genesis as Dialogue*, 332.

[170] Cf. Waltke, *Genesis*, 448; Brueggemann, *Genesis*, 267; Curtis, "Structure, Style and Context," 130.

difficult to reconcile with the blessing that follows.[171] The ambiguity regarding the identity of Jacob's opponent seems to be part of a strategy or reticence by the narrator. It seems as if "the narrative does not want us to know too much."[172]

Something else that adds to the ambiguity in this passage is that in two places the subjects of the verbs are not clearly identified. In vs. 26 it is only when we read that it was Jacob's hip that was dislocated that we can identify the actors of the preceding actions retroactively. The same happens in vs. 27–28 when it is only after Jacob's disclosure of his name that we know who does what in the preceding exchange.[173]

> The lack of proper nouns is not unusual in Hebrew narrative but here it adds to the tension and the picture of the two combatants being evenly matched. It also increases the confusion over the event and the outcome.[174]

It might also suggest that the painful dislocation of Jacob's hip has something to say about Jacob being forced to utter his own name. Jacob is confronted with himself. Jacob's opponent strikes him where it hurts! Weber's suggestion of a wordplay between 'bless' (וַיְבָרֶךְ) and 'hip' (יָרֵךְ) seems to give further credence to this.[175]

When the man realizes that he is not able to defeat Jacob, he 'touched' or 'struck' (וַיִּגַּע) Jacob's 'hip socket' or 'hollow of his thigh' (כַּף־יְרֵכוֹ).[176] Scholarly opinion differs regarding the translation of both phrases. Alter firmly states that to render the verb as 'struck' is unwarranted. Alter suggests that in the Qal נָגַע always means 'to touch,' and that only in the Piel it can mean 'to afflict.'[177] However, in Hamilton's opinion it is difficult, if not impossible to decide whether נָגַע should be rendered touched or struck.[178] Either way, one wonders why 'the

---

[171] "God mediating of a blessing through a demon would be without parallel" (Waltke, *Genesis*, 445). See also Hendel, *The Epic of the Patriarch*, 105.

[172] Brueggemann, *Genesis*, 267. Similarly Sternberg, *Poetics*, 239 who speaks of 'the permanence of ambiguity'; Mann, *The Book of the Torah*, 63; Alter, *Genesis*, 181.

[173] Cf. Gunkel, *Genesis*, 349; Hamilton, *Genesis 18–50*, 330; Humphreys, *The Character of God*, 191; Hartley, *Genesis*, 283.

[174] Walton, *Thou Traveller Unknown*, 80. Geller, "The Struggle at the Jabbok" suggests that enigma and ambiguity are 'fundament characteristics' in the narration of Jacob's struggle (cf. Hamilton, *Genesis 18–50*, 330 n. 21).

[175] Weber, "Nomen est Omen," 79–80; Pennant, "Genesis 32," 180.

[176] 'Touched': ESV; JPS; NIV. 'Struck': NRSV.

[177] Alter, *Genesis*, 181. See also Westermann, *Genesis 12–36*, 517.

[178] Hamilton, *Genesis 18–50*, 330–331. Hamilton seems to have the better argument here. HALOT 5973 for example, gives 'touch violently' as a translation option in the Qal.

man' did not resort to this option before![179] The second phrase has been interpreted differently as well. Some commentators opt for 'hip socket.' Others prefer 'hollow of his thigh,' which according to some has sexual connotations, implying that Jacob's progeny is at stake.[180] Whatever interpretation is preferred, two things are clear from the immediate context. First, the man's 'touch' results in Jacob limping away (vs. 32), which suggests a painful physical effect. Second, despite this handicap, Jacob clings on for a blessing.

32:27–30

The mysterious assailant requests to be let go. Jacob will not let him go unless he is blessed (אִם־בֵּרַכְתָּנִי). Jacob makes this demand despite an injury of which the full impact becomes clear in vs. 32.[181] The fact that Jacob demands a blessing, despite likely exhaustion and pain, shows Jacob's severe tenacity, an almost primal drive for 'being blessed.' Jacob is a struggler at heart. We think back to the struggle in the womb, which seems to have been equally violent (25:22). Then Jacob grasped Esau's heel, here Jacob is on the receiving end.[182]

What sort of blessing is Jacob after? It is interesting that several commentators omit to say anything about this at all. Scholars, who do comment on Jacob's request, are divided about its merit. Waltke interprets Jacob's request favourably: "God sanctifies Jacob's absolutely sincere and undivided commitment to the blessing."[183] Hamilton is more tentative: "it is not certain that Jacob's request is an act of piety."[184] Earlier in the Jacob-cycle the reader had ample opportunity to reflect on the increase of Jacob's offspring and wealth as expressions of God's blessing. Here, Jacob is separated from all that he has. Is he merely asking for more? Fokkelman seems to suggest he does: "That is Jacob all over! From the most miserable situation he wants to emerge

---

[179] This is just one of many questions that remain unanswered (cf. Ross, *Creation and Blessing*, 547).

[180] Cf. Smith, "'Heel' and 'Thigh'"; Gevirtz, "Of Patriarchs and Puns," 52; Miller, *Mysterious Encounters at Mamre and Jabbok*, 103; Geller, "The Struggle at the Jabbok," 50; Pennant, "Genesis 32," 179 (referring to Gen 46:26); Hamilton, *Genesis 18–50*, 331 n. 24 for further references. I will leave that discussion aside because it is not relevant for my topic of interest.

[181] This is just one of several things the reader comes to realize as the narrative unfolds.

[182] Cf. Janzen, *Genesis 12–50*, 130–131.

[183] Waltke, *Genesis*, 447.

[184] Hamilton, *Genesis 18–50*, 333. Similarly before him von Rad, *Genesis*, 316.

an enriched man."[185] This strikes me as an unlikely scenario. Gen 32 shows that material abundance cannot buy Jacob peace of mind. In his prayer, Jacob asks for deliverance (32:11) and his inner-thoughts first and foremost express Jacob's desire to be accepted by his brother (32:21). It seems reasonable to assume that Jacob's request is in some way linked with these concerns, not with a desire to be further enriched in a material sense. However, it is true that protection from Esau's wrath would not only safeguard Jacob, but also his family and possessions. Alternatively, scholars have suggested that Jacob seeks strength to stand against his brother.[186] Maybe in view here are the covenantal blessings of Lev 26 and Deut 28 that speak about Israel's ability to stand against its enemies.[187] Westermann firmly states about Jacob's demand: "this can only mean that he ['the man'] transfers something of his supernatural power to him [Jacob]."[188] After all, Jacob has experienced the dislocation of his hip (or however we want to interpret that) and he now starts to realize that he is dealing with someone more powerful than a mere mortal.[189] Jacob's full realization about his opponent's identity may only have come after the event (vs. 31).[190] Similar to Westermann, but slightly more tentative, Hamilton suggests that "it would appear that what Jacob desires in such a blessing is the strength of his assailant."[191] Alternatively, Terrien suggests that Jacob asks to be blessed "because he needed a renewal of his being in order to face the ordeal of the next day."[192] Although these proposals have their attraction, Jacob's motives are not disclosed by the narrator. As a result, it seems impossible to determine with certainty what Jacob means with 'bless me.'

Despite this uncertainty, there are several things we *can* say. Considering the challenging circumstances in which Jacob finds himself, this episode again demonstrates Jacob's immense drive to 'be blessed.' Gen 25 and 27 show how far Jacob was willing to go, in order to obtain his

---

[185] Fokkelman, *Narrative Art in Genesis*, 215.
[186] Hamilton, *Genesis 18–50*, 332–333; Waltke, *Genesis*, 446.
[187] As understood by the original audience of the Jacob narrative.
[188] Westermann, *Genesis 12–36*, 518. Comments in brackets by me.
[189] Cf. Ross, *Creation and Blessing*, 553; Kidner, *Genesis*, 169; Curtis, "Structure, Style and Context," 133–134.
[190] Sarna notes parallels with the appearance of the angel of the LORD to Manoah in Jdg 13 (Sarna, *Genesis*, 228).
[191] Hamilton, *Genesis 18–50*, 332.
[192] S. Terrien, *The Elusive Presence: Toward a New Biblical Theology* (New York, USA: Harper & Row, 1978), 88.

father's blessing. Here, with a multitude of children and vast wealth at risk, Jacob's drive to be blessed is unabated. As argued above, it seems reasonable to connect Jacob's request with what he most urgently needs at this very moment. Possibly, we will discover more when it becomes clear how Jacob's request is answered. However, we must allow for the possibility that the blessing Jacob receives is different from the blessing he asked for. It would not be the first time that God and Jacob converse on a different level (cf. Gen 28:13–22). If we look ahead, the narrative seems to suggest that Jacob is indeed able to face what lies ahead because of what took place at Peniel. However, this could be irrespective of the original intentions behind Jacob's request.

In reply, Jacob's opponent asks for Jacob's name. Speiser suggests this is merely 'rhetorical;' "the object is to contrast the old name with the new and thereby mark the change in Jacob's status."[193] However, the text may well aim deeper. The fact that vv. 26–28 do not contain subjects (see above), means that besides ambiguity, there is an almost singular focus on the name 'Jacob.' As soon as Jacob is forced to say his own name, the reader is reminded of Jacob's first naming that took place after another struggle; the one with his brother in the womb; Jacob—'heel-grabber' and 'supplanter.'[194] Thus Jacob's answer functions like a confession.[195] Jacob is confronted with the meaning of his name.[196] According to Hamilton "the acknowledgement of the old name, and its unfortunate suitability, paves the way for a new name."[197] In addition, the restricted use of Jacob's name in this episode may suggest that the painful dislocation of Jacob's hip has something to say about Jacob being forced to utter his own name. Jacob's opponent strikes him where it hurts, but this has a higher aim. From this

---

[193] Speiser, *Genesis*, 255. Similarly Sarna, *Genesis*, 227.
[194] Cf. See *Section* 2.2.
[195] Kodell, "Jacob Wrestles with Esau (Gen 32:23–32)," 69; Fokkelman, *Narrative Art in Genesis*, 215; Wenham, *Genesis 16–50*, 296; Hamilton, *Genesis 18–50*, 333; Ross, *Creation and Blessing*, 553; Hartley, *Genesis*, 284; Taschner, *Verheissung und Erfüllung*, 157 n. 82; Waltke, *Genesis*, 446. Many scholars refer to work by M. Buber in 1936, who spoke about Jacob's 'Namenbekenntnis der Schuld' (M. Buber, "Leitwort Style in Pentateuch Narrative," in *Scripture and Translation* (eds. M. Buber and F. Rosenzweig; Indianapolis, Indiana, USA: Indiana University Press, 1994).
[196] "Is he not rightly called Jacob? For he has cheated me these two times. He took away my birthright and behold, now he has taken away my blessing" (27:36) Cf. Wenham, *Genesis 16–50*, 296.
[197] Hamilton, *Genesis 18–50*, 333.

moment of painful confession, blessing flows. Jacob's opponent takes Jacob's name and relegates it to the past, giving Jacob a new destiny: Israel. "Your name shall no longer be called Jacob, but Israel, for you have striven with God and with men, and have prevailed" (vs. 29).[198]

> It is the bestowal of the new name that constitutes the essence of the blessing and the climax of the entire episode. Jacob had feared for his posterity; now he is tacitly assured that he will become the patriarch of a nation named Israel.[199]

Much has been written about the meaning of the name Israel.[200] According to Fokkelman "the original sense of the name of Israel may never be established for certain by scientific research."[201] For Coats "the explanation for the name is rooted in the story, not in scientific etymology."[202] Ross suggests that the name is relevant for the self-understanding of the nation Israel as fighting with man and God. "The name served to evoke the memory of the fight," and is therefore "significant for future struggles."[203] If Jacob's intention was to find additional strength by means of a blessing, the name change suggests that what he really needs is a change in personality, a re-orientation. Thus, Jacob's opponent might not give Jacob what he asks, but what he most urgently needs. And by enabling a change on the inside, Jacob's destiny is changed into his destiny as Israel.

---

[198] This pronouncement resembles biblical idiom that indicates 'spiritual metamorphosis of some kind' (Hamilton, *Genesis 18–50*, 333. Cf. Jer 3:16; 23:7; 31:29). See also Waltke, *Genesis*, 446, following M. Weinfeld, "Jeremiah and the Spiritual Metamorphosis of Israel," *ZAW* 88 (1976): 17–56, 18–19.

[199] Sarna, *Genesis*, 227.

[200] Cf. Ross, "Studies in the Life of Jacob—Part 2 Peniel," 348–349; Ross, *Creation and Blessing*, 554–555; Wenham, *Genesis 16–50*, 296; Hamilton, *Genesis 18–50*, 334–335; H. Marks, "Biblical Naming and Poetic Etymology," *JBL* 114, no. 1 (1995): 21–42, 35–36 and 40; Walton, *Thou Traveller Unknown*, 81–87.

[201] Fokkelman, *Narrative Art in Genesis*, 216.

[202] Coats, *Genesis*, 229.

[203] Ross, *Creation and Blessing*, 555–556. Similarly Walton, *Thou Traveller Unknown*, 95–96 and S.L. McKenzie, "'You Have Prevailed': The Function of Jacob's Encounter at Peniel in the Jacob Cycle," *ResQ* 23 (1980): 225–31, who discerns the editorial hand of P: "In Jacob, P saw the hope that exiled Israel would also return to the land of their heritage and again prevail over their opponents" (p. 231). H.A. McKay, "Jacob Makes It Across the Jabbok: An Attempt to Solve the Success/Failure Ambivalence in Israel's Self-consciousness," *JSOT* 12, no. 38 (1987): 3–13. also suggests this episode was meant to give hope to the post-exilic community (cf. 10–11).

Since names in the Bible are inextricably intertwined with personality and destiny, the change here signifies a final purging of the unsavoury character traits with which *ya'akov* has come to be associated.[204]

This encounter might also have had the objective to show Jacob who is in charge. According to Humphreys, in much of the Genesis narrative before Peniel, God is often "'God' as constructed by Jacob (...) Perhaps it is time in God's eyes for him to take Jacob on. It is time for God to reconstruct Jacob."[205] However, Sarna's phrase 'final purging' is probably a bit too optimistic! Unlike Abraham and Sarah after their re-naming (Gen 17),[206] Jacob is still referred to as Jacob regularly.[207] This might suggest that instead of a 'final purging,' Jacob's life remains a complex battle in which a winner is difficult to declare:

> The special significance of Jacob's becoming Israel is the purification of character. Peniel marks the triumph of the higher elements of his life over the lower elements; but if it is a triumph for the higher elements, it is a defeat for the lower. The outcome of the match is a paradox.[208]

Indeed, as the Peniel episode is a strange combination of victory and defeat, there is plenty of paradox in the remainder of Jacob's life. For example, in his encounter with Esau in Gen 33, Jacob seems to be a changed man in some aspects, but appears to be fairly 'unreformed' in others.[209] I think Kodell is right to describe Jacob's Peniel experience as the "culmination of a process rather than a sudden about-face."[210] As a result, "we must not expect, of course, to find a drastic difference in the Jacob who meets Esau the following day."[211]

---

[204] Sarna, *Genesis*, 227. Similarly, Fokkelman speaks of a "completely renewed, purified relationship with God" (Fokkelman, *Narrative Art in Genesis*, 222). Waltke speaks of a 'reorientation,' not necessarily a change of character (Waltke, *Genesis*, 446, also referring to Roop, *Genesis*, 215). See also Hamilton, *Genesis 18–50*, 335 and Holmgren, "Holding Your Own Against God!," 9–10.

[205] Humphreys, *The Character of God*, 193–194.

[206] "Abraham and Sarah's new names in Gen 17 signified their new stature under God's promise" (Janzen, *Genesis 12–50*, 129). See also Weiss, "Jacob's Struggle: A Psycho-Existential Exegesis," 30.

[207] Cf. Alter, *Genesis*, 182; Hartley, *Genesis*, 287; Humphreys, *The Character of God*, 194; Taschner, *Verheissung und Erfüllung*, 159.

[208] Ross, *Creation and Blessing*, 557. "It was defeat and victory in one" (Kidner, *Genesis*). See also Brueggemann, *Genesis*, 269. von Rad, *Genesis*, 320 notes that Jacob's 'inner purification' probably was incomplete. Cf. Humphreys, *The Character of God*, 195.

[209] Armstrong describes Jacob in Gen 33 as 'not an entirely reformed character' (Armstrong, *In the Beginning*, 92). See also Mann, *The Book of the Torah*, 61; Hartley, *Genesis*, 284. See *Section 4.4*.

[210] Kodell, "Jacob Wrestles with Esau (Gen 32:23–32)," 69.

[211] Kodell, "Jacob Wrestles with Esau (Gen 32:23–32)," 69.

When Jacob asks the name of his opponent, Jacob is answered by a question. "Why is it that you ask my name?"[212] Maybe another way of saying "don't you realize who I am?"[213] As in Judges 13:17–18 it is "only after the disappearance of the deity that the protagonist fully realizes that he has encountered the deity."[214] The short note 'and there he blessed him' brings the dialogue to a close and is the climax of the episode.[215] "The blessing is the new name itself, and this is followed by a parting blessing."[216] What Jacob had longed for so hard, now happens. After this the narrator does not make mention of the man nor his departure. In 35:9ff. God appears to Jacob again and confirms his new name 'Israel.' In addition, the Abrahamic blessing is repeated emphatically.[217] There seems to be a genuine progression of the blessing theme in the Jacob-cycle. I will comment on that in more detail in *Section* 4.5.

32:31–33

Jacob's first response is to name the place Peniel; "For I have seen God face to face, and yet my life has been delivered" (וַתִּנָּצֵל).[218] The word 'face' (פָּנֶה) points backwards and forwards. When the cattle droves were on their way to Esau, Jacob expressed the hope "afterwards I shall see his *face*. Perhaps he will accept me" (32:21). In 33:10, at the climax of the encounter with Esau, Jacob will exclaim "for I have seen your *face*, which is like seeing the *face* of God, and you have accepted me."[219] The verb נָצַל connects the naming of Peniel with Jacob's prayer

---

[212] לָמָּה זֶּה תִּשְׁאַל לִשְׁמִי; the identical phrase appears in Judges 13:8 where the angel of the LORD replies to Manoah's request. Cf. Waltke, *Genesis*, 447; Wenham, *Genesis 16–50*, 297; Hamilton, *Genesis 18–50*, 335–336; Kidner, *Genesis*, 169.

[213] Hamilton, *Genesis 18–50*, 336. "Think, and you will know the answer!" (Fokkelman, *Narrative Art in Genesis*, 218). Cp. Sternberg, *Poetics*, 241.

[214] Waltke, *Genesis*, 447. See vs. 30.

[215] This phrase seems to function similarly to the closing phrase in 33:11 ("thus he urged him and he took it"), which also concludes the main dialogue.

[216] Hamilton, *Genesis 18–50*, 336. Some translators opt for "and he bade him farewell/took leave of him", because the angel had already blessed Jacob in changing his name (Waltke, *Genesis*, 447; e.g. NJPS; Speiser, *Genesis*, 255; Sarna, *Genesis*, 228; Hamilton, *Genesis 18–50*, 327).

[217] In view of Gen 35:9ff. Eising concludes that the blessing in Gen 32:29 and Jacob's change into Israel must be seen in conjunction with the Abrahamic blessing (Eising, *Formgeschichtliche Untersuching*, 128; also referred to by Fokkelman, *Narrative Art in Genesis*, 217 n. 21).

[218] Cf. von Rad, *Genesis*, 318.

[219] Cf. Armstrong, *In the Beginning*, 91; Brett, *Genesis*, 99. The Hebrew phrases for 'accept me' and 'accepted me' in 32:21 and 33:10 are different.

for deliverance (32:12).[220] Interestingly, the God whom Jacob assumed
was on his side (cf. 32:10–13), he encounters in a bruising struggle; the
brother whom he assumed to be a fierce opponent, will turn out to be
a warm and gracious brother. In 32:4–22 Jacob makes preparations to
meet with Esau. At Peniel, Jacob himself is prepared for this meeting
by God.[221] As mentioned above, these two encounters are linked in
various ways. It is almost as if the encounters blend into each other.[222]
It seems reasonable to suggest that Jacob's expression of surprise, having survived his encounter with God (cf. Ex 33:20), becomes a basis for
hope that he will survive his meeting with Esau as well.[223] Hence Ross
concludes "his prayer for deliverance (Gen 32:10–13) was answered.
Meeting God face to face meant that he could now look Esau directly
in the eye."[224] In addition, the explanation of Jacob's new name 'Israel,'
"for you have striven with God and with men and have prevailed,"
would undoubtedly add to his hope as well.[225] Finally, the fact that
it was possible for a man like Jacob to be changed carries with it the
potential that Esau could be changed as well.

The sun that had set in 28:10 now rises upon Jacob, as he passes
Penuel.[226] Jacob's limp and the dietary requirement that flow from

---

[220] הַצִּילֵנִי נָא, the climax of Jacob's prayer (see *Section* 4.2). See also von Rad, *Gen-esis*, 315; Fokkelman, *Narrative Art in Genesis*, 220; Hamilton, *Genesis 18–50*, 337.

[221] Alter suggests that what was 'crooked' (Jacob), is "bent, permanently lamed (…)
in order to be made straight before his reunion with Esau" (Alter, *Genesis*, 181. Similarly Kahn, "Jacob's Choice in Genesis 25:19–28:9," 85–86). There are similarities with
Ex 4:24ff., where the LORD has a violent meeting with Moses in order to prepare him
for his meeting with Pharaoh (Cf. Gunkel, *Genesis*, 349; von Rad, *Genesis*, 319; Ross,
Creation and Blessing, 558; Waltke, *Genesis*, 445; Hendel, *The Epic of the Patriarch*,
105–106; Pennant, "Genesis 32," 178).

[222] Mann, *The Book of the Torah*, 60–61; Brueggemann, *Genesis*, 272–273; Taschner,
"Mit Wem Ringt Jakob in der Nacht?," 371ff.; Armstrong, *In the Beginning*, 91.

[223] See *Section* 4.3. Cf. Westermann, *Genesis 12–36*, 521 Baldwin, *The Message of
Genesis 12–50*, 138; Armstrong, *In the Beginning*, 92. Hamilton, *Genesis 18–50*, 337
puts more emphasis on Jacob's prayer to be delivered and its answer.

[224] Ross, *Creation and Blessing*, 556; Ross, "Studies in the Life of Jacob—Part 2:
Jacob at the Jabbok, Israel at Peniel," 349 Similarly Hartley, *Genesis*, 285.

[225] Wenham, *Genesis 16–50*, 297.

[226] Cf. Jdg 8:8–9; 1 Kgs 12:25. "The latter spelling may have been used in vs. 30, for
it captures the wordplay on God's face better" (Hartley, *Genesis*, 287 and von Rad,
Genesis, 318 before him). As noted in *Section* 2.4, the sun had set, only to rise again
in the narrative when Jacob's twenty-year exile would be over (32:32); "so the happenings of nature attend, underline and symbolize what happens between God and
man" (Fokkelman, *Narrative Art in Genesis*, 48–49). "The sun symbolizes salvation,
deliverance" (Fokkelman, *Narrative Art in Genesis*, 221).

it are lasting reminders of what happened during the night.[227] And
so, struggle turns into transition. Darkness turns into light. Jacob has
crossed from one side of the river to the other. And as Jacob moves
from struggle to blessed release he becomes Israel. Although much
mystery remains, Jacob's 'crossing over' or 'passing by' appears to be
a major turning point in the Jacob narrative.[228]

4.3.3   *Concluding Remarks*

Theologically, the passage is very complex.[229] The reader is left with
many questions; some hard to contemplate.[230] Is it even possible to
consider the possibility that God would enter into a struggle with a
human being and not overcome him?[231] Several other issues evade closure as well. Clearly, my reading does not resolve such questions, and
maybe they are not meant to be 'resolved.'[232] However, this episode
makes an important contribution to our understanding of the nature
and role of material possessions and their associated attitudes and
actions in the Jacob-cycle. Apart from a desperate prayer in 32:10–13,
Jacob has been absorbed by practical strategies and actions to appease
Esau ('the gift'). However, uncertainty remained about their efficacy
(32:21).[233] When Jacob is separated from all he has, 'a man' struggles
with him and Jacob clings on for a blessing. Although Jacob's request
may be linked with his desperate need for self-preservation, the blessing he receives comes in the form of a name change. Again, blessing
finds expression in the context of struggle. Jacob's new name, Israel,
is testimony of this. However, this blessing is quite different from the
expressions of blessing, as encountered before in the Jacob-cycle (offspring and wealth). In a way, the man breaks Jacob's self-sufficiency,

---

[227] This dietary requirement does not reappear in the OT, but may have featured
in later Judaism (Cf. Waltke, *Genesis*, 448; Kidner, *Genesis*, 170; Westermann, *Genesis
12–36*, 520; Wenham, *Genesis 16–50*, 297; Ross, *Creation and Blessing*, 557).

[228] Cf. Sarna, *Understanding Genesis*, 206; Curtis, "Structure, Style and Context,"
135; Walton, *Thou Traveller Unknown*, 94.

[229] "The narrative reflects some of Israel's most sophisticated theology" (Brueggemann, *Genesis*, 270).

[230] Many other questions remain. Cf. Ross, "Studies in the Life of Jacob—Part 2:
Jacob at the Jabbok, Israel at Peniel," 339.

[231] von Rad, *Genesis*, 320; Walton, *Thou Traveller Unknown*, 87.

[232] Cf. Pennant, "Genesis 32," 182. Similarly Geller, "The Struggle at the Jabbok,"
54, who speaks of 'pregnant ambiguity'.

[233] Cf. Weiss, "Jacob's Struggle: A Psycho-Existential Exegesis," 29.

as epitomized in Jacob's injury and limp. "Jacob's ego must undergo a horrible death."[234] Jacob's painful confession of his own name, leads to a name change which is the essence of the blessing he receives, the climax of the episode. This name change opens the possibility for Jacob to be freed from his deceitful and self-sufficient past.[235] The name Israel also points to the birth of great nation. Therefore, Jacob's name change must also be seen in connection with the promise of nationhood made to Abraham in Gen 12:2.

When Jacob names Peniel, it becomes clear that this change of identity will enable Jacob to 'face' Esau and to survive that encounter as well. Jacob's new identity (in the context of relationships) forms the heart of the matter. Outside expressions of blessing (offspring and wealth) have moved to the periphery of the narrative. At the heart of the blessing Jacob now receives lies a change in how Jacob can view himself, both in relationship with God and men. Janzen describes this as 'rebirth.'[236] In a way, Jacob comes to terms with himself in the light of God, and this enables him to face his brother.[237] This resonates with McKeown's statement that blessing and curses in the Pentateuch should primarily "be understood in terms of the relationships involved. The contents are secondary and may vary depending on the context."[238] The blessing Jacob receives at Peniel is different from the blessing of offspring and wealth he struggled for before. The blessing Jacob receives here is more intangible.

4.4   Jacob Meets Esau (Gen 33:1–20)

4.4.1   Introduction

In the light of sunrise that signifies a new chapter in Jacob's life, Jacob limps towards Esau. The long dreaded meeting can no longer be

---

[234] Fokkelman, "Genesis.", 51. See also Ross, *Creation and Blessing*, 552.

[235] Cf. Weiss, "Jacob's Struggle: A Psycho-Existential Exegesis," 29.

[236] "The combination of darkness, a river, wrestling all night, and a new name at daybreak implies that at Jabbok Jacob 'enters into the womb a second time' (John 3:4) to undergo rebirth" (Janzen, *Genesis 12–50*, 130). Jacob's grabbing of Esau's heel at birth, and Jacob being touched at the thigh has been interpreted as another link between these two birth episodes (e.g. Janzen, *Genesis 12–50*, 131).

[237] The Peniel episode has inspired many psycho-analytical interpretations: e.g. Janzen, *Genesis 12–50*, 130–132; Armstrong, *In the Beginning*, 91; Alter, *Genesis*, 181; J.M. Cohen, "Struggling with Angels and Men," *JBQ* 31, no. 2 (2003): 126–28; Weiss, "Jacob's Struggle: A Psycho-Existential Exegesis."

[238] McKeown, "Blessings and Curses," 87.

avoided.[239] How will he be received? The narrator keeps us in suspense just a little longer before Esau runs up to his brother to embrace and kiss him. Following this surprising development, focus shifts to a three-part dialogue between the brothers:[240]

Narrative—setting the scene:
Vv. 1–3: focus on Jacob
Vv. 4–5a: focus on Esau (release of tension)
    Dialogue 1 (opening the conversation; engagement):
    Vs. 5b: Esau
    Vs. 5c: Jacob
        Vv. 6–7 Narrative: wives, female servants and children
        Dialogue 2 (the heart of the matter):
        Vs. 8a: Esau
        Vs. 8b: Jacob
        Vs. 9: Esau
        Vv. 10–11a: Jacob: (note length!) climax & blessing returned
        Vs. 11b Narrative: Esau accepts
    Dialogue 3 (disengagement):
    Vs. 12: Esau
    Vv. 13–14: Jacob (note length!)
    Vs. 15a: Esau
    Vs. 15b: Jacob
Narrative—the aftermath:
Vs. 16: Esau's destination (Seir)
Vs. 17: Jacob's destination (Succoth)
Vv. 18–20: Jacob at Shechem (transition with the next episode)[241]

At the centre of this grand scene stands Jacob's statement "for I have seen your face, which is like seeing the face of God, and you have accepted me" (vs. 10), which connects this encounter with the one at Peniel.[242] Jacob presses Esau to accept 'my blessing' (בִּרְכָתִי) and Esau finally accepts (vs. 11).[243] What follows reflects a 'process of

---

[239] "The long-dreaded meeting of Jacob with Esau" (Wenham, *Genesis 16–50*, 298). After all, Esau last recorded words constituted a murderous threat (27:41) (Sailhamer, *Genesis, ad loc*).

[240] As with the previous episode, and the one that follows, dialogue stands at the centre of the proceedings (cf. Ross, *Creation and Blessing*, 562).

[241] For another helpful structure including the use of key-words, see Ross, *Creation and Blessing*, 562–563.

[242] Cf. Waltke, *Genesis*, 452. von Rad, *Genesis*, 322; Brueggemann, *Genesis*, 272–273; Hamilton, *Genesis 18–50*, 345–346; Brett, *Genesis*, 99–100; Mann, *The Book of the Torah*, 61; Brodie, *Genesis as Dialogue*, 332–333.

[243] Cf. Fokkelman, *Narrative Art in Genesis*, 226; Janzen, *Genesis 12–50*, 133; Waltke, *Genesis*, 452.

disengagement.'[244] The relative length of Jacob's replies in dialogue 2 and 3 illustrate his considerable effort; first to convince Esau to accept his gift/blessing and then to disengage himself from him.[245] Characteristic for this scene is the way the brothers address each other. Esau speaks to Jacob as 'my brother' (vs. 9),[246] whereas Jacob persists in referring to Esau as 'lord' (vv. 8, 13, 14x2, 15), while referring to himself as 'servant' (vv. 5, 14).[247] Despite Esau's generous embrace, Jacob seems ill at ease. In the end, Jacob promises to follow his brother to Seir, which he never does. Vv. 18–20 brings this episode to a close and sets the scene for the events of Gen 34.[248] Material possessions are an important feature in this scene (vv. 8, 9, 11), but the main emphasis is on the reconciliation between the two brothers (e.g. vv. 4, 10–11). I will investigate how important a factor material possessions are in this reconciliation.

4.4.2   Commentary

33:1–3

Esau's arrival, which Jacob greatly feared (32:7), is now imminent.[249] The reader is kept in suspense a little longer.[250] Jacob divides his family according to status and affection.[251] Some things have not changed. Whether Jacob splits his party as a preventive measure in case of attack,

---

[244] Sarna, *Genesis*, 229.

[245] Cf. Ross, *Creation and Blessing*, 563.

[246] "The familial term with the first-person possessive suffix is generally a form of *affectionate* address in biblical Hebrew" (Alter, *Genesis*, 185).

[247] von Rad, *Genesis*, 323; Westermann, *Genesis 12–36*, 524; Wenham, *Genesis 16–50*, 298; 'court etiquette' (Alter, *Genesis*, 185); Hamilton, *Genesis 18–50*, 345; Sarna, *Genesis*, 230; Brett, *Genesis*, 100; Ross, *Creation and Blessing*, 560–561; Janzen, *Genesis 12–50*, 133; Brodie, *Genesis as Dialogue*, 321; Waltke, *Genesis*, 454. According to Bar-Efrat this reflects Jacob's feelings of guilt towards his brother and the desire to appease him (Bar-Efrat, *Narrative Art*, 67).

[248] Wenham, *Genesis 16–50*, 287.

[249] "Behold, Esau was coming, and four hundred men with him" (cf. 32:6). One of the many ways chapters 32 and 33 are connected with each other (Taschner, *Verheissung und Erfüllung*, 160; Brett, *Genesis*, 99–100; Hamilton, *Genesis 18–50*, 345; referring to S.L. McKenzie, "The Jacob Tradition in Hosea xii 4–5," *VT* 36 (1986): 311–22).

[250] Cf. Fokkelman, *Narrative Art in Genesis*, 223.

[251] The two female servants and their children go first, followed by Leah and hers, with Rachel and Joseph at the end of the line. "The same word חָצָה 'split' as in 32:8. Is Jacob still acting out of craven fear?" (Wenham, *Genesis 16–50*, 298). See also Fokkelman, *Narrative Art in Genesis*, 223; Taschner, *Verheissung und Erfüllung*, 160; Hamilton, *Genesis 18–50*, 343.

or whether this is merely for 'presentation purposes' we do not know.[252] Mann notes that "part of the richness of this story is that it tells us absolutely nothing about the motivation of the characters."[253] However, instead of staying behind, Jacob now 'went on before them' (vs. 3).[254] As Jacob approaches his brother, he bows himself to the ground seven times, as a vassal would approach his lord.[255] How very different from Isaac's prediction (27:29).[256] Throughout this scene, Jacob seems to make every effort to reverse the events of Gen 27.[257] This is most evident in Jacob's insistence towards Esau to accept 'my blessing' and Esau's compliance (vs. 11).[258]

33:4–5

The release of tension comes in vs. 4. Esau runs up to Jacob and embraces him, falls on his neck and kisses him, and they weep.[259] This

---

[252] Cf. Wenham, *Genesis 16–50*, 298; Alter, *Genesis*, 184; Waltke, *Genesis*, 453; Mann, *The Book of the Torah*, 61. Sarna thinks it is just for presentation purposes (Sarna, *Genesis*, 229). Similarly Westermann, *Genesis 12–36*, 524–525.

[253] Mann, *The Book of the Torah*, 61. For some interesting 'gap-filling' cf. Cohen, "The Jacob-Esau Reunion" and Reiss, "Archetypes in the Patriarchal Family"; e.g. "the two brothers now understood that each had been blessed by God, each had what he wanted, and they no longer need resent one another" (Reiss, "Archetypes in the Patriarchal Family," 18).

[254] Geller, "The Struggle at the Jabbok," 43; Fokkelman, *Narrative Art in Genesis*, 223; Janzen, *Genesis 12–50*, 132; Wenham, *Genesis 16–50*, 298; Hamilton, *Genesis 18–50*, 343. At this point, this is the only textual evidence of change in Jacob's behaviour following Peniel (cf. Fokkelman, *Narrative Art in Genesis*, 223; Taschner, *Verheissung und Erfüllung*, 160). See also *Section 4.2*.

[255] A full length bow "as a symbol of submission to a superior authority" (Sarna, *Genesis*, 229 and ANE references there). See also Gunkel, *Genesis*, 354; Speiser, *Genesis*, 259; von Rad, *Genesis*, 322; Westermann, *Genesis 12–36*, 524 and 530; Wenham, *Genesis 16–50*, 298; Alter, *Genesis*, 184; Brodie, *Genesis as Dialogue*, 333; Waltke, *Genesis*, 453.

[256] 'An ironic reversal' (Gammie, "Theological Interpretation," 124). Cf. Brueggemann, *Genesis*, 271; Sarna, *Genesis*, 229; Turner, *Announcements of Plot in Genesis*, 122; Taschner, *Verheissung und Erfüllung*, 161; Walton, *Thou Traveller Unknown*, 187; Humphreys, *The Character of God*, 196.

[257] Wenham, *Genesis 16–50*, 298; Fokkelman, *Narrative Art in Genesis*, 223; Waltke, *Genesis*, 453.

[258] Wenham, *Genesis 16–50*, 298. Besides bowing to the ground, Jacob also consistently refers to Esau as 'my lord' (see below).

[259] The plural *waw* at the end of this verb may be a dittography, which implies that Esau alone weeps (Hamilton, *Genesis 18–50*, 340 n. 6; Alter, *Genesis*, 185). Kissing would also feature in a reconciliation scene in the next generation (cf. 45:14–15; Hamilton, *Genesis 18–50*, 343). Hamilton draws attention to the phonetic similarity between 'wrestle' in Gen 32 (אָבַק) and 'embrace' in Gen 33 (חָבַק), yet another link between these chapters (Hamilton, *Genesis 18–50*, 329 and 343; Wenham, *Genesis 16–50*, 295).

sequence alludes both to the sale of the birthright (Gen 25) and to the acquisition of the blessing (Gen 27). The sale of the birthright concluded with a remarkable sequence of five short verbs (25:34). According to Sarna "the story of their final reconciliation is correspondingly described through a unique concentration of five amplified verbs."[260] Janzen wonders, "does Esau's embrace and kiss trigger a shameful memory in Jacob—of how he had disguised his neck to feel like Esau (27:16) when he kissed his father (vv. 26–27)—and then erase the shame?"[261] The verbs נָגַשׁ ('come near') and שָׁחָה ('bow down') provide another link with Gen 27.[262] Clearly, this scene is full of reversal. Hamilton suggests that the kiss "is possibly not just a display of joyous feelings but an indication of forgiveness (cf. 2 Sam 14:33)."[263] When Jacob arrived in Haran, Laban had been the one to run up to him, embrace and kiss him (29:13). Back then, Jacob had told Laban 'all these things.' Now, we see a much more restrained and diplomatic Jacob.[264] Following their emotional reunion, Esau's attention is caught by the approaching groups of wives and children. "Who are these with you?" Jacob's response is short but filled with panache. "They are the children with whom God has favoured (אֲשֶׁר־חָנַן) your servant."[265] In this short reply, Jacob does three things. Jacob focuses on the children; he draws God into the conversation by referring to his favour; and Jacob continues his deference towards Esau by describing himself as 'your servant.' Humphreys calls Jacob's sole mention of the children 'a nice touch.' "Jacob singles out the most fragile and vulnerable of his sizable establishment."[266] Hamilton suggests that Jacob wants to avoid mentioning the wives, because finding a wife was the official reason for Jacob's departure twenty years ago. "The more the past remains entombed, the better for Jacob."[267] In this first exchange,

---

[260] Sarna, *Genesis*, 229.

[261] Janzen, *Genesis 12–50*, 133. See also Sarna, *Genesis*, 229.

[262] נָגַשׁ in 27:21, 22, 25x2, 26, 27 and 33:3, 6, 7x2 and שָׁחָה in 27:29x3 and 33:3, 6, 7x2. Cf. Taschner, *Verheissung und Erfüllung*, 160–162.

[263] Hamilton, *Genesis 18–50*, 344. On Esau's forgiveness see also von Rad, *Genesis*, 322; Westermann, *Genesis 12–36*, 525; Ross, *Creation and Blessing*, 564.

[264] Good even describes Jacob here as 'uptight Israel' instead of 'upright Israel' (Good, "Deception and Women: A Response," 129 as quoted by Hamilton, *Genesis 18–50*, 347 n. 32). Similarly Goldingay, *Old Testament Theology: Israel's Gospel*, 279.

[265] Wenham, *Genesis 16–50*, 298; Hamilton, *Genesis 18–50*, 340; Janzen, *Genesis 12–50*, 133.

[266] Humphreys, *The Character of God*, 196.

[267] Hamilton, *Genesis 18–50*, 344.

Jacob employs the verb חָנַן ('favoured').[268] As noted in *Section* 4.2, the concept חֵן ('favour') that was introduced in Gen 32, permeates this scene (vv. 8, 10 and 15).[269] The wordplay of חֵן with 'camp' (מַחֲנֶה) and 'gift/tribute' (מִנְחָה), reappears as well (vv. 8, 10).[270] Jacob hopes that Esau will show him favour in the same way God did (vs. 8). Taschner makes an interesting observation about the use of these words in this scene:

חנן (von Gott) (33,5)
    מחנה (V.8) (so nennt Esau die Herden, die ihm entgegengekommen waren)
        חן (V.8) (in den Augen Esaus)
        חן (V.10) (in den Augen Esaus)
    מנחה (V.10) (so nennt Jakob die Herden, die er Esau entgegenge-schickt hatte)
חנן (von Gott) (V.11)[271]

Clearly, חֵן a relationship phrase *par excellence* is the focal point of this passage.[272] Jacob seeks Esau's חֵן by means of מַחֲנֶה given as a מִנְחָה, all within the context of God's gracious provisions towards Jacob (חָנַן). This concentric structure also demonstrates the intricate entanglement of material possessions with relationship issues that are clearly of a higher order. As noted before, the reader of the Jacob-narrative is not meant to consider the nature and role of material possessions apart from these relationship concerns. Finally, Janzen draws attention to the 'overtones of cultic offering' in this passage.[273] I will discuss the importance of that observation below.

33:6–7

The women and children come near and bow down before Esau. Again, we are reminded of the order of 'social status and affection.'[274]

---

[268] "According to Flack the verb describes 'an action from a superior to an inferior who has no real claim for gracious treatment'" (TWOT 694g). See also Westermann, *Genesis 12–36*, 525.

[269] Westermann, *Genesis 12–36*, 530; Wenham, *Genesis 16–50*, 298.

[270] Cf. Wenham, *Genesis 16–50*, 289; Taschner, *Verheissung und Erfüllung*, 146; Fokkelman, *Narrative Art in Genesis*, 205; Alter, *Genesis*, 177; Hartley, *Genesis*, 280; Waltke, *Genesis*, 439.

[271] Taschner, *Verheissung und Erfüllung*, 164. See also Fokkelman, *Narrative Art in Genesis*, 226; Janzen, *Genesis 12–50*, 133.

[272] Ross, *Creation and Blessing*, 565.

[273] Janzen, *Genesis 12–50*, 133–134.

[274] Sarna, *Genesis*, 230.

"And last Joseph and Rachel drew near and they bowed down."
Joseph is the only child mentioned by name (vv. 2 and 7), and he is
the only one who is mentioned before his mother (vs. 7). The narrator is already laying the groundwork for the next phase in this family
drama.[275] Another observation must be made here. In *Section* 2.4 I
argued that it is not certain how to interpret Isaac's deathbed blessing.
I showed how scholarly opinion is divided on whether it is Isaac who
does 'transfer the blessing of Abraham' or not. Taschner notes that the
verbs נָגַשׁ and שָׁחָה (vv. 3, 6 and 7) provide an important link with
Gen 27. According to Taschner, in this scene of bowing wives and
children, the narrator juxtaposes the deathbed blessing of Isaac (that
is reversed), with the promise of offspring by God at Bethel (that has
been fulfilled):

> Es wird dem Leser oder der Leserin an dieser Stelle der Erzählung deut-
> lich vor Augen geführt, welche der höchst unterschiedlichen Aussagen
> über die Zukunft, die zu Beginn der Jakobserzählung gemacht wurden,
> tatsächlich eintreffen und welche nicht. Dabei lassen sich auf der einen
> Seite Orakel und Sterbesegen und auf der anderen die in Bethel ergan-
> gene Verheißung eindeutig einander antithetisch gegenüberstellen. Die
> Erfüllung der Mehrungsverheißung (28,14) wird als das genaue Gegent-
> eil der im Sterbesegen gemachten Zukunftaussagen in Szene gesetzt.
> Dadurch macht der Erzähler unmissverständlich klar, was er unter
> 'Segen' versteht und was nicht.[276]

This supports what I suggested before. Again, the narrator seems to
suggest that what Jacob struggled for so hard in Gen 25 and 27, turns
out to be un-important in relation to offspring and wealth. What really
mattered were God's promises in Bethel (Gen 28) and God's faithfulness in keeping them.

33:8–11

Esau now switches the conversation to 'all this camp' that he met.[277] As
in the Jacob-Laban narrative, the attention now shifts from children to
flocks. This part of the dialogue brings us to the heart of the matter.
The mention of 'camp' recalls Jacob's decision to split his people and

---

[275] Cf. Ross, *Creation and Blessing*, 564.

[276] Taschner, *Verheissung und Erfüllung*, 162. It can be argued that an embryonic
form of this observation was made by Westermann, *Genesis 12–36*, 530, who discerned a juxtaposition between חָנַן and בְּרָכָה. See also Brett, *Genesis*, 98.

[277] 'All this company' (ESV); 'all these droves' (NIV). See *Section* 4.2 on the wordplay between 'camp' (מַחֲנֶה) and 'gift' (מִנְחָה).

herds into two camps out of fear (32:7–8).[278] It also recalls Jacob's lavish gift, which Jacob sent 'before him' (32:20–21). Although Esau has taken note of the 'camp,' we cannot ascertain from the text to what extent Jacob's gift was the reason for Esau's generous embrace (see below).[279] Jacob answers "to find favour in the sight of my lord" (cf. 32:5!).[280] Finding Esau's favour, restoring the relationship, seems to be Jacob's sole concern.[281] The favour Jacob received from God (vs. 5) Jacob now hopes to receive from his brother.[282] Jacob frames this hope by mentioning God's gracious dealing with him (vv. 5 and 11).[283] The question, whether this is mere rhetoric or whether these are the words of a changed man, I will leave aside for the moment.[284] Esau declines, "I have much, my brother, keep what you have for yourself."[285] "Despite his loss of birthright and blessing (…) he can speak to Jacob in princely generosity."[286] This statement confirms the impression that was created with the mention of 'four hundred men.' Esau has indeed done quite well for himself (cf. 36:6–7).[287] Hamilton notes that Esau

---

[278] Wenham, *Genesis 16–50*, 299; Fokkelman, *Narrative Art in Genesis*, 225.

[279] Cf. Mann, *The Book of the Torah*, 61 on the lack of information on the motivation of the characters (as quoted above).

[280] This phrase (or something very similar) occurs three times in this scene (vv. 8, 10, 15).

[281] "Not only is the post-Peniel Jacob courageous (…) he is honest as well" (Hamilton, *Genesis 18–50*, 345).

[282] Fokkelman, *Narrative Art in Genesis*, 225; Janzen, *Genesis 12–50*, 133; McKeown, *Genesis*, 156.

[283] Cf. Taschner, *Verheissung und Erfüllung*, 164.

[284] "To stand against Jacob is again to stand against God as he now construes it for Esau" (Humphreys, *The Character of God*, 196). Others think these are the words of a changed man (e.g. Waltke, *Genesis*, 454).

[285] Esau's statement יֶשׁ־לִי רָב and Jacob's statement יֶשׁ־לִי־כֹל ('I have everything;' vs. 11) form the outer ring of a concentric structure, with Jacob's statement about seeing the face of God at its centre (Waltke, *Genesis*, 452; Janzen, *Genesis 12–50*, 133). The ESV and JPS opt for 'I have enough' in both instances. The NIV ('I have all I need') and the NRSV ('I have everything I want') try to bring out the difference. Cf. Alter, *Genesis*, 186. Rabbinic commentators have interpreted this as Esau's final concession of the birthright (cf. Sarna, *Genesis*, 230 and 366 n. 5). Some interpret Esau's refusal as Near Eastern courtesy (Hartley, *Genesis*, 289).

[286] Alter, *Genesis*, 185.

[287] Turner, *Announcements of Plot in Genesis*, 127; Westermann, *Genesis 12–36*, 526; R.J.D. Knauth, "Esau, Edomites," in *Dictionary of the Old Testament: Pentateuch* (eds. T.D. Alexander and D.W. Baker; Leicester, UK: Inter-Varsity Press, 2003), 222. In addition, Brodie draws attention to Esau's genealogy in Gen 36: "the sons of Esau form a glorious parade, and not only of sons but of chieftains and kings (36:1—37:1)" (Brodie, "Genesis as Dialogue," 307, and his reference to G. Hoekveld-Meijer, *Esau: Salvation in Disguise—Genesis 36: A Hidden Polemic Between Our Teacher and the*

"lost out on the first son's double portion. But missing that two-thirds share did not reduce him to a pauper."[288] Although it is true that Esau did not receive Isaac's blessing, Hamilton's observation does not seem to be correct. It is unlikely that Esau and Jacob did receive any share of the inheritance before Isaac's death (35:29).[289] At the time of their meeting in Gen 33, Jacob had not received his share, so it seems unlikely that Esau would have received his. Interestingly, no mention is made of the division of Isaac's estate at the time of Isaac's death either (cf. 25:5–6).[290] Isaac's inheritance does not seem to matter in explaining Esau's and Jacob's riches.

Jacob presses on. Every phrase is geared to obtain Esau's acceptance.[291] Hamilton notes that Jacob's "'I will not let you go unless you bless me' now becomes, in effect, 'I will not let you go unless you accept my gift.'"[292] The climax of Jacob's appeal is vs. 10; "for I have seen your face, which is like seeing the face of God, and you have accepted me" (vs. 10).[293] Brett suggests that this shows Jacob's surprise and relief about surviving his encounter with Esau, just as he survived his encounter with God:

> Israelites commonly thought that it was not possible to see God and live (Ex. 33:20; Jdg 6:22–23; 13:22), so Jacob's dialogue in Gen 33 is meant to evoke a similar assumption: he no more expected to survive a meeting with Esau than he expected to survive a fight with God.[294]

The decisive point in Jacob's appeal seems to be his switch from speaking about a 'gift' to 'my blessing' (בִּרְכָתִי); yet another reference to the events in Gen 27.[295] According to Mann, Jacob's release of his

Prophets about Edom's role in Post-Exilic Israel through Leitwort Names (Kampen, The Netherlands: Pharos, 1996)).

[288] Hamilton, *Genesis 18–50*, 345.

[289] See my discussion on inheritance related issues in Chapter 2.

[290] See also *Section 4.6*.

[291] Note Jacob's double 'please' at the beginning (אַל־נָא אִם־נָא); the second occurrence of 'if I have found favour in your sight;' and the second occurrence of 'God has favoured me.'

[292] Hamilton, *Genesis 18–50*, 346. It would be even more apt if Hamilton had used the phrase 'my blessing' instead of 'my gift.'

[293] Cf. Waltke, *Genesis*, 452.

[294] Brett, *Genesis*, 99. Similarly Hamilton, *Genesis 18–50*, 346; Alter, *Genesis*, 186; Walton, *Thou Traveller Unknown*, 192; "a new relationship enlivened by affection and genuine reconciliation" (I. Selvanayagam, "Jacob and the Nature of Blessing," 13, no. Jul–Dec (1994): 94–98, 98).

[295] "In effect, the gift becomes compensation for the blessing Jacob had stolen from Esau" (Brett, *Genesis*, 98). See also Westermann, *Genesis 12–36*, 530; Sarna, *Genesis*, 230; Wenham, *Genesis 16–50*, 299; Wenham, *Story as Torah*, 76; Waltke, *Genesis*, 455.

blessing "marks the most dramatic conversion of his character up to this point."[296] Alter makes an interesting observation:

> But the term chosen brilliantly echoes a phrase Jacob could not have actually heard, which Esau pronounced to their father two decades earlier: "he has taken my blessing" (27:36). In offering the tribute, Jacob is making restitution for his primal theft, unwittingly using language that confirms the act of restitution.[297]

The narrator succinctly summarizes the conclusion of Jacob's appeal: "thus he urged him and he took it."[298] Most commentators interpret this moment as reconciliation between the two brothers, or at least as a resolution of their conflict.[299] Opinions are divided about the importance of Jacob's gift to achieve this. Vawter thinks it was Jacob's gift and servility that mollified an angry Esau.[300] Also Thompson seems to suggest that Jacob's gift was important:

> Esau has become a people and has achieved his independence, threatening Jacob when he crosses the Jabbok on his return home. The threat is overcome and the passage is peaceful as a result of the cleverness of Jacob (32:13–31).[301]

However, several hints are made by the narrator that Jacob's gift was *not* the decisive factor in explaining Esau's attitude towards Jacob. Esau had not accepted the 'droves' that were offered to him in Gen 32.[302] In addition, Esau's behaviour towards Jacob seems gracious and genuine, from beginning to end.[303] Waltke suggests that the "narrator indicates the sincerity of Esau's refusal by editorializing 'because Jacob insisted' (33:14)."[304] Kidner's assessment about Jacob's gift is entirely

---

[296] Mann, *The Book of the Torah*, 62.

[297] Alter, *Genesis*, 186. I think we cannot be certain of this, but a similar thing happened in Gen 29, where Laban says "it is not done in our country to give the younger before the firstborn," a similar surprising switch of terms (see *Section* 3.3).

[298] "'He pressed him' is a very strong term, as its use elsewhere (19:3, 9; Jdg 19:7; 2 Kgs 2:17; 5:16) shows" (Wenham, *Genesis 16–50*, 299).

[299] Sarna, *Genesis*, 230; Hamilton, *Genesis 18–50*, 346; Wenham, *Genesis 16–50*, 298; Waltke, *Genesis*, 455; Brett, *Genesis*, 100.

[300] Vawter, *On Genesis*, 353.

[301] Thompson, "Conflict Themes in the Jacob Narratives," 17. Thompson also sees this as editorial action to reflect the later journey of Israel through Edom territory.

[302] Jacob's anxiety (Gen 32) and the significance of his nocturnal struggle also seem to deny such a self-reliant interpretation.

[303] Some rabbinic interpretations view Esau from an entirely different perspective (cf. A. Butterweck, "Die Begegnung zwischen Esau und Jakob (Gen 33, 1–18) im Spiegel rabbinischer Ausdeutungen," *BN* 116 (2003): 15–27).

[304] Waltke, *Genesis*, 455.

negative. He compares Jacob with "a pagan who approaches his deity
with a gift" allegedly in order to bribe him for a favour. Kidner adds
"Jacob would soon discover, grace, not negotiation, is the only solvent
of guilt."[305] Conversely, Ross calls Jacob's gift 'an unnecessary attempt
at appeasement.'[306] According to Ross, Gen 32 and 33 together "show
that this reconciliation was a work of God in answer to Jacob's prayer,
not a result of Jacob's attempt to appease his brother with a gift."[307] So,
is Jacob's gift entirely irrelevant? Although Esau's acceptance might
well be an answer to prayer, I am not willing to go as far as Ross.
The gift might not be the decisive factor in explaining Esau's magnanimity, but I think we cannot disregard it altogether. It is true that
the text does not say anything about the effect of the gift on Esau,
nevertheless we may assume that the approaching droves must have
made an impression.[308] Jacob's offering of a gift/blessing, and Esau's
acceptance, are probably significant in a different way. I mentioned
Janzen's observation about the 'overtones of cultic offering'[309] in this
passage. Similarly, Wenham notes that the "verb 'accept' (רָצָה) is an
important sacrificial term used to describe God's receiving of sacrifice
(e.g. Lev 1:4; 7:18; 19:7)."[310] Also the verb 'favour' (חָנַן) and the words
'face' (פָּנֶה) and 'gift' (מִנְחָה) have cultic connotations.[311] The sacrificial resonance of these various phrases might prove to be decisive in
how to assess Jacob's gift and Esau's acceptance. Just as with a sacrifice offered to God, the sacrifice does not *cause* God's acceptance, but
signifies it. This is a crucial difference. The same may be true for what
takes place between Jacob and Esau. Waltke notes that "if Esau accepts
his gift, then Jacob knows he has found acceptance, even as when God
accepts the tribute of his people."[312] Although the text does not give
any clues to what extent Jacob's 'camp'/'gift' was responsible for Esau's
warm embrace, his acceptance of the 'gift'/'blessing' is *indicative* of his

---

[305] Kidner, *Genesis*, 168.
[306] Ross, *Creation and Blessing*, 536 ff.
[307] Ross, *Creation and Blessing*, 537. Fokkelman also notes the answer to Jacob's
prayer (cf. Fokkelman, *Narrative Art in Genesis*, 227–228).
[308] See *Section 4.1*.
[309] Janzen, *Genesis 12–50*, 133–134 (see above).
[310] Wenham, *Genesis 16–50*, 299. See also Wenham's commentary on Gen 32. See
also Janzen, *Genesis 12–50*, 233; Brett, *Genesis*, 99; Taschner, *Verheissung und Erfüllung*, 165.
[311] Cf. Janzen, *Genesis 12–50*, 133–134; Brett, *Genesis*, 99; Waltke, *Genesis*, 455. See
also *Section 4.2*.
[312] Waltke, *Genesis*, 452.

'acceptance' of Jacob. Hence, Jacob has been forgiven, although that is never explicitly stated (in the same way Jacob never explicitly asks to be forgiven).[313] Thus Janzen concludes:

> There is deep wisdom here, in which Jacob's pertinent self-abasement is followed by Esau's acceptance of Jacob's gift, which becomes a blessing. Esau's acceptance of Jacob's gift and Jacob's blessing of Esau are a combined sign of Jacob's full restoration to a bilateral relation.[314]

Although it is impossible to determine to what extent material possessions are responsible for the change in the relationship dynamics between Esau and Jacob, the fact that Esau accepts Jacob's gift indicates that a change in their relationship has taken place.[315] The various allusions that are made in this passage to the ritual of sacrifice seem to favour such an interpretation. This passage also illustrates the fact that although material possessions and their associated attitudes and actions are a key-ingredient to the narrative, relationship concerns (both human and divine), are considered of higher importance.

33:12–15

The narrator does not dwell long on this dramatic moment.[316] The process of disengagement is about to start. Esau invites Jacob to journey together, but Jacob uses the vulnerable children and nursing flocks to make a polite excuse not to do so. Jacob even resorts to exaggeration: "If they are driven hard for one day, all the flocks will die" (vs. 13). Jacob also reverts to where he was in Gen 32, behind the flocks (vs. 14).[317] Cattle that was used to bridge a divide, here is used to create another. Jacob promises to follow Esau to Seir, but he never does. When Esau offers to leave some men behind, Jacob politely declines yet again. The phrase "let me find favour in the sight of my lord" are the last recorded words between the brothers. Jacob never manages to address Esau as 'brother.'[318] Not surprisingly, there is great diversity in the interpretations of this passage. Jacob's behaviour has been

---

[313] Cf. Westermann, *Genesis 12–36*, 530; Hamilton, *Genesis 18–50*, 346; Ross, *Creation and Blessing*, 561; Walton, *Thou Traveller Unknown*, 188.

[314] Janzen, *Genesis 12–50*, 134. See also Waltke, *Genesis*, 455.

[315] Cf. Fokkelman, *Narrative Art in Genesis*, 226: "If Esau accepts it then Jacob knows for sure that the reconciliation has been accomplished."

[316] "The climactic exchange falls away quickly" (Janzen, *Genesis 12–50*, 134).

[317] Hamilton, *Genesis 18–50*, 347.

[318] The final word in Hebrew 'my lord' (Alter, *Genesis*, 187).

interpreted as varied as 'fearful,' 'deceitful,' 'wise' and 'obedient' or a complex mix of these. According to von Rad, Jacob's replies show "the mistrust of one, who himself has often deceived."[319] Brett calls Jacob's behaviour 'deliberately misleading'[320] and comments that "one might have thought that Yahweh's command to Jacob in 31:3 ('Return to the land of your fathers and to your kin') should have included a more significant reconciliation with Esau."[321] Mann describes Jacob's conversion as 'not complete' and adds 'true conversion rarely, if ever, is.'[322] Brueggemann calls the text 'realistic:'

> Reconciliations are seldom as unambiguous as we anticipate. Jacob's encounter with God left him an empowered, renamed cripple. His reconciliation with his brother included deception. The two meetings belong together in promise and in caution.[323]

Wenham suggests there also may have been a theological reason for Jacob's hesitance. God commanded Jacob to return to Canaan, which does not include Seir (cf. 31:3, 13; 32:10).[324] According to Wenham "these different motives are not mutually exclusive" and he calls the uncertainty in which the narrative leaves us 'deliberate.' After all, "relations between Israel and Edom were uncertain at the best of times."[325] Similarly, Janzen allows for multiple factors:

> Do we see here yet another deception—a sign of a not yet fully resolved fear? That may be. Or it may be that Jacob has arrived at a wisdom at which impulsive Esau, for all his own transformation, has not yet

---

[319] von Rad, *Genesis*, 323 (also quoted by Wenham, *Genesis 16–50*, 299). Similarly, Fokkelman explains Jacob's fear in Gen 32 as a projection of Jacob's own bad conscience (Fokkelman, *Narrative Art in Genesis*, 224).

[320] Brett, *Genesis*, 100. Interestingly, Williams does not list this as a deception episode (Williams, *Deception in Genesis*). G.W. Coats, "Strife Without Reconciliation: A Narrative Theme in the Jacob Traditions," in *Werden und Wirken des alten Testaments: Festschrift für Claus Westermann zum 70 Geburtstag* (Göttingen, Germany: Vandenhoeck & Ruprecht, 1980), 103 and Ross, *Creation and Blessing*, 563 see it as deception. Westermann, *Genesis 12–36*, 526–7 does not. Cf. Sternberg, *Poetics*, 244–245; Williams, *Deception in Genesis*, 37 n. 41.

[321] Brett, *Genesis*, 100. Similarly Coats, "Strife Without Reconciliation" and Coats, *Genesis*, 227. For a useful survey of the various interpretations of this matter, cf. Walton, *Thou Traveller Unknown*, 189ff.

[322] Mann, *The Book of the Torah*, 62. Similarly Ross, *Creation and Blessing*, 561.

[323] Brueggemann, *Genesis*, 273.

[324] Wenham, *Genesis 16–50*, 299. Similarly Fokkelman, *Narrative Art in Genesis*, 229 and Ross, *Creation and Blessing*, 565, who calls Jacob's decision not to join Esau 'wise,' although he does not approve of Jacob's deception.

[325] Wenham, *Genesis 16–50*, 299. Similarly Walton, *Thou Traveller Unknown*, 197.

arrived. In some cases, reconciliation may lead, not to cohabitation, but to separation on good terms.[326]

Fokkelman interprets this episode as part of a larger development in Genesis of how fraternal conflicts are resolved. In Gen 4 there is murder. In Gen 32–33 there is some form of reconciliation but brothers do not dwell together. However, at the end of Genesis, there is reconciliation between brothers who eventually dwell together (Gen 47–50). "Thus the theme of brotherhood, metonymy for the bond that links humanity, is handled with growing complexity from the beginning of Genesis to the end."[327] In Gen 36:6–7 another reason is given for the separation between Esau and Jacob; "for their possessions were too great for them to dwell together" (see *Section* 4.6). That phrase recalls the rationale for the split between Abram and Lot (13:6).[328] In the story line of Genesis that suggests that we also must see the separation between Esau and Jacob as yet another split between the 'chosen' and the 'un-chosen' (Abram-Lot; Isaac-Ishmael; Jacob-Esau).[329] Eventually, Jacob's sons, brothers-in-conflict who will be reconciled in Gen 45, will live together and will become one people: Israel.

33:16–17

So Jacob and Esau separate.[330] Esau travels southwards towards Seir, but Jacob journeyed to Succoth.[331] According to Sarna this means that Jacob first returned North (the opposite direction of Esau!), before going West.[332] The mention of building a house and booths suggests permanent settlement. The reader might wonder whether this means that Jacob does not plan to return to Bethel. Sarna suggests that Jacob wants to recuperate his losses in the fertile valley.[333] This may well

---

[326] Janzen, *Genesis 12–50*, 134. "Esau probably knows that this is Jacob's polite way of declining his proposal" (Waltke, *Genesis*, 456). Similarly Hartley, *Genesis*, 290.

[327] Fokkelman, "Genesis," 53. Note that murder was also considered by Esau and Joseph's brothers. Cf. Wenham, *Story as Torah*, 148.

[328] Cf. Janzen, *Genesis 12–50*, 134, who mentions Abram and Lot as a similar amiable split.

[329] Cf. Malul, "'Āqēb 'Heel' and 'Āqab'," 205.

[330] Fokkelman draws attention to the similarities between 32:1–2a and 33:16–17a. Laban separates from Jacob, as did Esau.

[331] סֻכֹּת (booths). Cf. Long, *The Problem of Etiological Narrative*, 11–12; Wenham, *Genesis 16–50*, 300; Hamilton, *Genesis 18–50*, 348.

[332] Sarna, *Genesis*, 231; Alter, *Genesis*, 187. See also Hamilton, *Genesis 18–50*, 348 and references in n. 34.

[333] Sarna, *Genesis*, 231.

be possible, but there is nothing in the text that suggests this. Ross calls it a "perpetual reminder of Jacob's prosperous return and peaceful settlement in the land."[334] In contrast, Kidner calls it a "backward step, spiritually as well as geographically (…): it is difficult to reconcile the call to Bethel with the prolonged stay involved in building cattle sheds (…) and a house East of the Jordan."[335] Events in Gen 34 and 35 will shed further light on this matter.

33:18–20

Following his stay at Succoth, Jacob comes safely (שָׁלֵם) to the city of Shechem.[336] This short passage bridges two larger narrative units. It brings Jacob's return to Canaan to a close and it sets the scene for the events that follow in Gen 34.[337] Jacob's 'home-coming' has several strands to it. First, it recalls Jacob's flight from Laban (31:18), which was initiated by God (31:3) and is now concluded.[338] Jacob's absence from the land of 'his fathers' that started in Gen 28 now comes to a close as well.[339] In light of God's promises to Jacob at Bethel, and Jacob's response, it is clear that God has returned Jacob to the land 'in peace' (בְּשָׁלוֹם).[340] It is fitting that mention of this is made immediately after Jacob's reconciliation with Esau.[341] When Jacob erects an altar and calls it El-Elohe-Israel, it is clear that Jacob has accepted his new name[342] and that 'God is indeed his God.'[343] However, his

---

[334] Ross, *Creation and Blessing*, 566.

[335] Kidner, *Genesis*, 171–172.

[336] Hamilton notes that this involved crossing the Jordan river (Hamilton, *Genesis 18–50*, 349).

[337] Wenham, *Genesis 16–50*, 287; Walton, *Thou Traveller Unknown*, 192–193; Parry, *Old Testament Story and Christian Ethics*, 134–135.

[338] Note the phrase "the land of Canaan, on his way from Paddan-Aram." Paddan-Aram is mentioned in 25:20; 28:2, 5, 6, 7; 31:18; 39:9, 26; 46:15.

[339] He 'arrived' (vs. 18) balances 'departed' (28:10) (Sarna, *Genesis*, 231).

[340] Sarna, *Genesis*, 232; Fokkelman, *Narrative Art in Genesis*, 229; Hamilton, *Genesis 18–50*, 350; Alter, *Genesis*, 187; Janzen, *Genesis 12–50*, 134; Taschner, *Verheissung und Erfüllung*, 140. Some commentators interpret שׁלם as the place of a town (e.g. Westermann, *Genesis 12–36*, 528; Wenham, *Genesis 16–50*, 300). Following Parry, *Old Testament Story and Christian Ethics*, 134–135 n. 32, I tentatively favour to translate this as an adverb. Most translations favour this option as well (cf. ESV, JPS, NIV, NRSV).

[341] Kodell, "Jacob Wrestles with Esau (Gen 32:23–32)," 69; Fokkelman, *Narrative Art in Genesis*, 230.

[342] Fokkelman, *Narrative Art in Genesis*, 230; Janzen, *Genesis 12–50*, 135; Hamilton, *Genesis 18–50*, 350.

[343] Hamilton, *Genesis 18–50*, 350. See also Fokkelman, *Narrative Art in Genesis*, 230; Baldwin, *The Message of Genesis 12–50*, 142; Ross, *Creation and Blessing*, 566–567; Humphreys, *The Character of God*, 195; Walton, *Thou Traveller Unknown*, 193.

homecoming is not as yet complete. Jacob does not return to 'his father Isaac' (31:18), or to his 'father's house' (28:21), or to his 'kindred' (31:3).[344] This might signal that Jacob's journey is not quite over yet (35:27). Having arrived at Shechem, Jacob camps before the city and buys a piece of land from the sons of Hamor, 'Shechem's father.' The events of Gen 34 are set in the context of an economic transaction, and economic considerations are a pervasive feature of that passage (see below). Mention of Jacob's peaceful arrival puts the events of Gen 34 in a shameful light (34:21).[345]

Besides bridging two larger narrative units and recalling various earlier episodes, the scene contains various allusions to the Abraham-cycle. Like his grandfather, Jacob buys a plot of land from Canaanites, and the price of the transaction is recorded.[346] Jacob also erects an altar. According to Parry, it is no coincidence that Jacob arrives in Shechem before moving to Bethel and Mamre:[347]

> Jacob, as Abraham, may have set his feet on the land but he, like his ancestor, was not alone: the Canaanites were in the land. This parallel with Abraham explains the significance of Shechem and Bethel in the plot. The very places draw our attention to the promises of land and descendants.[348]

Besides similarities with the Abraham-narrative, there are also differences. Unlike Abraham, it seems that Jacob intends to make Shechem his permanent residence.[349] Waltke draws attention to the similarities with the description of Lot's settlement in the vicinity of Sodom (13:18). According to Waltke, Jacob puts his daughter at risk as Lot did with his daughters.[350] If that is true, this might well be an implicit criticism of Jacob by the narrator.

---

[344] Brodie, *Genesis as Dialogue*, 334.

[345] Cf. von Rad, *Genesis*, 323; Sarna, *Genesis*, 232.

[346] "The exact price is given, as in the case of the purchase of Machpelah in chapter 23, because the real estate is to be acquired in perpetuity and the sale must be final and incontestable" (Sarna, *Genesis*, 232). "The purchase of real estate, as with Abraham at Hebron, signals making a claim to permanent residence" (Alter, *Genesis*, 188). See also Hamilton, *Genesis 18–50*, 349.

[347] Parry, *Old Testament Story and Christian Ethics*, 134.

[348] Parry, *Old Testament Story and Christian Ethics*, 135.

[349] Hamilton, *Genesis 18–50*, 349.

[350] Waltke, *Genesis*, 460.

4.4.3   *Concluding Remarks*

There are several allusions in the text that connect this scene with almost every other part of the Jacob cycle.[351] When we try to understand the nature and role of material possessions in this passage, these various contexts must be taken into consideration. This suggests that putting all interpretive weight on one context at the exclusion of all others must be avoided.[352] In my view, the interpretations offered by scholars in relation to these various contexts can be complementary. For example, an interpretation that sees Jacob's actions as a reversal of events in Gen 25 and 27 can be complementary with a view that interprets the outcome of this scene as an answer to Jacob's prayer in Gen 32 (e.g. Ross). So, how are we to interpret the nature and role of material possessions in this passage? As noted before, material possessions are an important feature in the dialogue between Esau and Jacob that leads towards reconciliation. They are also used as an excuse by Jacob not to join Esau. As discussed, we cannot be certain how important Jacob's gifts were in the appeasement of his brother. However, they do fit the pattern that material possessions and/or associated attitudes or actions are often at the heart of conflict in Genesis and that material concessions are made (and accepted) to restore a damaged relationship. The various 'connotations of cultic offering' (Janzen) in this passage seem to support the view that what happens with Jacob's gift/blessing and Esau's acceptance is *indicative* of their restored relationship.

If we consider this episode in conjunction with Jacob's encounter at Peniel it seems right to describe this as a twin-peak climax to the Jacob-cycle. Here we have the most important juxtaposition between the horizontal and vertical elements in the Jacob-cycle. The two encounters are entwined in several ways.[353] According to Brueggemann the

---

[351] The sale of the birthright; the deception in Gen 27; God's appearance at Bethel; several events in the Jacob-Laban narrative; Jacob's anxious preparations in Gen 32, including his prayer to God, and Jacob's struggle at Peniel. This scene also prepares us for the events in the Joseph-cycle.

[352] Such as the suggestion by Ross that "this reconciliation was a work of God in answer to Jacob's prayer, not a result to Jacob's attempt to appease his brother with a gift" (Ross, *Creation and Blessing*, 537). Similarly Elliger, "Der Jakobskampf am Jabbok," 26; Sailhamer, *Genesis, ad loc.*

[353] See also von Rad, *Genesis*, 322–323; Fokkelman, *Narrative Art in Genesis*, 230–231; Mann, *The Book of the Torah*, 61; Walton, *Thou Traveller Unknown*, 191–192 and 195–197.

two encounters almost flow into each other: "it is hard to identify the players. In the *holy God*, there is something of the *estranged brother*. And the *forgiving brother*, there is something of the *blessing God*."[354] Jacob expresses relief about surviving both encounters.[355] Both episodes demonstrate the intricate entanglement of material possessions with relationship issues. As noted before, the reader of the Jacob-narrative is not meant to consider the nature and role of material possessions apart from these relationship concerns. Both episodes show that relationship concerns are of a higher order. Both episodes also feature blessing in the context of struggle. Having received God's blessing, Jacob is now able to give (return) his blessing to his brother.

Finally, the purchase of land by Jacob draws comparisons with Abraham's purchases of land. The plot of land becomes a place of worship, which is indicative of Jacob's developing relationship with God. Some commentators have suggested that this is how Jacob fulfils his vow to tithe (28:22).[356] However, none of the other patriarchal altars required the purchase of land.[357] Sarna suggests that like Abraham, Jacob intends to establish a family burial ground. Eventually, Joseph's bones would be buried there.[358] However, this transaction initiates a relationship between Jacob's family and Shechem's, which will end disastrously.

4.5 Jacob's Family and the Shechemites (Gen 34)

4.5.1 *Introduction*

An apparent innocent visit by Dinah to 'the daughters of the land' takes an ugly turn as she is 'humiliated' by Shechem, son of Hamor

---

[354] Brueggemann, *Genesis*, 272 (italics by Brueggemann). Jacob struggles with God, whom he assumed was on his side. And Jacob is reconciled with his brother with whom he had struggled in the womb (Mann, *The Book of the Torah*, 63).

[355] Alter, *Genesis*, 186. Indeed, "there will be no cheap reconciliations" (Brueggemann, *Genesis*, 272).

[356] Cf. Sailhamer, *Genesis*, *ad loc* following C.F. Keil, *Genesis und Exodus. 3d edition.* (Berlin, Germany: Brunnen Verlag, 1878).

[357] Sarna, *Genesis*, 232.

[358] "The portion of land purchased by Jacob at Shechem plays an important role in the later biblical narratives. This was the portion of land where the Israelites buried the bones of Joseph (Josh 24:32) and thus represented their hope in God's ultimate fulfillment of his promise of the land" (Sailhamer, *Genesis*, *ad loc*). See also Sarna, *Genesis*, 232.

'the prince of the land.'[359] Negotiations that follow result in the agreement by the men of Shechem to be circumcised. When they are still
suffering the effects of the 'procedure,' Simeon and Levi put them to
the sword and the (other) sons of Jacob plunder the entire city. The
episode closes with a fierce exchange between Jacob, Simeon and Levi,
which leaves this episode somewhat open-ended, with plenty of tension unresolved (34:30–31).[360]

Source critics have found this a difficult passage to analyze.[361] For
those who focus on the text in its final form, several other challenges
remain. "Interpreting this narrative is fraught with difficulties."[362]
Although the text has great literary coherence,[363] there are important
challenges how to interpret the story and its place within the Jacob-
cycle and wider context(s). These issues have generated lively academic
debate.[364] The way the narrator seems to influence opinions in different
ways at different times presents the reader with various complexities.[365]
I will comment on such matters to some extent, but it is inappropriate

---

[359] The sense of relief after Jacob's encounter with Esau and his safe arrival (שָׁלֵם)
at Shechem (33:18) lasts a mere few verses although it is likely that several years have
passed between Jacob's arrival in the land and the events of Gen 34 (cf. Sarna, *Genesis*,
233; Kidner, *Genesis*, 172).

[360] Some commentators draw comparisons with the ending of Jonah (e.g. Sarna,
Genesis, 238).

[361] E.g. Westermann, *Genesis 12–36*, 535–537. See Wenham, *Genesis 16–50*, 309 for
a comprehensive survey.

[362] Jeansonne, *The Women of Genesis*, 87–88. Similarly T. Frymer-Kensky, "Virginity in the Bible," in *Gender and Law in the Hebrew Bible and the Ancient Near East*
(eds. V.H. Matthews, B.M. Levinson and T. Frymer-Kensky; JSOTSup 262; Sheffield,
UK: Sheffield Academic Press, 1998), 86.

[363] Cf. Sternberg, *Poetics*, 445–475; Wenham, *Genesis 16–50*, 307; Parry, *Old Testament Story and Christian Ethics*, 123ff. According to Alter, Gen 34 presents us with
a deformed betrothal type-scene (Alter, *The Art of Biblical Narrative*, 51–62; Brodie,
Genesis as Dialogue, 334–335, Parry, *Old Testament Story and Christian Ethics*, 153–
154). In addition, the story is part of Jacob's journey to return to Bethel (itinerary)
(Parry, *Old Testament Story and Christian Ethics*, 134).

[364] E.g. the debate between Sternberg, Fewell and Gunn (cf. Sternberg, *Poetics*,
445–481; D.N. Fewell and D.M. Gunn, "Tipping the Balance: Sternberg's Reader and
the Rape of Dinah," *JBL* 110, no. 2 (1991): 193–211; M. Sternberg, "Biblical Poetics
and Sexual Politics: From Reading to Counterreading," *JBL* 111, no. 3 (1992): 463–88;
P. Noble, "A 'Balanced' Reading of the Rape of Dinah: Some Exegetical and Methodological Observations" *BI* 4, no. 2 (1996): 173–203). Cf. Wenham, *Story as Torah*, 109–
119 and Parry, *Old Testament Story and Christian Ethics*, 122 for helpful overviews.

[365] A prime example of this is the fact that the reader only finds out in 34:26 that
Dinah was held in Shechem's house all the time. This sheds a very different light
on the negotiations between Hamor, Shechem and Jacob's family (Sternberg, *Poetics*,
456). Cf. Armstrong, *In the Beginning*, 96; Wenham, *Story as Torah*, 110.

within the confines of my study to comment on them in the same depth as other scholars have done.

It is probably not immediately clear to the reader how Gen 34 relates to its immediate and wider contexts.[366] Over the last thirty years, various insights have been generated to clarify this issue. Fishbane and Rendsburg demonstrate that Gen 26 and 34 stand opposite each other in the palistrophic structure of the Jacob-cycle and appear to fulfil a similar function in that they create an 'interlude' for the events that stand on either side.[367] In addition, Gen 26 and 34 have various elements in common.[368] Fokkelman notes that both these chapters are about generations other than Jacob's: his parents in Gen 26 and his children in Gen 34.[369] "The effect of this is to tie the Jacob-cycle into the book of Genesis."[370] Wenham demonstrates that Gen 34 is an integral part of the Jacob-cycle by analyzing how the narrative "presupposes what precedes it and is itself presupposed in what follows."[371] Parry, building on the work of Longacre, Wenham and Brueggemann, has analyzed the literary structure of this chapter.[372] His analysis demonstrates the importance of key-words in the narrative.[373] In addition, Parry comments on the similarities between Jacob's arrival at Shechem (33:18–20) and Abraham before him (12:5–9).[374] "It is here that the very first explicit promise of land is given."[375] Parry alerts us to the mention in 12:6 that "at that time the Canaanites were in the land." The Hivites/Shechemites seem to fulfil that role in Gen 34.[376] Pulling these various threats together, Parry is convinced that "the issue of

---

[366] Brueggemann, *Genesis*, 274.

[367] Fishbane, *Text and Texture*, 46–48; Rendsburg, *The Redaction of Genesis*, 56–59. See *Section* 2.1 and 2.2.

[368] Cf. Wenham, *Genesis 16–50*, 186; Parry, *Old Testament Story and Christian Ethics*, 130–133.

[369] Fokkelman, *Narrative Art in Genesis*, 240–241. "Action begins to pass to the next generation" (Janzen, *Genesis 12–50*, 136).

[370] As discussed by Parry, *Old Testament Story and Christian Ethics*, 131.

[371] Wenham, *Genesis 16–50*, 308–309, as also discussed by Parry, *Old Testament Story and Christian Ethics*, 130–131. See also E. Neufeld, "The Rape of Dinah," *JBQ* 25, no. 4 (1997): 220–24.

[372] Parry, *Old Testament Story and Christian Ethics*, 124 (referring to R.E. Longacre, *Joseph: A Story of Divine Providence* (Winona Lake, IN, USA: Eisenbrauns, 1989), 87) and 127. Cf. Wenham, *Genesis 16–50*, 307; Brueggemann, *Genesis*, 274. See Waltke, *Genesis*, 458 for an alternative outline.

[373] See also Wenham, *Genesis 16–50*, 307; Noble, "A 'Balanced' Reading."

[374] Parry, *Old Testament Story and Christian Ethics*, 134–135.

[375] Parry, *Old Testament Story and Christian Ethics*, 134.

[376] Mann, *The Book of the Torah*, 64.

exogamy and its implications for the divine promise of descendants
and land inheritance is relevant to the story's interpretation."[377] Ross
thinks that the story is about "the problem of intermarriage with the
Canaanites and the decision to destroy them (Deut 7:1–5)."[378] Building
on the work of these various scholars, I will investigate how this tale of
rape and pillage adds to our understanding of the nature and role of
material possessions in the Jacob-cycle. This will confirm our previous
findings to some extent, but there is also an unexpected twist.

4.5.2   Commentary

34:1–4

The story seems to start innocently enough. Dinah 'went out' (וַתֵּצֵא)
to see the 'daughters of the land.' The verb 'going out' (יָצָא) is one of
the key-words in the narrative (vs. 1, 6, 24x2, and 26).[379] It is striking
that it is the very first word on vs. 1 and the very last word in vs. 26,
the possible relevance of which I will discuss below. Dinah is referred
to as the "daughter of Leah, whom she had born to Jacob." Rarely
does the OT trace lineage through a woman.[380] Simeon and Levi, two
of Leah's sons (29:31–34), are the only sons of Jacob who are referred
to by name in this episode. They are the ones who lead the assault on
Shechem (vs. 25ff.). This suggests that the difficult relationship between
Jacob and Leah (and their children) is one of the factors to consider as
the story unfolds.[381] In rabbinic thought "there are two ways to view
Dinah's fate. One blames her for 'going out,' the other views her as
pure victim."[382] A similar diversity can be discerned among Christian commentators. Some take the phrases 'went out' and 'daughters
of the land' as implied criticism.[383] Although there might be hints of
Dinah's 'imprudence, if not impropriety,'[384] we must be careful not to

---

[377] Parry, *Old Testament Story and Christian Ethics*, 136.

[378] Ross, *Creation and Blessing*, 568. Cf. Westermann, *Genesis 12–36*, 544.

[379] Sternberg, *Poetics*, 469–470. Similarly Sarna, *Genesis*, 238; Wenham, *Genesis 16–50*, 307; Hamilton, *Genesis 18–50* and Parry, *Old Testament Story and Christian Ethics*, 127.

[380] Hamilton, *Genesis 18–50*, 353 n. 14.

[381] Note the meaning of the names Simeon and Levi (see *Section 3.2*). Cf. Armstrong, *In the Beginning*, 97; Jeansonne, *The Women of Genesis*, 91; Parry, *Old Testament Story and Christian Ethics*, 136–137.

[382] Graetz, "Dinah the Daughter," 314.

[383] Cf. Sarna, *Genesis*, 233; Graetz, "Dinah the Daughter," 312; Frymer-Kensky, "Virginity in the Bible," 87; Waltke, *Genesis*, 461–462.

[384] Wenham, *Genesis 16–50*, 310. See also Jeansonne, *The Women of Genesis*, 91.

put too much blame on Dinah, as the narrator seems to put the blame squarely on Shechem (vs. 2).[385] Ross seems to occupy middle ground in this matter: "her excursion into their circles loosened the stone for the slide. Avoidance of the Canaanites would have been far safer."[386] According to Parry this opening scene draws 'attention to the issue of exogamy.'[387] Abraham did not want Isaac to marry 'from the daughters of the Canaanites' (24:3). Rebekah did not want Jacob to marry from 'the women of the land' (27:46; 28:6),[388] a request that must be seen in the context of Esau's marriages to two Hittite 'daughters' (26:34).[389]

Daughter Dinah's 'seeing' the 'daughters of the land' (vs. 1)[390] is juxtaposed by the 'seeing' of Shechem, "son of Hamor, the Hivite, the prince of the land" (vs. 2).[391] Shechem's ethnicity and social standing will prove to be complicating factors. This could hint as to how the events that follow should be interpreted.[392] This is the fourth time in Genesis that a female of the patriarchal family finds herself as a (potential) object of foreign desire.[393] This time the outcome will be much more dramatic. Shechem's 'seeing' leads to 'taking' (from לָקַח), another key-word in the narrative.[394] The frequent use of this word perfectly illustrates the centrality of 'acquisition' as key motivator in this episode. The narrator paints the scene with three harsh strokes that scream outrage: "He took her and lay with her and humiliated her."[395] "Just as the reader expects violence but surprisingly finds peace

---

[385] Parry, *Old Testament Story and Christian Ethics*, 231. Jacob might not have done enough to protect Dinah (cf. Graetz, "Dinah the Daughter," 311).

[386] Ross, *Creation and Blessing*, 572. Maybe it would have been better if Jacob had not purchased the land and gone straight to Bethel (cf. 35:1) (cf. Waltke, *Genesis*, 468). See *Section 4.5*.

[387] Parry, *Old Testament Story and Christian Ethics*, 136. See also Sarna, *Genesis*, 233.

[388] Sailhamer, *Genesis, ad loc*; Waltke, *Genesis*, 462.

[389] The closing verse of chapter 26, which stands opposite Gen 34 in the Jacob cycle!

[390] Hamilton translates 'to be seen' (Hamilton, *Genesis 18–50*, 353).

[391] Alter, *Genesis*, 189.

[392] Cf. Parry, *Old Testament Story and Christian Ethics*, 137; Ross, *Creation and Blessing*, 568–569.

[393] Sarna, *Genesis*, 233; Janzen, *Genesis 12–50*, 135–136.

[394] Parry discusses the potential sinfulness of 'seeing' and 'taking' (cf. Gen 3:6; 6:2; Josh 7:21) (Parry, *Old Testament Story and Christian Ethics*, 137). Similarly Hamilton, *Genesis 18–50*, 354; Waltke, *Genesis*, 462. This key-word occurs in vs. 2, 4, 9, 16, 17, 21, 25, 26, 28! Cf. Parry, *Old Testament Story and Christian Ethics*, 127.

[395] "Three Hebrew verbs of increasing severity underscore the brutality of Shechem's assault on Dinah" (Sarna, *Genesis*, 233–234). Note the quick succession of verbs in 25:34, which characterized 'carnal' Esau (see *Section 2.2*). See also Alter, *Genesis*, 189; Jeansonne, *The Women of Genesis*, 91–92.

when Jacob meets Esau, the reader expects peace at Shechem, but instead finds violence."[396] In view of Gen 2:24, Ross calls it "a clear violation of all moral law."[397] Besides it being intercourse before marriage, the text suggests that this happens against Dinah's will.[398] Much scholarly ink has flown over the nature of Shechem's crime. Besides the clear condemnation by the narrator,[399] it is clear that it was considered 'a heinous crime' by Dinah's brothers (vs. 7).[400] Parry identifies three aspects "that may single or together be the cause of offence:"[401] "Gen 34 is about the rape[402] of an unbetrothed Israelite girl by a *Hivite* man. *It was a triple-layered crime.*"[403] For Sarna this exemplifies, "once again, a major theme of the patriarchal stories: the sexual depravity of the inhabitants of the land."[404]

The narrator clearly condemns Shechem,[405] but he complicates matters by telling about Shechem's love for Dinah (vs. 3).[406] This love is

---

[396] Jeansonne, *The Women of Genesis*, 90.

[397] Ross, *Creation and Blessing*, 572. See also Hamilton, *Genesis 18–50*, 355 with some interesting observations on word-order.

[398] M.M. Caspi, "The Story of the Rape of Dinah: The Narrator and the Reader" *HS* 26 (1985): 25–45, 32; Ross, *Creation and Blessing*, 572; Parry, *Old Testament Story and Christian Ethics*, 146; J. Fleishman, "Shechem and Dinah—in the Light of Non-Biblical and Biblical Sources," *ZAW* 116, no. 1 (2004): 12–32, 28; Y. Shemesh, "Rape is Rape is Rape: The Story of Dinah and Shechem (Gensis 34)," *ZAW* 119, no. 1 (2007): 2–21, 2.

[399] Wenham, *Genesis 16–50*, 311; Waltke, *Genesis*, 468.

[400] Parry, *Old Testament Story and Christian Ethics*, 140.

[401] Parry, *Old Testament Story and Christian Ethics*, 140ff.

[402] Lyn M. Bechtel, "What If Dinah Is Not Raped? (Genesis 34)," *JSOT* 19, no. 62 (1994): 19–36, 26–27 thinks that Dinah was not raped. See also J. Fleishman, "Why Did Simeon and Levi Rebuke Their Father in Genesis 34:31?," *JNSL* 26, no. 2 (2000): 101–16, 112; Fleishman, "Shechem and Dinah"; Graetz, "Dinah the Daughter," 307. Although Hebrew does not have a word for 'rape' (S. Gravett, "Reading 'Rape' in the Hebrew Bible: A Consideration of Language," *JSOT* 28, no. 3 (2004): 279–99, 279), I agree with Parry that 'rape' is the most plausible interpretation (cf. Parry, *Old Testament Story and Christian Ethics*, 140–146). See also Westermann, *Genesis 12–36*, 538 ('a forceful violation'); Noble, "A 'Balanced' Reading," 178; Waltke, *Genesis*, 462, who refers to HALOT 853; Gravett, "Reading 'Rape' in the Hebrew Bible: A Consideration of Language," 281–284; R. Clark, "The Silence of Dinah's Cry," 1 (2006), 3ff.; Shemesh, "Rape is Rape is Rape." Goldingay notes that this rape is different from the way the Sodomites might have raped Lot's daughters (Judg 19–20) (Goldingay, *Old Testament Theology: Israel's Gospel*, 277).

[403] Parry, *Old Testament Story and Christian Ethics*, 146.

[404] Sarna, *Genesis*, 233.

[405] Sternberg, *Poetics*, 446; Westermann, *Genesis 12–36*, 179; Wenham, *Genesis 16–50*, 310; Noble, "A 'Balanced' Reading," 179; Waltke, *Genesis*, 468; Parry, *Old Testament Story and Christian Ethics*, 149.

[406] Caspi, "The Story of the Rape of Dinah," 33. Cf. Frymer-Kensky, "Virginity in the Bible," 87–88; Hamilton, *Genesis 18–50*, 355 and n. 23, who suggests the literal

so strong that he wants to marry her (vs. 8). This "complicates the moral balance of the story."[407] Noble rightly states, that "nothing can be inferred about how Dinah responded to Shechem's expression of love."[408] In case the reader might sympathize too much with young Shechem, the narrator proceeds to report how Shechem instructs his father ("get me this girl for my wife," vs. 4). He uses "the bluntest form of imperative without even a 'please.'"[409] This short report characterizes Shechem quite effectively. First impressions seem to be confirmed by what follows. In the negotiation with Jacob's family, Shechem interjects his father's speech, and his boisterous willingness to be circumcised gives the impression of an impetuous young man, who is used to getting his way.[410] After all, 'he was the most honoured of all his father's house' (vs. 19). Shechem is not rebuked for his behaviour by his father, whose compliance is immediate (vs. 6). Shechem's lack of restraint, which is not confronted by parental rebuke, is one of the elements that contribute to the disastrous developments that follow.[411] Already in these few verses the narrator presents the reader with a complex mix of facts and feelings. This suggests that the situation might not be as simple as the reader might expect.[412]

34:5–7

The next scene offers the stark contrast between Jacob's reaction on hearing the news, and the reaction of his sons. Jacob hears that Shechem had 'defiled' (טמא) his daughter. This phrase is also used

---

expression can have "a sense of guilt or repentance." Amnon hated Tamar following his rape (2 Sam 13:15–17) (cf. Wenham, *Genesis 16–50*, 310). For other comparisons between these two rapes, see Graetz, "Dinah the Daughter," 309ff.; Hamilton, *Genesis 18–50*, 362.

[407] Alter, *Genesis*, 190.

[408] Noble, "A 'Balanced' Reading," 179.

[409] Wenham, *Genesis 16–50*, 311. See also Jeansonne, *The Women of Genesis*, 92; Waltke, *Genesis*, 463. Commentators disagree about Shechem's use of the phrase ילדה. According to Wenham he describes Dinah rather disparagingly as 'this child' (Wenham, *Genesis 16–50*, 311). Similarly L. Brisman, *The Voice of Jacob: On the Composition of Genesis* (Bloomington & Indianapolis, Indiana, USA: Indiana University Press, 1990), 97. In contrast, Alter thinks this "suggests her vulnerability and the tenderness he now feels for her" (Alter, *Genesis*, 190).

[410] Cf. Brodie, *Genesis as Dialogue*, 340; Parry, *Old Testament Story and Christian Ethics*, 159.

[411] A similar thing can be said of the rape of Tamar. David is angry but no mention is made of any disciplinary action towards Amnon (2 Sam 13:21ff.).

[412] Jeansonne speaks of "the permanent ambiguity that the narrator has created in this account" (Jeansonne, *The Women of Genesis*, 88).

in vs. 13 and 27.[413] Sarna notes that "the dastardly act is now defined in religio-moral terms."[414] The narrator seems to utilize this phrase to capture the essence of what has taken place.

> The term 'defiled' is probably used on two levels of meaning. The more obvious is 'dishonored,' 'violated,' 'disgraced.' At a deeper level the term is no doubt used because Dinah was forced to have sex with an uncircumcised Canaanite.[415]

While Jacob's sons are still in the field "Jacob held his peace (or 'kept quiet')." Some commentators consider Jacob's silence a sign of wise restraint (e.g. B. Jacob).[416] Sarna moves away from that position by commenting that "the need to exercise restraint, pending the arrival of his sons, is understandable, but his passivity throughout the entire incident is remarkable."[417] In contrast, Armstrong cites 2 Sam 19:11 and Esther 4:14 to suggest that the phrase 'held his peace' (וְהֶחֱרִשׁ) "connotes culpable inertia or negligence."[418] Although that is not necessarily the case (e.g. 24:21),[419] the text suggests that there is every reason to be very angry.[420] Jacob, however, never mentions Dinah's name or fate (cf. vs. 30). The text does not contain any sign of Jacob's concern about Dinah or her honour.[421] One wonders whether this is because she is Leah's daughter or whether there are other reasons (see below).[422]

The mention that Hamor went out to speak with him (Jacob) provides a foil for the deep anger of Jacob's sons. Interestingly, Hamor came out to speak with 'him,' yet in vs. 8 he 'spoke with them.' As soon as Jacob's angry sons appear no mention is made of Jacob's

---

[413] Cf. Noble, "A 'Balanced' Reading," 191.

[414] Sarna, *Genesis*, 234. Similarly Brueggemann, *Genesis*, 275.

[415] Reyburn, *A Handbook on Genesis*, 788. See also Hamilton, *Genesis 18–50*, 356.

[416] E.g. Jacob, *Genesis*, 650–651; Hartley, *Genesis*, 293.

[417] Sarna, *Genesis*, 234.

[418] Armstrong, *In the Beginning*, 94–95. Very similar to Sternberg, *Poetics*, 448.

[419] Cf. Fewell, "Tipping the Balance," 198 and n. 8, as also cited by Noble, "A 'Balanced' Reading," 179.

[420] Compare this with David's reaction when he heard about Tamar being raped by Amnon; he was 'very angry' (2 Sam 13:21). However, like Jacob, David did not take the matter further (cf. Hamilton, *Genesis 18–50*, 356). See also Graetz, "Dinah the Daughter," 309; Waltke, *Genesis*, 463.

[421] Wenham, *Genesis 16–50*, 311. 'Callous indifference' (Armstrong, *In the Beginning*, 95). Note the difference with Jacob's reaction to the news of Joseph's death (37:34–35) (Hamilton, *Genesis 18–50*, 356; Waltke, *Genesis*, 463).

[422] Armstrong, *In the Beginning*, 95; Jeansonne, *The Women of Genesis*, 92.

involvement until vs. 30. It seems as if Jacob abdicates his patriarchal responsibility.[423] Some suggest Jacob is paralyzed by anxiety about his security (vs. 30; 35:5),[424] others think that he is merely pragmatic and is willing to go along with Hamor's proposal, considering it the best solution for a difficult situation.[425] However, up to vs. 30, the text does not disclose Jacob's thoughts or feelings.

When the sons of Jacob hear the news, they are 'indignant' and 'very angry,' "because he had done an outrageous thing (נְבָלָה) in Israel."[426] According to Phillips, נְבָלָה "indicates an action which is to be utterly deplored."[427] Wenham notes that elsewhere it is used "of crimes warranting the death penalty."[428] It is reasonable to assume that "the narrator thinks the grief and anger of the brothers is a natural and correct reaction to the incident."[429] At this point, the narrator seems to 'elicit maximum support for [the sons].'[430]

Noteworthy is the mention of 'Israel.'[431] Although Jacob has been renamed Israel and his sons have accepted that change, Jacob is consistently referred to as Jacob in the story and his sons as 'the sons of Jacob' (vs. 7, 13, 25, and 27).[432] The relevance of this becomes clear later.

---

[423] Ross, *Creation and Blessing*, 573; Waltke, *Genesis*, 467.

[424] Jeansonne, *The Women of Genesis*, 92. See also Brodie, *Genesis as Dialogue*, 336.

[425] Fleishman, "Why Did Simeon and Levi Rebuke Their Father in Genesis 34:31?," 112. See also Brueggemann, *Genesis*, 207.

[426] It is not entirely clear when and how the sons of Jacob hear the news. Scholarly opinion is divided (cf. Sarna, *Genesis*, 234; Jeansonne, *The Women of Genesis*, 93; Wenham, *Genesis 16–50*, 311; Hamilton, *Genesis 18–50*, 356). On the anger of Jacob's sons, cf. Parry, *Old Testament Story and Christian Ethics*, 157. Note the description of God's anger in 6:6 (Waltke, *Genesis*, 464).

[427] A. Phillips, "Nebalah: A Term for Seriously Disorderly and Unruly Conduct," *VT* 25, no. 2 (1975): 237–42, 237. Cf. 238–239 concerning Gen 34. See also von Rad, *Genesis*, 327; Brueggemann, *Genesis*, 276; Sarna, *Genesis*, 234; Hamilton, *Genesis 18–50*, 357; Alter, *Genesis*, 190; Ross, *Creation and Blessing*, 569.

[428] Wenham, *Genesis 16–50*, 311.

[429] Parry, *Old Testament Story and Christian Ethics*, 158. Similarly Ross, *Creation and Blessing*, 573; Waltke, *Genesis*, 464.

[430] Sternberg, *Poetics*, 455. Also quoted by Parry, *Old Testament Story and Christian Ethics*, 157. Similarly Jeansonne, *The Women of Genesis*, 93.

[431] Sarna calls it an anachronism, because Israel is not a nation yet (Sarna, *Genesis*, 234). According to Wenham this "suggests that the brothers' view of what is right and proper has abiding validity in national life" (Wenham, *Genesis 16–50*, 312). There is the possibility that Israel refers to Jacob himself (Sternberg, *Poetics*, 453; Hamilton, *Genesis 18–50*, 357; Alter, *Genesis*, 190).

[432] Janzen, *Genesis 12–50*, 136; Waltke, *Genesis*, 459; Humphreys, *The Character of God*, 197.

34:8–12

In this tense setting, Hamor formally addresses Jacob and his sons.
Vv. 8–12 contain two speeches that are joined together. Hamor opens
with a plea regarding Dinah to 'give her to him to be his wife' (vs. 8).
Shechem interjects with his own passionate plea in vs. 11 and closes
with a similar request:

תְּנוּ נָא אֹתָהּ לוֹ לְאִשָּׁה
vs. 8

וּתְנוּ־לִי אֶת־הַנַּעֲרָ לְאִשָּׁה
vs. 11

Various economic considerations stand at the heart of the combined
speeches. Both Hamor and Shechem do not mention what has occurred
nor express regret in any way.[433] Instead, Hamor opens with the mention of Shechem's longing (cf. vs. 3). This again shows Hamor's full
compliance with Shechem's request. Hamor then paints the bigger picture. The proposed marriage of one couple becomes intermarriage on
a large scale (vs. 9).[434] The associated benefit for Jacob's family will be
that they shall dwell together with the Shechemites and that the land
shall be open to them (vs. 10). "Hamor, in effect, offers what God has
promised."[435] Hamor finishes with a strong appeal, consisting of three
imperatives; "dwell and trade in it and get property in it."[436] According to Sarna "this last is the most valuable of the privileges offered,
even as it is also a subtle and pointed reminder to Jacob of his present
alien and disadvantaged position."[437] This clause also seems somewhat
strange. Jacob has already been able to acquire property, without inter-
marrying. Could this be a subtle threat? Overall, Hamor's proposal
appears to be polite and generous. His rhetoric is very confident as he
pushes for agreement. However, he appears to be completely insensitive to "the moral offence his son has caused."[438] His focus on the

---

[433] Jeansonne, *The Women of Genesis*, 93; Hartley, *Genesis*, 293–294.
[434] Cf. Guenther, "A Typology of Israelite Marriage," 390–391.
[435] Wenham, *Genesis 16–50*, 312. Similarly Ross, *Creation and Blessing*, 574.
[436] וּסְחָרוּהָ is translated by most English translations as 'trade in it' (e.g. EVS, NIV, NRSV, JPS). Probably it is better to translate it as 'move about freely' (E.A. Speiser, "The Verb SHR in Genesis and Early Hebrew Movements," *BASOR* 164 (1961): 23–28; Speiser, *Genesis*, 264–265; Westermann, *Genesis 12–36*, 539; Sarna, *Genesis*, 235; Wenham, *Genesis 16–50*, 311; Alter, *Genesis*, 191).
[437] Sarna, *Genesis*, 235.
[438] Parry, *Old Testament Story and Christian Ethics*, 159.

economic benefits of an alliance, while ignoring the atrocity, leaves the genuine and deep-felt anger of Jacob's sons (and the danger that is associated with that) unaddressed. This undoubtedly contributes to his downfall.[439]

Jacob's family does not get much time to dwell on Hamor's grand scheme. Shechem's interruption draws the attention back to the initial request to give Dinah to Shechem as his wife. Shechem's request is a mix of politeness and urgency: "let me find favor in your eyes, and whatever you say to me I will give" (vs.11). 'Taking' is now balanced with 'giving.'[440] Do we hear an echo of Laban's apparently generous offer in that other negotiation (30:28)? Shechem offers to pay whatever bride-price is demanded. For some this not only demonstrates how much Shechem wants to marry Dinah, but also "how eager he is to make restitution for what he has done."[441] I agree with Noble that the strength of Shechem's love for Dinah is the *only* motive that can be found in the text to explain Shechem's offer (cf. vs. 19).[442] Shechem, like Hamor, never expresses remorse.

How is the reader to evaluate these proposals? At this point it is too early to answer fully that question.[443] Hamor and Shechem avoid mentioning the atrocity nor express any form of regret, but they do offer concessions of a material nature to resolve the conflict. Hamor's 'land promise' stands at the heart of that offer. Regarding the 'bride-price,' Parry notes that if the issue were money, Jacob's family could not "have got a better deal anywhere else."[444] Brett suggests that Shechem "is in effect showing willingness to abide by the terms of the Deuteronomic law."[445] (Deut 22:28–29). Although that would be adherence *avant la lettre*, the story's original audience could well have understood it that way.[446] Although Shechem might show compliance to the

---

[439] Cf. Parry, *Old Testament Story and Christian Ethics*, 159.

[440] Alter, *Genesis*, 191.

[441] Fewell, "Tipping the Balance," 200–201, also cited by Noble, "A 'Balanced' Reading," 181.

[442] Noble, "A 'Balanced' Reading," 181.

[443] Jeansonne, *The Women of Genesis*, 94; Parry, *Old Testament Story and Christian Ethics*, 155–157.

[444] Parry, *Old Testament Story and Christian Ethics*, 159.

[445] Brett, *Genesis*, 101. Alternatively, Deut 22:28–29 can be considered "an internal commentary on the story of Dinah" (Carmichael, *Women, Law and the Genesis Traditions*, as referred to by Graetz, "Dinah the Daughter," 309).

[446] Alternatively, it has been suggested that "Shechem was willing to obey the law of the land as decreed by Mesopotamian legal sources" (Graetz, "Dinah the Daughter," 308 and n. 1 referring to J.J. Finkelstein. See also *Sarna, Genesis*, 235).

Torah, and even agrees to be circumcised, he never makes the God
of Israel his God, neither is that something that is explained to him.[447]
Unfortunately (for the Shechemites) it is not a matter of money. When
Shechem concludes his appeal, he repeats "I will give whatever you say
to me." And indeed he will!

The original audience of this story would have known there is
another fundamental problem:

> It sounds a generous proposal, but it is just such an arrangement that
> Deut 7:3 prohibits: "You shall not make marriages with them, giving
> your daughters to their sons or taking their daughters for your sons," a
> stance later endorsed by Josh 23:12; Ezra 9:14.[448]

The full implications of Hamor's proposal become clear in his speech to
the Shechemites (vv. 21–23). The fact that it is Hamor who makes the
'land promise,' instead of God, and that intermarriage would absorb
Jacob's family, so that they will never become an independent nation,
sits very uneasy with God's promises to the Patriarchs (12:2).[449]

> Will Israel become a great nation by becoming "one people" with the
> Canaanite population? Will they gain possession of the land by inter-
> marriage (vs. 10)? Throughout the Pentateuchal narrative the answer to
> such questions is always a resounding no.[450]

More light will be shed on these issues by events that follow. For
example, it is only revealed in vs. 26 that Dinah is held in Shechem's
house. According to Sternberg "the soft-spoken Hivites negotiate from
a strong position unfairly obtained."[451] Parry argues that Dinah is not
used as a hostage but as a *potential* hostage.[452] The difference may well
be too difficult to tell for Jacob's family! Dinah's absence must have
been acutely difficult for Jacob's family. This was probably aggravated
by the difference in status between the two parties. Jacob and his sons
are foreign settlers, a status of which they are reminded by Hamor,

---

[447] Cf. Brodie, *Genesis as Dialogue*, 340. See below.
[448] Wenham, *Genesis 16–50*, 312; Ross, *Creation and Blessing*, 568–569; Taschner, *Verheissung und Erfüllung*, 208; Waltke, *Genesis*, 464.
[449] Waltke calls it 'cultural genocide' (Waltke, *Genesis*, 466).
[450] Mann, *The Book of the Torah*, 64. See also Jeansonne, *The Women of Genesis*, 94.
[451] Sternberg, *Poetics*, 456. See also Sarna, *Genesis*, 235.
[452] Parry, *Old Testament Story and Christian Ethics*, 162.

the local ruler from whom they have just bought property.[453] There is a real power-imbalance between the two parties.[454] Although Hamor and Shechem make material concessions to resolve the conflict, which seems positive, the fact that Dinah is still in their 'possession' and that they never mention what has taken place, raise questions about their attitude and intentions. However, we should not attempt to close 'gaps' prematurely.[455]

34:13–17

Jacob's sons now take centre stage.[456] It is disclosed immediately that they answer Shechem and Hamor deceitfully (בְּמִרְמָה). They are indeed the sons of Jacob![457] Although the reader does not yet know the nature of the deceit, it is clear that what follows must not necessarily be taken at face value.[458] Then the reason for their deceit is given: "because he had defiled their sister Dinah." This, to some extent, softens the deceit.[459] Also, "by retaining this complexity of the action, the narrator continues to force the reader to remain conscious of the moral ambiguity of their actions."[460] Jacob's sons immediately decline the offer. Neither economic advancement nor the size of the bride-price is said to be the issue.[461] Only if all male Shechemites are circumcised (cf. 17:10) will Jacob's family agree to intermarry and dwell together with them.[462] Note the resonance with Hamor's proposal in vv. 9–10. The end result will be that they become 'one people' (vs. 22!). If the Shechemites do not agree, there will be no intermarriage with all the associated

---

[453] Sarna, *Genesis*, 235.

[454] Cf. Jeansonne, *The Women of Genesis*, 92; Hartley, *Genesis*, 293.

[455] Parry, *Old Testament Story and Christian Ethics*, 155–157.

[456] Jeansonne, *The Women of Genesis*, 94. For an alternative explanation involving the institution of fratriarchy, cf. Sarna, *Understanding Genesis*, 174 and Speiser, *Genesis*, 267, as discussed by Neufeld, "The Rape of Dinah," 221. Similarly Gunkel, *Genesis*, 363; Westermann, *Genesis 12–36*, 538. However, this appears to be a minority opinion.

[457] Cf. 27:35. Deceit has moved to the next generation. Cf. Armstrong, *In the Beginning*, 95; Alter, *Genesis*, 191; cf. Janzen, *Genesis 12–50*, 137–138.

[458] Wenham, *Genesis 16–50*, 313.

[459] Sternberg, *Poetics*, 459; Wenham, *Genesis 16–50*, 313; Noble, "A 'Balanced' Reading," 184.

[460] Jeansonne, *The Women of Genesis*, 94.

[461] Cf. Noble, "A 'Balanced' Reading," 184. Sarna takes the statement of the sons at face value (Sarna, *Genesis*, 236).

[462] "They then cite the key stipulation of the Abrahamic covenant: 'all your males must be circumcised' (17:10)" (Wenham, *Genesis 16–50*, 313). See Sailhamer, *Genesis ad loc*, who lists various thematic links between Gen 17 and 34.

benefits. "Then we will take our daughter and we will be gone" is a thinly veiled threat as it anticipates the eventual outcome of the encounter (vs. 26).[463] The text does not reveal the inner thoughts of Jacob's sons. Did they ask such a high price in order to be declined? Or were they planning the massacre from the beginning.[464] Noble makes and important observation:

> This is hardly the approach of people who are ideologically resolved to prevent intermarriage by all means possible; rather, the prospect of intermarriage is used as bait to induce the Hivites to circumcise themselves, for ulterior motives which the sequel makes clear.[465]

This interpretation gains further credence with Brett's observation that Simeon was married to a Canaanite wife at some point (46:10): "Simeon emerges as a man given to extravagant violence and, hypocritically, he is quite capable of exogamous marriage himself."[466] If there never was a principled objection against intermarriage, I agree with Parry that a premeditated massacre would be "a calculated overreaction to the situation."[467] Alternatively, a straightforward refusal to intermarry might not have been a viable alternative considering the power-imbalance between the two parties.[468] For Sarna this makes the deceit more or less acceptable.[469] The text does not fully disclose why Jacob's sons took this particular course of action, but we must not forget that they answered Hamor and Shechem 'deceitfully.'

34:18–24
Possibly to the surprise of Jacob's sons, Hamor and Shechem wholeheartedly agree with the proposal, and Shechem does not delay in being circumcised.[470] The fact that the narrator focuses on Shechem's circumcision (what about Hamor's?) may be relevant. Sarna detects

---

[463] Jacob, *Genesis*, 655. "Its use here has an ominous ring" (Sarna, *Genesis*, 236).
[464] Cf. Wenham, *Genesis 16–50*, 313; Janzen, *Genesis 12–50*, 137.
[465] Noble, "A 'Balanced' Reading," 184.
[466] Brett, *Genesis*, 102.
[467] Parry, *Old Testament Story and Christian Ethics*, 164.
[468] Cf. Sternberg, *Poetics*, 468; Wenham, *Genesis 16–50*, 315.
[469] Sarna, *Genesis*, 236. Cf. Wenham, *Story as Torah*, 112. Fleishman suggests that "Jacob felt he had no choice but to agree to the marriage of Dinah to Shechem on the condition that the men in Shechem undergo circumcision" (Fleishman, "Why Did Simeon and Levi Rebuke Their Father in Genesis 34:31?," 112). However, there is nothing in the text that clarifies this. This is yet another gap in the narrative that entices to be filled.
[470] Cf. Jeansonne, *The Women of Genesis*, 95.

a note of irony: "the part of the body used by Shechem in his violent passion will itself become the source of his own punishment!"[471]
Ouch!

Hamor and Shechem now must obtain agreement from their fellow
citizens. In their speech they speak with one voice (vs. 20). It is interesting to analyze their speech in light of what has actually happened and
what has been said so far.[472] What is mentioned and what is omitted?
First thing to note is that Hamor and Shechem never mention what
has transpired between Shechem and Dinah. Neither do they mention
Shechem's desire to marry Dinah nor that this is how the proposal for
an alliance with Jacob's family came to be. Those are big omissions!
Their opening statement is that "these men are at peace with us."
Indeed, the encounter between Jacob's family and the Shechemites
started peacefully (33:18), but after Shechem's deed, with Dinah still
in Shechem's house, this is not how Jacob's family would describe the
situation. Hamor and Shechem are either totally blind to the emotions
of Jacob's sons, or willfully ignore them. Then the familiar phrases
'dwell in the land', and 'trade in it' reappear followed by the proposal
to intermarry. They omit to mention the fact that Jacob's family has
been offered the right to buy land.[473] When the vista has been painted
the tricky issue of circumcision is brought up (vs. 22). Hamor and
Shechem utilize the phrase 'one people,' used by Jacob's sons. This
signals the efficacy of the rhetoric by Jacob's sons at this key-junction.
As soon as circumcision is mentioned, attention is immediately drawn
to the upside of the agreement: "will not their livestock, their property
and all their beasts be ours?" "With a knowledge of human nature, he
appeals to the greed of his compatriots."[474] This part of the speech is
completely new. If this is what it means to be 'one people' this whole
arrangement looks very unattractive for Jacob's family. Although it
is logical that Hamor and Shechem will present their proposal in the
most favorable way,[475] this particular twist makes us wonder whether

---

[471] Sarna, *Genesis*, 236. See also Alter, *Genesis*, 192.
[472] Cf. Berlin, *Poetics*, 76–79; Caspi, "The Story of the Rape of Dinah," 37; Parry, *Old Testament Story and Christian Ethics*, 165–168.
[473] Sarna, *Genesis*, 237; Waltke, *Genesis*, 466; Hartley, *Genesis*, 295.
[474] Gunkel, *Genesis*, 365.
[475] Cf. von Rad, *Genesis*, 328 ('a little diplomatic masterpiece'); Gunkel, *Genesis*, 364; Westermann, *Genesis 12–36*, 542; Alter, *Genesis*, 193; Ross, *Creation and Blessing*, 574.

they can be trusted.[476] An exhortation to conform to the condition put by the sons of Jacob closes their speech. The appeal is successful. All males agree to be circumcised. The material upside of the agreement held out as bait, proves to be very effective indeed. As a result, circumcision, sign of the Abrahamic covenant, is degraded to a mere means for material gain. Jeansonne rightly notes that "when the men of the city agree to be circumcised they know nothing of the covenant but agree for economic reasons alone."[477]

Ironically it will be the livestock and possessions of the Shechemites that will be taken away (vs. 28–29).[478] If the reader is meant to see this as ironic, or as 'poetic justice,' or as an example of *lex talionis*, the narrator seems to imply that Hamor and Shechem have not negotiated in good faith.[479] Maybe we should not judge the men of Shechem too harshly. Although they might have a keen eye for economic progress, their reasoning is not necessarily evil. They might not know anything about what happened between Shechem and Dinah. Also, if they had evil intent, would it not have been much easier to just conquer Jacob's family?[480] Parry concludes "at least they seem sincere, even if selfish."[481]

34:25–29

On 'the third day,' when the males of Shechem are still in pain, Simeon and Levi (Dinah's brothers) kill all males by the sword. Waltke speaks of a 'Lamech-like revenge.'[482] After killing Hamor and Shechem they "took Dinah out of Shechem's house and went away" (vs. 26).[483]

---

[476] Cf. Jeansonne, *The Women of Genesis*, 95; Berlin, *Poetics*, 78; Coats, *Genesis*, 235; Sarna, *Genesis*, 237; Hamilton, *Genesis 18–50*, 365–366; Wenham, *Story as Torah*, 113; Waltke, *Genesis*, 466; Goldingay, *Old Testament Theology: Israel's Gospel*, 222. I find the assessment of Hamor by Speiser, Armstrong and Brett too positive (cf. Speiser, *Genesis*, 268; Armstrong, *In the Beginning*, 95; Brett, *Genesis*, 102).

[477] Jeansonne, *The Women of Genesis*, 95. Similarly Ross, *Creation and Blessing*, 574.

[478] Cf. Caspi, "The Story of the Rape of Dinah," 41; Sarna, *Genesis*, 238; Jeansonne, *The Women of Genesis*, 95; Goldingay, *Old Testament Theology: Israel's Gospel*, 222.

[479] Cf. Sternberg, *Poetics*, 464ff.; Wenham, *Genesis 16–50*, 314; Hamilton, *Genesis 18–50*, 366; Waltke, *Genesis*, 467; Parry, *Old Testament Story and Christian Ethics*, 170.

[480] Fewell, "Tipping the Balance," 204; Parry, *Old Testament Story and Christian Ethics*, 167.

[481] Parry, *Old Testament Story and Christian Ethics*, 167. Similarly Alter, *Genesis*, 193. On the other hand, Jer 26:15 seems to suggest that the actions of a small group (Hamor and Shechem in this case) can lead to corporate guilt (vs. 27).

[482] Waltke, *Genesis*, 460.

[483] The palistrophic arrangement of the scene is also visible in the order of killing

Phrases that were used in the opening scene are now used to bring the narrative to a close (see above). This balance in phraseology implicitly raises the question whether the death of all Shechemite males is a fitting punishment for Dina's rape.[484] The narrator does not really help the reader to answer that question.[485] Instead, he proceeds by reporting what happens next. With all men dead, the (other) sons of Jacob come to plunder the entire city.[486] The narrator seems to dwell on the description of their booty.[487] According to Noble,

> The brothers' true motives are shown by the way the narrative lingers over the booty they capture (vv. 27–29), which is listed in far greater detail than the story line would otherwise require. The actions of these brothers, then, have degenerated into a self-interested plundering of the defenceless.[488]

Wenham notes that the description of the booty is similar to 12:16: "another occasion on which a patriarch was enriched despite his own sin."[489]

> Here we see that despite Jacob's lack of affection, moral principle, and courage, he survives. Indeed, he prospers in an unexpected way from his sons' fierce anger. He is greatly enriched by the seizure of the Shechemites' flocks, herds, wives, and other properties. His grandfather, Abraham, and his father, Isaac, had both failed to protect their women-folk because they feared for their own skin (12:10–20; 20; 26:6–14), yet they had prospered greatly. Here Jacob has a similar experience.[490]

At the end of *Section* 1.1 I noted that Mazor suggests that the listing of Abraham's riches in 12:16 serves as a 'deliberate rhetorical signpost'

---

and its conclusion. The episode had opened with Dinah, Shechem and Hamor, with the men from Shechem mentioned last. Now these players are killed in reversed order, with Dinah being taken from Shechem's house as a conclusion.

[484] Cf. Parry, *Old Testament Story and Christian Ethics*, 170; Waltke, *Genesis*, 467.

[485] "Unfortunately the matter is highly ambiguous" (Parry, *Old Testament Story and Christian Ethics*, 170).

[486] Sternberg, *Poetics*, 470; Sarna, *Genesis*, 238.

[487] Cf. Hamilton, *Genesis 18–50*, 370. According to Gunkel the narrator reports this "with pleasure" (Gunkel, *Genesis*, 365), but I do not think that is the case.

[488] Noble, "A 'Balanced' Reading," 193. Similarly Brueggemann, *Genesis*, 278; Westermann, *Genesis 12–36*, 543; Sternberg, *Poetics*, 472. Armstrong even compares Jacob's sons with 'scavenging wild beasts' (Armstrong, *In the Beginning*, 96). Similarly Hamilton, *Genesis 18–50*, 370.

[489] Wenham, *Genesis 16–50*, 316. See my comments on Gen 12:16 in *Section* 1.1.

[490] Wenham, *Genesis 16–50*, 318.

which "causes the reader to become much more alert and sensitive to the narrator's latent criticism."[491] Possibly the same is true here.

It is interesting that in the book Esther, when the Jews are allowed to take revenge on their attackers, there is the repeated mention that "they laid no hands on the plunder" (Esther 9:10, 15, 16), as if to stress that the Jews kept the ethical high ground, and that their actions could not be explained as a result of desire for material gain.[492]

The mention 'and they went' (וַיֵּצֵאוּ), which is the very last phrase in vs. 26, balances the very first word in vs. 1 (וַתֵּצֵא). "The plot ends where it began."[493] One wonders whether the narrator signals that he considers the pillage beyond the bounds of retribution.[494]

> That the narrator devotes the same length of description to both acts suggests that he evaluates equally the massacre and the looting. Thus the narrator may be distancing himself from Jacob, who is terribly distressed about the slaughtering but says nothing to the looters (vs. 30).[495]

Of course that still leaves the question whether the rape of one woman warrants the killing of the entire male population of Shechem. The conclusion of this encounter is in sharp contrast with other encounters in Genesis between Abraham and Isaac and the inhabitants of the land.[496] Instead of covenantal peace, the massacre at Shechem results in severe anxiety for Jacob's family (34:30; 35:5). Although the narrative suggests a certain level of selfishness on behalf of the Shechemites, the expansive description of the plunder seems to place question marks over the motives of Jacob's sons. One wonders whether this encounter would have ended less disastrously, if economic motives had not been brought into the equation in the way they were. Desire for gain caused the Shechemites to be incapacitated, and a similar desire may have prompted the sons of Jacob to kill the entire male populace. The description of the plunder resembles later occurrences of holy war (e.g. Num 31),[497] but God's sanction for such war is entirely absent

---

[491] Mazor, "Scolding Aesthetics," 304.

[492] I am indebted to my supervisor, Revd Dr Ernest Lucas for this insight. See also A. Berlin, *Esther* (JPS Torah Commentary; Philadelphia, USA: Jewish Publication Society, 2001), 85.

[493] Sternberg, *Poetics*, 469–470. Similarly Sarna, *Genesis*, 238.

[494] Cf. Sternberg, *Poetics*, 471; Ross, *Creation and Blessing*, 575.

[495] Hamilton, *Genesis 18–50*, 370.

[496] Gen 21:22–34 and Gen 26.

[497] Cf. Wenham, *Genesis 16–50*, 315; Waltke, *Genesis*, 467.

here.[498] Wenham's observation that "Num 31:9 repeats Gen 34:29 almost word-for-word in reverse order" is intriguing in that sense.[499] The narrator leaves us pondering various questions without offering too much help to resolve them. The reader's dilemma is not helped much by the exchange that concludes the episode.

34:30–31

Jacob rebukes Simeon and Levi, but his outburst seems entirely self-centred: "You have brought trouble on *me* by making *me* stink to the inhabitants of the land (…). *My* numbers are few, and if they gather themselves against *me* and attack *me*, I shall be destroyed, both *I* and *my* household."[500] According to Noble, Jacob is "concerned only with the possible *consequences* of their behaviour; the *injustice* of their actions is not an issue he addresses."[501]

Like Hamor and Shechem, Jacob never refers to Dinah's fate. Hepner suggests that Jacob's use of the phrase עֲכַרְתֶּם in 34:30 ('you have caused me anguish') implies that

> Jacob is not protesting the violence of Simeon and Levi, but the way they have violated the Deuteronomic law of proscription (Dt 7:25–26) in the same way that Achan does in the book of Joshua in the valley of עָכוֹר ('Achor,' Josh 7:24, 26). His anguish is caused by the fact that they have not fulfilled this law by removing alien gods, which he commands them to do (Gen 35:2).[502]

---

[498] Waltke, *Genesis*, 467.

[499] Wenham, *Genesis 16–50*, 316. See also discussion by Westermann, *Genesis 12–36*, 543 and Parry, *Old Testament Story and Christian Ethics*, 196 (and quote below).

[500] Cf. Noble, "A 'Balanced' Reading," 184. On Jacob's pragmatism, see Brueggemann, *Genesis*, 207.

[501] Noble, "A 'Balanced' Reading," 184. See also Sternberg, *Poetics*, 473; Hamilton, *Genesis 18–50*, 371; Waltke, *Genesis*, 467. Hepner, referring to Josh 7:24 and 26 comes with an entirely different explanation. He suggests that "the word עֲכַרְתֶּם implies that Jacob is not protesting the violence of Simeon and Levi but the way they have violated the Deuteronomic law of proscription (Dt 7:25–26) (…) His anguish is caused by the fact that they have not fulfilled this law by removing alien gods, which he commands them to do (Gen 35:2)" (Hepner, "Verbal Resonance in the Bible and Intertextuality," 6). However, it seems hard to find support for this in the rest of Jacob's speech. McKeown also picks up on the allusion of עָכַר: "Jacob's sons brought trouble by taking the law into their own hands and breaking the rules of normal civilized behaviour" (McKeown, *Genesis*, 159).

[502] Hepner, "Verbal Resonance in the Bible and Intertextuality," 6.

Simeon and Levi's fierce rebuke brings the episode to a close "should he treat our sister like a prostitute?"[503] Their question gives this episode an almost Jonah-like ending.[504] How is the reader to evaluate this final stand-off? "The text, which does not explicitly criticize the brothers for their violent act of revenge or Jacob for being a silent father, is left wide open to interpretation."[505] Kidner comments that "the appeaser and the avengers, mutually exasperated, and swayed respectively with fear and fury, were perhaps equidistant from true justice."[506] Although Jacob's passivity throughout the episode and his fearful and selfish speech opens him up to severe criticism, the violence of the brothers does indeed endanger the entire family.[507] Gen 35:5 indicates that if God had not intervened supernaturally, Jacob's family would have suffered the consequences.[508] Simeon and Levi seem to have the last word, but their violence seems excessive.[509] The motives of Jacob's (other) sons were probably not entirely pure either. According to Noble the "use of Dinah's defilement as a pretext for the rapacious acquisition of the entire wealth of the city again transforms Dinah's situation into a 'sex for money' deal."[510] Although the anger of Jacob's sons is justified, their deceit and desecration of the sign of the covenant, combined with their excessive violence, must be viewed negatively.[511] Graetz rightly objects to the view that *one woman's rape* justifies the wholesale killing of *entire town*.[512]

Simeon and Levi may have had the last word in Gen 34, but the last word in Genesis belongs to Jacob, who will condemn both brothers on

---

[503] Fleishman, "Why Did Simeon and Levi Rebuke Their Father in Genesis 34:31?," 112.

[504] Sarna, *Genesis*, 238.

[505] Graetz, "Dinah the Daughter," 308.

[506] Kidner, *Genesis*, 174.

[507] On Jacob's stance: "The tale's least sympathetic character" (Sternberg, *Poetics*, 473). Cf. Noble, "A 'Balanced' Reading," 184; Armstrong, *In the Beginning*, 97; Waltke, *Genesis*, 468.

[508] Cf. Noble, "A 'Balanced' Reading," 185; Wenham, *Story as Torah*, 119.

[509] "The sons' instinct for justice was correct, but their methods were ruthless and excessive" (Ross, *Creation and Blessing*, 575).

[510] Noble, "A 'Balanced' Reading," 195.

[511] Cf. Mann, *The Book of the Torah*, 64; Ross, *Creation and Blessing*, 575–576. See also Williams, *Deception in Genesis*, 23–24 and 35 n. 27 and Waltke, *Genesis*, 465, who evaluate the sons' deception negatively.

[512] Graetz, "Dinah the Daughter," 315. See also Brett, *Genesis*, 102.

his death bed.[513] Gen 49:5–7 is "usually understood by most exegetes to be a commentary on the episode in Gen 34."[514]

4.5.3   Concluding Remarks

Various themes feature in this sordid tale. There is the issue of crime and punishment entwined with the proposal for intermarriage between Jacob's family and the inhabitants of the land.[515] In the context of these larger concerns, material possessions and associated attitudes are important elements that explain the dynamics of the story. As we survey a bloody scene, what contribution does Gen 34 make to our overall understanding of the nature and role of material possessions and their associated attitudes and actions in the Jacob-cycle? I will summarize my thoughts under now familiar headings:

Relationships
"No one in this story escapes censure."[516] "In both families, the fathers fail to give leadership" and the sons fail to honour boundaries.[517] No wonder that the various relationships, which provide the context(s) against which events unfold, prove troublesome. All these relationships get compromised, damaged or destroyed:

- The troubled relationship between Jacob and Leah's children, with deep roots in the past (Gen 29), features at the start and at

---

[513] These events are recalled by Jacob in Gen 49, thus "Genesis 34 is therefore the permanent record of what was, to the Israelites, an unforgettable crime. It was preserved among the tribes as a permanent bar against Simeon or Levi becoming the leader in Israel. They above all others could not take the position of first-born" (Garrett, *Rethinking Genesis*, 157). See also Wenham, *Story as Torah*, 119.

[514] Graetz, "Dinah the Daughter," 308. See also Parry, *Old Testament Story and Christian Ethics*, Chapter 5 and Clark, "The Silence of Dinah's Cry," 2. Jacob's pronouncement in Gen 49 is not viewed positively by Sternberg (Sternberg, *Poetics*, 473). Parry suggests that we should interpret Gen 34 in an even wider context: "Genesis 34 records the act which brings down Jacob's curse in Gen 49:5–7. Exodus 32 is the turning point in the fortunes of the tribe of Levi whilst Numbers 25 is the final act of Levitical zeal for God which transforms and guarantees the new status of the tribe. As the violence is transformed so too is the curse" (Parry, *Old Testament Story and Christian Ethics*, 196). Although I cannot discuss Parry's suggestion in detail here, I think it is important to mention this. See also Waltke, *Genesis*, 467.

[515] Sternberg, *Poetics*, 445; Noble, "A 'Balanced' Reading," 203.

[516] Waltke, *Genesis*, 458. Similarly Noble, "A 'Balanced' Reading," 195.

[517] Waltke, *Genesis*, 458.

the end of the story. The consequences of this fracture will return
to haunt Jacob in the Joseph-cycle;[518]

- The relationship between Shechem and Dinah is one of rapist and
victim.[519] Although there is mention of 'love', marriage does not
follow. Instead, there are echoes of prostitution;

- The relationship between Jacob's family and the inhabitants of
the land is complex. Unlike Abraham and Isaac, who managed to
come to terms with the local population, Jacob's relationship with
them develops entirely differently.[520] It starts peacefully, but the
volatile combination of crime that is not acknowledged, rhetoric
that betrays a power imbalance, deceit and implied covetousness
on both sides, lead to a massacre with women and children taken
as spoils. Jacob's family does not act as a blessing to the nations,
although Hamor and Shechem can by no means be acquitted;[521]

- Finally, God seems to be entirely absent in this episode, but Gen
34 sheds light on the relationship between God and Jacob's family
in various ways. I will reflect on this in more detail below.

Material Possessions

The main plot in Gen 34 is centred on the violation of Dinah and the
fierce revenge by her brothers. However, material possessions and associated attitudes and actions play an important role. The story unfolds
against the settlement of Jacob's family in the vicinity of Shechem
and an economic transaction; the purchase of land (33:19). Although
the conflicts in Gen 34 are not about material possessions as such,
material advancement is used as an important incentive by various
parties. The frequent mention of 'taking' (from לָקַח), illustrates the
centrality of 'acquisition' in Gen 34. Hamor and Shechem use material incentives to persuade Jacob's family to allow Shechem to marry
Dinah, and to intermarry on a large scale.[522] Hamor and Shechem
use economic advancement in general (and Jacob's possessions in
particular) to entice their fellow citizens to be circumcised (34:23).[523]

---

[518] Cf. Alter, *Genesis*, 194.
[519] Noble, "A 'Balanced' Reading," 194.
[520] Cf. Armstrong, *In the Beginning*, 96; Mann, *The Book of the Torah*, 63.
[521] Cf. Turner, *Announcements of Plot in Genesis*, 140; Humphreys, *The Character of God*, 197.
[522] Cf. Sarna, *Genesis*, 235.
[523] Hamilton, *Genesis 18–50*, 365–366; Armstrong, *In the Beginning*, 95.

This appears to be crucial in obtaining agreement.[524] There clearly is a risk in making material gain the ultimate guiding principle for one's actions. In the end, all the male inhabitants of Shechem get killed and *their* possessions are dragged away. A tragic example of patriarchal wealth that is tainted (cf. 12:16)! When material gain is considered to be more important than relationships, accidents are bound to happen. Unlike other conflict situations in Genesis, the material concessions offered in Gen 34 do not lead to conflict resolution. Hamor and Shechem make them, but Jacob's sons never accept them. The plunder taken from Shechem is indicative of the state of a relationship that has deteriorated dramatically. Of course, the reader may have doubt whether these concessions were entirely sincere. Maybe Hamor's and Shechem's mistake was that they never addressed the real relationship issues. Their attempt to address the serious damage caused by concessions of a mere material nature appears to have been a vain attempt to 'paper over the cracks.' In the Jacob-cycle, concessions of a material nature are often part of conflict resolution, but rarely are the sole means to restore a broken relationship.

In addition, one wonders if the encounter between Jacob's family and the Shechemites would have ended less disastrously, if economic motives had not been brought into the equation in the way they were. Desire for gain caused the Shechemites to be incapacitated. A similar desire might have contributed to the decision by Jacob's sons to kill the entire male populace of Shechem and take excessive plunder.[525] The pillage of Shechem in which women, children, cattle and wealth are taken away, stands out as a remarkable anomaly within the patriarchal narratives. Although this particular narrative is extremely complex, I think that the absence of conflict resolution supports the view that the pillage of Shechem is not viewed positively by the narrator.

It is instructive to reflect on the interplay between Gen 26 and 34. In Gen 26, God's blessing results in Isaac's extreme wealth (26:12–14). Isaac's riches in turn led to envy and strife. In Gen 26 envy and strife turn into peace (26:31) as soon as God is acknowledged as the source of blessing.[526] Also, a covenant is made that includes an implicit compromise regarding the sharing of wells. In contrast, Gen 34 starts

---

[524] Garrett has analysed Gen 34 as a so-called 'negotiation-tale' (Garrett, *Rethinking Genesis*, 156).
[525] Cf. Brueggemann, *Genesis*, 279.
[526] Cf. Mann, *The Book of the Torah*, 63.

peacefully, but ends in killing and plunder, because covetousness has become a guiding principle for various parties. Material concessions are offered, but not accepted. One party takes all. Various relationships have moved from bad to worse. In contrast to Gen 26, God seems entirely absent and he is not acknowledged by anybody. Whereas Gen 26 probably features the most attractive occurrence of material possessions in the Jacob-cycle (26:12–14a), the plunder of Shechem shows material possessions in their least attractive form.

God

Although God seems entirely absent from the scene,[527] various aspects of Gen 34 cause us to reflect on the relationship between God and Jacob's family and humanity as a whole. God's promises of land, offspring and protection provide the backdrop against which events unfold. However, several of God's promises and intentions get seriously deformed in the hands of man. Hamor's proposal to intermarry is set over against God's promise of land, offspring and nationhood. God's intentions for marriage (2:24) get marred by rape and are compromised by desire for economic gain. Likewise, circumcision, sign of God's covenant with Abraham, gets marred beyond recognition. "The sacral institutions of marriage and circumcision are debased into weapons in the struggle for revenge and goods."[528] Both parties have to take their share of the blame for that. There might be another problem too. Although Jacob's gesture to build an altar near Shechem appears to be noble, one wonders whether he built it in the wrong place (35:1)![529] It probably would have much better if Jacob had gone straight to Bethel to fulfil his vow. All in all, the events at Shechem provide a new threat to the family, through whom God intends to work his plan of redemption for all of humanity. The pillage of Shechem appears to be the reverse of God's intention that through Abraham's line "all the families of the earth shall be blessed" (12:3).[530] Anticipating the

---

[527] Waltke, *Genesis*, 459; Brodie, *Genesis as Dialogue*, 335; Humphreys, *The Character of God*, 197.

[528] Janzen, *Genesis 12–50*, 137–138. See also Ross, *Creation and Blessing*, 574; Brett, *Genesis*, 102.

[529] Cf. Waltke, *Genesis*, 459 and 468; Kidner, *Genesis*, 172. See *Section 4.5*.

[530] "Although Jacob and his family were threatened by the actions of the Shechemites against Dinah, the response by Jacob's sons has not helped their situation. The covenantal promise continues to be threatened by outside forces" (Jeansonne, *The Women of Genesis*, 97).

events in Gen 35, Sailhamer comments that "the ultimate purpose of these narratives is to show that in spite of the fact that such plans run counter to God's own, they cannot thwart the eventual outworking of his intentions."[531] So Janzen ponders "what will it take for the children of Jacob to become the children of Israel?"[532]

4.6 The End of the Jacob-Cycle (Gen 35)

4.6.1 *Introduction*

Gen 35 brings the Jacob-cycle to a close.[533] Its climax is God's appearance to Jacob after his return to Bethel (35:9–13). It is at that point that the promises God made to Abraham and Isaac are most emphatically restated. The chapter closes with the death of Isaac and his burial by Esau and Jacob (35:29). Following the 'generations' of Esau in Gen 36, the attention shifts to Jacob's descendants (37:2). Jacob remains a strong presence in the background and his deathbed 'blessing' forms the climax of the Joseph-cycle. On first reading, Gen 35 might appear to be incoherent.[534] Skinner describes it as 'a series of fragmentary excerpts.'[535] According to Gunkel "the passage is not a coherent account, but a loosely piled 'heap.'"[536] In contrast Westermann, based on the arrangement of itinerary and genealogical sections, argues that the chapter follows 'a carefully conceived plan.'[537] This argument is strengthened by Wenham's observations that Gen 35 "presupposes most, if not all, of the other Jacob stories contained in Genesis"[538] and that there are great similarities with the way the Abraham- and Joseph-cycle are brought to a close.[539] The passage can be sub-divided in roughly three sections:

---

[531] Sailhamer, *Genesis*, commenting on Gen 34. See also Wenham, *Story as Torah*, 119.

[532] Janzen, *Genesis 12–50*, 138.

[533] Fishbane, *Text and Texture*, 43–46; Rendsburg, *The Redaction of Genesis*, 54–56.

[534] Cf. Wenham, *Genesis 16–50*, 321.

[535] Skinner, *Genesis*, 422. Brueggemann, *Genesis*, 280; '…a collection of miscellaneous notices' (Alter, *Genesis*, 195).

[536] Gunkel, *Genesis*, 366.

[537] Westermann, *Genesis 12–36*, 549. See also Parry, *Old Testament Story and Christian Ethics*, 134.

[538] Mann, *The Book of the Torah*, 65. See also Sarna, *Genesis*, 239.

[539] Wenham, *Genesis 16–50*, 321. See also Janzen, *Genesis 12–50*, 138–139.

Vv. 1–8 (journey from Shechem to Bethel);
Vv. 9–15 (at Bethel);
Vv. 16–29 (journey from Bethel to Hebron).[540]

The first two sections are initiated by divine speech, followed by a response from Jacob.[541] Hamilton notes that vv. 1–8 are set in the context of 'flight' (vs. 1 and 7; from בָּרַח), whereas vv. 9–15 are dominated by 'blessing' (בָּרַךְ).[542] Material possessions and associated attitudes and actions do not feature in a major way in this section.

4.6.2   Commentary

35:1–8

God was absent in Gen 34, but here he takes the initiative from the word 'go.'[543] God's instruction 'arise, go up' echoes God's earlier instruction to Abraham in 12:1[544] and Rebekah's and Isaac's instructions to Jacob in 27:43 and 28:2.[545] However, the verb 'go up' (עָלָה) is different and has connotations of pilgrimage.[546] God's directive to build an altar in Bethel, followed by acts of purification and the journey there, culminating in God's appearance, all fit the pilgrimage theme.[547] The acts of purification in vv. 2–4 stand opposite the defilement of illicit sex and bloodshed in Gen 34.[548] Shechem was Jacob's place of (prospective) 'dwelling' (34:10x2, 16, 21, 22, 23) and altar building (33:20), but here God tells Jacob that Bethel is the place: 'dwell *there*' (וְשֶׁב־שָׁם) and 'make an altar *there*' (וַעֲשֵׂה־שָׁם).[549] It appears that Shechem never was

---

[540] For more detailed structures cf. Wenham, *Genesis 16–50*, 321.

[541] Cf. Waltke, *Genesis*, 469.

[542] Hamilton, *Genesis 18–50*, 380.

[543] Brodie, *Genesis as Dialogue*, 335 and 344, comments on the complementarity of Gen 34 and 35 in this matter.

[544] Westermann, *Genesis 12–36*, 550; Brodie, *Genesis as Dialogue*, 341.

[545] Cf. Wenham, *Genesis 16–50*, 323; Brodie, *Genesis as Dialogue*, 341; Hamilton, *Genesis 18–50*, 374. Note also the mention of Paddan-aram in vs. 9 (cf. 28:2, 6).

[546] Cf. von Rad, *Genesis*, 331; Westermann, *Genesis 12–36*, 550; Sarna, *Genesis*, 239; Wenham, *Genesis 16–50*, 323; Mann, *The Book of the Torah*, 65; Walton, *Thou Traveller Unknown*, 207.

[547] Cf. Fokkelman, *Narrative Art in Genesis*, 232; Waltke, *Genesis*, 472; Brodie, *Genesis as Dialogue*, 341. Alternatively, Rendsburg associates the washing and changing of clothes with the 'homecoming motif' in ANE epic literature (G.A. Rendsburg, "Notes on Genesis XXXV," *VT* 34, no. 3 (1984): 361–66, 363–364).

[548] Brueggemann, *Genesis*, 280–281; Sarna, *Genesis*, 239; Wenham, *Genesis 16–50*, 323; Brett, *Genesis*, 105; Brodie, *Genesis as Dialogue*, 341.

[549] Janzen notes that in ANE tradition, major cult places are often built in response to divine directives (Janzen, *Genesis 12–50*, 139).

the right place.[550] The section is framed by two references to Jacob's flight before Esau (vs. 1 and 7)[551]—one of several links with God's encounter with Jacob in Bethel in Gen 28.[552] Jacob repeats the essence of God's words in vs. 3, following his own instructions to put away foreign gods, to purify themselves and change garments (vs. 2). Jacob does not repeat God's words regarding his flight from Esau. Instead, Jacob speaks of the "God who answers me in the day of my distress and has been with me wherever I have gone." For some, this is vintage Jacob.[553] However, Jacob also states that God has indeed lived up to Jacob's conditions (28:20).[554] "The whole incident must be read as an illustration of Jacob's religious maturation."[555] God continues to protect Jacob on his way to Bethel (vs. 5). Jacob's entourage bury all their foreign gods and the rings in their ears and Jacob gets rid of them (vs. 4). These gods and earrings may have been part of the loot taken from Shechem,[556] or may originate from Paddan-Aram.[557] What is relevant is that defilement is left behind at Shechem. Jacob is now ready to 'go up' to Bethel. The removal of foreign gods and earrings;[558] the purification; the change of garments, and the altar (vs. 7), are all physical signs of a relationship change. "This visit (or pilgrimage) has the earmarks of a new beginning, a break with the past."[559] Everything is now in place for Jacob to fulfil his vow.[560]

---

[550] Waltke, *Genesis*, 471; S. Bakon, "Jacob: Father of a Nation," *JBQ* 28, no. 1 (2000): 38–44, 39.

[551] Before meeting with God at Bethel it was necessary for Jacob to be reconciled with his brother. That has now happened (cf. Kidner, *Genesis*, 167).

[552] Cf. Sarna, *Genesis*, 239; Wenham, *Genesis 16–50*, 321; Cartledge, *Vows*; Richter, "Das Gelübde als theologische Rahmung der Jakobsüberlieferungen"; Terino, "A Text Linguistic Study of the Jacob Narrative," 52; Spero, "Jacob's Growing Understanding of His Experience at Beth-El," 213. Flight also recurs in the Jacob-Laban narrative: 31:20, 21, 22 and 27.

[553] Sternberg, *Poetics*, 420; Hamilton, *Genesis 18–50*, 376.

[554] Fokkelman, *Narrative Art in Genesis*, 232; Alter, *Genesis*, 196.

[555] Hamilton, *Genesis 18–50*, 376.

[556] Sarna, *Genesis*, 239; Sailhamer, *Genesis, ad loc*; Alter, *Genesis*, 195.

[557] Sarna, *Genesis*, 240; Alter, *Genesis*, 195; Walton, *Thou Traveller Unknown*, 207.

[558] According to Sarna these are "talismans adorned with pagan symbols" (Sarna, *Genesis*, 240). This is refuted by Hurowitz, who argues that the earrings "may have been those worn by the idols, rather than the idols' owners" (V.A. Hurowitz, "Who Lost an Earring? Genesis 35:4 Reconsidered," *CathBQ* 62, no. 1 (2000): 28–32; V.A. Hurowitz, "Whose Earrings Did Jacob Bury?" *BR* 17, no. 4 (2001): 31–33, 54).

[559] Kodell, "Jacob Wrestles with Esau (Gen 32:23–32)," 70, referring to Vawter, *On Genesis*, 362. Cf. Joshua 24:23ff.; von Rad, *Genesis*, 331–332; Westermann, *Genesis 12–36*, 550–551; Kidner, *Genesis*, 175; Hamilton, *Genesis 18–50*, 375.

[560] Cf. Wenham, *Genesis 16–50*, 323; Spero, "Jacob's Growing Understanding of His Experience at Beth-El," 214.

35:8

After Jacob builds an altar and names 'the place'[561] El-bethel, the narrator mentions the death and burial of Deborah, Rebekah's nurse.[562]
Many commentators suggest that the narrator 'gaps' Rebekah's death,
to communicate condemnation concerning her role in the deception
of Isaac.[563] This oblique reference to Jacob's (and Rebekah's) deceit in
Gen 27 to obtain Isaac's blessing is juxtaposed with God's blessing in
the next scene. Sarna suggests that as the burial of idols signifies purging of idolatry, Deborah's burial signifies the severing of all bonds with
Mesopotamia.[564] God's pronouncement that follows, in which blessing
and life are paramount (vv. 9–13), is framed by two deaths; Deborah's
(vs. 8), and Rachel's in child-birth (vs. 17–19). I will discuss this in
more detail below.

35:9–15

God spoke to Jacob in a dream in Gen 28, but this is something more
special altogether. As noted in *Section* 2.3, there are only six times in
Genesis where it is mentioned that the LORD (or God) 'appeared'
(וַיֵּרָא). The LORD (or God) only appears to the patriarchs and the
frequency decreases from Abraham onwards: 12:7; 17:1; 18:1; to Isaac
in 26:2; 24; and only once to Jacob (וַיֵּרָא אֱלֹהִים) in 35:9.[565] Textually,
this section has close parallels with God's appearance to Abraham in
Gen 17,[566] and with Isaac's prayer in 28:3–4,[567] which is answered here.[568]

---

[561] See *Section* 2.5 on the recurrence of the word 'place' (מָקוֹם). See also Hamilton,
Genesis 18–50, 377.

[562] She is referred to only once elsewhere in Genesis, but not by name (24:59).

[563] U. Cassuto, *A Commentary on the Book of Genesis—From Noah to Abraham*
(vol. 2; Jerusalem, Israel: The Magnes Press, The Hebrew University, 1973), 63; Rendsburg, "Notes on Genesis XXXV," 364–365; Hamilton, *Genesis 18–50*, 378; Waltke,
Genesis, 471.

[564] Sarna, *Genesis*, 241.

[565] Cf. Dieckmann, *Segen für Isaak*, 211. In 46:2 "God spoke to Israel in visions of
the night."

[566] Cf. von Rad, *Genesis*, 334; Westermann, *Genesis 12–36*, 552; Sarna, *Genesis*,
241; Ross, *Creation and Blessing*, 581; Brett, *Genesis*, 105; Brodie, *Genesis as Dialogue*,
342–343.

[567] Fokkelman, *Narrative Art in Genesis*, 234; Sarna, *Genesis*, 240; Wenham, *Genesis
16–50*, 325; Ross, *Creation and Blessing*, 581; Walton, *Thou Traveller Unknown*, 209.

[568] Note the textual similarities between 35:11–12 and Isaac's prayer (28:3–4): "God
Almighty bless you and make you fruitful and multiply you, that you may become a
company of peoples. May he give the blessing of Abraham to you and to your offspring with you, that you may take possession of the land of your sojournings that
God gave to Abraham!" Cf. Gross, "Jakob, der Mann des Segens. Zu Traditionsge-

In relation to Gen 17 McKeown notes that "after the events of the preceding chapter, this is a reminder that the covenant still stands in spite
of the misuse of the rite of circumcision."[569] There are also similarities with God's emphatic promise to Abraham in 22:16–18, following
Abraham's test concerning Isaac.[570] Jacob's test (35:1) looks a lot easier
in comparison. When God appears to Jacob, he blesses him (vs. 9). In
contrast to Peniel, the divine blessing is freely given, instead of being
obtained through struggle and negotiation. Three blessing components
can be identified: Jacob's name change to Israel; offspring and land.
The short-term promises of protection and safe return are absent, possibly because they have all been fulfilled.[571] In contrast to Jacob's name
change in 32:28–29, there is no context of struggle, and any (negative)
connotation is omitted.[572] God's command 'be fruitful and multiply'
resonates with Isaac's prayer (28:3–4) and with God's ratification of
his covenant with Abraham in Gen 17, which in turn resonate with
God's intentions in creation (1:28).[573] When Jacob's family settles in
Goshen, there is a sense of fulfilment (47:27).[574] This is one of several
threads that link the Jacob narrative with Gen 1–11 and the rest of
the Pentateuch. God's promise that kings will come from Jacob's body
looks even further ahead. The fact that the birth of Benjamin soon
follows (35:18) may be relevant in this context. It is from the tribe of
Benjamin that Israel will get its first king (1Sam 9:1–2).[575]

This episode confirms that God's promises to Abraham and Isaac
have been transferred to Jacob. It is interesting to consider how
these promises progress through the Jacob-cycle, especially regarding the theme of 'blessing.' There is major development from 'blessing
obtained through struggle' towards 'blessing freely given.' The transfer
of the divine promises from Abraham to Isaac was very straightforward (26:2–5), but the transfer from Isaac to Jacob gets complicated
by Jacob's (and Rebekah's) acts to manipulate the blessing (Gen 27).

---

schichte und Theologie der priesterlichen Jakobsüberlieferungen," 340–341; Walton,
Thou Traveller Unknown, 121 n. 70; Mitchell, *The Meaning of BRK*, 99.

[569] McKeown, *Genesis*, 161.

[570] Cf. Mann, *The Book of the Torah*, 65.

[571] Wenham, *Genesis 16–50*, 325.

[572] Sailhamer, *Genesis, ad loc.*

[573] Westermann, *Genesis 12–36*, 553; Alter, *Genesis*, 197; Waltke, *Genesis*, 474; Hartley, *Genesis*, 300; Walton, *Thou Traveller Unknown*, 211.

[574] See also Ex 1:7.

[575] Fokkelman, *Narrative Art in Genesis*, 235.

God transfers the patriarchal promises to Jacob at Bethel in Gen 28:13–15, but God does not tell Jacob 'I will bless you' (cp. 26:3).[576] At Peniel, Jacob obtains divine blessing, but only after a painful struggle and negotiation. It is only in Gen 35 that God freely and emphatically blesses Jacob without struggle, without negotiation and without Jacob's prompting in any way or form.

After this climactic appearance, 'God went up from him' (vs. 13). This is the last time that God is said to have appeared to a human being in the book of Genesis.[577] Jacob responds by setting up a pillar 'in the place,'[578] pours oil on it and again names the place Bethel. All very similar to 28:18–19, but this time there is just the act of worship. Jacob does not need to spell out what God has promised. It seems as if he has moved on. "God has fulfilled his promise to be with Jacob. Now Jacob has fulfilled *his* vow."[579]

35:16–29

Events on the last leg of Jacob's itinerary form an anti-climax to Bethel. The tragedies that befall Jacob in Gen 35 (and beyond) might cause the reader to wonder what it means to be blessed.[580] First of all, Rachel dies giving birth to Benjamin.[581] Tragically, what she so strongly desired causes her demise (30:24).[582] Rachel's death has been associated with Jacob's oath in 31:32.[583] To mark Rachel's tomb, Jacob erects another pillar. These two scenes could be called the story of the two pillars, juxtaposing blessing and curse. In the first scene, God blesses Jacob and commands him 'be fruitful and multiply' (vs. 11; 1:28). In vs. 16–18 however, a woman suffers great pain in childbearing and is overruled by her husband. Great resonance with the judgment pronounced on

---

[576] Cf. Fokkelman, *Narrative Art in Genesis*, 234.

[577] Armstrong, *In the Beginning*, 93. In 46:2 "God spoke to Israel in visions of the night."

[578] Hamilton, *Genesis 18–50*, 377.

[579] Mann, *The Book of the Torah*, 66.

[580] Armstrong even labels Gen 35:1–29 as 'the fall of Jacob,' which completely ignores God's blessing at Bethel (Armstrong, *In the Beginning*, 98).

[581] Fokkelman draws a comparison with Rebekah's agony in 25:22, opposite Rachel's agony in the palistrophic structure of the Jacob-cycle (Fokkelman, *Narrative Art in Genesis*, 235).

[582] "The fulfilment of her uncompromising wish entails her death" (Alter, *Genesis*, 198).

[583] Daube, "Fraud on Law for Fraud on Law," 55; D. Daube, "The Night of Death," *HTR* 61, no. 4 (1968): 629–32; Tucker, "Jacob's Terrible Burden: In the Shadow of the Text," 25 ("Jacob was responsible for Rachel's death—and he knew it!").

the first woman in Gen 3:16! And so, the primeval clash of blessing and curse in Gen 1–3 recurs in the Jacob-cycle. This was apparent in the complex struggles regarding the increase of wealth and children at the centre of the Jacob-Laban narrative. And here at the close of the Jacob-cycle it returns with a vengeance. Is the clash of blessing and curse a stalemate or will one win out? The birth of new life hints in the direction of blessing's ultimate victory. The renaming of Benjamin might indicate Jacob's newfound strength. Death and disappointment will not conquer life and hope.[584] Although the grief of Rachel's loss remains for the rest of Jacob's life (48:7), God's blessing eventually conquers all. Gen 47:27 reports that Israel became fruitful and multiplied greatly. In Gen 48 Jacob will recall his grief, but all in the context of God's great faithfulness. At the end of his life, Jacob realizes that none of God's promises had failed, and that God's word would stand.

Jacob (now referred to as Israel, vs. 22) is confronted with another tragedy; Reuben lay with Bilhah, possibly an attempt to prevent Rachel's maid from succeeding Rachel as favourite wife,[585] and/or an attempt to confirm his status as firstborn.[586] If the latter were true, inheritance related concerns may have played a role. The struggle for primacy moves to the next generation. Jacob's ambitions resulted in plenty of hardship. Reuben's attempt will meet with frustration and failure.[587] A short genealogy listing Jacob's twelve sons follows. At the end of the Jacob-cycle, God's promise regarding 'seed' has made a significant step forward, certainly in comparison with the previous generation.[588] Reuben's act and the list of twelve sons provide hooks with the Joseph-cycle, in which the question of primacy among brothers will be a key-concern. This renewed struggle for primacy finds its climax in

---

[584] Cf. Brueggemann, *Genesis*, 283–284; Ross, *Creation and Blessing*, 583.

[585] Sarna, *Genesis*, 244; Wenham, *Genesis 16–50*, 327.

[586] Wenham, *Genesis 16–50*, 327; Alter, *Genesis*, 200; Brodie, *Genesis as Dialogue*, 346; Janzen, *Genesis 12–50*, 143; Hamilton, *Genesis 18–50*, 387. "He, not Benjamin should be the child of his father's right hand" (Armstrong, *In the Beginning*, 99). See also Baldwin, *The Message of Genesis 12–50*, 151 on 'son of my right hand.'

[587] 'And Israel heard of it,' cf. 34:5: "both narratives deal with a transgression and its punishment" (49:3–4) (Westermann, *Genesis 12–36*, 556). See also Brett, *Genesis*, 104 on the theme of 'genealogical superiority.'

[588] Brodie draws attention to the contrast with the thriving line of Esau in Gen 36 (Brodie, "Genesis as Dialogue," 307; Brodie, *Genesis as Dialogue*, 344). For more on Gen 36, cf. Brett, *Genesis*, 106–107 and Hoekveld-Meijer, *Esau: Salvation in Disguise—Genesis 36: A Hidden Polemic Between Our Teacher and the Prophets about Edom's role in Post-Exilic Israel through Leitwort Names*. I will not comment on this issue here.

Jacob's 'blessing' at the end of his life in Gen 49.[589] In this death-bed pronouncement, Joseph will receive a double portion, through Jacob's adoption of Ephraim and Manasseh, but also Judah's long-term primacy will be foretold.

The Jacob-cycle closes with Jacob's arrival at Mamre where Isaac breaths his last at the age of 180 years, old and full of years.[590] Esau and Jacob (word order!) bury him (35:28–29). This echoes Gen 25:7–9 where Ishmael and Isaac bury Abraham.[591] How Isaac's inheritance was divided remains completely unmentioned (a marked difference from the mention of Abraham's inheritance, 25:5–6!).[592] What was fought over so hard appears to have become entirely irrelevant. The drive for material blessing at the cost of relationship is very costly and might prove to be irrelevant in hindsight. What matters are God's promises. As Abraham and Lot parted because of their abundant possessions (13:6), so Jacob and Esau could not dwell together (36:7). Jacob's line is the chosen line through whom God wants to work his blessing for all of humanity.

4.7 Conclusions

It appears that what has been discovered about the nature and role of material possessions and their associated attitudes and actions in earlier parts of the Jacob-cycle is confirmed in Gen 32–35, although Gen 34 provides an unexpected twist. I will summarize my findings under the now familiar headings.

Relationships

In Gen 32–35, as in previous parts of the Jacob-cycle, divine encounters are juxtaposed with human ones. Jacob's 'vertical' encounters at Mahanaim, Peniel and Bethel are interspersed with 'horizontal' ones. Jacob deeply worries about Esau, before reconciliation takes place. In the disastrous encounter with the Shechemites God appears to be

---

[589] Cf. Wright, *The Mission of God*, 210–211.

[590] "…'old and full of days', an idiomatic expression denoting that he lived a full life" (McKeown, *Genesis*, 162). Similarly Brueggemann, *Genesis*, 285. For a different opinion: Armstrong, *In the Beginning*, 99.

[591] Wenham, *Genesis 16–50*, 328.

[592] "What became of the property remains gapped to the last" (Sternberg, *Poetics*, 350; also quoted in *Section 2.4.3*).

completely absent. There are also other human tragedies that contrast God's emphatic blessing in Gen 35. The various relationships in this part of the Jacob-cycle are complex. Jacob's relationship with Esau moves towards resolution, but the brothers will not dwell together. Jacob's relationship with God is one of struggle in which blessing prevails. Jacob's relationship with the inhabitants of the land takes a dramatic turn for the worse, and the various relationships within Jacob's family are troublesome. A whole range of possibilities and problems are presented, which are testimony to the complexities and challenges of human existence.[593]

Material Possessions

Again, material possessions and associated attitudes and actions are pervasive features of the narrative and are important in order to understand the relationship dynamics in these chapters. Much narrative time is spent on Jacob's preparations to appease his brother with a gift, and on his efforts to get Esau to accept his 'blessing.' I have shown how the narrative in Gen 32–33 keeps the 'gift' in perspective with respect to relationship concerns. Although we cannot be sure to what extent Esau's generosity was influenced by Jacob's gift, I take it that the gift *signifies* that the relationship was restored, rather than being entirely responsible for its restoration. The thesis developed in previous chapters that material possessions and associated attitudes are often at the heart of conflict in the Jacob-cycle, but that they also form an integral component in conflict resolution, is confirmed and strengthened by the events in Gen 33.

In Gen 34, material possessions and associated attitudes and concerns are extremely important for understanding the rhetoric of the various parties, and the actions that ensue. Material desires and concerns are mixed in with a conflict that has a different origin altogether. Although material concessions were offered to resolve that conflict (sincerely or insincerely), they were never fully accepted and the atrocities that follow result in the killing of all males in Shechem, while women, children and all their possession are being carried off by the sons of Jacob. Shechem's plunder is testimony to relationships that have gone disastrously wrong.

---

[593] Brodie, *Genesis as Dialogue*, xi. Similarly Goldingay, *Old Testament Theology: Israel's Gospel*, 275.

In two key-episodes, Jacob's struggle with God at Peniel, and God's appearance to Jacob at Bethel (Gen 35), Jacob's possessions are not really part of the picture. In Peniel, Jacob is even separated from all he has. The blessings Jacob receives at Peniel and Bethel seem of a very different nature from material wealth. It seems as if material possessions are a more important feature in human encounters than in those with God.

God

God's role in this part of the Jacob-cycle is complex. God confronts Jacob at Peniel, but he does not confront Jacob over events in Shechem. Instead, God's protection ensures that nothing happens to Jacob, his family or his possessions. God is faithful to all his promises and God moves his plan forward despite the sin of the human race and the complications that brings. God is working his purposes out, although the reader might only discern that if he/she steps back and surveys a larger part of the biblical story line. Now that we have reached the end of the Jacob-cycle, it is time to look at the entire landscape and reach some conclusions.

CHAPTER FIVE

CONCLUSIONS

Exegesis is a work of love—Eugene Peterson[1]

Various biblical studies on wealth and poverty have been published over the last thirty years. Some of these studies touch on the wealth of the patriarchs in Gen 12–50, but they focus predominantly on other parts of the Bible. Scholars who have studied the patriarchal narratives in detail comment on aspects of patriarchal wealth, but do not offer an in-depth analysis of this topic. My study on Jacob's wealth shows that such an analysis is warranted and that it contributes to a fuller understanding of the Jacob-cycle. In this final chapter, I will summarize my findings in relation to the larger (theological) concerns of the book of Genesis. I will also discuss how the Jacob-cycle functions as *Torah* on this particular topic and I will conclude with some methodological reflections.

5.1 Summary of Findings

It has been my aim to offer an integrated analysis regarding the nature and role of material possessions in the Jacob-cycle (Gen 25:19–35:29). It is clear from this study that material possession must be studied in conjunction with associated attitudes and actions. There is the risk with any topical study that something that is peripheral to the narrative is moved towards the centre.[2] I have tried to keep things in perspective. Material possessions and associated attitudes and actions are not the main concerns of the Jacob-cycle, but they are not unimportant either. I have also tried to avoid the tendency to 'extract the message' and 'discard the story.'[3] The references to material

---

[1] Peterson, *Eat This Book*, 55.
[2] Cf. Goldingay, *Models for Interpretation of Scripture*, 2.
[3] See the end of *Section* 1.3.2 (Cf. Barton, *Reading the Old Testament*, 163; Fokkelman, "Genesis," 36; Peterson, *Eat This Book*, 43; Goldingay, *Old Testament Theology: Israel's Gospel*, 287).

possessions in the Jacob-cycle occur within a narrative text of great beauty and sophistication, and we need to respect the text for what it is. It has been my aim to study material possessions and associated attitudes and actions within their appropriate contexts. I will summarize my findings under various subheadings that together constitute the major findings of this study.

5.1.1   *A Pervasive Feature of the Narrative*

Although material possessions and associated attitudes and actions are not the main concern of the Jacob-cycle, they are an important and pervasive feature of the narrative. At a basic level this is made evident by the vast number of nouns and verbs related to material possessions in Gen 12–50 (Appendix A). In addition, material possessions and/or associated attitudes and actions feature in almost every episode of the Jacob-cycle, often at the heart of the narrative action:

- It is likely that concerns about material advancement play a role in Jacob's actions to acquire Esau's birthright and his father's blessing;
- Philistine jealousy about Isaac's prosperity and the struggle about wells are major drivers of the events described in Gen 26;
- Laban's greed is an important feature of the Jacob-Laban narrative;
- The acquisition of wealth and the generation of Jacob's offspring stand at the heart of the Jacob-Laban narrative;
- The narrator dwells on the description of Jacob's wealth in 31:43, which forms the climax of that episode;
- Jacob is separated from all he has to experience the divine blessing in Gen 32;
- Jacob's possessions are an important feature of Jacob's endeavour to appease Esau;
- Economic incentives play a central role in the rhetoric between Jacob's family and the Shechemites in Gen 34;
- The narrator dwells on describing the plunder taken from Shechem (34:28–29).

It is clear from these examples that material possessions and associated attitudes and actions are integral features of the Jacob narrative. Instead of being peripheral to the narrative they often are major drivers for much of the narrative action.

5.1.2   *Best Understood in the Context of Various Relationships*

Within the Jacob-cycle, material possessions and associated attitudes and actions must be seen in the context of various relationships, both 'vertically' (with God) and 'horizontally' (with humans).[4] This framework is evident in the composition of the Jacob-cycle itself. The birth-oracle in Gen 25:23 stands at the beginning of the Jacob-cycle and Jacob's encounters with God at Bethel, Mahanaim and Peniel provide the structural pillars for the rest of the cycle. These divine encounters are juxtaposed with human struggles, especially those with Esau and Laban. There are other relationships to consider as well: the various relationships within Isaac's family; the relationships between Jacob and his wives, concubines and children; and various relationships with outsiders (Philistines, Shechemites). The portrayal of these relationships is sophisticated, and all these relationships are subject to development. Material possessions and associated attitudes and actions are best understood in the context of these relationships (human and divine) and are essential to understand the various relationship dynamics, (e.g. conflict and conflict resolution). Other scholars have noted the importance of considering blessing and/or material wealth within the context of relationship (e.g. Wright; McConville; McKeown).[5] My study contributes a complementary analysis of how material possessions and relationship concerns interact, and how important they are to explain the various relationship dynamics in the Jacob-cycle. Material possessions can feature before, during or after a change in relationship:

- <u>Before</u>: Isaac's prosperity leads to Philistine envy, which causes a change in relationship;
- <u>During</u>: The increase of Jacob's herds takes place in the midst of the Jacob-Laban struggle;
- <u>After</u>: The booty carried away from Shechem is the end result of the engagement between the Shechemites and Jacob's family.

---

[4] According to Cramp the notion of "persons in relationship" is "an important but neglected strand of Christian ethical thought" (A.B. Cramp, "Economic Ethics," in *New Dictionary of Christian Ethics & Pastoral Theology* (eds. D.J. Atkinson and D.H. Field; Leicester, UK: IVP, 1995), 116). See also J.G. McConville, "The Old Testament and the Enjoyment of Wealth," in *Christ and Consumerism* (eds. C. Bartholomew and T. Moritz; Carlisle, Cumbria, UK: Paternoster, 2001), 37.

[5] Cf. Wright, *The Mission of God*, 199ff. (especially 221); McConville, "The Old Testament and the Enjoyment of Wealth," 37; McKeown, "Blessings and Curses," 87; McKeown, *Genesis*, 221–223.

Material possessions may influence, or be merely indicative of the state of relationship. For the Philistines, for example, Isaac's wells and success are indicative of being blessed by God (26:28–29).

The various episodes in the Jacob-cycle portray relationship concerns as more important than material concerns. This is most evident in Gen 33 where Jacob seeks Esau's חֵן by means of מַחֲנֶה given as a מִנְחָה, all within the context of God's gracious provisions towards Jacob (חָנַן). I have demonstrated how the textual structure of 33:5–11 reflects the intricate entanglement of material possessions with relationship issues that are clearly of a higher order. This principle is also evident as we consider conflict and conflict resolution in the Jacob-cycle (see below). The reader of the Jacob-narrative is clearly not meant to consider the nature and role of material possessions apart from these relationship concerns. Material possessions can only be enjoyed if various relationships (both human and divine) are in order.[6]

The portrayal of human relationships and their development is sophisticated. The same can be said of God's relationship with humanity, especially the one with Jacob. There is plenty of development, both in terms of God's involvement in Jacob's life, and Jacob's growing understanding regarding God's character and actions. I will discuss this in more detail, as we consider Jacob's wealth in relation to God's blessing and promises.

5.1.3   *Source of Conflict*

Material possessions and associated attitudes and actions stand at the heart of various conflicts in the Jacob-cycle. These conflicts arise when desire for material advancement gains ascendancy over relationship concerns:

- In Gen 25 and 27, Jacob is more concerned about the acquisition of the birthright and blessing than his relationship with, and the fate of, his brother and father;
- Philistine envy over Isaac's prosperity results in expulsion. The dispute continues over the ownership of various wells. Isaac's

---

[6] Cf. McKeown, "Blessings and Curses," 87.

naming of these wells reflects the conflict and its eventual resolution;

- Desire for material gain stands at the heart of the fierce struggle between Laban and Jacob;
- Desire for material gain was a factor in the escalation of the conflict with the Shechemites (Gen 34).

Various scholars have noted that struggle and conflict are central features of the patriarchal narratives.[7] It has also been noted that conflict resolution is portrayed as desirable in Genesis.[8] What scholars have largely ignored is the important role material possessions and associated attitudes and actions play to explain many of the conflicts in the Jacob-cycle, and their role in conflict resolution.

5.1.4 *Integral Part of Conflict Resolution*

The root ריב occurs in three places in Genesis: In 13:7 (Abraham-Lot); 26:20, 21, 22 (Isaac-Philistines); and 31:36 (Jacob-Laban). In every one of these episodes, material possessions and/or concerns about material security or wellbeing (e.g. wells) are at the heart of the conflict. Every one of these conflicts is eventually resolved, and each resolution involves a concession of a material nature. A paradigmatic example of conflict resolution is Gen 13, where Abraham's and Lot's herdsmen quarrel over wells.[9] Abraham takes the initiative to resolve that conflict by a generous offer to Lot (13:8–9). Abraham values the relationship with Lot as more important than the material advancement he might lose. God's approval may be inferred by the fact that God immediately appears to Abraham following the conflict resolution with an emphatic confirmation of God's promises to him.

In the Jacob-cycle, besides a source of conflict, material possessions are also an integral component in conflict resolution. In several conflicts, a concession is made of a material nature to resolve the conflict, restoring the proper balance between material and relationship concerns:

---

[7] E.g. Steinmetz, *From Father to Son*, 11. See also Gammie, "Theological Interpretation," 118: "there can be little question that the dominant motif in Genesis 25–26 is the motif of strife."

[8] Cf. Wenham, *Story as Torah*, 39.

[9] Janzen, *Old Testament Ethics*, 9–12.

- The settlement between Isaac and the Philistines includes the implicit sharing of wells;
- The turning point in the conflict between Leah and Rachel comes when Jacob is offered as a material concession. Maybe it is the low-point in the Jacob-cycle for Jacob. The son who is born as a result, Issachar, bears lasting witness to the exchange;
- When Jacob and Laban settle their dispute, Jacob can keep all he has taken with him;
- When Jacob returns the blessing to Esau with great acts of deference, Jacob insists that Esau accepts his generous gift ('my blessing'). I have argued that the textual evidence suggests that the acceptance of the gift signifies Esau's forgiveness.

In contrast to these various episodes that result in conflict resolution stands the conflict in Gen 34. Unlike all the other conflicts in the Jacob-cycle this one is not resolved. Although concessions of a material nature are made, they are never accepted. The pillage of Shechem in which women, children, cattle and wealth are taken away, stands out as a remarkable anomaly within the patriarchal narratives. Although this particular narrative is extremely complex, I think that the absence of conflict resolution supports the view that the pillage of Shechem is not viewed positively by the narrator.

5.2 Material Possessions within the Larger Context of Genesis

The Jacob-cycle is a very coherent composition in its own right, which is well-integrated within the larger construct of the book of Genesis.[10] Therefore, the Jacob-cycle can be read in relation to God's wonderful work in creation (Gen 1–2), which is declared to be 'very good.' Material abundance is part of that good creation. However, relationships need to be right. Human rebellion caused curse to enter the blessed world. All relationships are damaged as a result.[11] According to Brodie "Genesis is primarily about human existence" and "the Jacob narrative (…) while full of historical echoes, it is primarily a sophisticated

---

[10] *Section* 1.3.2.
[11] God-human; human-human; human-ground (cf. Wright, *Walking in the Ways of the Lord*, 26–45).

portrayal of the progress and pitfalls of human life."[12] The Jacob-cycle provides ample illustrations! Various episodes show us the strivings, responsibilities and worries that come with possessions. When Jacob is not striving and toiling for wealth, he is worrying about how not to lose it all. It seems that nowhere in the Jacob-cycle is Jacob's wealth associated with unalloyed peace.

However, Genesis is also about God's ongoing involvement with humanity. Although God judges rebellion, what stands out in Genesis is his grace. It is within this setting and story-line that God calls Abraham and makes another new beginning. God's plan of redemption continues. Jacob's wealth must be considered in relation to larger theological concerns in Genesis like 'blessing' and God's promises regarding land, 'seed' and relationship.[13] Material possessions must be understood within a Creation/Fall perspective where the world is a place in which blessing and curse interact.[14] Jacob's wealth cannot be simply categorized as a "restoration of abundance and delight"[15] or "entering into the life of God."[16] A more balanced proposal is made by Wenham, who states that "whereas Genesis approves of wealth properly acquired and generously distributed, grasping at wealth or meanness towards God and man is implicitly criticised" and "...none of Genesis' examples of acquisitive behaviours can be taken as a recommendation of it."[17] Material possessions are not good or evil in themselves, but they must be understood in the context of various relationships; relationships that have been marred, but which can be healed. A world where God remains involved to progress his redemption for all of creation.

5.2.1   The Relationship between Blessing and Material Possessions

Blessing is an important theme in Genesis: "...*the* theme that runs through Genesis is that of God's blessing—originally given, deservedly

---

[12] Brodie, *Genesis as Dialogue*, xi. Similarly Goldingay, *Old Testament Theology: Israel's Gospel*, 275.

[13] Perriman, 157; Clines, *The Theme of the Pentateuch*.

[14] Cf. Wenham, *Story as Torah*, 23.

[15] The general thesis of Schneider, *The Good of Affluence*.

[16] B.C. Birch, "Moral Agency, Community, and the Character of God in the Hebrew Bible," *Semeia* 66 (1994): 119–35, 30 as quoted by Wenham, *Story as Torah*, 105.

[17] Wenham, *Story as Torah*, 93.

compromised, graciously promised, variously imperilled, partially experienced."[18] Elsewhere, Goldingay comments that "in English 'blessing' is apt to suggest something religious and/or interpersonal, but *běrākâ* implies something concrete and material."[19] However, the relational dimension must not be ignored:

> Blessing is initially and strongly connected with creation and all the good gifts God longs for people to enjoy in the world—abundance, fruitfulness and fertility, long life, peace and rest. Yet at the same time, these things are to be enjoyed in the context of healthy relationships with God and with others.[20]

Material possessions can be a result of divine blessing, but they are not always. In Gen 26 we see the clearest example of material wealth that results from divine blessing (26:12–14). God's involvement is specifically mentioned. However, this leads to envy, and the story moves towards strife before it concludes in reconciliation. The possessions taken from Shechem in Gen 34 are probably farthest removed from divine blessing. God seems entirely absent, and what happens there comes close to 'curse.' Although such terminology is absent from the text, Jacob's family is certainly not a blessing to the nations in this instance. Interestingly, Gen 26 and 34 stand opposite each other in the palistrophic structure of the Jacob-cycle. Newsom and Brodie might call this a dialogical presentation.[21] In between these two extremes, at the heart of the Jacob-Laban narrative and at the very heart of the Jacob-cycle, stands Jacob's increase of children and wealth (29:31–30:43). God's involvement in the child-bearing episodes is specifically mentioned, but the narrator does not specifically mention God's involvement in Jacob's increase of wealth, although God is referred to by Laban and Jacob. Traditionally, wealth and offspring are considered typical exponents of blessing in the OT.[22] However, the struggle between the women (cf. 3:16)[23] and the struggle between the men, with much hard labour for Jacob (cf. 3:19; 31:40), seems to present us with a clash between blessing and 'curse.' So, within the symmetry of the

---

[18] Goldingay, *Models for Interpretation of Scripture*, 23. See also Appendix B.

[19] Goldingay, *Old Testament Theology: Israel's Gospel*, 221.

[20] Wright, *The Mission of God*, 221.

[21] Newsom, "Bakhtin, the Bible and Dialogical Truth," 298; Brodie, "Genesis as Dialogue"; Brodie, *Genesis as Dialogue*. Cf. *Section* 1.3.3.

[22] Cf. Appendix B.

[23] Cf. Wenham, *Genesis 1–15*, 89; Ross, *Creation and Blessing*, 146; McKeown, *Genesis*, 36.

palistrophic structure of the Jacob-cycle, we are presented with all the options: wealth as a result of blessing (Gen 26); wealth as 'curse' (Gen 34); wealth as a result of the interaction between the two (Gen 29–30). The way the narrator mentions God's involvement in these episodes (or not) aligns with this extremely well. One thing is clear: the narrative does not simply equate blessing and material wealth.

However, the dialogical contrast of blessing and curse is by no means a static stand-off. Despite frustrations and set-backs, the Genesis story shows how God advances his plans. This progression, despite various frustrations, is also visible in the Jacob-cycle, maybe most clearly in the progression of the blessing theme. There is a major development from 'blessing obtained through struggle' towards 'blessing freely given.' The transfer of the divine promises from Abraham to Isaac was very straightforward (26:2–5), but the transfer from Isaac to Jacob gets complicated by human acts to manipulate blessing (Gen 27). God transfers the patriarchal promises to Jacob at Bethel in Gen 28:13–15, but God does not tell Jacob 'I will bless you' (cp. 26:3). At Peniel, Jacob obtains divine blessing, but only after a painful struggle and negotiation. It is only in Gen 35 that God freely and emphatically blesses Jacob without struggle, without negotiation and without Jacob's prompting. Despite receiving God's emphatic blessing in Gen 35, Jacob's life remains a struggle: Rachel's death and Reuben's act in Gen 35, and the loss of Joseph later on (cf. 47:9). Yet, towards the end of his life, Jacob knows that God's purposes will never fail (Gen 48–49). However, it takes much more of the biblical story line to fully appreciate that blessing will eventually overcome curse.

5.2.2 *Material Possessions in View of the Patriarchal Promises*

We must expand this discussion and consider the relation between material possessions and the other divine promises made to Abraham, Isaac and Jacob regarding land, 'seed' and assistance ('I will be with you') or relationship. The story line of the Pentateuch is very much about the progressive realisation of these promises (Clines). Various episodes in the Jacob-cycle show the contrast between God's long-term and high-level promises, and short-term or immediate human concerns.[24] Struggle over material advancement seems to be more associated with short-term human struggle than with the long-term

---

[24] See also Appendix B.

divine promises. However, Jacob's material wealth is not entirely dis-
connected from God's involvement either. I have discussed already
the relation between material possessions and blessing. In addition,
God's land promise can be seen as the most important promise God
makes regarding possessions.[25] Not much progress is made with the
fulfilment of the land promise in the Jacob-cycle.[26] However, God's
promise regarding 'seed' makes substantial progress in the Jacob-cycle
compared to the story of Abraham and Isaac, although there are recurrent threats to the chosen line. This promise takes a giant step forward
in the Joseph-cycle (47:27). In Genesis, God is consistently portrayed
as the one who keeps his promises.

Jacob's wealth seems subordinate to God's larger scale promises. I
propose that Jacob's possessions should be considered as a 'means to
an end' in relation to God's promises of 'seed' and 'land.'[27]. Jacob's
ability to buy grain in Egypt to feed his family is a good example.[28]
A subtler one is the ability of the Patriarchs to hold their ground in
semi-hostile territory over a long period of time.[29] Wealth in this case
equates with 'staying power' or 'preservation'. Joseph's success in
Egypt must be interpreted in this preservation context, serving larger
objectives (cf. 50:19–21).[30]

> The wealth of the patriarchs must therefore be understood within its
> clear covenantal context. This wealth is tied directly to God's plan to
> give his people a special land (...) The preservation of the patriarchs

---

[25] Interestingly, possession of the Promised Land can only be understood within a
relationship paradigm. "The land-gift functioned as *proof of the relationship between
God and Israel*" (Wright, *Old Testament Ethics*, 88, italics by the author). See also
Wright, *Old Testament Ethics*, 190 and J.G. Millar, "Land," in *New Dictionary of Bibli-
cal Theology* (eds. T.D. Alexander and B.S. Rosner; Leicester, England: Inter-Varsity
Press, 2000), 625.

[26] On the progress of God's promises in the Jacob-cycle, cf. Turner, *Announcements
of Plot in Genesis*, 135–141.

[27] B. Howland, "Retelling Genesis," *First Thinks* 138, Dec (2003): 20–27, 27.

[28] "Precious metals afford a measure of security and protection in times of famine"
(Waltke, *Genesis*, 216).

[29] See Gen 14 (See also D.J. Wiseman, "Abraham in History and Tradition Part II:
Abraham the Prince," *BSac* 134 (1977): 228–37). Wiseman notes that the Patriarchs
are dealing on equal footing with the various kings. "Abraham's rank and dignity
were also acknowledged by the Egyptian king (Gen 12:10–20) who would otherwise
have dismissed an insignificant foreigner, especially if he were a suppliant for relief
or a mere herdsman-nomad, whose action had affronted the court" (D.J. Wiseman,
"Abraham Reassessed," in *Essays on the Patriarchal Narratives* (eds. A.R. Millard and
D.J. Wiseman; Leicester, UK: Inter-Varsity Press, 1980), 145).

[30] Gen 45:5–8; 50:19–20.

throughout Genesis 12—50 is never an end in itself, or primarily a response to their levels of obedience to God, but rather God's sovereign method of fulfilling his promises to gather a unique people together in a unique land.[31]

"One theme that recurs frequently in the Genesis narratives is the contrast between the work of man and the work of God, and that theme appears to be important in interpreting the stories about Jacob."[32] The self-sufficiency of the tower builders in Gen 11 ("let us make a name for ourselves") is contrasted with God's plan for Abraham and his line in Gen 12 ("I will make your name great"). We see the same contrast in the Jacob-cycle, where Jacob's self-sufficiency utterly fails (Gen 27), yet where God 'builds' a staircase from heaven to earth to show Jacob a different way. Where men's plans fail, God's plans succeed.[33] The inadequacy of Jacob's self-sufficiency is also demonstrated by Jacob's flight from Laban (God's intervention proves to be crucial), and by Jacob's anxiety regarding the approaching Esau. I think it is right to associate Jacob's wealth as acquired in Haran with God's promise of assistance (although more is involved). In contrast, the acquisition of possessions by means of plunder in Gen 34 should not be associated with God's involvement. However, the fact that Jacob's family is not attacked, hence their possessions are protected, should be (35:5). Material possessions might display God's help, but that is not always the case. In cases where God's help may be inferred, it is right to call Jacob 'signally' blessed (30:27) as was Isaac (Gen 26:28; Grüneberg and Moberly).[34]

5.2.3 'Story as Torah'?

The conclusions I have reached in this study illustrate how effectively story can function as *Torah*. My observations and conclusions have emerged quite naturally and inductively without the need to 'extract the message' and 'discard the story.'[35] The Jacob-story demonstrates

---

[31] Blomberg, *Neither Poverty nor Riches*, 36–37. Possessions serve the bigger objective of land and the land is eventually meant for living in the presence of God (Wright, *Living as the People of God*, 47). See also Kidner, *Genesis*, 153–154 who states that despite their wealth, the Patriarchs are meant to remain 'pilgrims.'

[32] Curtis, "Structure, Style and Context," 130.

[33] Curtis, "Structure, Style and Context," 131.

[34] Grüneberg, *Abraham*, 244; Moberly, *The Bible, Theology and Faith: A Study of Abraham and Jesus*, 124. See *Section* 2.3.2.

[35] See above.

quite powerfully how all-consuming the battle for material advancement can be. It shows the costly consequences when material advancement is considered more important than relationship and that the
consequences of such human sin have serious repercussions. God does
not seem to make many ethical demands of Jacob, but Jacob has to live
with the consequences of his actions. Although the narrator does not
seem to make a lot of specific ethical evaluations, the discerning reader
will gain plenty from the Jacob narrative ethically.[36] The narrative
offers a realistic portrayal of how God's blessing finds expression in a
fallen world, in which God remains involved.[37] The Jacob-cycle holds
out conflict resolution as a desirable option, but it never becomes a
simple manual for conflict-resolution.[38] People have to find out themselves, often the costly way. The more we look into the mirror held up
by the Jacob story and consider the nature and role of material possessions and associated attitudes and actions, the better we understand
the human predicament and the more we find out about the great cost
of human sin and the certain hope that flows from God's grace.

5.3   Methodological Reflections

In the course of this project I have engaged with many different scholars, who have applied many different methodologies to address many
different issues related to the Jacob-cycle. Some of these studies are
quite un-related to my topic, but I have aimed to benefit from many
different insights. I intended to cast my net wide, and that is what I
have done. Although my focus has been on the text in its final form, I
have engaged with scholars who do not share that approach.[39] Despite
a plethora of methods and insights, my findings have appeared inductively and naturally from the text, and have not been extracted from the
text at the expense of ruining the story. The Jacob stories feature plenty
of 'gaps.' As demonstrated throughout this study, several commentators find it difficult to resist the temptation to fill these 'gaps,' often to
fit a particular pre-understanding or bias. However, it is important to

---

[36] Cf. Goldingay, *Old Testament Theology: Israel's Gospel*, 275 and 286.
[37] Cf. Westermann, *Genesis 12–36*, 468.
[38] Cf. Gammie, "Theological Interpretation," 130: "The traditions of Genesis 25–36
seem, rather, to provide a blueprint for the handling of the familial, ethnic, socioeco-
nomic strife it describes so fully."
[39] Cf. Walton, *Thou Traveller Unknown*, 219.

resist this enticement, especially when one carries out a topical study. I have highlighted several issues associated with material possessions that resist closure. Here are some examples:

- We do not know all the details concerning the birthright (Gen 25) and Isaac's blessing (Gen 27);
- We do not know whether or how Jacob fulfilled his commitment to tithe (28:22);
- We do not know whether the agreement between Jacob and Laban should be described as a herding-contract, a marriage-contract, or as a combination of the two;
- We do not know to what extent inheritance related concerns played a role in the battle between Leah and Rachel;
- We do not know to what extent Esau's magnanimity towards Jacob can be explained as a result of the droves that met him on the way;
- We cannot be sure what the Shechemites knew and didn't know, and to what extent their desire for material gain was malicious, or rather a fairly innocent example of self-interest;
- We do not know how Isaac's inheritance was divided between his sons.

Leaving speculation and 'gap-filling' aside, I have demonstrated that plenty can be discovered in the Jacob-cycle regarding the nature and role of material possessions and associated attitudes and actions. No unwarranted 'gap-filling' has been required to make my case. My approach is not the only appropriate one, but I think that the combination of keeping the text central, while engaging with the multitudes of available methods and insights is the way forward for topical studies like this.

NOUNS AND VERBS RELATED TO MATERIAL
POSSESSIONS IN GEN 12–50

Type of Possession	References in Gen 12–50
רְכוּשׁ (generic: possession, property)	Gen 12:5; 13:6; 14:11; 14:12; 14:16x2; 14:21; 15:14; 31:18; 36:7; 46:6
אֲחֻזָּה (property: landed or general)	Gen 17:8; 23:4; 23:9; 23:20; 36:43; 47:11; 48:4; 49:30; 50:13
כָּל־אֲשֶׁר־לוֹ ('all that he had/ owned')[1]	Gen 12:20; 13:1; 24:2; 24:36; 25:5; 31:21; 39:4; 39:5x2; 39:6; 46:1
קִנְיָן (thing got or acquired, acquisition)	Gen 31:18; 34:23; 36:6
צֹאן (sheep, cattle)	Gen 12:16; 13:5; 20:14; 21:27; 21:28; 24:35; 26:14; 27:9; 29:2; 29:3; 29:6; 29:7; 29:8; 29:9; 29:10x2; 30:31; 30:32; 30:36; 30:38x2; 30:39x2; 30:40x3; 30:41x2; 30:42; 30:43; 31:4; 31:8x2; 31:10x2; 31:12; 31:19; 31:38; 31:41; 31:43x2; 32:6; 32:8; 33:13x2; 34:28; 37:2; 37:12; 37:14; 38:12; 38:13; 38:17; 45:10; 46:32x2; 46:34; 47:1; 47:3; 47:4; 47:17; 50:8
בָּקָר (cattle, herd, ox)	Gen 12:16; 13:5; 18:7f; 20:14; 21:27; 24:35; 26:14; 32:8; 33:13; 34:28; 45:10; 46:32; 47:1, 17; 50:8
חֲמוֹר (donkey, (he-)ass)	Gen 12:16; 22:3, 5; 24:35; 30:43; 32:6; 34:28; 36:24; 42:26f; 43:18, 24; 44:3, 13; 45:23; 47:17

---

[1] Or a very similar phrase.

Appendix A (*cont.*)

Type of Possession	References in Gen 12–50
עֶבֶד (servant, slave)[2]	Gen 12:16; 14:15; 20:8; 20:14; 21:25; 24:2; 24:5; 24:9; 24:10; 24:14; 24:17; 24:34; 24:35; 24:52; 24:53; 24:59; 24:61; 24:65x2; 24:66; 25:23; 26:15; 26:19; 26:25; 26:32; 27:37; 30:43; 32:6; 32:17x2; 39:17; 39:19; 40:20x2; 41:10; 41:12; 41:37; 41:38; 44:9; 44:10; 44:16; 44:17; 44:33; 45:16; 47:19; 47:25; 49:15; 50:2; 50:7
שִׁפְחָה (slave girl, maid)	Gen 12:16; 16:1; 16:2; 16:3; 16:5; 16:6; 16:8; 20:14; 24:35; 25:12; 29:24x2; 29:29x2; 30:4; 30:7; 30:9; 30:10; 30:12; 30:18; 30:43; 32:6; 32:23; 33:1; 33:2; 33:6; 35:25; 35:26
אָתוֹן (she-ass)	Gen 12:16; 32:16; 45:23
גָּמָל (camel)	Gen 12:16; 24:10x2; 24:11; 24:14; 24:19; 24:20; 24:22; 24:30; 24:31; 24:32x2; 24:35; 24:44; 24:46x2; 24:61; 24:63; 24:64; 30:43; 31:17; 31:34; 32:8; 32:16; 37:25
מִקְנֶה (acquisition, purchase)	Gen 17:12; 17:13; 17:23; 17:27; 23:18
מִקְנֶה (livestock)	Gen 13:2; 13:7x2; 26:14x2; 29:7; 30:29; 31:9; 31:18x2; 33:17; 34:5; 34:23; 36:6; 36:7; 46:6; 46:32; 46:34; 47:6; 47:16x2; 47:17x4; 47:18; 49:32
כֶּסֶף (silver, money)	Gen 13:2; 17:12; 17:13; 17:23; 17:27; 20:16; 23:9; 23:13; 23:15; 23:16x2; 24:35; 24:53; 31:15; 31:30x2; 37:28; 42:25; 42:27; 42:28; 42:35x2; 43:12x2; 43:15; 43:18; 43:21x2; 43:22x2; 43:23; 44:1; 44:2x2; 44:8x2; 45:22; 47:14x2; 47:15x2; 47:16; 47:18
זָהָב (gold)[3]	Gen 13:2; 24:22, 35, 53; 41:42; 44:8

---

[2] Only references where slaves/servants are occur as possession. Other occurrences for example, include polite expressions like '...do not pass by your servant' (Abraham to the LORD in Gen 18:3).

[3] Contrary to livestock in its various forms, gold does not feature in any major way.

Possessions Related Verbs	Usage in Gen 12–50
מָכַר (to sell)	**Gen 25:31; 25:33; 31:15; 37:27; 37:28; 37:36; 45:4; 45:5; 47:20; 47:22**
יָרַשׁ (to take possession of, to be heir)	**Gen 15:3; 15:4x2; 15:7; 15:8; 21:10; 22:17; 24:60; 28:4; 45:11**
רָכַשׁ (to collect, gather)	**Gen 12:5; 31:18x2; 36:6; 46:6**
שָׁבַר (Qal: to buy grain; Hiphil: to sell grain)[4]	**Gen 41:56; 41:57; 42:1; 42:2x2; 42:3; 42:5; 42:6; 42:7; 42:10; 42:19; 42:26; 43:2x2; 43:4; 43:20; 43:22; 44:2; 44:25; 47:14x2**

Major Moves in Gen 12–50 Associated with רְכוּשׁ

Gen 12:5	: **Abraham moves with all he has to Canaan;**
Gen 13:6	: **Abraham's and Lot's possessions are too great for them to stay together;**
Gen 14:11	: **Possessions of Sodom and Gomorrah are taken away;**
Gen 14:12	: **Lot's possessions are included in that pillage;**
Gen 14:16x2	: **Abraham recovers possessions of Sodom, Gomorrah and Lot;**
Gen 14:21	: **The king of Sodom offers Abraham the possessions but demands the people for himself. Abraham however refuses to accept anything from his hand;**
Gen 15:14	: **God foretells Abraham that his offspring will be 'sojourners in a land that is not theirs and will be servants there.... and afterwards they will come out with great possessions;**
Gen 31:18	: **After his stay in Paddan-aram, Jacob goes to the land of Canaan to his father Isaac (in a way mirroring Abraham's first arrival);[5]**
Gen 36:7	: **Jacob and Esau's possessions are too great for them to stay together (mirroring Abraham and Lot in Gen 13:6);**
Gen 46:6	: **Jacob moves with all he has to Egypt (in the opposite direction of Abraham in Gen 12:20–13:1f.).**

Westermann suggests that this probably points to a time when silver was more valuable than gold (commenting on Gen 13:2, Westermann, *Genesis 12–36*, 175), which seems somewhat illogical as the order of items in 13:2 suggest a ranking from the lesser to the greater. However, the occurrence of gold is sparse indeed. It is interesting to consider however that gold appears at the beginning of narratives about 'a next phase': Abraham returning to Canaan; Rebecca 'lured' into the family; and, Joseph's start as governor of Egypt.

[4] To break; to buy grain (HALOT 9353: "originally referring to breaking off a piece of silver to make a purchase").

[5] Wenham, *Genesis 16–50*, 272.

APPENDIX B

THE RELATIONSHIP BETWEEN BLESSING
AND POSSESSIONS IN GEN 12–50

Blessing is a recurring theme in Genesis. According to Goldingay "...*the* theme that runs through Genesis is that of God's blessing—originally given, deservedly compromised, graciously promised, variously imperilled, partially experienced."[1] Wenham notes that "the root ברך occurs more frequently in Genesis than in any other part of the OT: 88 times in Genesis as against 310 times elsewhere."[2] Here is a chart of the occurrences of the verb בְּרַךְ and the substantive בְּרָכָה in Genesis as a whole:

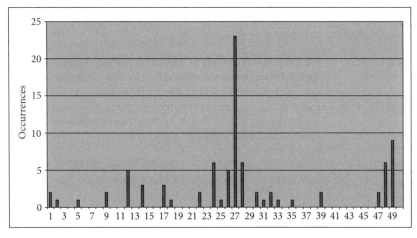

Occurrences of the verb בְּרַךְ and the substantive בְּרָכָה in Genesis 1–50.

---

[1] Goldingay, *Models for Interpretation of Scripture*, 23.
[2] Wenham, *Genesis 1–15*, 275. The 88 occurrences in Genesis, break down as follows: the verb בְּרַךְ Qal (8x); Niphal (3x); Piel (59x) Hithpael (2x) and the substantive בְּרָכָה (16x) (source: Keller, "ברך to bless," 267 TLOT; cf. M.L. Brown, "ברך." NIDOTTE #1385, 1:757–67.

Westermann and McKenzie have categorized these occurrences into four groups (see numbering in graph above): 1) God's blessing on creation; 2) God's blessing on Abraham (and Isaac); 3) the struggle for Isaac's blessing; and 4) Jacob's blessing of Pharaoh and his sons.[3] This is a helpful starting point, but for our purposes we need to refine the grid. When we study *all* references to blessing in Gen 12–50, it becomes clear that *various* parties speak about blessing, namely: God himself; the patriarchs; the narrator and others.[4] These parties do not necessarily speak about the same thing. For example, Abraham's servant in Gen 24 draws attention to God's blessing in relation to Abraham's prosperity.[5] Yet when God speaks in 12:1–3, blessing seems to transcend 'mere' possessions. To determine the meaning of 'blessing'/'bless' it is necessary to study each occurrence in context.

As we examine the various occurrences of bless* in the Abraham-, Jacob- and Joseph-cycle, it becomes clear that there is quite a number of differences between them.[6] In the Abraham-cycle it is predominantly God who talks about blessing, followed by those who comment on the (perceived) visible results of the divine blessing. But God's blessing speeches occur less and less and disappear altogether in the Joseph-cycle:[7]

'Blessing Speak'	God	Patriarchal Family	The Narrator	Others/ Bystanders
Abraham Cycle	52% (11)	0% (0)	14% (3)	33% (7)
Jacob Cycle	10% (4)	56% (23)	27% (11)	7% (3)
Joseph Cycle	0% (0)	47% (9)	53% (10)	0% (0)

---

[3] Westermann deserves credit for the first three categories, McKenzie for the last. See: B.A. McKenzie, "Jacob's Blessing on Pharaoh: An Interpretation of Gen 46:31–47:26," *WTJ* 45, no. 2 (1983): 386–99, 386. I already mentioned Fretheim's contribution to split God's blessing in two categories: blessing over all of creation, and specific blessing for the patriarchs (Fretheim, "Which Blessing?," 281).

[4] Melchizedek, Abimelech, Abraham's servant, Rebecca, Esau, Laban etc.

[5] A key-component to the servant's rhetorical strategy (24:34–36). Cf. Waltke, *Genesis*, 330; Wenham, *Genesis 16–50*, 147; Hamilton, *Genesis 18–50*, 15 and Brueggemann, *Genesis*, 198–200.

[6] The Abraham-cycle: 11:10–25:18; Jacob-cycle: 25:19–36; Joseph-cycle: 37–50.

[7] This aligns well with the decrease of 'appearances' by the LORD (or God) to the patriarchs (cf. Dieckmann, *Segen für Isaak*, 211; see above).

Keeping this in mind, we will first look at the various instances where *God himself* speaks of 'blessing' (or expresses his thoughts). Having considered both *context* and *content* of these divine blessing utterances, we will compare them with those expressed by others.[8]

BLESSING: GOD'S PERSPECTIVE

In Gen 12–50 there are various passages where God speaks about blessing:

- In these instances, God talks *exclusively* to the patriarchs (Abraham: 12:2–3; 17:16, 20; 22:17–18; Isaac: 26:3, 4, 24; Jacob: 28:14), the exception being 18:18 where God speaks to himself (as recorded by the narrator);
- In most cases, the beneficiaries of these blessings are: the patriarchs themselves; their 'seed;' and all the nations of the earth (12:1–3). Exceptions are 17:16 (Sarah) and 20 (Ishmael);
- These blessing utterances seem to take place at key moments in the storyline (crises),[9] and when God's promises are transferred to the next generation.[10]

In these instances, it is not straightforward to determine what God *exactly* means with 'I will bless you.' This is not helped by the fact that these utterances are fairly rare and generally short. The many interpretive challenges of 12:1–3 illustrate this point. A few comments in relation to our topic. On the macro-level, 12:1–3 is considered important for at least two reasons.[11] First of all, God's calling of Abraham can be considered programmatic for everything that follows in Genesis and the Pentateuch.[12] God's statements, which are high-level, conceptual and not yet 100% specific, combined with Abraham's response (12:4ff.), set this new phase of the story in motion. Abraham has

---

[8] There are instances in Gen 12–50 where men bless God (Melchizedek (14:20) and Abraham's servant (24:27)), but a discussion of these passages is beyond the scope of our particular study (cf. Grüneberg, *Abraham*, chapter 5).

[9] Sarna, *Understanding Genesis*, 102; e.g. the famine as experienced by Isaac (26:1–2) and Jacob's flight to Haran to avoid Esau's wrath.

[10] Wenham, *Genesis 1–15*, 275.

[11] A third reason is the way 12:1–3 links with Gen 1–11 (see below).

[12] Wenham, *Genesis 1–15*, 274; von Rad, *Genesis*, 161; Turner, *Announcements of Plot in Genesis*, 51 and Clines, *The Theme of the Pentateuch*, 29.

to leave his security in order to be blessed by God.[13] Because God's promises are not very specific yet, Abraham's response is interpreted as one of faith.[14] As the story unfolds, God's promises become more specific; clearly a case of progressive revelation. Regarding the promise of offspring to Abraham Alter notices: "*The promise becomes more and more definite* as it seems progressively more implausible to the aged patriarch, until Isaac is born."[15] Wenham makes a similar observation regarding all of God's promises in Genesis:

> To grasp the importance of the promises in Genesis the reader should look at all God's speeches in the book noting the changes in wording between one passage and the next (…) *These changes show that God makes the promises ever more specific and dogmatic as the patriarchs respond in faith and obedience.*[16]

Some promises are fulfilled in Abraham's lifetime (offspring), others not (land).[17] Mitchell's distinction between promises and blessings, where blessings are normally 'fulfilled in the recipients' lifetime' and where promise fulfilment goes beyond the lifetime of the recipient, clearly goes too far.[18] Divine blessing in Gen 12–50 might well be subject to progressive revelation as well.

Secondly, the phrase 'Go' (לֶךְ־לְךָ) in 12:1 and 22:2 is striking.[19] These passages can be seen as the two pillars on which the entire Abraham cycle rests. This again suggests that what really matters in Abraham's life is the interplay between God's instructions/promises and Abraham's response in faith.[20]

> The basic plot moves from profound tension to unexpected resolution. That movement occurs principally between the promise of 12:1–3 and the reiteration of that promise in 22:15–18.[21]

---

[13] A similar move takes place in Gen 22: Abraham's obedience results in a repeat of God's promises in the most strong blessing/promise language of the Abraham cycle (22:16–17).

[14] This is especially true for the promise of becoming a great nation (cf. Sarna, *Understanding Genesis*, 100).

[15] Alter, *Genesis*, 66, italics mine.

[16] Wenham, "Theology of Genesis 12–50," in *Genesis* (italics mine).

[17] Hence the 'partial fulfillment' of the patriarchal promises (cf. Clines, *The Theme of the Pentateuch*).

[18] Mitchell, *The Meaning of BRK*, 35 and 181.

[19] Waltke, *Genesis*, 195–196; Alter, *Genesis*, 50; Hamilton, *Genesis 1–17*, 370–371; Turner, *Announcements of Plot in Genesis*, 87; Sarna, *Understanding Genesis*, 160; Westermann, *Genesis 12–36*, 357.

[20] Brueggemann, *Genesis*, 111; Waltke, *Genesis*, 196.

[21] Brueggemann, *Genesis*, 109.

It is within this framework that we have to analyze all that pertains to possessions in the Abraham cycle.

On the micro-level, our focus in 12:1–3 is on the *meaning* of 'bless/ blessing,' the keyword in the passage:[22] "...and I will bless you" (12:2);" "...so that you will be a blessing" (12:2); "I will bless those who bless you" (12:3); "...and in you all the nations of the earth will be blessed" (12:3). The fact that different parties 'do the blessing' should alert us that different aspects of blessing might be in view. For example, if we take God's blessing as an assurance of fruitfulness, it is clear that this is something only God can do. So, we have to consider which parties are involved in the blessing: God, humanity, or both? Who is blessing and who is on the receiving end?

Before we proceed, we need to be aware of a number of translation issues, as they do have 'profound theological implications:'[23]

- The phrase וֶהְיֵה בְּרָכָה (12:2) can be interpreted as an imperative ('be a blessing!') or as a consequence of what has preceded ('so you will be a blessing');
- Secondly, the phrase וְנִבְרְכוּ בְךָ כֹּל מִשְׁפְּחֹת הָאֲדָמָה (12:3) can be interpreted as "and in you all nations of the earth will be blessed" or "find a blessing" or "...will bless themselves" (a passive, middle or reflexive reading).

I limit myself to the first issue.[24] Wenham notes that the expression וֶהְיֵה בְּרָכָה "occurs in only two other passages, Isa 19:24 and Zech 8:13" and that "its precise interpretation is uncertain."[25] Janzen suggests that "the shape or structure of the passage is a guide to its content and meaning (...): a twofold repetition of one *imperative* followed by three *result* clauses:" Abraham has to *go* (from his country etc.) and

---

[22] Westermann, *Genesis 12–36*, 149.

[23] Speiser, *Genesis*, 86.

[24] For an in-depth study on Gen 12:3, see Grüneberg, *Abraham*. For an excellent summary of the issues regarding the second translation, see Wenham, *Genesis 1–15*, 277. Cf. Chisholm, *From Exegesis to Exposition*, 85; Dumbrell, *The Faith of Israel*, 28 (who prefers a reflexive translation: 'win for themselves a blessing') and Turner, *Announcements of Plot in Genesis*, 55–57, who shows that a choice between these options is by no means straightforward.

[25] Wenham identifies the various issues and identifies how interpreters fall in different camps (Wenham, *Genesis 1–15*, 275).

he has to *be a blessing*.[26] The many promises made by God (in the result clauses) seem to be conditional upon Abraham's obedience to the imperatives. "'Showing the land' (12:1) becomes 'I will give this land' (12:7) only when Abraham makes his move."[27] We begin to see the interplay between command/promise, obedience in faith, and a clarified/firmer promise. "Genesis insists on the importance of both divine grace and human behaviour."[28] Although this explanation certainly has its merits, most commentators prefer the translation "…so that you will be a blessing."[29] Whatever interpretation is preferred, it is clear that there is balance in 12:1–3: Yes, Abraham is blessed, yet he "must be more than a recipient. He is both a receptacle for the divine blessing and a transmitter of that blessing."[30] This is underlined by the fact that the climactic seventh term of the utterance deals with the blessing for the nations.[31] As we examine the prosperity of the patriarchs we need to keep this balance in mind.

---

[26] Janzen, *Genesis 12–50*, 15. The imperatival translation ('be a blessing') is also favoured by Turner, *Announcements of Plot in Genesis*, 104 (who sees the clauses that follow as consequential) and Hamilton, *Genesis 1–17*, 369–370 (discussion in footnote). Contrary to this, Wenham argues that all clauses are subordinate to the command 'Go': "Grammatically, the main verbs—'make,' 'bless,' 'make great,' 'be,' 'bless,' 'curse,' 'find blessing'—are all subordinate to the imperative 'Go' (vs. 1). Most of them are imperfects or cohortatives prefixed by weak *waw* which indicates purpose or consequence. (The other grammatical forms used here have the same function). The divine intentionality could also be expressed by translating these verses 'Go…so that I may make you…bless you…etc.'" (Wenham, *Genesis 1–15*, 274).

[27] Hamilton, *Genesis 1–17*, 371. Specifying the land would have "detracted from the act of faith involved in heeding the simple command" (Sarna, *Understanding Genesis*, 101).

[28] Grüneberg, *Abraham*, 244.

[29] Wenham, *Genesis 1–15*, 266. This is based on GKC paragraph 110i, which states: "The imperative, when depending (with *waw copulative*) upon a jussive (cohortative), or an interrogative sentence, frequently expresses also a consequence which is to be expected with certainty, and often a consequence which is intended, or in fact an intention." See also Sailhamer, *Genesis* (on 12:2). Finally there is a minority that opts for a re-pointing of the 2nd masculine singular imperative into a 3rd masculine singular imperfect: "and it [your name] will be a blessing." See Turner, *Announcements of Plot in Genesis*, 53. This translation is followed by Skinner, *Genesis*, 244; Gunkel, *Genesis*, 164; Speiser, *Genesis*, 85–86.

[30] Hamilton, *Genesis 1–17*, 373. Turner states: "Abraham does little to bless the nations" (Turner, *Announcements of Plot in Genesis*, 111). Turner is probably a bit too harsh, especially in the light of Abraham's assessment in the NT (Gen 15:6!). For more on the 'ethics' of the patriarchs: cf. Westermann, *Genesis 12–36*, 167; T.D. Alexander, *Genesis 22 and the Covenant of Circumcision* (JSOTSup 25; Sheffield, UK: Sheffield Academic Press, 1983), 17 as quoted by Turner, *Announcements of Plot in Genesis*, 92; Wenham, *Story as Torah*, 106.

[31] Waltke, *Genesis*, 203. Cf. Hamilton, *Genesis 1–17*, 371.

The interpretations really start to diverge on the likely meaning of God's promise 'I will bless you' in 12:2. Most interpreters opt for a combination of these. Demarcation lines are not always clearly drawn or declared:

1. No specific meaning can be given yet;[32]
2. A bestowing of 'life-force for good;'[33]
3. Blessing as a summary phrase for the promises made in 12:1–3;[34]
4. Blessing linked with becoming a great nation;[35]
5. Blessing linked with getting a great name;[36]
6. Blessing linked with descendants;[37]
7. Blessing linked with land;[38]
8. God's blessing in a relational/spiritual sense;[39]
9. Blessing as a broad concept covering "happiness, success and increase of earthly possessions."[40] An explicit link is made between blessing and possessions or prosperity (not limited to 'land').[41]

It is instructive to examine these options in relation to expanding circles of literary context:

---

[32] Hamilton, *Genesis 1–17*, 372; R.A. Pyne, "The 'Seed', the Spirit and the Blessing of Abraham," *BSac* 152 (1995): 211–22, 212.

[33] Brueggemann, *Genesis*, 165 and 168; Davidson, *Genesis 12–50*, 20.

[34] Westermann, *Genesis 12–36*, 149.

[35] Hamilton alludes to that: Hamilton, *Genesis 1–17*, 372.

[36] Westermann, *Genesis 12–36*, 149.

[37] von Rad, *Genesis*, 155.

[38] Brown, "ברך." NIDOTTE #1385, 1:759: "there is little dispute as to the meaning of most of the promised blessing, referring to both posterity and land, and fully expressed in Gen 12:2–3."

[39] A minority view, but an important one: cf. Baldwin, *The Message of Genesis 12–50*, 31; Clines, *The Theme of the Pentateuch*, 34–37.

[40] Turner, *Announcements of Plot in Genesis*, 104 following a definition by J. Scharbert, "ברך; ברכה." TDOT Vol. 2, 293.

[41] Wenham, *Genesis 1–15*, 275. Waltke mentions prosperity as one of the 'three nuances of bless' (the other two being potency/fertility and victory). Waltke then links these three blessing nuances with a definition from Horst: "Blessing brings the power for life, the enhancement of life, and the increase of life" (F. Horst, *Gottes Recht: Gesammelte Studien zum Recht im Alten Testament* (Munich, Germany: Chr. Kaiser Verlag, 1961), 194 as quoted by Roop, *Genesis*, 98 and Waltke, *Genesis*, 205), which links with the 'life-force' category. Blomberg also links blessing with wealth (Blomberg, *Neither Poverty nor Riches*, 36). Elsewhere, Blomberg comments on 12:1–3 that "prosperity was part of the promise, and he refers to: Gen 12:7; 15:18; 17:8; 22:17" (C.L. Blomberg, "Wealth," in *Evangelical Dictionary of Biblical Theology* (ed. W.A. Elwell; Grand Rapids, Michigan, USA: Baker Books, 1996), 813). It must be noted however, that all these verses speak specifically about the land as possession.

- In 12:2, the meaning of 'blessing' cannot be determined. It is subject to progressive revelation;
- In the context of 12:1–3, blessing could be linked with *great name* and/or *great nation;*
- In the context of Gen 12 (and the rest of Gen 12–50) blessing could be linked to *seed* and *land;*
- Finally, from the rest of the Pentateuch[42] and the OT definitions for blessing can be derived, in aid of the interpretation of 12:1–3.

These 'context circles' however, must be applied in a particular order.[43] All commentators who interpret God's blessing in 12:2–3 in terms of wealth and prosperity seem to base this on later OT texts, while seemingly skipping or de-emphasizing intermediate context stages. One disadvantage of this approach is that, when the link between blessing and prosperity has been imposed on 12:1–3, the occurrences of patriarchal wealth that follow (13:2) are then linked back to the promise of blessing![44] Are we indeed to interpret the unethical ways of Abraham's enrichment in Gen 12 and 20 as blessed by God (see Chapter 1)? This seems undesirable. Maybe we are not yet meant to come up with a firm interpretation for 'blessing' in 12:1–3 yet. As with the progressive revelation regarding the land promise it might be better to follow the story line in Genesis and the Pentateuch to see what it means to be blessed by God. When we are told that "the Lord had blessed Abraham *in all things*" (24:1), we still have to be cautious in linking God's blessing too narrowly with wealth.[45]

> "Everything", we soon learn, includes not only great wealth but also a new lease of procreativity and the retention of spiritual powers (…) Yet

---

[42] Good examples of 4) and 5) are Wenham, *Genesis 1–15*, 275 and Clines, *The Theme of the Pentateuch*.

[43] Cf. Klein, *Introduction to Biblical Interpretation*, 161–162.

[44] Blomberg, *Neither Poverty nor Riches*, 36; Waltke, *Genesis*, 205.

[45] Most commentators link 24:1 with Abraham's wealth (cf. 24:35): Turner, *Announcements of Plot in Genesis*, 114; Wenham, *Genesis 16–50*, 140. Hamilton suggests we may also interpret Abraham's longevity as an aspect of God's blessing (also in 24:1). "Other manifestations of that blessing would include his material prosperity, his victory over the eastern kings, the restoration of fertility to Sarah's womb, the birth and survival of Isaac, Abraham's own survival through uncertain times, and the reception of divine promises that signal Abraham and his descendants as a light to the nations" (Hamilton, *Genesis 18–50*, 138). In addition, Abraham had enjoyed a relationship with God and had grown in that relationship (cf. Perriman, "Faith, Health and Prosperity," 125–126).

so blessed is Abraham that he can spend his last years raising a new family while taking measures (with his characteristic wisdom and foresight and fairness) to safeguard the interests of his old and divinely appointed one.[46]

At this stage it might be beneficial to take another step back in order to look at *all* the promises God makes to the Patriarchs.[47] Clines has analyzed "the textual evidence for the character and quantity of the promise material" (in the Pentateuch) and has identified promises relating to: a) descendants; b) relationship and c) land.[48] References to 'blessing' are categorized under 'relationship,' although Clines also links blessing with possession of the land (26:3 and 28:4) and with descendants.[49] Wenham summarizes the promise material as follows:

> There are four elements in these promises that keep recurring: 1) descendants/ nationhood; 2) land; 3) covenantal relationship; and 4) blessing to the nations (…) these promise elements of land, descendants and covenantal relationship are the most visible components of the blessing, which is the overarching concept in the book of Genesis.[50]

I will study the nature and function of material possessions in relation to these promises. Interestingly, most commentators pick up on the themes of 'land'[51] and 'seed,'[52] and indeed God's *tangible* promises mostly deal with these big themes, but many miss the 'promise of relationship:' "The importance of the 'relationship promise' follows from the recurring promise by God to be with the various patriarchs: Gen 26:3, 24: 28:15; 31:3; 31:5; 35:3; 31:42: 48:21."[53] Maybe this omission

---

[46] Sternberg, *Poetics*, 349.

[47] Realizing that promise and blessing are not necessarily the same thing: Westermann, *The Promises to the Fathers*, 74–78; Westermann, *Genesis 12–36*, 408–409; Brueggemann, *Genesis*, 206–207 and Mitchell, *The Meaning of BRK*, 35 and 181.

[48] Clines, *The Theme of the Pentateuch*, 32. Clines helpfully organizes the numerous passages from the Pentateuch under these three headings: Clines, *The Theme of the Pentateuch*, 32–47. For alternative categorizations, cf. V.P. Hamilton, "Genesis: Theology of," in NIDOTTE, 667.

[49] "…blessing should be most frequently linked with the promise of descendants" (Clines, *The Theme of the Pentateuch*, 36).

[50] Wenham, *Story as Torah*, 22.

[51] "In its present form, the governing promise concerns the land" (Brueggemann, *Genesis*, 109). See also Wright, *Living as the People of God*, 46.

[52] See Kidner, *Genesis*, 113; Waltke, *Genesis*, 196. See also Clines reference to Westermann, "Promises to the Patriarchs," 691a) who states that "the most frequent promise of Gen 12–50 is that of posterity, with that of the land as a distant second" (Westermann as quoted by Clines, *The Theme of the Pentateuch*, 36 and 146).

[53] Clines, *The Theme of the Pentateuch*, 36; cf. Vetter, *Jahwes Mit-Sein* and Vetter, "עם with את."

illustrates the human tendency to focus on the visible and the material at the cost of the intangible and spiritual. Schneider's statement that 'God's promises have always been material in nature', is clearly too narrow.[54] Grüneberg's proposal is more attractive: "Blessing often conveys benefits. It is not simply a commendation, or an acknowledgement of relationship, but (at least commonly) makes a material difference in the world."[55] Goldingay comments that "in English 'blessing' is apt to suggest something religious and/or interpersonal, but *bĕrākâ* implies something concrete and material."[56] These are helpful summaries, as long as the importance of relationship as an integral element of blessing is not undervalued. Mitchell's conclusions regarding blessing in the OT however, might go too far:

> Fertility, as well as the other benefits such as prosperity and dominion, are really not essential elements of blessing at all. The factor that makes a blessing a blessing is the relationship between God and the person blessed. (…) A blessing is any benefit or utterance which God freely bestows in order to make known to the recipient and to others that he is favourably disposed toward the recipient. The type of benefit God actually bestows when he blesses is of secondary importance.[57]

I prefer an intermediate position: Although blessing is a concept that must be studied in the context of relationship, it is reasonable to ask how that blessing finds its expression. Therefore, when we study patriarchal wealth in relation to God's promises to the patriarchs, we must therefore consider both the various relational aspects and the practical outworking of the blessing. Wright strikes the right balance:

> Blessing is initially and strongly connected with creation and all the good gifts God longs for people to enjoy in the world—abundance, fruitfulness and fertility, long life, peace and rest. Yet at the same time, these things are to be enjoyed in the context of healthy relationships with God and with others.[58]

Alternatively, we can examine what God exactly promises to *give* (in Gen 12–50). When we look at all occurrences of the verb 'to give' (נָתַן in the sense of 'give') in passages of direct divine speech, in which God (or the Lord God) is the subject (e.g. 'I will give to you….'), the

---

[54] Schneider, *The Good of Affluence*, 60.
[55] Grüneberg, *Abraham*, 99. Similarly "…life and well-being within every sphere of existence" (Fretheim, *The Pentateuch*, 97).
[56] Goldingay, *Old Testament Theology: Israel's Gospel*, 221.
[57] Mitchell, *The Meaning of BRK*, 165.
[58] Wright, *The Mission of God*, 221.

result is fascinating.[59] God seems to focus almost exclusively on the *land* he intends to give to Abraham and his descendants: 12:7; 13:15; 13:17; 15:18; 17:18; 24:7; 26:3; 26:4; 28:13; 35:12 (3x).[60] God is looking centuries ahead to the moment he can give the land as a possession to the descendants of the Patriarchs.[61]

The Patriarchs have quite different concerns. When God promises to Abraham that his reward shall be very great (15:1), Abraham replies by asking "O Lord God, what will you *give* me…?" (15:2), "behold, you have *given me no offspring*…" (15:3). Thankfully, God is not indifferent to Abraham's concerns. We see another striking contrast in Gen 28. God has just announced the glorious promises of land, offspring and relationship in a dream to Jacob 'on the run' (28:13–15). When Jacob wakes up, he makes a vow: "*If* God will be with me and will keep me in this way that I go, *and will give me bread to eat and clothing to wear*, (…) *then* the Lord shall be my God (…) *and of all that you give me I will give a full tenth to you*" (28:20–22) (see Section 2.4). These passages show that God and humanity can have blessing perspectives that are quite different.

Finally, Janzen interprets 12:1–3 in light of the story of the tower builders (11:1–9). Is Abraham meant to use the same standard as the tower builders to determine what it means to have a great name or to become a great nation?

> If Abram is to be the means of healing what has gone wrong in the human community and in its care of creation (compare 1:28; 2:15 with 3:17–19; 6:5–7, 11–13), part of what will be called for is a re-education in what is meant by blessedness and greatness.[62]

---

[59] Brueggemann elsewhere discusses so called 'verbs of promise'. The main one is 'to swear' שָׁבַע ('to promise on oath' see Deut 6:23 NRSV). "The verbs that derive from or supply the substance of *sb*, the content of the oath, are most characteristically 'give' (*ntn*) and 'bless' (*brk*)." In the discussion that follows, Brueggemann seems to line up 'give' with 'land' and 'bless' with 'seed', which seems quite reasonable in light of the above (W. Brueggemann, *Theology of the Old Testament* (Minneapolis, USA: Fortress Press, 1997), 165–169).

[60] The only exception is 17:16 where God promises Abraham to give him a son by Sarah.

[61] 'There can be no fulfilment of the land promise unless there is an heir. The promise of the heir is always in the service of the land promise' (Brueggemann, *Genesis*, 109).

[62] Janzen, *Genesis 12–50*, 19–20. "The rest of the ancestral narratives give ample evidence (…) of the slowness and painfulness with which that re-education must proceed" (Janzen, *Genesis 12–50*, 20).

Maybe we are still in need of that re-education.

The above shows that it is not always straightforward to determine the meaning of blessing in Gen 12–50. It appears to be dependent on who speaks about blessing and where the 'blessing speech' occurs in the story line. Divine promises of blessing are subject to progressive revelation and become firmer and well defined as they interact with responses of faith by their recipients. Having predominantly considered God's perspective up till now, we now turn to humanity's perspective on blessing.

BLESSING: HUMANITY'S PERSPECTIVE

In the Abraham-cycle God does most of the blessing-talk. In the Jacob- and Joseph cycle the patriarchal family takes over and an apparent shift in meaning takes place: 'blessing' seems more closely linked with material blessing. Everything gets a more 'earthly and earthy feel' to it.[63] Take Isaac's blessing in Gen 27: "…dew of heaven and the fatness of the earth and plenty of grain and wine," plus dominion over people (27:27–29).[64] Although God is still the one who is supposed to bless, Isaac's blessing is quite different from the usual blessing upon the Patriarchs by God (see Section 2.3).[65] This does not mean that the material aspects of blessing in the Jacob-cycle (and Joseph-cycle) are contrary to God's intentions. However, blessing speech by the patriarchal family might not represent the full blessing picture. This might be explained to some extent by the level of relationship a person has with God. Take Jacob's life-story: He grows from a person who anxiously grasps his brother's birthright and his father's blessing, to someone who *receives* God's blessing (28:10–22), although he does not comprehend its content right away (see Section 2.4). He then develops from a person who understands God's involvement in his material blessing (Gen 30–31) to a person who lives in an awareness of God's faithfulness throughout his life (48:15). At the end of his life, Jacob has

---

[63] Brueggemann, *Genesis*, 206–207.

[64] In the Jacob-cycle the first person to speak about blessing is God (26:3–4). In Gen 27 the patriarchal family takes over: Isaac: 27:4, 7, 25, 27, 29x2, 33x2, 35; Rebecca: 27:10; Jacob: 27:12, 19; Esau: 27:31, 34, 36x2, 38x2; Narrator: 27:23, 27, 30, 41x2.

[65] von Rad, *Genesis*, 273; Wenham, *Genesis 16–50*, 209.

grown tremendously in his relationship with God and he dies 'a man of hope,'[66] having a much clearer grasp of God's promises (48:3–4).

The fact that something special is at work in the lives of the Patriarchs does not go by unnoticed. At various points in Gen 12–50 'outsiders' make comments like: "God is with you in all that you do" (21:22);[67] "We see plainly that the Lord has been with you (…) You are now the blessed of the Lord" (26:28–29);[68] "I have learned by divination that the Lord has blessed me because of you" (30:27).

> That all the families of the earth will be blessed through Abraham and his offspring is central to the patriarchal promises (e.g., 12:3; 22:18; 28:14), and this is one of several incidents where outsiders admit that God's blessing very apparently rests on Abraham's family and those associated with them (14:19–20; 21:22–23; 26:12–16, 28–29; 39:5, 23).[69]

In these cases it is predominantly material advancement or tangible patriarchal success that elicits such responses. Similarly, we have seen various instances where the narrator draws our attention to God being at work in the lives of the Patriarchs and the resulting (visible) increase of their wealth (and success) (24:1; 26:12–13; 31:4–18; 39:2–6).

In Gen 12–50 God's promises of blessing and relationship often seem conceptual and intangible, yet the tangible effects of God's presence attract the attention of various other parties (see commentary on Gen 26:28–29 below). Sometimes, God's perspective and the world's seem to align (Gen 26), but sometimes they do not, and we have already seen examples of that.[70] This suggests that the human players who speak about blessing in Gen 12–50 may only be able to see part of the (divine) blessing picture:

---

[66] Take for example 48:21. "The old man died steady in the promise" (Brueggemann, *Genesis*, 358).

[67] Abimelech and Phicol to Abraham, 21:22. Baldwin links this statement with Abraham's 'prospering' (Baldwin, *The Message of Genesis 12–50*, 88). "God (the LORD) was with the other patriarchs (עִם, 26:3; 28:15; 31:3; 46:4; or אֶת 39:3) (…) What success is being referred to here is obscure: it could be Abraham's intercession (20:17) or the successful birth and weaning of Isaac (21:2, 8). The use of the participle 'doing' may suggest continued success, so that neither of these specific achievements is referred to but, rather, the whole tenor of Abraham's life expresses the blessing of God" (Wenham, *Genesis 16–50*, 92). Hamilton links this statement with 20:17 where Abimelech had witnessed Abraham's answered prayer (Hamilton, *Genesis 18–50*, 88).

[68] Abimelech plus advisors to Isaac, 26: 28–29.

[69] Laban to Jacob in Gen 30:27 (Wenham, *Genesis 16–50*, 255).

[70] E.g. Abraham's wealth upon his return from Egypt (see *Section* 1.1).

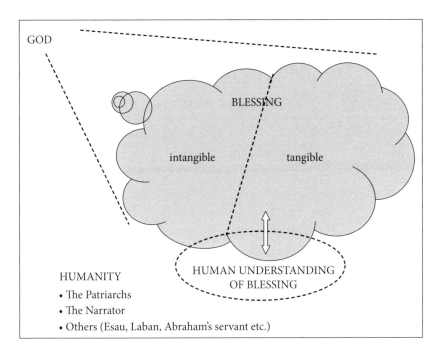

In Gen 12–50 different parties speak about blessing and they do not necessarily mean the same thing. Blessing seems to cover quite a range of issues. Exegesis of Gen 12:1–3 has shown that we have to be careful with defining 'blessing' too quickly and too tightly, as divine promises and blessing appear to be subject to progressive revelation. Although God certainly shows that he is involved in humanity's concerns, God's concerns differ in places from his human counterparts, who tend to focus on the tangible aspects of blessing instead of the intangible (relationship) and long-term ones (land). Furthermore, human understanding of blessing seems to depend on the degree of relationship a person has with God: the better that relation, the better the understanding (arrow in picture above).[71] Possessions (as blessing) are best understood within this relationship context. Although it is reasonable to link blessing with possessions in *certain* passages, this does not necessarily mean that *all* possessions are a blessing from God.[72] Blessing is always more than just possessions.

---

[71] As illustrated so well by Jacob (see above).
[72] See picture: This is illustrated by the part of 'human understanding' that does not overlap with the divine definition of blessing.

BIBLIOGRAPHY

Alexander, T.D. "Are the Wife/Sister Incidents of Genesis Literary Compositional Variants?" *Vetus Testamentum* 42, no. 2 (1992): 145–53.
——. *From Paradise to the Promised Land.* Carlisle, UK: Paternoster Press, 2002.
——. "Genealogies, Seed and the Compositional Unity of Genesis." *Tyndale Bulletin* 44, no. 2 (1993): 255–70.
——. *Genesis 22 and the Covenant of Circumcision.* Journal for the Study of the Old Testament Supplement Series 25. Sheffield, UK: Sheffield Academic Press, 1983.
Allen, C.G. "On Me Be the Curse, My Son!" Pages 159–72 in *Encounter with the Text: Form and History in the Hebrew Bible.* Edited by M.J. Buss. Philadelphia, Pennsylvania, USA: Fortress Press, 1979.
Alter, R. and F. Kermode, eds. *The Literary Guide to the Bible.* London, UK: Collins, 1987.
Alter, R. *The Art of Biblical Narrative.* New York: Basic Books, 1981.
——. *Genesis.* New York, USA: W.W. Norton & Company, 1996.
Amit, Y. "The Dual Causality Principle and its Effect on Biblical Literature." *Vetus Testamentum* 37, no. 4 (1987): 385–400.
——. *Reading Biblical Narratives.* Minneapolis, USA: Fortress Press, 2001.
Armstrong, K. *In the Beginning: A New Interpretation of Genesis.* New York, USA: Ballantine Books, 1996.
Arnold, B.T. "בכר #1144." Pages 658–59 of vol. 1 in the *New International Dictionary of Old Testament Theology and Exegesis.* Edited by W.A. VanGemeren. 5 vols. Carlisle, Cumbria, England: Paternoster Press, 1998.
Averbeck, R.E. "מַעֲשֵׂר #5130." Pages 1035–55 in vol. 2 of the *New International Dictionary of Old Testament Theology and Exegesis.* Edited by W.A. VanGemeren. 5 vols. Carlisle, Cumbria, England: Paternoster Press, 1997.
Baker, D.L. "Safekeeping, Borrowing and Rental." *Journal for the Study of the Old Testament* 31, no. 1 (2006): 27–42.
Baker, D.W. "Diversity and Unity in the Literary Structure of Genesis." Pages 189–205 in *Essays on the Patriarchal Narratives.* Edited by A.R. Millard and D.J. Wiseman. Leicester, UK: Inter-Varsity Press, 1980.
Bakon, S. "Jacob: Father of a Nation." *Jewish Bible Quarterly* 28, no. 1 (2000): 38–44.
Bal, M. "Tricky Thematics." *Semeia* 42 (1988): 133–55.
Baldwin, J.G. *The Message of Genesis 12–50.* Edited by J.A. Motyer and J.R.W. Stott Motyer. The Bible Speaks Today. Leicester, UK: Inter-Varsity Press, 1986.
Bar-Efrat, S. *Narrative Art in the Bible.* London, UK: T&T Clark International, 1989.
Barr, James. *The Semantics of Biblical Language.* London, UK: SCM, 1983.
Barthes, R. "La lutte avec l'ange: analyse textuelle de Gen 32:23–33." Pages 27–39 in *Analyse structurale et exégèse biblique.* Edited by R. Barthes and T. Bovon Barthes. Neuchâtel: Delachaux et Niestlé, 1971.
Barton, J. *Ethics and the Old Testament.* London, UK: SCM Press, 2002.
——. *Reading the Old Testament.* London, UK: Darton, Long and Todd Ltd., 2003.
Bechtel, Lyn M. "What If Dinah Is Not Raped? (Genesis 34)." *Journal for the Study of the Old Testament* 19, no. 62 (1994): 19–36.
Ben-Reuven, S. "Mandrakes as Retribution for Buying the Birthright (Hebrew)." *Beth Mikra* 28 (1982/83): 230–31.
Berge, K. *Die Zeit des Jahwisten, Ein Beitrag zur Datierung jahwistischer Vätertexte.* Beihefte zur Zeitschrift für die alttestamentliche Wissenschaft. Berlin 186, Germany: Walter de Gruyter, 1990.

Berlin, A. *Esther*. The JPS Torah Commentary. Philadelphia, USA: Jewish Publication Society, 2001.

——. *Poetics and Interpretation of Hebrew Narrative*. Sheffield, UK: Sheffield Academic Press, 1983.

Birch, B.C. "Moral Agency, Community, and the Character of God in the Hebrew Bible." *Semeia* 66 (1994): 119–35.

Bland, K.P. "The Rabbinic Method and Literary Criticism." Pages 16–23 in *Literary Interpretations of Biblical Narratives*. Edited by K.R.R. Gros Louis. Nashville, Tennessee, USA: Abingdon Press, 1974.

Bledstein, A.J. "Binder, Trickster, Heel and Hairy Man: Rereading Genesis 27 as a Trickster Tale Told by a Woman." Pages 282–95 in *A Feminist Companion to Genesis*. Edited by A. Brenner. Sheffield, UK: Sheffield Academic Press, 1993.

Blomberg, C.L. *Neither Poverty nor Riches*. Leicester, UK: Apollos, 1999.

——. "The Unity and Diversity of Scripture." Pages 64–72 in *New Dictionary of Biblical Theology*. Edited by T.D. Alexander and B.S. Rosner. Leicester, England: InterVarsity Press, 2000.

——. "Wealth." Pages 813–16 in *Evangelical Dictionary of Biblical Theology*. Edited by W.A. Elwell. Grand Rapids, Michigan, USA: Baker Books, 1996.

Blum, E. *Die Komposition der Vätergeschichte*. Vol. 57, Wissenschaftliche Monographien zum Alten und Neuen Testament. Neukirchen-Vluyn, Germany: Neukirchener Verlag, 1984.

——. "Noch einmal: Jakobs Traum in Bethel—Genesis 28, 10–22." Pages 33–54 in *Rethinking the Foundations: Historiography in the Ancient World and in the Bible—Essays in Honour of John van Seters*. Beihefte zur Zeitschrift für die alttestamentliche Wissenschaft 294. Berlin, Germany: Walter de Gruyter, 2000.

Boase, E. "Life in the Shadows: The Role and Function of Isaac in Genesis—Synchronic and Diachronic Readings." *Vetus Testamentum* 51, no. 3 (2001): 312–35.

Breitbart, S. "The Problem of Deception in Genesis 27." *Jewish Bible Quarterly* 29, no. 1 (2001): 45–47.

Brenner, A., ed. *A Feminist Companion to Genesis*. Sheffield, UK: Sheffield Academic Press, 1993.

Brenner, A. *Colour Terms in the Old Testament*. Journal for the Study of the Old Testament Supplement Series 21. Sheffield, UK: Sheffield Academic Press, 1982.

——. "Female Social Behaviour: Two Descriptive Patterns within the 'Birth of Hero' Paradigm." *Vetus Testamentum* 36, no. 3 (1986): 257–73.

Brett, M.G. *Genesis: Procreation and the politics of identity*. London, UK: Routledge, an imprint of the Taylor and Francis Group, 2000.

Brichto, H.C. "Kin, cult, land and afterlife: a biblical complex." Pages 1–54 in *Hebrew Union College Annual 44*, 1973.

——. *The Problem of "Curse" in the Hebrew Bible*, Journal of Biblical Literature Monograph Series 13. Philadelphia, USA: Society of Biblical Literature and Exegesis, 1963.

Brisman, L. *The Voice of Jacob: On the Composition of Genesis*. Bloomington & Indianapolis, Indiana, USA: Indiana University Press, 1990.

Brodie, T.L. *Genesis as Dialogue: A Literary, Historical and Theological Commentary*. Oxford, UK: Oxford University Press, 2001.

——. "Genesis as Dialogue: Genesis' Twenty-six Diptychs as a Key to Narrative Unity and Meaning." Pages 297–314 in *Studies in the Book of Genesis—Literature, Redaction and History*. Edited by A. Wénin. Leuven, Belgium: Leuven University Press, 2001.

Brown, M.L. "ברך #1385." Pages 757–67 in vol. 1 of *New International Dictionary of Old Testament Theology and Exegesis*. Edited by W.A. VanGemeren. 5 vols. Carlisle, Cumbria, England: Paternoster Press, 1997.

Brueggemann, W. *The Land*, Overtures to Biblical Theology. London, UK: SPCK, 1978.

——. "Of the Same Flesh and Bone (Gen 2, 23a)." *Catholic Biblical Quarterly* 32 (1970): 532–42.

——. *Theology of the Old Testament*. Minneapolis, USA: Fortress Press, 1997.

——. *Genesis*. Edited by J.L. Mays, Interpretation—A Bible Commentary for Teaching and Preaching. Atlanta, Georgia, USA: John Knox Press, 1982.

——. "Biblical Theology Appropriately Postmodern." Pages 97–108 in *Jews, Christians and the Theology of the Hebrew Scriptures*. Edited by A. Ogden Bellis and J.S. Kaminsky. Atlanta, Georgia, USA: Society of Biblical Literature, 2000.

Buber, M. "Leitwort Style in Pentateuch Narrative." Pages 114–28 in *Scripture and Translation*. Edited by M. Buber and F. Rosenzweig. Indianapolis, Indiana, USA: Indiana University Press, 1994.

Bultmann, R. *Existence and Faith: Shorter Writings of Rudolph Bultmann*. London, UK: Fontana, 1964.

Burrows, M. "The Complaint of Laban's Daughters." *Journal of the American Oriental Society* 57, no. 3 (1937): 259–76.

Butterweck, A. "Die Begegnung zwischen Esau und Jakob (Gen 33, 1–18) im Spiegel rabbinischer Ausdeutungen." *Biblische Notizen* 116 (2003): 15–27.

Calvin, J. *Institutio Christianae Religionis*. Geneva, 1559.

Carmichael, C.M. *Women, Law and the Genesis Traditions*. Edinburgh, UK: Edinburgh University Press, 1979.

Carpenter, E. "עָבַד #6268." Pages 304–09 in vol. 3 of the *New International Dictionary of Old Testament Theology and Exegesis*. Edited by W.A. VanGemeren. 5 vols. Carlisle, Cumbria, England: Paternoster Press, 1998.

Carr, D.M. *Reading the Fractures of Genesis—Historical and Literary Approaches*. Louisville, Kentucky, USA: Westminster John Knox Press, 1996.

Carroll, R.P. "The Reader and the Text." Pages 3–34 in *Text in Context: Essays by Members of the Society for Old Testament Study*. Edited by A.D.H. Mayes. Oxford, UK: Oxford University Press, 2000.

Cartledge, T.W. *Vows in the Hebrew Bible and the Ancient Near East*. Journal for the Study of the Old Testament Supplement Series 147. Sheffield, UK: Sheffield Academic Press, 1992.

Caspi, M.M. "The Story of the Rape of Dinah: The Narrator and the Reader." *Hebrew Studies* 26 (1985): 25–45.

Cassuto, U. *A Commentary on the Book of Genesis—From Noah to Abraham*. Vol. 2, A Commentary on the Book of Genesis. Jerusalem, Israel: The Magnes Press, The Hebrew University, 1973.

Chapman, C. *Whose Promised Land?* Oxford, UK: Lion Publishing, 2002.

Chirichigno, G. *Debt-Slavery in Israel and the Ancient Near East*. Sheffield, UK: Continuum Publishing, 1993.

Chisholm, R.B. "Does God 'Change His Mind'?" *Bibliotheca Sacra* 152, no. 608 (1995): 387–99.

——. *From Exegesis to Exposition*. Grand Rapids, Michigan, USA: Baker Books, 1998.

Church, B.P. *The Israel Saga*. New York, USA: Macmillan, 1932.

Clark, R. "The Silence of Dinah's Cry." *lectio difficilior* 1 (2006).

Clifford, R.J. "Genesis 25:19–34." *Interpretation* 45, no. October (1991): 397–401.

Clines, D.J.A. *The Theme of the Pentateuch*. Sheffield, UK: Sheffield Academic Press, 1997.

——. "The Ancestor in Danger: But not the Same Danger." Pages 67–84 in *What Does Eve do to Help? And other Readerly Questions in the Old Testament*. Edited by D.J.A. Clines. Sheffield, UK: Sheffield University Press, 1990.

Clines, D.J.A. and J.C. Exum. "The New Literary Criticism." Pages 11–24 in *The New Literary Criticism and the Hebrew Bible*. Edited by J.C. Exum and D.J.A. Clines. Journal for the Study of the Old Testament Supplement Series 143. Sheffield, UK: Sheffield Academic Press, 1993.

Coats, G.W. *Genesis—With an Introduction to Narrative Literature.* Grand Rapids, MI, USA: Eerdmans Publishing Company, 1983.

——. "Strife Without Reconciliation: A Narrative Theme in the Jacob Traditions." Pages 82–106 in *Werden und Wirken des alten Testaments: Festschrift für Claus Westermann zum 70 Geburtstag.* Göttingen, Germany: Vandenhoeck & Ruprecht, 1980.

Cohen, J.M. "The Jacob-Esau Reunion." *Jewish Bible Quarterly* 21, no. July (1993): 159–63.

——. "Struggling with Angels and Men." *Jewish Bible Quarterly* 31, no. 2 (2003): 126–28.

Cramp, A.B. "Economic Ethics." Pages 115–21 in *New Dictionary of Christian Ethics & Pastoral Theology.* Edited by D.J. Atkinson and D.H. Field. Leicester, UK: IVP, 1995.

Curtis, E.M. "Structure, Style and Context as a Key to Interpreting Jacob's Encounter at Peniel." *Journal of the Evangelical Theological Society* 30 (1987): 129–37.

Daniel, L. "Can we talk? About money? Affluent Christians." *Christian Century* February 8 (2003): 26–30.

Daube, D. "Fraud on Law for Fraud on Law." *Oxford Journal of Legal Studies* 1, no. 1 (1981): 51–60.

——. "The Night of Death." *Harvard Theological Review* 61, no. 4 (1968): 629–32.

——. *Studies in Biblical Law.* Cambridge, UK: Cambridge University Press, 1947.

Daube, D. and R. Yaron. "Jacob's Reception by Laban." *Journal of Semitic Studies* 1 (1956): 60–61.

Davidson, R. *Genesis 12–50.* Cambridge Bible Commentary. Edited by P.R. Ackroyd, A.R.C. Leaney and J.W. Packer. The Cambridge, UK: Cambridge University Press, 1979.

Davies, E.W. *The Dissenting Reader: Feminist Approaches to the Hebrew Bible.* Aldershot, UK: Ashgate, 2003.

de Hoop, R. "The Use of the Past to Address the Present: The Wife-Sister Incidents (Gen. 12:10–20; 20:1–18; 26:1–16)." Pages 359–70 in *Studies in the Book of Genesis—Literature, Redaction and History.* Edited by A. Wénin. Leuven, Belgium: Leuven University Press, 2001.

de Moor, J.C., ed. *Synchronic or Diachronic? A Debate on Method in Old Testament Exegesis.* Leiden, The Netherlands: Brill, 1995.

de Pury, A. "Jakob am Jabbok, Gen. 32, 23–33 im Licht einer alt-irischen Erzählung." *Theologische Zeitschrift* 35 (1979): 18–34.

——. *Promesse divine et légende cultuelle dans le cycle de Jacob: Gen 28 et les traditions patriarcales. études bibliques.* Paris, France: Gabalda, 1975.

de Regt, L.J. "Hebrew Syntactic Inversions and their Literary Equivalence in English: Robert Alter's Translations of Genesis and 1 and 2 Samuel." *Journal for the Study of the Old Testament* 30, no. 3 (2006): 287–314.

de Vaux, R. *Ancient Israel.* Translated by J. McHugh. London, UK: Darton, Longman & Todd Ltd., 1968.

Diamond, J.A. "The Deception of Jacob: A New Perspective on an Ancient Solution to the Problem." *Vetus Testamentum* 34, no. 2 (1984): 211–13.

Dieckmann, D. *Segen für Isaak—Eine rezeptionsästhetische Auslegung von Gen 26 und Kotexten.* Beihefte zur Zeitschrift für die alttestamentliche Wissenschaft 329. Berlin, Germany: Walter de Gruyter, 2003.

Dillmann, A. *Genesis.* Edinburgh, UK: T&T Clark, 1897.

Donaldson, M.E. "Kinship Theory and the Patriarchal Narratives: The Case of the Barren Wife." *Journal of the American Academy of Religion* 49, no. 1 (1981): 77–87.

Driver, S.R. *The Book of Genesis.* London, UK: Methuen, 1916.

Dumbrell, W.J. *Covenant & Creation.* Exeter, UK: Paternoster Press, 1984.

——. *The Faith of Israel.* Leicester, UK: Apollos, 2002.

——. *The Search for Order.* Grand Rapids, Michigan, USA: Baker Books, 1994.

Eising, H. *Formgeschichtliche Untersuching zur Jakobserzählung der Genesis*. Emsdetten, Germany: Dissertations-Druckenei Heinr. & J. Lechte, 1940.

Elliger, K. "Der Jakobskampf am Jabbok." *Zeitschrift für Theologie und Kirche* 48 (1951): 1–31.

Evans, C.D. "The Patriarch Jacob—An Innocent Man." *Bible Review* 2, no. 1 (1987): 32–37.

Exum, J.C. *Fragmented Women: Feminist (Sub)versions of Biblical Narratives*. Journal for the Study of the Old Testament Supplement Series 163. Sheffield, UK: Sheffield Academic Press, 1993.

——. "Who's Afraid of 'the Endangered Ancestress'?" Pages 91–113 in *The New Literary Criticism and the Hebrew Bible*. Edited by J.C. Exum and D.J.A. Clines. Sheffield, UK: Sheffield Academic Press, 1993.

——. "Feminist Study of the Old Testament." Pages 86–115 in *Text in Context: Essays by Members of the Society for Old Testament Study*. Edited by A.D.H. Mayes. Oxford, UK: Oxford University Press, 2000.

Fee, G.D. *Listening to the Spirit in the Text*. Grand Rapids, Michigan, USA: Wm. B. Eerdmans Publishing Co., 2000.

Feliks, J. "Biology." Pages 1024–27 in *Encyclopaedia Judaica (electronic ed.)*. Vol. 4. Brooklyn, NY, USA: Lambda Publishers, 1997.

Fewell, D.N. and D.M. Gunn. "Tipping the Balance: Sternberg's Reader and the Rape of Dinah." *Journal of Biblical Literature* 110, no. 2 (1991): 193–211.

Finkelstein, J.J. "An Old Babylonian Herding Contract and Genesis 31:38f." *Journal of the American Oriental Society* 88 (1968): 30–36.

Fischer, G. "Jakobs Rolle in der Genesis." *Biblische Zeitschrift* 47, no. 2 (2003): 269–80.

Fischer, I. *Die Erzeltern Israels: Feministisch-theologische Studien zu Genesis 12–36*. Edited by O. Kaiser. Beihefte zur Zeitschrift für die alttestamentliche Wissenschaft 222. Berlin, Germany: Walter de Gruyter, 1994.

Fishbane, M. "Composition and Structure in the Jacob Cycle (Gen 25:19–25:22)." *Journal of Jewish Studies* 26 (1975): 15–38.

——. *Text and Texture*. New York, USA: Schocken Books Inc., 1979.

Fisher, L.R. "Two Projects at Claremont." *Ugarit Forschungen* 3 (1971): 27–31.

Fleishman, J. "Shechem and Dinah—in the Light of Non-Biblical and Biblical Sources." *Zeitschrift für die alttestamentliche Wissenschaft* 116, no. 1 (2004): 12–32.

——. "Why Did Simeon and Levi Rebuke Their Father in Genesis 34:31?" *Journal of Northwest Semitic Languages* 26, no. 2 (2000): 101–16.

Fokkelman, J.P. *Reading Biblical Narrative: An Introductory Guide*. Translated by Ineke Smit. Louisville, Kentucky, USA: Westminster John Knox Press, 1999.

——. "Genesis." Pages 36–55 in *The Literary Guide to the Bible*. Edited by R. Alter and F. Kermode. London, UK: Collins, 1987.

——. *Narrative Art in Genesis*. Edited by D.E. Orton. Vol. 12, The Biblical Seminar. Sheffield, UK: JSOT Press (an inprint of Sheffield Academic Press Ltd.), 1991.

Foster, R. *Money, Sex and Power*. London, UK: Hodder & Stoughton, 1985.

Fox, E. *Genesis and Exodus: A New English Rendition with Commentary and Notes*. New York, USA: Schocken Books, 1983.

Frankel, R. "The Matriarchal Groupings of the Tribal Eponyms: A Reappraisal." Pages 121–27 in *The World of Genesis. Persons, Places, Perspectives*. Edited by P.R. Davies and D.J.A. Clines. Journal for the Study of the Old Testament Supplement Series 257. Sheffield, UK: Sheffield Academic Press, 1998.

Frankena, R. "Some Remarks on the Semitic Background of Chapters xxix–xxxi of the Book of Genesis." *Oudtestamentische Studiën* 17 (1972): 53–64.

Fretheim, T.E. *The Pentateuch*. Nashville, Tennessee, USA Abingdon Press, 1996.

——. "Which Blessing Does Isaac Give Jacob?" Pages 279–91 in *Jews, Christians and the Theology of the Hebrew Scriptures*. Edited by A. Ogden Bellis and J.S. Kaminsky, Atlanta, Georgia, USA: Society of Biblical Literature, 2000.

Frettlöh, M.L. *Theologie des Segens: biblische und dogmatishe Wahrnehmungen.* Gütersloh, Germany: Gütersloher Verlagshaus, 2005.

Frey, H. *Das Buch des Kampfes.* Stuttgart, Germany: Calwer Verlag, 1938.

Frolov, S. "The Other Side of the Jabbok: Genesis 32 as a Fiasco of Patriarchy." *Journal for the Study of the Old Testament* 91 (2000): 41–59.

Frymer-Kensky, T. "Patriarchal Family Relationships and Near Eastern Law." *The Biblical Archaeologist* 44, no. 4 (1981): 209–14.

——. *Reading the Women of the Bible.* New York, USA: Schocken Books, 2002.

——. *Studies in Bible and Feminist Criticism*, JPS Scholar of Distinction Series. Philadelphia, USA: The Jewish Publication Society, 2006.

——. "Virginity in the Bible." Pages 79–96 in *Gender and Law in the Hebrew Bible and the Ancient Near East.* Edited by V.H. Matthews, B.M. Levinson and T. Frymer-Kensky. Journal for the Study of the Old Testament Supplement Series 262. Sheffield, UK: Sheffield Academic Press, 1998.

Fuchs, E. "For I Have the Way of Women: Deception, Gender, and Ideology in Biblical Narrative." *Semeia* 42 (1988): 68–83.

——. "Who is hiding the truth? Deceptive Women and Biblical Androcentrism." Pages 137–44 in *Feminist Perspectives on Biblical Scholarship.* Edited by A. Yarbro Collins. Atlanta, USA: Society of Biblical Literature, 1985.

Gammie, J.G. "Theological Interpretation by way of Literary and Tradition Analysis: Genesis 25–36." Pages 117–34 in *Encounter with the Text: Form and History in the Hebrew Bible.* Edited by M.J. Buss. Philadelphia, Pennsylvania, USA: Fortress Press, 1979.

Garrett, D. *Rethinking Genesis.* Grand Rapids, Michigan, USA: Baker Book House, 1991.

Gaster, T.H. *Myth, Legend, and Custom in the Old Testament: A Comparative Study with Chapters from Sir James G. Frazer's Folklore in the Old Testament.* New York, USA: Harper & Row, 1969.

Geller, S.A. "The Struggle at the Jabbok: The Uses of Enigma in a Biblical Narrative." *Journal of the Ancient Near Eastern Society* 14 (1982): 37–60.

Gerleman, G. "שׁלם to have enough." Pages 1337–48 in *Theological Lexicon of the Old Testament.* Edited by E. Jenni and C. Westermann. Peabody, Massachusetts, USA: Hendrickson Publishers, Inc., 1997.

Gevirtz, S. "Of Patriarchs and Puns: Joseph at the Fountain, Jacob at the Ford." *Hebrew Union College Annual* 46 (1975): 33–54.

Gillmayr-Bucher, S. "The Woman of their Dreams: The Image of Rebekah in Genesis 24." Pages 90–101 in *The World of Genesis. Persons, Places, Perspectives.* Edited by P.R. Davies and D.J.A. Clines. Journal for the Study of the Old Testament Supplement Series 257. Sheffield, UK: Sheffield Academic Press, 1998.

Global Issues. Cited 25th August 2010. Online: www.globalissues.org.

Goldingay, J. *After Eating the Apricot.* Carlisle, Cumbria, United Kingdom: Solway, 1996.

——. *Models for Interpretation of Scripture.* Toronto, Canada: Clements Publishing, 1995.

——. *Old Testament Theology: Israel's Gospel.* 2 vols. Vol. 1. Milton Keynes, UK: Paternoster, 2003.

——. "The Study of Old Testament Theology: Its Aims and Purpose." *Tyndale Bulletin*, no. 2 (1975): 37–39.

Goldsworthy, Graeme. *According to Plan.* Leicester, UK: Inter-Varsity Press, 1991.

Golka, F.W. "Bechorah und Berachah: Erstgeburtsrecht und Segen." Pages 133–44 in *Recht und Ethos im Alten Testament-Gestalt und Wirkung.* Edited by S. Beyerle, G. Mayer and H. Strauss. Neukirchener, Germany: Neukirchen-Vluyn, 1999.

Good, E.M. "Deception and Women: A Response." *Semeia* 42 (1988): 117–32.

Goodnick, B. "Jacob's Deception of his Father." *Jewish Bible Quarterly* 22, no. 4 (1994): 237–40.

Gordon, C.H. "Biblical Customs and the Nuzu Tablets." *The Biblical Archaeologist* 3, no. 1 (1940): 1–12.

Gradwohl, R. "Waren Leas Augen hässlich?" *Vetus Testamentum* 49, no. 1 (1999): 119–24.

Graetz, N. "Dinah the Daughter." Pages 306–17 in *A Feminist Companion to Genesis*. Edited by A. Brenner. Sheffield, UK: Sheffield Academic Press, 1993.

Gravett, S. "Reading 'Rape' in the Hebrew Bible: A Consideration of Language." *Journal for the Study of the Old Testament* 28, no. 3 (2004): 279–99.

Greenberg, M. "Another Look at Rachel's Theft of the Teraphim." *Journal of Biblical Literature* 81 (1962): 239–48.

——. *Biblical Prose Prayer*. Berkeley, USA: University of California, 1983.

Greenfield, J. "Našu-nadānu and Its Congeners." in *Essays on the Ancient Near East in Memory of J.J. Finkelstein*. Edited by M. de Jong Ellis. Hamden, Conn., USA: Archon, 1977.

Griffiths, J.G. "The Celestial Ladder and the Gate of Heaven (Gen 28:12 and 17)." *Expository Times* 76 (1964/65): 229–30.

Gross, W. "Jakob, der Mann des Segens. Zu Traditionsgeschichte und Theologie der priesterlichen Jakobsüberlieferungen." *Biblica* 49 (1968): 340–41.

Grüneberg, K.N. *Abraham, Blessing and the Nations: A Philological and Exegetical Study of Genesis 12:3 in its Narrative Context*. Beihefte zur Zeitschrift für die alttestamentliche Wissenschaft 332. Berlin, Germany: Walter de Gruyter, 2003.

Guenther, Allen. "A Typology of Israelite Marriage: Kinship, Socio Economic, and Religious Factors." *Journal for the Study of the Old Testament* 29, no. 4 (2005): 387–407.

Gunkel, H. *Genesis*. Translated by M.E. Biddle. Macon, Georgia, USA: Mercer University Press, 1997.

Gunn, D.M. "Hebrew Narrative." Pages 223–52 in *Text in Context: Essays by Members of the Society for Old Testament Study*. Edited by A.D.H. Mayes. Oxford, UK: Oxford University Press, 2000.

Gunn, D.M. and D.N. Fewell. *Narrative in the Hebrew Bible*. Oxford, UK: Oxford University Press, 1993.

Hafemann, S.J. and P.R. House eds. *Central Themes in Biblical Theology: Mapping Unity in Diversity*. Nottingham, UK: Apollos, 2007.

Hamilton, V.P. *The Book of Genesis Chapters 1–17*. Edited by R.K. Harrison, The New International Commentary on the Old Testament. Grand Rapids, Michigan, USA: William B. Eerdmans Publishing Company, 1990.

——. *The Book of Genesis Chapters 18–50*. Edited by R.K. Harrison, The New International Commentary on the Old Testament. Grand Rapids, Michigan, USA: William B. Eerdmans Publishing Company, 1995.

——. "Genesis: Theology of." Pages 663–75 in vol. 1 of the *New International Dictionary of Old Testament Theology and Exegesis*. Edited by W.A. VanGemeren. 5 vols. Carlisle, Cumbria, England: Paternoster Press, 1997.

Hartley, J.E. *Genesis*. New International Bible Commentary 1. Carlisle, Cumbria, UK: Paternoster Press, 2000.

Hauge, M.R. "The Struggles of the Blessed in Estrangement." *Studia Theologica* 29 (1975): 1–30; 113–46.

Hays, R.B. *The Conversion of the Imagination: Paul as Interpreter of Israel's Scripture*. Grand Rapids, Michigan, USA: Wm. B. Eerdmans Publishing Company, 2005.

Hempel, J. *Die israelisch Anschauungen von Segen und Fluch im Lichte altorientalischer Parallelen*. Beihefte zur Zeitschrift für die alttestamentliche Wissenschaft 81. Berlin, Germany: Walter de Gruyter, 1961.

Hendel, R.S. *The Epic of the Patriarch: The Jacob Cycle and the Narrative Traditions of Canaan and Israel.* Atlanta, Georgia, USA: Scholars Press, 1987.

Hengel, M. *Property and Riches in the Early Church.* London, UK: SCM Press, 1974.

Hepner, G. "Verbal Resonance in the Bible and Intertextuality." *Journal for the Study of the Old Testament* 26, no. 2 (2001): 3–27.

Hiers, R.H. "Transfer of Property by Inheritance and Bequest in Biblical Law and Tradition." *Journal of Law and Religion* 10, no. 1 (1993–1994): 121–55.

Hoebel, E.H. *The Law of Primitive Man. A Study of Comparative Legal Dynamics.* Cambridge, UK, 1967.

Hoekveld-Meijer, G. *Esau: Salvation in Disguise—Genesis 36: A Hidden Polemic Between Our Teacher and the Prophets about Edom's role in Post-Exilic Israel through Leitwort Names.* Kampen, The Netherlands: Pharos, 1996.

Hoftijzer, J. *Die Verheissungen an die drei Erzväter.* Leiden, The Netherlands: Brill, 1956.

——. "Holistic or Compositional Approach? Linguistic Remarks to the Problem." in *Synchronic or Diachronic? A Debate on Method in Old Testament Exegesis.* Edited by J.C. De Moor. Leiden, The Netherlands: E.J. Brill, 1995.

Holladay, W.L. *A Concise Hebrew and Aramaic Lexicon of the Old Testament—Based upon the Lexical Work of Ludwig Koehler and Walter Baumgartner.* Leiden, The Netherlands: Brill, 2000.

Holmgren, F.C. "Holding Your Own Against God! Genesis 32:22–32 (In the Context of Genesis 31–33)." *Interpretation* 44 (1990): 5–17.

Hoppe, L.J. *There shall be no poor among you: Poverty in the Bible.* Nashville, Tennesee, USA: Abingdon Press, 2004.

Horst, F. *Gottes Recht: Gesammelte Studien zum Recht im Alten Testament.* Munich, Germany: Chr. Kaiser Verlag, 1961.

Houtman, C. "What Did Jacob See in His Dream at Bethel?" *Vetus Testamentum* 27 (1977): 337–51.

——. "What Did Jacob See in His Dream at Mahanaim?" *Vetus Testamentum* 28 (1978): 37–44.

Howland, B. "Retelling Genesis." *First Thinks* 138, no. Dec (2003): 20–27.

Hughes, D. "Book review of 'Neither Poverty nor Riches: A Biblical Theology of Possessions' by Craig Blomberg." *Themelios* 25, no. 2 (2000): 74.

——. "Book review of 'There shall be no poor among you: Poverty in the Bible' by Leslie J. Hoppe." *Themelios* 30, no. 3 (2005): 107–08.

Humphreys, W.L. *The Character of God in the Book of Genesis: A Narrative Appraisal.* Louisville, Kentucky, USA: Westminster John Knox Press, 2001.

Hurowitz, V.A. "Who Lost an Earring? Genesis 35:4 Reconsidered." *Catholic Biblical Quarterly* 62, no. 1 (2000): 28–32.

——. "Whose Earrings Did Jacob Bury?" *Bible Review* 17, no. 4 (2001): 31–33, 54.

Jacob, B. *Das Erste Buch der Tora—Genesis.* Berlin, Germany: Schocken Verlag, 1934.

Jamieson, R., A.R. Fausset, and D. Brown. *Commentary Critical and Explanatory on the Whole Bible.* Oak Harbor, WA, USA: Logos Research Systems, Inc., 1871.

Janzen, J.G. *Genesis 12–50,* International Theological Commentary. Grand Rapids, Michigan, USA: Wm. B. Eerdmans Publishing Company, 1993.

——. "Land." Pages 143–54 in *Anchor Bible Dictionary.* Edited by D.N. Freedman. New York, USA: Doubleday, 1996.

Janzen, W. *Old Testament Ethics.* Louisville, Kentucky, USA: Westminster/John Knox Press, 1994.

Jay, N. "Sacrifice, Descent and the Patriarchs." *Vetus Testamentum* 38, no. 1 (1988): 52–70.

Jeansonne, S.P. *The Women of Genesis.* Minneapolis, USA: Fortress Press, 1990.

Johnston, P. and P. Walker eds. *The Land of Promise.* Leicester, UK: Apollos, 2000.

Kahn, P. "Jacob's Choice in Genesis 25:19–28:9." *Jewish Bible Quarterly* 29, no. 2 (2001): 80–86.

Kaiser, W.C. jr. *A History of Israel: From the Bronze Age Through the Jewish Wars.* Nashville, TN, USA: Broadman & Holman Publishers, 1998.

Kass, L.R. "Love of Woman and Love of God." *Commentary* 107, no. March (1999): 46–54.

Keil, C.F. *Genesis und Exodus. 3rd edition.* Berlin, Germany: Brunnen Verlag, 1878.

Keller, C.A. "'Die Gefährdung der Ahnfrau': Ein Beitrag zur gattungs- und motivgeschichtlichen Erforschung alttestamentlicher Erzählungen." *Zeitschrift für die alttestamentliche Wissenschaft* 66 (1954): 181–91.

Keller, C.A., Wehmeier, G. "ברך to bless." Pages 266–82 in vol. 1 *Theological Lexicon of the Old Testament* (3 vols.). Edited by E. Jenni and C. Westermann. Peabody, Massachusetts, USA: Hendrickson Publishers, Inc., 1997.

Keukens, K.H. "Der irreguläre Sterbesegen Isaaks—Bemerkungen zur Interpretation von Genesis 27, 1–45." *Biblische Notizen* 19 (1982): 43–56.

Kidner, D. *Genesis.* Edited by D.J. Wiseman, Tyndale Old Testament Commentaries. London, UK: The Tyndale Press, 1967.

Kitchen, K.A. *On the Reliability of the Old Testament.* Grand Rapids, Michigan, USA: Wm. B. Eerdmans Publishing Co., 2003.

——. "Genesis 12–50 in the Near Eastern World." Pages 67–92 in *He Swore an Oath—Biblical Themes from Genesis 12–50.* Edited by R.S. Hess, G.J. Wenham and P.E. Satterthwaite. Carlisle, Cumbria, UK: The Paternoster Press, 1994.

Klein, W.W., C.L. Blomberg and R.L. Hubbard Jr. *Introduction to Biblical Interpretation.* Nashville, Tennessee, USA: W Publishing Group, 1993.

Knauth, R.J.D. "Esau, Edomites." Pages 219–24 in *Dictionary of the Old Testament: Pentateuch.* Edited by T.D. Alexander and D.W. Baker. Leicester, UK: Inter-Varsity Press, 2003.

Knight, D.A. "Introduction: Ethics, Ancient Israel and the Hebrew Bible." *Semeia* 66 (1994): 1–8.

——. "The Pentateuch." Pages 263–96 in *The Hebrew Bible and it's Modern Interpreters.* Edited by D.A. Knight and G.M. Tucker. Philadelphia, Pennsylvania, USA: Fortress Press, 1985.

Knoppers, G.N. "The Preferential Status of the Eldest Son Revoked?" Pages 115–26 in *Rethinking the Foundations: Historiography in the Ancient World and in the Bible—Essays in Honour of John van Seters.* Beihefte zur Zeitschrift für die alttestamentliche Wissenschaft 294. Berlin, Germany: Walter de Gruyter, 2000.

Koch, K. *The Growth of Biblical Tradition: The Form Critical Method.* Translated by S.M. Cupitt. New York, USA: Charles Scribner's Sons, 1969.

Kodell, J. "Jacob Wrestles with Esau (Gen 32:23–32)." *Biblical Theology Bulletin* 10, no. 2 (1980): 65–70.

Kselman, J.S. "Semantic-Sonant Chiasmus in Biblical Poetry." *Biblica* 58 (1977): 220.

——. "Birthright." Page 134 in *Harper's Bible Dictionary.* Edited by P.J. Achtermeier. San Fransisco, USA: Harper & Row, 1985.

LaCocque, A. "Une Descendance Manipulée et Ambiguë (Genèse 29, 31–30, 24)." Pages 109–27 in *Jacob: Commentaire à Plusieurs Voix de Gen 25–36—Mèlanges offerts à Albert de Pury.* Edited by J.-D. Macchi and T. Römer. Geneva, Swiss: Labor et Fides, 2001.

Leupold, H.C. *Exposition of Genesis.* Grand Rapids, Michigan, USA: Baker Book House, 1942.

Levine, B.A. "Firstborn." Pages 1308 in *Encyclopaedia Judaica (electronic ed.).* Vol. 6. Brooklyn, NY, USA: Lambda Publishers, 1997.

Levine, Nachman. "The Curse and the Blessing: Narrative Discourse Syntax and Literary Form." *Journal for the Study of the Old Testament* 27, no. 2 (2002): 189–99.

Lipton, D. *Revisions of the Night: Politics and Promises in the Patriarchal Dreams of Genesis.* Edited by D.J.A. Clines and P.R. Davies. Journal for the Study of the Old Testament Supplement Series 288. Sheffield, UK: Sheffield Academic Press, 1999.

Long, B.O. *The Problem of Etiological Narrative.* Beihefte zur Zeitschrift für die alttestamentliche Wissenschaft 108. Berlin, Germany: Töpelmann, 1968.

Longacre, R.E. *Joseph: A Story of Divine Providence.* Winona Lake, IN, USA: Eisenbrauns, 1989.

Longman III, T. "Literary Approaches to Old Testament Study." Pages 97–115 in *The Face of Old Testament Studies: A Survey of Contemporary Approaches.* Edited by D.W. Baker and B.T. Arnold. Grand Rapids, Michigan, USA: Baker Books, 2004.

——. "Literary Approaches and Interpretation." Pages 103–24 in vol. 1 *New International Dictionary of Old Testament Theology and Exegesis.* Edited by W.A. VanGemeren. 5 vols. Carlisle, Cumbria, England: Paternoster Press, 1998.

Lucas, E. "Proverbs: The Act-Consequence Nexus." Pages in *Postgraduate Seminar, 6th February 2007.* Trinity College Bristol, 2007.

Lutz, D.A. "The Isaac Tradition in the Book of Genesis." Drew University, 1969.

Mabee, C. "Jacob and Laban: The Structure of Judicial Proceedings (Genesis XXXI 25–42)." *Vetus Testamentum* 30 (1980): 192–207.

Macchi, J.-D. and T. Römer eds. *Jacob: Commentaire à Plusieurs Voix de Gen 25–36—Mèlanges offerts à Albert de Pury.* Geneva, Swiss: Labor et Fides, 2001.

Malul, M. "'Āqēb 'Heel' and 'Āqab' 'To Supplant' and the Concept of Successions in the Jacob-Esau Narratives." *Vetus Testamentum* 46, no. 2 (1996): 190–212.

Mann, T.W. "'All the Families of the Earth': The Theological Unity of Genesis." *Interpretation* 45, no. 4 (1991): 341–53.

——. *The Book of the Torah: The Narrative Integrity of the Pentateuch.* Atlanta, USA: John Knox Press, 1988.

Marcus, D. "Traditional Jewish Responses to the Question of Deceit in Genesis 27." Pages 293–305 in *Jews, Christians and the Theology of the Hebrew Scriptures.* Edited by A. Ogden Bellis and J.S. Kaminsky. Atlanta, Georgia, USA: Society of Biblical Literature, 2000.

Marks, H. "Biblical Naming and Poetic Etymology." *Journal of Biblical Literature* 114, no. 1 (1995): 21–42.

Martens, E.A. *God's Design: A Focus on Old Testament Theology.* Leicester, UK: Apollos, 1994.

——. "Tackling Old Testament Theology." *Journal of the Evangelical Theological Society* 20, no. 2 (1977): 123–32.

Martin-Achard, R. "Remarques sur Genèse 26." *Zeitschrift für die alttestamentliche Wissenschaft* 100 Supplement (1988): 22–46.

——. "Un exégète devant Gen 32:23–33." Pages 41–62 in *Analyse structurale et exégèse biblique.* Edited by R. Barthes and T. Bovon. Neuchâtel: Delachaux et Niestlé, 1971.

Marx, A. "Genèse 26, 1–14A." Pages 22–33 in *Jacob: Commentaire à Plusieurs Voix de Gen 25–36—Mèlanges offerts à Albert de Pury.* Edited by J.-D. Macchi and T. Römer. Geneva, Swiss: Labor et Fides, 2001.

Matthews, V.H. "The Wells of Gerar." *The Biblical Archaeologist* 49, no. 2 (1986): 118–26.

Matthews, V.H., M.W. Chavalas and J.H. Walton, *The IVP Bible Background Commentary: Old Testament (electronic ed.)* Downers Grove, IL, USA: Inter-Varsity Press, 2000.

Mazor, Y. "Scolding Aesthetics." *Scandinavian Journal of the Old Testament* 9 (1995): 297–313.

McConville, J.G. "The Old Testament and the Enjoyment of Wealth." Pages 34–53 in *Christ and Consumerism.* Edited by C. Bartholomew and T. Moritz. Carlisle, Cumbria, UK: Paternoster, 2001.

McCree, W.T. "The Covenant Meal in the Old Testament." *Journal of Biblical Literature* 45, no. 1/2 (1923): 120–28.

McKay, H.A. "Jacob Makes It Across the Jabbok: An Attempt to Solve the Success/ Failure Ambivalence in Israel's Self-consciousness." *Journal for the Study of the Old Testament* 12, no. 38 (1987): 3–13.

McKenzie, B.A. "Jacob's Blessing on Pharaoh: An Interpretation of Gen 46:31–47:26." *Westminster Theological Journal* 45, no. 2 (1983): 386–99.

McKenzie, S.L. "The Jacob Tradition in Hosea xii 4–5." *Vetus Testamentum* 36 (1986): 311–22.

——. "'You Have Prevailed': The Function of Jacob's Encounter at Peniel in the Jacob Cycle." *Restoration Quarterly* 23 (1980): 225–31.

McKenzie, S.L. and S.R. Haynes eds. *To Each Its Own Meaning*. Louisville, Kentucky, USA: Westminster John Knox Press 1999.

McKeown, J. *Genesis*, The Two Horizons Old Testament Commentary. Grand Rapids, MI, USA: Eerdmans, 2008.

——. "Blessings and Curses." Pages 83–87 in *Dictionary of the Old Testament: Pentateuch*. Edited by T.D. Alexanderand D.W. Baker. Leicester, UK: Inter-Varsity Press, 2003.

Mendelsohn, I. "On the Preferential Status of the Eldest Son." *Bulletin of the American Schools of Oriental Research* 156 (1959): 38–40.

Merrill, E.H. "Fixed Dates in Patriarchal Chronology." *Bibliotheca Sacra* 137, no. 547 (1980): 241–51.

Milgrom, J. *Numbers*, The JPS Torah Commentary. Philadelphia, USA: Jewish Publication Society, 1990.

Millar, J.G. "Land." Pages 623–27 in *New Dictionary of Biblical Theology*. Edited by T.D. Alexander and B.S. Rosner. Leicester, England: Inter-Varsity Press, 2000.

Millard, A.R. "The Celestial Ladder and the Gate of Heaven (Gen 28:12,17)." *Expository Times* 78 (1966/67): 86–87.

——. "The Meaning of the Name Judah." *Zeitschrift für die alttestamentliche Wissenschaft* 86, no. 216–218 (1974).

Millard, A.R. and D.J. Wiseman eds. *Essays on the Patriarchal Narratives*. Leicester, UK: Inter-Varsity Press, 1980.

Miller, G.P. "Contracts of Genesis." *Journal of Legal Studies* 22, no. 1 (1993): 15–45.

Miller, J.M., Hayes, J.H. *A History of Ancient Israel and Judah*. London, UK: SCM Press, 1999.

Miller, W.T. *Mysterious Encounters at Mamre and Jabbok*. Edited by J. Neusner, Brown Judaic Studies 50. Chico, Ca, USA: Scholars Press, 1984.

Miscall, P.D. "Jacob and Joseph Story Analogies." *Journal for the Study of the Old Testament* 6 (1978): 28–40.

——. "Literary Unity in Old Testament Narrative." *Semeia* 15 (1979): 26–43.

——. *The Workings of Old Testament Narrative*, The Society of Biblical Literature Semeia Studies. Philadelphia, Pennsylvania, USA: Fortress Press, 1983.

Mitchell, C.W. *The Meaning of BRK "To Bless" in the Old Testament*, Society of Biblical Literature Dissertation Series 95. Atlanta, Georgia, USA: Scholars Press, 1987.

Moberly, R.W.L. *The Bible, Theology and Faith: A Study of Abraham and Jesus*. Edited by C. Gunton and D.W. Hardy. Cambridge Studies in Christian Doctrine. Cambridge, UK: Cambridge University Press, 2000.

Mobley, G. "The Wild Man in the Bible and the Ancient Near East." *Journal of Biblical Literature* 116, no. 2 (1997): 217–33.

Mongold, S. "Color Genetics in Icelandic Sheep." *The Shepherd* 42, no. 6 (1997): 11–16.

Morrison, M.A. "The Jacob and Laban Narrative in Light of Near Eastern Sources." *The Biblical Archaeologist* 46, no. 3 (1983): 155–64.

Munk, E. *The Call of the Torah: An Anthology of Interpretation and Commentary on the Five Books of Moses*. Jerusalem, Israel: Feldheim, 1980.

Nel, P.J. "The Talion Principles in Old Testament Narratives." *Journal of Northwest Semitic Languages* 20, no. 1 (1994): 21–29.
———. "שׁלם #8966." Pages 130–35 in vol. 4 of the *New International Dictionary of Old Testament Theology and Exegesis.* Edited by W.A. VanGemeren. 5 vols. Carlisle, Cumbria, England: Paternoster Press, 1997.
Neufeld, E. "The Rape of Dinah." *Jewish Bible Quarterly* 25, no. 4 (1997): 220–24.
Newsom, C.A. "Bakhtin, the Bible and Dialogical Truth." *Journal of Religion* 76, no. 2 (1996): 290–306.
Nicol, G.C. "The Chronology of Genesis: Genesis XXVI 1–33 as 'Flashback'." *Vetus Testamentum* 46, no. 3 (1996): 330–38.
———. "Jacob as Oedipus—Old Testament Narrative as Mythology." *Expository Times* 108, no. Nov (1996): 43–44.
———. "The Narrative Structure and Interpretation of Gen XXVI 1–33." *Vetus Testamentum* 46, no. 3 (1996): 339–60.
———. "Story-patterning in Genesis." Pages 215–33 in *Text as Pretext.* Edited by R.P. Carroll. Journal for the Study of the Old Testament Supplement Series 138. Sheffield, UK: JSOT Press, 1992.
Niditch, S. *Underdogs and Tricksters: A Prelude to Biblical Folklore.* San Fransisco, USA: Harper and Row, 1987.
Nielsen. Cited 25th August 2010. Online: http://www.broadcastingcable.com.
Noble, P. "A 'Balanced' Reading of the Rape of Dinah: Some Exegetical and Methodological Observations" *Biblical Interpretation* 4, no. 2 (1996): 173–203.
Noegel, S.B. "Sex, Sticks and the Trickster in Gen 30:31–43." *Journal of the Ancient Near Eastern Society* 25 (1997): 7–17.
———. "Drinking Feasts and Deceptive Feats: Jacob and Laban's Double Talk." Pages 163–79 in *Puns and Pundits: Wordplay in the Hebrew Bible and Ancient Near Eastern Literature.* Edited by S.B. Noegel. Bethesda, Maryland, USA: CDL Press, 2000.
Novak, S. "Jacob's Two Dreams." *Jewish Bible Quarterly* 24, no. 3 (1996): 189–90.
Oblath, M. "'To Sleep, Perchance to Dream…': What Jacob Saw at Bethel (Genesis 28:10–22)." *Journal for the Study of the Old Testament* 95 (2001): 117–26.
Oden, R.A. Jr. "Jacob as Father, Husband and Nephew: Kinship Studies and the Patriarchal Narratives." *Journal of Biblical Literature* 102, no. 2 (1983): 189–205.
Ogden Bellis, A. "A sister is a forever friend: reflections on the story of Rachel and Leah." *Journal of Religious Thought* 55–56, no. 2–1 (1999): 109–15.
Osborne, G.R. *The Hermeneutical Spiral.* Downers Grove, Illinois, USA: Inter-Varsity Press, 1991.
Otto, E. "Jakob in Bet-El: Ein Beitrag zur Geschichte der Jakobsüberlieferung." *Zeitschrift für die alttestamentliche Wissenschaft* 88 (1976): 165–90.
———. *Theologische Ethik des Alten Testaments.* Stuttgart, Germany: Kohlhammer, 1994.
Packer, J.I. "Hermeneutics and Biblical Authority." Pages 137–54 in *Solid Ground.* Edited by C.R. Trueman, T.J. Gray and C.L. Blomberg. Leicester, UK: Apollos, 1975.
Pagolu, A. *The Religion of the Patriarchs,* Journal for the Study of the Old Testament Supplement Series 277. Sheffield, UK: Sheffield Academic Press, 1998.
Parker, S.B. "The Vow in Ugaritic and Israelite Narrative Literature." *Ugarit Forschungen* 11 (1979): 693–700.
Parry, R. *Old Testament Story and Christian Ethics—The Rape of Dinah as Case Study.* Milton Keynes, United Kingdom: Paternoster Press, 2004.
Patterson, R.D. "The Old Testament Use Of An Archetype: The Trickster." *Journal of the Evangelical Theological Society* 42, no. 3 (1999): 385–94.
Pearson, J.D. "A Mendelian Interpretation of Jacob's Sheep." *Sixteenth Century Journal* 13, no. 1 (2001): 51–58.
Pedersen, J. *Israel: Its Life and Culture.* London, UK: Geoffrey Cumberledge, 1926.

Peleg, Y. "Going Up and Going Down: A Key to Interpreting Jacob's Dream (Gen 28, 10–22)." *Zeitschrift für die alttestamentliche Wissenschaft* 116, no. 1 (2004): 1–11.

Pennant, D.F. "Genesis 32: Lighten Our Darkness, Lord We Pray." Pages 175–83 in *He Swore an Oath—Biblical Themes from Genesis 12–50*. Edited by R.S. Hess, G.J. Wenham and P.E. Satterthwaite. Carlisle, Cumbria, UK: The Paternoster Press, 1994.

Perriman, A. "Faith, Health and Prosperity." The Evangelical Alliance (UK) Commission on Unity and Truth among Evangelicals. Carlisle, Cumbria, UK: Paternoster Press, 2003.

Peterson, E.H. *Eat This Book: The Art of Spiritual Reading*. London, UK: Hodder & Stoughton, 2006.

Pfeiffer, C.F. *The Patriarchal Age*. Grand Rapids, Michigan, USA: Baker Book House, 1961.

Philips Long, V. "Reading the Old Testament as Literature." Pages 85–124 in *Interpreting the Old Testament: A Guide for Exegesis*. Edited by C.C. Broyles. Grand Rapids, MI, USA: Baker Academic, 2001.

Phillips, A. "Nebalah: A Term for Seriously Disorderly and Unruly Conduct." *Vetus Testamentum* 25, no. 2 (1975): 237–42.

Piper, L. and A. Ruvinski. *The Genetics of Sheep*. Wallingford Oxfordshire, UK: CABI Publishing, 1997.

Pollak, A. "Laban and Jacob." *Jewish Bible Quarterly* 29, no. 1 (2001): 60–62.

Polzin, R. "'The Ancestress of Israel in Danger' In Danger." *Semeia* 3 (1975): 81–96.

———. "Literary Unity in Old Testament Narrative: A Response." *Semeia* 15 (1979): 45–49.

Postgate, J.N. "Some Old Babylonian Shepherds and Their Flocks." *Journal of Semitic Studies* 20 (1975): 1–20.

Preuss, H.D. "Ich will mit dir sein." *Zeitschrift für die alttestamentliche Wissenschaft* 80 (1968): 139–73.

Provan, I., V. Philips Long and T. Longman III. *A Biblical History of Israel*. London, UK: Westminster John Knox Press, 2003.

Pyne, R.A. "The 'Seed', the Spirit and the Blessing of Abraham." *Bibliotheca Sacra* 152 (1995): 211–22.

Ramm, B. "Biblical Interpretation." Pages 18–28 in *Hermeneutics*. Edited by B. Ramm. Grand Rapids, Michigan, USA: Baker Books, 1987.

Rand, H. "Switching Brides: Conspiracy and Cover-Up." *Jewish Bible Quarterly* 29, no. 3 (2001): 190–92.

Recker, C. *Die Erzählungen vom Patriarchen Jakob—ein Beitrag zur mehrperspektivischen Bibelauslegung*. Münster, Germany: Lit Verlag, 2000.

Reiss, M. "Archetypes in the Patriarchal Family." *Jewish Bible Quarterly* 28, no. 1 (2000): 12–19.

Rendsburg, G.A. "Notes on Genesis XXXV." *Vetus Testamentum* 34, no. 3 (1984): 361–66.

———. *The Redaction of Genesis*. Winona Lake, Indiana, USA: Eisenbrauns, 1986.

Rendtorff, R. *The Canonical Hebrew Bible: A Theology of the Old Testament*. Translated by D. Orton. Leiden, The Netherlands: Deo Publishing, 2005.

———. *Das überlieferungsgeschichtliche Problem des Pentateuch*. Beihefte zur Zeitschrift für die alttestamentliche Wissenschaft 147. Berlin, Germany: Walter de Gruyter, 1977.

———. "Jakob in Bethel: Beobachtungen zum Aufbau and zur Quellenfrage in Gen 28:10–22." *Zeitschrift für die alttestamentliche Wissenschaft* 94 (1982): 511–23.

———. *The Old Testament: An Introduction*. Translated by J. Bowden. London, UK: SCM Press Ltd., 1985.

Reyburn, W.D., and E.M. Fry, *A Handbook on Genesis*, UBS Handbook Series. New York, USA: United Bible Societies, 1997.

Richter, H.F. "'Auf den Knien eines andern gebären'? (Zur Deutung von Gen 30:3 und 50:23)." *Zeitschrift für die alttestamentliche Wissenschaft* 91 (1979): 436–37.

Richter, W. "Das Gelübde als theologische Rahmung der Jakobsüberlieferungen." *Biblische Zeitschrift* 11 (1967): 21–52.

Rogerson, J.W. "Old Testament Ethics." Pages 116–37 in *Text in Context: Essays by Members of the Society for Old Testament Study*. Edited by A.D.H. Mayes. Oxford, UK: Oxford University Press, 2000.

Ronning, J. "The Naming of Isaac: The Role of the Wife/Sister Episodes in the Redaction of Genesis." *Westminster Theological Journal* 53, no. 1 (1991): 1–28.

Roop, E.F. *Genesis*. Kitchener, Ontario, Canada: Herald, 1987.

Rosner, B.S. "Biblical Theology." Pages 3–11 in *New Dictionary of Biblical Theology*. Edited by T.D. Alexander and B.S. Rosner, Leicester, England: Inter-Varsity Press, 2000.

Ross-Burstall, J. "Leah and Rachel: A Tale of Two Sisters." *Word & World* 14, Spring (1994): 162–70.

Ross, A.P. *Creation and Blessing: A Guide to the Study and Exposition of Genesis*. Grand Rapids, MI, USA: Baker Books, 1996.

——. "Studies in the Life of Jacob—Part 1: Jacob's Vision: The Founding of Bethel." *Bibliotheca Sacra* 142, no. 568 (1985): 224–37.

——. "Studies in the Life of Jacob—Part 2: Jacob at the Jabbok, Israel at Peniel." *Bibliotheca Sacra* 142, no. 568 (1985): 338–54.

——. *Genesis*. Edited by J.F. Walvoord and R.B. Zuck, Bible Knowledge Commentary vol. 1. Wheaton, IL, USA: Victor Books, 1983–c1985.

Ryken, L. "Literary Criticism of the Bible: Some Fallacies." Pages 24–40 in *Literary Interpretations of Biblical Narratives*. Edited by K.R.R. Gros Louis. Nashville, Tennessee, USA: Abingdon Press, 1974.

Ryken, L., J. Wilhoit, T. Longman et al., eds. "Vow, Oath." Dictionary of Biblical Imagery. Downers Grove, IL, USA: InterVarsity Press, 2000.

Safren, J.D. "Balaam and Abraham." *Vetus Testamentum* 38 (1988): 105–28.

Sailhamer, J.H. *Genesis*. Edited by F.E. Gaebelein, Expositor's Bible Commentary 2. Grand Rapids, Michigan, USA: Zondervan, 1992.

Sarna, N.M. *Genesis*, The JPS Torah Commentary. Philadelphia, USA: Jewish Publication Society, 1989.

——. *Understanding Genesis*, The Melton Research Series—The Heritage of Biblical Israel 1. New York, UK: Schocken Books, 1970.

Scharbert, J. "ברך; ברכה." Pages 279–308 in vol. 2 *Theological Dictionary of the Old Testament*. Edited by G.J. Botterweck and H. Ringgren. Grand Rapids, MI, USA: Eerdmans, 1975.

Scherman, N. and M. Zlotowitz, *Bereishis/Genesis: A New Translation with a Commentary anthologized from Talmudic, Midrashic and Rabbinic Sources*. 2nd ed. 4 vols. Vol. 3, Artscroll Tanach Series. New York, USA: Mesorah, 1980.

Schmidt, L. "Jakob erschleicht sich den väterlichen Segen: Literaturkritik und Redaktion von Genesis 27, 1–45." *Zeitschrift für die alttestamentliche Wissenschaft* 100, no. 2 (1988): 159–83.

Schnabel, E.J. "Scripture." Pages 34–43 in *New Dictionary of Biblical Theology*. Edited by T.D. Alexander and B.S. Rosner, Leicester, England: Inter-Varsity Press, 2000.

Schneider, J.R. *Godly Materialism: Rethinking Money and Possessions*. Downers Grove, USA: IVP, 1994.

——. *The Good of Affluence*. Grand Rapids, Michigan, USA: William B. Eerdmans Publishing Company, 2002.

Schwartz, J. "Jubilees, Bethel and the Temple of Jacob." *Hebrew Union College Annual* 56 (1985): 63–85.

Scobie, C.H.H. *The ways of our God: An Approach to Biblical Theology*. Grand Rapids, Mich.: W.B. Eerdmans Pub., 2003.

Sedgwick, C.J. "Victory through Defeat." *Expository Times* 110, no. 10 (1999): 325–26.

Selman, M.J. "Comparative Customs and the Patriarchal Age." Pages 93–138 in *Essays on the Patriarchal Narratives.* Edited by A.R. Millard and D.J. Wiseman. Leicester, UK: Inter-Varsity Press, 1980.

Selvanayagam, I. "Jacob and the Nature of Blessing." *Bulletin of the Henry Martyn Institute of Islamic Studies* 13, no. Jul–Dec (1994): 94–98.

Shemesh, Y. "Rape is Rape is Rape: The Story of Dinah and Shechem (Gensis 34)." *Zeitschrift für die alttestamentliche Wissenschaft* 119, no. 1 (2007): 2–21.

Sheridan, M., ed. *Ancient Christian Commentary on Scripture: Genesis 12–50.* Edited by T.C. Oden. Downers Grove, Illinois, USA: Inter-Varsity Press, 2002.

Sherwood, S.K. *"Had God Not Been on My Side": An Examination of the Narrative Technique of the Story of Jacob and Laban (Genesis 29, 1–32, 2).* Series XXIII, Theology, Vol. 400, European University Studies. Frankfurt am Main, Germany: Peter Lang, 1990.

Sider, R.J. *Rich Christians in an Age of Hunger.* 4th ed. Dallas, TX, USA: Word, 1997.

Ska, J.L. "Genèse 25, 19–34—Ouverture du Cycle de Jacob." Pages 11–21 in *Jacob: Commentaire à Plusieurs Voix de Gen 25–36—Mèlanges offerts à Albert de Pury.* Edited by J.-D. Macchi and T. Römer. Geneva, Swiss: Labor et Fides, 2001.

Skinner, J. *Genesis.* The International Critical Commentary. Edinburgh, UK: T&T Clark, 1910.

Smith, S.H. "'Heel' and 'Thigh:' The Concept of Sexuality in the Jacob-Esau Narratives." *Vetus Testamentum* 40, no. 4 (1990): 464–73.

Snijders, L.A. "Genesis 27: Het bedrog van Jacob." *Nederlands Theologisch Tijdschrift* 45 (1991): 183–92.

Spanier, K. "Rachel's Theft of the Teraphim: Her Struggle for Family Primacy." *Vetus Testamentum* 42, no. 3 (1992): 404–12.

Speiser, E.A. *Genesis,* The Anchor Bible. Garden City, NY, USA: Doubleday & Company, Inc., 1964.

——. "I Know Not the Day of My Death." *Journal of Biblical Literature* 74, no. 4 (1955): 252–56.

——. "New Kirkuk Documents Relating to Family Laws." *Annual of the American Schools of Oriental Research* 10, no. 8 (1930): 39.

——. "The Verb SHR in Genesis and Early Hebrew Movements." *Bulletin of the American Schools of Oriental Research* 164 (1961): 23–28.

Spero, S. "Jacob's Growing Understanding of His Experience at Beth-El." *Jewish Bible Quarterly* 26, no. 4 (1998): 211–15.

Steinberg, N. "The Genealogical Framework of the Family Stories in Genesis." *Semeia* 46 (1989): 41–50.

——. "Israelite Tricksters: Their Analogues and Cross-Cultural Study." *Semeia* 42 (1988): 1–13.

Steinmetz, D. *From Father to Son: Kinship, Conflict and Continuity in Genesis,* Literary Currents in Biblical Interpretation. Louisville, Kentucky, USA: Westminster/ John Knox Press, 1991.

Sternberg, M. "Biblical Poetics and Sexual Politics: From Reading to Counterreading." *Journal of Biblical Literature* 111, no. 3 (1992): 463–88.

——. *The Poetics of Biblical Narrative: Ideological Literature and the Drama of Reading.* Bloomington, Indiana, USA: Indiana University Press, 1987.

Stott, J.R.W. *Issues Facing Christians Today.* London, UK: William Collins Sons & Co. Ltd., 1990.

Strickman, H.N. and A.M. Silver (trans.). *Ibn Ezra's Commentary on the Pentateuch: Genesis.* New York, USA: Menorah Publishing Company, 1988.

Strus, A. "Étymologies des noms propres dans Gen 29:32–30:24: valeurs littéraires et fonctionelles." *Salesianum* 40 (1978): 57–72.

Syrén, R. *The Forsaken First-Born: A Study of a Recurrent Motif in the Patriarchal Narratives*, Journal for the Study of the Old Testament Supplement Series 133. Sheffield, UK: Sheffield Academic Press, 1993.

Taschner, J. "Mit Wem Ringt Jakob in der Nacht?—Oder: Der Versuch, mit Rembrandt eine Leerstelle anzuleuchten." *Biblical Interpretation* 6, no. 3/4 (1998): 367–80.

——. *Verheissung und Erfüllung in der Jakoberzählung (Gen 25, 19–33, 17): Eine Analyse Ihres Spunnungsbogens*, Herders Biblishe Studien 27. Freiburg, Germany: Herder, 2000.

Tate, W.R. *Biblical Interpretation*. Peabody, Massachusetts, USA: Hendrickson Publishers Inc., 1997.

Terino, J. "A Text Linguistic Study of the Jacob Narrative." *Vox Evangelica* 18 (1988): 45–62.

Terrien, S. *The Elusive Presence: Toward a New Biblical Theology*. New York, USA: Harper & Row, 1978.

Thiselton, A.J. *New Horizons in Hermeneutics*. Grand Rapids, Michigan, USA: Zondervan, 1992.

——. "The Supposed Power of Words in the Biblical Writings." *Journal of Theological Studies* 25 (1974): 283–99.

Thompson, T.L. "The Background of the Patriarchs: A Reply to William Dever and Malcolm Clark." *Journal for the Study of the Old Testament* 9 (1978): 25.

——. "Conflict Themes in the Jacob Narratives." *Semeia* 15 (1979): 5–25.

——. *The Historicity of the Patriarchal Narratives: The Quest for the Historical Abraham*. Beihefte zur Zeitschrift für die alttestamentliche Wissenschaft 133. Berlin, Germany: Walter de Gruyter, 1974.

Toorn, K. van der. "The Nature of the Biblical Teraphim in the Light of the Cuneiform Evidence." *Catholic Biblical Quarterly* 52 (1990): 203–22.

Tsevat, M. "בכור." Pages 121–27 in *Theological Dictionary of the Old Testament*. Edited by G. Botterweck and H. Ringgren. Grand Rapids, MI, USA: Eerdmans, 1977–1990.

Tucker, G. "Jacob's Terrible Burden: In the Shadow of the Text." *Bible Review* 10, June (1994): 20–28, 54.

Tucker, G.M. "Covenant Forms and Contract Forms." *Vetus Testamentum* 15, no. 4 (1965): 487–503.

Turner, L.A. *Announcements of Plot in Genesis*, Journal for the Study of the Old Testament Supplement Series 96. Sheffield, UK: Sheffield Academic Press, 1990.

van Seters, J. *Abraham in History and Tradition*. New Haven: Yale University Press, 1975.

——. "Divine Encounter at Bethel (Gen 28:10–22) in Recent Literary-Critical Study of Genesis." *Zeitschrift für die alttestamentliche Wissenschaft* 110, no. 4 (1998): 503–13.

——. "Jacob's Marriages and Near East Customs: A Re-examination." *Harvard Theological Review* 62, no. 4 (1969): 377–95.

——. *Prologue to History: The Yahwist as Historian in Genesis*. Louisville, Kentucky, USA: Westminster/John Knox Press, 1992.

Vanhoozer, K.J. *Is There Meaning in This Text?* Leicester, UK: Apollos, 1998.

Vawter, B. *On Genesis: A New Reading*. London, UK: Geoffrey Chapman, 1977.

Vermeylen, J. "De Guérar à Béer-Shéva—Genèse 26, 14B-25." Pages 34–50 in *Jacob: Commentaire à Plusieurs Voix de Gen 25–36—Mélanges offerts à Albert de Pury*. Edited by J.-D. Macchi and T. Römer, Geneva, Swiss: Labor et Fides, 2001.

Vetter, D. *Jahwes Mit-Sein: Ein Ausdruck des Segens*. Stuttgart, Germany: Calwer Verlag, 1971.

——. "עם with את." Pages 919–21 in the *Theological Lexicon of the Old Testament*. Edited by E. Jenni and C. Westermann. Peabody, Massachusetts, USA: Hendrickson Publishers, Inc., 1997.

von Rad, G. *Genesis*. Translated by J.H. Marks. London, UK: SCM Press Ltd., 1961.
——. *Old Testament Theology*. 3rd ed. Vol. 1. London, UK: SCM Press Ltd., 1979.
Wakely, R. "נָדַר #5623." Pages 37–42 in vol. 3 of the *New International Dictionary of Old Testament Theology and Exegesis*. Edited by W.A. VanGemeren. 5 vols. Carlisle, Cumbria, England: Paternoster Press, 1998.
Waldman, N.M. "A Note on Genesis 30:27b." *Jewish Quarterly Review* 55 (1964): 164–65.
Waltke, B.K. *Genesis*. Grand Rapids, Michigan, USA: Zondervan, 2001.
——. O'Connor, M. *An Introduction to Biblical Hebrew Syntax*. Winona Lake, Indiana, USA: Eisenbrauns, 1990.
Walton, K. *Thou Traveller Unknown: The Presence and Absence of God in the Jacob Narrative*, Paternoster Biblical and Theological Monographs. Carlisle, United Kingdom: Paternoster Press, 2003.
Waterman, L. "Jacob the Forgotten Supplanter." *The American Journal of Semitic Languages and Literatures* 55, no. 1 (1938): 25–43.
Weber, B. "Nomen est Omen: Einige Erwägungen zu Gen 32:23–33 und seinem Kontext." *Biblische Notizen* 61 (1992): 76–83.
Wehmeier, G. *Der Segen im Alten Testament*, Theologische Dissertationen 6. Basel: Friedrich Reinhardt, 1970.
Weinfeld, M. "Jeremiah and the Spiritual Metamorphosis of Israel." *Zeitschrift für die alttestamentliche Wissenschaft* 88 (1976): 17–56.
Weiser, A. *Pirushe Ha-Torah Le-Rabbenu Avraham ibn Ezra*. Jerusalem, Israel, 1976.
Weiss, A. "Jacob's Struggle: A Psycho-Existential Exegesis." *Journal of Psychology and Judaism* 18, no. 1 (1994): 19–31.
Wenham, G.J. *Genesis 1–15*. Edited by B.M. Metzger, D.A. Hubbard, and G.W. Barker, Vol. 1, Word Biblical Commentary. Dallas, Texas, USA: Word Books, Publisher, 1987.
——. *Genesis 16–50*. Edited by B.M. Metzger, D.A. Hubbard, and G.W. Barker, Vol. 2, Word Biblical Commentary. Dallas, Texas, USA: Word Books, Publisher, 1994.
——. *Genesis*. 4th ed, New Bible Commentary. Leicester, UK: Inter-Varsity Press, 1994.
——. *Story as Torah: Reading the Old Testament Ethically*. Grand Rapids, Michigan, USA: Baker Academic, 2000.
——. "Pondering the Pentateuch: The Search for a New Paradigm." Pages 116–44 in *The Face of Old Testament Studies: A Survey of Contemporary Approaches*. Edited by D.W. Baker and B.T. Arnold. Grand Rapids, Michigan, USA: Baker Books, 2004.
——. "The Face at the Bottom of the Well: Hidden Agendas of the Pentateuchal Commentator." Pages 185–209 in *He Swore an Oath—Biblical Themes from Genesis 12–50*. Edited by R.S. Hess, G.J. Wenham and P.E. Satterthwaite, Carlisle, Cumbria, UK: The Paternoster Press, 1994.
Wénin, A., ed. *Studies in the Book of Genesis—Literature, Redaction and History*. Leuven, Belgium: Leuven University Press, 2001.
West, S.A. "The Nuzi Tablets—Reflections on the Patriarchal Narratives." *Bible and Spade* 10, no. 3–4 (1981): 65–73.
Westermann, C. *Blessing in the Bible and the Life of the Church*. Philadelphia, USA: Fortress, 1978.
——. *Genesis 1–11*. Translated by J.J. Scullion S.J. London, UK: SPCK, 1984.
——. *Genesis 12–36*. Translated by J.J. Scullion S.J. London, UK: SPCK, 1985.
——. *The Promises to the Fathers: Studies on the patriarchal narrative* Philadelphia, USA: Fortress 1980.
——. "Promises to the Patriarchs." in *Interpreter's Dictionary of the Bible (Supplementary Volume)*. Edited by K. Crim. Nashville, Tennessee, USA: Abingdon, 1976.
——. "Peace (*Shalom*) in the Old Testament." Pages 16–48 in *The Meaning of Peace: Biblical Studies*. Edited by P.B. Yoder and W.M. Swartley, Louisville, Kentucky, USA: Westminster/John Knox, 1992.

Whartenby Jr., T.J. "Genesis 28:10–22." *Interpretation* 45, no. October (1991): 402–05.

Wheeler, S.E. *Wealth as Peril and Obligation: The New Testament on Possessions.* Grand Rapids, Michigan, USA: Eerdmans, 1995.

White, H. "French Structuralism and OT Narrative Analysis: Roland Barthes." *Semeia* 3 (1975): 99–127.

——. *Narration and Discourse in the Book of Genesis.* Cambridge, United Kingdom: Cambridge University Press, 1991.

Whybray, R.N. *Introduction to the Pentateuch.* Grand Rapids, MI, USA: Eerdmans Publishing Company, 1995.

——. *The Making of the Pentateuch.* Journal for the Study of the Old Testament Supplement Series 53. Sheffield, UK: Sheffield Academic Press, 1987.

Willi-Plein, I. "Genesis 27 als Rebekka-geschichte: Zu einem historiographischen Kunstgriff der biblischen Vätergeschichten." *Theologishe Zeitschrifr* 45 (1989): 315–34.

Williams, M.J. *Deception in Genesis: An Investigation into the Morality of a Unique Biblical Phenomenon.* Edited by H. Gossai, Studies in Biblical Literature 32. New York, USA: Peter Lang Publishing Inc., 2001.

Wilson, J.R. "Theology and the Old Testament." Pages 245–64 in *Interpreting the Old Testament: A Guide for Exegesis.* Edited by C.C. Broyles. Grand Rapids, MI, USA: Baker Academic, 2001.

Wiseman, D.J. "Abraham in History and Tradition Part I: Abraham the Hebrew." *Bibliotheca Sacra* 134 (1977): 123–30.

——. "Abraham in History and Tradition Part II: Abraham the Prince." *Bibliotheca Sacra* 134 (1977): 228–37.

——. "'Is it Peace?' Covenant and Diplomacy." *Vetus Testamentum* 32 (1982): 325.

——. "Abraham Reassessed." Pages 139–56 in *Essays on the Patriarchal Narratives.* Edited by A.R. Millard and D.J. Wiseman. Leicester, UK: Inter-Varsity Press, 1980.

Wright, C.J.H. *God's People in God's Land.* Exeter, UK: Paternoster Press Ltd., 1990.

——. *Living as the People of God.* Leicester, UK: Inter-Varsity Press, 1998.

——. *The Mission of God.* Leicester, UK: Inter-Varsity Press, 2006.

——. *Old Testament Ethics for the People of God.* Leicester, UK: Inter-Varsity Press, 2004.

——. *Walking in the Ways of the Lord: The Ethical Authority of the Old Testament.* Leicester, UK: Inter-Varsity Press, 1995.

——. "אֶרֶץ #824." Pages 518–24 in vol. 1 *New International Dictionary of Old Testament Theology and Exegesis.* Edited by W.A. VanGemeren. 5 vols. Grand Rapids, Michigan, USA: Zondervan, 1998.

Wyatt, N. "There and Back Again: The Significance of Movement in the Priestly Work." *Scandinavian Journal of the Old Testament* 1 (1990): 61–80.

——. "Where Did Jacob Dream His Dream?" *Scandinavian Journal of the Old Testament* 2 (1990): 44–57.

Yarbrough, R.W. "Biblical Theology." Pages 61–66 in *Evangelical Dictionary of Biblical Theology.* Edited by W.A. Elwell. Grand Rapids, Michigan, USA: Baker Books, 2000.

Zakowitz, Y. "Through the Looking Glass: Reflections/Inversions of Genesis Stories in the Bible." *Biblical Interpretation* 2 (1993): 139–52.

Zimmerli, W. *The Old Testament and the World.* London, UK: SPCK, 1976.

Zuck, R.B., E.H. Merrill, and D.L. Bock. *A Biblical Theology of the Old Testament.* Chicago, USA: Moody Press, 1996.

AUTHOR INDEX

SCRIPTURE INDEX

SUPPLEMENTS TO VETUS TESTAMENTUM

97. Lo, A. *Job 28 as Rhetoric.* An Analysis of Job 28 in the Context of Job 22-31. 2003. ISBN 90 04 13320 8
98. TRUDINGER, P.L. *The Psalms of the Tamid Service.* A Liturgical Text from the Second Temple. 2004. ISBN 90 04 12968 5
99. FLINT, P.W. and P.D. MILLER, JR. (eds.) with the assistance of A. Brunell. *The Book of Psalms.* Composition and Reception. 2004. ISBN 90 04 13842 8
100. WEINFELD, M. *The Place of the Law in the Religion of Ancient Israel.* 2004. ISBN 90 04 13749 1
101. FLINT, P.W., J.C. VANDERKAM and E. TOV. (eds.) *Studies in the Hebrew Bible, Qumran, and the Septuagint.* Essays Presented to Eugene Ulrich on the Occasion of his Sixty-Fifth Birthday. 2004. ISBN 90 04 13738 6
102. MEER, M.N. VAN DER. *Formation and Reformulation.* The Redaction of the Book of Joshua in the Light of the Oldest Textual Witnesses. 2004. ISBN 90 04 13125 6
103. BERMAN, J.A. *Narrative Analogy in the Hebrew Bible.* Battle Stories and Their Equivalent Non-battle Narratives. 2004. ISBN 90 04 13119 1
104. KEULEN, P.S.F. VAN. *Two Versions of the Solomon Narrative.* An Inquiry into the Relationship between MT 1 Kgs. 2-11 and LXX 3 Reg. 2-11. 2004. ISBN 90 04 13895 1
105. MARX, A. *Les systèmes sacrificiels de l'Ancien Testament.* Forms et fonctions du culte sacrificiel à Yhwh. 2005. ISBN 90 04 14286 X
106. ASSIS, E. *Self-Interest or Communal Interest.* An Ideology of Leadership in the Gideon, Abimelech and Jephthah Narritives (Judg 6-12). 2005. ISBN 90 04 14354 8
107. WEISS, A.L. *Figurative Language in Biblical Prose Narrative.* Metaphor in the Book of Samuel. 2006. ISBN 90 04 14837 X
108. WAGNER, T. *Gottes Herrschaft.* Eine Analyse der Denkschrift (Jes 6, 1-9,6). 2006. ISBN 90 04 14912 0
109. LEMAIRE, A. (ed.). *Congress Volume Leiden 2004.* 2006. ISBN 90 04 14913 9
110. GOLDMAN, Y.A.P., A. van der Kooij and R.D. Weis (eds.). *Sôfer Mahîr.* Essays in Honour of Adrian Schenker Offered by Editors of *Biblia Hebraica Quinta.* 2006. ISBN 90 04 15016 1
111. WONG, G.T.K. *Compositional Strategy of the Book of Judges.* An Inductive, Rhetorical Study. 2006. ISBN 90 04 15086 2
112. HØYLAND LAVIK, M. *A People Tall and Smooth-Skinned.* The Rhetoric of Isaiah 18. 2006. ISBN 90 04 15434 5
113. REZETKO, R., T.H. LIM and W.B. AUCKER (eds.). *Reflection and Refraction.* Studies in Biblical Historiography in Honour of A. Graeme Auld. 2006. ISBN 90 04 14512 5
114. SMITH, M.S. and W.T. PITARD. *The Ugaritic Baal Cycle.* Volume II. Introduction with Text, Translation and Commentary of KTU/CAT 1.3–1.4. 2009. ISBN 978 90 04 15348 6
115. BERGSMA, J.S. *The Jubilee from Leviticus to Qumran.* A History of Interpretation. 2006. ISBN-13 978 90 04 15299 1. ISBN-10 90 04 15299 7
116. GOFF, M.J. *Discerning Wisdom.* The Sapiential Literature of the Dead Sea Scrolls. 2006. ISBN-13 978 90 04 14749 2. ISBN-10 90 04 14749 7
117. DE JONG, M.J. *Isaiah among the Ancient Near Eastern Prophets.* A Comparative Study of the Earliest Stages of the Isaiah Tradition and the Neo-Assyrian Prophecies. 2007. ISBN 978 90 04 16161 0
118. FORTI, T.L. *Animal Imagery in the Book of Proverbs.* 2007. ISBN 978 90 04 16287 7
119. PINÇON, B. *L'énigme du bonheur.* Étude sur le sujet du bien dans le livre de Qohélet. 2008. ISBN 978 90 04 16717 9

120. ZIEGLER, Y. *Promises to Keep.* The Oath in Biblical Narrative. 2008.
ISBN 978 90 04 16843 5

121. VILLANUEVA, F.G. *The 'Uncertainty of a Hearing'.* A Study of the Sudden Change of Mood in the Psalms of Lament. 2008. ISBN 978 90 04 16847 3

122. CRANE, A.S. *Israel's Restoration.* A Textual-Comparative Exploration of Ezekiel 36–39. 2008. ISBN 978 90 04 16962 3

123. MIRGUET, F. *La représentation du divin dans les récits du Pentateuque.* Médiations syntaxiques et narratives. 2009. ISBN 978 90 04 17051 3

124. RUITEN, J. VAN and J.C. Vos DE (eds.). *The Land of Israel in Bible, History, and Theology.* Studies in Honour of Ed Noort. 2009. ISBN 978 90 04 17515 0

125. EVANS, P.S. *The Invasion of Sennacherib in the Book of Kings.* A Source-Critical and Rhetorical Study of 2 Kings 18-19. 2009. ISBN 978 90 04 17596 9

126. GLENNY, W.E. *Finding Meaning in the Text.* Translation Technique and Theology in the Septuagint of Amos. 2009. ISBN 978 90 04 17638 6

127. COOK, J. (ed.). *Septuagint and Reception.* Essays prepared for the Association for the Study of the Septuagint in South Africa. 2009. ISBN 978 90 04 17725 3

128. KARTVEIT, M. *The Origin of the Samaritans.* 2009. ISBN 978 90 04 17819 9

129. LEMAIRE, A., B. HALPERN and M.J. ADAMS (eds.). *The Books of Kings.* Sources, Composition, Historiography and Reception. 2010. ISBN 978 90 04 17729 1

130. GALIL, G., M. GELLER and A. MILLARD (eds.). *Homeland and Exile.* Biblical and Ancient Near Eastern Studies in Honour of Bustenay Oded. 2009.
ISBN 978 90 04 17889 2

131. ANTHONIOZ, S. *L'eau, enjeux politiques et théologiques, de Sumer à la Bible.* 2009.
ISBN 978 90 04 17898 4

132. HUGO, P. and A. SCHENKER (eds.). *Archaeology of the Books of Samuel.* The Entangling of theTextual and Literary History. 2010. ISBN 978 90 04 17957 8

133. LEMAIRE, A. (ed.). *Congress Volume Ljubljana.* 2007. 2010. ISBN 978 90 04 17977 6

134. ULRICH, E. (ed.). *The Biblical Qumran Scrolls.* Transcriptions and Textual Variants. 2010. ISBN 978 90 04 18038 3

135. DELL, K.J., G. DAVIES and Y. VON KOH (eds.). *Genesis, Isaiah and Psalms.* A Festschrift to honour Professor John Emerton for his eightieth birthday. 2010.
ISBN 978 90 04 18231 8

136. GOOD, R. *The Septuagint's Translation of the Hebrew Verbal System in Chronicles.* 2010. ISBN 978 90 04 15158 1

137. REYNOLDS, K.A. *Torah as Teacher.* The Exemplary Torah Student in Psalm 119. 2010. ISBN 978 90 04 18268 4

138. VAN DER MEER, M., P. VAN KEULEN, W. Th. VAN PEURSEN and B. TER HAAR ROMENY (eds.). *Isaiah in Context.* Studies in Honour of Arie van der Kooij on the Occasion of his Sixty-Fifth Birthday. 2010. ISBN 978 90 04 18657 6

139. TIEMEYER, L.-S. *For the Comfort of Zion.* The Geographical and Theological Location of Isaiah 40-55. 2011. ISBN 978 90 04 18930 0

140/1. LANGE, A., E. TOV and M. WEIGOLD (eds.). *The Dead Sea Scrolls In Context.* Integrating the Dead Sea Scrolls in the Study of Ancient Texts, Languages, and Cultures. 2011. ISBN 978 90 04 18903 4

141. HALVORSON-TAYLOR, M.A. *Enduring Exile.* The Metaphorization of Exile in the Hebrew Bible. 2011. ISBN 978 90 04 16097 2

142. JOACHIMSEN, K. *Identities in Transition.* The Pursuit of Isa. 52:13–53:12. 2011.
ISBN 978 90 04 20106 4

143. GILMOUR, R. *Representing the Past.* A Literary Analysis of Narrative Historiography in the Book of Samuel. 2011. ISBN 978 90 04 20340 2

144. BARBIERO, G. and M. TAIT (trans). *Song of Songs.* A Close Reading. 2011.
ISBN 978 90 04 20325 9

145. KOOWON, K. *Incubation as a Type-Scene in the 'Aqhatu, Kirta, and Hannah Stories.* A Form-Critical and Narratological Study of KTU 1.14 I-1.15 III, 1.17 I-II, and 1 Samuel 1:1-2:11. 2011. ISBN 978 90 04 20239 9

145. VROLIJK, P.D. *Jacob's Wealth.* An Examination into the Nature and Role of Material Possessions in the Jacob-Cycle (Gen 25:19-35:29). 2011. ISBN 978 90 04 20329 9